The Oxford Dictionary of

Twentieth
Century
Quotations

The Oxford Dictionary of

Twentieth Century Quotations

Edited by **Elizabeth Knowles**

OXFORD
UNIVERSITY PRESS

OXFORD
UNIVERSITY PRESS

Great Clarendon Street, Oxford OX2 6DP

Oxford University Press is a department of the University of Oxford.
It furthers the University's objective of excellence in research, scholarship,
and education by publishing worldwide in
Oxford NewYork

Athens Auckland Bangkok Bogotá Buenos Aires Calcutta
CapeTown Chennai DaresSalaam Delhi Florence HongKong Istanbul
Karachi KualaLumpur Madrid Melbourne MexicoCity Mumbai
Nairobi Paris SãoPaulo Singapore Taipei Tokyo Toronto Warsaw
with associated companies in Berlin Ibadan

Published in the United States
by Oxford University Press Inc., New York

First published 1998
First published in USA 1999

British Library Cataloguing in Publication Data
Data available

Library of Congress Cataloging in Publication Data
The Oxford dictionary of twentieth century quotations /
edited by Elizabeth Knowles
Includes indexes.
1. Quotations.   I. Knowles, Elizabeth (Elizabeth M.)
PN6080.0955   1998   808.88'2—dc21   98-17511
ISBN 0-19-860103-4

10 9 8 7 6 5 4 3 2

Designed by Jane Stevenson
Typeset in Monotype Photina and Meta
by Interactive Services Ltd, Gloucester
Printed in Great Britain
on acid-free paper by
Biddles Ltd
Guildford and King's Lynn

Contents

Project Team

Managing Editor   Elizabeth Knowles

Senior Editor   Susan Ratcliffe

Index Editor   Christina Malkowska Zaba

Library Research   Ralph Bates
Marie G. Diaz

Reading Programme   Charlotte Graves Taylor
Jean Harker
Verity Mason
Penelope Newsome
Helen Rappaport

Data Capture   Sandra Vaughan

Proof-reading   Fabia Claris
Penny Trumble

We are grateful to Gerald Blick for additional research.

Introduction

The *Oxford Dictionary of Twentieth Century Quotations* brings together quotations crucial to a picture of the twentieth century, offering the reader an overview of the social, political, cultural, and scientific concerns of succeeding decades. 1914, the year of the outbreak of the First World War, is taken as the cultural watershed of the century; the book concentrates on writers who were alive in or after that year. All quotations are from the twentieth century; this gives an interesting perspective on a writer like Thomas Hardy who is thus represented by the poetry which was the chief literary form of his later work, rather than by the novels which he wrote in the nineteenth century.

The opportunity to chart some of the ebbs and flows of cultural change is one of the main pleasures of working on a book of this kind; another is to listen to the multiplicity of voices which contribute to this picture of the century. It is possible to see different forms of source becoming dominant. In the first half of the century the major sources of quotation came from the written word in poetry, plays, novels (Auden, Hardy, James, Kipling, Larkin, and Shaw all represent this tradition), or the spoken word through the medium of major speeches on formal occasions (Churchill, Lloyd George, and Roosevelt are examples here). Latterly however the possible canon has widened to include what might be thought of as more ephemeral material: soundbites, online sources, films, television, and advertisements.

A number of writers give their own view of the century, and of its key points. Virginia Woolf, for example, believes that the year which saw the death of Edward VII and the first Post-Impressionist Exhibition was of supreme cultural importance:

> On or about December 1910 human nature changed . . . All human relations shifted—those between masters and servants, husbands and wives, parents and children. And when human relations change there is at the same time a change in religion, conduct, politics, and literature.

D. H. Lawrence, on the other hand, thinks the key year came five years later: 'It was in 1915 the old world ended.' In a paper written just after the First World War Jan Christiaan Smuts sees the founding of the League of Nations as crucial, 'The tents have been struck, and the great caravan of humanity is once more on the march.'

The precise nature of the twentieth century is also widely commented on. To Derek Tangye, it 'decorates life like a Christmas cake, but . . . still cannot do anything about the basic ingredients.' The American historian Arthur Schlesinger has an ingenious speculation as to how those ingredients could have been changed:

> Suppose . . . that Lenin had died of typhus in Siberia in 1895
> and Hitler had been killed on the western front in 1916.
> What would the twentieth century have looked like now?

Others attempt to catch an identity by coining a phrase. 'It is a period between two wars—the long week-end it has been called,' says E. M. Forster of the interwar years. In the 1950s Evelyn Waugh, through the character of Gilbert Pinfold, sums up his view of modernity:

> He abhorred plastics, Picasso, sunbathing and jazz—
> everything in fact that had happened in his lifetime.

He would have disliked even more, had he lived to see it, the period summed up by Mary Quant, 'This latter half of the twentieth century belongs to Youth,' and by Tom Wolfe, 'We are now in the Me Decade.' Robert Hewison looks towards the millennium without much optimism; 'The end game of the 1990s promises neither nirvana nor Armageddon, but entropy'.

Although 1914 is taken as the watershed, there are of course events from before the First World War which echo down the century, such as the loss of the *Titanic* in 1912 ('We are putting passengers off in small boats' runs the last recorded message in the section for **Last words**), described by Hardy in his 1914 poem 'The Convergence of the Twain':

> And as the smart ship grew
> In stature, grace, and hue,
> In shadowy silent distance grew the Iceberg too.

The *Titanic* has given us an image of inescapable disaster, as in 'I'm not going to rearrange the furniture on the deck of the Titanic' (Gerald Ford's campaign manager in 1976, having lost five out of six primaries). Yet we are still in touch with the event itself; in 1997 the youngest survivor, Millvina Dean, was offered an iced drink while visiting the American house in which she and her family would have lived had her father not drowned in 1912: 'I can't bear iced drinks . . . the iceberg, you know. Perhaps some champagne.' In fact, as Pat Barker tells us, some events never move wholly into the past:

> The Somme is like the Holocaust. It revealed things about
> mankind that we cannot come to terms with and cannot
> forget. It can never become the past.

Most recently, the single event which has generated most questions is the death of Diana, Princess of Wales, the 'People's Princess' (popularized if not coined by Tony Blair), who according to her brother was by the time of her death 'the most hunted person of the modern age'.

Journalism as a field of activity is of course extremely productive of quotations; the popular press, particularly towards the end of the century, comes in for some harsh words. 'Dabbling their fingers in the stuff of other people's souls' (Lord McGregor), 'drinking in the last chance saloon' (David Mellor, in a somewhat premature judgement), 'When seagulls follow a trawler, it is because they think sardines will be thrown into the sea' (Eric Cantona), 'dogs of war' (Catherine Deneuve), 'blood on their hands' (Lord Spencer). But other voices speak up for the serious side of journalism. 'You can only love one war; afterward, I suppose, you do your duty' (Martha Gellhorn, on reporting the Spanish Civil War). 'Go to where the silence is and say something' advises Amy Goodman, accepting an award for her coverage of the 1991 massacre in East Timor. The power of the press in our century is further reflected in our section for **Newspaper headlines and leaders**: 'Gotcha!', 'It *is* a moral issue', 'Whose finger do you want on the trigger?', 'Winter of Discontent'.

The influence of developing technology is a constant theme, although many would agree with David Hockney that 'The thing with high-tech is that you always end up using scissors.' Genetic engineering is with us (James Watson suggests that one day a child born with genetic defects will 'sue its parents for being born'). In 1997 the ability of British geneticists to clone a lamb alarms the American politician John Marchi, 'We ought not to permit a cottage industry in the God business'. Randall E. Stross speaks up in the context of computing technology for Bill Gates, who 'embodies what was supposed to be impossible—the practical intellectual.'

Arthur Eddington's speculation in 1928, 'If an army of monkeys were strumming on typewriters they *might* write all the books in the British Museum', is tartly answered by Robert Wilensky nearly 70 years later:

> We've all heard that a million monkeys banging on a million
> typewriters will eventually reproduce the entire work of
> Shakespeare. Now, thanks to the Internet, we know this is
> not true.

And while the Internet is increasingly a fact of life for many people, Noam Chomsky reminds us that it is also 'an élite organization; most of the population of the world has never even made a phone call.' To Timothy Leary, on the other hand, 'The PC is the LSD of the 1990s'. Godfrey Smith, addressing a new grandchild, wishes, 'In a world full of audio visual marvels, may words matter to you and be full of magic.' It is salutary to be reminded, in the words of Michael Lynton, that,

> The book is the greatest interactive medium of all time. You
> can underline it, write in the margins, fold down a page, skip
> ahead. And you can take it anywhere.

Television ('The word is half Greek, half Latin. No good can come of it.'—C. P. Scott) has been another major twentieth century development. In Shimon Peres's view, it has 'made dictatorship impossible, but democracy unbearable'. The development of cable prompts a succinct summary from Kelvin Mackenzie, 'We are surfers' food.' Often the subject of criticism ('the malign accomplishments of television'—J. K. Galbraith, 'Television . . . thrives on unreason'—Robin Day, 'Stupidvision'—Polly Toynbee on daytime television), it receives a more balanced assessment from Clive James:

> Television is simultaneously blamed, often by the same
> people, for worsening the world and for being powerless to
> change it.

The world of sport, particularly football ('The beautiful game' to Pele, more serious than a matter of life and death to Bill Shankly) is well represented here.

Jimmy Connors ruefully contrasts playing in the American and British tennis championships: 'New Yorkers love it when you spill your guts out there. Spill your guts at Wimbledon and they make you clear it up.' Tom Stoppard, a cricket enthusiast, doubts his ability to enjoy baseball: 'I don't think I can be expected to take seriously any game which takes less than three days to reach its conclusion.'

Politicians, of course, are here in force, often giving their views from what Theodore Roosevelt calls his 'bully pulpit'. 'It is fun to be in the same decade as you,' cables Franklin Roosevelt, acknowledging Winston Churchill's congratulations on his sixtieth birthday. A more modern statesman looks forward to the next century: 'The policy of European integration is in reality a question of war and peace in the 21st century' (Helmut Kohl). Signing the Dayton Accord, the Bosnian President gives his bleak summary of what had been achieved: 'not . . . a just peace, but . . . more just than a continuation of war.' There are some disappointments: Deng Xiaoping fails to achieve his ambition 'to be around in 1997 to see with my own eyes Hong Kong's return to China.' Mary Robinson, however, can rightly celebrate the achievement of the women of Ireland in electing the first woman President of the Republic in 1990: 'Instead of rocking the cradle, they rocked the system.' The section for **Political slogans** runs from 'All the way with LBJ' and 'Ban the bomb' to 'Yes it hurt, yes it worked' and 'Yesterday's men (they failed before)'.

The electorate also have their voice; the cartoonist Mike Peters wonders,

> When I go into the voting booth, do I vote for . . . the best
> President? Or the slime bucket who'll make my life as a
> cartoonist wonderful?

Politicians' wives make their mark, if not necessarily from the 'white glove pulpit' envisaged by Nancy Reagan. 'The one thing I do not want to be called is First Lady. It sounds like a saddle horse' asserts Jacqueline Kennedy. 'I could have stayed home and baked cookies and had teas' says Hillary Clinton, insisting on her right to her own professional life. Barbara Bush, on the other hand, looks forward to a change of gender in the White House:

> Somewhere out in this audience may even be someone who
> will one day follow in my footsteps and preside over the White
> House as the President's spouse. I wish him well.

Edna Healey provides a notable personal assessment of Margaret Thatcher, 'She has no hinterland. In particular, she has no sense of history.'

One of the interests of a collection like this is to see views of a topic changing over a period of years. Thus in the entry for Robert McNamara we move from his 1964 statement on the Vietnam War, 'I don't object to it's being called McNamara's War . . . It is a very important war and I am pleased to be identified with it,' to his 1995 reassessment, 'We were wrong. We were terribly wrong.' Germaine Greer, in the mid 1980s, is seemingly dissatisfied with some of the results of her earlier efforts, 'I didn't fight to get women out from behind the vacuum cleaner to get them onto the board of Hoover.' David Bailey looks back detachedly at his success, 'I never cared for fashion much. Amusing little seams and witty pleats. It was the girls I liked.' On the other hand, Mary Quant, who once saw the end of the century as 'belonging to Youth', is encouraged by the present rather than the past:

> Being young is greatly overestimated . . . Any failure seems so
> total. Later on you realize you can have another go.

Catch-phrases and **Sayings and slogans** contribute to the sound of the twentieth century, and we have sections for both integrated in the main author sequence of the book. 'Evening, all,' is Sergeant Dixon's opening to *Dixon of Dock Green*, first spoken in 1956; a contrast to the 1990s aggression of 'I'm Bart Simpson: who the hell are you?' **Official advice** ranges from the earliest road safety slogan, 'Stop-look-and-listen' (current in the US from 1912), through the wartime admonitions, 'Careless talk costs lives,' 'Dig for victory,' 'Make do and mend,' to current concerns: 'Don't die of ignorance,' 'Slip, slap, slop.' The question put to civil servants planning to travel home for Christmas in 1939 is, 'Is your journey *really* necessary?'; in 1996 the 'Gardener's Water Code' suggests persuasively, 'Tradition dictates that we have a lawn—but do we really need one?' Perhaps, looking at the plethora of advice, we can only conclude with *The X Files* that 'The truth is out there,' while remembering hopefully with the British National Lottery that 'It could be you.'

'Wars and rumours of wars' echo through the century. 'The lamps are going out all over Europe,' says Lord Grey in 1914. 'This is not a peace treaty, it is an armistice for twenty years,' is Foch's assessment of the Versailles Treaty in 1919. In 1936 the Spanish Civil War erupted, and many British and American writers went to support the embattled Republic against the insurgents and the 'fifth column' of General Mola (although the story of the advice given by the Communist Harry Pollitt to Stephen Spender, 'Go to Spain and get killed. The movement needs a Byron,' is probably apocryphal). The Second World War (especially in such Churchillian phrases as 'their finest hour' and 'fight on the beaches'), Vietnam (of which Muhammad Ali declared, 'I ain't got no quarrel with the Viet Cong'), the Falklands ('a fight between two bald men over a comb', to quote Jorge Luis Borges's application of a proverbial phrase), and the Gulf War (in which 'the mother of battles,' threatened by Saddam Hussein, added a new phrase to the language) are all to be found within these pages.

The more mundane concerns of ordinary life are of course also here, with many contributors speaking feelingly on the subject of food and drink. Compton Mackenzie criticizes a traditional tea:

> You are offered a piece of bread and butter that feels like a
> damp handkerchief and sometimes, when cucumber is added,
> like a wet one.

Peter Fleming, writing from Yunnanfu on an evening when he has eaten a Chinese dinner at six followed by a French dinner at nine, complains of feeling 'the sharks' fins navigating unhappily in the burgundy.' Virginia Woolf, wrestling with wartime rations, prepares to cook 'Haddock and sausage meat'. Nearer our own time, food is more consciously associated with health. Diana, Princess of Wales, comments on the temporary effects of 'bingeing' when suffering from bulimia, 'It gives you a feeling of comfort . . . like having a pair of arms around you.' Joan Bakewell takes a breezy approach to current dietary concerns, 'I'm afraid I'm addicted to fat and love British beef,' while Marianne Jean-Baptiste sees an essential cultural change, 'The national dish is no longer fish and chips, it's curry.'

Advertisements and films are major sources for quotations, and we thus have sections for **Advertising slogans** ('an ace caff with quite a nice museum attached', 'beans meanz Heinz', 'Go to work on an egg', 'It's good to talk', 'Stop me and buy one', 'Tell Sid') and **Film lines** ('E.T. phone home', 'Go ahead, make my day', 'May the force be with you').

One of the features of popular culture is that quoted material is often modified by the quoter. We have brought together in one section the best-known **Misquotations** of the century, from 'Beam me up, Scotty', and 'Crisis? What crisis?', through 'Play it again, Sam', to 'the white heat of technology', and 'Why don't you come up and see me sometime?'

In compiling this text we have drawn on the substantial resources of Oxford Quotations Dictionaries: our existing published texts, and our growing bank of new quotations. Fed by our reading programme, this is constantly enhanced by the generosity of those who write to us with questions, comments, and suggestions; a practice which we hope will long continue. Among those who have contributed to our resources and replied to questions, thanks are especially due to Archie Burnett, Antony Jay, Peter Kemp, Nigel Rees, Ned Sherrin, and Hilary Spurling. Particular help with this book is also warmly and gratefully acknowledged: Peter Hennessy was kind enough to read and comment on an earlier draft of the text, and Bernard O'Donoghue gave valuable advice as to the poetry content. Rexton Bunnett provided the background history of Herbert Farjeon's 'I've danced with a man who's danced with a girl.' Colleagues in the Dictionary Department have, as always, supplied us with quotations that they have come across. We hope that not only our contributors, but all those who read and use the book, will be rewarded by some of the pleasure and interest that the editorial staff have felt in working on it.

ELIZABETH KNOWLES

Oxford 1998

How to Use the Dictionary

The sequence of entries is by alphabetical order of author, usually by surname but with occasional exceptions such as members of royal families (e.g. **Diana, Princess of Wales** and **Elizabeth II**), and Popes (**John Paul II**), or authors known by a pseudonym ('**Saki**'). In general authors' names are given in the form by which they are best known, so that we have **Harold Macmillan** (not Lord Stockton), **Tony Blair** (not Anthony Charles Lynton Blair), **Iris Murdoch** (not Jean Iris Murdoch), and **H. G. Wells** (not Herbert George Wells). **Anonymous** quotations are included under that heading, or in one of the special category sections (see below).

Author names are followed by dates of birth and death (where known) and brief descriptions; where appropriate, cross-references are then given to quotations about that author elsewhere in the text (*on Capote: see* **Vidal** 317:15). Cross-references are also made to other entries in which the author appears, e.g. '*see also* **Epitaphs** 105:7' and '*see also* **Lennon and McCartney**'. Within each author entry, quotations are separated by literary form (novels, plays, poems: see further below) and within each group arranged by alphabetical order of title, 'a' and 'the' being ignored. Foreign-language text is given if it is felt that the quotation is familiar in the language of origin ('*Vorsprung durch Technik*').

Quotations from diaries, letters, and speeches are given in chronological order and usually follow the literary or published works quoted, with the form for which the author is best known taking precedence. Thus in the case of political figures, speeches appear first, just as poetry quotations precede those in prose for poets, and poetry quotations come second for an author regarded primarily as a novelist.

Quotations from secondary sources such as biographies and other writers' works come at the end of the entry. Quotations to which a date in the author's lifetime can be assigned are arranged in chronological order, in sequence with diary entries, letters, and speeches. Attributed quotations which cannot be so dated are arranged in alphabetical order of quotation text.

Within the alphabetical sequence there are a number of special category entries: **Advertising slogans**, **Catch-phrases**, **Epitaphs**, **Film lines**, **Film titles**, **Last words**, **Misquotations**, **Newspaper headlines and leaders**, **Official advice**, **Political slogans**, **Sayings and slogans**, and **Telegrams**. Quotations in these sections are arranged alphabetically according to the first word of the quotation (ignoring 'a' and 'the').

Contextual information regarded as essential to a full appreciation of the quotation precedes the text in an italicized note; information seen as providing useful amplification follows in an italicized note. Each quotation is accompanied by a bibliographical note as to the source from which the quotation is taken; titles and dates of publication are given, but full finding references are not. Titles of published volumes (*Autumn Journal* by Louis MacNeice and *Long Walk to Freedom* by Nelson Mandela) appear in italics; titles of short stories and poems not published as volumes in their own right, and individual song titles, are given in roman type inside inverted commas ('Big Yellow Taxi' by Joni Mitchell and 'A Call' by Seamus Heaney).

Cross-references to specific quotations are used to direct the reader to another related item. In each case a reference is given to an author's name or to the title of the special category entry, followed by the page number and then the unique quotation number on that page ('see **Film lines** 110:9' and 'cf. **Reagan** 262:4'). The use of 'see' indicates that following up the cross-reference will supply essential information; 'cf.' indicates information that will amplify what is already given. In some cases, a quotation dating from before 1900 constitutes a direct source; when this happens, the source quotation is given directly below the quotation to which it relates. Authors who have their own entries are typographically distinguished by the use of bold ('*of Peter* **Cook**', '*by Mae* **West**') in context or source notes.

Indexes

Keyword Index

The most significant words from each quotation appear in the keyword index, allowing individual quotations to be traced. Both the keywords and the entries following each keyword, including those in foreign languages, are in strict alphabetical order. Singular and plural nouns (with their possessive forms) are grouped separately. References are to the author's name (often in abbreviated form, as AUNG for Aung San Suu Kyi) followed by the page number and the number of the unique quotation on the page. Thus AUNG 19:18 means quotation number 19 on page 18, in the entry for Aung San Suu Kyi.

Thematic Index

In addition, a selection of quotations on designated subjects can be traced through the thematic index. Each subject heading is followed by a short line from each of the quotations on the theme. References are to the author's name and page and quotation number, as in the keyword index.

Diane Abbott 1953–
British Labour politician

1 Being an MP is the sort of job all
working-class parents want for their
children—clean, indoors and no heavy
lifting.
   in *Independent* 18 January 1994

George Abbott 1887–1995
American director, producer, and dramatist

2 If you want to be adored by your peers
and have standing ovations wherever
you go—live to be over ninety.
   in *The Times* 2 February 1995; obituary

Dannie Abse 1923–
Welsh-born doctor and poet

3 I know the colour rose, and it is lovely,
But not when it ripens in a tumour;
And healing greens, leaves and grass, so
   springlike
In limbs that fester are not springlike.
   'Pathology of Colours' (1968)

Bella Abzug 1920–98
American politician

4 Richard Nixon impeached himself. He
gave us Gerald Ford as his revenge.
   in *Rolling Stone*; Linda Botts *Loose Talk* (1980)

Goodman Ace 1899–1982
American humorist

5 TV—a clever contraction derived from
the words Terrible Vaudeville . . . we call
it a medium because nothing's well done.
   letter, to Groucho Marx, in *The Groucho Letters*
   (1967)

Chinua Achebe 1930–
Nigerian novelist

6 In such a regime, I say, you died a good
death if your life had inspired someone to
come forward and shoot your murderer
in the chest—without asking to be paid.
   A Man of the People (1966)

Dean Acheson 1893–1971
American statesman, Secretary of State
1949–53

7 I will undoubtedly have to seek what is
happily known as gainful employment,
which I am glad to say does not describe
holding public office.
   in *Time* 22 December 1952

8 Great Britain has lost an empire and has
not yet found a role.
   speech at the Military Academy, West Point, 5
   December 1962

9 A memorandum is written not to inform
the reader but to protect the writer.
   in *Wall Street Journal* 8 September 1977

Giuseppe Adami 1878–1946 and Renato Simoni 1875–1952

10 *Nessun dorma.*
None shall sleep.
   Turandot (1926 opera, music by Puccini)
   closing lines (after Gozzi's drama, 1762)

Douglas Adams 1952–
English science fiction writer

11 Don't panic.
   The Hitch Hiker's Guide to the Galaxy (1979)
   preface

12 The Answer to the Great Question Of . . .
Life, the Universe and Everything . . . [is]
Forty-two.
   The Hitch Hiker's Guide to the Galaxy (1979)

Franklin P. Adams 1881–1960
American journalist and humorist

13 Years ago we discovered the exact point,
the dead centre of middle age. It occurs
when you are too young to take up golf
and too old to rush up to the net.
   Nods and Becks (1944)

14 Elections are won by men and women
chiefly because most people vote against
somebody rather than for somebody.
   Nods and Becks (1944); cf. **Fields** 108:12

Gerry Adams 1948–

Northern Irish politician; President of Sinn Fein

1 It might or might not be right to kill, but sometimes it is necessary.
   view of the protagonist in a short story; *Before the Dawn* (1996)

Harold Adamson 1906–80

American songwriter

2 Comin' in on a wing and a pray'r.
   derived from the contemporary comment of a war pilot, speaking from a disabled plane to ground control
   title of song (1943)

Alfred Adler 1870–1937

Austrian psychologist and psychiatrist

3 The truth is often a terrible weapon of aggression. It is possible to lie, and even to murder, for the truth.
   The Problems of Neurosis (1929)

Polly Adler 1900–62

American writer

4 A house is not a home.
   title of book (1954)

Theodor Adorno 1903–69

German philosopher, sociologist, and musicologist

5 It is barbarous to write a poem after Auschwitz.
   I. Buruma *Wages of Guilt* (1994)

■ Advertising slogans

see box opposite

Æ (George William Russell) 1867–1935

Irish poet and essayist

6 In ancient shadows and twilights
Where childhood had strayed,
The world's great sorrows were born
And its heroes were made.
In the lost boyhood of Judas
Christ was betrayed.
   'Germinal' (1931)

Herbert Agar 1897–1980

American poet and writer

7 The truth which makes men free is for the most part the truth which men prefer not to hear.
   A Time for Greatness (1942); see below

   And ye shall know the truth, and the truth shall make you free.
   Bible St John

James Agate 1877–1947

British drama critic and novelist

8 Shaw's plays are the price we pay for Shaw's prefaces.
   diary, 10 March 1933

9 My mind is not a bed to be made and re-made.
   diary, 9 June 1943

10 A professional is a man who can do his job when he doesn't feel like it. An amateur is a man who can't do his job when he does feel like it.
   diary, 19 July 1945

11 Diary-writing isn't wholly good for one . . . It leads to living for one's diary instead of living for the fun of living as ordinary people do.
   letter, 7 December 1946

Spiro T. Agnew 1918–96

American Republican politician

12 I didn't say I wouldn't go into ghetto areas. I've been in many of them and to some extent I would have to say this: If you've seen one city slum you've seen them all.
   in *Detroit Free Press* 19 October 1968; see below

Advertising slogans

1 Access—your flexible friend.
Access credit card, 1981 onwards

2 An ace caff with quite a nice museum attached.
the Victoria and Albert Museum, February 1989

3 All human life is there.
the *News of the World*; used by Maurice Smelt in the late 1950s; see below

Cats and monkeys—monkeys and cats—all human life is there!
Henry James *The Madonna of the Future* (1879)

4 American Express? . . . That'll do nicely, sir.
American Express credit card, 1970s

5 And all because the lady loves Milk Tray.
Cadbury's Milk Tray chocolates, 1968 onwards

6 Australians wouldn't give a XXXX for anything else.
Castlemaine lager, 1986 onwards

7 Beanz meanz Heinz.
Heinz baked beans, c.1967; coined by Maurice Drake

8 Bovril . . . Prevents that sinking feeling.
Bovril, 1920; coined by H. H. Harris (1920)

9 . . . But I know a man who can.
Automobile Association, 1980s

10 Can you tell Stork from butter?
Stork margarine, from c.1956

11 Cool as a mountain stream.
Consulate menthol cigarettes, early 1960s onwards

12 A diamond is forever.
De Beers Consolidated Mines, 1940s onwards; coined by Frances Gerety; cf. **Loos** 194:7

13 Does she . . . or doesn't she?
Clairol hair colouring, 1950s

14 Don't be vague, ask for Haig.
Haig whisky, c.1936

15 Don't forget the fruit gums, Mum.
Rowntree's Fruit gums, 1958–61

16 Drinka Pinta Milka Day.
British Milk Marketing Board, 1958; coined by Bertrand Whitehead

17 Even your closest friends won't tell you.
Listerine mouthwash, US, in *Woman's Home Companion* November 1923

18 Full of Eastern promise.
Fry's Turkish Delight, 1950s onwards

19 Go to work on an egg.
British Egg Marketing Board, from 1957; perhaps written by Fay **Weldon** or Mary Gowing

20 Guinness is good for you.
reply universally given to researchers asking people why they drank Guinness
adopted by Oswald Greene, c.1929; cf. **Advertising slogans** 4:11

21 Happiness is a cigar called Hamlet.
Hamlet cigars; cf. **Ephron** 104:3, **Lennon** 187:13, **Schulz** 280:13

22 Have a break, have a Kit-Kat.
Rowntree's Kit-Kat, from c.1955

23 Heineken refreshes the parts other beers cannot reach.
Heineken lager, 1975 onwards; coined by Terry Lovelock

24 Horlicks guards against night starvation.
Horlicks malted milk drink, 1930s

25 If you want to get ahead, get a hat.
the Hat Council, 1965

26 I'm only here for the beer.
Double Diamond beer, 1971 onwards; coined by Ros Levenstein

27 It beats as it sweeps as it cleans.
Hoover vacuum cleaners, devised in 1919 by Gerald Page-Wood

28 It's finger lickin' good.
Kentucky fried chicken, from 1958

29 It's good to listen.
British Telecom, from 1997; cf. **Advertising slogans** 4:1

▶

▶ Advertising slogans continued

1 It's good to talk.
British Telecom, from 1994; cf. **Advertising slogans** 3:29

2 It's tingling fresh. It's fresh as ice.
Gibbs toothpaste; the first advertising slogan heard on British television, 22 September 1955

3 I was a seven-stone weakling.
Charles Atlas body-building, originally in US

4 Just when you thought it was safe to go back in the water.
publicity for *Jaws 2* (1978 film)

5 Keep that schoolgirl complexion.
Palmolive soap, from 1917; coined by Charles S. Pearce

6 Kills all known germs.
Domestos bleach, 1959

7 Let the train take the strain.
British Rail, 1970 onwards

8 Let your fingers do the walking.
Bell system Telephone Directory Yellow Pages, 1960s

9 A Mars a day helps you work, rest and play.
Mars bar, *c*.1960 onwards; coined by Norman Gaff (d. 1988)

10 The mint with the hole.
Life-Savers, US, 1920; and Rowntree's Polo mints, UK, from 1947

11 My Goodness, My Guinness.
Guinness stout, 1935; coined by Dicky Richards; cf. **Advertising slogans** 3:20

12 Never knowingly undersold.
motto of the John Lewis Partnership, from *c*.1920; coined by John Lewis (1885–1963)

13 Nice one, Cyril.
taken up by supporters of Cyril Knowles, Tottenham Hotspur footballer; the Spurs team later made a record featuring the line
Wonderloaf, 1972

14 No manager ever got fired for buying IBM.
IBM

15 Oxo gives a meal man-appeal.
Oxo beef extract, *c.* 1960

16 Persil washes whiter—and it shows.
Persil washing powder, 1970s

17 Put a tiger in your tank.
Esso petrol, 1964

18 Say it with flowers.
Society of American Florists, 1917; coined by Patrick O'Keefe (1872–1934)

19 Sch . . . you know who.
Schweppes mineral drinks, 1960s

20 Someone, somewhere, wants a letter from you.
British Post Office, 1960s

21 Stop me and buy one.
Wall's ice cream, from spring 1922; coined by Cecil Rodd

22 Tell Sid.
privatization of British Gas, 1986

23 Things go better with Coke.
Coca-Cola, 1963

24 Top people take *The Times*.
The Times newspaper, from January 1959

25 *Vorsprung durch Technik.*
Progress through technology.
Audi cars, from 1986

26 We are the Ovaltineys,
Little [*or* Happy] girls and boys.
'We are the Ovaltineys' (song from *c*.1935); Ovaltine drink

27 We're number two. We try harder.
Avis car rentals

28 We won't make a drama out of a crisis.
Commercial Union insurance

29 Where's the beef?
Wendy's Hamburgers, from January 1984; coined by Cliff Freeman; cf. **Mondale** 219:11

30 You're never alone with a Strand.
Strand cigarettes, 1960; coined by John May

▶▶ Spiro T. Agnew continued

See one promontory (said Socrates of old), one mountain, one sea, one river, and see all.

Robert Burton (1577–1640) *The Anatomy of Melancholy* (1621–51)

1 In the United States today, we have more than our share of the nattering nabobs of negativism.

speech in San Diego, 11 September 1970

Anna Akhmatova 1889–1966

Russian poet

2 It was a time when only the dead smiled, happy in their peace.

Requiem (1935–40)

3 Stars of death stood over us, and innocent Russia squirmed under the bloody boots, under the wheels of black Marias.

Requiem (1935–40)

4 They took you away at dawn, I walked after you as though you were being borne out, the children were crying in the dark room, the candle swam by the ikon-stand. The cold of the ikon on your lips. Death sweat on your brow . . . Do not forget! I will howl by the Kremlin towers like the wives of the Streltsy.

on the arrest of her friend N. N. Punin during the Stalinist purges

Requiem (1935–40)

5 In the young century's cool nursery, In its chequered silence, I was born.

'Willow' (1940)

Zoë Akins 1886–1958

6 The Greeks had a word for it.

title of play (1930)

Alain (Émile-Auguste Chartier) 1868–1951

French poet and philosopher

7 Nothing is more dangerous than an idea, when you have only one idea.

Propos sur la religion (1938)

Edward Albee 1928–

American dramatist

8 Who's afraid of Virginia Woolf?

title of play (1962); cf. **Churchill** 65:3

Richard Aldington 1892–1962

English poet, novelist, and biographer

9 Patriotism is a lively sense of collective responsibility. Nationalism is a silly cock crowing on its own dunghill.

The Colonel's Daughter (1931)

Brian Aldiss 1925–

English science fiction writer

10 Science Fiction is no more written for scientists than ghost stories are written for ghosts.

introduction to *Penguin Science Fiction* (1962)

11 Keep violence in the mind Where it belongs.

Barefoot in the Head (1969) 'Charteris'

Buzz Aldrin 1930–

American astronaut; second man on the moon

12 Beautiful! Beautiful! Magnificent desolation.

of the lunar landscape

on the first moon walk, 20 July 1969

Nelson Algren 1909–

American novelist

13 A walk on the wild side.

title of novel (1956)

14 Never play cards with a man called Doc. Never eat at a place called Mom's. Never

sleep with a woman whose troubles are worse than your own.
in *Newsweek* 2 July 1956

Muhammad Ali (Cassius Clay) 1942–

American boxer

1 I'm the greatest.
catch-phrase used from 1962, in *Louisville Times* 16 November 1962

2 Float like a butterfly, sting like a bee.
summary of his boxing strategy
G. Sullivan *Cassius Clay Story* (1964); probably originated by Drew 'Bundini' Brown

3 I ain't got no quarrel with the Viet Cong.
refusing to be drafted to fight in Vietnam
at a press conference in Miami, Florida, February 1966

Fred Allen 1894–1956

American humorist

4 California is a fine place to live—if you happen to be an orange.
in *American Magazine* December 1945

5 A celebrity is a person who works hard all his life to become well known, and then wears dark glasses to avoid being recognized.
Laurence J. Peter (ed.) *Quotations for our Time* (1977)

6 Committee—a group of men who individually can do nothing but as a group decide that nothing can be done.
attributed

Woody Allen 1935–

American film director, writer, and actor
on Allen: see **Farrow** 106:11

7 That [sex] was the most fun I ever had without laughing.
Annie Hall (1977 film, with Marshall Brickman)

8 Don't knock masturbation. It's sex with someone I love.
Annie Hall (1977 film, with Marshall Brickman)

9 Is sex dirty? Only if it's done right.
Everything You Always Wanted to Know about Sex (1972 film)

10 My brain? It's my second favourite organ.
Sleeper (1973 film, with Marshall Brickman)

11 Take the money and run.
title of film (1968)

12 It's not that I'm afraid to die. I just don't want to be there when it happens.
Death (1975)

13 More than any other time in history, mankind faces a crossroads. One path leads to despair and utter hopelessness. The other, to total extinction. Let us pray we have the wisdom to choose correctly.
Side Effects (1980) 'My Speech to the Graduates'

14 A fast word about oral contraception. I asked a girl to go to bed with me and she said 'no'.
at a nightclub in Chicago, March 1964, recorded on *Woody Allen Volume Two*

15 Not only is there no God, but try getting a plumber on weekends.
in *New Yorker* 27 December 1969 'My Philosophy'

16 If only God would give me some clear sign! Like making a large deposit in my name at a Swiss bank.
'Selections from the Allen Notebooks' in *New Yorker* 5 November 1973

17 On bisexuality: It immediately doubles your chances for a date on Saturday night.
in *New York Times* 1 December 1975

18 I don't want to achieve immortality through my work . . . I want to achieve it through not dying.
Eric Lax *Woody Allen and his Comedy* (1975)

19 I recently turned sixty. Practically a third of my life is over.
in *Observer* 'Sayings of the Week' 10 March 1996

Svetlana Alliluyeva 1925–

daughter of Joseph **Stalin**

20 He is gone, but his shadow still stands over all of us. It still dictates to us and we, very often, obey.
of her father, Joseph **Stalin**
Twenty Letters to a Friend (1967)

Robert Altman 1922–

American film director

1 What's a cult? It just means not enough people to make a minority.

in *Guardian* 11 April 1981

Lord Altrincham

see **John Grigg**

Luis Walter Alvarez 1911–88

American physicist

2 There is no democracy in physics. We can't say that some second-rate guy has as much right to opinion as Fermi.

D. S. Greenberg *The Politics of Pure Science* (1969)

Leo Amery 1873–1955

British Conservative politician

3 For twenty years he has held a season-ticket on the line of least resistance and has gone wherever the train of events has carried him, lucidly justifying his position at whatever point he has happened to find himself.

*on Herbert **Asquith***

in *Quarterly Review* July 1914

4 Speak for England.

to Arthur Greenwood in the House of Commons, 2 September 1939: see **Boothby** 41:8

5 I will quote certain other words. I do it with great reluctance, because I am speaking of those who are old friends and associates of mine, but they are words which, I think, are applicable to the present situation. This is what Cromwell said to the Long Parliament when he thought it was no longer fit to conduct the affairs of the nation: 'You have sat too long here for any good you have been doing. Depart, I say, and let us have done with you. In the name of God, go.'

speech, House of Commons, 7 May 1940; see below

You have sat too long here for any good you have been doing. Depart, I say, and let us have done with you. In the name of God, go!

Oliver Cromwell (1599–1658) addressing the Rump Parliament, 20 April 1653, oral tradition

Hardy Amies 1909–

English couturier

6 It is totally impossible to be well dressed in cheap shoes.

The Englishman's Suit (1994)

7 She is only 5ft 4in, and to make someone that height look regal is difficult. Fortunately she holds herself very well.

of the Queen

interview in *Sunday Telegraph* 9 February 1997

Kingsley Amis 1922–95

English novelist and poet

8 His mouth had been used as a latrine by some small creature of the night, and then as its mausoleum.

Lucky Jim (1953)

9 Alun's life was coming to consist more and more exclusively of being told at dictation speed what he knew.

The Old Devils (1986)

10 Outside every fat man there was an even fatter man trying to close in.

One Fat Englishman (1963); cf. **Orwell** 237:14

11 Should poets bicycle-pump the human heart
Or squash it flat?
Man's love is of man's life a thing apart;
Girls aren't like that.

'A Bookshop Idyll' (1956); see below

Man's love is of man's life a thing apart,
'Tis woman's whole existence.

Lord Byron (1788–1824) *Don Juan* (1819–24)

12 Women are really much nicer than men:
No wonder we like them.

'A Bookshop Idyll' (1956)

13 Death has got something to be said for it:
There's no need to get out of bed for it.

'Delivery Guaranteed' (1979)

1 The women of that ever-fresh terrain,
The night after tonight.
'A Dream of Fair Women' (1956)

2 The delusion that there are thousands of
young people about who are capable of
benefiting from university training, but
have somehow failed to find their way
there, is . . . a necessary component of
the expansionist case . . . More will mean
worse.
in *Encounter* July 1960

3 If you can't annoy somebody with what
you write, I think there's little point in
writing.
in *Radio Times* 1 May 1971

4 A bad review may spoil your breakfast
but you shouldn't allow it to spoil your
lunch.
Giles Gordon *Aren't We Due a Royalty
Statement?* (1993); attributed

5 No pleasure is worth giving up for the
sake of two more years in a geriatric
home in Weston-super-Mare.
in *The Times* 21 June 1994; attributed

Martin Amis 1949–

English novelist

6 To be more interested in the writer than
the writing is just eternal human
vulgarity.
on BBC2 *Bookmark*, 9 March 1996

7 You are living in a land you no longer
recognize. You don't know the language.
on his 'cataclysmic mid-life crisis'
in *Times* 21 August 1997

Maxwell Anderson 1888–1959

American dramatist

8 But it's a long, long while
From May to December;
And the days grow short
When you reach September.
'September Song' (1938 song)

Maxwell Anderson 1888–1959 and Lawrence Stallings 1894–1968

American dramatists

9 What price glory?
title of play (1924)

Robert Anderson 1917–

American dramatist

10 Tea and sympathy.
title of play (1957)

Maya Angelou 1928–

American novelist and poet

11 In all my work what I try to say is that as
human beings we are more alike than we
are unalike.
interview in *New York Times* 20 January 1993

Noel Annan 1916–

English historian and writer

12 The day of the jewelled epigram is passed
and, whether one likes it or not, one is
moving into the stern puritanical era of
the four-letter word.
in the House of Lords, 1966; George Greenfield
Scribblers for Bread (1989)

13 The cardinal virtue was no longer to love
one's country. It was to feel compassion
for one's fellow men and women.
of his own generation
Our Age (1990)

Anonymous

see also **Advertising slogans, Newspaper
headlines, Official advice, Political
slogans, Sayings and slogans**

14 An abomination unto the Lord, but a
very present help in time of trouble.
definition of a lie
an amalgamation of the *Bible* Proverbs 12.22
and Psalms 46.1, often attributed to Adlai
Stevenson

15 All human beings are born free and equal
in dignity and rights.
Universal Declaration of Human Rights (1948)
article 1

1 Anyone here been raped and speaks English?

shouted by a British TV reporter in a crowd of Belgian civilians waiting to be airlifted out of the Belgian Congo, c.1960

   Edward Behr *Anyone Here been Raped and Speaks English?* (1981)

2 *Arbeit macht frei.*

Work liberates.

   words inscribed on the gates of Dachau concentration camp, 1933, and subsequently on those of Auschwitz

3 The best defence against the atom bomb is not to be there when it goes off.

   contributor to *British Army Journal*, in *Observer* 20 February 1949

4 Bigamy is having one husband too many. Monogamy is the same.

   Erica Jong *Fear of Flying* (1973) epigraph

5 A bigger bang for a buck.

   description of Charles E. **Wilson**'s defence policy, in *Newsweek* 22 March 1954

6 Can't act. Slightly bald. Also dances.

   studio official's comment on Fred Astaire
   Bob Thomas *Astaire* (1985)

7 Cathedral time is five minutes later than standard time.

   order of service leaflet, Christ Church Cathedral, Oxford, 1990s

8 A community in which power, wealth and opportunity are in the hands of the many not the few, where the rights we enjoy reflect the duties we owe . . . in which the enterprise of the market and the rigour of competition are joined with the forces of partnership and cooperation.

   new Clause Four of the Labour Party constitution, passed at a special conference 29 April 1995; cf. **Anonymous** 11:14

9 Do not stand at my grave and weep:
I am not there. I do not sleep.
I am a thousand winds that blow.
I am the diamond glints on snow.
I am the gentle autumn's rain.
When you awaken in the morning's hush,
I am the swift uplifting rush
Of quiet birds in circled flight.
I am the soft stars that shine at night.
Do not stand at my grave and cry;

I am not there, I did not die.

quoted in letter left by British soldier Stephen Cummins when killed by the IRA, March 1989
   origin uncertain; attributed to various authors

10 Expletive deleted.

*frequent editorial amendment of transcripts of Richard **Nixon** during the Watergate inquiry*
   Submission of Recorded Presidential Conversations . . . by President Richard M. Nixon 30 April 1974

11 Exterminate . . . the treacherous English, walk over General French's contemptible little army.

*annexe to British Expeditionary Force Routine Orders, 24 September 1914 (allegedly quoting Kaiser **Wilhelm II** but probably fabricated by the British)*
   A. Ponsonby *Falsehood in Wartime* (1928)

12 Faster than a speeding bullet! . . . Look! Up in the sky! It's a bird! It's a plane! It's Superman! Yes, it's Superman! . . . who—disguised as Clark Kent, mild-mannered reporter for a great metropolitan newspaper—fights a never ending battle for truth, justice and the American way!

   Superman (US radio show, 1940 onwards) preamble

13 God is not dead but alive and working on a much less ambitious project.

   graffito quoted in *Guardian* 26 November 1975; cf. **Anonymous** 10:5

14 Hark the herald angels sing
Mrs Simpson's pinched our king.

   children's rhyme at the time of the Abdication in 1936, quoted in letter from Clement Attlee, 26 December 1938; see below

   Hark! the herald-angels sing
   Glory to the new born king.

   alteration, in George Whitefield's *Hymns for Social Worship* (1753), of Charles Wesley's 'Hymn for Christmas' (1739)

15 Here we go, here we go, here we go.

   song sung especially by football supporters, 1980s

16 I don't like the family Stein!
There is Gert, there is Ep, there is Ein.
Gert's writings are punk,
Ep's statues are junk,
Nor can anyone understand Ein.

   1920s rhyme; R. Graves and A. Hodge *The Long Weekend* (1940)

1 If I should die and leave you here awhile,
Be not like others, sore undone, who keep
Long vigils by the silent dust, and weep.
For my sake—turn again to life and smile,
Nerving thy heart and trembling hand to do
Something to comfort other hearts than thine.
Complete those dear unfinished tasks of mine
And I, perchance, may therein comfort you.

read at the funeral of **Diana**, Princess of Wales; variously attributed (origins discussed in Nigel Rees 'Quote . . . Unquote' Newsletter October 1997)

2 If you really want to make a million . . . the quickest way is to start your own religion.

previously attributed to L. Ron Hubbard 1911–86 in B. Corydon and L. Ron Hubbard Jr. *L. Ron Hubbard* (1987), but attribution subsequently rejected by L. Ron Hubbard Jr., who also dissociated himself from this book

3 The iron lady.

*name given to Margaret **Thatcher**, then Leader of the Opposition, by the Soviet defence ministry newspaper* Red Star, *which accused her of trying to revive the cold war*

in *Sunday Times* 25 January 1976

4 It became necessary to destroy the town to save it.

statement issued by US Army, referring to Ben Tre in Vietnam; in *New York Times* 8 February 1968

5 Jacques Brel is alive and well and living in Paris.

title of musical entertainment (1968–72) which triggered numerous imitations; cf. **Anonymous** 9:13

6 *Jedem das Seine.*
To each his own.

often quoted as 'Everyone gets what he deserves'
inscription on the gate of Buchenwald concentration camp, *c.* 1937; cf. **Bold** 41:1

7 *Je suis Marxiste—tendance Groucho.*
I am a Marxist—of the Groucho tendency.

slogan found at Nanterre in Paris, 1968

8 Kilroy was here.

graffito popularized by American servicemen in the Second World War

9 Liberty is always unfinished business.

title of 36th Annual Report of the American Civil Liberties Union, 1 July 1955–30 June 1956

10 Life is a sexually transmitted disease.

graffito found on the London Underground; D. J. Enright (ed.) *Faber Book of Fevers and Frets* (1989)

11 Lloyd George knew my father,
My father knew Lloyd George.

sung to the tune of 'Onward, Christian Soldiers'; possibly by Tommy Rhys Roberts (1910–75)

12 Mademoiselle from Armenteers,
Hasn't been kissed for forty years,
Hinky, dinky, parley-voo.

song of the First World War, variously attributed to Edward Rowland and to Harry Carlton

13 The noise, my dear! And the people!
of the retreat from Dunkirk, May 1940
A. Rhodes *Sword of Bone* (1942)

14 No more Latin, no more French,
No more sitting on a hard board bench.
No more beetles in my tea
Making googly eyes at me;
No more spiders in my bath
Trying hard to make me laugh.

children's rhyme for the end of school term, in Iona and Peter Opie *Lore and Language of Schoolchildren* (1959); variants include 'No more Latin, no more Greek, / No more cares to make me squeak'

15 Nostalgia isn't what it used to be.

graffito, taken as title of book by Simone Signoret, 1978

16 Not so much a programme, more a way of life!

title of satirical BBC television series, 1964

17 O Death, where is thy sting-a-ling-a-ling,
O grave, thy victory?
The bells of Hell go ting-a-ling-a-ling
For you but not for me.

'For You But Not For Me' sung by British soldiers during the First World War; see below

O death, where is thy sting? O grave, where is thy victory?
Bible I Corinthians

1 Once again we stop the mighty roar of London's traffic.
> *In Town Tonight* (BBC radio series, 1933–60) preamble

2 The [*or* A] quick brown fox jumps over the lazy dog.
> used by keyboarders to ensure that all letters of the alphabet are functioning; R. H. Templeton Jr. *The Quick Brown Fox* (1945)

3 The rabbit has a charming face:
Its private life is a disgrace.
I really dare not name to you
The awful things that rabbits do.
> 'The Rabbit' in *The Week-End Book* (1925)

4 Science finds, industry applies, man conforms.
> subtitle of guidebook to 1933 Chicago World's Fair

5 See the happy moron,
He doesn't give a damn,
I wish I were a moron,
My God! perhaps I am!
> in *Eugenics Review* July 1929

6 She was poor but she was honest
Victim of a rich man's game.
First he loved her, then he left her,
And she lost her maiden name . . .

It's the same the whole world over,
It's the poor wot gets the blame,
It's the rich wot gets the gravy.
Ain't it all a bleedin' shame?
> 'She was Poor but she was Honest' sung by British soldiers in the First World War

7 The singer not the song.
> from a West Indian calypso; title of a novel (1959) by Audrey Erskine Lindop

8 Some television programmes are so much chewing gum for the eyes.
> *John Mason Brown quoting a friend of his young son, interview, 28 July 1955*
> J. B. Simpson *Best Quotes* (1957)

9 There is so much good in the worst of us,
And so much bad in the best of us,
That it hardly becomes any of us
To talk about the rest of us.
> attributed, among others, to E. W. Hoch (1849–1945) on the grounds of it having appeared in his Kansas publication, the *Marion Record*, though in fact disclaimed by him ('behoves' sometimes substituted for 'becomes')

10 There was a young lady of Riga
Who went for a ride on a tiger;
They returned from the ride
With the lady inside,
And a smile on the face of the tiger.
> R. L. Green (ed.) *A Century of Humorous Verse* (1959)

11 [This film] is so cryptic as to be almost meaningless. If there is a meaning, it is doubtless objectionable.
> *banning Jean **Cocteau**'s film* The Seashell and the Clergyman *(1929)*
> The British Board of Film Censors, in J. C. Robertson *Hidden Cinema* (1989)

12 This is a rotten argument, but it should be good enough for their lordships on a hot summer afternoon.
> *annotation to a ministerial brief, said to have been read out inadvertently in the House of Lords*
> Lord Home *The Way the Wind Blows* (1976)

13 Though I yield to no one in my admiration for Mr Coolidge, I do wish he did not look as if he had been weaned on a pickle.
> anonymous remark, in Alice Roosevelt Longworth *Crowded Hours* (1933)

14 To secure for the workers by hand or by brain the full fruits of their industry and the most equitable distribution thereof that may be possible upon the basis of the common ownership of the means of production, distribution, and exchange.
> Clause Four of the Labour Party's Constitution of 1918 (revised 1929); the commitment to common ownership of services was largely removed in 1995; cf. **Anonymous** 9:8

15 We do not need a loose cannon like her.
> *an unidentified junior minister commenting on the intervention into the campaign against landmines by **Diana**, Princess of Wales*
> in *Times* 15 January 1997

16 We're here
Because
We're here.
> sung to the tune of 'Auld Lang Syne' by British soldiers in the First World War

17 When cult is added to power
even the chairman makes mistakes
Xiaoping suffered criticism (in the
    Cultural Revolution)
and the people raised him up.
Now he represents bureaucracy
and official corruption.

The country does not want him,
the people do not want him.
*poem put up in the Forbidden City in 1989,
shortly before the tanks moved into Tiananmen
Square*
> quoted in obituary of **Deng** Xiaoping, in
> *Guardian* 20 February 1997

1 Winston is back.
*Board of Admiralty signal to the Fleet on Winston
Churchill's reappointment as First Sea Lord, 3
September 1939*
> Martin Gilbert *Winston S. Churchill* (1976)

2 You should make a point of trying every
experience once, excepting incest and
folk-dancing.
> Arnold Bax (1883–1953), quoting 'a
> sympathetic Scot' in *Farewell My Youth* (1943)

Jean Anouilh 1910–87
French dramatist

3 The spring is wound up tight. It will
uncoil of itself. That is what is so
convenient in tragedy. The least little
turn of the wrist will do the job.
Anything will set it going.
> *Antigone* (1944, tr. L. Galantiere, 1957)

4 Tragedy is clean, it is restful, it is
flawless.
> *Antigone* (1944, tr. L. Galantiere, 1957)

5 Dying is nothing. So start by living. It's
less fun and it lasts longer.
> *Roméo et Jeannette* (1946)

6 There will always be a lost dog
somewhere that will prevent me from
being happy.
> *La Sauvage* (1938)

Guillaume Apollinaire
1880–1918
French poet
*on Apollinaire: see **Logue** 193:6*

7 *Les souvenirs sont cors de chasse
Dont meurt le bruit parmi le vent.*

Memories are hunting horns
Whose sound dies on the wind.
> 'Cors de Chasse' (1912)

8 When man wanted to make a machine
that would walk he created the wheel,
which does not resemble a leg.
> *Les Mamelles de Tirésias* (1918)

9 One can't carry one's father's corpse
about everywhere.
> *Les peintres cubistes* (1965)

Louis Aragon 1897–1982
French poet, essayist, and novelist

10 *Ô mois des floraisons mois des
      métamorphoses
Mai qui fut sans nuage et Juin poignardé
Je n'oublierai jamais les lilas ni les roses
Ni ceux que le printemps dans ses plis a
      gardé.*

O month of flowerings, month of
      metamorphoses,
May without cloud and June that was
      stabbed,
I shall never forget the lilac and the roses
Nor those whom spring has kept in its
      folds.
> 'Les lilas et les roses' (1940)

Diane Arbus 1923–71
American photographer

11 A photograph is a secret about a secret.
The more it tells you the less you know.
> Patricia Bosworth *Diane Arbus: a Biography*
> (1985)

Robert Ardrey 1908–80
American dramatist and evolutionist

12 Not in innocence, and not in Asia, was
mankind born.
> *African Genesis* (1961)

Hannah Arendt 1906–75
American political philosopher

13 It was as though in those last minutes he
[Eichmann] was summing up the lessons
that this long course in human
wickedness had taught us—the lesson of
the fearsome, word-and-thought-defying
banality of evil.
> *Eichmann in Jerusalem* (1963)

1 The most radical revolutionary will become a conservative on the day after the revolution.

in *New Yorker* 12 September 1970

2 Under conditions of tyranny it is far easier to act than to think.

W. H. Auden *A Certain World* (1970)

Louis Armstrong 1901–71

American singer and jazz musician
see also **Misquotations** 218:9

3 All music is folk music, I ain't never heard no horse sing a song.

in *New York Times* 7 July 1971

Neil Armstrong 1930–

American astronaut; first man on the moon

4 That's one small step for a man, one giant leap for mankind.

landing on the moon; as the craft touched down, Armstrong had radioed 'Houston, Tranquillity Base here. The Eagle has landed'

in *New York Times* 21 July 1969; interference in transmission obliterated 'a'

Robert Armstrong 1927–

British civil servant, Head of the Civil Service, 1981–7

5 It contains a misleading impression, not a lie. It was being economical with the truth.

*referring to a letter during the 'Spycatcher' trial, Supreme Court, New South Wales; the expression 'over-economical with the truth' had been applied to Harold **Wilson** by the Earl of Dalkeith in the House of Commons, 4 July 1968*

in *Daily Telegraph* 19 November 1986; see below; cf. **Clark** 69:14

As in the exercise of all the virtues, there is an economy of truth.

Edmund Burke (1729–97) *Two letters on Proposals for Peace* (1796)

William Armstrong 1915–80

British civil servant, Head of the Civil Service 1968–74

6 The business of the Civil Service is the orderly management of decline.

in 1973: Peter Hennessy *Whitehall* (1990)

Roseanne Arnold 1953–

American comedian

7 I used to think I was an interesting person, but I must tell you how sobering a thought it is to realize your life's story fills about thirty-five pages and you have, actually, not much to say.

Roseanne (1990)

8 If I were Her what would really piss me off the worst is that they cannot even get My gender right for Christsakes.

Roseanne (1990)

L. A. Artsimovich 1909–73

9 The joke definition according to which 'Science is the best way of satisfying the curiosity of individuals at government expense' is more or less correct.

in *Novy Mir* January 1967

George Asaf 1880–1951

British songwriter

10 What's the use of worrying?
It never was worth while,
So, pack up your troubles in your old kit-bag,
And smile, smile, smile.

'Pack up your Troubles' (1915 song)

Isaac Asimov 1920–92

Russian-born biochemist and science fiction writer

11 The three fundamental Rules of Robotics . . . One, a robot may not injure a human being, or, through inaction, allow a human being to come to harm . . . Two . . . a robot must obey the orders given it by human beings except where such orders would conflict with the First Law . . . three, a robot must protect its own existence as long as such protection does not conflict with the First or Second Laws.

I, Robot (1950) 'Runaround'

12 A public that does not understand how science works can all too easily fall prey to those ignoramuses like Senator

Proxmire who make fun of what they do not understand, or to the sloganeers who proclaim scientists to be the mercenary warriors of today, and the tools of the military.

in *Nature* 10 November 1963

1 Science fiction writers foresee the inevitable, and although problems and catastrophes may be inevitable, solutions are not.

'How Easy to See the Future' in *Natural History* April 1975

2 When, however, the lay public rallies around an idea that is denounced by distinguished but elderly scientists and supports that idea with great fervour and emotion—the distinguished but elderly scientists are then, after all, probably right.

corollary to Arthur C. **Clarke**'s law; cf. **Clarke** 70:5
Arthur C. Clarke 'Asimov's Corollary' in K. Frazier (ed.) *Paranormal Borderlands of Science* (1981)

3 The first law of dietetics seems to be: if it tastes good, it's bad for you.

attributed

Cynthia Asquith 1887–1960

English writer

4 I am beginning to rub my eyes at the prospect of peace . . . One will at last fully recognize that the dead are not only dead for the duration of the war.

diary, 7 October 1918

Herbert Henry Asquith
1852–1928

British Liberal statesman; Prime Minister, 1908–16; husband of Margot **Asquith**
on Asquith: see **Amery** 7:3; see also **Telegrams** 305:4

5 We had better wait and see.

referring, in 1910, to the rumour that the House of Lords was to be flooded with new Liberal peers to ensure the passage of the Finance Bill
Roy Jenkins *Asquith* (1964)

6 Youth would be an ideal state if it came a little later in life.

in *Observer* 15 April 1923

7 It is fitting that we should have buried the Unknown Prime Minister [Bonar Law] by the side of the Unknown Soldier.

R. Blake *The Unknown Prime Minister* (1955)

8 [The War Office kept three sets of figures:] one to mislead the public, another to mislead the Cabinet, and the third to mislead itself.

A. Horne *Price of Glory* (1962)

Margot Asquith 1864–1945

British political hostess; wife of Herbert **Asquith**
on Asquith: see **Parker** 243:10

9 I may be wrong, but I have never found deserting friends conciliates enemies.

Lay Sermons (1927)

10 Kitchener is a great poster.

More Memories (1933)

11 I always knew the living talked rot, but it's nothing to the rot the dead talk.

on spiritualism
Henry 'Chips' Channon, diary, 20 December 1937

12 He can't see a belt without hitting below it.

of **Lloyd George**
in *Listener* 11 June 1953

13 She tells enough white lies to ice a wedding cake.

of Lady Desborough
in *Listener* 11 June 1953

14 The *t* is silent, as in *Harlow*.

to Jean Harlow, who had mispronounced her name
T. S. Matthews *Great Tom* (1973)

Nancy Astor 1879–1964

American-born British Conservative politician
on Astor: see **Churchill** 69:2

15 One reason why I don't drink is because I wish to know when I am having a good time.

in *Christian Herald* June 1960

16 I married beneath me, all women do.

in *Dictionary of National Biography* (1917–)

Brooks Atkinson 1894–1984

American journalist and critic

1 After each war there is a little less democracy to save.

Once Around the Sun (1951) 7 January

2 In every age 'the good old days' were a myth. No one ever thought they were good at the time. For every age has consisted of crises that seemed intolerable to the people who lived through them.

Once Around the Sun (1951) 8 February

David Attenborough 1926–

English naturalist and broadcaster

3 I'm not over-fond of animals. I am merely astounded by them.

in *Independent* 14 January 1995

Clement Attlee 1883–1967

British Labour statesman; Prime Minister, 1945–51
on Attlee: see **Churchill** 67:15, 69:6, **de Gaulle** 86:13, **Jay** 160:3, **Nicolson** 230:8, **Orwell** 239:10

4 I must remind the Right Honourable Gentleman that a monologue is not a decision.

*to Winston **Churchill**, who had complained that a matter had been raised several times in Cabinet, c.1945*

Francis Williams *A Prime Minister Remembers* (1961)

5 The voice we heard was that of Mr Churchill but the mind was that of Lord Beaverbrook.

*on **Churchill**'s accusing the Labour Party of planning to set up a Gestapo*

speech on radio, 5 June 1945

6 You have no right whatever to speak on behalf of the Government. Foreign Affairs are in the capable hands of Ernest Bevin . . . I can assure you there is widespread resentment in the Party at your activities and a period of silence on your part would be welcome.

letter to Harold Laski, 20 August 1945

7 I should be a sad subject for any publicity expert. I have none of the qualities which create publicity.

Harold Nicolson diary, 14 January 1949

8 Few thought he was even a starter
There were many who thought
  themselves smarter
But he ended PM
CH and OM
An earl and a knight of the garter.

describing himself

letter to Tom Attlee, 8 April 1956

9 [Russian Communism is] the illegitimate child of Karl Marx and Catherine the Great.

speech at Aarhus University, 11 April 1956

10 Democracy means government by discussion, but it is only effective if you can stop people talking.

speech at Oxford, 14 June 1957

11 Often the 'experts' make the worst possible Ministers in their own fields. In this country we prefer rule by amateurs.

speech at Oxford, 14 June 1957

12 If the King asks you to form a Government you say 'Yes' or 'No', not 'I'll let you know later!'

Kenneth Harris *Attlee* (1982)

W. H. Auden 1907–73

English poet
on Auden: see **Orwell** 239:2, **Spender** 294:2

13 Sob, heavy world,
Sob as you spin
Mantled in mist, remote from the happy.

The Age of Anxiety (1947) pt. 4 'The Dirge'

14 Blessed Cecilia, appear in visions
To all musicians, appear and inspire:
Translated Daughter, come down and
  startle
Composing mortals with immortal fire.

Anthem for St Cecilia's Day (1941) pt. 1; set to music by Benjamin Britten, to whom it was dedicated, as *Hymn to St Cecilia* op. 27 (1942)

15 I'll love you, dear, I'll love you
Till China and Africa meet
And the river jumps over the mountain
And the salmon sing in the street,

I'll love you till the ocean

Is folded and hung up to dry
And the seven stars go squawking
Like geese about the sky.
'As I Walked Out One Evening' (1940)

1 The glacier knocks in the cupboard,
The desert sighs in the bed,
And the crack in the tea-cup opens
A lane to the land of the dead.
'As I Walked Out One Evening' (1940)

2 At the far end of the enormous room
An orchestra is playing to the rich.
'At the far end of the enormous room' (1933)

3 The desires of the heart are as crooked as
corkscrews
Not to be born is the best for man.
'Death's Echo' (1937); see below

Not to be born is, past all prizing, best.
Sophocles (c.496–406 BC) Oedipus Coloneus
(translation by R. C. Jebb); cf. **Yeats** 337:14

4 Happy the hare at morning, for she
cannot read
The Hunter's waking thoughts.
Dog beneath the Skin (with Christopher
Isherwood, 1935)

5 To save your world you asked this man
to die:
Would this man, could he see you now,
ask why?
'Epitaph for the Unknown Soldier' (1955)

6 When he laughed, respectable senators
burst with laughter,
And when he cried the little children died
in the streets.
'Epitaph on a Tyrant' (1940); see below

As long as he lived, he was the
guiding-star of a whole brave nation,
and when he died the little children
cried in the streets.
of William of Orange; John Lothrop Motley
(1814–77) *The Rise of the Dutch Republic*
(1856)

7 Altogether elsewhere, vast
Herds of reindeer move across
Miles and miles of golden moss,
Silently and very fast.
'The Fall of Rome' (1951)

8 He was my North, my South, my East
and West,
My working week and my Sunday rest,
My noon, my midnight, my talk, my
song;

I thought that love would last for ever: I
was wrong.
'Funeral Blues' (1936)

9 To us he is no more a person
now but a whole climate of opinion.
'In Memory of Sigmund Freud' (1940)

10 You were silly like us; your gift survived
it all:
The parish of rich women, physical
decay,
Yourself. Mad Ireland hurt you into
poetry.
'In Memory of W. B. Yeats' (1940)

11 For poetry makes nothing happen: it
survives
In the valley of its saying where
executives
Would never want to tamper.
'In Memory of W. B. Yeats' (1940)

12 Earth, receive an honoured guest:
William Yeats is laid to rest.
Let the Irish vessel lie
Emptied of its poetry.
'In Memory of W. B. Yeats' (1940)

13 In the nightmare of the dark
All the dogs of Europe bark,
And the living nations wait,
Each sequestered in its hate;

Intellectual disgrace
Stares from every human face,
And the seas of pity lie
Locked and frozen in each eye.
'In Memory of W. B. Yeats' (1940)

14 Time that with this strange excuse
Pardoned Kipling and his views,
And will pardon Paul Claudel,
Pardons him for writing well.
'In Memory of W. B. Yeats' (1940)

15 Look, stranger, at this island now.
title of poem (1936)

16 Lay your sleeping head, my love,
Human on my faithless arm.
'Lullaby' (1940)

17 But in my arms till break of day
Let the living creature lie,
Mortal, guilty, but to me
The entirely beautiful.
'Lullaby' (1940)

1 About suffering they were never wrong,
  The Old Masters: how well they
      understood
  Its human position; how it takes place
  While someone else is eating or opening
      a window or just walking dully along.
      'Musée des Beaux Arts' (1940)

2 Even the dreadful martyrdom must run
      its course
  Anyhow in a corner, some untidy spot
  Where the dogs go on with their doggy
      life and the torturer's horse
  Scratches its innocent behind on a tree.
      'Musée des Beaux Arts' (1940)

3 To the man-in-the-street, who, I'm sorry
      to say,
  Is a keen observer of life,
  The word 'Intellectual' suggests straight
      away
  A man who's untrue to his wife.
      New Year Letter (1941)

4 This is the Night Mail crossing the
      Border,
  Bringing the cheque and the postal order,
  Letters for the rich, letters for the poor,
  The shop at the corner, the girl next
      door.
      'Night Mail' (1936)

5 And make us as Newton was, who in his
      garden watching
  The apple falling towards England,
      became aware
  Between himself and her of an eternal tie.
      'O Love, the interest itself' (1936)

6 Private faces in public places
  Are wiser and nicer
  Than public faces in private places.
      Orators (1932) dedication

7 Out on the lawn I lie in bed,
  Vega conspicuous overhead.
      'Out on the lawn I lie in bed' (1936)

8 Some thirty inches from my nose
  The frontier of my Person goes,
  And all the untilled air between
  Is private *pagus* or demesne.
  Stranger, unless with bedroom eyes
  I beckon you to fraternize,
  Beware of rudely crossing it:
  I have no gun, but I can spit.
      'Prologue: the Birth of Architecture' (1966)

9 I and the public know
  What all schoolchildren learn,
  Those to whom evil is done
  Do evil in return.
      'September 1, 1939' (1940)

10 All I have is a voice
   To undo the folded lie,
   The romantic lie in the brain
   Of the sensual man-in-the-street
   And the lie of Authority
   Whose buildings grope the sky:
   There is no such thing as the State
   And no one exists alone;
   Hunger allows no choice
   To the citizen or the police;
   We must love one another or die.
      'September 1, 1939' (1940)

11 A shilling life will give you all the facts.
      title of poem (1936)

12 Each year brings new problems of Form
      and Content,
   new foes to tug with: at Twenty I tried to
   vex my elders, past Sixty it's the young
      whom
   I hope to bother.
      'Shorts I' (1969)

13 A poet's hope: to be,
   like some valley cheese,
   local, but prized elsewhere.
      'Shorts II' (1976)

14 Sir, no man's enemy.
      title of poem (1930)

15 Harrow the house of the dead; look
      shining at
   New styles of architecture, a change of
      heart.
      'Sir, No Man's Enemy' (1930)

16 To-morrow for the young the poets
      exploding like bombs,
   The walks by the lake, the weeks of
      perfect communion;
   To-morrow the bicycle races
   Through the suburbs on summer
      evenings: but to-day the struggle.
      'Spain 1937' (1937)

17 History to the defeated
   May say Alas but cannot help or pardon.
      'Spain 1937' (1937)

18 To ask the hard question is simple.
      title of poem (1933)

1 Was he free? Was he happy? The
question is absurd:
Had anything been wrong, we should
certainly have heard.
'The Unknown Citizen' (1940)

2 Of course, Behaviourism 'works'. So does
torture. Give me a no-nonsense, down-
to-earth behaviourist, a few drugs, and
simple electrical appliances, and in six
months I will have him reciting the
Athanasian Creed in public.
A Certain World (1970) 'Behaviourism'

3 It is a sad fact about our culture that a
poet can earn much more money writing
or talking about his art than he can by
practising it.
The Dyer's Hand (1963) foreword

4 Man is a history-making creature who
can neither repeat his past nor leave it
behind.
The Dyer's Hand (1963) 'D. H. Lawrence'

5 Almost all of our relationships begin and
most of them continue as forms of
mutual exploitation, a mental or physical
barter, to be terminated when one or
both parties run out of goods.
The Dyer's Hand (1963) 'Hic et Ille'

6 When I find myself in the company of
scientists, I feel like a shabby curate who
has strayed by mistake into a drawing
room full of dukes.
The Dyer's Hand (1963) 'The Poet and the City'

7 Some books are undeservedly forgotten;
none are undeservedly remembered.
The Dyer's Hand (1963) 'Reading'

8 One cannot review a bad book without
showing off.
The Dyer's Hand (1963) 'Reading'

9 It takes little talent to see clearly what
lies under one's nose, a good deal of it to
know in which direction to point that
organ.
The Dyer's Hand (1963) 'Writing'

10 Routine, in an intelligent man, is a sign
of ambition.
'The Life of That-There Poet' (1958)

11 What do you think about England, this
country of ours where nobody is well?
The Orators (1932) 'Address for a Prize-Day'

12 Art is born of humiliation.
Stephen Spender *World Within World* (1951)

13 Geniuses are the luckiest of mortals
because what they must do is the same
as what they most want to do.
Dag Hammarskjöld *Markings* (1964) foreword

14 LSD? Nothing much happened, but I did
get the distinct impression that some
birds were trying to communicate with
me.
George Plimpton (ed.) *The Writer's Chapbook*
(1989)

15 My face looks like a wedding-cake left out
in the rain.
Humphrey Carpenter *W. H. Auden* (1981)

16 Nothing I wrote in the thirties saved one
Jew from Auschwitz.
attributed

Stan Augarten

17 Computers are composed of nothing
more than logic gates stretched out to the
horizon in a vast numerical irrigation
system.
*State of the Art: A Photographic History of the
Integrated Circuit* (1983)

Aung San Suu Kyi 1945–

Burmese political leader

18 It's very different from living in academia
in Oxford. We called someone vicious in
the *Times Literary Supplement*. We didn't
know what vicious was.
on returning to Burma (Myanmar)
in *Observer* 25 September 1988 'Sayings of the
Week'

19 In societies where men are truly
confident of their own worth, women are
not merely tolerated but valued.
videotape speech at NGO Forum on Women,
China, early September 1995

George Austin 1931–

British Anglican clergyman, Archdeacon of
York

20 We're now paying the price for the
Eighties and Lord Runcie's kind of effete,
liberal elitism amongst bishops which

also spread into the theological colleges. There is now a big gap between the faith of those in the pulpit and those in the pews.

in *Guardian* 7 February 1997

Revd W. Awdry 1911–97
English writer of children's books

1 You've a lot to learn about trucks, little Thomas. They are silly things and must be kept in their place. After pushing them about here for a few weeks you'll know almost as much about them as Edward. Then you'll be a Really Useful Engine.

Thomas the Tank Engine (1946)

2 I should like my epitaph to say, 'He helped people see God in the ordinary things of life, and he made children laugh.'

in *Independent* 'Obituaries' 22 March 1997

Alan Ayckbourn 1939–
English dramatist

3 My mother used to say, Delia, if s-e-x ever rears its ugly head, close your eyes before you see the rest of it.

Bedroom Farce (1978)

4 This place, you tell them you're interested in the arts, you get messages of sympathy.

Chorus of Disapproval (1986)

A. J. Ayer 1910–89
English philosopher
on Ayer: see **Priestley** 256:14

5 No moral system can rest solely on authority.

Humanist Outlook (1968) introduction

6 It seems that I have spent my entire time trying to make life more rational and that it was all wasted effort.

in *Observer* 17 August 1986

7 If I had been someone not very clever, I would have done an easier job like publishing. That's the easiest job I can think of.

attributed

8 Why should you mind being wrong if someone can show you that you are?

attributed

Pam Ayres 1947–
English writer of humorous verse

9 Medicinal discovery,
It moves in mighty leaps,
It leapt straight past the common cold
And gave it us for keeps.

'Oh no, I got a cold' (1976)

Isaac Babel 1894–1940
Russian short-story writer

10 A phrase is born into the world both good and bad at the same time. The secret lies in a slight, an almost invisible twist. The lever should rest in your hand, getting warm, and you can only turn it once, not twice.

Guy de Maupassant (1932)

11 No iron can stab the heart with such force as a full stop put just at the right place.

Guy de Maupassant (1932)

12 Now a man talks frankly only with his wife, at night, with the blanket over his head.

remark *c.*1937; Solomon Volkov *St Petersburg* (1996)

13 They didn't let me finish.

to his wife, on the day of his arrest by the NKVD, 16 May 1939

Lauren Bacall 1924–
American actress
see also **Film lines** 111:7

14 I think your whole life shows in your face and you should be proud of that.

in *Daily Telegraph* 2 March 1988

Lord Baden-Powell
1857–1941
English soldier; founder of the Boy Scouts, 1908

15 The scouts' motto is founded on my initials, it is: BE PREPARED.

Scouting for Boys (1908)

David Bailey 1938–

English photographer
see also **Sayings and slogans** 278:22

1 It takes a lot of imagination to be a good
  photographer. You need less imagination
  to be a painter, because you can invent
  things. But in photography everything is
  so ordinary; it takes a lot of looking
  before you learn to see the ordinary.
    interview in *The Face* December 1984

2 I never cared for fashion much. Amusing
  little seams and witty little pleats. It was
  the girls I liked.
    in *Independent* 5 November 1990

3 Women love scallywags, but some marry
  them and then try to make them wear a
  blazer.
    in *Mail on Sunday* 16 February 1997 'Quotes of
    the Week'

Beryl Bainbridge 1933–

English novelist

4 Nobody ever, unless he is very wicked,
  deliberately tries to hurt anybody. It's
  just that men cannot help not loving you
  or behaving badly.
    interview in *Daily Telegraph* 10 September
    1996

5 Women are programmed to love
  completely, and men are programmed to
  spread it around.
    interview in *Daily Telegraph* 10 September
    1996

Bruce Bairnsfather 1888–1959

British cartoonist

6 Well, if you knows of a better 'ole, go to
  it.
    Fragments from France (1915) cartoon caption

Joan Bakewell 1933–

English broadcaster and writer
on Bakewell: see **Muir** 225:4

7 I'm afraid I'm addicted to fat and love
  British beef. BSE holds no terror for me

because . . . I am as likely to get it as win
the National Lottery.
  on her main difficulty in following a healthy diet
    in *Independent* 30 August 1997 'Quote
    Unquote'

James Baldwin 1924–87

American novelist and essayist

8 Children have never been very good at
  listening to their elders, but they have
  never failed to imitate them. They must,
  they have no other models.
    Nobody Knows My Name (1961) 'Fifth Avenue,
    Uptown: a letter from Harlem'

9 Anyone who has ever struggled with
  poverty knows how extremely expensive
  it is to be poor.
    Nobody Knows My Name (1961) 'Fifth Avenue,
    Uptown: a letter from Harlem'

10 At the root of the American Negro
   problem is the necessity of the American
   white man to find a way of living with
   the Negro in order to be able to live with
   himself.
    in *Harper's Magazine* October 1953 'Stranger in
    a Village'

11 Money, it turned out, was exactly like
   sex, you thought of nothing else if you
   didn't have it and thought of other things
   if you did.
    in *Esquire* May 1961 'Black Boy looks at the
    White Boy'

12 If the concept of God has any validity or
   any use, it can only be to make us larger,
   freer, and more loving. If God cannot do
   this, then it is time we got rid of Him.
    in *New Yorker* 17 November 1962 'Down at the
    Cross'

13 It comes as a great shock around the age
   of 5, 6 or 7 to discover that the flag to
   which you have pledged allegiance,
   along with everybody else, has not
   pledged allegiance to you. It comes as a
   great shock to see Gary Cooper killing off
   the Indians and, although you are
   rooting for Gary Cooper, that the Indians
   are you.
    *speaking for the proposition that 'The American
    Dream is at the expense of the American Negro'*
      speech at the Cambridge Union, England, 17
      February 1965

1 If they take you in the morning, they will
be coming for us that night.

> in *New York Review of Books* 7 January 1971
> 'Open Letter to my Sister, Angela Davis'

Stanley Baldwin 1867–1947

British Conservative statesman; Prime
Minister, 1923–4, 1924–9, 1935–7
on Baldwin: see **Beaverbrook** 25:6,
Churchill 67:12, **Curzon** 82:11; *see also*
Kipling 175:17, **Misquotations** 218:11

2 They [parliament] are a lot of hard-faced
men who look as if they had done very
well out of the war.

> J. M. Keynes *Economic Consequences of the
> Peace* (1919)

3 A platitude is simply a truth repeated
until people get tired of hearing it.

> speech, House of Commons, 29 May 1924

4 There are three classes which need
sanctuary more than others—birds, wild
flowers, and Prime Ministers.

> in *Observer* 24 May 1925

5 'Safety first' does not mean a smug self-
satisfaction with everything as it is. It is a
warning to all persons who are going to
cross a road in dangerous circumstances.

> in *The Times* 21 May 1929

6 Had the employers of past generations all
of them dealt fairly with their men there
would have been no unions.

> speech in Birmingham, 14 January 1931

7 The bomber will always get through. The
only defence is in offence, which means
that you have to kill more women and
children more quickly than the enemy if
you want to save yourselves.

> speech, House of Commons, 10 November
> 1932

8 Since the day of the air, the old frontiers
are gone. When you think of the defence
of England you no longer think of the
chalk cliffs of Dover; you think of the
Rhine. That is where our frontier lies.

> speech, House of Commons, 30 July 1934

9 This House today is a theatre which is
being watched by the whole world. Let us
conduct ourselves with that dignity
which His Majesty is showing in this
hour of his trial.

> speech, House of Commons, 10 December
> 1936

10 Do not run up your nose dead against
the Pope or the NUM!

> Lord Butler *The Art of Memory* (1982); cf.
> **Macmillan** 202:7

Arthur James Balfour
1848–1930

British Conservative statesman; Prime
Minister, 1902–5
on Balfour: see **Churchill** 68:3, **Lloyd
George** 192:5, 192:12

11 His Majesty's Government view with
favour the establishment in Palestine of a
national home for the Jewish people, and
will use their best endeavours to facilitate
the achievement of this object, it being
clearly understood that nothing shall be
done which may prejudice the civil and
religious rights of existing non-Jewish
communities in Palestine, or the rights
and political status enjoyed by Jews in
any other country.

> *known as the 'Balfour Declaration'; cf.* **Weizmann**
> 322:8
>
> letter to Lord Rothschild 2 November 1917

12 Christianity, of course . . . but why
journalism?

> *replying to the remark that 'all the faults of the
> age come from Christianity and journalism'*
> Margot Asquith *Autobiography* (1920)

13 Biography should be written by an acute
enemy.

> in *Observer* 30 January 1927

14 [Our] whole political machinery presupposes a people so fundamentally at
one that they can safely afford to bicker.

> introduction to Walter Bagehot *The English
> Constitution* (World Classics ed., 1928)

15 I thought he was a young man of
promise, but it appears he is a young
man of promises.

> *of* **Churchill**
> Winston Churchill *My Early Life* (1930)

J. G. Ballard 1930–

British writer

1 Everything is becoming science fiction.
From the margins of an almost invisible
literature has sprung the intact reality of
the 20th century.
'Fictions of Every Kind' in *Books and Bookmen*
February 1971

2 A car crash harnesses elements of
eroticism, aggression, desire, speed,
drama, kinaesthetic factors, the stylizing
of motion, consumer goods, status—all
these in one event. I myself see the car
crash as a tremendous sexual event
really: a liberation of human and
machine libido (if there is such a thing).
interview in *Penthouse* September 1970

3 Some refer to it as a cultural Chernobyl. I
think of it as a cultural Stalingrad.
of Euro Disney
in *Daily Telegraph* 2 July 1994; cf. **Mnouchkine**
219:9

Whitney Balliett 1926–

American writer

4 A critic is a bundle of biases held loosely
together by a sense of taste.
Dinosaurs in the Morning (1962) introductory
note

5 The sound of surprise.
title of book on jazz (1959)

Pierre Balmain 1914–82

French couturier

6 The trick of wearing mink is to look as
though you were wearing a cloth coat.
The trick of wearing a cloth coat is to
look as though you are wearing mink.
in *Observer* 25 December 1955

E. Digby Baltzell 1915–

7 There is a crisis in American leadership
in the middle of the twentieth century
that is partly due, I think, to the
declining authority of an establishment
which is now based on an increasingly
castelike White-Anglo Saxon-Protestant
(WASP) upper class.
The Protestant Establishment (1964)

Lord Bancroft 1922–96

British civil servant; Head of the Civil
Service 1978–81

8 Conviction politicians, certainly:
conviction civil servants, no.
'Whitehall: Some Personal Reflections', lecture
at the London School of Economics 1
December 1983

Tallulah Bankhead 1903–68

American actress
on Bankhead: see **Campbell** 52:6

9 Cocaine habit-forming? Of course not. I
ought to know. I've been using it for
years.
Tallulah (1952)

10 There is less in this than meets the eye.
describing a revival of Maeterlinck's play
Aglavaine and Selysette
Alexander Woollcott *Shouts and Murmurs*
(1922)

11 I'm as pure as the driven slush.
in *Saturday Evening Post* 12 April 1947

12 I read Shakespeare and the Bible and I
can shoot dice. That's what I call a
liberal education.
attributed

13 They used to shoot her through gauze.
You should shoot me through linoleum.
on Shirley Temple
attributed

Imamu Amiri Baraka 1934–

American poet and dramatist

14 God has been replaced, as he has all over
the West, with respectability and air
conditioning.
Midstream (1963)

15 A rich man told me recently that a liberal
is a man who tells other people what to
do with their money.
in *Kulchur* Spring 1962 'Tokenism'

16 A man is either free or he is not. There
cannot be any apprenticeship for
freedom.
in *Kulchur* Spring 1962 'Tokenism'

Pat Barker 1943–

English novelist

1 The Somme is like the Holocaust. It revealed things about mankind that we cannot come to terms with and cannot forget. It can never become the past.
on winning the Booker Prize 1995
  in *Athens News* 9 November 1995

Ronnie Barker 1929–

English comedian

2 The marvellous thing about a joke with a double meaning is that it can only mean one thing.
Sauce (1977)

Frederick R. Barnard

3 One picture is worth ten thousand words.
in *Printers' Ink* 10 March 1927

Clive Barnes 1927–

British journalist and critic

4 This is the kind of show to give pornography a dirty name.
of Oh, Calcutta!
  in *New York Times* 18 June 1969

Julian Barnes 1946–

English novelist

5 Do not imagine that Art is something which is designed to give gentle uplift and self-confidence. Art is not a *brassière*. At least, not in the English sense. But do not forget that *brassière* is the French for life-jacket.
Flaubert's Parrot (1984)

6 Books say: she did this because. Life says: she did this. Books are where things are explained to you; life is where things aren't.
Flaubert's Parrot (1984)

7 Does history repeat itself, the first time as tragedy, the second time as farce? No, that's too grand, too considered a process. History just burps, and we taste again that raw-onion sandwich it swallowed centuries ago.
A History of the World in 10½ Chapters (1989); see below

Hegel says somewhere that all great events and personalities in world history reappear in one fashion or another. He forgot to add: the first time as tragedy, the second as farce.
Karl Marx (1818–83) *The Eighteenth Brumaire of Louis Bonaparte* (1852)

8 Love is just a system for getting someone to call you darling after sex.
Talking It Over (1991)

J. M. Barrie 1860–1937

Scottish writer and dramatist
on Barrie: see **Guedalla** 135:3, **Hope** 152:2

9 His lordship may compel us to be equal upstairs, but there will never be equality in the servants' hall.
The Admirable Crichton (performed 1902)

10 When the first baby laughed for the first time, the laugh broke into a thousand pieces and they all went skipping about, and that was the beginning of fairies.
Peter Pan (1928)

11 Every time a child says 'I don't believe in fairies' there is a little fairy somewhere that falls down dead.
Peter Pan (1928)

12 To die will be an awfully big adventure.
Peter Pan (1928); cf. **Last words** 183:3

13 Do you believe in fairies? Say quick that you believe! If you believe, clap your hands!
Peter Pan (1928)

14 Charm . . . it's a sort of bloom on a woman. If you have it, you don't need to have anything else; and if you don't have it, it doesn't much matter what else you have.
What Every Woman Knows (performed 1908)

15 There are few more impressive sights in the world than a Scotsman on the make.
What Every Woman Knows (performed 1908)

16 The tragedy of a man who has found himself out.
What Every Woman Knows (performed 1908)

1 Someone said that God gave us memory
so that we might have roses in December.
Rectorial Address at St Andrew's, 3 May 1922

2 Courage is the thing. All goes if courage
goes!
Rectorial Address at St Andrews, 3 May 1922;
cf. **Lewis** 190:7

Ethel Barrymore 1879–1959
American actress

3 For an actress to be a success, she must
have the face of a Venus, the brains of a
Minerva, the grace of Terpsichore, the
memory of a Macaulay, the figure of
Juno, and the hide of a rhinoceros.
George Jean Nathan *The Theatre in the Fifties*
(1953)

John Barrymore 1882–1942
American actor

4 My only regret in the theatre is that I
could never sit out front and watch me.
Eddie Cantor *The Way I See It* (1959)

Karl Barth 1886–1968
Swiss Protestant theologian

5 Men have never been good, they are not
good and they never will be good.
Christian Community (1948)

6 He will not be like an ant which has
foreseen everything in advance, but like
a child in a forest, or on Christmas Eve:
one who is always rightly astonished by
events, by the encounters and
experiences which overtake him.
of the justified man
Church Dogmatics (1936)

7 It may be that when the angels go about
their task of praising God, they play only
Bach. I am sure, however, that when
they are together *en famille*, they play
Mozart.
Wolfgang Amadeus Mozart (1956)

Roland Barthes 1915–80
French writer and critic

8 I think that cars today are almost the
exact equivalent of the great Gothic
cathedrals: I mean the supreme creation
of an era, conceived with passion by
unknown artists, and consumed in image
if not in usage by a whole population
which appropriates them as a purely
magical object.
Mythologies (1957) 'La nouvelle Citroën'

Bernard Baruch 1870–1965
American financier and presidential adviser

9 We are today in the midst of a cold war.
*'cold war' was suggested to him by H. B. **Swope**,
former editor of the* New York World
speech to South Carolina Legislature 16 April
1947

10 To me old age is always fifteen years
older than I am.
in *Newsweek* 29 August 1955

11 Vote for the man who promises least;
he'll be the least disappointing.
M. Berger *New York* (1960)

12 A political leader must keep looking over
his shoulder all the time to see if the boys
are still there. If they aren't still there,
he's no longer a political leader.
in *New York Times* 21 June 1965

Jacques Barzun 1907–
American historian and educationist

13 If it were possible to talk to the unborn,
one could never explain to them how it
feels to be alive, for life is washed in the
speechless real.
The House of Intellect (1959)

Jean Baudrillard 1929–
French sociologist and cultural critic

14 The microwave, the waste disposal, the
orgasmic elasticity of the carpets, this soft
resort-style civilization irresistibly evokes
the end of the world.
America (1986)

Lord Bauer 1915–

British economist

1 Foreign aid is a system of taking money from poor people in rich countries and giving it to rich people in poor countries.
   attributed; not recollected by Lord Bauer but not repudiated by him

L. Frank Baum

see **Harburg** 138:13

Beverley Baxter 1891–1964

British journalist and Conservative politician

2 Beaverbrook is so pleased to be in the Government that he is like the town tart who has finally married the Mayor!
   Henry ('Chips') Channon diary, 12 June 1940

John Bayley 1925–

English academic

3 It is rather like falling from stair to stair in a series of bumps.
   *on his wife Iris **Murdoch**'s progressive loss of memory from Alzheimer's disease*
   in an interview, *Daily Telegraph* 8 February 1997

Lord Beatty 1871–1936

British Admiral of the Fleet, 1916–19

4 There's something wrong with our bloody ships today.
   at the Battle of Jutland, 1916
   Winston Churchill *The World Crisis 1916–1918* (1927)

Lord Beaverbrook 1879–1964

Canadian-born British newspaper proprietor and Conservative politician
*on Beaverbrook: see **Attlee** 15:5, **Baxter** 25:2, **Kipling** 175:17, **Muggeridge** 224:10, **Wells** 323:14*

5 Our cock won't fight.
   *of **Edward VIII**, during the abdication crisis of 1936*
   F. Donaldson *Edward VIII* (1974)

6 The Flying Scotsman is no less splendid a sight when it travels north to Edinburgh than when it travels south to London. Mr Baldwin denouncing sanctions was as dignified as Mr Baldwin imposing them.
   in *Daily Express* 29 May 1937

7 Now who is responsible for this work of development on which so much depends? To whom must the praise be given? To the boys in the back rooms. They do not sit in the limelight. But they are the men who do the work.
   in *Listener* 27 March 1941

8 I ran the paper [*Daily Express*] purely for propaganda, and with no other purpose.
   evidence to Royal Commission on the Press, 18 March 1948, in A. J. P. Taylor *Beaverbrook* (1972)

9 With the publication of his Private Papers in 1952, he committed suicide 25 years after his death.
   *of Earl **Haig***
   Men and Power (1956)

10 Often undecided whether to desert a sinking ship for one that might not float, he would make up his mind to sit on the wharf for a day.
   *of Lord **Curzon***
   Men and Power (1956)

11 [He] did not seem to care which way he travelled providing he was in the driver's seat.
   *of **Lloyd George***
   The Decline and Fall of Lloyd George (1963)

Samuel Beckett 1906–89

Irish dramatist, novelist, and poet

12 It is suicide to be abroad. But what is it to be at home, Mr Tyler, what is it to be at home? A lingering dissolution.
   All That Fall (1957)

13 We could have saved sixpence. We have saved fivepence. (*Pause*) But at what cost?
   All That Fall (1957)

14 CLOV: Do you believe in the life to come?
   HAMM: Mine was always that.
   Endgame (1958)

15 Where I am, I don't know, I'll never know, in the silence you don't know, you must go on, I can't go on, I'll go on.
   The Unnamable (1959)

1 Nothing to be done.
  Waiting for Godot (1955)

2 There's a man all over for you, blaming
  on his boots the faults of his feet.
  Waiting for Godot (1955)

3 One of the thieves was saved. (*Pause*) It's
  a reasonable percentage.
  Waiting for Godot (1955)

4 ESTRAGON: Charming spot. Inspiring
  prospects. Let's go.
  VLADIMIR: We can't.
  ESTRAGON: Why not?
  VLADIMIR: We're waiting for Godot.
  Waiting for Godot (1955)

5 Nothing happens, nobody comes, nobody
  goes, it's awful!
  Waiting for Godot (1955)

6 He can't think without his hat.
  Waiting for Godot (1955)

7 VLADIMIR: That passed the time.
  ESTRAGON: It would have passed in any
  case.
  VLADIMIR: Yes, but not so rapidly.
  Waiting for Godot (1955)

8 Habit is a great deadener.
  Waiting for Godot (1955)

9 Ever tried. Ever failed. No matter. Try
  again. Fail again. Fail better.
  Worstward Ho (1983)

10 I couldn't have done it otherwise, gone
  on I mean. I could not have gone on
  through the awful wretched mess of life
  without having left a stain upon the
  silence.
  Deirdre Bair *Samuel Beckett* (1978)

11 Even death is unreliable: instead of zero it
  may be some ghastly hallucination, such
  as the square root of minus one.
  attributed

Harry Bedford and Terry Sullivan

British songwriters

12 I'm a bit of a ruin that Cromwell knocked
  about a bit.
  'It's a Bit of a Ruin that Cromwell Knocked
  about a Bit' (1920 song, written for Marie
  Lloyd)

Thomas Beecham 1879–1961

English conductor

13 Good music is that which penetrates the
  ear with facility and quits the memory
  with difficulty.
  speech, *c.*1950, in *New York Times* 9 March
  1961

14 The English may not like music, but they
  absolutely love the noise it makes.
  in *New York Herald Tribune* 9 March 1961

15 At a rehearsal I let the orchestra play as
  they like. At the concert I make them
  play as *I* like.
  Neville Cardus *Sir Thomas Beecham* (1961)

16 A kind of musical Malcolm Sargent.
  of Herbert von Karajan
  H. Atkins and A. Newman *Beecham Stories*
  (1978)

17 There are two golden rules for an
  orchestra: start together and finish
  together. The public doesn't give a damn
  what goes on in between.
  H. Atkins and A. Newman *Beecham Stories*
  (1978)

18 Too much counterpoint; what is worse,
  Protestant counterpoint.
  of J. S. Bach
  in *Guardian* 8 March 1971

19 Two skeletons copulating on a
  corrugated tin roof.
  describing the harpsichord
  H. Atkins and A. Newman *Beecham Stories*
  (1978)

Max Beerbohm 1872–1956

English critic, essayist, and caricaturist

20 She was one of the people who say 'I
  don't know anything about music really,
  but I know what I like.'
  Zuleika Dobson (1911)

21 The Socratic manner is not a game at
  which two can play.
  Zuleika Dobson (1911)

22 Vulgarity has its uses. Vulgarity often
  cuts ice which refinement scrapes at
  vainly.
  letter, 21 May 1921

23 Have you noticed . . . there is never any
  third act in a nightmare? They bring you

to a climax of terror and then leave you
there. They are the work of poor
dramatists.

S. N. Behrman *Conversations with Max* (1960)

Brendan Behan 1923–64

Irish dramatist

1 PAT: He was an Anglo-Irishman.
MEG: In the blessed name of God what's
that?
PAT: A Protestant with a horse.

The Hostage (1958)

2 When I came back to Dublin, I was
courtmartialled in my absence and
sentenced to death in my absence, so I
said they could shoot me in my absence.

The Hostage (1958)

*on being asked 'What was the message of your
play' after a performance of* The Hostage:
3 Message? Message? What the hell do you
think I am, a bloody postman?

Dominic Behan *My Brother Brendan* (1965); cf.
Goldwyn 130:11

4 There's no such thing as bad publicity
except your own obituary.

Dominic Behan *My Brother Brendan* (1965)

Clive Bell 1881–1964

English art critic

5 Art and Religion are, then, two roads by
which men escape from circumstance to
ecstasy.

Art (1914)

6 I will try to account for the degree of my
aesthetic emotion. That, I conceive, is the
function of the critic.

Art (1914)

7 Only reason can convince us of those
three fundamental truths without a
recogniton of which there can be no
effective liberty: that what we believe is
not necessarily true; that what we like is
not necessarily good; and that all
questions are open.

Civilization (1928)

George Bell 1883–1958

Anglican clergyman, Bishop of Chichester

8 The policy is obliteration, openly
acknowledged. This is not a justifiable act
of war.

of the saturation bombing of Berlin
speech, House of Lords, 9 February 1944

Gertrude Bell 1868–1926

English traveller, archaeologist, and
government servant

9 I feel at times like the Creator about the
middle of the week. He must have
wondered what it was going to be like, as
I do.

creating Iraq, at the Cairo Conference 1921;
attributed

Hilaire Belloc 1870–1953

British poet, essayist, historian, novelist,
and Liberal politician

10 Believing Truth is staring at the sun.

title of poem (1938)

11 Physicians of the Utmost Fame
Were called at once; but when they came
They answered, as they took their Fees,
'There is no Cure for this Disease.'

Cautionary Tales (1907) 'Henry King'

12 And always keep a-hold of Nurse
For fear of finding something worse.

Cautionary Tales (1907) 'Jim'

13 Sir! you have disappointed us!
We had intended you to be
The next Prime Minister but three:
The stocks were sold; the Press was
     squared;
The Middle Class was quite prepared.
But as it is! . . . My language fails!
Go out and govern New South Wales!

Cautionary Tales (1907) 'Lord Lundy'

14 Matilda told such Dreadful Lies,
It made one Gasp and Stretch one's Eyes.

Cautionary Tales (1907) 'Matilda'

15 For every time She shouted 'Fire!'
They only answered 'Little Liar!'

Cautionary Tales (1907) 'Matilda'

16 I said to Heart, 'How goes it ?' Heart
replied:

'Right as a Ribstone Pippin!' But it lied.
'The False Heart' (1910)

1 I'm tired of Love: I'm still more tired of
   Rhyme.
   But Money gives me pleasure all the time.
   'Fatigued' (1923)

2 Remote and ineffectual Don
   That dared attack my Chesterton.
   'Lines to a Don' (1910)

3 Lord Finchley tried to mend the Electric
   Light
   Himself. It struck him dead: And serve
   him right!
   It is the business of the wealthy man
   To give employment to the artisan.
   More Peers (1911) 'Lord Finchley'

4 Like many of the Upper Class
   He liked the Sound of Broken Glass.
   New Cautionary Tales (1930) 'About John'; cf.
   Waugh 320:13

5 The accursed power which stands on
   Privilege
   (And goes with Women, and
   Champagne, and Bridge)
   Broke—and Democracy resumed her
   reign:
   (Which goes with Bridge, and Women
   and Champagne).
   'On a Great Election' (1923)

6 I am a sundial, and I make a botch
   Of what is done much better by a watch.
   'On a Sundial' (1938)

7 When I am dead, I hope it may be said:
   'His sins were scarlet, but his books were
   read.'
   'On His Books' (1923)

8 Pale Ebenezer thought it wrong to fight,
   But Roaring Bill (who killed him)
   thought it right.
   'The Pacifist' (1938)

9 Do you remember an Inn,
   Miranda?
   Do you remember an Inn? . . .
   And the fleas that tease in the High
   Pyrenees
   And the wine that tasted of the tar?
   'Tarantella' (1923)

10 Balliol made me, Balliol fed me,
   Whatever I had she gave me again:
   And the best of Balliol loved and led me.

God be with you, Balliol men.
'To the Balliol Men Still in Africa' (1910)

11 Be content to remember that those who
   can make omelettes properly can do
   nothing else.
   A Conversation with a Cat (1931)

Saul Bellow 1915–

American novelist

12 If I am out of my mind, it's all right with
   me, thought Moses Herzog.
   Herzog (1961) opening sentence

13 Psychoanalysis pretends to investigate
   the Unconscious. The Unconscious by
   definition is what you are not conscious
   of. But the Analysts already know what's
   in it—they should, because they put it all
   in beforehand.
   The Dean's December (1982)

14 In the greatest confusion there is still an
   open channel to the soul. It may be
   difficult to find because by midlife it is
   overgrown, and some of the wildest
   thickets that surround it grow out of
   what we describe as our education. But
   the channel is always there, and it is our
   business to keep it open, to have access
   to the deepest part of ourselves.
   Allan Bloom The Closing of the American Mind
   (1987)

15 Nobody likes being written about in their
   lifetime, it's as though the FBI and the
   CIA were suddenly to splash your files in
   the paper.
   on his forthcoming biography
   in Guardian 10 September 1997

Nora Beloff 1919–97

British journalist

16 I had the necessary qualifications:
   inexhaustible stamina, insatiable
   curiosity and a thick skin.
   on being a journalist
   in Guardian 15 February 1997; obituary

Robert Benchley 1889–1945

American humorist
see also **Film lines** 111:1, **Telegrams** 305:6

1 The biggest obstacle to professional writing is the necessity for changing a typewriter ribbon.
    Chips off the old Benchley (1949) 'Learn to Write'

2 The surest way to make a monkey of a man is to quote him.
    My Ten Years in a Quandary (1936)

3 In America there are two classes of travel—first class, and with children.
    Pluck and Luck (1925)

4 I do most of my work sitting down; that's where I shine.
    R. E. Drennan Algonquin Wits (1968)

5 It took me fifteen years to discover that I had no talent for writing, but I couldn't give it up because by that time I was too famous.
    Nathaniel Benchley Robert Benchley (1955)

6 One square foot less and it would be adulterous.
    of the cramped office he shared with Dorothy **Parker**
    in New Yorker 5 January 1946

Julien Benda 1867–1956

French philosopher and novelist

7 La trahison des clercs.
    The treachery of the intellectuals.
    title of book (1927)

Stephen Vincent Benét

1898–1943

American poet and novelist

8 I have fallen in love with American names,
The sharp, gaunt names that never get fat.
    'American Names' (1927)

9 Bury my heart at Wounded Knee.
    'American Names' (1927)

10 And kept his heart a secret to the end
From all the picklocks of biographers.
    of Robert E. Lee
    John Brown's Body (1928)

William Rose Benét

1886–1950

American poet

11 Blake saw a treefull of angels at Peckham Rye,
And his hands could lay hold on the tiger's terrible heart.
Blake knew how deep is Hell, and Heaven how high,
And could build the universe from one tiny part.
    'Mad Blake' (1918)

Tony Benn 1925–

British Labour politician, who in 1963 succeeded in disclaiming his hereditary peerage to return to the Commons
on Benn: see **Levin** 189:11

12 Not a reluctant peer but a persistent commoner.
    at a Press Conference, 23 November 1960

13 The British House of Lords is the British Outer Mongolia for retired politicians.
    in Observer 4 February 1962

14 Some of the jam we thought was for tomorrow, we've already eaten.
    attributed, 1969; see below

    The rule is, jam to-morrow and jam yesterday—but never jam today.
    Lewis Carroll (1832–98) Through the Looking-Glass (1872)

on seeing Harold **Wilson**, who had resigned as Prime Minister in March, looking 'absolutely shrunk':
15 Office is something that builds up a man only if he is somebody in his own right.
    diary, 12 April 1976

of the influence of Parliament:
16 Through talk, we tamed kings, restrained tyrants, averted revolution.
    Anthony Sampson The Changing Anatomy of Britain (1982)

1 The distortion of the Marxist idea that developed in Russia was as great, and of the same character, as the distortion of the Christian teaching at the time of the Inquisition. But it is as wholly wrong to blame Marx for what was done in his name, as it is to blame Jesus for what was done in his.

Alan Freeman *The Benn Heresy* (1982)

2 I did not enter the Labour Party forty-seven years ago to have our manifesto written by Dr Mori, Dr Gallup and Mr Harris.

in *Guardian* 13 June 1988

3 A faith is something you die for; a doctrine is something you kill for: there is all the difference in the world.

in *Observer* 16 April 1989 'Sayings of the Week'

4 The rights that are entrusted to us are not for us to give away. Even if I agree with everything that is proposed, I cannot hand away powers lent to me for five years by the people of Chesterfield. I just could not do it.

on the essential impediment to the Maastricht Treaty

speech, London, 20 November 1991

questions habitually asked by Tony Benn on meeting somebody in power:

5 What power have you got? Where did you get it from? In whose interests do you exercise it? To whom are you accountable? How do we get rid of you?

'The Independent Mind', lecture at Nottingham, 18 June 1993

6 If you file your waste-paper basket for 50 years, you have a public library.

in *Daily Telegraph* 5 March 1994

7 A quotation is what a speaker wants to say—unlike a soundbite which is all that an interviewer allows you to say.

letter to Antony Jay, August 1996

8 We should put the spin-doctors in spin clinics, where they can meet other spin patients and be treated by spin consultants. The rest of us can get on with the proper democratic process.

in *Independent* 25 October 1997 'Quote Unquote'

Alan Bennett 1934–

English actor and dramatist

9 I go to the theatre to be entertained, I want to be taken out of myself, I don't want to see lust and rape and incest and sodomy and so on, I can get all that at home.

Beyond the Fringe (1963) 'Man of Principles'

10 The real solvent of class distinction is a proper measure of self-esteem—a kind of unselfconsciousness. Some people are at ease with themselves, so the world is at ease with them. My parents thought this kind of ease was produced by education . . . they didn't see that what disqualified them was temperament—just as, though educated up to the hilt, it disqualifies me. What keeps us in our place is embarrassment.

Dinner at Noon (BBC television, 1988)

11 Outside Shakespeare the word treason to me means nothing. Only, you pissed in our soup and we drank it.

Coral Browne to Guy Burgess
An Englishman Abroad (1989)

12 I don't want to give you the idea I'm trying to hide anything, or that anything unorthodox goes on between my wife and me. It doesn't. Nothing goes on at all . . . No foreplay. No afterplay. And fuck all in between.

Enjoy (1980)

13 I have never understood this liking for war. It panders to instincts already catered for within the scope of any respectable domestic establishment.

Forty Years On (1969)

14 Memories are not shackles, Franklin, they are garlands.

Forty Years On (1969)

15 Standards are always out of date. That is what makes them standards.

Forty Years On (1969)

16 Don't swear, boy. It shows a lack of vocabulary.

Forty Years On (1969)

17 I'm all in favour of free expression provided it's kept rigidly under control.

Forty Years On (1969)

1 Sapper, Buchan, Dornford Yates, practitioners in that school of Snobbery with Violence that runs like a thread of good-class tweed through twentieth-century literature.

Forty Years On (1969)

2 To be Prince of Wales is not a position. It is a predicament.

The Madness of King George (1995 film); in the 1992 play *The Madness of George III* the line was 'To be heir to the throne . . . '

3 Brought up in the provinces in the forties and fifties one learned early the valuable lesson that life is generally something that happens elsewhere.

Talking Heads (1988) introduction

4 Here I sit, alone and sixty,
Bald, and fat, and full of sin,
Cold the seat and loud the cistern,
As I read the Harpic tin.

'Place Names of China'

5 He proved that a life of self-indulgence, if led with a whole heart, may also bring a certain wisdom.

of Peter **Cook**

in *Observer* 31 December 1995

6 But I loathe Classic FM more and more for its cosiness, its safety and its wholehearted endorsement of the post-Thatcher world, with medical insurance and Saga holidays rammed down your throat between every item.

diary, 3 July 1996

7 People always complain about muck-raking biographers saying 'Leave us our heroes.' 'Leave us our villains' is just as important.

of an attempt to rehabilitate Earl **Haig**

diary, 11 February 1996

Arnold Bennett 1867–1931

English novelist

8 Seventy minutes had passed before Mr Lloyd George arrived at his proper theme. He spoke for a hundred and seventeen minutes, in which period he was detected only once in the use of an argument.

Things that have Interested Me (1921) 'After the March Offensive.'

9 The price of justice is eternal publicity.

Things that have Interested Me (2nd series, 1923) 'Secret Trials'

10 A cause may be inconvenient, but it's magnificent. It's like champagne or high heels, and one must be prepared to suffer for it.

The Title (1918)

11 Being a husband is a whole-time job. That is why so many husbands fail. They cannot give their entire attention to it.

The Title (1918)

12 Journalists say a thing that they know isn't true, in the hope that if they keep on saying it long enough it *will* be true.

The Title (1918)

13 Literature's always a good card to play for Honours. It makes people think that Cabinet ministers are educated.

The Title (1918)

Jill Bennett 1931–90

English actress; former wife of John **Osborne**

14 Never marry a man who hates his mother, because he'll end up hating you.

in *Observer* 12 September 1982 'Sayings of the Week'

A. C. Benson 1862–1925

English writer

15 Land of Hope and Glory, Mother of the Free,
How shall we extol thee who are born of thee?
Wider still and wider shall thy bounds be set;
God who made thee mighty, make thee mightier yet.

'Land of Hope and Glory' written to be sung as the Finale to Elgar's *Coronation Ode* (1902)

Stella Benson 1892–1933

English novelist

1 Call no man foe, but never love a
stranger.
This is the End (1917)

Edmund Clerihew Bentley
1875–1956

English writer

2 The Art of Biography
Is different from Geography.
Geography is about Maps,
But Biography is about Chaps.
Biography for Beginners (1905) introduction

3 George the Third
Ought never to have occurred.
One can only wonder
At so grotesque a blunder.
'George the Third' (1929)

4 Sir Humphrey Davy
Abominated gravy.
He lived in the odium
Of having discovered Sodium.
'Sir Humphrey Davy' (1905)

5 Sir Christopher Wren
Said, 'I am going to dine with some men.
If anybody calls
Say I am designing St Paul's.'
'Sir Christopher Wren' (1905)

Eric Bentley 1916–

6 Ours is the age of substitutes: instead of
language, we have jargon; instead of
principles, slogans; and, instead of
genuine ideas, Bright Ideas.
in *New Republic* 29 December 1952

Lloyd Bentsen 1921–

American Democratic politician

*responding to Dan **Quayle**'s claim to have 'as
much experience in the Congress as Jack **Kennedy**
had when he sought the presidency':*
7 Senator, I served with Jack Kennedy. I
knew Jack Kennedy. Jack Kennedy was a
friend of mine. Senator, you're no Jack
Kennedy.
in the vice-presidential debate, 5 October 1988

Ingmar Bergman 1918–

Swedish film director

8 After years of playing with images of life
and death, life has made me shy.
*message sent when his daughter Linn Ullman
collected the Palme of Palmes for him at the
Cannes Film Festival*
in *Observer* 18 May 1997 'Soundbites'

Irving Berlin 1888–1989

American songwriter

9 Anything you can do, I can do better,
I can do anything better than you.
'Anything You Can Do' (1946 song)

10 Heaven—I'm in Heaven—And my heart
beats so that I can hardly speak;
And I seem to find the happiness I seek
When we're out together dancing cheek-
to-cheek.
'Cheek-to-Cheek' (1935 song)

11 God bless America,
Land that I love,
Stand beside her and guide her
Thru the night with a light from above.
From the mountains to the prairies,
To the oceans white with foam,
God bless America,
My home sweet home.
'God Bless America' (1939 song)

12 There may be trouble ahead,
But while there's moonlight and music
and love and romance,
Let's face the music and dance.
'Let's Face the Music and Dance' (1936 song)

13 Oh! how I hate to get up in the morning,
Oh! how I'd love to remain in bed;
For the hardest blow of all,
Is to hear the bugler call,
You've got to get up, you've got to get
up,
You've got to get up this morning!
'Oh! How I Hate to Get Up in the Morning'
(1918 song)

14 A pretty girl is like a melody
That haunts you night and day.
'A Pretty Girl is like a Melody' (1919 song)

15 The song is ended (but the melody lingers
on).
title of song (1927)

1 There's no business like show business.
  title of song (1946)

2 I'm puttin' on my top hat,
  Tyin' up my white tie,
  Brushin' off my tails.
  'Top Hat, White Tie and Tails' (1935 song)

3 I'm dreaming of a white Christmas,
  Just like the ones I used to know.
  'White Christmas' (1942 song)

4 Listen, kid, take my advice, never hate a
  song that has sold half a million copies.
  to Cole **Porter,** *of the song 'Rosalie'*
  Philip Furia *Poets of Tin Pan Alley* (1990)

Isaiah Berlin 1909–97
British philosopher

5 There exists a great chasm between
  those, on one side, who relate everything
  to a single central vision . . . and, on the
  other side, those who pursue many ends,
  often unrelated and even
  contradictory . . . The first kind of
  intellectual and artistic personality
  belongs to the hedgehogs, the second to
  the foxes.
  The Hedgehog and the Fox (1953); see below

  The fox knows many things—the
  hedgehog one *big* one.
  Archilochus (7th century BC) fragment

6 Liberty is liberty, not equality or fairness
  or justice or human happiness or a quiet
  conscience.
  Two Concepts of Liberty (1958)

7 Few new truths have ever won their way
  against the resistance of established ideas
  save by being overstated.
  Vico and Herder (1976)

8 Rousseau was the first militant lowbrow.
  in *Observer* 9 November 1952

J. D. Bernal 1901–71
Irish-born physicist

9 Men will not be content to manufacture
  life: they will want to improve on it.
  The World, the Flesh and the Devil (1929)

Georges Bernanos 1888–1948
French novelist and essayist

10 The wish for prayer is a prayer in itself.
  Journal d'un curé de campagne (1936)

11 Hell, madam, is to love no more.
  Journal d'un curé de campagne (1936)

Jeffrey Bernard 1932–97
English journalist
see also **Waterhouse** 320:6

12 It may be more difficult to make new
  friends as you get older but it is some
  consolation to know how easy it is to lose
  them when you are young.
  in *The Spectator* 17 August 1985

13 Oh, the self-importance of fading stars.
  Never mind, they will be black holes one
  day.
  in *The Spectator* 18 July 1992

Eric Berne 1910–70
American psychiatrist

14 Games people play: the psychology of
  human relationships.
  title of book (1964)

Lord Berners 1883–1950
English composer, artist, and writer

15 He's always backing into the limelight.
  of T. E. **Lawrence**
  oral tradition

Carl Bernstein 1944–
and Bob Woodward 1943–
American journalists

16 All the President's men.
  title of book (1974) on the Watergate scandal

Yogi Berra 1925–
American baseball player

17 It ain't over till it's over.
  comment on National League pennant race,
  1973, quoted in many versions

18 The future ain't what it used to be.
  attributed

1 If people don't want to come out to the ball park, nobody's going to stop 'em.
of baseball games
attributed

2 It was déjà vu all over again.
attributed

Daniel Berrigan

American anti-Vietnam War activist

3 This is a war run to show the world, and particularly the Third World, where exactly it stands in relation to our technology.
attributed, 1973

Chuck Berry 1931–

American rock and roll singer

4 Roll over, Beethoven, and tell Tchaikovsky the news.
'Roll Over, Beethoven' (1956 song)

John Berryman 1914–72

American poet

5   People will take balls,
Balls will be lost always, little boy,
And no one buys a ball back.
'The Ball Poem' (1948)

6 We must travel in the direction of our fear.
'A Point of Age' (1942)

7 Life, friends, is boring. We must not say so . . .
And moreover my mother taught me as a boy
(repeatedly) 'Ever to confess you're bored
means you have no

Inner Resources.'
77 Dream Songs (1964) no. 14

8 I seldom go to films. They are too exciting,
said the Honourable Possum.
77 Dream Songs (1964) no. 53

Pierre Berton 1920–

Canadian writer

9 Somebody who knows how to make love in a canoe.
definition of a Canadian
in *Toronto Star, Canadian Magazine* 22 December 1973

Theobald von Bethmann Hollweg 1856–1921

Chancellor of Germany, 1909–17

10 Just for a word 'neutrality'—a word which in wartime has so often been disregarded—just for a scrap of paper, Great Britain is going to make war on a kindred nation who desires nothing better than to be friends with her.
summary of a report by Sir Edward Goschen to Sir Edward Grey in *British Documents on Origins of the War 1898–1914* (1926)

John Betjeman 1906–84

English poet
on Betjeman: see **Ewart** 104:10

11 He sipped at a weak hock and seltzer
As he gazed at the London skies
Through the Nottingham lace of the curtains
Or was it his bees-winged eyes?
'The Arrest of Oscar Wilde at the Cadogan Hotel' (1937)

12 And girls in slacks remember Dad,
And oafish louts remember Mum,
And sleepless children's hearts are glad,
And Christmas-morning bells say 'Come!'
'Christmas' (1954)

13 And is it true? And is it true,
This most tremendous tale of all,
Seen in a stained-glass window's hue,
A Baby in an ox's stall?
'Christmas' (1954)

14 Oh! Chintzy, Chintzy cheeriness,
Half dead and half alive!
'Death in Leamington' (1931)

15 Spirits of well-shot woodcock, partridge, snipe
Flutter and bear him up the Norfolk sky.
'Death of King George V' (1937)

1 Old men who never cheated, never
    doubted,
  Communicated monthly, sit and stare
  At the new suburb stretched beyond the
    run-way
  Where a young man lands hatless from
    the air.
    'Death of King George V' (1937)

2 Oh shall I see the Thames again?
  The prow-promoted gems again,
  As beefy ATS
  Without their hats
  Come shooting through the bridge?
  And 'cheerioh' or 'cheeri-bye'
  Across the waste of waters die
  And low the mists of evening lie
  And lightly skims the midge.
    'Henley-on-Thames' (1945)

3 Phone for the fish-knives, Norman
  As Cook is a little unnerved;
  You kiddies have crumpled the serviettes
  And I must have things daintily served.
    'How to get on in Society' (1954)

4 It's awf'lly bad luck on Diana,
  Her ponies have swallowed their bits;
  She fished down their throats with a
    spanner
  And frightened them all into fits.
    'Hunter Trials' (1954)

5 The Church's Restoration
  In eighteen-eighty-three
  Has left for contemplation
  Not what there used to be.
    'Hymn' (1931)

6 Think of what our Nation stands for,
  Books from Boots' and country lanes,
  Free speech, free passes, class distinction,
  Democracy and proper drains.
    'In Westminster Abbey' (1940)

7 In the licorice fields at Pontefract
  My love and I did meet
  And many a burdened licorice bush
  Was blooming round our feet.
    'The Licorice Fields at Pontefract' (1954)

8 Belbroughton Road is bonny, and pinkly
    bursts the spray
  Of prunus and forsythia across the public
    way.
    'May-Day Song for North Oxford' (1945)

9 Gaily into Ruislip Gardens
  Runs the red electric train,

With a thousand Ta's and Pardon's
Daintily alights Elaine;
Hurries down the concrete station
With a frown of concentration,
Out into the outskirt's edges
Where a few surviving hedges
Keep alive our lost Elysium—rural
  Middlesex again.
  'Middlesex' (1954)

10 Official designs are aggressively neuter,
   The Puritan work of an eyeless computer.
     'The Newest Bath Guide' (1974)

11 Pam, I adore you, Pam, you great big
     mountainous sports girl,
   Whizzing them over the net, full of the
     strength of five:
   That old Malvernian brother, you zephyr
     and khaki shorts girl,
   Although he's playing for Woking,
   Can't stand up to your wonderful
     backhand drive.
     'Pot Pourri from a Surrey Garden' (1940)

12 Come, friendly bombs, and fall on
     Slough!
   It isn't fit for humans now,
   There isn't grass to graze a cow.
   Swarm over, Death!
     'Slough' (1937)

13 Miss J. Hunter Dunn, Miss J. Hunter
     Dunn,
   Furnish'd and burnish'd by Aldershot
     sun.
     'A Subaltern's Love-Song' (1945)

14 Love-thirty, love-forty, oh! weakness of
     joy,
   The speed of a swallow, the grace of a
     boy,
   With carefullest carelessness, gaily you
     won,
   I am weak from your loveliness, Joan
     Hunter Dunn.
     'A Subaltern's Love-Song' (1945)

15 By roads 'not adopted', by woodlanded
     ways,
   She drove to the club in the late summer
     haze.
     'A Subaltern's Love-Song' (1945)

16 The dread of beatings! Dread of being
     late!

And, greatest dread of all, the dread of games!
Summoned by Bells (1960)

1 Broad of Church and 'broad of Mind',
Broad before and broad behind,
A keen ecclesiologist,
A rather dirty Wykehamist.
'The Wykehamist' (1931)

2 Ghastly good taste, or a depressing story of the rise and fall of English architecture.
title of book (1933)

Bruno Bettelheim 1903–90
Austrian-born American psychologist

3 The most extreme agony is to feel that one has been utterly forsaken.
Surviving and other essays (1979)

Aneurin Bevan 1897–1960
British Labour politician
on Bevan: see **Bevin** 37:10, **Churchill** 67:8, **Macmillan** 202:2

4 This island is made mainly of coal and surrounded by fish. Only an organizing genius could produce a shortage of coal and fish at the same time.
speech at Blackpool, 24 May 1945

5 No amount of cajolery, and no attempts at ethical or social seduction, can eradicate from my heart a deep burning hatred for the Tory Party . . . So far as I am concerned they are lower than vermin.
speech at Manchester, 4 July 1948

6 The language of priorities is the religion of Socialism.
speech at Labour Party Conference, 8 June 1949

7 [Winston Churchill] does not talk the language of the 20th century but that of the 18th. He is still fighting Blenheim all over again. His only answer to a difficult situation is send a gun-boat.
speech at Labour Party Conference, 2 October 1951

8 We know what happens to people who stay in the middle of the road. They get run down.
in *Observer* 6 December 1953

9 Damn it all, you can't have the crown of thorns *and* the thirty pieces of silver.
on his position in the Labour Party, c.1956
Michael Foot *Aneurin Bevan* vol. 2 (1973)

10 I am not going to spend any time whatsoever in attacking the Foreign Secretary . . . If we complain about the tune, there is no reason to attack the monkey when the organ grinder is present.
on the Suez crisis
speech, House of Commons, 16 May 1957

11 If you carry this resolution you will send Britain's Foreign Secretary naked into the conference chamber.
on a motion proposing unilateral nuclear disarmament by the UK
speech at Labour Party Conference, 3 October 1957

12 I know that the right kind of leader for the Labour Party is a desiccated calculating machine who must not in any way permit himself to be swayed by indignation. If he sees suffering, privation or injustice he must not allow it to move him, for that would be evidence of the lack of proper education or of absence of self-control. He must speak in calm and objective accents and talk about a dying child in the same way as he would about the pieces inside an internal combustion engine.
generally taken as referring to Hugh **Gaitskell**, *although Bevan specifically denied it in an interview with Robin* **Day** *on 28 April 1959*
Michael Foot *Aneurin Bevan* (1973) vol. 2

13 This so-called affluent society is an ugly society still. It is a vulgar society. It is a meretricious society. It is a society in which priorities have gone all wrong.
speech in Blackpool, 29 November 1959; cf. **Galbraith** 123:2

14 I read the newspapers avidly. It is my one form of continuous fiction.
in *The Times* 29 March 1960

15 Fascism is not in itself a new order of society. It is the future refusing to be born.
Leon Harris *The Fine Art of Political Wit* (1965)

1 I stuffed their mouths with gold.

on his handling of the consultants during the establishment of the National Health Service

B. Abel-Smith *The Hospitals 1800–1948* (1964)

William Henry Beveridge

1879–1963

British economist

2 Ignorance is an evil weed, which dictators may cultivate among their dupes, but which no democracy can afford among its citizens.

Full Employment in a Free Society (1944)

3 Want is one only of five giants on the road of reconstruction . . . the others are Disease, Ignorance, Squalor and Idleness.

Social Insurance and Allied Services (1942)

4 The state is or can be master of money, but in a free society it is master of very little else.

Voluntary Action (1948)

Ernest Bevin 1881–1951

British Labour politician and trade unionist
on Bevin: see **Foot** 114:14, **Jenkins** 161:2

5 The most conservative man in this world is the British Trade Unionist when you want to change him.

speech, Trades Union Congress, 8 September 1927

6 I hope you will carry no resolution of an emergency character telling a man with a conscience like Lansbury what he ought to do . . . It is placing the Executive in an absolutely wrong position to be taking your conscience round from body to body to be told what you ought to do with it.

often quoted as 'hawking his conscience round the Chancellories of Europe'

Labour Party Conference Report (1935)

7 My [foreign] policy is to be able to take a ticket at Victoria Station and go anywhere I damn well please.

in *Spectator* 20 April 1951

8 I didn't ought never to have done it. It was you, Willie, what put me up to it.

to Lord Strang, after officially recognizing Communist China

C. Parrott *Serpent and Nightingale* (1977)

9 If you open that Pandora's Box, you never know what Trojan 'orses will jump out.

on the Council of Europe

Roderick Barclay *Ernest Bevin and the Foreign Office* (1975)

on the observation that Aneurin **Bevan** *was sometimes his own worst enemy:*

10 Not while I'm alive 'e ain't!

also attributed to Bevin of Herbert **Morrison**

Roderick Barclay *Ernest Bevin and Foreign Office* (1975)

Steve Biko 1946–77

South African anti-apartheid campaigner

11 The liberal must understand that the days of the Noble Savage are gone; that the blacks do not need a go-between in this struggle for their own emancipation. No true liberal should feel any resentment at the growth of black consciousness. Rather, all true liberals should realize that the place for their fight for justice is within their white society. The liberals must realize that they themselves are oppressed if they are true liberals and therefore they must fight for their own freedom and not that of the nebulous 'they' with whom they can hardly claim identification. The liberal must apply himself with absolute dedication to the idea of educating his white brothers.

'Black Souls in White Skins?' (written 1970), in *Steve Biko—I Write What I Like* (1978)

12 The most potent weapon in the hands of the oppressor is the mind of the oppressed.

statement as witness, 3 May 1976

Laurence Binyon 1869–1943

English poet

13 They shall grow not old, as we that are left grow old.
Age shall not weary them, nor the years condemn.

At the going down of the sun and in the
　morning
We will remember them.
*regularly recited as part of the ritual for
Remembrance Day parades; cf.* **Epitaphs** 106:2
'For the Fallen' (1914)

1 Now is the time for the burning of the
leaves.
'The Ruins' (1942)

Nigel Birch 1906–81

British Conservative politician

2 My God! They've shot our fox!
on hearing of the resignation of Hugh **Dalton**,
*Labour Chancellor of the Exchequer, after the leak
of Budget secrets*
comment, 13 November 1947

John Bird 1936–

English actor and satirist

3 That was the week that was.
title of satirical BBC television series, 1962–3

Harrison Birtwhistle 1934–

English composer

4 You can't stop. Composing's not
voluntary, you know. There's no choice,
you're not free. You're landed with an
idea and you have responsibility to that
idea.
in *Observer* 14 April 1996 'Sayings of the Week'

Elizabeth Bishop 1911–79

American poet

5 The state with the prettiest name,
the state that floats in brackish water,
held together by mangrove roots.
'Florida' (1946)

6 Topography displays no favourites;
　North's as near as West.
More delicate than the historians' are the
　map-makers' colours.
'The Map' (1946)

7 The armoured cars of dreams, contrived
　to let us do
so many a dangerous thing.
'Sleeping Standing Up' (1946)

Björk 1965–

Icelandic pop star

8 Icelandic peoples were the ones who
memorized sagas . . . We were the first
rappers of Europe.
attributed, January 1996

James Black 1924–

British analytical pharmacologist; winner of
the Nobel prize for medicine

9 In the culture I grew up in you did your
work and you did not put your arm
around it to stop other people from
looking—you took the earliest possible
opportunity to make knowledge
available.
on modern scientific research
in *Daily Telegraph* 11 December 1995

Tony Blair 1953–

British Labour statesman; Prime Minister
since 1997

10 Labour is the party of law and order in
Britain today. Tough on crime and tough
on the causes of crime.
as Shadow Home Secretary
speech at the Labour Party Conference, 30
September 1993

11 The art of leadership is saying no, not
yes. It is very easy to say yes.
in *Mail on Sunday* 2 October 1994

12 Those who seriously believe we cannot
improve on words written for the world
of 1918 when we are now in 1995 are
not learning from our history but living
it.
on the proposed revision of Clause IV
in *Independent* 11 January 1995; cf.
Anonymous 9:8, 11:14

13 We need to build a relationship of trust
not just within a firm but within a
society. By trust, I mean the recognition
of a mutual purpose for which we work
together and in which we all benefit. It is
a Stakeholder Economy in which
opportunity is available to all,

advancement is through merit and from which no group or class is set apart or excluded.

> speech (press release) in Singapore, 8 January 1996

1 Ask me my three main priorities for Government, and I tell you: education, education and education.

> speech at the Labour Party Conference, 1 October 1996

2 Enough of talking—it is time now to do.

taking office as Prime Minister

> on the steps of 10 Downing Street, 2 May 1997

3 We are not the masters. The people are the masters. We are the servants of the people . . . What the electorate gives, the electorate can take away.

addressing Labour MPs on the first day of the new Parliament, 7 May 1997

> in *Guardian* 8 May 1997; cf. **Misquotations** 219:3

4 She was the People's Princess, and that is how she will stay . . . in our hearts and in our memories forever.

> on hearing of the death of **Diana,** Princess of Wales, 31 August 1997; in *The Times* 1 September 1997

5 I am from the Disraeli school of Prime Ministers in their relations with the Monarch.

at the Queen's golden wedding celebration, 20 November 1997; cf. **Elizabeth II** 103:1

> in *Daily Telegraph* 21 November 1997

Eubie Blake 1883–1983

American ragtime pianist

at the age of ninety-seven, Blake was asked at what age the sex drive goes:

6 You'll have to ask somebody older than me.

> attributed

7 If I'd known I was gonna live this long, I'd have taken better care of myself.

on reaching the age of 100

> in *Observer* 13 February 1983 'Sayings of the Week'

Lesley Blanch 1907–

British writer

8 She was an Amazon. Her whole life was spent riding at breakneck speed towards the wilder shores of love.

> *The Wilder Shores of Love* (1954)

Danny Blanchflower 1926–93

English footballer

9 The great fallacy is that the game is first and last about winning. It is nothing of the kind. The game is about glory, it is about doing things in style and with a flourish, about going out and beating the lot, not waiting for them to die of boredom.

> attributed, 1972

Arthur Bliss 1891–1975

English composer

10 What is called the serenity of age is only perhaps a euphemism for the fading power to feel the sudden shock of joy or sorrow.

> *As I Remember* (1970)

Edmund Blunden 1896–1974

English poet

11 All things they have in common being so
      poor,
   And their one fear, Death's shadow at
      the door.

> 'Almswomen' (1920)

12 I am for the woods against the world,
   But are the woods for me?

> 'The Kiss' (1931)

13 I have been young, and now am not too
      old;
   And I have seen the righteous forsaken,
   His health, his honour and his quality
      taken.
   This is not what we were formerly told.

> 'Report on Experience' (1929)

Alfred Blunt 1879–1957

English Protestant cleric, Bishop of Bradford

1 The benefit of the King's Coronation depends, under God, upon two elements: First, on the faith, prayer, and self-dedication of the King himself, and on that it would be improper for me to say anything except to commend him, and ask you to commend him, to God's grace, which he will so abundantly need . . . if he is to do his duty faithfully. We hope that he is aware of his need. Some of us wish that he gave more positive signs of his awareness.

*referring to **Edward VIII**'s relationship with Mrs Simpson, which until then had not been publicly mentioned; cf. **Anonymous** 9:14*

speech to Bradford Diocesan Conference, 1 December 1936

Robert Bly 1926–

American writer

2 Every modern male has, lying at the bottom of his psyche, a large, primitive being covered with hair down to his feet. Making contact with this Wild Man is the step the Eighties male or the Nineties male has yet to take.

Iron John (1990)

Ronald Blythe 1922–

English writer

3 An industrial worker would sooner have a £5 note but a countryman must have praise.

Akenfield (1969)

4 With full-span lives having become the norm, people may need to learn how to be aged as they once had to learn how to be adult.

The View in Winter (1979)

David Boaz 1953–

American lawyer

5 Alcohol didn't cause the high crime rates of the '20s and '30s, Prohibition did.

Drugs don't cause today's alarming crime rates, but drug prohibition does.

quoted by Judge James C. Paine, addressing the Federal Bar Association in Miami, 1991

'The Legalization of Drugs' 27 April 1988

Ivan F. Boesky 1937–

American businessman

6 Greed is all right . . . Greed is healthy. You can be greedy and still feel good about yourself.

commencement address, Berkeley, California, 18 May 1986; cf. **Film lines** 110:8

Louise Bogan 1897–1970

American poet

7 Women have no wilderness in them,
They are provident instead,
Content in the tight hot cell of their hearts
To eat dusty bread.

'Women' (1923)

Humphrey Bogart

see **Film lines** 110:9, 110:11, 111:11

John B. Bogart 1848–1921

American journalist

8 When a dog bites a man, that is not news, because it happens so often. But if a man bites a dog, that is news.

F. M. O'Brien *Story of the* [New York] *Sun* (1918); often attributed to Charles A. Dana

Niels Bohr 1885–1962

Danish physicist

9 Of course not, but I am told it works even if you don't believe in it.

when asked whether he really believed a horseshoe hanging over his door would bring him luck, c.1930

A. Pais *Inward Bound* (1986)

10 Anybody who is not shocked by this subject has failed to understand it.

of quantum mechanics

attributed; *Nature* 23 August 1990

11 One of the favourite maxims of my father was the distinction between the two sorts

of truths, profound truths recognized by the fact that the opposite is also a profound truth, in contrast to trivialities where opposites are obviously absurd.

S. Rozental *Niels Bohr* (1967)

Alan Bold 1943–

Scottish poet

1 This happened near the core
Of a world's culture. This
Occurred among higher things.
This was a philosophical conclusion.
Everybody gets what he deserves.

The bare drab rubble of the place.
The dull damp stone. The rain.
The emptiness. The human lack.

'June 1967 at Buchenwald' (1969); cf.
Anonymous 10:6

2 Scotland, land of the omnipotent No.

'A Memory of Death' (1969)

3 Our job is to try
To change things.
After Hiroshima
You ask a poet to sing.

'Recitative' (1965)

Robert Bolt 1924–95

English dramatist

4 Morality's *not* practical. Morality's a gesture. A complicated gesture learned from books.

A Man for All Seasons (1960)

5 It profits a man nothing to give his soul for the whole world . . . But for Wales—!

A Man for All Seasons (1960); see below

For what shall it profit a man, if he shall gain the whole world, and lose his own soul?

Bible St Mark

Violet Bonham Carter

see **Telegrams** 305:4

Dietrich Bonhoeffer 1906–45

German Lutheran theologian and pastor

6 It is the nature, and the advantage, of strong people that they can bring out the

crucial questions and form a clear opinion about them. The weak always have to decide between alternatives that are not their own.

Widerstand und Ergebung (1951)

Bono 1960–

Irish rock star, member of U2

7 They didn't have Kalashnikovs but U2 tickets in their hands.

of the audience at the U2 concert in Sarajevo, 24 September 1997

in *Daily Telegraph* 25 September 1997

Connie Booth

see John **Cleese** and Connie Booth

Robert Boothby 1900–86

British Conservative politician

8 *You* speak for Britain!

*to Arthur Greenwood, acting Leader of the Labour Party, after Neville **Chamberlain** had failed to announce an ultimatum to Germany; perhaps taking up an appeal already voiced by Leo **Amery***

Harold Nicolson diary, 2 September 1939; cf. **Amery** 7:4

Betty Boothroyd 1929–

Labour politician; Speaker of the House of Commons since 1992

9 My desire to get here was like miners' coal dust, it was under my fingers and I couldn't scrub it out.

of Parliament

Glenys Kinnock and Fiona Millar (eds.) *By Faith and Daring* (1993)

James H. Boren 1925–

American bureaucrat

10 Guidelines for bureaucrats: (1) When in charge, ponder. (2) When in trouble, delegate. (3) When in doubt, mumble.

in *New York Times* 8 November 1970

Jorge Luis Borges 1899–1986

Argentinian writer

1 I come from a vertiginous country where the lottery forms a principal part of reality.
Fictions (1956) 'The Babylon Lottery'

2 The original is unfaithful to the translation.
of Henley's translation of Vathek
Sobre el 'Vathek' de William Beckford; in *Obras Completas* (1974)

3 For one of those gnostics, the visible universe was an illusion or, more precisely, a sophism. Mirrors and fatherhood are abominable because they multiply it and extend it.
Tlön, Uqbar, Orbis Tertius (1941)

4 The Falklands thing was a fight between two bald men over a comb.
application of a proverbial phrase
in *Time* 14 February 1983

Horatio Bottomley 1860–1933

British newspaper proprietor and financier

5 What poor education I have received has been gained in the University of Life.
speech at the Oxford Union, 2 December 1920

reply to a prison visitor who asked if he were sewing:
6 No, reaping.
S. T. Felstead *Horatio Bottomley* (1936)

Louis Bousquet

French songwriter

7 *Nous en rêvons la nuit, nous y pensons le jour,*
Ce n'est que Madelon, mais pour nous, c'est l'amour.
We dream of her by night, we think of her by day,
It's only Madelon, but for us, it's love.
'Quand Madelon' (1914), French soldiers' song of the First World War

Elizabeth Bowen 1899–1973

Anglo-Irish novelist

8 It is about five o'clock in an evening that the first hour of spring strikes—autumn arrives in the early morning, but spring at the close of a winter day.
The Death of the Heart (1938)

9 The heart may think it knows better: the senses know that absence blots people out. We have really no absent friends.
The Death of the Heart (1938)

10 I suppose art is the only thing that can go on mattering once it has stopped hurting.
Heat of the Day (1949)

11 There is no end to the violations committed by children on children, quietly talking alone.
The House in Paris (1935)

12 Fate is not an eagle, it creeps like a rat.
The House in Paris (1935)

13 Jealousy is no more than feeling alone against smiling enemies.
The House in Paris (1935)

14 It is not only our fate but our business to lose innocence, and once we have lost that, it is futile to attempt a picnic in Eden.
'Out of a Book' in *Orion III* (ed. Rosamund Lehmann et al, 1946)

15 A high altar on the move.
of Edith **Sitwell**
V. Glendinning *Edith Sitwell* (1981)

David Bowie 1947–

English rock musician

16 Ground control to Major Tom.
'Space Oddity' (1969 song)

17 The 1970s for me started the 21st century—it was the beginning of a true pluralism in social attitudes.
An Earthling at 50 ITV programme; in *Sunday Times* 12 January 1997

Boy George 1961–

English pop singer and songwriter

18 She's a gay man trapped in a woman's body.
of **Madonna**
Take It Like a Man (1995)

Charles Boyer

see **Misquotations** 218:2

Omar Bradley 1893–1981

American general

1 The way to win an atomic war is to make certain it never starts.
     speech on Armistice Day, 1948

2 We have grasped the mystery of the atom and rejected the Sermon on the Mount.
     speech on Armistice Day, 1948

3 The world has achieved brilliance without wisdom, power without conscience. Ours is a world of nuclear giants and ethical infants.
     speech on Armistice Day, 1948

4 Red China is not the powerful nation seeking to dominate the world. Frankly, in the opinion of the Joint Chiefs of Staff, this strategy would involve us in the wrong war, at the wrong place, at the wrong time, and with the wrong enemy.
     US Congress Senate Committee on Armed Services (1951)

Marlon Brando

see **Film lines** 110:10; *see also* **Glass**

Richard Branson 1950–

English businessman

5 We spend most of our lives working. So why do so few people have a good time doing it? Virgin is the possibility of good times.
     interview in *New York Times* 28 February 1993

Georges Braque 1882–1963

French painter

6 Art is meant to disturb, science reassures.
     Le Jour et la nuit: Cahiers 1917–52

7 Truth exists; only lies are invented.
     Le Jour et la nuit: Cahiers 1917–52

John W. Bratton

see Jimmy **Kennedy** and John W. Bratton

Werner von Braun 1912–77

German-born American rocket engineer

8 Don't tell me that man doesn't belong out there. Man belongs wherever he wants to go—and he'll do plenty well when he gets there.
     on space
         in *Time* 17 February 1958

9 Basic research is what I am doing when I don't know what I am doing.
     R. L. Weber *A Random Walk in Science* (1973)

Bertolt Brecht 1898–1956

German dramatist

10 Terrible is the temptation to be good.
     The Caucasian Chalk Circle (1948)

11 ANDREA: Unhappy the land that has no heroes! . . .
GALILEO: No. Unhappy the land that needs heroes.
     The Life of Galileo (1939)

12 The aim of science is not to open the door to infinite wisdom, but to set a limit to infinite error.
     The Life of Galileo (1939)

13 They have gone too long without a war here. Where is morality to come from in such a case, I ask? Peace is nothing but slovenliness, only war creates order.
     Mother Courage (1939)

14 The finest plans are always ruined by the littleness of those who ought to carry them out, for the Emperors can actually do nothing.
     Mother Courage (1939)

15 Don't tell me peace has broken out, when I've just bought fresh supplies.
     Mother Courage (1939)

16 The resistible rise of Arturo Ui.
     title of play (1941)

1 Oh, the shark has pretty teeth, dear,
And he shows them pearly white.
Just a jack-knife has Macheath, dear
And he keeps it out of sight.
The Threepenny Opera (1928)

2 Food comes first, then morals.
The Threepenny Opera (1928)

3 What is robbing a bank compared with
founding a bank?
The Threepenny Opera (1928)

4 Who built Thebes of the seven gates?
In the books you will find the names of
kings.
Did the kings haul up the lumps of
rock? . . .
Where, the evening that the wall of
China was finished
Did the masons go?
'Questions From A Worker Who Reads' (1935)

5 Would it not be easier
In that case for the government
To dissolve the people
And elect another?
*on the uprising against the Soviet occupying
forces in East Germany in 1953*
'The Solution' (1953)

Sydney Brenner 1927–

British scientist

6 A modern computer hovers between the
obsolescent and the nonexistent.
attributed in *Science* 5 January 1990

Aristide Briand 1862–1932

French statesman

7 The high contracting powers solemnly
declare . . . that they condemn recourse
to war and renounce it . . . as an
instrument of their national policy
towards each other . . . The settlement or
the solution of all disputes or conflicts of
whatever nature or of whatever origin
they may be which may arise . . . shall
never be sought by either side except by
pacific means.
draft, 20 June 1927, later incorporated into the
Kellogg Pact, 1928

Edward Bridges 1892–1969

British civil servant, Cabinet Secretary and
Head of the Civil Service

8 I confidently expect that we shall
continue to be grouped with mothers-
in-law and Wigan Pier as one of the
recognized objects of ridicule.
of civil servants
Portrait of a Profession (1950)

Vera Brittain 1893–1970

English writer

9 Politics are usually the executive
expression of human immaturity.
Rebel Passion (1964)

Russell Brockbank 1913–

British cartoonist

10 Fog in Channel—Continent isolated.
newspaper placard in cartoon, *Round the Bend
with Brockbank* (1948); the phrase 'Continent
isolated' was quoted as already current by
John Gunther *Inside Europe* (1938)

Harold Brodkey 1930–96

American writer

11 The American daydream, as in Twain
(and Hemingway), is about re-building
after the flood, about being better off
than before, about outwitting this or that
challenge, up to and including death.
Well, how do you manage to be
optimistic for the moment? Without
hope?
This Wild Darkness: The Story of My Death
(1996)

12 But the horror was I had no strength to
respond or pretend after only a short
while, less than an hour. I am not able to
be present for him and never will be
anymore.
*on a visit from his four-year-old grandson, while
dying of Aids*
This Wild Darkness: The Story of My Death
(1996)

Joseph Brodsky 1940–96

Russian-born American poet

1 As a form of moral insurance, at least, literature is much more dependable than a system of beliefs or a philosophical doctrine.
> 'Uncommon Visage', Nobel lecture 1987, in *On Grief and Reason* (1996)

2 There is no other antidote to the vulgarity of the human heart than doubt and good taste, which one finds fused in works of great literature.
> 'Letter to a President [Václav Havel]' (1993), in *On Grief and Reason* (1996)

Jacob Bronowski 1908–74

Polish-born mathematician and humanist

3 The world can only be grasped by action, not by contemplation . . . The hand is the cutting edge of the mind.
> *The Ascent of Man* (1973)

4 The essence of science: ask an impertinent question, and you are on the way to a pertinent answer.
> *The Ascent of Man* (1973)

5 The wish to hurt, the momentary intoxication with pain, is the loophole through which the pervert climbs into the minds of ordinary men.
> *The Face of Violence* (1954)

6 Therapy has become what I think of as the tenth American muse.
> attributed

Rupert Brooke 1887–1915

English poet
on Brooke: see **Cornford** 77:7, **James** 159:13, **Leavis** 186:1

7 Blow out, you bugles, over the rich Dead!
There's none of these so lonely and poor of old,
But, dying, has made us rarer gifts than gold.
These laid the world away; poured out the red
Sweet wine of youth; gave up the years to be
Of work and joy, and that unhoped serene,

That men call age; and those that would have been,
Their sons, they gave, their immortality.
> 'The Dead' (1914)

8 Then, the cool kindliness of sheets, that soon
Smooth away trouble; and the rough male kiss
Of blankets.
> 'The Great Lover' (1914)

9 Fish say, they have their stream and pond;
But is there anything beyond?
> 'Heaven' (1915)

10 Unkempt about those hedges blows
An English unofficial rose.
> 'The Old Vicarage, Grantchester' (1915)

11 God! I will pack, and take a train,
And get me to England once again!
For England's the one land, I know,
Where men with Splendid Hearts may go.
> 'The Old Vicarage, Grantchester' (1915)

12 For Cambridge people rarely smile,
Being urban, squat, and packed with guile.
> 'The Old Vicarage, Grantchester' (1915)

13 Stands the Church clock at ten to three?
And is there honey still for tea?
> 'The Old Vicarage, Grantchester' (1915)

14 Now, God be thanked Who has matched us with His hour,
And caught our youth, and wakened us from sleeping,
With hand made sure, clear eye, and sharpened power,
To turn, as swimmers into cleanness leaping.
> 'Peace' (1914)

15 If I should die, think only this of me:
That there's some corner of a foreign field
That is for ever England. There shall be
In that rich earth a richer dust concealed;
A dust whom England bore, shaped, made aware.
> 'The Soldier' (1914)

Anita Brookner 1938–

British novelist and art historian

1 Good women always think it is their fault when someone else is being offensive. Bad women never take the blame for anything.
Hotel du Lac (1984)

2 They were reasonable people, and no one was to be hurt, not even with words.
Hotel du Lac (1984)

3 I have reached the age when a woman begins to perceive that she is growing into the person she least plans to resemble: her mother.
Incidents in the Rue Laugier (1995)

4 Dr Weiss, at forty, knew that her life had been ruined by literature.
A Start in Life (1981)

Gwendolyn Brooks 1917–

American poet

5 Exhaust the little moment. Soon it dies. And be it gash or gold it will not come Again in this identical disguise.
'Exhaust the little moment' (1949)

6 The time
cracks into furious flower. Lifts its face all unashamed. And sways in wicked grace.
'The Second Sermon on the Warpland' (1968)

J. Brooks

7 A four-legged friend, a four-legged friend, He'll never let you down.
sung by Roy Rogers about his horse Trigger
'A Four Legged Friend' (1952)

Heywood Broun 1888–1939

American journalist

8 Men build bridges and throw railroads across deserts, and yet they contend successfully that the job of sewing on a button is beyond them. Accordingly, they don't have to sew buttons.
Seeing Things at Night (1921) 'Holding a Baby'

9 Posterity is as likely to be wrong as anybody else.
Sitting on the World (1924) 'The Last Review'

10 Everybody favours free speech in the slack moments when no axes are being ground.
in *New York World* 23 October 1926

11 Just as every conviction begins as a whim so does every emancipator serve his apprenticeship as a crank. A fanatic is a great leader who is just entering the room.
in *New York World* 6 February 1928

Craig Brown 1957–

English humorist

12 The world dwindles daily for the humorist . . . Jokes are fast running out, for a joke must transform real life in some perverse way, and real life has begun to perform the same operation perfectly professionally upon itself.
Craig Brown's Greatest Hits (1993)

H. Rap Brown 1943–

American Black Power leader

13 I say violence is necessary. It is as American as cherry pie.
speech, 27 July 1967

Lew Brown 1893–1958

American songwriter
see also **De Sylva** 88:12

14 Life is just a bowl of cherries.
title of song (1931)

Cecil Browne 1932–

American businessman

15 But not so odd
As those who choose

A Jewish God,
But spurn the Jews.

> reply to verse by William Norman Ewer; cf.
> **Ewer** 106:4

Frederick 'Boy' Browning
1896–1965
British soldier

1 I think we might be going a bridge too far.

> *expressing reservations about the Arnhem 'Market Garden' operation to Field Marshal* **Montgomery**
>
> > on 10 September 1944; R. E. Urquhart *Arnhem* (1958)

Lenny Bruce 1925–66
American comedian

2 The liberals can understand everything but people who don't understand them.

> John Cohen (ed.) *The Essential Lenny Bruce* (1967)

3 I'll die young, but it's like kissing God.

> *on his drug addiction*
> > attributed

Frank Bruno 1961–
English boxer

4 Boxing's just show business with blood.

> in *Guardian* 20 November 1991

5 Know what I mean, Harry?

> supposed to have been said in interview with sports commentator Harry Carpenter, possibly apocryphal

Anita Bryant 1940–

6 If homosexuality were the normal way, God would have made Adam and Bruce.

> in *New York Times* 5 June 1977

Bill Bryson 1951–
American travel writer

7 I had always thought that once you grew up you could do anything you wanted—stay up all night or eat ice-cream straight out of the container.

> *The Lost Continent* (1989)

8 What an odd thing tourism is. You fly off to a strange land, eagerly abandoning all the comforts of home, and then expend vast quantities of time and money in a largely futile attempt to recapture the comforts that you wouldn't have lost if you hadn't left home in the first place.

> *Neither Here Nor There* (1991)

Zbigniew Brzezinski 1928–
US Secretary of State and National Security Advisor

9 Russia can be an empire or a democracy, but it cannot be both.

> in *Foreign Affairs* March/April 1994 'The Premature Partnership'

Martin Buber 1878–1965
Austrian-born religious philosopher and Zionist

10 Through the Thou a person becomes I.

> *Ich und Du* (1923)

John Buchan 1875–1940
Scottish novelist; Governor-General of Canada, 1935–40
on Buchan: see **Bennett** 31:1

11 To live for a time close to great minds is the best kind of education.

> *Memory Hold-the-Door* (1940)

12 It's a great life if you don't weaken.

> *Mr Standfast* (1919)

13 An atheist is a man who has no invisible means of support.

> H. E. Fosdick *On Being a Real Person* (1943)

Frank Buchman 1878–1961

American evangelist; founder of the Moral
Re-Armament movement

1 There is enough in the world for
everyone's need, but not enough for
everyone's greed.
  Remaking the World (1947)

2 I thank heaven for a man like Adolf
Hitler, who built a front line of defence
against the anti-Christ of Communism.
  in *New York World-Telegram* 26 August 1936

Art Buchwald 1925–

American humorist

3 War is too serious a business to be left to
computers.
  in *International Herald Tribune* 14/15 June 1980

Gene Buck 1885–1957 and Herman Ruby 1891–1959

4 That Shakespearian rag,—
Most intelligent, very elegant.
  'That Shakespearian Rag' (1912 song); cf. **Eliot**
  101:12

Edward Bullard 1907–80

English geophysicist

5 Rutherford was a disaster. He started the
'something for nothing' tradition . . . the
notion that research can always be done
on the cheap . . . The war taught us
differently. If you want quick and
effective results you must put the money
in.
  P. Grosvenor and J. McMillan *The British Genius*
  (1973); cf. **Rutherford** 272:15

Arthur Buller 1874–1944

British botanist and mycologist

6 There was a young lady named Bright,
Whose speed was far faster than light;
She set out one day
In a relative way
And returned on the previous night.
  'Relativity' in *Punch* 19 December 1923

Ivor Bulmer-Thomas 1905–93

British Conservative politician

7 If he ever went to school without any
boots it was because he was too big for
them.
  *of Harold **Wilson**, who had claimed in a speech
  the previous year that more than half the children
  with whom he went to school had been unable to
  afford boots or shoes (and had therefore worn
  clogs)*
    speech at the Conservative Party Conference,
    in *Manchester Guardian* 13 October 1949; cf.
    Long 193:10

Basil Bunting 1900–85

English poet

8 Praise the green earth. Chance has
    appointed her
home, workshop, larder, middenpit.
Her lousy skin scabbed here and there by
cities provides us with name and nation.
  'Attis: or, Something Missing' (1931)

9 Dance tiptoe, bull,
black against may.
  'Briggflatts' (1965)

10   Our doom
is, to be sifted by the wind,

heaped up, smoothed down like silly
    sands.
We are less permanent than thought.
  'Villon' (1925)

Luis Buñuel 1900–83

Spanish film director
see also **Film titles** 112:7

11 Thanks to God, I am still an atheist.
  in *Le Monde* 16 December 1959

Julie Burchill 1960–

English journalist and writer

12 The freedom women were supposed to
have found in the Sixties largely boiled
down to easy contraception and
abortion: things to make life easier for
men, in fact.
  Damaged Goods (1986) 'Born Again Cows'

13 Now, at last, this sad, glittering century
has an image worthy of it: a wandering,

wondering girl, a silly Sloane turned secular saint, coming home in her coffin to RAF Northolt like the good soldier she was.

in *Guardian* 2 September 1997

Anthony Burgess 1917–
English novelist and critic

1 A clockwork orange.
   title of novel (1962)

2 It was the afternoon of my eighty-first birthday, and I was in bed with my catamite when Ali announced that the archbishop had come to see me.
   Earthly Powers (1980)

3 He said it was artificial respiration, but now I find I am to have his child.
   Inside Mr Enderby (1963)

4 The ideal reader of my novels is a lapsed Catholic and a failed musician, short-sighted, colour-blind, auditorily biased, who has read the books that I have read. He should also be about my age.
   George Plimpton (ed.) *Writers at Work* (4th Series, 1977)

5 The US presidency is a Tudor monarchy plus telephones.
   George Plimpton (ed.) *Writers at Work* (4th Series, 1977)

Johnny Burke 1908–64
American songwriter

6 Every time it rains, it rains
   Pennies from heaven.
   Don't you know each cloud contains
   Pennies from heaven?
   'Pennies from Heaven' (1936 song); cf. **Thatcher** 305:8

7 Like Webster's Dictionary, we're Morocco bound.
   'The Road to Morocco' (1942 song)

Burnum Burnum 1936–97
Australian political activist

8 We wish no harm to England's native people. We are here to bring you good

manners, refinement and an opportunity to make a *Koompartoo*, a fresh start.
in 1988, the year of Australia's bicentenary, on planting an Aboriginal flag on the white cliffs of Dover and 'claiming' England for the Aboriginal people
   on 26 January 1988; in obituary, *Independent* 20 August 1997

William S. Burroughs 1914–97
American novelist
see also **Last words** 182:12

9 Kerouac opened a million coffee bars and sold a million pairs of Levis to both sexes. Woodstock rises from his pages.
   The Adding Machine (1985) 'Remembering Jack Kerouac'

10 Junk is the ideal product . . . the ultimate merchandise. No sales talk necessary. The client will crawl through a sewer and beg to buy.
   The Naked Lunch (1959) introduction

11 The face of 'evil' is always the face of total need.
   The Naked Lunch (1959)

Benjamin Hapgood Burt 1880–1950
American songwriter

12 'You can tell a man who "boozes" by the company he chooses'
   And the pig got up and slowly walked away.
   'The Pig Got Up and Slowly Walked Away' (1933 song)

13 When you're all dressed up and no place to go.
   title of song (1913)

Nat Burton

14 There'll be bluebirds over the white cliffs of Dover,
   Tomorrow, just you wait and see.
   'The White Cliffs of Dover' (1941 song)

Barbara Bush 1925–

wife of George Bush; First Lady, 1989–93

1 Somewhere out in this audience may even be someone who will one day follow in my footsteps, and preside over the White House as the President's spouse. I wish him well!

remarks at Wellesley College Commencement, 1 June 1990

George Bush 1924–

American Republican statesman; 41st President of the US, 1989–93; husband of Barbara **Bush**
on Bush: see **Richards** 264:7

2 Oh, the vision thing.
responding to the suggestion that he turn his attention from short-term campaign objectives and look to the longer term
in *Time* 26 January 1987

3 What's wrong with being a boring kind of guy?
during the campaign for the Republican nomination; in *Daily Telegraph* 28 April 1988

4 Read my lips: no new taxes.
campaign pledge on taxation
in *New York Times* 19 August 1988

5 And now, we can see a new world coming into view. A world in which there is the very real prospect of a new world order.
speech, in *New York Times* 7 March 1991

Nicholas Murray Butler
1862–1947

President of Columbia University, 1901–45

6 An expert is one who knows more and more about less and less.
Commencement address at Columbia University; attributed

R. A. ('Rab') Butler 1902–82

British Conservative politician

on hearing of the appointment of Winston Churchill as Prime Minister in succession to Neville Chamberlain:
7 The good clean tradition of English politics, that of Pitt as opposed to Fox,

has been sold to the greatest adventurer of modern political history.
John Colville diary, 10 May 1940

8 REPORTER: Mr Butler, would you say that this [Anthony Eden] is the best Prime Minister we have?
R. A. BUTLER: Yes.
interview at London Airport, 8 January 1956

9 I think a Prime Minister has to be a butcher and know the joints. That is perhaps where I have not been quite competent, in knowing all the ways that you can cut up a carcass.
in *Listener* 28 June 1966

10 Politics is the Art of the Possible. That is what these pages show I have tried to achieve—not more—and that is what I have called my book.
The Art of the Possible (1971); see below; cf. **Galbraith** 123:14

Politics is the art of the possible.
Bismarck (1815–98) conversation with Meyer von Waldeck, 11 August 1867

11 In politics you must always keep running with the pack. The moment that you falter and they sense that you are injured, the rest will turn on you like wolves.
Dennis Walters *Not Always with the Pack* (1989)

A. S. Byatt 1936–

English novelist

12 What literature can and should do is change the people who teach the people who don't read the books.
interview in *Newsweek* 5 June 1995

James Branch Cabell
1879–1958

American novelist and essayist

13 The optimist proclaims that we live in the best of all possible worlds; and the pessimist fears this is true.
The Silver Stallion (1926); see below

In this best of possible worlds . . . all is for the best.
Voltaire (1694–1778) *Candide* (1759)

Irving Caesar 1895–

American songwriter

1 Picture you upon my knee,
Just tea for two and two for tea.
'Tea for Two' (1925 song)

John Cage 1912–92

American composer, pianist, and writer

2 I have nothing to say
and I am saying it and that is
poetry.
'Lecture on nothing' (1961)

James Cagney

see Film lines 110:1, Misquotations 219:6

James M. Cain 1892–1977

American novelist

3 The postman always rings twice.
title of novel (1934)

Michael Caine 1933–

English film actor

4 Not many people know that.
title of book (1984)

Joseph Cairns 1920–

British industrialist and politician

5 The betrayal of Ulster, the cynical and
entirely undemocratic banishment of its
properly elected Parliament and a
relegation to the status of a fuzzy wuzzy
colony is, I hope, a last betrayal
contemplated by Downing Street because
it is the last that Ulster will countenance.
speech on retiring as Lord Mayor of Belfast, 31
May 1972

Charles Calhoun 1897–1972

6 Shake, rattle and roll.
title of song (1954)

Antônio Callado 1917–97

Brazilian novelist

7 To live beyond eighty is an exaggeration,
almost an excess.
just before his 80th birthday (he died on 28
January, aged 80 years and 2 days)
in Independent 1 February 1997; obituary

James Callaghan 1912–

British Labour statesman; Prime Minister
1976–9
on Callaghan: see Jenkins 161:1, see also
Misquotations 218:3

8 You cannot now, if you ever could,
spend your way out of a recession.
speech at Labour Party Conference, 28
September 1976

9 You never reach the promised land. You
can march towards it.
in a television interview, 20 July 1978

10 I had known it was going to be a 'winter
of discontent'.
television interview, 8 February 1979; in Daily
Telegraph 9 February 1979; see below; cf.
Newspaper headlines 231:2

Now is the winter of our discontent
Made glorious summer by this sun of
York.
William Shakespeare (1564–1616) Richard III
(1591)

11 It's the first time in recorded history that
turkeys have been known to vote for an
early Christmas.
in the debate resulting in the fall of the Labour
government, when the pact between Labour and
the Liberals had collapsed, and the Scottish and
Welsh Nationalists had also withdrawn their
support
in the House of Commons, 28 March 1979

12 There are times, perhaps once every
thirty years, when there is a sea-change
in politics. It then does not matter what
you say or what you do. There is a shift
in what the public wants and what it
approves of. I suspect there is now such a
sea-change—and it is for Mrs Thatcher.
during the election campaign of 1979
Kenneth O. Morgan Callaghan (1997)

*of the popularity of Margaret **Thatcher**:*

1 The further you got from Britain, the more admired you found she was.
in *Spectator* 1 December 1990

Helder Camara 1909–

Brazilian priest

2 When I give food to the poor they call me a saint. When I ask why the poor have no food they call me a communist.
attributed

Mrs Patrick Campbell

1865–1940

English actress
*on Campbell: see **Woollcott** 335:17*

3 I'm out of a job. London wants flappers, and I can't flap.
of the theatre of 1927
Margot Peters *Mrs Pat* (1984)

4 The deep, deep peace of the double-bed after the hurly-burly of the chaise-longue.
on her recent marriage
Alexander Woollcott *While Rome Burns* (1934)
'The First Mrs Tanqueray'

5 It doesn't matter what you do in the bedroom as long as you don't do it in the street and frighten the horses.
Daphne Fielding *The Duchess of Jermyn Street* (1964)

6 Tallulah [Bankhead] is always skating on thin ice. Everyone wants to be there when it breaks.
in *The Times* 13 December 1968

Roy Campbell 1901–57

South African poet

7 Giraffes!—a People
Who live between the earth and skies,
Each in his lone religious steeple,
Keeping a light-house with his eyes.
'Dreaming Spires' (1946)

8 Of all the clever people round me here
I most delight in Me—
Mine is the only voice I care to hear,
And mine the only face I like to see.
'Home Thoughts in Bloomsbury' (1930)

9 You praise the firm restraint with which they write—
I'm with you there, of course:
They use the snaffle and the curb all right,
But where's the bloody horse?
'On Some South African Novelists' (1930)

10 South Africa, renowned both far and wide
For politics and little else beside.
The Wayzgoose (1928)

11 I hate 'Humanity' and all such abstracts: but I love *people*. Lovers of 'Humanity' generally hate *people and children*, and keep parrots or puppy dogs.
Light on a Dark Horse (1951)

Albert Camus 1913–60

French novelist, dramatist, and essayist

12 You know what charm is: a way of getting the answer yes without having asked any clear question.
The Fall (1957)

13 We are all special cases. We all want to appeal against something! Everyone insists on his innocence, at all costs, even if it means accusing the rest of the human race and heaven.
The Fall (1957)

14 I'll tell you a big secret, *mon cher*. Don't wait for the last judgement. It takes place every day.
The Fall (1957)

15 Poor people's memory is less nourished than that of the rich; it has fewer landmarks in space because they seldom leave the place where they live, and fewer reference points in time . . . Of course, there is the memory of the heart that they say is the surest kind, but the heart wears out with sorrow and labour, it forgets sooner under the weight of fatigue.
The First Man (1994)

16 The struggle itself towards the heights is enough to fill a human heart. One must imagine that Sisyphus is happy.
The Myth of Sisyphus (1942)

17 Politics and the fate of mankind are formed by men without ideals and

without greatness. Those who have greatness within them do not go in for politics.
Notebooks 1935–42 (1963)

1 An intellectual is someone whose mind watches itself.
Notebooks 1935–42 (1963)

2 What is a rebel? A man who says no.
The Rebel (1953)

3 All modern revolutions have ended in a reinforcement of the State.
The Rebel (1953)

4 Mother died today. Or perhaps it was yesterday, I don't know.
The Stranger (1944)

5 What I know most surely about morality and the duty of man I owe to sport.
often quoted as '. . . I owe to football'
Herbert R. Lottman *Albert Camus* (1979)

6 Without work, all life goes rotten, but when work is soulless, life stifles and dies.
attributed; E. F. Schumacher *Good Work* (1979)

Elias Canetti 1905–94

Bulgarian-born writer and novelist

7 All the things one has forgotten scream for help in dreams.
Die Provinz der Menschen (1973)

Eric Cantona 1966–

French footballer

8 When seagulls follow a trawler, it is because they think sardines will be thrown into the sea.
to the media at the end of a press conference, 31 March 1995

Al Capone 1899–1947

Italian-born American gangster

9 Once in the racket you're always in it.
in *Philadelphia Public Ledger* 18 May 1929

10 Don't you get the idea I'm one of these goddam radicals. Don't get the idea I'm knocking the American system.
interview, *c.*1929, with Claud Cockburn; Claud Cockburn *In Time of Trouble* (1956)

Truman Capote 1924–84

American writer and novelist
on Capote: see **Vidal** 317:15

11 Other voices, other rooms.
title of novel (1948)

Al Capp 1907–79

American cartoonist

12 A product of the untalented, sold by the unprincipled to the utterly bewildered.
on abstract art
in *National Observer* 1 July 1963

Neville Cardus 1889–1975

English critic and writer

13 If everything else in this nation of ours were lost but cricket—her Constitution and the laws of England of Lord Halsbury—it would be possible to reconstruct from the theory and practice of cricket all the eternal Englishness which has gone to the establishment of that Constitution and the laws aforesaid.
Cricket (1930)

George Carey 1935–

British Anglican clergyman, Archbishop of Canterbury from 1991

14 I see it as an elderly lady, who mutters away to herself in a corner, ignored most of the time.
on the Church of England
in *Readers Digest* (British ed.) March 1991

15 We must recall that the Church is always 'one generation away from extinction.'
Working Party Report *Youth A Part: Young People and the Church* (1996) foreword

Stokely Carmichael 1941–98

American Black Power leader

16 The only position for women in SNCC is prone.
response to a question about the position of women
at a Student Nonviolent Coordinating Committee conference, November 1964

Stokely Carmichael 1941–98 and Charles Vernon Hamilton 1929–
American Black Power leaders

1 The adoption of the concept of Black Power is one of the most legitimate and healthy developments in American politics and race relations in our time. . . . It is a call for black people in this country to unite, to recognize their heritage, to build a sense of community. It is a call for black people to begin to define their own goals, to lead their own organizations and to support those organizations. It is a call to reject the racist institutions and values of this society.

Black Power (1967)

Dale Carnegie 1888–1955
American writer and lecturer

2 How to win friends and influence people.

title of book (1936)

J. L. Carr 1912–
English novelist

3 *You* have not had thirty years' experience . . . *You* have had one year's experience 30 times.

to a teacher
The Harpole Report (1972)

Lord Carrington 1919–
British Conservative politician

4 Q: If Mrs Thatcher were run over by a bus . . . ?
LORD CARRINGTON: It wouldn't dare.

during the Falklands War
Russell Lewis *Margaret Thatcher* (1984)

Edward Carson 1854–1935
Northern Irish lawyer and politician

5 From the day I first entered parliament up to the present, devotion to the union has been the guiding star of my political life.

in *Dictionary of National Biography* (1917–)

6 My only great qualification for being put at the head of the Navy is that I am very much at sea.

I. Colvin *Life of Lord Carson* (1936)

Rachel Carson 1907–64
American zoologist

7 Over increasingly large areas of the United States, spring now comes unheralded by the return of the birds, and the early mornings are strangely silent where once they were filled with the beauty of bird song.

The Silent Spring (1962)

Angela Carter 1940–92
English novelist

8 Clothes are our weapons, our challenges, our visible insults.

Nothing Sacred (1982) 'Notes for a Theory of Sixties Style'

9 Comedy is tragedy that happens to *other* people.

Wise Children (1991)

10 If *Miss* means respectably unmarried, and *Mrs* respectably married, then *Ms* means nudge, nudge, wink, wink.

'The Language of Sisterhood' in Christopher Ricks (ed.) *The State of the Language* (1980); cf. **Monty Python's Flying Circus** 221:1

Howard Carter 1874–1939
English archaeologist

11 Yes, wonderful things.

when asked what he could see on first looking into the tomb of Tutankhamun, 26 November 1922; his notebook records the words as 'Yes, it is wonderful'

H. V. F. Winstone *Howard Carter and the discovery of the tomb of Tutankhamun* (1993)

Jimmy Carter 1924–

American Democratic statesman, 39th President of the US, 1977–81

1 I'm Jimmy Carter, and I'm going to be your next president.
to the son of a campaign supporter, November 1975
  I'll Never Lie to You (1976)

2 We should live our lives as though Christ were coming this afternoon.
speech to Bible class at Plains, Georgia, March 1976
  in *Boston Sunday Herald Advertiser* 11 April 1976

3 I've looked on a lot of women with lust. I've committed adultery in my heart many times. This is something that God recognizes I will do—and I have done it—and God forgives me for it.
  in *Playboy* November 1976

Sydney Carter 1915–

English folk-song writer

4 It's God they ought to crucify
Instead of you and me,
I said to the carpenter
A-hanging on the tree.
  'Friday Morning' (1967)

5 Dance then wherever you may be,
I am the Lord of the Dance, said he,
And I'll lead you all, wherever you may be
And I'll lead you all in the dance, said he.
  'Lord of the Dance' (1967)

Barbara Cartland 1901–

English writer

6 After forty a woman has to choose between losing her figure or her face. My advice is to keep your face, and stay sitting down.
  Libby Purves 'Luncheon à la Cartland'; in *The Times* 6 October 1993; similar remarks have been attributed since *c.*1980

Pablo Casals 1876–1973

Spanish cellist, conductor, and composer

7 It is like a beautiful woman who has not grown older, but younger with time, more slender, more supple, more graceful.
of the cello
  in *Time* 29 April 1957

8 The man who works and is not bored is never old.
  J. Lloyd Webber (ed.) *Song of the Birds* (1985)

Roger Casement 1864–1916

Irish nationalist; executed for treason in 1916

9 Self-government is our right, a thing born in us at birth, a thing no more to be doled out to us, or withheld from us, by another people than the right to life itself— than the right to feel the sun, or smell the flowers, or to love our kind.
  statement at the conclusion of his trial, the Old Bailey, London, 29 June 1916

10 Where all your rights become only an accumulated wrong; where men must beg with bated breath for leave to subsist in their own land, to think their own thoughts, to sing their own songs, to garner the fruits of their own labours . . . then surely it is a braver, a saner and truer thing, to be a rebel in act and deed against such circumstances as these than tamely to accept it as the natural lot of men.
  statement at the conclusion of his trial, the Old Bailey, London, 29 June 1916

Hugh Casson 1910–

English architect

11 We have now to plan no longer for soft little animals pottering about on their own two legs, but for hard steel canisters hurtling about with these same little animals inside them.
  C. Williams-Ellis *Around the World in 90 Years* (1978)

Ted Castle 1907–79

British journalist

1 In place of strife.

*title of Government White Paper, 17 January 1969,
suggested by Castle to his wife, Barbara Castle,
then Secretary of State for Employment*

Barbara Castle diary, 15 January 1969

Fidel Castro 1927–

Cuban statesman, Prime Minister 1959–76
and President since 1976
on Castro: see **Ceauşescu** 56:9

2 Capitalism is using its money; we
socialists throw it away.

in *Observer* 8 November 1964

■ Catch-phrases

see box opposite
see also **Grenfell** 133:11, **Laurel** 181:12

Willa Cather 1873–1947

American novelist

3 Oh, the Germans classify, but the French
arrange!

Death Comes For the Archbishop (1927))

Mr Justice Caulfield 1914–

British lawyer

4 Remember Mary Archer in the witness
box. Your vision of her will probably
never disappear. Has she elegance? Has
she fragrance? Would she have—without
the strain of this trial—a radiance?

summing up of court case between Jeffrey
Archer and the *News of the World*, July 1987, in
The Times 24 July 1987

Charles Causley 1917–

English poet and schoolmaster

5 Timothy Winters comes to school
With eyes as wide as a football-pool,
Ears like bombs and teeth like splinters:
A blitz of a boy is Timothy Winters.

'Timothy Winters' (1957)

Constantine Cavafy
1863–1933

Greek poet

6 What are we waiting for, gathered in the
market-place?
The barbarians are to arrive today.

'Waiting for the Barbarians' (1904)

7 And now, what will become of us
without the barbarians?
Those people were a kind of solution.

'Waiting for the Barbarians' (1904)

Edith Cavell 1865–1915

English nurse

8 Patriotism is not enough. I must have no
hatred or bitterness towards anyone.

*on the eve of her execution by the Germans for
assisting in the escape of British soldiers from
occupied Belgium*

in *The Times* 23 October 1915

Nicolae Ceauşescu 1918–89

Romanian Communist statesman, first
President of the Socialist Republic of
Romania 1974–89

9 Fidel Castro is right. You do not quieten
your enemy by talking with him like a
priest, but by burning him.

at a Communist Party meeting 17 December 1989

in *Guardian* 11 January 1990

Paul Celan 1920–70

German poet

10 A man lives in the house he plays with
his vipers he writes
he writes when it grows dark to
Deutschland your golden hair
Margareta
Your ashen hair Shulamith we shovel a
grave in the air there you won't lie too
cramped.

'Deathfugue' (written 1944)

▶▶

Catch-phrases

1 CECIL: After you, Claude.
CLAUDE: No, after you, Cecil.

> *ITMA* (BBC radio programme, 1939–49),
> written by Ted Kavanagh (1892–1958)

2 And now for something completely different.

> *Monty Python's Flying Circus* (BBC TV
> programme, 1969–74)

3 Anyone for tennis?

> said to be typical of drawing-room comedies,
> much associated with Humphrey Bogart
> (1899–1957); perhaps from George Bernard
> Shaw 'Anybody on for a game of tennis?'
> *Misalliance* (1914)

4 Are yer courtin'?

> *Have a Go!* (BBC radio quiz programme,
> 1946–67), used by Wilfred Pickles (1904–)

5 Are you sitting comfortably? Then I'll begin.

> *sometimes 'Then we'll begin'*
>
> *Listen with Mother* (BBC radio programme
> for children, 1950–82), used by Julia Lang
> (1921–)

6 The butler did it!

> *a solution for detective stories*
>
> Nigel Rees, in *Sayings of the Century* (1984),
> quotes a correspondent who recalls hearing
> it at a cinema *c.*1916 but the origin of the
> phrase has not been traced

7 Can I do you now, sir?

> *spoken by 'Mrs Mopp'*
>
> *ITMA* (BBC radio programme, 1939–49),
> written by Ted Kavanagh (1892–1958)

8 Can you hear me, mother?

> used by Sandy Powell (1900–82)

9 The day war broke out.

> *customary preamble to radio monologues in the
> role of a Home Guard, used by Robb Wilton
> (1881–1957)*
>
> from *c.*1940

10 Didn't she [*or* he *or* they] do well?

> used by Bruce Forsyth (1928–) in 'The
> Generation Game' on BBC Television, 1973
> onwards

11 Don't forget the diver.

> *spoken by 'The Diver'; based on 'a memory of
> the pier at New Brighton where Tommy Handley
> used to go as a child . . . A man in a bathing
> suit . . . whined "Don't forget the diver, sir."'*
>
> *ITMA* (BBC radio programme, 1939–49),
> written by Ted Kavanagh (1892–1958)

12 Eat my shorts!

> *The Simpsons* (American TV series, 1990–),
> created by Matt Groening

13 Ee, it was agony, Ivy.

> *Ray's a Laugh* (BBC radio programme,
> 1949–61), written by Ted Ray (1906–77)

14 Evening, all.

> opening words spoken by Jack Warner as
> Sergeant Dixon in *Dixon of Dock Green* (BBC
> television series, 1956–76), written by Ted
> Willis (1918–)

15 Everybody wants to get inta the act!

> used by Jimmy Durante (1893–1980)

16 An everyday story of country folk.

> introduction to *The Archers* (BBC radio serial,
> 1950 onwards), written by Geoffrey Webb
> and Edward J. Mason

17 Exterminate! Exterminate!

> the Daleks in *Dr Who* (BBC television series,
> from 1963), written by Terry Nation

18 A good idea—son.

> *Educating Archie*, 1950–3 BBC radio comedy
> series, written by Eric Sykes (1923–) and
> Max Bygraves (1922–)

19 Good morning, sir—was there something?

> used by Sam Costa in radio comedy series
> *Much-Binding-in-the-Marsh*, written by
> Richard Murdoch (1907–90) and Kenneth
> Horne (1900–69), started 2 January 1947

20 Goodnight, children . . . everywhere.

> *closing words normally spoken by 'Uncle Mac'
> in the 1930s and 1940s*
>
> on *Children's Hour* (BBC Radio programme);
> written by Derek McCulloch (1892–1978)

▶

> ## Catch-phrases continued

1 Have you read any good books lately?

used by Richard Murdoch in radio comedy series *Much-Binding-in-the-Marsh*, written by Richard Murdoch (1907–90) and Kenneth Horne (1900–69), started 2 January 1947

2 Hello, good evening, and welcome.

used by David Frost (1939–) in 'The Frost Programme' on BBC Television, 1966 onwards

3 Here come de judge.

from the song-title 'Here comes the judge' (1968); written by Dewey 'Pigmeat' Markham, Dick Alen, Bob Astor, and Sarah Harvey

4 Here's one I made earlier.

culmination to directions for making a model out of empty yoghurt pots, coat-hangers, and similar domestic items

children's BBC television programme *Blue Peter*, 1963 onwards

5 I didn't get where I am today without . . . .

used by the manager C. J. in BBC television series *The Fall and Rise of Reginald Perrin*, 1976–80); based on David Nobbs *The Death of Reginald Perrin* (1975)

6 I don't like this game, let's play another game—let's play doctor and nurses.

phrase first used by Bluebottle in 'The Phantom Head-Shaver' in *The Goon Show* (BBC radio series) 15 October 1954, written by Spike **Milligan**; the catch-phrase was often 'I do not like this game'

7 I don't mind if I do.

spoken by 'Colonel Chinstrap'

ITMA (BBC radio programme, 1939–49), written by Ted Kavanagh (1892–1958)

8 I go—I come back.

spoken by 'Ali Oop'

ITMA (BBC radio programme, 1939–49), written by Ted Kavanagh (1892–1958)

9 I have a cunning plan.

Baldrick's habitual over-optimistic promise in *Blackadder II* (1987 television series), written by Richard Curtis and Ben Elton (1959–)

10 I'm Bart Simpson: who the hell are you?

The Simpsons (American TV series, 1990–), created by Matt Groening

11 I'm in charge.

used by Bruce Forsyth (1928–) in 'Sunday Night at the London Palladium' on ITV, 1958 onwards

12 I'm worried about Jim.

frequent line in *Mrs Dale's Diary*, BBC radio series 1948–69

13 It all depends what you mean by . . .

habitually used by C. E. M. **Joad** when replying to questions on 'The Brains Trust' (formerly 'Any Questions'), BBC radio (1941–8)

14 It's being so cheerful as keeps me going.

spoken by 'Mona Lott'

ITMA (BBC radio programme, 1939–49), written by Ted Kavanagh (1892–1958)

15 I've arrived and to prove it I'm here!

Educating Archie, 1950–3 BBC radio comedy series, written by Eric Sykes (1923–) and Max Bygraves (1922–)

16 I've started so I'll finish.

said when a contestant's time runs out while a question is being put

Magnus Magnusson (1929–) *Mastermind*, BBC television (1972–97)

17 Just like that!

used by Tommy Cooper (1921–84)

18 Keep on truckin'.

used by Robert Crumb (1943–) in cartoons from *c.*1972

19 Left hand down a bit!

The Navy Lark (BBC radio series, 1959–77), written by Laurie Wyman

20 Let's be careful out there.

Hill Street Blues (television series, 1981 onwards), written by Steven Bochco and Michael Kozoll

▶

▶ Catch-phrases continued

1 Mind my bike!
used by Jack Warner (1895–1981) in the BBC radio series *Garrison Theatre*, 1939 onwards

2 Nice to see you—to see you, nice.
used by Bruce Forsyth (1928–) in 'The Generation Game' on BBC Television, 1973 onwards

3 Oh, calamity!
used by Robertson Hare (1891–1979)

4 Pass the sick bag, Alice.
used by John Junor (1919–97); in *Sunday Express* and elsewhere

5 Seriously, though, he's doing a grand job!
used by David Frost (1939–) in 'That Was The Week That Was', on BBC Television, 1962-3

6 Shome mishtake, shurely?
in *Private Eye* magazine, 1980s

7 So farewell then . . .
frequent opening of poems by 'E. J. Thribb' in Private Eye *magazine, usually as an obituary* 1970s onwards

8 Take me to your leader.
from science-fiction stories

9 The truth is out there.
The X Files (American television series, 1993–), created by Chris Carter

10 Very interesting . . . but stupid.
Rowan and Martin's Laugh-In (American television series, 1967–73), written by Dan Rowan (1922–87) and Dick Martin (1923–)

11 The weekend starts here.
Ready, Steady, Go, British television series, c.1963

12 We have ways of making you talk.
perhaps originating in the line 'We have ways of making men talk' in *Lives of a Bengal Lancer* (1935 film), written by Waldemar Young et al.

13 What's up, Doc?
Bugs Bunny cartoons, written by Tex Avery (1907–80), from c.1940

14 Who loves ya, baby?
used by Telly Savalas (1926–) in American TV series *Kojak* (1973-8)

15 You bet your sweet bippy.
Rowan and Martin's Laugh-In (American television series, 1967–73), written by Dan Rowan (1922–87) and Dick Martin (1923–)

16 You might very well think that. I couldn't possibly comment.
the Chief Whip's habitual response to questioning
House of Cards (televised 1990); written by Michael Dobbs (1948–)

17 You're going to like this . . . not a lot . . . but you'll like it!
used by Paul Daniels (1938–) in his conjuring act, especially on television from 1981 onwards

18 You rotten swines. I told you I'd be deaded.
phrase first used by Bluebottle in 'Hastings Flyer' in *The Goon Show* (BBC radio series) 3 January 1956, written by Spike **Milligan**

19 Your starter for ten.
phrase often used by Bamber Gascoigne (1935–) in *University Challenge* (ITV quiz series, 1962–87)

20 You silly twisted boy.
phrase first used in 'The Dreaded Batter Pudding Hurler' in *The Goon Show* (BBC radio series) 12 October 1954, written by Spike **Milligan**

▶▶ Paul Celan continued

21 He shouts play death more sweetly this
Death is a master from Deutschland
he shouts scrape your strings darker
you'll rise then as smoke to the sky

you'll have a grave then in the clouds
there you won't lie too cramped.
'Deathfugue' (written 1944)

22 *Der Tod ist ein Meister aus Deutschland.*
Death is a master from Germany.
'Deathfugue' (written 1944)

1 There's nothing in the world for which a poet will give up writing, not even when he is a Jew and the language of his poems is German.

letter to relatives, 2 August 1948

Neville Chamberlain

1869–1940

British Conservative statesman; Prime Minister, 1937–40
on Chamberlain: see **Channon** 61:7, **Churchill** 65:13, **Nicolson** 230:5

2 In war, whichever side may call itself the victor, there are no winners, but all are losers.

speech at Kettering, 3 July 1938

3 How horrible, fantastic, incredible it is that we should be digging trenches and trying on gas-masks here because of a quarrel in a far away country between people of whom we know nothing.

on Germany's annexation of the Sudetenland
radio broadcast, 27 September 1938

4 This is the second time in our history that there has come back from Germany to Downing Street peace with honour. I believe it is peace for our time.

speech from 10 Downing Street, 30 September 1938; see below

Lord Salisbury and myself have brought you back peace—but a peace I hope with honour.

Benjamin Disraeli (1804–81) speech on returning from the Congress of Berlin, 16 July 1878

5 This morning, the British Ambassador in Berlin handed the German government a final Note stating that, unless we heard from them by eleven o'clock that they were prepared at once to withdraw their troops from Poland, a state of war would exist between us. I have to tell you now that no such undertaking has been received, and that consequently this country is at war with Germany.

radio broadcast, 3 September 1939

6 Whatever may be the reason—whether it was that Hitler thought he might get away with what he had got without fighting for it, or whether it was that after all the preparations were not sufficiently complete—however, one thing is certain—he missed the bus.

speech at Central Hall, Westminster, 4 April 1940

Raymond Chandler

1888–1959

American writer of detective fiction

7 It was a blonde. A blonde to make a bishop kick a hole in a stained glass window.

Farewell, My Lovely (1940)

8 A big hard-boiled city with no more personality than a paper cup.

of Los Angeles
The Little Sister (1949)

9 Crime isn't a disease, it's a symptom. Cops are like a doctor that gives you aspirin for a brain tumour.

The Long Good-Bye (1953)

10 Down these mean streets a man must go who is not himself mean, who is neither tarnished nor afraid.

in *Atlantic Monthly* December 1944 'The Simple Art of Murder'

11 If my books had been any worse, I should not have been invited to Hollywood, and if they had been any better, I should not have come.

letter to Charles W. Morton, 12 December 1945

12 Would you convey my compliments to the purist who reads your proofs and tell him or her that I write in a sort of broken-down patois which is something like the way a Swiss waiter talks, and that when I split an infinitive, God damn it, I split it so it will stay split.

letter to Edward Weeks, 18 January 1947

13 When in doubt have a man come through the door with a gun in his hand.

attributed

Coco Chanel 1883–1971

French couturière

14 Clothes by a man who doesn't know women, never had one, and dreams of being one!

of Dior's New Look
in *Vanity Fair* June 1994

1 Passion always goes, and boredom stays.
> Frances Kennett *Coco: the Life and Loves of Gabrielle Chanel* (1989)

2 You ask if they were happy. This is not a characteristic of a European. To be contented—that's for the cows.
> A. Madsen *Coco Chanel* (1990)

3 Youth is something very new: twenty years ago no one mentioned it.
> Marcel Haedrich *Coco Chanel, Her Life, Her Secrets* (1971)

Henry ('Chips') Channon
1897–1958
American-born British Conservative politician and diarist

4 I like my 'abroad' to be Catholic and sensual.
> diary, 18 January 1924

5 What is more dull than a discreet diary? One might just as well have a discreet soul.
> diary, 26 July 1935

6 There is nowhere in the world where sleep is so deep as in the libraries of the House of Commons.
> diary, 16 December 1937

7 He is winning through and will probably be Premier for years to come.
> *of Neville* **Chamberlain**
> diary, 15 January 1939

8 I gather it has now been decided not to embrace the Russian bear, but to hold out a hand and accept its paw gingerly. No more. The worst of both worlds.
> diary, 16 May 1939

Charlie Chaplin 1889–1977
English film actor and director

9 All I need to make a comedy is a park, a policeman and a pretty girl.
> *My Autobiography* (1964)

10 Words are cheap. The biggest thing you can say is 'elephant'.
> *on the universality of silent films*
> B. Norman *The Movie Greats* (1981)

Arthur Chapman 1873–1935
American poet

11 Out where the handclasp's a little stronger,
Out where the smile dwells a little longer,
That's where the West begins.
> *Out Where the West Begins* (1916)

Charles, Prince of Wales
1948–
Heir apparent to the British throne; former husband of **Diana**, Princess of Wales

when asked if he was 'in love':
12 Yes . . . whatever that may mean.
> *after the announcement of his engagement*
> interview, 24 February 1981; cf. **Duffy** 92:8

13 A monstrous carbuncle on the face of a much-loved and elegant friend.
> *on the proposed extension to the National Gallery*
> speech in London, 30 May 1984

14 I just come and talk to the plants, really—very important to talk to them, they respond I find.
> television interview, 21 September 1986

Lord Charteris 1913–
the Queen's former private secretary

15 The Duchess of York is a vulgarian. She is vulgar, vulgar, vulgar, and that is that.
> in *Spectator* 5 January 1995

G. K. Chesterton 1874–1936
English essayist, novelist, and poet
on Chesterton: see **Belloc** 28:2, **Epitaphs** 105:12; *see also* **Telegrams** 305:1

16 Are they clinging to their crosses, F. E. Smith?
> *satirizing F. E.* **Smith**'s *response to the Welsh Disestablishment Bill*
> 'Antichrist' (1915)

17 Talk about the pews and steeples
And the Cash that goes therewith!
But the souls of Christian peoples . . .
Chuck it, Smith!
> 'Antichrist' (1915)

18 I tell you naught for your comfort,
Yea, naught for your desire,

Save that the sky grows darker yet
And the sea rises higher.
The Ballad of the White Horse (1911)

1 For the great Gaels of Ireland
Are the men that God made mad,
For all their wars are merry,
And all their songs are sad.
The Ballad of the White Horse (1911)

2 The thing on the blind side of the heart,
On the wrong side of the door,
The green plant groweth, menacing
Almighty lovers in the Spring;
There is always a forgotten thing,
And love is not secure.
The Ballad of the White Horse (1911)

3 The gallows in my garden, people say,
Is new and neat and adequately tall.
I tie the noose on in a knowing way
As one that knots his necktie for a ball;
But just as all the neighbours—on the
wall—
Are drawing a long breath to shout
'Hurray!'
The strangest whim has seized me . . . .
After all
I think I will not hang myself today.
'Ballade of Suicide' (1915)

4 When fishes flew and forests walked
And figs grew upon thorn,
Some moment when the moon was blood
Then surely I was born.

With monstrous head and sickening cry
And ears like errant wings,
The devil's walking parody
On all four-footed things.
'The Donkey' (1900)

5 Fools! For I also had my hour;
One far fierce hour and sweet:
There was a shout about my ears,
And palms before my feet.
'The Donkey' (1900)

6 They died to save their country and they
only saved the world.
'English Graves' (1922)

7 Why do you rush through the fields in
trains,
Guessing so much and so much.
Why do you flash through the flowery
meads,
Fat-head poet that nobody reads;

And why do you know such a frightful
lot
About people in gloves and such?
'The Fat White Woman Speaks' (1933); cf.
Cornford 77:6

8 From all that terror teaches,
From lies of tongue and pen,
From all the easy speeches
That comfort cruel men,
From sale and profanation
Of honour and the sword,
From sleep and from damnation,
Deliver us, good Lord!
'A Hymn' (1915)

9 Strong gongs groaning as the guns boom
far,
Don John of Austria is going to the war.
'Lepanto' (1915)

10 The folk that live in Liverpool, their heart
is in their boots;
They go to hell like lambs, they do,
because the hooter hoots.
'Me Heart' (1914)

11 Before the Roman came to Rye or out to
Severn strode,
The rolling English drunkard made the
rolling English road.
A reeling road, a rolling road, that
rambles round the shire,
And after him the parson ran, the sexton
and the squire;
A merry road, a mazy road, and such as
we did tread
The night we went to Birmingham by
way of Beachy Head.
'The Rolling English Road' (1914)

12 For there is good news yet to hear and
fine things to be seen,
Before we go to Paradise by way of
Kensal Green.
'The Rolling English Road' (1914)

13 Smile at us, pay us, pass us; but do not
quite forget.
For we are the people of England, that
never have spoken yet.
'The Secret People' (1915)

14 Tea, although an Oriental,
Is a gentleman at least;
Cocoa is a cad and coward,

Cocoa is a vulgar beast.

'Song of Right and Wrong' (1914)

1 Lancashire merchants whenever they like
Can water the beer of a man in Klondike
Or poison the meat of a man in Bombay;
And that is the meaning of Empire Day.

'Songs of Education: II Geography' (1922)

2 And Noah he often said to his wife when he sat down to dine,
'I don't care where the water goes if it doesn't get into the wine.'

'Wine and Water' (1914)

3 An adventure is only an inconvenience rightly considered. An inconvenience is only an adventure wrongly considered.

All Things Considered (1908) 'On Running after one's Hat'

4 The rich are the scum of the earth in every country.

The Flying Inn (1914)

5 There is no such thing on earth as an uninteresting subject; the only thing that can exist is an uninterested person.

Heretics (1905)

6 Bigotry may be roughly defined as the anger of men who have no opinions.

Heretics (1905)

7 After the first silence the small man said to the other: 'Where does a wise man hide a pebble?'
And the tall man answered in a low voice: 'On the beach.'
The small man nodded, and after a short silence said: 'Where does a wise man hide a leaf?'
And the other answered: 'In the forest.'

The Innocence of Father Brown (1911)

8 One sees great things from the valley; only small things from the peak.

The Innocence of Father Brown (1911)

9 Thieves respect property. They merely wish the property to become their property that they may more perfectly respect it.

The Man who was Thursday (1908)

10 The human race, to which so many of my readers belong, has been playing at children's games from the beginning, and will probably do it till the end, which is a nuisance for the few people who grow up.

Napoleon of Notting Hill (1904)

11 The men who really believe in themselves are all in lunatic asylums.

Orthodoxy (1908)

12 Poets do not go mad; but chess-players do. Mathematicians go mad, and cashiers; but creative artists very seldom. I am not, as will be seen, in any sense attacking logic: I only say that this danger does lie in logic, not in imagination.

Orthodoxy (1908)

13 Tradition means giving votes to the most obscure of all classes, our ancestors. It is the democracy of the dead.

Orthodoxy (1908)

14 Democrats object to men being disqualified by the accident of birth; tradition objects to their being disqualified by the accident of death.

Orthodoxy (1908)

15 All conservatism is based upon the idea that if you leave things alone you leave them as they are. But you do not. If you leave a thing alone you leave it to a torrent of change.

Orthodoxy (1908)

16 Angels can fly because they take themselves lightly.

Orthodoxy (1908)

17 It isn't that they can't see the solution. It is that they can't see the problem.

The Scandal of Father Brown (1935)

18 They say travel broadens the mind; but you must have the mind.

'The Shadow of the Shark' (1921)

19 Lying in bed would be an altogether perfect and supreme experience if only one had a coloured pencil long enough to draw on the ceiling.

Tremendous Trifles (1909)

1 Hardy went down to botanize in the swamp, while Meredith climbed towards the sun. Meredith became, at his best, a sort of daintily dressed Walt Whitman: Hardy became a sort of village atheist brooding and blaspheming over the village idiot.

Victorian Age in Literature (1912)

2 The Christian ideal has not been tried and found wanting. It has been found difficult; and left untried.

What's Wrong with the World (1910) pt. 1 'The Unfinished Temple'

3 The prime truth of woman, the universal mother . . . that if a thing is worth doing, it is worth doing badly.

What's Wrong with the World (1910) pt. 4 'Folly and Female Education'

4 To be clever enough to get all that money, one must be stupid enough to want it.

The Wisdom of Father Brown (1914)

5 Journalism largely consists in saying 'Lord Jones Dead' to people who never knew that Lord Jones was alive.

The Wisdom of Father Brown (1914)

6 Democracy means government by the uneducated, while aristocracy means government by the badly educated.

in *New York Times* 1 February 1931

7 When men stop believing in God they don't believe in nothing; they believe in anything.

widely attributed, although not traced in his works; first recorded as 'The first effect of not believing in God is to believe in anything' in Emile Cammaerts *Chesterton: The Laughing Prophet* (1937)

Maurice Chevalier 1888–1972

French singer and actor

8 Considering the alternative, it's not too bad at all.

on being asked what he felt about the advancing years, on his seventy-second birthday

Michael Freedland *Maurice Chevalier* (1981)

Erskine Childers 1870–1922

Anglo-Irish writer and Irish nationalist
see also **Last words** 182:2

9 The riddle of the sands.

title of novel (1903)

Lawton Chiles 1930–

American politician

10 You are misunderstood, maligned, viewed by the press as a Pulitzer Prize ready to be won.

on the problems of investigative journalism for politicians

in *St Petersburg (Florida) Times* 6 March 1991

Jaques Chirac 1932–

French statesman, Prime Minister 1974–6 and 1986–8, President since 1995

11 For its part, France wants you to take part in this great undertaking.

on European Monetary Union

speech to both Houses of Parliament, 15 May 1996

Melanie ('Mel C.') Chisholm

English pop singer, member ('Sporty Spice') of The Spice Girls
see also **Rowbottom**

12 If Oasis are bigger than God, what does that make us? Bigger than Buddha?

asserting that the Spice Girls are 'a darn sight bigger than Oasis'

in *Independent* 16 August 1997 'Quote Unquote'; cf. **Gallagher** 124:2, **Lennon** 187:16

Noam Chomsky 1928–

American linguistics scholar

13 Colourless green ideas sleep furiously.

illustrating that grammatical structure is independent of meaning

Syntactic Structures (1957)

14 The Internet is an élite organization; most of the population of the world has never even made a phone call.

on the limitations of the World Wide Web

in *Observer* 18 February 1996

Agatha Christie 1890–1976

English writer of detective fiction
on Christie: see **Thomas** 307:20

1 He [Hercule Poirot] tapped his forehead.
'These little grey cells. It is "up to
them".'

   The Mysterious Affair at Styles (1920)

2 I'm a sausage machine, a perfect sausage
machine.

   G. C. Ramsey *Agatha Christie* (1972)

Frank E. Churchill 1901–1942

3 Who's afraid of the big bad wolf?

   title of song (1933; probably written in
   collaboration with Ann Ronell)

Winston Churchill 1874–1965

British Conservative statesman; Prime
Minister, 1940–5, 1951–5
on Churchill: see **Anonymous** 12:1, **Attlee**
15:4, 15:5, **Balfour** 21:15, **Bevan** 36:7,
Butler 50:7, **Muggeridge** 224:9, **Murrow**
226:5, **Nicolson** 230:8; *see also*
Misquotations 219:1

4 It cannot in the opinion of His Majesty's
Government be classified as slavery in the
extreme acceptance of the word without
some risk of terminological inexactitude.

   speech in the House of Commons, 22 February
   1906

5 He is one of those orators of whom it was
well said, 'Before they get up, they do not
know what they are going to say; when
they are speaking, they do not know
what they are saying; and when they
have sat down, they do not know what
they have said.'

   of Lord Charles Beresford

   speech in the House of Commons, 20
   December 1912

6 Business carried on as usual during
alterations on the map of Europe.

   on the self-adopted 'motto' of the British people

   speech at Guildhall, 9 November 1914

7 The whole map of Europe has been
changed . . . but as the deluge subsides
and the waters fall short we see the
dreary steeples of Fermanagh and Tyrone
emerging once again.

   speech in the House of Commons, 16 February
   1922

8 Anyone can rat, but it takes a certain
amount of ingenuity to re-rat.

   *on rejoining the Conservatives twenty years after
   leaving them for the Liberals, c.1924*

   Kay Halle *Irrepressible Churchill* (1966)

9 I decline utterly to be impartial as
between the fire brigade and the fire.

   replying to complaints of his bias in editing the
   British Gazette *during the General Strike*

   speech in the House of Commons, 7 July 1926

10 I remember, when I was a child, being
taken to the celebrated Barnum's circus,
which contained an exhibition of freaks
and monstrosities, but the exhibit on the
programme which I most desired to see
was the one described as 'The Boneless
Wonder'. My parents judged that that
spectacle would be too revolting and
demoralizing for my youthful eyes, and I
have waited 50 years to see the boneless
wonder sitting on the Treasury Bench.

   of Ramsay **MacDonald**

   speech in the House of Commons, 28 January
   1931

11 [The Government] go on in strange
paradox, decided only to be undecided,
resolved to be irresolute, adamant for
drift, solid for fluidity.

   speech in the House of Commons, 12
   November 1936

12 Dictators ride to and fro upon tigers
which they dare not dismount. And the
tigers are getting hungry.

   letter, 11 November 1937

13 The utmost he [Neville Chamberlain] has
been able to gain for Czechoslovakia and
in the matters which were in dispute has
been that the German dictator, instead of
snatching his victuals from the table, has
been content to have them served to him
course by course.

   speech, House of Commons, 5 October 1938

1 I cannot forecast to you the action of Russia. It is a riddle wrapped in a mystery inside an enigma.

radio broadcast, 1 October 1939

2 I have nothing to offer but blood, toil, tears and sweat.

speech in the House of Commons, 13 May 1940

3 What is our policy? . . . to wage war against a monstrous tyranny, never surpassed in the dark, lamentable catalogue of human crime.

speech in the House of Commons, 13 May 1940

4 What is our aim? . . . Victory, victory at all costs, victory in spite of all terror; victory, however long and hard the road may be; for without victory, there is no survival.

speech in the House of Commons, 13 May 1940

5 We shall not flag or fail. We shall go on to the end. We shall fight in France, we shall fight on the seas and oceans, we shall fight with growing confidence and growing strength in the air, we shall defend our island, whatever the cost may be. We shall fight on the beaches, we shall fight on the landing grounds, we shall fight in the fields and in the streets, we shall fight in the hills; we shall never surrender.

speech in the House of Commons, 4 June 1940

6 What General Weygand called the 'Battle of France' is over. I expect that the Battle of Britain is about to begin. Upon this battle depends the survival of Christian civilization. Upon it depends our own British life and the long continuity of our institutions and our Empire. The whole fury and might of the enemy must very soon be turned on us. Hitler knows that he will have to break us in this island or lose the war. If we can stand up to him all Europe may be free and the life of the world may move forward into broad, sunlit uplands; but if we fail then the whole world, including the United States, and all that we have known and cared for, will sink into the abyss of a new dark age made more sinister, and perhaps more prolonged, by the lights of a perverted science. Let us therefore brace ourselves to our duty, and so bear ourselves that, if the British Commonwealth and its Empire lasts for a thousand years, men will still say, 'This was their finest hour.'

speech in the House of Commons, 18 June 1940

7 Never in the field of human conflict was so much owed by so many to so few.

on the Battle of Britain

speech in the House of Commons, 20 August 1940

8 No one can guarantee success in war, but only deserve it.

letter to Lord Wavell, 26 November 1940

9 As far as I can see you have used every cliché except 'God is Love' and 'Please adjust your dress before leaving'.

*on a long-winded report from Anthony **Eden***

in *Life* 9 December 1940; when this story was repeated in the *Daily Mirror*, Churchill denied that it was true

10 Give us the tools and we will finish the job.

*addressing President **Roosevelt***

radio broadcast, 9 February 1941

11 The British nation is unique in this respect. They are the only people who like to be told how bad things are, who like to be told the worst.

speech in the House of Commons, 10 June 1941

12 The people of London with one voice would say to Hitler: 'You have committed every crime under the sun . . . .We will have no truce or parley with you, or the grisly gang who work your wicked will. You do your worst— and we will do our best.'

speech at County Hall, London, 14 July 1941

13 Do not let us speak of darker days; let us rather speak of sterner days. These are not dark days: these are great days—the greatest days our country has ever lived; and we must all thank God that we have been allowed, each of us according to our stations, to play a part in making these days memorable in the history of our race.

speech at Harrow School, 29 October 1941

14 It becomes still more difficult to reconcile Japanese action with prudence or even

with sanity. What kind of a people do they think we are?

speech to US Congress, 26 December 1941

1 When I warned them [the French Government] that Britain would fight on alone whatever they did, their generals told their Prime Minister and his divided Cabinet, 'In three weeks England will have her neck wrung like a chicken.' Some chicken! Some neck!

speech to Canadian Parliament, 30 December 1941

2 A medal glitters, but it also casts a shadow.

a reference to the envy caused by the award of honours

in 1941; Kenneth Rose *King George V* (1983)

3 We mean to hold our own. I have not become the King's First Minister in order to preside over the liquidation of the British Empire.

speech in London, 10 November 1942

4 Now this is not the end. It is not even the beginning of the end. But it is, perhaps, the end of the beginning.

on the Battle of Egypt

speech at the Mansion House, London, 10 November 1942

5 National compulsory insurance for all classes for all purposes from the cradle to the grave.

radio broadcast, 21 March 1943

6 There is no finer investment for any community than putting milk into babies.

radio broadcast, 21 March 1943

7 The empires of the future are the empires of the mind.

speech at Harvard, 6 September 1943

8 Unless the Right Hon. Gentleman changes his policy and methods and moves without the slightest delay, he will be as great a curse to this country in time of peace, as he was a squalid nuisance in time of war.

*of Aneurin **Bevan***

speech in the House of Commons, 6 December 1945

9 From Stettin in the Baltic to Trieste in the Adriatic an iron curtain has descended across the Continent.

'iron curtain' previously had been applied by others to the Soviet Union or her sphere of influence, e.g. Ethel Snowden Through Bolshevik Russia *(1920), Dr **Goebbels** Das Reich (25 February 1945), and by Churchill himself in a cable to President **Truman** (4 June 1945)*

speech at Westminster College, Fulton, Missouri, 5 March 1946

10 Democracy is the worst form of Government except all those other forms that have been tried from time to time.

speech in the House of Commons, 11 November 1947

11 This is the sort of English up with which I will not put.

Ernest Gowers *Plain Words* (1948) 'Troubles with Prepositions'

12 No, not dead. But the candle in that great turnip has gone out.

*in reply to the comment 'One never hears of **Baldwin** nowadays—he might as well be dead'*

Harold Nicolson diary, 17 August 1950

13 Naval tradition? Monstrous. Nothing but rum, sodomy, prayers, and the lash.

often quoted as 'rum, sodomy, and the lash', as in Peter Gretton Former Naval Person *(1968)*

Harold Nicolson diary, 17 August 1950

14 To jaw-jaw is always better than to war-war.

speech at White House, 26 June 1954

15 A modest man who has a good deal to be modest about.

*of Clement **Attlee***

in *Chicago Sunday Tribune Magazine of Books* 27 June 1954

16 I am prepared to meet my Maker. Whether my Maker is prepared for the great ordeal of meeting me is another matter.

at a news conference in Washington, 1954, in *New York Times* 25 January 1965

17 I have never accepted what many people have kindly said—namely, that I inspired the nation . . . It was the nation and the race dwelling all round the globe that had the lion's heart. I had the luck to be

called upon to give the roar. I also hope that I sometimes suggested to the lion the right place to use his claws.

speech at Westminster Hall, 30 November 1954

1 I have taken more out of alcohol than alcohol has taken out of me.

Quentin Reynolds *By Quentin Reynolds* (1964)

2 In defeat unbeatable: in victory unbearable.

*of Lord **Montgomery***

E. Marsh *Ambrosia and Small Beer* (1964)

3 Like a powerful graceful cat walking delicately and unsoiled across a rather muddy street.

*of **Balfour's** moving from **Asquith's** Cabinet to that of **Lloyd George***

Great Contemporaries (1937)

*of the career of Lord **Curzon**:*

4 The morning had been golden; the noontide was bronze; and the evening lead. But all were solid, and each was polished till it shone after its fashion.

Great Contemporaries (1937)

5 I wrote my name at the top of the page. I wrote down the number of the question '1'. After much reflection I put a bracket round it thus '(1)'. But thereafter I could not think of anything connected with it that was either relevant or true. . . . It was from these slender indications of scholarship that Mr Welldon drew the conclusion that I was worthy to pass into Harrow. It is very much to his credit.

My Early Life (1930)

6 By being so long in the lowest form [at Harrow] I gained an immense advantage over the cleverer boys. They all went on to learn Latin and Greek . . . . But I was taught English. . . . Thus I got into my bones the essential structure of the ordinary British sentence—which is a noble thing. . . . Naturally I am biased in favour of boys learning English. I would make them all learn English: and then I would let the clever ones learn Latin as an honour, and Greek as a treat.

My Early Life (1930)

7 Headmasters have powers at their disposal with which Prime Ministers have never yet been invested.

My Early Life (1930)

8 Mr Gladstone read Homer for fun, which I thought served him right.

My Early Life (1930)

9 It is a good thing for an uneducated man to read books of quotations.

My Early Life (1930)

10 In war: resolution. In defeat: defiance. In victory: magnanimity. In peace: goodwill.

The Second World War (1948) vol. 1 epigraph

11 I felt as if I were walking with destiny, and that all my past life had been but a preparation for this hour and this trial.

The Second World War (1948) vol. 1

12 The loyalties which centre upon number one are enormous. If he trips he must be sustained. If he makes mistakes they must be covered. If he sleeps he must not be wantonly disturbed. If he is no good he must be pole-axed. But this last extreme process cannot be carried out every day; and certainly not in the days just after he has been chosen.

The Second World War (1949) vol. 2

13 If Hitler invaded hell I would make at least a favourable reference to the devil in the House of Commons.

The Second World War (1950) vol. 3

14 I did not suffer from any desire to be relieved of my responsibilities. All I wanted was compliance with my wishes after reasonable discussion.

The Second World War (1951) vol. 4

15 It may almost be said, 'Before Alamein we never had a victory. After Alamein we never had a defeat.'

The Second World War (1951) vol. 4

16 Jellicoe was the only man on either side who could lose the war in an afternoon.

The World Crisis (1927)

17 The ability to foretell what is going to happen tomorrow, next week, next month, and next year. And to have the

ability afterwards to explain why it didn't happen.

describing the qualifications desirable in a prospective politician

> B. Adler *Churchill Wit* (1965)

1 I am fond of pigs. Dogs look up to us. Cats look down on us. Pigs treat us as equals.

> attributed, in M. Gilbert *Never Despair* (1988)

2 NANCY ASTOR: If I were your wife I would put poison in your coffee!
CHURCHILL: And if I were your husband I would drink it.

> Consuelo Vanderbilt Balsan *Glitter and Gold* (1952)

3 A remarkable example of modern art. It certainly combines force with candour.

on the notorious 80th birthday portrait by Graham Sutherland, later destroyed by Lady Churchill

> Martin Gilbert *Churchill: A Life* (1991)

4 The only recorded instance in history of a rat swimming *towards* a sinking ship.

of a former Conservative who proposed to stand as a Liberal

> Leon Harris *The Fine Art of Political Wit* (1965)

5 The Prime Minister has nothing to hide from the President of the United States

*on stepping from his bath in the presence of a startled President **Roosevelt***

> recalled by Roosevelt's son in *Churchill* (BBC television series presented by Martin Gilbert, 1992)

6 A sheep in sheep's clothing.

*of Clement **Attlee***

> Lord Home *The Way the Wind Blows* (1976)

7 Take away that pudding—it has no theme.

> Lord Home *The Way the Wind Blows* (1976)

8 We are all worms. But I do believe that I am a glow-worm.

> Violet Bonham-Carter *Winston Churchill as I Knew Him* (1965)

9 BESSIE BRADDOCK: Winston, you're drunk.
CHURCHILL: Bessie, you're ugly. But tomorrow I shall be sober.

> J. L. Lane (ed.) *Sayings of Churchill* (1992)

Count Galeazzo Ciano
1903–44

Italian fascist politician; son-in-law of Mussolini

10 Victory has a hundred fathers, but no-one wants to recognise defeat as his own.

often quoted as '. . . but defeat is an orphan'

> diary, 9 September 1942

E. M. Cioran 1911–95

Romanian-born French philosopher

11 Without the possibility of suicide, I would have killed myself long ago.

> in *Independent* 2 December 1989

12 I do nothing, granted. But I see the hours pass—which is better than trying to fill them.

> in *Guardian* 11 May 1993

Alan Clark 1928–

British Conservative politician, son of Kenneth **Clark**; husband of Jane **Clark**
*on Clark: see **Parris** 244:15*

13 There are no true friends in politics. We are all sharks circling, and waiting, for traces of blood to appear in the water.

> diary, 30 November 1990

14 Our old friend economical . . . with the *actualité*.

under cross-examination at the Old Bailey during the Matrix Churchill case

> in *Independent* 10 November 1992; cf. **Armstrong** 13:5

15 If you have bright plumage, people will take pot shots at you.

> in *Independent* 25 June 1994

16 Safe is spelled D-U-L-L. Politics has got to be a fun activity, otherwise people turn their back on it.

on being selected as parliamentary candidate for Kensington and Chelsea, 24 January 1997

> in *Daily Telegraph* 25 January 1997

Jane Clark

wife of Alan **Clark**

1 If you bed people of below-stairs class, they will go to the papers.

in *Daily Telegraph* 31 May 1994

Kenneth Clark 1903–83

English art historian, father of Alan **Clark**

2 It's a curious fact that the all-male religions have produced no religious imagery—in most cases have positively forbidden it. The great religious art of the world is deeply involved with the female principle.

Civilisation (1969)

3 Perrault's façade reflects the triumph of an authoritarian state . . . the work not of craftsmen, but of wonderfully gifted civil servants.

of the Louvre

Civilisation (1969)

Arthur C. Clarke 1917–

English science fiction writer

4 Any sufficiently advanced technology is indistinguishable from magic.

The Lost Worlds of 2001 (1972)

5 If an elderly but distinguished scientist says that something is possible he is almost certainly right, but if he says that it is impossible he is very probably wrong.

in *New Yorker* 9 August 1969; cf. **Asimov** 14:2

6 How inappropriate to call this planet Earth when it is clearly Ocean.

in *Nature* 8 March 1990

7 The only genuine consciousness-expanding drug.

of science fiction

letter claiming coinage in *New Scientist* 2 April 1994

Kenneth Clarke 1940–

British Conservative politician, Chancellor of the Exchequer

8 Tell your kids to get their scooters off my lawn.

allegedly said to the Party Chairman, Brian Mawhinney, of young Central Office personnel; cf. **Wilson** 331:9

television report, 5 December 1996; in *Guardian* 7 December 1996

9 The Government doesn't have a hostile attitude to the single currency. It was a slip of the tongue.

in response to a statement by fellow Conservative Malcolm Rifkind, 19 February 1997

in *Guardian* 20 February 1997

Philip 'Tubby' Clayton
1885–1972

Australian-born British clergyman, founder of Toc H

10 CHAIRMAN: What is service?
CANDIDATE: The rent we pay for our room on earth.

admission ceremony of Toc H, a society founded after the First World War to provide Christian fellowship and social service

Tresham Lever *Clayton of Toc H* (1971)

Eldridge Cleaver 1935–

American political activist

11 You're either part of the solution or you're part of the problem.

speech in San Francisco, 1968, in R. Scheer *Eldridge Cleaver, Post Prison Writings and Speeches* (1969)

John Cleese 1939–
and Connie Booth

British comedy writer and actor; British comedy actress
on Cleese: see **Thomson** 309:4; *see also* **Monty Python's Flying Circus**

12 They're Germans. Don't mention the war.

Fawlty Towers 'The Germans' (BBC TV programme, 1975)

Georges Clemenceau

1841–1929

French statesman; Prime Minister of France,
1906–9, 1917–20
on Clemenceau: see **Lloyd George** 192:10

1 My home policy: I wage war; my foreign
policy: I wage war. All the time I wage
war.
> speech to French Chamber of Deputies, 8
> March 1918

2 What do you expect when I'm between
two men of whom one [Lloyd George]
thinks he is Napoleon and the other
[Woodrow Wilson] thinks he is Jesus
Christ?
> *to André Tardieu, on being asked why he always
> gave in to* **Lloyd George** *at the Paris Peace
> Conference, 1918*
>> letter from Harold Nicolson to his wife, Vita
>> Sackville-West, 20 May 1919

3 It is easier to make war than to make
peace.
> speech at Verdun, 20 July 1919

4 Oh, to be seventy again!
> *on seeing a pretty girl on his eightieth birthday*
> James Agate diary, 19 April 1938

5 War is too serious a matter to entrust to
military men.
> attributed to Clemenceau, e.g. in Hampden
> Jackson *Clemenceau and the Third Republic*
> (1946), but also to Briand and Talleyrand; cf.
> **Buchwald** 48:3, **de Gaulle** 86:13

Harlan Cleveland 1918–

American government official

6 The revolution of rising expectations.
> phrase coined, 1950; Arthur Schlesinger *A
> Thousand Days* (1965)

Hillary Rodham Clinton

1947–

American lawyer, wife of Bill **Clinton**, First
Lady of the US since 1993

7 I could have stayed home and baked
cookies and had teas. But what I decided
was to fulfil my profession, which I
entered before my husband was in public
life.
> comment on questions raised by rival
> Democratic contender Edmund G. Brown Jr.; in
> *Albany Times-Union* 17 March 1992

8 There is no such thing as other people's
children.
> in *Newsweek* 15 January 1996

William Jefferson ('Bill') Clinton 1946–

American Democratic statesman; 42nd
President of the US from 1993; husband of
Hillary Rodham **Clinton**
see also **Political slogans** 251:15

9 I experimented with marijuana a time or
two. And I didn't like it, and I didn't
inhale.
> in *Washington Post* 30 March 1992

10 The comeback kid!
> *description of himself after coming second in the
> New Hampshire primary in the* 1992 *presidential
> election (since* 1952, *no presidential candidate
> had won the election without first winning in New
> Hampshire)*
>> Michael Barone and Grant Ujifusa *The Almanac
>> of American Politics 1994*

Brian Clough 1935–

English football player and manager

11 If I'm ever feeling a bit uppity, whenever
I get on my high horse, I go and take
another look at my dear Mam's mangle
that has pride of place in the dining-
room.
> *Clough: The Autobiography* (1994)

Kurt Cobain 1967–94

American rock singer, guitarist, and
songwriter, husband of Courtney **Love**
see also **Young** 340:6

12 I'd rather be dead than cool.
> 'Stay Away' (1991 song)

Claud Cockburn 1904–81

British writer and journalist

1 Reality goes bounding past the satirist like a cheetah laughing as it lopes ahead of the greyhound.
    Crossing the Line (1958)

2 Small earthquake in Chile. Not many dead.
    winning entry for a dullest headline competition at The Times
    In Time of Trouble (1956)

Jean Cocteau 1889–1963

French dramatist and film director
on Cocteau: see **Anonymous** 11:11

3 Life is a horizontal fall.
    Opium (1930)

4 Victor Hugo was a madman who thought he was Victor Hugo.
    Opium (1930)

5 Being tactful in audacity is knowing how far one can go too far.
    Le Rappel à l'ordre (1926)

6 The worst tragedy for a poet is to be admired through being misunderstood.
    Le Rappel à l'ordre (1926)

7 If it has to choose who is to be crucified, the crowd will always save Barabbas.
    Le Rappel à l'ordre (1926)

Denise Coffey

British actress

8 I am that twentieth-century failure, a happy undersexed celibate.
    Ned Sherrin *Cutting Edge* (1984)

George M. Cohan 1878–1942

American actor-manager and dramatist

9 Over there, over there,
    Send the word, send the word over there
    That the Yanks are coming, the Yanks are coming,
    The drums rum-tumming everywhere.
    So prepare, say a prayer,
    Send the word, send the word to beware.
    We'll be over, we're coming over

And we won't come back till it's over, over there.
    'Over There' (1917 song)

10 I don't care what you say about me, as long as you say *something* about me, and as long as you spell my name right.
    to a newspaperman who wanted some information about Broadway Jones *in* 1912
    John McCabe *George M. Cohan* (1973)

Leonard Cohen 1934–

Canadian singer and writer

11 I don't consider myself a pessimist. I think of a pessimist as someone who is waiting for it to rain. And I feel soaked to the skin.
    in *Observer* 2 May 1993 'Sayings of the Week'

David Coleman 1926–

British sports commentator

12 He just can't believe what isn't happening to him.
    in *Guardian* 24 December 1980 'Sports Quotes of the Year'

13 That's the fastest time ever run—but it's not as fast as the world record.
    Barry Fantoni (ed.) *Private Eye's Colemanballs 3* (1986)

Colette 1873–1954

French novelist

14 The world of the emotions that are so lightly called physical.
    Le Blé en herbe (1923)

15 Her childhood, then her adolescence, had taught her patience, hope, silence and the easy manipulation of the weapons and virtues of all prisoners.
    Chéri (1920)

16 Let's buy a pack of cards, good wine, bridge scores, knitting needles, all the paraphernalia needed to fill an enormous void, everything needed to hide that horror—the old woman.
    Chéri (1920)

R. G. Collingwood 1889–1943

English philosopher and archaeologist

1 Perfect freedom is reserved for the man who lives by his own work and in that work does what he wants to do.
   Speculum Mentis (1924)

Charles Collins

English songwriter

2 My old man said, 'Follow the van,
   Don't dilly-dally on the way!'
   'Don't Dilly-Dally on the Way' (1919 song, with Fred Leigh); popularized by Marie Lloyd

Michael Collins 1890–1922

Irish nationalist leader and politician

3 Think—what I have got for Ireland? Something which she has wanted these past seven hundred years. Will anyone be satisfied at the bargain? Will anyone? I tell you this—early this morning I signed my death warrant.
   on signing the treaty establishing the Irish Free State; he was shot from ambush in the following year
      letter, 6 December 1921

   on arriving at Dublin Castle for the handover by British forces on 16 January 1922, and being told that he was seven minutes late:
4 We've been waiting seven hundred years, you can have the seven minutes.
   Tim Pat Coogan *Michael Collins* (1990); attributed

John Robert Colombo 1936–

Canadian writer

5 Canada could have enjoyed:
   English government,
   French culture,
   and American know-how.

   Instead it ended up with:
   English know-how,
   French government,
   and American culture.
   'O Canada' (1965)

Betty Comden 1919–
and Adolph Green 1915–

American songwriters

6 The party's over, it's time to call it a day.
   'The Party's Over' (1956 song)

Henry Steele Commager
1902–

American historian

7 It was observed half a century ago that what is a stone wall to a layman, to a corporate lawyer is a triumphant arch. Much the same might be said of civil rights and freedoms. To the layman the Bill of Rights seems to be a stone wall against the misuse of power. But in the hands of a congressional committee, or often enough of a judge, it turns out to be so full of exceptions and qualifications that it might be a whole series of arches.
   'The Right to Dissent' in *Current History* October 1955; see below

   A law, Hinnissey, that might look like a wall to you or me wud look like a triumphal arch to th'expeeryenced eye iv a lawyer.
   Peter Finley Dunne (1867–1936) 'Mr Dooley on the Power of the Press' in *American Magazine* 1906

Denis Compton 1918–97

British cricketer

8 I couldn't bat for the length of time required to score 500. I'd get bored and fall over.
   to Brian Lara, who had recently scored 501 not out, a world record in first-class cricket
   in *Daily Telegraph* 27 June 1994

Ivy Compton-Burnett
1884–1969

English novelist

9 Time has too much credit . . . It is not a great healer. It is an indifferent and perfunctory one. Sometimes it does not heal at all. And sometimes when it seems to, no healing has been necessary.
   Darkness and Day (1951)

1 Well, of course, people are only human . . . But it really does not seem much for them to be.
A Family and a Fortune (1939)

2 People don't resent having nothing nearly as much as too little.
A Family and a Fortune (1939)

3 'The more we ask, the more we have. And, it is fair enough: asking is not always easy.'
'And it is said to be hard to accept . . . So no wonder we have so little.'
The Mighty and their Fall (1961)

4 There are different kinds of wrong. The people sinned against are not always the best.
The Mighty and their Fall (1961)

5 A leopard does not change his spots, or change his feeling that spots are rather a credit.
More Women than Men (1933)

6 We must use words as they are used or stand aside from life.
Mother and Son (1955)

7 There is more difference within the sexes than between them.
Mother and Son (1955)

8 My point is that it [wickedness] is not punished, and that is why it is natural to be guilty of it. When it is likely to be punished, most of us avoid it.
in *Orion* (1945) 'A Conversation between I. Compton-Burnett and M. Jourdain'

Gerry Conlon

first member of the Guildford Four to be released from prison

9 The life sentence goes on. It's like a runaway train that you can't just get off.
of life after his conviction was quashed by the Court of Appeal
in *Irish Post* 13 September 1997

Billy Connolly 1942–

Scottish comedian

10 Marriage is a wonderful invention; but, then again, so is a bicycle repair kit.
Duncan Campbell *Billy Connolly* (1976)

Cyril Connolly 1903–74

English writer

11 Literature is the art of writing something that will be read twice; journalism what will be read once.
Enemies of Promise (1938)

12 As repressed sadists are supposed to become policemen or butchers, so those with an irrational fear of life become publishers.
Enemies of Promise (1938)

13 Whom the gods wish to destroy they first call promising.
Enemies of Promise (1938)

14 There is no more sombre enemy of good art than the pram in the hall.
Enemies of Promise (1938)

15 I have called this style the Mandarin style, since it is beloved by literary pundits, by those who would make the written word as unlike as possible to the spoken one. It is the style of those writers whose tendency is to make their language convey more than they mean or more than they feel, it is the style of most artists and all humbugs.
Enemies of Promise (1938)

16 In the eighteenth century he would have become Prime Minister before he was thirty; as it was he appeared honourably ineligible for the struggle of life.
*of Alec Douglas-**Home***
Enemies of Promise (1938)

17 Imprisoned in every fat man a thin one is wildly signalling to be let out.
The Unquiet Grave (1944); cf. **Amis** 7:10, **Orwell** 237:14

18 Our memories are card-indexes consulted, and then put back in disorder by authorities whom we do not control.
during the Blitz
The Unquiet Grave (1944)

19 M is for Marx
And Movement of Masses
And Massing of Arses.
And Clashing of Classes.
'Where Engels Fears to Tread' (1945)

20 It is closing time in the gardens of the West and from now on an artist will be

judged only by the resonance of his solitude or the quality of his despair.

in *Horizon* December 1949—January 1950

1 It is the one war in which everyone changes sides.

on the generation gap

Tom Driberg, speech in House of Commons, 30 October 1959

2 He could not blow his nose without moralising on the state of the handkerchief industry.

of George **Orwell**

in *Sunday Times* 29 September 1968

James Connolly 1868–1916

Irish nationalist and labour leader; executed after the Easter Rising, 1916

3 The worker is the slave of capitalist society, the female worker is the slave of that slave.

The Re-conquest of Ireland (1915)

Jimmy Connors 1952–

American tennis player

4 New Yorkers love it when you spill your guts out there. Spill your guts at Wimbledon and they make you stop and clean it up.

at Flushing Meadow

in *Guardian* 24 December 1984 'Sports Quotes of the Year'

Joseph Conrad 1857–1924

Polish-born British novelist

5 The horror! The horror!

Heart of Darkness (1902)

6 The terrorist and the policeman both come from the same basket.

The Secret Agent (1907)

7 Reality, as usual, beats fiction out of sight.

commenting on 'this wartime atmosphere'

letter 11 August 1915

Shirley Conran 1932–

English writer

8 Life is too short to stuff a mushroom.

Superwoman (1975)

9 First things first, second things never.

Superwoman (1975)

10 Conran's Law of Housework—it expands to fill the time available plus half an hour.

Superwoman 2 (1977); cf. **Parkinson** 244:6

Terence Conran 1931–

British designer and businessman

11 The figure is unbelievable—just because she cooked a few meals now and again and wrote a few books.

on the £10 million divorce settlement awarded to Caroline Conran

in *Mail on Sunday* 6 July 1997 'Quotes of the Week'

A. J. Cook 1885–1931

English labour leader; Secretary of the Miners' Federation of Great Britain, 1924–31

12 Not a penny off the pay, not a second on the day.

often quoted with 'minute' substituted for 'second'

speech at York, 3 April 1926

Peter Cook 1937–95

English satrist and actor
on Cook: see **Bennett** 31:5

13 I'm glad it hasn't changed him. He's still selfish, vain, greedy. In other words a fully-rounded human being.

of Dudley Moore's success in the US

in *Guardian* 10 January 1994

14 Life is a matter of passing the time enjoyably. There may be other things in life, but I've been too busy passing my time enjoyably to think very deeply about them.

in *Guardian* 10 January 1994

Calvin Coolidge 1872–1933

American Republican statesman, 30th President of the US, 1923–9
on Coolidge: see **Anonymous** 11:13, **Mencken** 213:4, **Parker** 243:17

1 There is no right to strike against the public safety by anybody, anywhere, any time.
> telegram to Samuel Gompers, 14 September 1919

2 Civilization and profits go hand in hand.
> speech in New York, 27 November 1920

3 The chief business of the American people is business.
> speech in Washington, 17 January 1925

4 I do not choose to run for President in nineteen twenty-eight.
> statement issued at Rapid City, South Dakota, 2 August 1927

when asked by Mrs Coolidge what a sermon had been about:
5 'Sins,' he said. 'Well, what did he say about sin?' 'He was against it.'
> John H. McKee *Coolidge: Wit and Wisdom* (1933); perhaps apocryphal

6 They hired the money, didn't they?
> *on war debts incurred by England and others*
> J. H. McKee *Coolidge: Wit and Wisdom* (1933)

7 Nothing in the world can take the place of persistence. Talent will not; nothing is more common than unsuccessful men with talent. Genius will not; unrewarded genius is almost a proverb. Education will not; the world is full of educated derelicts. Persistence and determination are omnipotent. The slogan 'press on' has solved and always will solve the problems of the human race.
> attributed in the programme of a memorial service for Coolidge in 1933

Diana Cooper 1892–1986

wife of Duff **Cooper**

8 It's nerve and brass, *audace* and disrespect, and leaping-before-you-look and what-the-hellism, that must be developed.
> *on speaking French fluently rather than correctly*
> Philip Ziegler *Diana Cooper* (1981)

Duff Cooper 1890–1954

British Conservative politician, diplomat, and writer; husband of Diana **Cooper**

9 Your two stout lovers frowning at one another across the hearth rug, while your small, but perfectly formed one kept the party in a roar.
> *letter to Lady Diana Manners, later his wife, October 1914*
> Artemis Cooper *Durable Fire* (1983)

Wendy Cope 1945–

English poet

10 Bloody men are like bloody buses—
You wait for about a year
And as soon as one approaches your stop
Two or three others appear.
> 'Bloody Men' (1992)

11 They say that men suffer,
As badly, as long.
I worry, I worry,
In case they are wrong.
> 'I Worry' (1992)

12 Making cocoa for Kingsley Amis.
> title of poem (1986)

13 It was a dream I had last week
And some kind of record seemed vital.
I knew it wouldn't be much of a poem
But I love the title.
> 'Making Cocoa for Kingsley Amis' (1986)

14 What makes men so tedious
Is the need to show off and compete.
They'll bore you to death for hours and hours
Before they'll admit defeat.
> 'Men and their boring arguments' (1988)

15 I used to think all poets were Byronic—
Mad, bad and dangerous to know.
And then I met a few. Yes it's ironic—
I used to think all poets were Byronic.
They're mostly wicked as a ginless tonic
And wild as pension plans.
> 'Triolet' (1986); see below

> Mad, bad, and dangerous to know.
> Lady Caroline Lamb (1785–1828) writing of Byron in her journal after their first meeting at a ball in March 1812; Elizabeth Jenkins *Lady Caroline Lamb* (1932)

Aaron Copland 1900–90

American composer, pianist, and conductor

1 The whole problem can be stated quite
simply by asking, 'Is there a meaning to
music?' My answer to that would be,
'Yes.' And 'Can you state in so many
words what the meaning is?' My answer
to that would be, 'No.'
  What to Listen for in Music (1939)

Ralph Cornes

2 Computers are anti-Faraday machines.
He said he couldn't understand anything
until he could count it, while computers
count everything and understand
nothing.
  in *Guardian* 28 March 1991

Bernard Cornfeld 1927–

American businessman

3 Do you sincerely want to be rich?
  stock question to salesmen
    C. Raw et al. *Do You Sincerely Want to be Rich?*
    (1971)

Frances Cornford 1886–1960

English poet; wife of Francis M. **Cornford**
on Cornford: see **Chesterton** 62:7

4 Whoso maintains that I am humbled
    now
(Who wait the Awful Day) is still a liar;
I hope to meet my Maker brow to brow
And find my own the higher.
  'Epitaph for a Reviewer' (1954)

5 How long ago Hector took off his plume,
Not wanting that his little son should
    cry,
Then kissed his sad Andromache
    goodbye—
And now we three in Euston waiting-
    room.
  'Parting in Wartime' (1948)

6 O fat white woman whom nobody loves,
Why do you walk through the fields in
    gloves,
When the grass is soft as the breast of
    doves
And shivering-sweet to the touch?

O why do you walk through the fields in
    gloves,
Missing so much and so much?
  'To a Fat Lady seen from the Train' (1910); cf.
  Chesterton 62:7

7 A young Apollo, golden-haired,
Stands dreaming on the verge of strife,
Magnificently unprepared
For the long littleness of life.
  of Rupert **Brooke**
  'Youth' (1910)

Francis M. Cornford
1874–1943

English classical scholar; husband of
Frances **Cornford**

8 Every public action, which is not
customary, either is wrong, or, if it is
right, is a dangerous precedent. It follows
that nothing should ever be done for the
first time.
  Microcosmographia Academica (1908)

9 That branch of the art of lying which
consists in very nearly deceiving your
friends without quite deceiving your
enemies.
  on propaganda
    Microcosmographia Academica (1922 ed.)

Baron Pierre de Coubertin
1863–1937

French sportsman and educationist, founder
of the modern Olympics

10 The important thing in life is not the
victory but the contest; the essential
thing is not to have won but to have
fought well.
  speech in London, 24 July 1908

Émile Coué 1857–1926

French psychologist
on Coué: see **Inge** 156:10

11 Every day, in every way, I am getting
better and better.
  to be said 15 to 20 times, morning and evening
    De la suggestion et de ses applications (1915)

Douglas Coupland 1961–

Canadian author

1 Generation X: tales for an accelerated culture.

   title of book (1991)

Noël Coward 1899–1973

English dramatist, actor, and composer
on Coward: see **Tynan** 314:5

2 Dance, dance, dance, little lady!
   Leave tomorrow behind.

   'Dance, Little Lady' (1928 song)

3 Don't let's be beastly to the Germans
   When our Victory is ultimately won.

   'Don't Let's Be Beastly to the Germans' (1943 song)

4 I believe that since my life began
   The most I've had is just
   A talent to amuse.

   'If Love Were All' (1929 song)

5 I'll see you again,
   Whenever spring breaks through again.

   'I'll See You Again' (1929 song)

6 London Pride has been handed down to us.
   London Pride is a flower that's free.
   London Pride means our own dear town to us,
   And our pride it for ever will be.

   'London Pride' (1941 song)

7 Mad about the boy,
   It's pretty funny but I'm mad about the boy.
   He has a gay appeal
   That makes me feel
   There may be something sad about the boy.

   'Mad about the Boy' (1932 song)

8 Mad dogs and Englishmen
   Go out in the midday sun.
   The Japanese don't care to,
   The Chinese wouldn't dare to,
   The Hindus and Argentines sleep firmly from twelve to one,
   But Englishmen detest a siesta.

   'Mad Dogs and Englishmen' (1931 song)

9 Don't put your daughter on the stage,
   Mrs Worthington,

   Don't put your daughter on the stage.

   'Mrs Worthington' (1935 song)

10 Poor little rich girl
   You're a bewitched girl,
   Better beware!

   'Poor Little Rich Girl' (1925 song)

11 Someday I'll find you,
   Moonlight behind you,
   True to the dream I am dreaming.

   'Someday I'll Find You' (1930 song)

12 The Stately Homes of England,
   How beautiful they stand,
   To prove the upper classes
   Have still the upper hand.

   'The Stately Homes of England' (1938 song); see below

   The stately homes of England,
   How beautiful they stand!
   Amidst their tall ancestral trees,
   O'er all the pleasant land.

   Felicia Hemans (1793–1835) 'The Homes of England' (1849)

13 There are bad times just around the corner,
   There are dark clouds travelling through the sky
   And it's no good whining
   About a silver lining
   For we know from experience that they won't roll by.

   'There are Bad Times Just Around the Corner' (1953 song)

14 I believe we should all behave quite differently if we lived in a warm, sunny climate all the time.

   Brief Encounter (1945)

15 Very flat, Norfolk.

   Private Lives (1930)

16 Extraordinary how potent cheap music is.

   Private Lives (1930)

17 Certain women should be struck regularly, like gongs.

   Private Lives (1930)

18 Dear 338171 (May I call you 338?).

   letter to T. E. Lawrence, 25 August 1930

19 The age of the common man has taken over a nation which owes its very existence to uncommon men.

   diary, 31 December 1956

1 Just say the lines and don't trip over the
furniture.
advice on acting
> D. Richards *The Wit of Noël Coward* (1968)

2 Television is for appearing on, not
looking at.
> D. Richards *The Wit of Noël Coward* (1968)

3 It would be nice if sometimes the kind
things I say were considered worthy of
quotation. It isn't difficult, you know, to
be witty or amusing when one has
something to say that is destructive, but
damned hard to be clever and quotable
when you are singing someone's praises.
> William Marchant *The Pleasure of His Company*
> (1981)

4 Two wise acres and a cow.
*of Edith, Osbert, and Sacheverell **Sitwell**; the
phrase 'Three acres and a cow' was associated
with Jesse Collings and his land reform
propaganda, c. 1886, though already proverbial
then*
> J. Pearson *Façades* (1978)

Hart Crane 1899–1932
American poet

5 Stars scribble on our eyes the frosty
sagas,
The gleaming cantos of unvanquished
space.
> 'Cape Hatteras' (1930)

6 Cowslip and shad-blow, flaked like
tethered foam
Around bared teeth of stallions, bloomed
that spring
When first I read thy lines, rife as the
loam
Of prairies, yet like breakers cliffward
leaping!
. . . My hand
in yours,
Walt Whitman—
so—
> 'Cape Hatteras' (1930)

7 We have seen
The moon in lonely alleys make
A grail of laughter of an empty ash can.
> 'Chaplinesque' (1926)

8 Ah, madame! truly it's not right
When one isn't the real Gioconda,

To adapt her methods and deportment
For snaring the poor world in a blue
funk.
> 'Locutions des Pierrots' (1933)

9   So the 20th Century—so
whizzed the Limited—roared by and left
three men, still hungry on the tracks,
ploddingly
watching the tail lights wizen and
converge, slipping
gimleted and neatly out of sight.
> 'The River' (1930)

10 O Sleepless as the river under thee,
Vaulting the sea, the prairies' dreaming
sod,
Unto us lowliest sometime sweep,
descend
And of the curveship lend a myth to God.
> 'To Brooklyn Bridge' (1930)

11 You who desired so much—in vain to
ask—
Yet fed your hunger like an endless task,
Dared dignify the labor, bless the quest—
Achieved that stillness ultimately best,

Being, of all, least sought for: Emily,
hear!
> 'To Emily Dickinson' (1927)

Ivor Crewe 1945–
British political scientist

12 The British public has always displayed a
healthy cynicism of MPs. They have
taken it for granted that MPs are self-
serving impostors and hypocrites who
put party before country and self before
party.
*addressing the Nolan inquiry into standards in
public life*
> in *Guardian* 18 January 1995

Francis Crick 1916–
English biophysicist
*on Crick: see **Wolpert** 334:9*

13 'You' your joys and your sorrows, your
memories and ambitions, your sense of
personal identity and free will, are in fact
no more than the behaviour of a vast

assembly of nerve cells and their
associated molecules.
*The Astonishing Hypothesis: The Scientific
Search for the Soul* (1994)

1 Almost all aspects of life are engineered
at the molecular level, and without
understanding molecules we can only
have a very sketchy understanding of life
itself.
What Mad Pursuit (1988)

Francis Crick 1916–
and James D. Watson 1928–
English biophysicist; American biologist

2 It has not escaped our notice that the
specific pairing we have postulated
immediately suggests a possible copying
mechanism for the genetic material.
*proposing the double helix as the structure of
DNA, and hence the chemical mechanism of
heredity*
in *Nature* 25 April 1953

Quentin Crisp 1908–
English writer

3 There was no need to do any housework
at all. After the first four years the dirt
doesn't get any worse.
The Naked Civil Servant (1968)

4 An autobiography is an obituary in serial
form with the last instalment missing.
The Naked Civil Servant (1968)

Julian Critchley 1930–
British Conservative politician and journalist

5 Humming, Hawing and Hesitation are
the three Graces of contemporary
Parliamentary oratory.
Westminster Blues (1985)

6 The only safe pleasure for a
parliamentarian is a bag of boiled sweets.
in *Listener* 10 June 1982

7 She cannot see an institution without
hitting it with her handbag.
*of Margaret **Thatcher***
in *The Times* 21 June 1982

Richmal Crompton 1890–1969
English author of books for children

8 I'll thcream and thcream and thcream till
I'm thick. I can.
Violet Elizabeth's habitual threat
Still—William (1925)

Bing Crosby 1903–77
American singer and film actor
*on Crosby: see also **Epitaphs** 105:8*

9 Where the blue of the night
Meets the gold of the day,
Someone waits for me.
'Where the Blue of the Night' (1931 song); with
Roy Turk and Fred Ahlert

Anthony Crosland 1918–77
British Labour politician; Foreign Secretary
1976–7

10 Total abstinence and a good filing system
are not now the right signposts to the
socialist Utopia; or at least, if they are,
some of us will fall by the wayside.
The Future of Socialism (1956)

11 If it's the last thing I do, I'm going to
destroy every fucking grammar school in
England. And Wales, and Northern
Ireland.
*c.1965, while Secretary of State for Education and
Science*
Susan Crosland *Tony Crosland* (1982)

12 In the blood of the socialist there should
always run a trace of the anarchist and
the libertarian, and not too much of the
prig and the prude.
Susan Crosland *Tony Crosland* (1982)

13 Harold knows best. Harold is a bastard,
but he is a genius. He's like Odysseus.
Odysseus was a bastard, but he managed
to steer the ship between Scylla and
Charybdis.
*on Harold **Wilson***
Susan Crosland *Tony Crosland* (1982)

14 The party's over.
*cutting back central government's support for
rates, as Minister of the Environment in the 1970s*
Anthony Sampson *The Changing Anatomy of
Britain* (1982); cf. **Comden** 73:6

Amanda Cross 1926–

American crime writer and academic

1 'What . . . is a text course?' 'One that uses books, of course . . . You remember books? They're what we used to read before we started discussing what we ought to read.'
   Poetic Justice (1970)

2 In former days, everyone found the assumption of innocence so easy; today we find fatally easy the assumption of guilt.
   Poetic Justice (1970)

Douglas Cross

American songwriter

3 I left my heart in San Francisco
   High on a hill it calls to me.
   To be where little cable cars climb half-
      way to the stars,
   The morning fog may chill the air—
   I don't care!
   'I Left My Heart in San Francisco' (1954 song)

Richard Crossman 1907–74

British Labour politician
on Crossman: see **Dalton** 83:3

4 While there is death there is hope.
   on the death of Hugh **Gaitskell** *in* 1963
   Tam Dalyell *Dick Crossman* (1989)

5 The Civil Service is profoundly deferential—'Yes, Minister! No, Minister! If you wish it, Minister!'
   diary, 22 October 1964

6 There is a cracking sound in the political atmosphere: the sound of the consensus breaking up.
   in 1970; Anthony Sampson *The Changing Anatomy of Britain* (1982)

Aleister Crowley 1875–1947

English diabolist

7 Do what thou wilt shall be the whole of the Law.
   Book of the Law (1909); see below

   Do what you like.
   François Rabelais (c.1494–c.1553) *Gargantua* (1534)

e. e. cummings 1894–1962

Amercian poet

8 anyone lived in a pretty how town
   (with up so floating many bells down)
   spring summer autumn winter
   he sang his didn't he danced his did.
   50 Poems (1949) no. 29

9 'next to of course god america i
   love you land of the pilgrims' and so
      forth oh
   say can you see by the dawn's early my
   country 'tis of centuries come and go
   and are no more what of it we should
      worry.
   is 5 (1926)

10 Humanity i love you because
    when you're hard up you pawn your
    intelligence to buy a drink.
    'La Guerre' no. 2 (1925)

11 o to be a metope
    now that triglyph's here.
    'Memorabilia' (1926); see below

    Oh, to be in England
    Now that April's there.
    Robert Browning (1812–89) 'Home-Thoughts, from Abroad' (1845)

12 a politician is an arse upon
    which everyone has sat except a man.
    1 x 1 (1944) no. 10

13 plato told

    him: he couldn't
    believe it (jesus

    told him; he
    wouldn't believe
    it).
    1 x 1 (1944) no. 13

14 pity this busy monster, manunkind,
    not. Progress is a comfortable disease.
    1 x 1 (1944) no. 14

15 We doctors know
    a hopeless case if—listen: there's a hell
    of a good universe next door; let's go.
    1 x 1 (1944) no. 14

16 when man determined to destroy
    himself he picked the was
    of shall and finding only why
    smashed it into because.
    1 x 1 (1944) no. 26

1 (i do not know what it is about you that
closes
and opens; only something in me
understands
the voice of your eyes is deeper than all
roses)
nobody, not even the rain, has such
small hands.
'somewhere I have never travelled' (1931)

2 i like my body when it is with your
body. It is so quite new a thing.
Muscles better and nerves more.
'Sonnets–Actualities' no. 8 (1925)

3 the Cambridge ladies who live in
furnished souls
are unbeautiful and have comfortable
minds.
'Sonnets–Realities' no. 1 (1923)

William Thomas Cummings
1903–45
American priest

4 There are no atheists in the foxholes.
C. P. Romulo I Saw the Fall of the Philippines
(1943)

Mario Cuomo 1932–
American Democratic politician

5 You campaign in poetry. You govern in
prose.
in New Republic, Washington, DC, 8 April 1985

Don Cupitt 1934–
British theologian

6 Christmas is the Disneyfication of
Christianity.
in Independent 19 December 1996

Edwina Currie 1946–
British Conservative politician

7 My message to the businessmen of this
country when they go abroad on
business is that there is one thing above
all they can take with them to stop them
catching Aids—and that is the wife.
speech at Runcorn, 12 February 1987

Tony Curtis 1925–
American actor

8 It's like kissing Hitler.
when asked what it was like to kiss Marilyn
Monroe
A. Hunter Tony Curtis (1985)

Michael Curtiz 1888–1962
Hungarian-born American film director

9 Bring on the empty horses!
while directing The Charge of the Light Brigade
(1936 film)
David Niven Bring on the Empty Horses (1975)

Lord Curzon 1859–1925
British Conservative politician; Viceroy of
India 1898–1905
on Curzon: see **Beaverbrook** 25:10,
Churchill 68:4, **Nehru** 229:5

10 When a group of Cabinet Ministers
begins to meet separately and to discuss
independent action, the death-tick is
audible in the rafters.
in November 1922, shortly before the fall of **Lloyd
George**'s Coalition Government
David Gilmour Curzon (1994)

11 Not even a public figure. A man of no
experience. And of the utmost
insignificance.
of Stanley **Baldwin**, appointed Prime Minister in
1923 in succession to Bonar Law
Harold Nicolson Curzon: the Last Phase (1934)

12 Dear me, I never knew that the lower
classes had such white skins.
supposedly said by Curzon when watching troops
bathing during the First World War
K. Rose Superior Person (1969)

13 Gentlemen do not take soup at luncheon.
E. L. Woodward Short Journey (1942)

Richard J. Daley 1902–76

American Democratic politician and Mayor of Chicago

1 The policeman isn't there to create disorder; the policeman is there to preserve disorder.
to the press, on the riots during the Democratic Convention in 1968
> Milton N. Rakove *Don't Make No Waves: Don't Back No Losers* (1975)

Salvador Dali 1904–89

Spanish painter

2 Picasso is Spanish, I am too. Picasso is a genius. I am too. Picasso will be seventy-two and I about forty-eight. Picasso is known in every country of the world; so am I. Picasso is a Communist; I am not.
> lecture in Madrid, 12 October 1951; Meredith Etherington Smith *Dali* (1992)

Hugh Dalton 1887–1962

British Labour politician
on Dalton: see **Birch** 38:2

3 He is loyal to his own career but only incidentally to anything or anyone else.
of Richard **Crossman**
> diary, 17 September 1941

Joe Darion 1917–

American songwriter

4 Dream the impossible dream.
> 'The Quest' (1965 song)

Bill Darnell

Canadian environmentalist

5 Make it a *green* peace.
at a meeting of the Don't Make a Wave Committee, which preceded the formation of Greenpeace
> in Vancouver, 1970; Robert Hunter *The Greenpeace Chronicle* (1979); cf. **Hunter** 154:12

Clarence Darrow 1857–1938

American lawyer

6 I do not consider it an insult, but rather a compliment to be called an agnostic. I do not pretend to know where many ignorant men are sure—that is all that agnosticism means.
> speech at trial of John Thomas Scopes for teaching Darwin's theory of evolution in school, 15 July 1925

7 I would like to see a time when man loves his fellow man and forgets his colour or his creed. We will never be civilized until that time comes. I know the Negro race has a long road to go. I believe that the life of the Negro race has been a life of tragedy, of injustice, of oppression. The law has made him equal, but man has not.
> speech in Detroit, 19 May 1926

8 When I was a boy I was told that anybody could become President. I'm beginning to believe it.
> Irving Stone *Clarence Darrow for the Defence* (1941)

Francis Darwin 1848–1925

English botanist; son of Charles Darwin

9 In science the credit goes to the man who convinces the world, not to the man to whom the idea first occurs.
> in *Eugenics Review* April 1914

Robertson Davies 1913–95

Canadian novelist

10 I see Canada as a country torn between a very northern, rather extraordinary, mystical spirit which it fears and its desire to present itself to the world as a Scotch banker.
> *The Enthusiasms of Robertson Davies* (1990)

11 It's an excellent life of somebody else. But I've really lived inside myself, and she can't get in there.
on a biography of himself
> interview in *The Times* 4 April 1995

W. H. Davies 1871–1940

Welsh poet

12 A rainbow and a cuckoo's song
May never come together again;
May never come

This side the tomb.
'A Great Time' (1914)

1 It was the Rainbow gave thee birth,
And left thee all her lovely hues.
'Kingfisher' (1910)

2 What is this life if, full of care,
We have no time to stand and stare.
'Leisure' (1911)

3 Come, lovely Morning, rich in frost
On iron, wood and glass . . .

Come, rich and lovely Winter's Eve,
That seldom handles gold;
And spread your silver sunsets out,
In glittering fold on fold.
'Silver Hours' (1932)

Bette Davis

see **Film lines** 110:2, 110:5, 112:1

Sammy Davis Jnr. 1925–90

American entertainer

4 Being a star has made it possible for me
to get insulted in places where the
average Negro could never *hope* to go
and get insulted.
Yes I Can (1965)

Richard Dawkins 1941–

English biologist

5 [Natural selection] has no vision, no
foresight, no sight at all. If it can be said
to play the role of watchmaker in nature,
it is the *blind* watchmaker.
The Blind Watchmaker (1986); see below

Suppose I had found a *watch* upon the
ground, and it should be enquired how
the watch happened to be in that
place . . . the inference, we think, is
inevitable; that the watch must have
had a maker.
William Paley (1743–1805) *Natural Theology*
(1802)

6 However many ways there may be of
being alive, it is certain that there are
vastly more ways of being dead.
The Blind Watchmaker (1986)

7 The essence of life is statistical
improbability on a colossal scale.
The Blind Watchmaker (1986); cf. **Fisher** 109:12

8 The selfish gene
title of book (1976)

9 They are in you and in me; they created
us, body and mind; and their
preservation is the ultimate rationale for
our existence . . . they go by the name of
genes, and we are their survival
machines.
The Selfish Gene (1976)

10 Science offers the best answers to the
meaning of life. Science offers the
privilege of understanding before you die
why you were ever born in the first place.
in *Break the Science Barrier with Richard
Dawkins* (Channel Four) 1 September 1996

11 I think it is likely that there is life out
there. I fear we shall never know about
it.
Seven Wonders of the World (BBC TV) 9 April
1997

Christopher Dawson
1889–1970

English historian of ideas and social culture

12 As soon as men decide that all means are
permitted to fight an evil, then their good
becomes indistinguishable from the evil
that they set out to destroy.
The Judgement of the Nations (1942)

Lord Dawson of Penn
1864–1945

English doctor; physician to King George V
on Dawson: see **Moynihan** 224:6

13 The King's life is moving peacefully
towards its close.
bulletin, 20 January 1936; K. Rose *King George
V* (1983)

Robin Day 1923–

British broadcaster
on Day: see **Howerd** 153:2

14 Television . . . thrives on unreason, and
unreason thrives on television . . . -

[Television] strikes at the emotions rather than the intellect.

Grand Inquisitor (1989)

Moshe Dayan 1915–81
Israeli statesman and general

1 War is the most exciting and dramatic thing in life. In fighting to the death you feel terribly relaxed when you manage to come through.

in *Observer* 13 February 1972

C. Day-Lewis 1904–72
Anglo-Irish poet and critic

2 Do not expect again a phoenix hour,
  The triple-towered sky, the dove
    complaining,
  Sudden the rain of gold and heart's first
    ease
  Traced under trees by the eldritch light of
    sundown.

'From Feathers to Iron' (1935)

3 Tempt me no more; for I
  Have known the lightning's hour,
  The poet's inward pride,
  The certainty of power.

The Magnetic Mountain (1933)

4 You that love England, who have an ear
    for her music,
  The slow movement of clouds in
    benediction,
  Clear arias of light thrilling over her
    uplands,
  Over the chords of summer sustained
    peacefully.

The Magnetic Mountain (1933)

5 It is the logic of our times,
  No subject for immortal verse—
  That we who lived by honest dreams
  Defend the bad against the worse.

'Where are the War Poets?' (1943)

6 Every good poem, in fact, is a bridge built from the known, familiar side of life over into the unknown. Science too, is always making expeditions into the unknown. But this does not mean that science can supersede poetry. For poetry enlightens us in a different way from science; it speaks directly to our feelings or

imagination. The findings of poetry are no more and no less true than science.

Poetry for You (1944)

John Dean 1938–
American lawyer and White House counsel during the Watergate affair

7 We have a cancer within, close to the Presidency, that is growing.

from the [Nixon] Presidential Transcripts, 21 March 1973

Millvina Dean 1911–
English youngest survivor of the Titanic disaster

8 I can't bear iced drinks . . . the iceberg, you know. Perhaps some champagne, though.

while visiting the house in Kansas City, Missouri, in which her family would have lived if her father had not drowned

in *Times* 20 August 1997

Simone de Beauvoir 1908–86
French novelist and feminist

9 Garbo's visage had a kind of emptiness into which anything could be projected— nothing can be read into Bardot's face.

Brigitte Bardot and the Lolita Syndrome (1959)

10 It is not in giving life but in risking life that man is raised above the animal; that is why superiority has been accorded in humanity not to the sex that brings forth but to that which kills.

The Second Sex (1949)

11 One is not born a woman: one becomes one.

The Second Sex (1949)

12 Few tasks are more like the torture of Sisyphus than housework, with its endless repetition . . . The housewife wears herself out marking time: she makes nothing, simply perpetuates the present.

The Second Sex (1949)

Edward de Bono 1933–

British writer and physician

1 Some people are aware of another sort of thinking which . . . leads to those simple ideas that are obvious only after they have been thought of . . . the term 'lateral thinking' has been coined to describe this other sort of thinking; 'vertical thinking' is used to denote the conventional logical process.

The Use of Lateral Thinking (1967)

2 Unhappiness is best defined as the difference between our talents and our expectations.

in *Observer* 12 June 1977

Guy Debord 1931–94

French philosopher

3 Villages, unlike towns, have always been ruled by conformism, isolation, petty surveillance, boredom and repetitive malicious gossip about the same families. Which is a precise enough description of the global spectacle's present vulgarity.

on the concept of the 'global village'; see **McLuhan** 201:2

Comments on the Society of the Spectacle (1988)

Régis Debray 1940–

French Marxist theorist

4 International life is right-wing, like nature. The social contract is left-wing, like humanity.

Charles de Gaulle (1994)

Eugene Victor Debs
1855–1926

Founder of the Socialist party of America

5 When great changes occur in history, when great principles are involved, as a rule the majority are wrong. The minority are right.

speech at his trial for sedition in Cleveland, Ohio, 11 September 1918

6 While there is a lower class , I am in it; while there is a criminal element, I am of it; while there is a soul in prison, I am not free.

speech at his trial for sedition, in Cleveland, Ohio, 14 September 1918

Edgar Degas 1834–1917

French artist

7 Art is vice. You don't marry it legitimately, you rape it.

P. Lafond *Degas* (1918)

Charles de Gaulle 1890–1970

French general; President of France, 1959–69

8 France has lost a battle. But France has not lost the war!

proclamation, 18 June 1940

9 Faced by the bewilderment of my countrymen, by the disintegration of a government in thrall to the enemy, by the fact that the institutions of my country are incapable, at the moment, of functioning, I General de Gaulle, a French soldier and military leader, realize that I now speak for France.

speech in London, 19 June 1940

10 Since they whose duty it was to wield the sword of France have let it fall shattered to the ground, I have taken up the broken blade.

speech, 13 July 1940

11 *Je vous ai compris.*

I have understood you.

speech at Algiers, 4 June 1958

12 Yes, it is Europe, from the Atlantic to the Urals, it is Europe, it is the whole of Europe, that will decide the fate of the world.

speech to the people of Strasbourg, 23 November 1959

13 Politics are too serious a matter to be left to the politicians.

replying to **Attlee***'s remark that 'De Gaulle is a very good soldier and a very bad politician'*

Clement Attlee *A Prime Minister Remembers* (1961); cf. **Clemenceau** 71:5

1 *Europe des patries.*
A Europe of nations.
widely associated with De Gaulle, c.1962, and
taken as encapsulating his views, although
perhaps not coined by him
    J. Lacouture *De Gaulle: the Ruler* (1991)

2 How can you govern a country which
has 246 varieties of cheese?
    E. Mignon *Les Mots du Général* (1962)

3 Since a politician never believes what he
says, he is quite surprised to be taken at
his word.
    Ernest Mignon *Les Mots du Général* (1962)

4 Treaties, you see, are like girls and roses:
they last while they last.
    speech at Elysée Palace, 2 July 1963

5 *Vive Le Québec Libre.*
Long Live Free Quebec.
    speech in Montreal, 24 July 1967

6 Authority doesn't work without prestige,
or prestige without distance.
    Le Fil de l'épée (1932)

7 The sword is the axis of the world and its
power is absolute.
    Vers l'armée de métier (1934)

8 What we think about death only matters
for what death makes us think about life.
    A. Malraux *Les Chênes qu'on abat* (1971)

9 And now she is like everyone else.
on the death of his daughter, who had been born
with Down's syndrome
    attributed

10 One does not put Voltaire in the Bastille.
*when asked to arrest **Sartre**, in the 1960s*
    in *Encounter* June 1975

J. de Knight 1919–
and M. Freedman 1893–1962

11 (We're gonna) rock around the clock.
    title of song (1953)

Walter de la Mare 1873–1956
English poet and novelist

12 Oh, no man knows
Through what wild centuries
Roves back the rose.
    'All That's Past' (1912)

13 He is crazed with the spell of far Arabia,
They have stolen his wits away.
    'Arabia' (1912)

14 Beauty vanishes; beauty passes;
However rare—rare it be.
    'Epitaph' (1912)

15 Look thy last on all things lovely,
Every hour.
    'Fare Well' (1918)

16 'Is there anybody there?' said the
Traveller,
Knocking on the moonlit door.
    'The Listeners' (1912)

17 'Tell them I came, and no one answered,
That I kept my word,' he said.
    'The Listeners' (1912)

18 Softly along the road of evening,
In a twilight dim with rose,
Wrinkled with age, and drenched with
dew,
Old Nod, the shepherd, goes.
    'Nod' (1912)

19 Slowly, silently, now the moon
Walks the night in her silver shoon.
    'Silver' (1913)

20 Behind the blinds I sit and watch
The people passing—passing by;
And not a single one can see
My tiny watching eye.
    'The Window' (1913)

Shelagh Delaney 1939–
English dramatist

21 Women never have young minds. They
are born three thousand years old.
    A Taste of Honey (1959)

Frederick Delius 1862–1934
English composer, of German and
Scandinavian descent

22 It is only that which cannot be expressed
otherwise that is worth expressing in
music.
    in *Sackbut* September 1920 'At the Crossroads'

Jack Dempsey 1895–1983

American boxer

1 Honey, I just forgot to duck.

*to his wife, on losing the World Heavyweight title, 23 September 1926; after a failed attempt on his life in 1981, Ronald **Reagan** quipped 'I forgot to duck'*

J. and B. P. Dempsey *Dempsey* (1977)

Catherine Deneuve 1943–

French actress

2 The paparazzi are nothing but dogs of war.

*after the death in a car crash of **Diana**, Princess of Wales*

in *Daily Telegraph* 3 September 1997

Deng Xiaoping 1904–97

Chinese Communist statesman, from 1977 paramount leader of China
*on Deng: see **Anonymous** 11:17*

3 It doesn't matter if a cat is black or white, as long as it catches mice.

in the early 1960s; in *Daily Telegraph* 20 February 1997, obituary

4 I should love to be around in 1997 to see with my own eyes Hong Kong's return to China.

in 1984; in *Daily Telegraph* 20 February 1997, obituary

Lord Denning 1899–

British judge

5 The Treaty [of Rome] is like an incoming tide. It flows into the estuaries and up the rivers. It cannot be held back.

in 1975; Anthony Sampson *The Essential Anatomy of Britain* (1992)

6 To every subject of this land, however powerful, I would use Thomas Fuller's words over three hundred years ago, 'Be ye never so high, the law is above you.'

in a High Court ruling against the Attorney-General, January 1977; see below

Be ye never so high, the law is above you.

Thomas Fuller (1654–1734) *Gnomologia* (1732)

7 The keystone of the rule of law in England has been the independence of judges. It is the only respect in which we make any real separation of powers.

The Family Story (1981)

8 Properly exercised the new powers of the executive lead to the welfare state; but abused they lead to the totalitarian state.

Anthony Sampson *The Changing Anatomy of Britain* (1982)

9 As a moth is drawn to the light, so is a litigant drawn to the United States. If he can only get his case into their courts, he stands to win a fortune. At no cost to himself; and at no risk of having to pay anything to the other side.

Smith Kline & French Laboratories Ltd. v. Bloch 1983

10 We shouldn't have all these campaigns to get the Birmingham Six released if they'd been hanged. They'd have been forgotten and the whole community would be satisfied.

in *Spectator* 18 August 1990

Jacques Derrida 1930–

French philosopher and critic

11 *Il n'y a pas de hors-texte.*
There is nothing outside of the text.

Of Grammatology (1967)

Buddy De Sylva 1895–1950 and Lew Brown 1893–1958

12 The moon belongs to everyone,
The best things in life are free,
The stars belong to everyone,
They gleam there for you and me.

'The Best Things in Life are Free' (1927 song)

Peter De Vries 1910–

American novelist

13 Gluttony is an emotional escape, a sign something is eating us.

Comfort Me With Apples (1956)

14 The value of marriage is not that adults produce children but that children produce adults.

The Tunnel of Love (1954)

Lord Dewar 1864–1930

British industrialist

1 [There are] only two classes of
pedestrians in these days of reckless
motor traffic—the quick, and the dead.
   George Robey *Looking Back on Life* (1933)

Thomas E. Dewey 1902–71

American politician and presidential
candidate
see also **Newspaper headlines** 231:3

2 That's why it's time for a change!
   *phrase used extensively in campaigns of 1944,
   1948, and 1952*
      campaign speech in San Francisco, 21
      September 1944

Sergei Diaghilev 1872–1929

Russian ballet impresario

3 *Étonne-moi.*
   Astonish me.
   to Jean **Cocteau**
      W. Fowlie (ed.) *Journals of Jean Cocteau* (1956)

4 Tchaikovsky thought of committing
suicide for fear of being discovered as a
homosexual, but today, if you are a
composer and *not* homosexual, you
might as well put a bullet through your
head.
   Vernon Duke *Listen Here!* (1963)

Diana, Princess of Wales
1961–97

former wife of **Charles**, Prince of Wales
on Diana: see **Blair** 39:4, **Dowd** 91:10, **Duffy**
92:8, **Elizabeth II** 102:13, **John** 162:3,
Motion 223:15, **Spencer** 292:15

5 If men had to have babies, they would
only ever have one each.
   in *Observer* 29 July 1984 'Sayings of the Week'

6 It gives you a feeling of comfort. It's like
having a pair of arms around you, but
it's temporary. Then you're disgusted at
the bloatedness of your stomach, and
then you bring it all up again.
   on bulimia
      interview on *Panorama*, BBC1 TV, 20 November
      1995

7 I'd like to be a queen in people's hearts
but I don't see myself being Queen of this
country.
   interview on *Panorama*, BBC1 TV, 20 November
   1995

8 There were three of us in this marriage,
so it was a bit crowded.
   interview on *Panorama*, BBC1 TV, 20 November
   1995

9 I'm not a political figure . . . I'm a
humanitarian figure. I always have been
and I always will be.
   on taking part in the campaign against landmines
      in *Daily Telegraph* 17 January 1997

10 You are going to get a big surprise with
the next thing I do.
   to reporters at St Tropez
      in *Guardian* 16 July 1997

11 The press is ferocious. It forgives nothing,
it only hunts for mistakes . . . In my
position anyone sane would have left a
long time ago.
   contrasting British and foreign press reporting
      in *Le Monde* 27 August 1997

Paul Dickson 1939–

American writer

12 Rowe's Rule: the odds are five to six that
the light at the end of the tunnel is the
headlight of an oncoming train.
   in *Washingtonian* November 1978

Joan Didion 1934–

American writer

13 Was there ever in anyone's life span a
point free in time, devoid of memory, a
night when choice was any more than
the sum of all the choices gone before?
   Run River (1963)

Howard Dietz 1896–1983

American songwriter

14 *Ars gratia artis.*
   Art for art's sake.
   *motto of Metro-Goldwyn-Mayer film studios,
   apparently intended to say 'Art is beholden to the
   artists'*
      Bosley Crowthier *The Lion's Share* (1957); see
      below

L'art pour l'art.
Art for art's sake.
Benjamin Constant (1767–1834) *Journal intime*
11 February 1804

Ernest Dimnet
French priest, writer, and lecturer

1 Architecture, of all the arts, is the one
which acts the most slowly, but the most
surely, on the soul.
What We Live By (1932)

Isak Dinesen (Karen Blixen)
1885–1962
Danish novelist and short-story writer

2 A herd of elephant . . . pacing along as if
they had an appointment at the end of
the world.
Out of Africa (1937)

3 What is man, when you come to think
upon him, but a minutely set, ingenious
machine for turning, with infinite
artfulness, the red wine of Shiraz into
urine?
Seven Gothic Tales (1934) 'The Dreamers'

Paul Dirac 1902–84
British theoretical physicist, of Swiss
descent

4 It is more important to have beauty in
one's equations than to have them fit
experiment . . . It seems that if one is
working from the point of view of getting
beauty in one's equations, and if one has
a really sound insight, one is on a sure
line of progress. If there is not complete
agreement between the results of one's
work and experiment, one should not
allow oneself to be too discouraged,
because the discrepancy may well be due
to minor features that are not properly
taken into account and that will get
cleared up with further developments of
the theory.
in Scientific American May 1963

5 It is nice, but in one of the chapters the
author made a mistake. He describes the
sun as rising twice on the same day.
on the novel Crime and Punishment
G. Gamow *Thirty Years that Shook Physics*
(1966)

Ken Dodd 1931–
British comedian

6 Freud's theory was that when a joke
opens a window and all those bats and
bogeymen fly out, you get a marvellous
feeling of relief and elation. The trouble
with Freud is that he never had to play
the old Glasgow Empire on a Saturday
night after Rangers and Celtic had both
lost.
in *Guardian* 30 April 1991; quoted in many
forms since the mid-1960s

Robert ('Bob') Dole 1923–
American Republican politician

*announcing his decision to relinquish his Senate
seat and step down as majority leader:*
7 I will seek the presidency with nothing to
fall back on but the judgement of the
people and with nowhere to go but the
White House or home.
on Capitol Hill, 15 May 1996; in *Daily Telegraph*
16 May 1996

8 A corps of the elite who never grew up,
never did anything real, never sacrificed,
never suffered, and never learned.
of the Clinton administration
nomination acceptance speech at Republican
convention in San Diego, 15 August 1996

9 It's a lot more fun winning. It hurts to
lose.
*conceding the US presidential election, 6
November 1996*
in *Daily Telegraph* 7 November 1996

J. P. Donleavy 1926–
Irish-American novelist

10 When you don't have any money, the
problem is food. When you have money,
it's sex. When you have both, it's health.
The Ginger Man (1955)

Mark Doty 1953–

American poet

1 and I swear sometimes
   when I put my head to his chest
   I can hear the virus humming

   like a refrigerator.
     'Atlantis' (1996)

2 *In one of those,* he says, *is the virus,*
   a box of AIDS. And if I open it . . .
     'Grosse Fuge' (1996)

Keith Douglas 1920–44

English poet

3 And all my endeavours are unlucky
      explorers
   come back, abandoning the expedition.
     'On Return from Egypt, 1943–4' (1946)

4 Remember me when I am dead
   And simplify me when I'm dead.
     'Simplify me when I'm Dead' (1941)

5 For here the lover and killer are mingled
   who had one body and one heart.
   And death, who had the soldier singled
   has done the lover mortal hurt.
     'Vergissmeinnicht, 1943'

Norman Douglas 1868–1952

Scottish-born novelist and essayist

6 To find a friend one must close one eye.
   To keep him—two.
     Almanac (1941)

7 You can tell the ideals of a nation by its
   advertisements.
     South Wind (1917)

O. Douglas (Anna Buchan)
1877–1948

Scottish writer, sister of John **Buchan**

8 It is wonderful how much news there is
   when people write every other day; if
   they wait for a month, there is nothing
   that seems worth telling.
     Penny Plain (1920)

William O. Douglas
1898–1980

American lawyer

9 Free speech is not to be regulated like
   diseased cattle and impure butter. The
   audience . . . that hissed yesterday may
   applaud today, even for the same
   performance.
     dissenting opinion in *Kingsley Books, Inc. v.*
     Brown 1957

Maureen Dowd 1952–

American journalist

10 The Princess of Wales was the queen of
   surfaces, ruling over a kingdom where
   fame was the highest value and glamour
   the most cherished attribute.
     in *New York Times* 3 September 1997

Arthur Conan Doyle
1859–1930

Scottish-born writer of detective fiction
see also **Misquotations** 218:5

11 Matilda Briggs . . . was a ship which is
   associated with the giant rat of Sumatra,
   a story for which the world is not yet
   prepared.
     The Case-Book of Sherlock Homes (1927)

12 Good old Watson! You are the one fixed
   point in a changing age.
     His Last Bow (1917)

13 The vocabulary of 'Bradshaw' is nervous
   and terse, but limited. The selection of
   words would hardly lend itself to the
   sending of general messages.
     The Valley of Fear (1915)

14 Mediocrity knows nothing higher than
   itself, but talent instantly recognizes
   genius.
     The Valley of Fear (1915)

Margaret Drabble 1939–

English novelist

15 Lord knows what incommunicable small
   terrors infants go through, unknown to
   all. We disregard them, we say they

forget, because they have not the words to make us remember . . . By the time they learn to speak they have forgotten the details of their complaints, and so we never know. They forget so quickly we say, because we cannot contemplate the fact that they never forget.
The Millstone (1965)

1 England's not a bad country . . . It's just a mean, cold, ugly, divided, tired, clapped-out, post-imperial, post-industrial slag-heap covered in polystyrene hamburger cartons.
A Natural Curiosity (1989)

2 Affluence was, quite simply, a question of texture . . . The threadbare carpets of infancy, the coconut matting, the ill-laid linoleum, the utility furniture . . . had all spoken of a life too near the bones of subsistence, too little padded, too severely worn.
The Needle's Eye (1972)

3 Perhaps the rare and simple pleasure of being seen for what one is compensates for the misery of being it.
A Summer Bird-Cage (1963)

John Drinkwater 1882–1937
English poet and dramatist

4   Deep is the silence, deep
On moon-washed apples of wonder.
'Moonlit Apples' (1917)

Alexander Dubček 1921–92
Czechoslovak statesman; First Secretary of the Czechoslovak Communist Party, 1968–9

5 In the service of the people we followed such a policy that socialism would not lose its human face.
describing the Prague Spring, 1968
in *Rudé Právo* 19 July 1968

W. E. B. Du Bois 1868–1963
American social reformer and political activist

6 The problem of the twentieth century is the problem of the colour line—the relation of the darker to the lighter races

of men in Asia and Africa, in America and the islands of the sea.
The Souls of Black Folk (1905)

7 One thing alone I charge you. As you live, believe in life! Always human beings will live and progress to greater, broader and fuller life. The only possible death is to lose belief in this truth simply because the great end comes slowly, because time is long.
last message, written 26 June, 1957, and read at his funeral, 1963

Carol Ann Duffy 1965–
English poet

8 Whatever 'in love' means,
true love is talented.
Someone vividly gifted in love has gone.
*on the death of **Diana**, Princess of Wales*
'September, 1997' (1997); cf. **Charles** 61:12

John Foster Dulles 1888–1959
American international lawyer and politician

9 The ability to get to the verge without getting into the war is the necessary art . . . We walked to the brink and we looked it in the face.
in *Life* 16 January 1956; cf. **Stevenson** 298:7

Daphne Du Maurier 1907–89
English novelist

10 Last night I dreamt I went to Manderley again.
Rebecca (1938)

Isadora Duncan
see **Last words** 182:3

Ronald Duncan 1914–82
English dramatist

11 Where in this wide world can man find nobility without pride,

Friendship without envy, or beauty
    without vanity?

'In Praise of the Horse' (1962)

Ian Dunlop 1925–

British art historian

1 The shock of the new.

title of book about modern art (1972)

Douglas Dunn 1942–

Scottish poet

2 In a country like this
   Our ghosts outnumber us . . .

'At Falkland Palace' (1988)

3 My poems should be Clyde-built, crude
     and sure,
   With images of those dole-deployed
   To honour the indomitable Reds,
   Clydesiders of slant steel and angled
     cranes;
   A poetry of nuts and bolts, born, bred,
   Embattled by the Clyde, tight and
     impure.

'Clydesiders' (1974)

4 They ruined us. They conquered
     continents.
   We filled their uniforms. We cruised the
     seas.
   We worked their mines and made their
     histories.
   You work, we rule, they said. We worked;
     they ruled.
   They fooled the tenements. All men were
     fooled.

'Empires' (1979)

5 I am light with meditation, religiose
   And mystic with a day of solitude.

'Reading Pascan in the Lowlands' (1985)

Paul Durcan 1944–

Irish poet

6   Some of us made it
   To the forest edge, but many of us did not

Make it, although their unborn children
    did—
Such as you whom the camp
    commandant branded
Sid Vicious of the Sex Pistols. Jesus, break
    his fall:

There—but for the clutch of luck—go we
    all.

'The Death by Heroin of Sid Vicious' (1980)

Ray Durem 1915–63

American poet

7 Some of my best friends are white boys.
   when I meet 'em
   I treat 'em
   just the same as if they was people.

'Broadminded' (written 1951)

Leo Durocher 1906–91

American baseball coach

8 Nice guys. Finish last.

casual remark at a practice ground, July 1946

   Nice Guys Finish Last (as the remark generally
   is quoted, 1975)

Lawrence Durrell 1912–90

English novelist, poet, and travel writer

9 No history much? Perhaps. Only this
     ominous
   Dark beauty flowering under veils,
   Trapped in the spectrum of a dying style:
   A village like an instinct left to rust,
   Composed around the echo of a pistol-
     shot.

'Sarajevo' (1951)

Friedrich Dürrenmatt 1921–

Swiss writer

10 What was once thought can never be
   unthought.

The Physicists (1962)

Ian Dury 1942–

British rock singer and songwriter

1 Sex and drugs and rock and roll.
  title of song (1977)

Robert Duvall

see **Film lines** 110:13

Andrea Dworkin 1946–

American feminist and writer

2 Seduction is often difficult to distinguish
  from rape. In seduction, the rapist
  bothers to buy a bottle of wine.
    speech to women at *Harper & Row*, 1976; in
    Letters from a War Zone (1988)

Bob Dylan 1941–

American singer and songwriter

3 How many roads must a man walk down
  Before you can call him a man? . . .
  The answer, my friend, is blowin' in the
  wind,
  The answer is blowin' in the wind.
    'Blowin' in the Wind' (1962 song)

4 Don't think twice, it's all right.
  title of song (1963)

5 I saw ten thousand talkers whose
  tongues were all broken,
  I saw guns and sharp swords, in the
  hands of young children . . .
  And it's a hard rain's a gonna fall.
    'A Hard Rain's A Gonna Fall' (1963 song)

6 Money doesn't talk, it swears.
    'It's Alright, Ma (I'm Only Bleeding)' (1965
    song)

7 She takes just like a woman, yes, she
  does
  She makes love just like a woman, yes,
  she does
  And she aches just like a woman
  But she breaks like a little girl.
    'Just Like a Woman' (1966 song)

8 How does it feel
  To be on your own
  With no direction home
  Like a complete unknown

Like a rolling stone?
    'Like a Rolling Stone' (1965 song)

9 She knows there's no success like failure
  And that failure's no success at all.
    'Love Minus Zero / No Limit' (1965 song)

10 Hey! Mr Tambourine Man, play a song
  for me.
  I'm not sleepy and there is no place I'm
  going to.
    'Mr Tambourine Man' (1965 song)

11 Ah, but I was so much older then,
  I'm younger than that now.
    'My Back Pages' (1964 song)

12 Señor, señor, do you know where we're
  headin'?
  Lincoln County Road or Armageddon?
    'Señor (Tale of Yankee Power)' (1978 song)

13 All that foreign oil controlling American
  soil.
    'Slow Train' (1979 song)

14 Come mothers and fathers,
  Throughout the land
  And don't criticize
  What you can't understand.
  Your sons and your daughters
  Are beyond your command
  Your old road is
  Rapidly agin'
  Please get out of the new one
  If you can't lend your hand
  For the times they are a-changin'!
    'The Times They Are A-Changing' (1964 song)

15 But I can't think for you
  You'll have to decide,
  Whether Judas Iscariot
  Had God on his side.
    'With God on our Side' (1963 song)

Clint Eastwood

see **Film lines** 110:7

Abba Eban 1915–

Israeli diplomat

16 History teaches us that men and nations
  behave wisely once they have exhausted
  all other alternatives.
    speech in London, 16 December 1970

Arthur Eddington 1882–1944

British astrophysicist

1 I shall use the phrase 'time's arrow' to express this one-way property of time which has no analogue in space.
   The Nature of the Physical World (1928)

2 If an army of monkeys were strumming on typewriters they *might* write all the books in the British Museum.
   The Nature of the Physical World (1928); cf. **Wilensky** 329:1

3 If someone points out to you that your pet theory of the universe is in disagreement with Maxwell's equations—then so much the worse for Maxwell's equations. If it is found to be contradicted by observation—well, these experimentalists do bungle things sometimes. But if your theory is found to be against the second law of thermodynamics I can give you no hope; there is nothing for it but to collapse in deepest humiliation.
   The Nature of the Physical World (1928)

4 I am standing on the threshold about to enter a room. It is a complicated business. In the first place I must shove against an atmosphere pressing with a force of fourteen pounds on every square inch of my body. I must make sure of landing on a plank travelling at twenty miles a second round the sun— a fraction of a second too early or too late, the plank would be miles away. I must do this whilst hanging from a round planet, head outward into space, and with a wind of aether blowing at no one knows how many miles a second through every interstice of my body.
   The Nature of the Physical World (1928)

5 I ask you to look both ways. For the road to a knowledge of the stars leads through the atom; and important knowledge of the atom has been reached through the stars.
   Stars and Atoms (1928)

6 Science is an edged tool, with which men play like children, and cut their own fingers.
   attributed; R. L. Weber *More Random Walks in Science* (1982)

Anthony Eden 1897–1977

British Conservative statesman; Prime Minister, 1955–7; husband of Clarissa **Eden** on Eden: see **Butler** 50:8, **Churchill** 66:9, **Muggeridge** 224:13, **Paget** 241:10

7 We are in an armed conflict; that is the phrase I have used. There has been no declaration of war.
   on the Suez crisis
      speech in the House of Commons, 1 November 1956

8 Long experience has taught me that to be criticized is not always to be wrong.
   during the Suez crisis
      speech at Lord Mayor's Guildhall banquet; in *Daily Herald* 10 November 1956

Clarissa Eden 1920–

wife of Anthony **Eden**

9 For the past few weeks I have really felt as if the Suez Canal was flowing through my drawing room.
      speech at Gateshead, 20 November 1956

Marriott Edgar 1880–1951

10 There's a famous seaside place called Blackpool,
   That's noted for fresh air and fun,
   And Mr and Mrs Ramsbottom
   Went there with young Albert, their son.
      'The Lion and Albert' (1932)

Edward VIII (Duke of Windsor) 1894–1972

King of the United Kingdom, 1936; husband of the Duchess of **Windsor** on Edward: see **Anonymous** 9:14, **Beaverbrook** 25:5, **Blunt** 40:1, **George V** 126:8, **Mary** 209:11; see also **Misquotations** 219:2

11 At long last I am able to say a few words of my own . . . you must believe me when I tell you that I have found it

impossible to carry the heavy burden of responsibility and to discharge my duties as King as I would wish to do without the help and support of the woman I love.

following his abdication

radio broadcast, 11 December 1936

1 The thing that impresses me most about America is the way parents obey their children.

in *Look* 5 March 1957

Barbara Ehrenreich 1941–
American sociologist and writer

2 Exercise is the yuppie version of bulimia.

The Worst Years of Our Lives (1991) 'Food Worship'

Paul Ralph Ehrlich 1932–
American biologist

3 The first rule of intelligent tinkering is to save all the parts.

in *Saturday Review* 5 June 1971

John Ehrlichman 1925–
American government official in the **Nixon** administration

4 I think we ought to let him hang there. Let him twist slowly, slowly in the wind.

Nixon had withdrawn his support for Patrick Gray, nominated as director of the FBI, although Gray himself had not been informed

in *Washington Post* 27 July 1973

Max Ehrmann 1872–1945

5 Go placidly amid the noise and the haste, and remember what peace there may be in silence.

often wrongly dated to 1692, the date of foundation of a church in Baltimore whose vicar circulated the poem in 1956

'Desiderata' (1948)

Albert Einstein 1879–1955
German-born theoretical physicist; originator of the theory of relativity
on Einstein: see **Anonymous** 9:16, **Picasso** 249:5, **Squire** 295:2

6 Science without religion is lame, religion without science is blind.

Science, Philosophy and Religion (1941)

7 $E = mc^2$.

the usual form of Einstein's original statement: 'If a body releases the energy L in the form of radiation, its mass is decreased by L/V^2'

in *Annalen der Physik* 18 (1905)

8 God is subtle but he is not malicious.

remark made during a week at Princeton beginning 9 May 1921, later carved above the fireplace of the Common Room of Fine Hall (the Mathematical Institute), Princeton University

9 I am convinced that *He* [God] does not play dice.

letter to Max Born, 4 December 1926

10 I am an absolute pacifist . . . It is an instinctive feeling. It is a feeling that possesses me, because the murder of men is disgusting.

interview with Paul Hutchinson, in *Christian Century* 28 August 1929

11 If my theory of relativity is proven correct, Germany will claim me as a German and France will declare that I am a citizen of the world. Should my theory prove untrue, France will say that I am a German and Germany will declare that I am a Jew.

address at the Sorbonne, Paris, possibly early December 1929, in *New York Times* 16 February 1930

12 I never think of the future. It comes soon enough.

in an interview, given on the *Belgenland*, December 1930

13 I am not only a pacifist but a militant pacifist. I am willing to fight for peace. Nothing will end war unless the people themselves refuse to go to war.

interview with G. S. Viereck, January 1931

14 As a human being, one has been endowed with just enough intelligence to be able to see clearly how utterly

inadequate that intelligence is when confronted with what exists.

letter to Queen Elisabeth of Belgium, 19 September 1932

1 The eternal mystery of the world is its comprehensibility . . . The fact that it is comprehensible is a miracle.

usually quoted as 'The most incomprehensible fact about the universe is that it is comprehensible'

in *Franklin Institute Journal* March 1936 'Physics and Reality'

2 Some recent work by E. Fermi and L. Szilard, which has been communicated to me in manuscript, leads me to expect that the element uranium may be turned into a new and important source of energy in the immediate future. Certain aspects of the situation which has arisen seem to call for watchfulness and, if necessary, quick action on the part of the Administration.

warning of the possible development of an atomic bomb, and leading to the setting up of the Manhattan Project

letter to Franklin **Roosevelt**, 2 August 1939, drafted by Leo Szilard and signed by Einstein

3 The unleashed power of the atom has changed everything save our modes of thinking and we thus drift toward unparalleled catastrophe.

telegram to prominent Americans, 24 May 1946

4 If *A* is a success in life, then *A* equals *x* plus *y* plus *z*. Work is *x*; *y* is play; and *z* is keeping your mouth shut.

in *Observer* 15 January 1950

5 Common sense is nothing more than a deposit of prejudices laid down in the mind before you reach eighteen.

Lincoln Barnett *The Universe and Dr Einstein* (1950 ed.)

6 The grand aim of all science [is] to cover the greatest number of empirical facts by logical deduction from the smallest possible number of hypotheses or axioms.

Lincoln Barnett *The Universe and Dr Einstein* (1950 ed.)

7 If I would be a young man again and had to decide how to make my living, I would not try to become a scientist or scholar or teacher. I would rather choose to be a plumber or a peddler in the hope to find that modest degree of independence still available under present circumstances.

in *Reporter* 18 November 1954

8 The distinction between past, present and future is only an illusion, however persistent.

letter to Michelangelo Besso, 21 March 1955

9 One must divide one's time between politics and equations. But our equations are much more important to me.

C. P. Snow 'Einstein'; M. Goldsmith et al. (eds.) *Einstein* (1980)

10 Nationalism is an infantile sickness. It is the measles of the human race.

Helen Dukas and Banesh Hoffman *Albert Einstein, the Human Side* (1979)

11 When I was young, I found out that the big toe always ends up making a hole in a sock. So I stopped wearing socks.

to Philippe Halsman; A. P. French *Einstein: A Centenary Volume* (1979)

Dwight D. Eisenhower
1890–1969

American general and Republican statesman, 34th President of the US, 1953–61
on Eisenhower: see **Joplin** 164:3, **Political slogans** 251:12

12 Every gun that is made, every warship launched, every rocket fired signifies, in the final sense, a theft from those who hunger and are not fed, those who are cold and are not clothed. This world in arms is not spending money alone. It is spending the sweat of its labourers, the genius of its scientists, the hopes of its children.

speech in Washington, 16 April 1953

13 You have broader considerations that might follow what you might call the 'falling domino' principle. You have a row of dominoes set up. You knock over the first one, and what will happen to the last one is that it will go over very quickly.

speech at press conference, 7 April 1954

14 I think that people want peace so much that one of these days governments had better get out of the way and let them have it.

broadcast discussion, 31 August 1959

1 In preparing for battle I have always found that plans are useless, but planning is indispensable.

Richard Nixon *Six Crises* (1962); attributed

T. S. Eliot 1888–1965

Anglo-American poet, critic, and dramatist
on Eliot: see **Leavis** 186:3, **Lewis** 190:5

2 Because I do not hope to turn again
Because I do not hope
Because I do not hope to turn.

Ash-Wednesday (1930) pt. 1

3 Teach us to care and not to care
Teach us to sit still.

Ash-Wednesday (1930) pt. 1

4 Lady, three white leopards sat under a juniper-tree
In the cool of the day.

Ash-Wednesday (1930) pt. 2

5 What is hell?
Hell is oneself,
Hell is alone, the other figures in it
Merely projections.

The Cocktail Party (1950)

6 Success is relative:
It is what we can make of the mess we have made of things.

The Family Reunion (1939)

7 Round and round the circle
Completing the charm
So the knot be unknotted
The cross be uncrossed
The crooked be made straight
And the curse be ended.

The Family Reunion (1939)

8 How unpleasant to meet Mr Eliot!
With his features of clerical cut,
And his brow so grim
And his mouth so prim
And his conversation, so nicely
Restricted to What Precisely
And If and Perhaps and But.

'Five-Finger Exercises' (1936); see below

'How pleasant to know Mr Lear!'
Edward Lear (1812–88) *Nonsense Songs* (1871) preface

9 Time present and time past
Are both perhaps present in time future,
And time future contained in time past.

Four Quartets 'Burnt Norton' (1936) pt. 1

10 Footfalls echo in the memory
Down the passage which we did not take
Towards the door we never opened
Into the rose-garden.

Four Quartets 'Burnt Norton' (1936) pt. 1

11   Human kind
Cannot bear very much reality.

Four Quartets 'Burnt Norton' (1936) pt. 1.

12 At the still point of the turning world.

Four Quartets 'Burnt Norton' (1936) pt. 2

13   Words strain,
Crack and sometimes break, under the burden,
Under the tension, slip, slide, perish,
Decay with imprecision, will not stay in place,
Will not stay still.

Four Quartets 'Burnt Norton' (1936) pt. 5

14 In my beginning is my end.

Four Quartets 'East Coker' (1940) pt. 1; see below

In my end is my beginning.

Mary, Queen of Scots (1542–87) motto embroidered with an emblem of her mother, Mary of Guise

15 That was a way of putting it—not very satisfactory:
A periphrastic study in a worn-out poetical fashion,
Leaving one still with the intolerable wrestle
With words and meanings.

Four Quartets 'East Coker' (1940) pt. 2

16 The houses are all gone under the sea.
The dancers are all gone under the hill.

Four Quartets 'East Coker' (1940) pt. 2

17 O dark dark dark. They all go into the dark,
The vacant interstellar spaces, the vacant into the vacant.

Four Quartets 'East Coker' (1940) pt. 3

18 The wounded surgeon plies the steel
That questions the distempered part;
Beneath the bleeding hands we feel
The sharp compassion of the healer's art

Resolving the enigma of the fever chart.
Four Quartets 'East Coker' (1940) pt. 4

1   Each venture
Is a new beginning, a raid on the
    inarticulate
With shabby equipment always
    deteriorating
In the general mess of imprecision of
    feeling.
Four Quartets 'East Coker' (1940) pt. 5

2 Trying to learn to use words, and every
    attempt
Is a wholly new start, and a different
    kind of failure.
Four Quartets 'East Coker' (1940) pt. 5

3 I do not know much about gods; but I
    think that the river
Is a strong brown god.
Four Quartets 'The Dry Salvages' (1941) pt. 1

4 We had the experience but missed the
    meaning.
Four Quartets 'The Dry Salvages' (1941) pt. 2

5 And what the dead had no speech for,
    when living,
They can tell you, being dead: the
    communication
Of the dead is tongued with fire beyond
    the language of the living.
Four Quartets 'Little Gidding' (1942) pt. 1

6 Ash on an old man's sleeve
Is all the ash the burnt roses leave.
Four Quartets 'Little Gidding' (1942) pt. 2

7 The death of hope and despair,
This is the death of air.
Four Quartets 'Little Gidding' (1942) pt. 2

8 Since our concern was speech, and
    speech impelled us
To purify the dialect of the tribe.
Four Quartets 'Little Gidding' (1942) pt. 2

9 And the end of all our exploring
Will be to arrive where we started
And know the place for the first time.
Four Quartets 'Little Gidding' (1942) pt. 5

10 What we call the beginning is often the
    end
And to make an end is to make a
    beginning.
The end is where we start from.
Four Quartets 'Little Gidding' (1942) pt. 5

11 A people without history
Is not redeemed from time, for history is
    a pattern
Of timeless moments. So, while the light
    fails
On a winter's afternoon, in a secluded
    chapel
History is now and England.
Four Quartets 'Little Gidding' (1942) pt. 5

12 And all shall be well and
All manner of thing shall be well
When the tongues of flame are in-folded
Into the crowned knot of fire
And the fire and the rose are one.
Four Quartets 'Little Gidding' (1942) pt. 5; see
below

Sin is behovely, but all shall be well
and all shall be well and all manner of
thing shall be well.
Julian of Norwich (1343–after 1416) *Revelations
of Divine Love*

13 Here I am, an old man in a dry month
Being read to by a boy, waiting for rain.
'Gerontion' (1920)

14 After such knowledge, what forgiveness?
'Gerontion' (1920)

15 Tenants of the house,
Thoughts of a dry brain in a dry season.
'Gerontion' (1920)

16 We are the hollow men
We are the stuffed men
Leaning together
Headpiece filled with straw. Alas!
'The Hollow Men' (1925)

17 Here we go round the prickly pear
Prickly pear prickly pear.
'The Hollow Men' (1925)

18 Between the idea
And the reality
Between the motion
And the act
Falls the Shadow.
'The Hollow Men' (1925)

19 This is the way the world ends
Not with a bang but a whimper.
'The Hollow Men' (1925)

20 A cold coming we had of it,
Just the worst time of the year
For a journey, and such a long journey:
The ways deep and the weather sharp,

The very dead of winter.
'Journey of the Magi' (1927); see below

It was no summer progress. A cold coming they had of it, at this time of the year; just, the worst time of the year, to take a journey, and specially a long journey, in. The ways deep, the weather sharp, the days short, the sun farthest off *in solstitio brumali*, the very dead of Winter.
Lancelot Andrewes (1555–1626) *Of the Nativity* (1622)

1   There was a Birth, certainly,
We had evidence and no doubt. I had seen birth and death
But had thought they were different.
'Journey of the Magi' (1927)

2 With an alien people clutching their gods.
'Journey of the Magi' (1927)

3 Let us go then, you and I,
When the evening is spread out against the sky
Like a patient etherized upon a table.
'Love Song of J. Alfred Prufrock' (1917); cf.
Lewis 190:5

4 In the room the women come and go
Talking of Michelangelo.
'Love Song of J. Alfred Prufrock' (1917)

5 The yellow fog that rubs its back upon the window-panes.
'Love Song of J. Alfred Prufrock' (1917)

6 I have measured out my life with coffee spoons.
'Love Song of J. Alfred Prufrock' (1917)

7 I should have been a pair of ragged claws
Scuttling across the floors of silent seas.
'Love Song of J. Alfred Prufrock' (1917)

8 I have seen the moment of my greatness flicker,
And I have seen the eternal Footman hold my coat, and snicker,
And in short, I was afraid.
'Love Song of J. Alfred Prufrock' (1917)

9 No! I am not Prince Hamlet, nor was meant to be;
Am an attendant lord, one that will do
To swell a progress, start a scene or two,
Advise the prince.
'Love Song of J. Alfred Prufrock' (1917)

10 I grow old . . . I grow old . . .
I shall wear the bottoms of my trousers rolled.

Shall I part my hair behind? Do I dare to eat a peach?
I shall wear white flannel trousers, and walk upon the beach.
I have heard the mermaids singing, each to each.

I do not think that they will sing to me.
'Love Song of J. Alfred Prufrock' (1917); see below

Teach me to hear mermaids singing.
John Donne (1572–1631) *Songs and Sonnets*
'Song: Go and catch a falling star'

11 I am aware of the damp souls of housemaids
Sprouting despondently at area gates.
'Morning at the Window' (1917)

12 Yet we have gone on living,
Living and partly living.
Murder in the Cathedral (1935)

13 The last temptation is the greatest treason:
To do the right deed for the wrong reason.
Murder in the Cathedral (1935)

14 Clear the air! clean the sky! wash the wind!
Murder in the Cathedral (1935)

15 He always has an alibi, and one or two to spare:
At whatever time the deed took place—
MACAVITY WASN'T THERE!
Old Possum's Book of Practical Cats (1939)
'Macavity: the Mystery Cat'

16 The winter evening settles down
With smell of steaks in passageways.
Six o'clock.
The burnt-out ends of smoky days.
'Preludes' (1917)

17 Midnight shakes the memory
As a madman shakes a dead geranium.
'Rhapsody on a Windy Night' (1917)

18 Where is the Life we have lost in living?
Where is the wisdom we have lost in knowledge?
Where is the knowledge we have lost in information?
The Rock (1934)

1 . . . Here were decent godless people:
   Their only monument the asphalt road
   And a thousand lost golf balls.
   The Rock (1934)

2 Birth, and copulation, and death.
   That's all the facts when you come to
     brass tacks.
   Sweeney Agonistes (1932) 'Fragment of an
   Agon'

3 Any man has to, needs to, wants to
   Once in a lifetime, do a girl in.
   Sweeney Agonistes (1932) 'Fragment of an
   Agon'

4 I gotta use words when I talk to you.
   Sweeney Agonistes (1932) 'Fragment of an
   Agon'

5 The nightingales are singing near
   The Convent of the Sacred Heart,

   And sang within the bloody wood
   When Agamemnon cried aloud
   And let their liquid siftings fall
   To stain the stiff dishonoured shroud.
   'Sweeney among the Nightingales' (1919)

6 April is the cruellest month, breeding
   Lilacs out of the dead land.
   The Waste Land (1922) pt. 1

7 I read, much of the night, and go south
   in the winter.
   The Waste Land (1922) pt. 1

8 I will show you fear in a handful of dust.
   The Waste Land (1922) pt. 1

9 A crowd flowed over London Bridge, so
   many,
   I had not thought death had undone so
   many.
   The Waste Land (1922) pt. 1

10 And still she cried, and still the world
   pursues,
   'Jug Jug' to dirty ears.
   The Waste Land (1922) pt. 2; see below

   O 'tis the ravished nightingale.
   Jug, jug, jug, jug, tereu, she cries.
   John Lyly (*c*.1554–1606) *Campaspe* (1584)

11 I think we are in rats' alley
   Where the dead men lost their bones.
   The Waste Land (1922) pt. 2

12 O O O O that Shakespeherian Rag—
   It's so elegant

So intelligent.
   The Waste Land (1922) pt. 2; cf. **Buck** 48:4

13 Hurry up please it's time.
   The Waste Land (1922) pt. 2

14 But at my back from time to time I hear
   The sound of horns and motors, which
     shall bring
   Sweeney to Mrs Porter in the spring.
   O the moon shone bright on Mrs Porter
   And on her daughter
   They wash their feet in soda water.
   The Waste Land (1922) pt. 3; see below

   But at my back I always hear
   Time's wingèd chariot hurrying near.
   Andrew Marvell (1621–78) 'To His Coy Mistress'
   (1681)

15 At the violet hour, when the eyes and
     back
   Turn upward from the desk, when the
     human engine waits
   Like a taxi throbbing waiting.
   The Waste Land (1922) pt. 3

16 I Tiresias, old man with wrinkled dugs.
   The Waste Land (1922) pt. 3

17 One of the low on whom assurance sits
   As a silk hat on a Bradford millionaire.
   The Waste Land (1922) pt. 3

18 When lovely woman stoops to folly and
   Paces about her room again, alone,
   She smoothes her hair with automatic
     hand,
   And puts a record on the gramophone.
   The Waste Land (1922) pt. 3; see below

   When lovely woman stoops to folly
   And finds too late that men betray.
   Oliver Goldsmith (1728–74) *The Vicar of
   Wakefield* (1766)

19 Webster was much possessed by death
   And saw the skull beneath the skin.
   'Whispers of Immortality' (1919)

20 Uncorseted, her friendly bust
   Gives promise of pneumatic bliss.
   'Whispers of Immortality' (1919)

21 Culture may even be described simply as
   that which makes life worth living.
   Notes Towards a Definition of Culture (1948)

1 The only way of expressing emotion in the form of art is by finding an 'objective correlative'; in other words, a set of objects, a situation, a chain of events which shall be the formula of that *particular* emotion; such that when the external facts, which must terminate in sensory experience, are given, the emotion is immediately evoked.

> *The Sacred Wood* (1920) 'Hamlet and his Problems'

2 Immature poets imitate; mature poets steal.

> *The Sacred Wood* (1920) 'Philip Massinger'

3 Someone said: 'The dead writers are remote from us because we *know* so much more than they did.' Precisely, and they are that which we know.

> *The Sacred Wood* (1920) 'Tradition and Individual Talent'

4 Poetry is not a turning loose of emotion, but an escape from emotion; it is not the expression of personality but an escape from personality.

> *The Sacred Wood* (1920) 'Tradition and Individual Talent'

5 We know too much and are convinced of too little. Our literature is a substitute for religion, and so is our religion.

> *Selected Essays* (1932) 'A Dialogue on Dramatic Poetry' (1928)

6 In the seventeenth century a dissociation of sensibility set in, from which we have never recovered; and this dissociation, as is natural, was due to the influence of the two most powerful poets of the century, Milton and Dryden.

> *Selected Essays* (1932) 'The Metaphysical Poets' (1921)

7 Poets in our civilization, as it exists at present, must be *difficult*.

> *Selected Essays* (1932) 'The Metaphysical Poets' (1921)

8 [*The Waste Land*] was only the relief of a personal and wholly insignificant grouse against life; it is just a piece of rhythmical grumbling.

> *The Waste Land* (ed. Valerie Eliot, 1971) epigraph

Queen Elisabeth of Belgium
1876–1965
German-born consort of King Albert of the Belgians

9 Between them [Germany] and me there is now a bloody curtain which has descended forever.

> *on Germany's invasion of Belgium in* 1914
> attributed

Elizabeth II 1926–
Queen of the United Kingdom from 1952; wife of Prince **Philip**
on Elizabeth II: see **Grigg** 134:5, **Philip** 248:8

10 I declare before you all that my whole life, whether it be long or short, shall be devoted to your service and the service of our great Imperial family to which we all belong.

> broadcast speech, as Princess Elizabeth, to the Commonwealth from Cape Town, 21 April 1947

11 I think everybody really will concede that on this, of all days, I should begin my speech with the words 'My husband and I'.

> *speech at Guildhall, London, on her 25th wedding anniversary*
> in *The Times* 21 November 1972

12 In the words of one of my more sympathetic correspondents, it has turned out to be an 'annus horribilis'.

> speech at Guildhall, London, 24 November 1992

13 I for one believe that there are lessons to be drawn from her life and from the extraordinary and moving reaction to her death.

> *broadcast from Buckingham Palace on the evening before the funeral of **Diana**, Princess of Wales, 5 September 1997*
> in *The Times* 6 September 1997

14 I sometimes sense the world is changing almost too fast for its inhabitants, at least for us older ones.

> *on her tour of Pakistan, 8 October 1997*
> in *Times* 9 October 1997

1 Please don't be too effusive.

adjuration to the Prime Minister, at their weekly meeting on the speech he was to make to celebrate her golden wedding

in *Daily Telegraph* 21 November 1997; cf. **Blair** 39:5

2 Think what we would have missed if we had never . . . used a mobile phone or surfed the Net—or, to be honest, listened to other people talking about surfing the Net.

reflecting on developments in the past 50 years

in *Daily Telegraph* 21 November 1997

Elizabeth, the Queen Mother 1900–

Queen Consort of **George VI**

3 I'm glad we've been bombed. It makes me feel I can look the East End in the face.

to a London policeman, 13 September 1940

J. Wheeler-Bennett *King George VI* (1958)

4 The Princesses would never leave without me and I couldn't leave without the King, and the King will never leave.

on the suggestion that the royal family be evacuated during the Blitz

Penelope Mortimer *Queen Elizabeth* (1986)

5 How small and selfish is sorrow. But it bangs one about until one is senseless.

letter to Edith Sitwell, shortly after the death of **George VI**

Victoria Glendinning *Edith Sitwell* (1983)

Elizabeth, Countess von Arnim 1866–1941

Australian-born British writer

6 Guests can be, and often are, delightful, but they should never be allowed to get the upper hand.

All the Dogs in My Life (1936)

Alf Ellerton

7 Belgium put the kibosh on the Kaiser.

title of song (1914)

Duke Ellington 1899–1974

American jazz pianist, composer, and band-leader

see also **Mills** 216:3

8 Playing 'Bop' is like scrabble with all the vowels missing.

in *Look* 10 August 1954

Alice Thomas Ellis 1932–

English novelist

9 Claudia's the sort of person who goes through life holding on to the sides.

The Other Side of the Fire (1983)

10 Our only hope rests on the off-chance that God does exist.

Unexplained Laughter (1985)

Havelock Ellis 1859–1939

English sexologist

11 What we call 'progress' is the exchange of one nuisance for another nuisance.

Impressions and Comments (1914) 31 July 1912

12 All civilization has from time to time become a thin crust over a volcano of revolution.

Little Essays of Love and Virtue (1922)

Paul Éluard 1895–1952

French poet

13 *Adieu tristesse*
Bonjour tristesse.
Farewell sadness
Good-day sadness.

'À peine défigurée' (1932)

William Empson 1906–84

English poet and literary critic

14 Just a smack at Auden.

title of poem, 1940

15 Waiting for the end, boys, waiting for the end.

'Just a smack at Auden' (1940)

16 You don't want madhouse and the whole thing there.

'Let it Go' (1955)

1 Slowly the poison the whole blood stream
  fills.
  It is not the effort nor the failure tires.
  The waste remains, the waste remains
  and kills.
    'Missing Dates' (1935)

2 Seven types of ambiguity.
    title of book (1930)

Nora Ephron 1941–
American writer and journalist

3 We have lived through the era when
  happiness was a warm puppy, and the
  era when happiness was a dry martini,
  and now we have come to the era when
  happiness is 'knowing what your uterus
  looks like'.
    Crazy Salad (1975) 'Vaginal Politics'; cf.
    Advertising slogans 3:21, **Lennon** 187:13,
    Schulz 280:13

4 I am continually fascinated at the
  difficulty intelligent people have in
  distinguishing what is controversial from
  what is merely offensive.
    in *Esquire* January 1976

■ Epitaphs
see box opposite

Jacob Epstein 1880–1959
British sculptor
on Epstein: see **Anonymous** 9:16

5 Why don't they stick to murder and
  leave art to us?
    on hearing that his statue of Lazarus in New
    College chapel, Oxford, kept **Khrushchev** *awake*
    at night
      attributed

Ludwig Erhard 1897–1977
German statesman, Chancellor of West
Germany (1963–6)

6 Without Britain Europe would remain
  only a torso.
    remark on W. German television, 27 May 1962;
    in *The Times* 28 May 1962

Susan Ertz 1894–1985
American writer

7 Millions long for immortality who don't
  know what to do with themselves on a
  rainy Sunday afternoon.
    Anger in the Sky (1943)

Lord Esher 1913–
English architect and planner

8 When politicians and civil servants hear
  the word 'culture' they feel for their blue
  pencils.
    speech, House of Lords, 2 March 1960; cf.
    Johst 163:13

9 Who would guess that those gloomy
  bunkers were built to celebrate the
  pleasures of the senses?
    of the Hayward Gallery complex, London
      A Broken Wave (1987)

Gavin Ewart 1916–95
British poet

10 So the last date slides into the bracket,
   that will appear in all future
       anthologies—
   And in quiet Cornwall and in London's
       ghastly racket
   We are now Betjemanless.
     'In Memoriam, Sir John Betjeman (1906–84)'
     (1985)

11 Is it Colman's smile
   That makes life worth while
   Or Crawford's significant form?
   Is it Lombard's lips
   Or Mae West's hips
   That carry you through the storm?
     'Verse from an Opera' (1939)

William Norman Ewer
1885–1976
British writer

12 I gave my life for freedom—This I know:
   For those who bade me fight had told me
       so.
     'Five Souls' (1917)

Epitaphs

1 Commander Jacques-Yves Cousteau has rejoined the world of silence.

announcement by the Cousteau Foundation, Paris, 25 June 1997; Cousteau (1910–97) published The Silent World *in 1953*

in *Daily Telegraph* 26 June 1997

2 Excuse My Dust.

Dorothy **Parker**'s suggested epitaph for herself (1925); Alexander Woollcott *While Rome Burns* (1934) 'Our Mrs Parker'

3 Free at last, free at last
Thank God almighty
We are free at last.

*epitaph of Martin Luther **King**, Atlanta, Georgia*

anonymous spiritual, with which he ended his 'I have a dream' speech; cf. **King** 172:6

4 God damn you all: I told you so.

*H. G. **Wells**' suggestion for his own epitaph, in conversation with Ernest Barker, 1939*

Ernest Barker *Age and Youth* (1953)

5 Hereabouts died a very gallant gentleman, Captain L. E. G. Oates of the Inniskilling Dragoons. In March 1912, returning from the Pole, he walked willingly to his death in a blizzard to try and save his comrades, beset by hardships.

epitaph on cairn erected in the Antarctic, 15 November 1912 by E. L. Atkinson (1882–1929) and Apsley Cherry-Garrard (1882–1959)

Apsley Cherry-Garrard *Worst Journey in the World* (1922); cf. **Last words** 182:6

6 Here lies Groucho Marx—and lies and lies and lies and lies. P.S. He never kissed an ugly girl.

his own suggestion for his epitaph

B. Norman *The Movie Greats* (1981)

7 Here lies W. C. Fields. I would rather be living in Philadelphia.

suggested epitaph for himself, in *Vanity Fair* June 1925

8 He was an average guy who could carry a tune.

Bing **Crosby**'s suggested epitaph for himself

in *Newsweek* 24 October 1977

9 His foe was folly and his weapon wit.

inscription for W. S. Gilbert's memorial on the Victoria Embankment, London (1915), by Anthony Hope (1863–1933)

10 I will return. And I will be millions.

inscription on the tomb of Eva **Perón,** Buenos Aires

11 John Le Mesurier wishes it to be known that he conked out on November 15th. He sadly misses family and friends.

obituary notice on the death of John Le Mesurier (1912–83), in *The Times* 16 November 1983

12 Poor G.K.C., his day is past—
Now God will know the truth at last.

*mock epitaph for G. K. **Chesterton**, by E. V. Lucas (1868–1938)*

Dudley Barker *G. K. Chesterton* (1973)

13 Rest in peace. The mistake shall not be repeated.

inscription on the cenotaph at Hiroshima, Japan

14 A soldier of the Great War known unto God.

standard epitaph for the unidentified dead of World War One

adopted by the War Graves Commission

15 Their name liveth for evermore.

*standard inscription on the Stone of Sacrifice in each military cemetery of World War One, proposed by Rudyard **Kipling** as a member of the War Graves Commission*

Charles Carrington *Rudyard Kipling* (rev. ed. 1978); see below

Their bodies are buried in peace; but their name liveth for evermore.

Bible (Apocrypha) Ecclesiasticus

▶

> ▶ **Epitaphs** continued

1 Timothy has passed . . .
message on his Internet web page announcing the death of Timothy Leary, 31 May 1996
  in Guardian 1 June 1996

2 When you go home, tell them of us and say,
'For your tomorrow we gave our today.'
Kohima memorial to the Burma campaign of the Second World War; in recent years used at Remembrance Day parades in the UK (cf. Binyon 37:13); see below

When you go home, tell them of us and say,
'For your tomorrows these gave their today.'
John Maxwell Edmonds (1875–1958)
Inscriptions Suggested for War Memorials (1919)

3 Without you, Heaven would be too dull to bear,
And Hell would not be Hell if you are there.
epitaph for Maurice Bowra by John Sparrow
  in Times Literary Supplement 30 May 1975

▶▶ **William Norman Ewer** continued

4 How odd
Of God
To choose
The Jews.
The Week-End Book (1924); cf. Browne 46:15

Richard Eyre 1943–
English theatre director

5 We exercise the ultimate sanction of switching off only in an extreme case, like a heroin addict rejecting the needle in the face of death.
on television as an agent of cultural destruction
  attributed, 1995

Clifton Fadiman 1904–
American critic

6 Milk's leap toward immortality.
of cheese
  Any Number Can Play (1957)

7 The mama of dada.
of Gertrude Stein
  Party of One (1955)

Eleanor Farjeon 1881–1965
English writer for children

8 Morning has broken
Like the first morning,

Blackbird has spoken
Like the first bird.
'A Morning Song (for the First Day of Spring)' (1957)

Herbert Farjeon 1887–1945
English writer and theatre critic

9 For I've danced with a man.
I've danced with a man
Who—well, you'll never guess.
I've danced with a man who's danced with a girl
Who's danced with the Prince of Wales!
'I've danced with a man who's danced with a girl'; first written for Elsa Lanchester and sung at private parties; later sung on stage by Mimi Crawford (1928)

King Farouk 1920–65
King of Egypt, 1936–52

10 Soon there will be only five Kings left—the King of England, the King of Spades, the King of Clubs, the King of Hearts and the King of Diamonds.
  said to Lord Boyd-Orr at a conference in Cairo, 1948; Lord Boyd-Orr *As I Recall* (1966)

Mia Farrow 1945–
American actress

11 He had polyester sheets and I wanted to get cotton sheets. He discussed it with his

shrink many times before he made the switch.

of the dependence of her former partner, Woody **Allen**, *on psychotherapists*
> in *Independent* 8 February 1997 'Quote Unquote'

William Faulkner 1897–1962
American novelist
see also **Film lines** 111:7, **Film titles** 112:11

1 He made the books and he died.
his own 'sum and history of my life'
> letter to Malcolm Cowley, 11 February 1949

2 He [the writer] must teach himself that the basest of all things is to be afraid and, teaching himself that, forget it forever, leaving no room in his workshop for anything but the old verities and truths of the heart, the old universal truths lacking which any story is ephemeral and doomed—love and honor and pity and pride and compassion and sacrifice.
> Nobel Prize speech, Stockholm, 10 December 1950

3 The poet's voice need not merely be the record of man; it can be one of the props, the pillars, to help him endure and prevail.
> Nobel prize acceptance speech, Stockholm, 10 December 1950

4 The writer's only responsibility is to his art. He will be completely ruthless if he is a good one. He has a dream. It anguishes him so much he must get rid of it. He has no peace until then. Everything goes by the board . . . If a writer has to rob his mother, he will not hesitate; the *Ode on a Grecian Urn* is worth any number of old ladies.
> in *Paris Review* Spring 1956

5 A man shouldn't fool with booze until he's fifty; then he's a damn fool if he doesn't.
> James M. Webb and A. Wigfall Green *William Faulkner of Oxford* (1965)

Dianne Feinstein 1933–
American Democratic politician, Mayor of San Francisco

6 Toughness doesn't have to come in a pinstripe suit.
> in *Time* 4 June 1984

7 There was a time when you could say the least government was the best—but not in the nation's most populous state.
> campaign speech, 15 March 1990

James Fenton 1949–
English poet

8 It is not what they built. It is what they knocked down.
It is not the houses. It is the spaces between the houses.
It is not the streets that exist. It is the streets that no longer exist.
> *German Requiem* (1981)

9 'I didn't exist at Creation
I didn't exist at the Flood,
And I won't be around for Salvation
To sort out the sheep from the cud—

'Or whatever the phrase is. The fact is
In soteriological terms
I'm a crude existential malpractice
And you are a diet of worms.'
> 'God, A Poem' (1983)

10 Yes
You have come upon the fabled lands
   where myths
Go when they die.
> 'The Pitt-Rivers Museum' (1983)

11 Windbags can be right. Aphorists can be wrong. It is a tough world.
> in *Times* 21 February 1985

Edna Ferber 1887–1968
American writer

12 Being an old maid is like death by drowning, a really delightful sensation after you cease to struggle.
> R. E. Drennan *Wit's End* (1973)

Enrico Fermi 1901–54
Italian-born American atomic physicist

13 If I could remember the names of all these particles I'd be a botanist.
> R. L. Weber *More Random Walks in Science* (1973)

14 Whatever Nature has in store for mankind, unpleasant as it may be, men

must accept, for ignorance is never better than knowledge.

Laura Fermi *Atoms in the Family* (1955)

Kathleen Ferrier

see **Last words** 182:13

Paul Feyerabend 1924–94

Austrian philosopher

1 The time is overdue for adding the separation of state and science to the by now customary separation of state and church. Science is only *one* of the many instruments man has invented to cope with his surroundings. It is not the only one, it is not infallible, and it has become too powerful, too pushy, and too dangerous to be left on its own.

Against Method (1975)

Richard Phillips Feynman 1918–88

American theoretical physicist

2 For a successful technology, reality must take precedence over public relations, for nature cannot be fooled.

Appendix to the *Rogers Commission Report on the Space Shuttle Challenger Accident* 6 June 1986

3 What I cannot create, I do not understand.

attributed

Frank Field 1942–

British Labour politician

4 The archbishop is usually to be found nailing his colours to the fence.

of Archbishop **Runcie***; a similar comment has been recorded on A. J.* **Balfour***, c.1904*

attributed in *Crockfords 1987/88* (1987)

Dorothy Fields 1905–74

American songwriter

5 The minute you walked in the joint,
I could see you were a man of distinction,

A real big spender . . .
Hey! big spender, spend a little time with me.

'Big Spender' (1966 song)

6 A fine romance with no kisses.
A fine romance, my friend, this is.

'A Fine Romance' (1936 song)

7 Grab your coat, and get your hat,
Leave your worry on the doorstep,
Just direct your feet
To the sunny side of the street.

'On the Sunny Side of the Street' (1930 song)

8 Pick yourself up,
Dust yourself off,
Start all over again.

'Pick Yourself Up' (1936 song)

W. C. Fields 1880–1946

American humorist
on Fields: see **Rosten** 269:7; *see also*
Epitaphs 105:7, **Film lines** 110:15

9 Some weasel took the cork out of my lunch.

You Can't Cheat an Honest Man (1939 film)

10 Never give a sucker an even break.

title of a W. C. Fields film (1941); the catch-phrase (Fields's own) is said to have originated in the musical comedy *Poppy* (1923)

11 It ain't a fit night out for man or beast.

adopted by Fields but claimed by him not to be original; letter, 8 February 1944

12 Hell, I never vote *for* anybody. I always vote *against*.

R. L. Taylor *W. C. Fields* (1950)

13 The funniest thing about comedy is that you never know why people laugh. I know *what* makes them laugh but trying to get your hands on the *why* of it is like trying to pick an eel out of a tub of water.

R. J. Anobile *A Flask of Fields* (1972)

14 If at first you don't succeed, try, try again. Then quit. No use being a damn fool about it.

attributed

15 Last week, I went to Philadelphia, but it was closed.

R. J. Anobile *Godfrey Daniels* (1975)

1 Never cry over spilt milk, because it may have been poisoned.

to Carlotta Monti

> Carlotta Monti with Cy Rice *W. C. Fields and Me* (1971)

■ Film lines

see box overleaf
see also Woody **Allen**, W. C. **Fields**, Greta **Garbo**, Stan **Laurel**, Mae **West**

■ Film titles

see box page 112

Michael Fish 1944–

British weather forecaster

2 A woman rang to say she heard there was a hurricane on the way. Well don't worry, there isn't.

weather forecast on the night before serious gales in southern England

> BBC TV, 15 October 1987

Carrie Fisher 1956–

American actress and writer

3 Here's how men think. Sex, work—and those are reversible, depending on age— sex, work, food, sports and lastly, begrudgingly, relationships. And here's how women think. Relationships, relationships, relationships, work, sex, shopping, weight, food.

> *Surrender the Pink* (1990)

H. A. L. Fisher 1856–1940

English historian

4 Men wiser and more learned than I have discerned in history a plot, a rhythm, a predetermined pattern. These harmonies are concealed from me. I can see only one emergency following upon another as wave follows upon wave.

> *A History of Europe* (1935)

5 Purity of race does not exist. Europe is a continent of energetic mongrels.

> *A History of Europe* (1935)

Lord Fisher 1841–1920

British admiral

6 Sack the lot!

on government overmanning and overspending

> letter to *The Times*, 2 September 1919

7 Never contradict. Never explain. Never apologize.

> letter to *The Times*, 5 September 1919

8 Yours till Hell freezes.

> attributed to Fisher, but not original; F. Ponsonby *Reflections of Three Reigns* (1951)

Marve Fisher

American songwriter

9 I like Chopin and Bizet, and the voice of Doris Day,
Gershwin songs and old forgotten carols.
But the music that excels is the sound of oil wells
As they slurp, slurp, slurp into the barrels.

> 'An Old-Fashioned Girl' (1954 song)

10 I want an old-fashioned house
With an old-fashioned fence
And an old-fashioned millionaire.

> 'An Old-Fashioned Girl' (1954 song)

R. A. Fisher 1890–1962

English statistician and geneticist

11 The best causes tend to attract to their support the worst arguments.

> *Statistical Methods and Scientific Inference* (1956)

12 It was Darwin's chief contribution, not only to Biology but to the whole of natural science, to have brought to light a process by which contingencies *a priori* improbable are given, in the process of time, an increasing probability, until it is their non-occurrence, rather than their occurence, which becomes highly probable.

sometimes quoted as 'Natural selection is a mechanism for generating an exceedingly high degree of improbability'

> 'Retrospect of the criticisms of the Theory of Natural Selection' in Julian Huxley *Evolution as a Process* (1954)

Film lines

1 Anyway, Ma, I made it . . . Top of the world!

White Heat (1949 film) written by Ivan Goff (1910–) and Ben Roberts (1916–84); last lines—spoken by James Cagney

2 Don't let's ask for the moon! We have the stars!

Now, Voyager (1942 film), from the novel (1941) by Olive Higgins Prouty (1882–1974); spoken by Bette Davis

3 Either he's dead, or my watch has stopped.

A Day at the Races (1937 film) written by Robert Pirosh, George Seaton, and George Oppenheimer; spoken by Groucho **Marx**

4 E.T. phone home.

E.T. (1982 film) written by Melissa Mathison (1950–)

5 Fasten your seat-belts, it's going to be a bumpy night.

All About Eve (1950 film) written by Joseph L. Mankiewicz (1909–); spoken by Bette Davis

6 Frankly, my dear, I don't give a damn!

Gone with the Wind (1939 film) written by Sidney Howard; spoken by Clark Gable; cf. **Mitchell** 217:8

7 Go ahead, make my day.

Sudden Impact (1983 film) written by Joseph C. Stinson (1947–); spoken by Clint Eastwood

8 Greed—for lack of a better word—is good. Greed is right. Greed works.

Wall Street (1987 film) written by Stanley Weiser and Oliver Stone (1946–); cf. **Boesky** 40:6

9 Here's looking at you, kid.

Casablanca (1942 film) written by Julius J. Epstein (1909–), Philip G. Epstein (1909–52), and Howard Koch (1902–); spoken by Humphrey Bogart to Ingrid Bergman; cf. **Film lines** 110:11, 111:3, 111:11

10 I could have had class. I could have been a contender.

On the Waterfront (1954 film) written by Budd Schulberg (1914–); spoken by Marlon Brando

11 If she can stand it, I can. Play it!

usually quoted as 'Play it again, Sam'

Casablanca (1942 film) written by Julius J. Epstein (1909–), Philip G. Epstein (1909–52), and Howard Koch (1902–); spoken by Humphrey Bogart; cf. **Film lines** 110:9, 111:3, 111:11, **Misquotations** 218:12

12 If you can't leave in a taxi you can leave in a huff. If that's too soon, you can leave in a minute and a huff.

Duck Soup (1933 film) written by Bert Kalmar (1884–1947), Harry Ruby (1895–1974), Arthur Sheekman (1891–1978), and Nat Perrin; spoken by Groucho **Marx**; cf. **Film lines** 111:14, 112:2

13 I love the smell of napalm in the morning. It smells like victory.

Apocalypse Now (1979 film) written by John Milius and Francis Ford Coppola (1939–); spoken by Robert Duvall

14 In Italy for thirty years under the Borgias they had warfare, terror, murder, bloodshed—they produced Michelangelo, Leonardo da Vinci and the Renaissance. In Switzerland they had brotherly love, five hundred years of democracy and peace and what did that produce . . . ? The cuckoo clock.

The Third Man (1949 film); words added by Orson **Welles** to Graham **Greene**'s screenplay

15 It's a funny old world—a man's lucky if he gets out of it alive.

You're Telling Me (1934 film), written by Walter de Leon and Paul M. Jones; spoken by W. C. **Fields**; cf. **Thatcher** 306:16

16 DRIFTWOOD (Groucho Marx): It's all right. That's—that's in every contract. That's—that's what they call a sanity clause.

FIORELLO (Chico Marx): You can't fool me. There ain't no Sanity Claus.

Night at the Opera (1935 film) written by George S. Kaufman (1889–1961) and Morrie Ryskind (1895–1985)

▶

▶ Film lines continued

1 Let's get out of these wet clothes and into a dry Martini.

> line coined in the 1920s by Robert **Benchley**'s press agent and adopted by Mae **West** in *Every Day's a Holiday* (1937 film)

2 Madness! Madness!

> *The Bridge on the River Kwai* (1957 film of the novel by Pierre Boulle) written by Carl Foreman (1914–), closing line

3 Major Strasser has been shot. Round up the usual suspects.

> *Casablanca* (1942 film) written by Julius J. Epstein (1909–), Philip G. Epstein (1909–52), and Howard Koch (1902–); spoken by Claude Rains; cf. **Film lines** 110:9, 110:11, 111:11

4 The man you love to hate.

> anonymous billing for Erich von Stroheim in the film *The Heart of Humanity* (1918)

5 Man your ships, and may the force be with you.

> *Star Wars* (1977 film) written by George Lucas (1944–)

6 Marriage isn't a word . . . it's a *sentence*!

> *The Crowd* (1928 film) written by King Vidor (1895–1982)

7 Maybe just whistle. You know how to whistle, don't you, Steve? You just put your lips together and blow.

> *To Have and Have Not* (1944 film) written by Jules Furthman (1888–1960) and William **Faulkner**; spoken by Lauren **Bacall**

8 Mr Kane was a man who got everything he wanted, and then lost it. Maybe Rosebud was something he couldn't get or something he lost. Anyway, it wouldn't have explained anything. I don't think any word can explain a man's life. No, I guess Rosebud is just a piece in a jigsaw puzzle, a missing piece.

> *Citizen Kane* (1941 film) written by Herman J. Mankiewicz (1897–1953) and Orson **Welles**

9 My momma always said life was like a box of chocolates . . . you never know what you're gonna get.

> *Forrest Gump* (1994 film), written by Eric Ross, based on the novel (1986) by Winston Groom; spoken by Tom Hanks

10 Nature, Mr Allnutt, is what we are put into this world to rise above.

> *The African Queen* (1951 film) written by James Agee 1909–55; not in the novel by C. S. Forester

11 Of all the gin joints in all the towns in all the world, she walks into mine.

> *Casablanca* (1942 film) written by Julius J. Epstein (1909–), Philip G. Epstein (1909–52), and Howard Koch (1902–); spoken by Humphrey Bogart; cf. **Film lines** 110:9, 110:11, 111:3

12 Oh no, it wasn't the aeroplanes. It was Beauty killed the Beast.

> *King Kong* (1933 film) written by James Creelman (1901–41) and Ruth Rose

13 The pellet with the poison's in the vessel with the pestle. The chalice from the palace has the brew that is true.

> *The Court Jester* (1955 film) written by Norman Panama (1914–) and Melvin Frank (1913–88); spoken by Danny Kaye

14 Remember, you're fighting for this woman's honour . . . which is probably more than she ever did.

> *Duck Soup* (1933 film) written by Bert Kalmar (1884–1947), Harry Ruby (1895–1974), Arthur Sheekman (1891–1978), and Nat Perrin; spoken by Groucho **Marx**; cf. **Film lines** 110:12, 112:2

15 The son of a bitch stole my watch!

> *The Front Page* (1931 film), from the play (1928) by Charles MacArthur (1895–1956) and Ben Hecht (1894–1964)

16 GERRY: We can't get married at all . . . I'm a man.
OSGOOD: Well, nobody's perfect.

> *Some Like It Hot* (1959 film) written by Billy **Wilder** and I. A. L. Diamond; closing words spoken by Jack Lemmon and Joe E. Brown

▶

▶ Film lines continued

1 What a dump!

Beyond the Forest (1949 film) written by Lenore Coffee (?1897–1984); line spoken by Bette Davis, entering a room

2 Why, a four-year-old child could understand this report. Run out and find me a four-year-old child. I can't make head or tail of it.

Duck Soup (1933 film) written by Bert Kalmar (1884–1947), Harry Ruby (1895–1974), Arthur Sheekman (1891–1978), and Nat Perrin; spoken by Groucho **Marx**; cf. **Film lines** 110:12, 111:14

3 You're going out a youngster but you've *got* to come back a star.

42nd Street (1933 film) written by James Seymour and Rian James

4 JOE GILLIS: You used to be in pictures. You used to be big.
NORMA DESMOND: I am big. It's the pictures that got small.

Sunset Boulevard (1950 film) written by Charles Brackett (1892–1969), Billy **Wilder**, and D. M. Marshman Jr.

Film titles

5 Back to the future.

written by Robert Zemeckis and Bob Gale, 1985

6 Close encounters of the third kind.

written by Steven Spielberg (1947–), 1977

7 The discreet charm of the bourgeoisie.

written by Luis **Buñuel**, 1972

8 The Empire strikes back.

written by George Lucas (1944–), 1980; the sequel to *Star Wars*

9 Every which way but loose.

written by Jeremy Joe Kronsberg, 1978; starring Clint Eastwood

10 The good, the bad, and the ugly.

written by Age Scarpelli, Luciano Vincenzoni (1926–), and Sergio Leone (1921–), 1966

11 The long hot summer.

written by Irving Ravetch and Harriet Frank, 1958; based on stories by William **Faulkner**

12 Naughty but nice.

written by Jerry Wald (1911–62) and Richard Macaulay, 1939

13 Never on Sunday.

written by Jules Dassin (1911–), 1959

14 Rebel without a cause.

written by R. M. Lindner (1914–56), 1959, based on his book (1944); starring James Dean

15 Sunday, bloody Sunday.

written by Penelope **Gilliatt**, 1971

16 Sweet smell of success.

written by Ernest Lehman, 1957

Gerry Fitt 1926–

Northern Irish politician

17 People [in Northern Ireland] don't march as an alternative to jogging. They do it to assert their supremacy. It is pure tribalism, the cause of troubles all over the world.

referring to the 'marching season' in Northern Ireland, leading up to the anniversary of the Battle of the Boyne on 12 July, when parades by Orange communities traditionally take place

in *The Times* 5 August 1994

F. Scott Fitzgerald 1896–1940

American novelist

18 Let me tell you about the very rich. They are different from you and me.

*to which Ernest **Hemingway** replied, 'Yes, they have more money'*

All the Sad Young Men (1926) 'Rich Boy'

19 The beautiful and damned.

title of novel (1922)

1 At eighteen our convictions are hills from which we look; at forty-five they are caves in which we hide.
   'Bernice Bobs her Hair' (1920)

2 Her voice is full of money.
   of Daisy
   The Great Gatsby (1925)

3 They were careless people, Tom and Daisy—they smashed up things and creatures and then retreated back into their money or their vast carelessness, or whatever it was that kept them together, and let other people clean up the mess they had made.
   The Great Gatsby (1925)

4 Gatsby believed in the green light, the orgastic future that year by year recedes before us. It eluded us then, but that's no matter . . . So we beat on, boats against the current, borne back ceaselessly into the past.
   The Great Gatsby (1925)

5 See that little stream—we could walk to it in two minutes. It took the British a month to walk it—a whole empire walking very slowly, dying in front and pushing forward behind. And another empire walked very slowly backward a few inches a day, leaving the dead like a million bloody rugs.
   Tender is the Night (1934)

6 The test of a first-rate intelligence is the ability to hold two opposed ideas in the mind at the same time, and still retain the ability to function.
   in *Esquire* February 1936 'The Crack-Up'

7 In a real dark night of the soul it is always three o'clock in the morning.
   'dark night of the soul' being a translation of the Spanish title of a work (1578–80) by St John of the Cross
   'Handle with Care' in *Esquire* March 1936

8 No grand idea was ever born in a conference, but a lot of foolish ideas have died there.
   Edmund Wilson (ed.) *The Crack-Up* (1945) 'Note-Books E'

9 Show me a hero and I will write you a tragedy.
   Edmund Wilson (ed.) *The Crack-Up* (1945) 'Note-Books E'

10 There are no second acts in American lives.
   Edmund Wilson (ed.) *The Last Tycoon* (1941) 'Hollywood, etc.'

11 My theory of writing I can sum up in one sentence. An author ought to write for the youth of his own generation, the critics of the next, and the schoolmasters of ever after.
   letter to the Booksellers' Convention, April 1920

Bud Flanagan 1896–1968

British comedian

12 Underneath the Arches,
   I dream my dreams away,
   Underneath the Arches,
   On cobble-stones I lay.
   'Underneath the Arches' (1932 song)

Michael Flanders 1922–75 and Donald Swann 1923–94

English songwriters

13 Have some Madeira, m'dear.
   title of song (c.1956)

14 Mud! Mud! Glorious mud!
   Nothing quite like it for cooling the blood.
   'The Hippopotamus' (1952 song)

15 Eating people is wrong!
   'The Reluctant Cannibal' (1956 song)

16 That monarch of the road,
   Observer of the Highway Code,
   That big six-wheeler
   Scarlet-painted
   London Transport
   Diesel-engined
   Ninety-seven horse power
   Omnibus!
   'A Transport of Delight' (c.1956 song)

James Elroy Flecker
1884–1915

English poet

17 West of these out to seas colder than the Hebrides
   I must go

Where the fleet of stars is anchored and
the young
Star captains glow.
  'The Dying Patriot' (1913)

1 The dragon-green, the luminous, the
dark, the serpent-haunted sea.
  'The Gates of Damascus' (1913)

2 For lust of knowing what should not be
known,
We take the Golden Road to Samarkand.
  The Golden Journey to Samarkand (1913) pt. 1,
  'Epilogue'

3 I have seen old ships sail like swans
asleep
Beyond the village which men still call
Tyre,
With leaden age o'ercargoed, dipping
deep
For Famagusta and the hidden sun
That rings black Cyprus with a lake of
fire.
  'Old Ships' (1915)

Ian Fleming 1908–64

English thriller writer
see also **Misquotations** 218:8

4 A medium Vodka dry Martini—with a
slice of lemon peel. Shaken and not
stirred.
  Dr No (1958)

5 From Russia with love.
  title of novel (1957)

6 Live and let die.
  title of novel (1954)

Peter Fleming 1907–71

English journalist and travel writer

7 São Paulo is like Reading, only much
farther away.
  Brazilian Adventure (1933)

8 Last night we went to a Chinese dinner
at six and a French dinner at nine, and I
can feel the sharks' fins navigating
unhappily in the Burgundy.
  letter from Yunnanfu, 20 March 1938

Dario Fo 1926–

Italian dramatist

9 *Non si paga, non si paga.*
We won't pay, we won't pay.
  title of play (1975; translated by Lino Pertile in
  1978 as 'We Can't Pay? We Won't Pay!' and
  performed in London in 1981 as *'Can't Pay?
  Won't Pay!'*); cf. **Political slogans** 251:7

Ferdinand Foch 1851–1929

French general

10 My centre is giving way, my right is
retreating, situation excellent, I am
attacking.
  *message during the first Battle of the Marne,
  September 1914*
    R. Recouly *Foch* (1919)

11 This is not a peace treaty, it is an
armistice for twenty years.
  at the signing of the Treaty of Versailles, 1919
    P. Reynaud *Mémoires* (1963)

J. Foley 1906–1970

British songwriter

12 Old soldiers never die,
They simply fade away.
  'Old Soldiers Never Die' (1920 song);
  copyrighted by Foley but possibly a folk-song
  from the First World War; cf. **MacArthur** 197:3

Jane Fonda 1937–

American actress

13 A man has every season, while a woman
has only the right to spring.
  in *Daily Mail* 13 September 1989

Michael Foot 1913–

British Labour politician

14 A speech from Ernest Bevin on a major
occasion had all the horrific fascination
of a public execution. If the mind was left
immune, eyes and ears and emotions
were riveted.
  Aneurin Bevan (1962)

1 Think of it! A second Chamber selected
by the Whips. A seraglio of eunuchs.
   speech in the House of Commons, 3 February
   1969

2 It is not necessary that every time he
rises he should give his famous imitation
of a semi-house-trained polecat.
   of Norman **Tebbit**
   speech in the House of Commons, 2 March
   1978

Anna Ford 1943–

English journalist and broadcaster

3 Let's face it, there are no plain women on
television.
   in *Observer* 23 September 1979

Gerald Ford 1909–

American Republican statesman, 38th
President of the US, 1974–7
on Ford: see **Abzug** 1:4

4 I am a Ford, not a Lincoln.
   on taking the vice-presidential oath, 6
   December 1973

5 Our long national nightmare is over. Our
Constitution works; our great Republic is
a Government of laws and not of men.
   on being sworn in as President, 9 August 1974;
   see below

   A government of laws, and not of men.
   John Adams (1735–1826) in *Boston Gazette*
   (1774)

6 If the Government is big enough to give
you everything you want, it is big
enough to take away everything you
have.
   J. F. Parker *If Elected* (1960)

Henry Ford 1863–1947

American car manufacturer

7 Any customer can have a car painted
any colour that he wants so long as it is
black.
   on the Model T Ford, 1909
   My Life and Work (with Samuel Crowther, 1922)

8 History is more or less bunk.
   in *Chicago Tribune* 25 May 1916

9 What we call evil is simply ignorance
bumping its head in the dark.
   n *Observer* 16 March 1930

10 Exercise is bunk. If you are healthy, you
don't need it: if you are sick you
shouldn't take it.
   attributed

Lena Guilbert Ford 1870–1916

English songwriter

11 Keep the Home-fires burning,
While your hearts are yearning,
Though your lads are far away
They dream of Home.
There's a silver lining
Through the dark cloud shining;
Turn the dark cloud inside out,
Till the boys come Home.
   'Till the Boys Come Home!' (1914 song); music
   by Ivor Novello

Howell Forgy 1908–83

American naval chaplain

12 Praise the Lord and pass the
ammunition.
   at Pearl Harbor, 7 December 1941, while sailors
   passed ammunition by hand to the deck
   in *New York Times* 1 November 1942 (later title
   of song by Frank Loesser, 1942)

E. M. Forster 1879–1970

English novelist
on Forster: see **Mansfield** 207:3

13 Everything must be like something, so
what is this like?
   Abinger Harvest (1936) 'Doll Souse'

14 [Public schoolboys] go forth into a world
that is not entirely composed of public-
school men or even of Anglo-Saxons, but
of men who are as various as the sands of
the sea; into a world of whose richness
and subtlety they have no conception.
They go forth into it with well-developed
bodies, fairly developed minds, and
undeveloped hearts.
   Abinger Harvest (1936) 'Notes on English
   Character'

15 Yes—oh dear yes—the novel tells a story.
   Aspects of the Novel (1927)

1 How can I tell what I think till I see what
I say?
  Aspects of the Novel (1927); cf. **Wallas** 319:2

2 A dogged attempt to cover the universe
with mud, an inverted Victorianism, an
attempt to make crossness and dirt
succeed where sweetness and light failed.
  *of James **Joyce's** Ulysses*
  Aspects of the Novel (1927); see below

  The pursuit of perfection, then, is the
  pursuit of sweetness and light . . . He
  who works for sweetness and light
  united, works to make reason and the
  will of God prevail.
  Matthew Arnold (1822–88) *Culture and Anarchy*
  (1869)

3 It is a period between two wars—the
long week-end it has been called.
  *The Development of English Prose between
  1918 and 1939* (1945)

4 Railway termini. They are our gates to
the glorious and the unknown. Through
them we pass out into adventure and
sunshine, to them, alas! we return.
  Howards End (1910)

5 It will be generally admitted that
Beethoven's Fifth Symphony is the most
sublime noise that has ever penetrated
into the ear of man.
  Howards End (1910)

6 To trust people is a luxury in which only
the wealthy can indulge; the poor cannot
afford it.
  Howards End (1910)

7 She felt that those who prepared for all
the emergencies of life beforehand may
equip themselves at the expense of joy.
  Howards End (1910)

8 Personal relations are the important
thing for ever and ever, and not this
outer life of telegrams and anger.
  Howards End (1910)

9 Only connect! . . . Only connect the prose
and the passion, and both will be exalted,
and human love will be seen at its
height.
  Howards End (1910)

10 Death destroys a man: the idea of death
saves him.
  Howards End (1910)

11 It's the worst thing that can ever happen
to you in all your life, and you've got to
mind it . . . They'll come saying, 'Bear
up—trust to time.' No, no; they're
wrong. Mind it.
  The Longest Journey (1907)

12 There is much good luck in the world,
but it is luck. We are none of us safe. We
are children, playing or quarrelling on
the line.
  The Longest Journey (1907)

13 The so-called white races are really
pinko-grey.
  A Passage to India (1924)

14 Nothing in India is identifiable, the mere
asking of a question causes it to
disappear or to merge in something else.
  A Passage to India (1924)

15 Pathos, piety, courage—they exist, but
are identical, and so is filth. Everything
exists, nothing has value.
  A Passage to India (1924)

16 Where there is officialism every human
relationship suffers.
  A Passage to India (1924)

17 God si [is] Love. Is this the final message
of India?
  A Passage to India (1924)

18 Think before you speak is criticism's
motto; speak before you think creation's.
  Two Cheers for Democracy (1951) 'Raison d'être
  of Criticism'

19 If I had to choose between betraying my
country and betraying my friend, I hope I
should have the guts to betray my
country.
  Two Cheers for Democracy (1951) 'What I
  Believe'

20 So Two cheers for Democracy: one
because it admits variety and two
because it permits criticism. Two cheers
are quite enough: there is no occasion to
give three. Only Love the Beloved
Republic deserves that.
  Two Cheers for Democracy (1951) 'What I
  Believe'; see below

  Even love, the beloved Republic, that
    feeds upon freedom lives.
  Algernon Charles Swinburne (1837–1909)
  'Hertha' (1871)

Margaret Forster 1938–

English novelist

1 But that perhaps is the point of any memoir—to walk with the dead and yet see them with our eyes, from our vantage point.

Hidden Lives: A Family Memoir (1995)

Frederick Forsyth 1938–

English novelist

2 Everyone seems to remember with great clarity what they were doing on November 22nd, 1963, at the precise moment they heard President Kennedy was dead.

The Odessa File (1972)

Harry Emerson Fosdick 1878–1969

American Baptist minister

3 I renounce war for its consequences, for the lies it lives on and propagates, for the undying hatred it arouses, for the dictatorships it puts in the place of democracy, for the starvation that stalks after it.

Armistice Day Sermon in New York, 1933

Gene Fowler

American screenwriter

4 Will Hays is my shepherd, I shall not want, He maketh me to lie down in clean postures.

on the establishment of the 'Hays Office' in 1922 to monitor the Hollywood film industry

Clive Marsh and Gaye Ortiz (eds.) *Explorations in Theology and Film* (1997); see below

The Lord's my shepherd, I'll not want.
He makes me down to lie
In pastures green.

Bible Psalm 23 (Scottish Metrical Psalms, 1650)

H. W. Fowler 1858–1933

English lexicographer and grammarian

5 The English speaking world may be divided into (1) those who neither know

nor care what a split infinitive is; (2) those who do not know, but care very much; (3) those who know and condemn; (4) those who know and approve; and (5) those who know and distinguish. Those who neither know nor care are the vast majority and are a happy folk, to be envied by most of the minority classes.

Modern English Usage (1926)

Norman Fowler 1938–

British Conservative politician

6 I have a young family and for the next few years I should like to devote more time to them.

often quoted as 'spend more time with my family'

resignation letter to the Prime Minister, in *Guardian* 4 January 1990; cf. **Thatcher** 306:13

Theodore Fox 1899–1989

English doctor

7 We shall have to learn to refrain from doing things merely because we know how to do them.

speech to Royal College of Physicians, 18 October 1965

Anatole France 1844–1924

French writer

8 Imitation lies at the root of most human actions. A respectable person is one who conforms to custom. People are called good when they do as others do.

Crainquebille (1923)

9 Without lies humanity would perish of despair and boredom.

La Vie en fleur (1922)

10 Make hatred hated!

to public school teachers

speech in Tours, August 1919; Carter Jefferson *Anatole France: The Politics of Scepticism.*

11 You think you are dying for your country; you die for the industrialists.

in *L'Humanité* 18 July 1922

Anne Frank 1929–45

German-born Jewish diarist

1 I want to go on living even after death!
  diary, 4 April 1944

Felix Frankfurter 1882–1965

American lawyer

2 It is a fair summary of history to say that
the safeguards of liberty have been forged
in controversies involving not very nice
people.
  dissenting opinion in *United States v.*
  Rabinowitz 1950

Lord Franks 1905–92

British philosopher and administrator

3 The Pentagon, that immense monument
to modern man's subservience to the
desk.
  in *Observer* 30 November 1952

  on the composition of such bodies as royal
  commissions and committees of inquiry:
4 There is a fashion in these things and
when you are in fashion you are asked to
do a lot.
  in conversation, 24 January 1977; Peter
  Hennessy *Whitehall* (1990)

5 A secret in the Oxford sense: you may tell
it to only one person at a time.
  in *Sunday Telegraph* 30 January 1977

Michael Frayn 1933–

English writer

6 To be absolutely honest, what I feel really
bad about is that I don't feel worse.
That's the ineffectual liberal's problem in
a nutshell.
  in *Observer* 8 August 1965

Arthur Freed 1894–1973

7 Singin' in the rain.
  title of song (1929)

Marilyn French 1929–

American writer

8 The truth is that it is not the sins of the
fathers that descend unto the third

generation, but the sorrows of the
mothers.
  Her Mother's Daughter (1987)

9 Whatever they may be in public life,
whatever their relations with men, in
their relations with women, all men are
rapists, and that's all they are. They rape
us with their eyes, their laws, and their
codes.
  The Women's Room (1977)

10 'I hate discussions of feminism that end
up with who does the dishes,' she said.
So do I. But at the end, there are always
the damned dishes.
  The Women's Room (1977)

Sigmund Freud 1856–1939

Austrian psychiatrist; originator of
psychoanalysis
on Freud: see **Auden** 16:9, **Dodd** 90:6

11 We are so made, that we can only derive
intense enjoyment from a contrast, and
only very little from a state of things.
  Civilization and its Discontents (1930)

12 Anatomy is destiny.
  Collected Writings (1924) vol. 5

13 The interpretation of dreams is the royal
road to a knowledge of the unconscious
activities of the mind.
  The Interpretation of Dreams (2nd ed., 1909);
  cf. **Misquotations** 218:4

14 Intolerance of groups is often, strangely
enough, exhibited more strongly against
small differences than against
fundamental ones.
  Moses and Monotheism (1938)

15 Analogies decide nothing, that is true,
but they can make one feel more at
home.
  New Introductory Lectures on Psychoanalysis
  (1933)

16 The great question that has never been
answered and which I have not yet been
able to answer, despite my thirty years of
research into the feminine soul, is 'What
does a woman want?'
  letter to Marie Bonaparte, in E. Jones *Sigmund*
  Freud (1955)

17 All that matters is love and work.
  attributed

1 Frozen anger.
his definition of depression
   attributed

2 Yes, America is gigantic, but a gigantic mistake.
   Peter Gay *Freud: A Life for Our Time* (1988)

Betty Friedan 1921–

American feminist

3 The problem that has no name.
being the fact that American women are kept from growing to their full human capacities
   The Feminine Mystique (1963); cf. 119:5

4 It is easier to live through someone else than to become complete yourself.
   The Feminine Mystique (1963)

5 Today the problem that has no name is how to juggle work, love, home and children.
   The Second Stage (1987); cf. 119:3

Milton Friedman 1912–

American economist and exponent of monetarism; policy adviser to President **Reagan** 1981–9
see also **Sayings** 279:8

6 There is an invisible hand in politics that operates in the opposite direction to the invisible hand in the market. In politics, individuals who seek to promote only the public good are led by an invisible hand to promote special interests that it was no part of their intention to promote.
   Bright Promises, Dismal Performance: An Economist's Protest (1983)

7 History suggests that capitalism is a necessary condition for political freedom. Clearly it is not a sufficient condition for it.
   Capitalism and Freedom (1962)

8 A society that puts equality—in the sense of equality of outcome—ahead of freedom will end up with neither equality nor freedom.
   Free to Choose (1980)

9 Inflation is the one form of taxation that can be imposed without legislation.
   in *Observer* 22 September 1974

10 Thank heavens we do not get all of the government that we are made to pay for.
   attributed; quoted by Lord Harris of High Cross in the House of Lords, 24 November 1994

Max Frisch 1911–

Swiss novelist and dramatist

11 Technology . . . the knack of so arranging the world that we need not experience it.
   Homo Faber (1957)

Charles Frohman

see **Last words** 183:3

Erich Fromm 1900–80

American philosopher and psychologist

12 Man's main task in life is to give birth to himself, to become what he potentially is. The most important product of his effort is his own personality.
   Man for Himself (1947)

13 In the nineteenth century the problem was that *God is dead*; in the twentieth century the problem is that *man is dead*. In the nineteenth century inhumanity meant cruelty; in the twentieth century it means schizoid self-alienation. The danger of the past was that men became slaves. The danger of the future is that men may become robots.
   The Sane Society (1955)

David Frost 1939–

English broadcaster and writer
on Frost: see **Muggeridge** 224:8; *see also* **Catch-phrases** 58:2, 59:5

14 Having one child makes you a parent; having two you are a referee.
   in *Independent* 16 September 1989

Robert Frost 1874–1963

American poet

15 I'd like to get away from earth awhile
And then come back to it and begin over.
May no fate wilfully misunderstand me
And half grant what I wish and snatch me away

Not to return. Earth's the right place for
  love:
I don't know where it's likely to go
  better.
  'Birches' (1916)

1 Most of the change we think we see in
  life
  Is due to truths being in and out of
  favour.
  'The Black Cottage' (1914)

2 Forgive, O Lord, my little jokes on Thee
  And I'll forgive Thy great big one on me.
  'Cluster of Faith' (1962)

3 And nothing to look backward to with
  pride,
  And nothing to look forward to with
  hope.
  'The Death of the Hired Man' (1914)

4 'Home is the place where, when you
  have to go there,
  They have to take you in.'
  'I should have called it
  Something you somehow haven't to
  deserve.'
  'The Death of the Hired Man' (1914)

5 They cannot scare me with their empty
  spaces
  Between stars—on stars where no
  human race is.
  I have it in me so much nearer home
  To scare myself with my own desert
  places.
  'Desert Places' (1936)

6 Some say the world will end in fire,
  Some say in ice.
  From what I've tasted of desire
  I hold with those who favour fire.
  But if it had to perish twice,
  I think I know enough of hate
  To say that for destruction ice
  Is also great
  And would suffice.
  'Fire and Ice' (1923)

7 The land was ours before we were the
  land's.
  'The Gift Outright' (1942)

8 Happiness makes up in height for what it
  lacks in length.
  title of poem (1942)

9 Never ask of money spent
  Where the spender thinks it went.

Nobody was ever meant
To remember or invent
What he did with every cent.
  'The Hardship of Accounting' (1936)

10 And were an epitaph to be my story
  I'd have a short one ready for my own.
  I would have written of me on my stone:
  I had a lover's quarrel with the world.
  'The Lesson for Today' (1942)

11 Something there is that doesn't love a
  wall,
  That sends the frozen-ground-swell under
  it.
  'Mending Wall' (1914)

12 My apple trees will never get across
  And eat the cones under his pines, I tell
  him.
  He only says, 'Good fences make good
  neighbours.'
  'Mending Wall' (1914)

13 Before I built a wall I'd ask to know
  What I was walling in or walling out,
  And to whom I was like to give offence.
  'Mending Wall' (1914)

14 I never dared be radical when young
  For fear it would make me conservative
  when old.
  'Precaution' (1936)

15 No memory of having starred
  Atones for later disregard,
  Or keeps the end from being hard.
  'Provide Provide' (1936)

16 Two roads diverged in a wood, and I—
  I took the one less travelled by,
  And that has made all the difference.
  'The Road Not Taken' (1916)

17 We dance round in a ring and suppose,
  But the Secret sits in the middle and
  knows.
  'The Secret Sits' (1942)

18 I've broken Anne of gathering bouquets.
  It's not fair to the child. It can't be helped
  though:
  Pressed into service means pressed out of
  shape.
  'The Self-Seeker' (1914)

19 The best way out is always through.
  'A Servant to Servants' (1914)

20 Whose woods these are I think I know.
  His house is in the village though;

He will not see me stopping here
To watch his woods fill up with snow.
> 'Stopping by Woods on a Snowy Evening'
> (1923); cf. **O'Rourke** 237:1

1 The woods are lovely, dark and deep.
But I have promises to keep,
And miles to go before I sleep.
> 'Stopping by Woods on a Snowy Evening'
> (1923)

2 It should be of the pleasure of a poem
itself to tell how it can. The figure a poem
makes. It begins in delight and ends in
wisdom. The figure is the same as for
love.
> *Collected Poems* (1939) 'The Figure a Poem
> Makes'

3 No tears in the writer, no tears in the
reader. No surprise for the writer, no
surprise for the reader.
> *Collected Poems* (1939) 'The Figure a Poem
> Makes'

4 Like a piece of ice on a hot stove the
poem must ride on its own melting. A
poem may be worked over once it is in
being, but may not be worried into being.
> *Collected Poems* (1939) 'The Figure a Poem
> Makes'

5 Poetry is a way of taking life by the
throat.
> E. S. Sergeant *Robert Frost* (1960)

6 I'd as soon write free verse as play tennis
with the net down.
> E. Lathem *Interviews with Robert Frost* (1966)

7 Poetry is what is lost in translation. It is
also what is lost in interpretation.
> L. Untermeyer *Robert Frost* (1964)

Christopher Fry 1907–

English dramatist

8 The dark is light enough.
> title of play (1954)

9 The lady's not for burning.
> title of play (1949); cf. **Thatcher** 305:12

10 I travel light; as light,
That is, as a man can travel who will
Still carry his body around because
Of its sentimental value.
> *The Lady's not for Burning* (1949)

11   What after all
Is a halo? It's only one more thing to
keep clean.
> *The Lady's not for Burning* (1949)

12 Where in this small-talking world can I
find
A longitude with no platitude?
> *The Lady's not for Burning* (1949)

13   The best
Thing we can do is to make wherever
we're lost in
Look as much like home as we can.
> *The Lady's not for Burning* (1949)

Roger Fry 1866–1934

English art critic
see also **Winterson** 332:12

14 Art is significant deformity.
> Virginia Woolf *Roger Fry* (1940)

15 Bach almost persuades me to be a
Christian.
> Virginia Woolf *Roger Fry* (1940)

Carlos Fuentes 1928–

Mexican novelist and writer

16 High on the agenda for the 21st century
will be the need to restore some kind of
tragic consciousness.
> Rushworth M. Kidder *An Agenda for the 21st
> Century* (1987)

Francis Fukuyama 1952–

American historian

17 What we may be witnessing is not just
the end of the Cold War but the end of
history as such: that is, the end point of
man's ideological evolution and the
universalism of Western liberal
democracy.
> in *Independent* 20 September 1989

J. William Fulbright 1905–

American politician

18 The Soviet Union has indeed been our
greatest menace, not so much because of
what it has done, but because of the

excuses it has provided us for our
failures.

> in *Observer* 21 December 1958 'Sayings of the
> Year'

John Fuller 1937–

English poet

1 You and I, when our days are done,
must say
Without exactly saying it, good-bye.

> 'Pyrosymphonie' (1996)

R. Buckminster Fuller
1895–1983

American designer and architect

2 God, to me, it seems,
is a verb
not a noun,
proper or improper.

> untitled poem written in 1940, in *No More
> Secondhand God* (1963)

3 Now there is one outstandingly
important fact regarding Spaceship
Earth, and that is that no instruction
book came with it.

> *Operating Manual for Spaceship Earth* (1969)

4 Either war is obsolete or men are.

> in *New Yorker* 8 January 1966

Sam Fuller 1912–

American film director

5 When you're in the battlefield, survival is
all there is. Death is the only great
emotion.

> in *Guardian* 26 February 1991

Alfred Funke b. 1869

German writer

6 *Gott strafe England!*
God punish England!

> *Schwert und Myrte* (1914); cf. **Squire** 295:3

Will Fyffe 1885–1947

7 I belong to Glasgow
Dear Old Glasgow town!
But what's the matter wi' Glasgow?
For it's going round and round.
I'm only a common old working chap,
As anyone can see,
But when I get a couple of drinks on a
Saturday,
Glasgow belongs to me.

> 'I Belong to Glasgow' (1920 song)

Rose Fyleman 1877–1957

English writer for children

8 There are fairies at the bottom of our
garden!

> 'The Fairies' (1918)

Clark Gable

see **Film lines** 110:6

Zsa Zsa Gabor 1919–

Hungarian-born film actress

9 I never hated a man enough to give him
diamonds back.

> in *Observer* 25 August 1957

10 A man in love is incomplete until he has
married. Then he's finished.

> in *Newsweek* 28 March 1960

11 You mean apart from my own?

> *when asked how many husbands she had had*
> K. Edwards *I Wish I'd Said That* (1976)

12 Not hard enough.

> *when asked how hard she had slapped a
> policeman*
> in *Independent* 21 September 1989

Hugh Gaitskell 1906–63

British Labour politician
on Gaitskell: see **Bevan** 36:12, **Crossman**
81:4

13 There are some of us . . . who will fight
and fight and fight again to save the
Party we love.

> speech at Labour Party Conference, 5 October
> 1960

14 It means the end of a thousand years of
history.

> *on a European federation; cf.* **Major** 205:2
> speech at Labour Party Conference, 3 October
> 1962

1 The subtle terrorism of words.
in a warning given to his Party, c.1957
Harry Hopkins *The New Look* (1963); attributed

J. K. Galbraith 1908–

Canadian-born American economist

2 The affluent society
title of book (1958)

3 The conventional wisdom.
*ironic term for 'the beliefs that are at any time
assiduously, solemnly and mindlessly traded
between the conventionally wise'*
The Affluent Society (1958)

4 These are the days when men of all social
disciplines and all political faiths seek the
comfortable and the accepted; when the
man of controversy is looked upon as a
disturbing influence; when originality is
taken to be a mark of instability; and
when, in minor modification of the
scriptural parable, the bland lead the
bland.
The Affluent Society (1958)

5 It is a far, far better thing to have a firm
anchor in nonsense than to put out on
the troubled seas of thought.
The Affluent Society (1958)

6 In a community where public services
have failed to keep abreast of private
consumption things are very different.
Here, in an atmosphere of private
opulence and public squalor, the private
goods have full sway.
The Affluent Society (1958)

We have public poverty and private
opulence.
Sallust (86–35 BC) *Catiline*

7 The greater the wealth, the thicker will
be the dirt.
The Affluent Society (1958)

8 It is not necessary to advertise food to
hungry people, fuel to cold people, or
houses to the homeless.
American Capitalism (1952)

9 The salary of the chief executive of the
large corporation is not a market reward
for achievement. It is frequently in the
nature of a warm personal gesture by the
individual to himself.
Annals of an Abiding Liberal (1979)

10 Trickle-down theory—the less than
elegant metaphor that if one feeds the
horse enough oats, some will pass
through to the road for the sparrows.
The Culture of Contentment (1992)

11 The reduction of politics to a spectator
sport . . . has been one of the more
malign accomplishments of television.
Television newsmen are breathless on
how the game is being played, largely
silent on what the game is all about.
A Life in Our Times (1981)

12 A wrong decision isn't forever; it can
always be reversed. The losses from a
delayed decision *are* forever; they can
never be retrieved.
A Life in our Times (1981)

of the defeat of Germany in World War Two:
13 That they were defeated is conclusive
testimony to the inherent inefficiencies of
dictatorship, the inherent efficiencies of
freedom.
in *Fortune* December 1945

14 Politics is not the art of the possible. It
consists in choosing between the
disastrous and the unpalatable.
letter to President Kennedy, 2 March 1962; see
below; cf. **Butler** 50:10

Politics is the art of the possible.
Bismarck (1815–98), conversation with Meyer
von Waldeck, 11 August 1867

15 If all else fails, immortality can always be
assured by a spectacular error.
attributed

Liam Gallagher 1972–

English pop singer

16 I'm not getting married today. I'm in bed.
*after his rumoured wedding to Patsy Kensit failed
to take place*
in *Independent* 15 February 1997

Noel Gallagher 1967–

English pop singer

17 We are lads. We have burgled houses
and nicked car stereos, and we like girls
and swear and go to the football and take
the piss.
interview in *Melody Maker* 30 March 1996

1 Drugs is like getting up and having a cup of tea in the morning.
in a radio interview, 28 January 1997
in *Daily Telegraph* 31 January 1997

2 I would hope we mean more to people than putting money in a church basket and saying ten Hail Marys on a Sunday. Has God played Knebworth recently?
on the drawing power of Oasis
in *New Musical Express* 12 July 1997; cf. **Chisholm** 64:12, **Lennon** 187:16

John Galsworthy 1867–1933
English novelist

3 He was afflicted by the thought that where Beauty was, nothing ever ran quite straight, which, no doubt, was why so many people looked on it as immoral.
In Chancery (1920)

4 A man of action forced into a state of thought is unhappy until he can get out of it.
Maid in Waiting (1931)

5 I know nothing—nobody tells me anything.
A Man of Property (1906)

Ray Galton 1930–
and Alan Simpson 1929–
English scriptwriters

6 I came in here in all good faith to help my country. I don't mind giving a reasonable amount [of blood], but a pint . . . why that's very nearly an armful.
Hancock's Half Hour 'The Blood Donor' (1961 television programme); words spoken by Tony Hancock

George Gamow 1904–68
Russian-born American physicist

7 We do not know why they [elementary particles] have the masses they do; we do not know why they transform into another the way they do; we do not know anything! The one concept that stands like the Rock of Gibraltar in our sea of confusion is the Pauli [exclusion] principle.
in *Scientific American* July 1959

8 With five free parameters, a theorist could fit the profile of an elephant.
attributed; in *Nature* 21 June 1990

Mahatma Gandhi 1869–1948
Indian statesman
on Gandhi: see **Naidu** 227:7, **Nehru** 229:1

9 What difference does it make to the dead, the orphans and the homeless, whether the mad destruction is wrought under the name of totalitarianism or the holy name of liberty or democracy?
Non-Violence in Peace and War (1942) vol. 1

10 The moment the slave resolves that he will no longer be a slave, his fetters fall. He frees himself and shows the way to others. Freedom and slavery are mental states.
Non-Violence in Peace and War (1949) vol. 2

11 Non-violence is the first article of my faith. It is also the last article of my creed.
speech on a charge of sedition
at Shahi Bag, 18 March 1922

12 In my humble opinion, non-cooperation with evil is as much a duty as is cooperation with good.
speech in Ahmadabad, 23 March 1922

on being asked what he thought of modern civilization:
13 That would be a good idea.
while visiting England in 1930
E. F. Schumacher *Good Work* (1979)

Greta Garbo 1905–90
Swedish film actress
on Garbo: see **de Beauvoir** 85:9, **Tynan** 314:6

14 I want to be alone.
Grand Hotel (1932 film)

15 I tank I go home.
on being refused a pay rise by Louis B. Mayer
Norman Zierold *Moguls* (1969)

Federico García Lorca
1899–1936

Spanish poet and dramatist

1 *A las cinco de la tarde.*
   Eran las cinco en punto de la tarde.
   Un niño trajo la blanca sábana
   a las cinco de la tarde.

   At five in the afternoon.
   It was exactly five in the afternoon.
   A boy brought the white sheet
   at five in the afternoon.
   > *Llanto por Ignacio Sánchez Mejías* (1935) 'La Cogida y la muerte'

2 *Verde que te quiero verde.*
   Verde viento. Verdes ramas.
   El barco sobre la mar
   y el caballo en la montaña.

   Green how I love you green.
   Green wind.
   Green boughs.
   The ship on the sea
   and the horse on the mountain.
   > *Romance sonámbulo* (1924–7)

Ed Gardner 1901–63

American radio comedian

3 Opera is when a guy gets stabbed in the back and, instead of bleeding, he sings.
   > *Duffy's Tavern* (US radio programme, 1940s)

John Nance Garner 1868–1967

American Democratic politician, vice-president 1933–41

4 The vice-presidency isn't worth a pitcher of warm piss.
   > O. C. Fisher *Cactus Jack* (1978)

Bill Gates 1955–

American computer entrepreneur
on Gates: see **Stross** 300:9

5 If they want we will give them a sleeping bag, but there is something romantic about sleeping under the desk. They want to do it.
   > *on his young software programmers*
   > in *Independent* 18 November 1995 'Quote Unquote'

6 Technology is just a tool. In terms of getting the kids working together and motivating them, the teacher is the most important.
   > in *Independent on Sunday* 12 October 1997 'For the Record'

Noel Gay 1898–1954

British songwriter

7 I'm leaning on a lamp-post at the corner of the street,
   In case a certain little lady comes by.
   > 'Leaning on a Lamp-Post' (1937); sung by George Formby

Eric Geddes 1875–1937

British politician and administrator

8 The Germans . . . are going to be squeezed as a lemon is squeezed—until the pips squeak.
   > speech at Cambridge, 10 December 1918

Bob Geldof 1954–

Irish rock musician

9 Most people get into bands for three very simple rock and roll reasons: to get laid, to get fame, and to get rich.
   > in *Melody Maker* 27 August 1977

Bob Geldof 1954–
and Midge Ure 1953–

Irish rock musician; Scottish rock musician

10 Feed the world
    Feed the world.
    Feed the world
    Let them know it's Christmas time again.
    > 'Do They Know it's Christmas?' (1984 song)

Martha Gellhorn 1908–98

American journalist

11 I believed that all one did about a war was go to it, as a gesture of solidarity, and get killed, or survive if lucky until the war was over . . . I had no idea you could be what I became, an unscathed tourist of wars.
    > *The Face of War* (1959)

of the defeat of the Spanish Republic:

1 I daresay we all became more competent press tourists because of it, since we never again cared so much. You can only love one war; afterward, I suppose, you do your duty.

The Honeyed Peace (1953)

Jean Genet 1910–86

French novelist, poet, and dramatist

2 What we need is hatred. From it our ideas are born.

The Blacks (1959); epigraph

3 Are you there . . . Africa of the millions of royal slaves, deported Africa, drifting continent, are you there? Slowly you vanish, you withdraw into the past, into the tales of castaways, colonial museums, the works of scholars.

The Blacks (1959)

4 Anyone who hasn't experienced the ecstasy of betrayal knows nothing about ecstasy at all.

Prisoner of Love (1986)

George V 1865–1936

King of Great Britain and Ireland from 1910
on George V: see **Nicolson** 230:10; *see also* **Last words** 182:1, 182:5

5 The Old Country must wake up if she intends to maintain her old position of pre-eminence in her Colonial trade against foreign competitors.

reprinted in 1911 with the title 'Wake up, England'

speech at Guildhall, 5 December 1901

6 I have many times asked myself whether there can be more potent advocates of peace upon earth through the years to come than this massed multitude of silent witnesses to the desolation of war.

message read at Terlincthun Cemetery, Boulogne, 13 May 1922

7 No more coals to Newcastle, no more Hoares to Paris.

following Samuel Hoare's resignation as Foreign Secretary on 18 December 1935

Earl of Avon *Facing the Dictators* (1962)

8 After I am dead, the boy will ruin himself in twelve months.

of his son, the future **Edward VIII**

K. Middlemas and J. Barnes *Baldwin* (1969)

on H. G. **Wells**'s *comment on 'an alien and uninspiring court':*

9 I may be uninspiring, but I'll be damned if I'm an alien!

Sarah Bradford *George VI* (1989); attributed

10 I will not have another war. *I will not.* The last one was none of my doing and if there is another one and we are threatened with being brought into it, I will go to Trafalgar Square and wave a red flag myself sooner than allow this country to be brought in.

Andrew Roberts *Eminent Churchillians* (1994)

11 My father was frightened of his mother; I was frightened of my father, and I am damned well going to see to it that my children are frightened of me.

attributed in Randolph S. Churchill *Lord Derby* (1959), but said by Kenneth Rose in *George V* (1983) to be almost certainly apocryphal; cf. **Morshead** 222:12

George VI 1895–1952

King of Great Britain and Northern Ireland from 1936
see also **Haskins** 142:2

12 I feel happier now that we have no allies to be polite to and to pamper.

to Queen Mary, 27 June 1940
J. Wheeler-Bennett *King George VI* (1958)

13 Abroad is bloody.

W. H. Auden *A Certain World* (1970) 'Royalty'; cf. **Mitford** 217:13

14 The family firm.

description of the British monarchy
attributed

Daniel George

English writer

15 O Freedom, what liberties are taken in thy name!

The Perpetual Pessimist (1963); see below

O liberty! what crimes are committed in thy name!

Mme Roland (1754–93) in A. de Lamartine *Histoire des Girondins* (1847)

Ira Gershwin 1896–1983

American songwriter
see also **Heyward**

1 I got rhythm,
I got music,
I got my man
Who could ask for anything more?
    'I Got Rhythm' (1930 song)

2 Lady, be good!
    title of musical (1924)

3 You like potato and I like po-tah-to,
You like tomato and I like to-mah-to;
Potato, po-tah-to, tomato, to-mah-to—
Let's call the whole thing off!
    'Let's Call the Whole Thing Off' (1937 song)

4 In time the Rockies may crumble,
Gibraltar may tumble,
They're only made of clay,
But our love is here to stay.
    'Love is Here to Stay' (1938 song)

5 Holding hands at midnight
'Neath a starry sky,
Nice work if you can get it,
And you can get it if you try.
    'Nice Work If You Can Get It' (1937 song)

6 The way you wear your hat,
The way you sip your tea,
The mem'ry of all that—
No, no! They can't take that away from
me!
    'They Can't Take That Away from Me' (1937 song)

J. Paul Getty 1892–1976

American industrialist

7 If you can actually count your money,
then you are not really a rich man.
    in *Observer* 3 November 1957

Stella Gibbons 1902–89

English novelist

8 Something nasty in the woodshed.
    Cold Comfort Farm (1932)

Wolcott Gibbs 1902–58

American critic

9 Backward ran sentences until reeled the
mind.
    satirizing the style of Time *magazine*
        in *New Yorker* 28 November 1936 'Time . . .
        Fortune . . . Life . . . Luce'

Kahlil Gibran 1883–1931

Syrian writer and painter

10 Are you a politician who says to himself:
'I will use my country for my own
benefit'? . . . Or are you a devoted patriot,
who whispers in the ear of his inner self:
'I love to serve my country as a faithful
servant.'
    The New Frontier (1931); cf. **Kennedy** 169:7

11 Your children are not your children.
They are the sons and daughters of Life's
    longing for itself.
They came through you but not from
    you
And though they are with you yet they
    belong not to you.
    The Prophet (1923) 'On Children'

12 Work is love made visible. And if you
cannot work with love but only with
distaste, it is better that you should leave
your work and sit at the gate of the
temple and take alms of those who work
with joy.
    The Prophet (1923) 'On Work'

13 An exaggeration is a truth that has lost
its temper.
    Sand and Foam (1926)

Wilfrid Wilson Gibson
1878–1962

English poet

14 But we, how shall we turn to little things
And listen to the birds and winds and
    streams
Made holy by their dreams,

Nor feel the heart-break in the heart of things?
'Lament' (1918)

André Gide 1869–1951

French novelist and critic
on Gide: see **Quennell** 258:11

1 What cleanliness everywhere! You dare not throw your cigarette into the lake. No graffiti in the urinals. Switzerland is proud of this; but I believe this is just what she lacks: manure.
diary, Lucerne, 10 August 1917

Eric Gill 1882–1940

English sculptor, engraver, and typographer

2 That state is a state of slavery in which a man does what he likes to do in his spare time and in his working time that which is required of him.
Art-nonsense and Other Essays (1929) 'Slavery and Freedom'

Penelope Gilliatt 1933–93

see **Film titles** 112:15

Hermione Gingold 1897–1987

English actress

3 Contrary to popular belief, English women do not wear tweed nightgowns.
in *Saturday Review* 16 April 1955

Newton Gingrich 1943–

American Republican politician; Speaker of the House of Representatives from 1995

4 No society can survive, no civilization can survive, with 12-year-olds having babies, with 15-year-olds killing each other, with 17-year-olds dying of Aids, with 18-year-olds getting diplomas they can't read.
in December 1994, *after the Republican electoral victory*
in *The Times* 9 February 1995

5 In a campaign, first you put up the façade, then you go around and build the building.
in *New Yorker* 9 October 1995

Allen Ginsberg 1926–97

American poet and novelist

6 What if someone gave a war & Nobody came?
'Graffiti' (1972); cf. **Sandburg** 275:3

7 I saw the best minds of my generation destroyed by madness, starving hysterical naked.
dragging themselves through the negro streets at dawn looking for an angry fix,
angelheaded hipsters burning for the ancient heavenly connection to the starry dynamo in the machinery of the night.
Howl (1956)

8 What peaches and what penumbras! Whole families shopping at night! Aisles full of husbands! Wives in the avocados, babies in the tomatoes!—and you, Garcia Lorca what were you doing down by the watermelons?
'A Supermarket in California' (1956)

George Gipp d. 1920

American footballer

9 Win just one for the Gipper.
attributed; the catch-phrase later became associated with Ronald **Reagan**, who uttered the immortal words in the 1940 film *Knute Rockne, All American*

Jean Giraudoux 1882–1944

French dramatist

10 As soon as war is declared it will be impossible to hold the poets back. Rhyme is still the most effective drum.
La Guerre de Troie n'aura pas lieu (1935); translated by Christopher Fry as *Tiger at the Gates*, 1955)

11 No poet ever interpreted nature as freely as a lawyer interprets the truth.
La Guerre de Troie n'aura pas lieu (1935)

Edna Gladney

American philanthropist

1 There are no illegitimate children, only illegitimate parents.
MGM paid her a large sum for the line for the 1941 film based on her life, 'Blossoms in the Dust'
A. Loos *Kiss Hollywood Good-Bye* (1978)

George Glass 1910–84

2 An actor is a kind of a guy who if you ain't talking about him ain't listening.
Bob Thomas *Brando* (1973); said to be often quoted by Marlon Brando, as in *Observer* 1 January 1956

David Glencross 1936–

British television executive

3 It is unlikely that the government reaches for a revolver when it hears the word culture. The more likely response is to search for a dictionary.
Royal Television Society conference on the future of television, 26–27 November 1988; cf. **Johst** 163:13

Victoria Glendinning 1937–

English biographer and novelist

4 There's no greater bliss in life than when the plumber eventually comes to unblock your drains. No writer can give that sort of pleasure.
in *Observer* 3 January 1993

Jean-Luc Godard 1930–

French film director

5 Photography is truth. The cinema is truth 24 times per second.
Le Petit Soldat (1960 film)

6 *Ce n'est pas une image juste, c'est juste une image.*
This is not a just image, it is just an image.
Colin MacCabe *Godard: Images, Sounds, Politics* (1980)

7 GEORGES FRANJU: Movies should have a beginning, a middle and an end.

JEAN-LUC GODARD: Certainly, but not necessarily in that order.
in *Time* 14 September 1981

A. D. Godley 1856–1925

English classicist

8 What is this that roareth thus?
Can it be a Motor Bus?
Yes, the smell and hideous hum
Indicat Motorem Bum!
letter, 10 January 1914, in *Reliquiae* (1926)

Joseph Goebbels 1897–1945

German Nazi leader

9 We can manage without butter but not, for example, without guns. If we are attacked we can only defend ourselves with guns not with butter.
speech in Berlin, 17 January 1936; cf. **Goering** 129:11

10 Making noise is an effective means of opposition.
Ernest K. Bramsted *Goebbels and National Socialist Propaganda 1925–45* (1965)

Hermann Goering 1893–1946

German Nazi leader
see also **Johst** 163:16

11 Would you rather have butter or guns? . . . preparedness makes us powerful. Butter merely makes us fat.
speech at Hamburg, 1936, in W. Frischauer *Goering* (1951); cf. **Goebbels** 129:9

12 I herewith commission you to carry out all preparations with regard to . . . a *total solution* of the Jewish question in those territories of Europe which are under German influence.
instructions to Reinhard **Heydrich**, 31 July 1941; W. L. Shirer *Rise and Fall of the Third Reich* (1962); cf. **Heydrich** 147:11

Isaac Goldberg 1887–1938

13 Diplomacy is to do and say
The nastiest thing in the nicest way.
in *The Reflex* October 1927

William Golding 1911–93

English novelist

1 Nothing is so impenetrable as laughter in a language you don't understand.
   An Egyptian Journal (1985)

Barry Goldwater 1909–98

American Republican politician

2 I would remind you that extremism in the defence of liberty is no vice! And let me remind you also that moderation in the pursuit of justice is no virtue!
   accepting the presidential nomination, 16 July 1964

Sam Goldwyn 1882–1974

American film producer
on Goldwyn: see **Hand** 138:4, **Hecht** 144:9; *see also* **Shaw** 286:4

3 Gentlemen, include me out.
   resigning from the Motion Picture Producers and Distributors of America, October 1933
   M. Freedland *The Goldwyn Touch* (1986)

4 A verbal contract isn't worth the paper it is written on.
   Alva Johnston *The Great Goldwyn* (1937)

5 'I can answer you in two words, "im-possible" ' is almost the cornerstone of the Goldwyn legend, but Sam did not say it. It was printed late in 1925 in a humorous magazine and credited to an anonymous Potash or Perlmutter.
   Alva Johnston *The Great Goldwyn* (1937)

6 That's the way with these directors, they're always biting the hand that lays the golden egg.
   Alva Johnston *The Great Goldwyn* (1937)

7 Why should people go out and pay to see bad movies when they can stay at home and see bad television for nothing?
   in *Observer* 9 September 1956

8 Any man who goes to a psychiatrist should have his head examined.
   Norman Zierold *Moguls* (1969)

9 I'll give you a definite maybe.
   attributed

10 Let's have some new clichés.
   attributed, perhaps apocryphal

11 Pictures are for entertainment, messages should be delivered by Western Union.
   A. Marx *Goldwyn* (1976); cf. **Behan** 27:3

12 What we need is a story that starts with an earthquake and works its way up to a climax.
   attributed, perhaps apocryphal

Amy Goodman 1957–

American journalist

13 Go to where the silence is and say something.
   accepting an award from Columbia University for her coverage of the 1991 massacre in East Timor by Indonesian troops
   in *Columbia Journalism Review* March/April 1994

Mikhail Sergeevich Gorbachev 1931–

Soviet statesman, General Secretary of the Communist Party of the USSR 1985–91 and President 1988–91
on Gorbachev: see **Gromyko** 134:11, **Thatcher** 306:6

14 The guilt of Stalin and his immediate entourage before the Party and the people for the mass repressions and lawlessness they committed is enormous and unforgivable.
   speech on the seventieth anniversary of the Russian Revolution, 2 November 1987

15 The idea of restructuring [perestroika] . . . combines continuity and innovation, the historical experience of Bolshevism and the contemporaneity of socialism.
   speech on the seventieth anniversary of the Russian Revolution, 2 November 1987

16 After leaving the Kremlin . . . my conscience was clear. The promise I gave to the people when I started the process of perestroika was kept: I gave them freedom.
   Memoirs (1995)

Mack Gordon 1904–59

American songwriter

17 Pardon me boy is that the Chattanooga Choo-choo,

Track twenty nine,
Boy you can gimme a shine.
'Chattanooga Choo-choo' (1941 song)

Maxim Gorky 1868–1936
Russian writer and revolutionary

1 The proletarian state must bring up
thousands of excellent 'mechanics of
culture', 'engineers of the soul'.
speech at the Writers' Congress 1934; cf.
Kennedy 169:15, **Stalin** 295:5

Stuart Gorrell 1902–63
American songwriter

2 Georgia, Georgia, no peace I find,
Just an old sweet song keeps Georgia on
my mind.
'Georgia on my Mind' (1930 song)

Stephen Jay Gould 1941–
American palaeontologist

3 A man does not attain the status of
Galileo merely because he is persecuted;
he must also be right.
Ever since Darwin (1977)

4 Science is an integral part of culture. It's
not this foreign thing, done by an arcane
priesthood. It's one of the glories of
human intellectual tradition.
in *Independent* 24 January 1990

Lew Grade 1906–
British television producer and executive

5 All my shows are great. Some of them
are bad. But they are all great.
in *Observer* 14 September 1975

D. M. Graham 1911–

6 That this House will in no circumstances
fight for its King and Country.
motion worded by Graham for a debate at the
Oxford Union, 9 February 1933

Bernie Grant 1944–
British Labour politician

7 The police were to blame for what
happened on Sunday night and what
they got was a bloody good hiding.
after a riot in which a policeman was killed
speech as leader of Haringey Council outside
Tottenham Town Hall, 8 October 1985

Cary Grant
see **Telegrams** 305:5

Robert Graves 1895–1985
English poet

8 Children are dumb to say how hot the
day is,
How hot the scent is of the summer rose.
'The Cool Web' (1927)

9 There's a cool web of language winds us
in,
Retreat from too much joy or too much
fear.
'The Cool Web' (1927)

10 Truth-loving Persians do not dwell upon
The trivial skirmish fought near
Marathon.
'The Persian Version' (1945)

11 As you are woman, so be lovely:
As you are lovely, so be various.
'Pygmalion to Galatea' (1927)

12 Love is a universal migraine.
A bright stain on the vision
Blotting out reason.
'Symptoms of Love'

13 'What did the mayor do?'
'I was coming to that.'
'Welsh Incident' (1938)

14 Goodbye to all that.
title of autobiography (1929)

15 If there's no money in poetry, neither is
there poetry in money.
speech at London School of Economics, 6
December 1963

16 Science has lost its virgin purity, has
become dogmatic instead of seeking for

enlightenment and has gradually fallen into the hands of the traders.

Bruno Friedman *Flawed science, damaged human life* (1969)

1 LSD reminds me of the minks that escape from mink-farms and breed in the forest and become dangerous and destructive. It has escaped from the drug factory and gets made in college laboratories.

George Plimpton (ed.) *The Writer's Chapbook* (1989)

Jimmy Greaves 1940–

English footballer

2 The thing about sport, any sport, is that swearing is very much part of it.

attributed, 1989

Graham Greene 1904–91

English novelist
see also **Film lines** 110:14

3 Catholics and Communists have committed great crimes, but at least they have not stood aside, like an established society, and been indifferent. I would rather have blood on my hands than water like Pilate.

The Comedians (1966)

4 He gave her a bright fake smile; so much of life was a putting-off of unhappiness for another time. Nothing was ever lost by delay.

The Heart of the Matter (1948)

5 They had been corrupted by money, and he had been corrupted by sentiment. Sentiment was the more dangerous, because you couldn't name its price. A man open to bribes was to be relied upon below a certain figure, but sentiment might uncoil in the heart at a name, a photograph, even a smell remembered.

The Heart of the Matter (1948)

6 Despair is the price one pays for setting oneself an impossible aim.

Heart of the Matter (1948)

7 Here you could love human beings nearly as God loved them, knowing the

worst; you didn't love a pose, a pretty dress, a sentiment artfully assumed.

The Heart of the Matter (1948)

8 He felt the loyalty we all feel to unhappiness—the sense that that is where we really belong.

The Heart of the Matter (1948)

9 Any victim demands allegiance.

The Heart of the Matter (1948)

10 His hilarity was like a scream from a crevasse.

The Heart of the Matter (1948)

11 What do we ever get nowadays from reading to equal the excitement and the revelation in those first fourteen years?

The Lost Childhood and Other Essays (1951) title essay

12 Goodness has only once found a perfect incarnation in a human body and never will again, but evil can always find a home there. Human nature is not black and white but black and grey.

The Lost Childhood and Other Essays (1951) title essay

13 There is always one moment in childhood when the door opens and lets the future in.

The Power and the Glory (1940)

14 Innocence always calls mutely for protection, when we would be so much wiser to guard ourselves against it: innocence is like a dumb leper who has lost his bell, wandering the world meaning no harm.

The Quiet American (1955)

15 For a writer, success is always temporary, success is only a delayed failure. And it is incomplete.

A Sort of Life (1971)

16 Success in journalism can be a form of failure. Freedom comes from lack of possessions. The truth-divulging paper must imitate the tramp and sleep under a hedge.

in *New Statesman* 31 May 1968

17 [I wanted] to discover what lies behind the dark, thick leaf of the aspidistra that

guards . . . the vulnerable gap between the lace curtains.

on early attempts to experience life outside his own social class

> Norman Sherry *Life of Graham Greene 1904–39* (1989)

Germaine Greer 1939–

Australian feminist

1 The stereotype is the Eternal Feminine. She is the Sexual Object sought by all men, and by all women. She is of neither sex, for she has herself no sex at all. Her value is solely attested by the demand she excites in others. All she must contribute is her existence. She need achieve nothing, for she is the reward of achievement.

> *The Female Eunuch* (1970)

2 Women have very little idea of how much men hate them.

> *The Female Eunuch* (1971)

3 You can now see the Female Eunuch the world over . . . spreading herself wherever blue jeans and Coca-Cola may go. Wherever you see nail varnish, lipstick, brassieres, and high heels, the Eunuch has set up her camp.

> *The Female Eunuch* (20th anniversary ed., 1991) foreword

4 Human beings have an inalienable right to invent themselves; when that right is pre-empted it is called brain-washing.

> in *The Times* 1 February 1986

5 I didn't fight to get women out from behind the vacuum cleaner to get them onto the board of Hoover.

> in *Guardian* 27 October 1986

6 Football is an art more central to our culture than anything the Arts Council deigns to recognize.

> in *Independent* 28 June 1996

Hubert Gregg 1914–

English songwriter

7 Maybe it's because I'm a Londoner That I love London so.

> 'Maybe It's Because I'm a Londoner' (1947 song)

Dick Gregory 1932–

American comedian

8 You gotta say this for the white race—its self-confidence knows no bounds. Who else could go to a small island in the South Pacific where there's no poverty, no crime, no unemployment, no war and no worry—and call it a 'primitive society'?

> *From the Back of the Bus* (1962)

9 Wouldn't it be a hell of a thing if all this was burnt cork and you people were being tolerant for nothing?

> *Nigger* (1965)

10 Baseball is very big with my people. It figures. It's the only way we can get to shake a bat at a white man without starting a riot.

> D. H. Nathan (ed.) *Baseball Quotations* (1991)

Joyce Grenfell 1910–79

English comedy actress and writer

11 George—don't do that.

recurring line in monologues about a nursery school

> from the 1950s; *George—Don't Do That* (1977)

12 So gay the band,
So giddy the sight,
Full evening dress is a must,
But the zest goes out of a beautiful waltz
When you dance it bust to bust.

> 'Stately as a Galleon' (1978 song)

Julian Grenfell 1888–1915

English soldier and poet

13 And Life is Colour and Warmth and Light And a striving evermore for these; And he is dead, who will not fight; And who dies fighting has increase.

> 'Into Battle' in *The Times* 28 May 1915

Clifford Grey 1887–1941

14 If you were the only girl in the world And I were the only boy.

> 'If You Were the Only Girl in the World' (1916 song)

Lord Grey of Fallodon
1862–1933

British Liberal politician

1 The lamps are going out all over Europe; we shall not see them lit again in our lifetime.
on the eve of the First World War
25 Years (1925)

John Grierson 1888–1972
English documentary film-maker
on Grierson: see **Swanson** 301:11

2 Art is not a mirror but a hammer.
H. Forsyth Hardy (ed.) *Grierson on Documentary* (1946, 1966)

3 In sponsored film work the price to be paid for the privilege of aesthetic experiment is the discipline of public service.
in *Dictionary of National Biography* (1917–)

Mervyn Griffith-Jones
1909–79

British lawyer

4 Is it a book you would even wish your wife or your servants to read?
of D. H. **Lawrence***'s* Lady Chatterley's Lover, *while appearing for the prosecution at the Old Bailey*
in *The Times* 21 October 1960

John Grigg 1924–
British writer and journalist, who as Lord Altrincham disclaimed his hereditary title in 1963

5 The personality conveyed by the utterances which are put into her mouth is that of a priggish schoolgirl, captain of the hockey team, a prefect, and a recent candidate for confirmation. It is not thus that she will be able to come into her own as an independent and distinctive character.
of Queen **Elizabeth II**
in *National and English Review* August 1958

6 Autobiography is now as common as adultery and hardly less reprehensible.
in *Sunday Times* 28 February 1962

Geoffrey Grigson 1905–85
English critic

7 The old ideas of nobility and sacrifice have become a howitzer squatting at Hyde Park like a petrified toad, and the hero has become a cabinet minister on a pedestal in bronze boots.
on modern sculpture
Henry Moore (1944)

Joseph ('Jo') Grimond
1913–93

British Liberal politician, Leader of the Liberal Party (1956–67)

8 In bygone days, commanders were taught that when in doubt, they should march their troops towards the sound of gunfire. I intend to march my troops towards the sound of gunfire.
speech to the Liberal Party Assembly, 14 September 1963

on the chance of a pact with the Labour Government:
9 Our teeth are in the real meat.
speech to the Liberal Party Assembly, 1965

10 The trouble with the Labour Party is that they don't really believe in Socialism, but they cannot wholeheartedly approve of private enterprise either.
attributed, 1965

Andrei Gromyko 1909–89
Soviet statesman, President of the USSR 1985–8

11 Comrades, this man has a nice smile, but he's got iron teeth.
of Mikhail **Gorbachev**
speech to Soviet Communist Party Central Committee, 11 March 1985

Andrew Grove 1936–
American businessman

12 Only the paranoid survive.
dictum on which he has long run his company, the Intel Corporation
in *New York Times* 18 December 1994

Philip Guedalla 1889–1944

British historian and biographer

1 Any stigma, as the old saying is, will serve to beat a dogma.

   Masters and Men (1923) 'Ministers of State'

2 The little ships, the unforgotten Homeric catalogue of *Mary Jane* and *Peggy IV*, of *Folkestone Belle*, *Boy Billy*, and *Ethel Maud*, of *Lady Haig* and *Skylark* . . . the little ships of England brought the Army home.

   on the evacuation of Dunkirk
   Mr Churchill (1941)

3 The cheerful clatter of Sir James Barrie's cans as he went round with the milk of human kindness.

   Supers and Supermen (1920) 'Some Critics'

4 The work of Henry James has always seemed divisible by a simple dynastic arrangement into three reigns: James I, James II, and the Old Pretender.

   Supers and Supermen (1920) 'Some Critics'

5 History repeats itself. Historians repeat each other.

   Supers and Supermen (1920) 'Some Historians'

Ernesto ('Che') Guevara 1928–67

Argentinian revolutionary and guerrilla leader

6 The Revolution is made by man, but man must forge his revolutionary spirit from day to day.

   Socialism and Man in Cuba (1968)

Hervé Guibert 1955–91

French writer

7 [AIDS was] an illness in stages, a very long flight of steps that led assuredly to death, but whose every step represented a unique apprenticeship. It was a disease that gave death time to live and its victims time to die, time to discover time, and in the end to discover life.

   To the Friend who did not Save my Life (1991)

Nubar Gulbenkian 1896–1972

British industrialist and philanthropist

8 The best number for a dinner party is two—myself and a dam' good head waiter.

   in *Daily Telegraph* 14 January 1965

Thom Gunn 1929–

English poet

9 My thoughts are crowded with death
   and it draws so oddly on the sexual
   that I am confused
   confused to be attracted
   by, in effect, my own annihilation.

   'In Time of Plague' (1992)

10 Their relationship consisted
   In discussing if it existed.

   'Jamesian' (1992)

Alan Guth 1947–

American physicist

11 It is often said that there is no such thing as a free lunch. The Universe, however, is a free lunch.

   in *Harpers* November 1994; cf. **Sayings** 279:8

Woody Guthrie 1912–67

American folksinger and songwriter

12 This land is your land, this land is my land,
   From California to the New York Island.
   From the redwood forest to the Gulf Stream waters
   This land was made for you and me.

   'This Land is Your Land' (1956 song)

Lord Haig 1861–1928

British soldier, Commander of British armies in France, 1915–18
on Haig: see **Beaverbrook** 25:9

13 A very weak-minded fellow I am afraid, and, like the feather pillow, bears the marks of the last person who has sat on him!

   describing the 17th Earl of Derby
   letter to Lady Haig, 14 January 1918

1 Every position must be held to the last man: there must be no retirement. With our backs to the wall, and believing in the justice of our cause, each one of us must fight on to the end.

> order to British troops, 12 April 1918; A. Duff Cooper *Haig* (1936)

Lord Hailsham (Quintin Hogg) 1907–

British Conservative politician
on Hailsham: see **Paget** 241:11

2 Conservatives do not believe that the political struggle is the most important thing in life . . . The simplest of them prefer fox-hunting—the wisest religion.

> *The Case for Conservatism* (1947)

3 We are a democratically governed republic with a wholly admirable head of state.

> *Values: Collapse and Cure* (1994)

4 A great party is not to be brought down because of a scandal by a woman of easy virtue and a proved liar.

> BBC television interview on the Profumo affair; in *The Times* 14 June 1963

5 If the British public falls for this, I think it will be stark, raving bonkers.

> *on the Labour party programme*
>
> in press conference at Conservative Central Office, 12 October 1964

6 I believe there is a golden thread which alone gives meaning to the political history of the West, from Marathon to Alamein, from Solon to Winston Churchill and after. This I chose to call the doctrine of liberty under the law.

> in 1975; Anthony Sampson *The Changing Anatomy of Britain* (1982)

7 The elective dictatorship.

> title of the Dimbleby Lecture, 19 October 1976

8 The English and, more latterly, the British, have the habit of acquiring their institutions by chance or inadvertence, and shedding them in a fit of absent-mindedness.

> 'The Granada Guildhall Lecture 1987' 10 November 1987; see below

We seem . . . to have conquered and peopled half the world in a fit of absence of mind.

> John Seeley (1834–95) *The Expansion of England* (1883)

J. B. S. Haldane 1892–1964

Scottish mathematical biologist

9 Now, my own suspicion is that the universe is not only queerer than we suppose, but queerer than we *can* suppose.

> *Possible Worlds* (1927)

10 If my mental processes are determined wholly by the motions of atoms in my brain, I have no reason for supposing that my beliefs are true. They may be sound chemically, but that does not make them sound logically. And hence I have no reason for supposing my brain to be composed of atoms.

> *Possible Worlds* (1927) 'When I am Dead'

11 I wish I had the voice of Homer
To sing of rectal carcinoma,
Which kills a lot more chaps, in fact,
Than were bumped off when Troy was sacked.

> 'Cancer's a Funny Thing'; Ronald Clark *J. B. S.* (1968)

12 The Creator, if He exists, has a special preference for beetles.

> *on observing that there are 400,000 species of beetles on this planet, but only 8,000 species of mammals*
>
> in *Journal of the British Interplanetary Society* (1951)

13 I'd lay down my life for two brothers or eight cousins.

> attributed; in *New Scientist* 8 August 1974

H. R. Haldeman 1929–93

Presidential assistant to Richard Nixon

14 Once the toothpaste is out of the tube, it is awfully hard to get it back in.

> *on the Watergate affair*
>
> to John Dean, 8 April 1973, in *Hearings Before the Select Committee on Presidential Campaign Activities of US Senate: Watergate and Related Activities* (1973)

Jerry Hall

American model, wife of Mick **Jagger**

1 My mother said it was simple to keep a man, you must be a maid in the living room, a cook in the kitchen and a whore in the bedroom. I said I'd hire the other two and take care of the bedroom bit.
in *Observer* 6 October 1985

Radclyffe Hall 1883–1943

English novelist

2 The well of loneliness.
title of novel (1928)

3 You're neither unnatural, nor abominable, nor mad; you're as much a part of what people call nature as anyone else; only you're unexplained as yet— you've not got your niche in creation.
The Well of Loneliness (1928)

Margaret Halsey 1910–

American writer

4 Englishwomen's shoes look as if they had been made by someone who had often heard shoes described but had never seen any.
With Malice Toward Some (1938)

5 The English never smash in a face. They merely refrain from asking it to dinner.
With Malice Toward Some (1938)

W. F. ('Bull') Halsey

1882–1959

American admiral

6 The Third Fleet's sunken and damaged ships have been salvaged and are retiring at high speed toward the enemy.
on hearing claims that the Japanese had virtually annihilated the US fleet
report, 14 October 1944; E. B. Potter *Bull Halsey* (1985)

Oscar Hammerstein II

1895–1960

American songwriter

7 Fish got to swim and birds got to fly
I got to love one man till I die,
Can't help lovin' dat man of mine.
'Can't Help Lovin' Dat Man of Mine' (1927 song)

8 Climb ev'ry mountain, ford ev'ry stream
Follow ev'ry rainbow, till you find your dream!
'Climb Ev'ry Mountain' (1959 song)

9 June is bustin' out all over.
title of song (1945)

10 The last time I saw Paris
Her heart was warm and gay,
I heard the laughter of her heart in ev'ry street café.
'The Last Time I saw Paris' (1941 song)

11 The corn is as high as an elephant's eye,
An' it looks like it's climbin' clear up to the sky.
'Oh, What a Beautiful Mornin' ' (1943 song)

12 Oh, what a beautiful mornin',
Oh, what a beautiful day!
I got a beautiful feelin'
Ev'rything's goin' my way.
'Oh, What a Beautiful Mornin' ' (1943 song)

13 Ol' man river, dat ol' man river,
He must know sumpin', but don't say nothin',
He jus' keeps rollin',
He jus' keeps rollin' along.
'Ol' Man River' (1927 song)

14 Some enchanted evening,
You may see a stranger,
You may see a stranger,
Across a crowded room.
'Some Enchanted Evening' (1949 song)

15 The hills are alive with the sound of music,
With songs they have sung for a thousand years.
The hills fill my heart with the sound of music,
My heart wants to sing ev'ry song it hears.
'The Sound of Music' (1959 song)

16 There is nothin' like a dame.
title of song (1949)

17 I'm as corny as Kansas in August,
High as a flag on the Fourth of July!
'A Wonderful Guy' (1949 song)

18 You'll never walk alone.
title of song (1945)

Christopher Hampton 1946–

English dramatist

1 Masturbation is the thinking man's television.
   Philanthropist (1970)

2 A definition of capitalism . . . the process whereby American girls turn into American women.
   Savages (1974)

Learned Hand 1872–1961

American judge

3 No plagiarist can excuse the wrong by showing how much of his work he did not pirate.
   in *Sheldon v. Metro-Goldwyn Pictures Corp.* 1936

4 A self-made man may prefer a self-made name.
   on Samuel Goldfish's changing his name to Samuel **Goldwyn**
   Bosley Crowther *Lion's Share* (1957)

Brian Hanrahan 1949–

British journalist

5 I counted them all out and I counted them all back.
   on the number of British aeroplanes joining the raid on Port Stanley
   BBC broadcast report, 1 May 1982

Lorraine Hansberry 1930–65

American dramatist

6 Though it be a thrilling and marvellous thing to be merely young and gifted in such times, it is doubly so, doubly dynamic—to be young, gifted and *black*.
   To be young, gifted and black: Lorraine Hansberry in her own words (1969) adapted by Robert Nemiroff; cf. **Irvine** 157:12

Otto Harbach 1873–1963

American songwriter

7 Now laughing friends deride tears I cannot hide,

So I smile and say 'When a lovely flame dies,
Smoke gets in your eyes.'
   'Smoke Gets in your Eyes' (1933 song)

E. Y. ('Yip') Harburg
1898–1981

American songwriter

8 Brother can you spare a dime?
   title of song (1932)

9 Say, it's only a paper moon,
Sailing over a cardboard sea.
   'It's Only a Paper Moon' (1933 song, with Billy Rose)

10 Wanna cry, wanna croon.
Wanna laugh like a loon.
It's that Old Devil Moon in your eyes.
   'Old Devil Moon' (1946 song)

11 Somewhere over the rainbow
Way up high,
There's a land that I heard of
Once in a lullaby.
   'Over the Rainbow' (1939 song)

12 When our organs have been transplanted
And the new ones made happy to lodge in us,
Let us pray one wish be granted—
We retain our zones erogenous.
   'Seated One Day at the Organ' (1965)

13 Follow the yellow brick road.
   'We're Off to See the Wizard' (1939 song); see below; cf. **John** 162:5

   The road to the City of Emeralds is paved with yellow brick.
   L. Frank Baum (1856–1919) *The Wonderful Wizard of Oz* (1900)

14 Words make you think a thought. Music makes you feel a feeling. A song makes you feel a thought . . . The greatest romance in the life of a lyricist is when the right word meets the right note; often however, a Park Avenue phrase elopes with a Bleeker Street chord resulting in a shotgun wedding and a quickie divorce.
   lecture given at the New York YMCA in 1970

Keir Hardie 1856–1915

Scottish Labour politician

1 Woman, even more than the working
  class, is the great unknown quantity of
  the race.
    speech at Bradford, 11 April 1914

D. W. Harding 1906–

British psychologist and critic

2 Regulated hatred.
    title of an article on the novels of Jane Austen
      in *Scrutiny* March 1940

Godfrey Harold Hardy
1877–1947

English mathematician

3 Beauty is the first test: there is no
  permanent place in the world for ugly
  mathematics.
    A Mathematician's Apology (1940)

Thomas Hardy 1840–1928

English novelist and poet
on Hardy: see **Chesterton** 64:1

4 When the Present has latched its postern
    behind my tremulous stay,
  And the May month flaps its glad green
    leaves like wings,
  Delicate-filmed as new-spun silk, will the
    neighbours say,
  'He was a man who used to notice such
    things'?
    'Afterwards' (1917)

5 The bower we shrined to Tennyson,
    Gentlemen,
  Is roof-wrecked; damps there drip upon
  Sagged seats, the creeper-nails are rust,
  The spider is sole denizen.
    'An Ancient to Ancients' (1922)

6 'Peace upon earth!' was said. We sing it,
  And pay a million priests to bring it.
  After two thousand years of mass
  We've got as far as poison-gas.
    'Christmas: 1924' (1928)

7 In a solitude of the sea
  Deep from human vanity

And the Pride of Life that planned her,
  stilly couches she . . .

Over the mirrors meant
To glass the opulent
The sea-worm crawls—grotesque,
  slimed, dumb, indifferent.
on the loss of the Titanic
    'Convergence of the Twain' (1914)

8 The Immanent Will that stirs and urges
  everything.
    'Convergence of the Twain' (1914)

9 And as the smart ship grew
  In stature, grace, and hue,
  In shadowy silent distance grew the
    Iceberg too . . .

Till the Spinner of the Years
Said 'Now!' And each one hears,
And consummation comes, and jars two
  hemispheres.
    'Convergence of the Twain' (1914)

10 An aged thrush, frail, gaunt, and small,
  In blast-beruffled plume.
    'The Darkling Thrush' (1902)

11 So little cause for carollings
  Of such ecstatic sound
  Was written on terrestrial things
  Afar or nigh around,
  That I could think there trembled
    through
  His happy good-night air
  Some blessed Hope, whereof he knew
  And I was unaware.
    'The Darkling Thrush' (1902)

12 If way to the Better there be, it exacts a
  full look at the worst.
    'De Profundis' (1902)

13 Well, World, you have kept faith with
    me,
  Kept faith with me;
  Upon the whole you have proved to be
  Much as you said you were.
    'He Never Expected Much' (1928)

14 I am the family face;
  Flesh perishes, I live on,
  Projecting trait and trace
  Through time to times anon,
  And leaping from place to place
  Over oblivion.
    'Heredity' (1917)

1 Only a man harrowing clods
In a slow silent walk
With an old horse that stumbles and
   nods
Half asleep as they stalk.
   'In Time of "The Breaking of Nations" ' (1917)

2 Yonder a maid and her wight
Come whispering by:
War's annals will cloud into night
Ere their story die.
   'In Time of "The Breaking of Nations" ' (1917)

3 Yes; quaint and curious war is!
You shoot a fellow down
You'd treat if met where any bar is,
Or help to half-a-crown.
   'The Man he Killed' (1909)

4 What of the faith and fire within us
Men who march away
Ere the barn-cocks say
Night is growing grey,
To hazards whence no tears can win us;
What of the faith and fire within us
Men who march away?
   'Men Who March Away' (1914)

5 In the third-class seat sat the journeying
   boy
And the roof-lamp's oily flame
Played down on his listless form and face,
Bewrapt past knowing to what he was
   going,
Or whence he came.
   'Midnight on the Great Western' (1917)

6 Woman much missed, how you call to
   me, call to me.
   'The Voice' (1914)

7 This is the weather the cuckoo likes,
And so do I.
   'Weathers' (1922)

8 And drops on gate-bars hang in a row,
And rooks in families homeward go.
   'Weathers' (1922)

9 When I set out for Lyonnesse,
A hundred miles away,
The rime was on the spray,
And starlight lit my lonesomeness.
   'When I set out for Lyonnesse' (1914)

10 War makes rattling good history; but
Peace is poor reading.
   The Dynasts (1904)

11 A local thing called Christianity.
   The Dynasts (1904)

W. F. Hargreaves 1846–1919

British songwriter

12 I'm Burlington Bertie
I rise at ten thirty and saunter along like
   a toff,
I walk down the Strand with my gloves
   on my hand,
Then I walk down again with them off.
   'Burlington Bertie from Bow' (1915 song)

13 I acted so tragic the house rose like
   magic,
The audience yelled 'You're sublime.'
They made me a present of Mornington
   Crescent
They threw it a brick at a time.
   'The Night I Appeared as Macbeth' (1922 song)

Lord Harlech 1918–85

British diplomat

14 Britain will be honoured by historians
more for the way she disposed of an
empire than for the way in which she
acquired it.
   in *New York Times* 28 October 1962; cf.
   Hailsham 136:8

Charles Eustace Harman
1894–1970

British judge

15 Accountants are the witch-doctors of the
modern world and willing to turn their
hands to any kind of magic.
   speech, February 1964, in A. Sampson *The New
   Anatomy of Britain* (1971)

Jimmy Harper et al.

16 The biggest aspidistra in the world.
   title of song (1938); popularized by Gracie
   Fields

Michael Harrington 1928–89

American writer and sociologist

17 For the urban poor the police are those
who arrest you. In almost any slum there

is a vast conspiracy against the forces of law and order.

The Other America: Poverty in the United States (1962)

Arthur Harris 1892–1984

British Air Force Marshal

1 I would not regard the whole of the remaining cities of Germany as worth the bones of one British Grenadier.

supporting the continued strategic bombing of German cities

letter to Norman Bottomley, deputy Chief of Air Staff, 29 March 1945; Max Hastings *Bomber Command* (1979); see below

Not worth the healthy bones of a single Pomeranian grenadier.

Bismarck (1815–98) in G. O. Kent *Bismarck and his Times* (1978)

George Harrison 1943–

English rock and pop guitarist, former member of The Beatles

2 The good thing about them is that you can look at them with the sound turned down.

of the Spice Girls

in *Independent* 28 August 1997

3 The more you jump around, the bigger your hat is, the more people listen to your music . . . The only important thing is to sell, and make money. It's nothing to do with talent.

of modern music as exemplified by Oasis and U2

in *Independent* 28 August 1997

Paul Harrison 1936–

American dramatist and director

4 The poor tread lightest upon the earth. The higher our income, the more resources we control and the more havoc we wreak.

in *Guardian* 1 May 1992

Josephine Hart 1942–

5 Damaged people are dangerous. They know they can survive.

Damage (1991); cf. **Starkie** 295:10

Lorenz Hart 1895–1943

American songwriter

6 Bewitched, bothered, and bewildered am I.

'Bewitched' (1941 song)

7 When love congeals
It soon reveals
The faint aroma of performing seals.

'I Wish I Were in Love Again' (1937 song)

8 I get too hungry for dinner at eight.
I like the theatre, but never come late.
I never bother with people I hate.
That's why the lady is a tramp.

'The Lady is a Tramp' (1937 song)

9 In a mountain greenery
Where God paints the scenery—
Just two crazy people together.

'Mountain Greenery' (1926 song)

10 Thou swell! Thou witty!
Thou sweet! Thou grand!
Wouldst kiss me pretty?
Wouldst hold my hand?

'Thou Swell' (1927 song)

Moss Hart 1904–61 and George Kaufman 1889–1961

11 You can't take it with you.

title of play (1936)

Dorothy Hartley 1893–1985

English writer

12 Hot on Sunday,
Cold on Monday,
Hashed on Tuesday,
Minced on Wednesday,
Curried Thursday,
Broth on Friday,
Cottage pie Saturday.

Food in England (1954) 'Vicarage Mutton'

L. P. Hartley 1895–1972

English novelist

13 The past is a foreign country: they do things differently there.

The Go-Between (1953) prologue

F. W. Harvey b. 1888

English poet

1 From troubles of the world
I turn to ducks
Beautiful comical things.
'Ducks' (1919)

Minnie Louise Haskins

1875–1957

English teacher and writer

2 And I said to the man who stood at the gate of the year: 'Give me a light that I may tread safely into the unknown.'
And he replied:
'Go out into the darkness and put your hand into the Hand of God. That shall be to you better than light and safer than a known way.'
quoted by **George VI** *in his Christmas broadcast, 1939*
Desert (1908) 'God Knows'

Václav Havel 1936–

Czech dramatist and statesman; President of Czechoslovakia 1989–92 and of the Czech Republic since 1993

3 That special time caught me up in its wild vortex and—in the absence of leisure to reflect on the matter— compelled me to do what had to be done.
on his election to the Presidency
Summer Meditations (1992)

4 Truth is not merely what we are thinking, but also why, to whom and under what circumstances we say it.
Temptation (1985)

5 To respond to evil by committing another evil does not eliminate evil but allows it to go on forever.
letter, 5 November 1989

6 Let us teach ourselves and others that politics can be not only the art of the possible, especially if this means the art of speculation, calculation, intrigue, secret deals, and pragmatic manoeuvring, but that it can even be the art of the

impossible, namely, the art of improving ourselves and the world.
speech, Prague, 1 January 1990; cf. **Butler** 50:10

7 The Gypsies are a litmus test not of democracy but of civil society.
attributed

Stephen Hawking 1942–

English theoretical physicist

8 Someone told me that each equation I included in the book would halve the sales.
A Brief History of Time (1988)

9 In effect, we have redefined the task of science to be the discovery of laws that will enable us to predict events up to the limits set by the uncertainty principle.
A Brief History of Time (1988)

10 What is it that breathes fire into the equations and makes a universe for them to describe . . . Why does the universe go to all the bother of existing?
A Brief History of Time (1988)

11 If we find the answer to that [why it is that we and the universe exist], it would be the ultimate triumph of human reason—for then we would know the mind of God.
A Brief History of Time (1988)

Ian Hay 1876–1952

Scottish novelist and dramatist

12 War is hell, and all that, but it has a good deal to recommend it. It wipes out all the small nuisances of peace-time.
The First Hundred Thousand (1915)

13 What do you mean, funny? Funny-peculiar or funny ha-ha?
The Housemaster (1938)

14 The dawn of legibility in his handwriting has revealed his utter inability to spell.
attributed; perhaps used in a dramatization of *The Housemaster* (1938)

Bill Hayden 1933–

Australian Labor politician

Hayden had resigned as Opposition leader in 1983 as Malcolm Fraser was in the process of calling the election, but remained convinced that he would have won:

1 I am not convinced the Labor Party could not win under my leadership. I believe a drover's dog could lead the Labor Party to victory the way the country is.
   John Stubbs *Hayden* (1989)

Alfred Hayes 1911–85

American songwriter

2 I dreamed I saw Joe Hill last night
   Alive as you and me.
   Says I, 'But Joe, you're ten years dead.'
   'I never died,' says he.
   'I Dreamed I Saw Joe Hill Last Night' (1936 song)

Lee Hazlewood 1929–

American singer and songwriter

3 These boots are made for walkin'.
   title of song (1966)

Denis Healey 1917–

British Labour politician

4 I warn you there are going to be howls of anguish from the 80,000 people who are rich enough to pay over 75% [tax] on the last slice of their income.
   speech at Labour Party Conference, 1 October 1973

5 It's no good ceasing to become the world's policeman in order to become the world's parson instead.
   at a meeting of the Cabinet at Chequers, 17 November 1974; Peter Hennessy *Whitehall* (1990)

6 Like being savaged by a dead sheep.
   *on being criticized by Geoffrey **Howe** in the House of Commons*
   in the House of Commons, 14 June 1978

7 While the rest of Europe is marching to confront the new challenges, the Prime Minister is shuffling along in the gutter in the opposite direction, like an old bag lady, muttering imprecations at anyone who catches her eye.
   *of Margaret **Thatcher***
   in the House of Commons, 22 February 1990

Edna Healey 1918–

British writer

8 She has no hinterland; in particular she has no sense of history.
   *of Margaret **Thatcher***
   Denis Healey *The Time of My Life* (1989)

Seamus Heaney 1939–

Irish poet

9 All agog at the plasterer on his ladder
   Skimming our gable and writing our
      name there
   With his trowel point, letter by strange
      letter.
   'Alphabets' (1987)

10 And found myself thinking: if it were
      nowadays,
   This is how Death would summon
      Everyman.
   'A Call' (1996)

11 How culpable was he
   That last night when he broke
   Our tribe's complicity?
   'Now you're supposed to be
   An educated man,'
   I hear him say. 'Puzzle me
   The right answer to that one.
   'Casualty' (1979)

12 Between my finger and my thumb
   The squat pen rests.
   I'll dig with it.
   'Digging' (1966)

13 Me waiting until I was nearly fifty
   To credit marvels.
   'Fosterling' (1991)

14 The annals say: when the monks of
      Clonmacnoise
   Were all at prayers inside the oratory
   A ship appeared above them in the air.
   'Lightenings viii' (1991)

15 Don't be surprised
   If I demur, for, be advised
   My passport's green.

No glass of ours was ever raised
To toast *The Queen*.

rebuking the editors of The Penguin Book of
Contemporary British Poetry *for including him
among its authors*
  Open Letter (1983)

1 Who would connive
   in civilised outrage
   yet understand the exact
   and tribal, intimate revenge.
   'Punishment' (1975)

2 My heart besieged by anger, my mind a
   gap of danger,
   I walked among their old haunts, the
   home ground where they bled;
   And in the dirt lay justice like an acorn
   in the winter
   Till its oak would sprout in Derry where
   the thirteen men lay dead.
   of Bloody Sunday, Londonderry, 30 January 1972
   'The Road to Derry'

3   Here is the News,
   Said the absolute speaker. Between him
   and us
   A great gulf was fixed where
   pronunciation
   Reigned tyrannically
   'A Sofa in the Forties' (1996)

4   The famous
   Northern reticence, the tight gag of place
   And times: yes, yes. Of the 'wee six' I
   sing
   Where to be saved you only must save
   face
   And whatever you say, you say nothing.
   'Whatever You Say Say Nothing' (1975)

Edward Heath 1916–

British Conservative statesman; Prime
Minister, 1970–4
on Heath: see Jenkins 161:6

5 This would, at a stroke, reduce the rise in
   prices, increase production and reduce
   unemployment.
   press release from Conservative Central Office,
   16 June 1970, never actually spoken by Heath

6 The unpleasant and unacceptable face of
   capitalism.
   on the Lonrho affair
   in the House of Commons, 15 May 1973

Fred Heatherton

7 I've got a loverly bunch of coconuts,
   There they are a-standing in a row.
   'I've Got a Lovely Bunch of Coconuts' (1944
   song; revised version 1948)

John Heath-Stubbs 1918–

English poet

8 Venerable Mother Toothache
   Climb down from the white battlements,
   Stop twisting in your yellow fingers
   The fourfold rope of nerves.
   'A Charm Against the Toothache' (1954)

Ben Hecht 1894–1964

American screenwriter
see also Film lines 111:15

9 [Goldwyn] filled the room with wonderful
   panic and beat at your mind like a man
   in front of a slot machine, shaking it for a
   jackpot.
   A. Scott Berg *Goldwyn* (1989)

Tippi Hedren 1935–

American actress

10 [Alfred Hitchcock] thought of himself as
   looking like Cary Grant. That's tough, to
   think of yourself one way and look
   another.
   interview in California, 1982; P. F. Boller and R.
   L. Davis *Hollywood Anecdotes* (1988)

Amanda Heggs

11 Sometimes I have a terrible feeling that I
   am dying not from the virus, but from
   being untouchable.
   of Aids
   in *Guardian* 12 June 1989

Werner Heisenberg 1901–76

German mathematical physicist

12 An expert is someone who knows some
   of the worst mistakes that can be made in
   his subject and who manages to avoid
   them.
   Der Teil und das Ganze (1969); tr. A. J.
   Pomerans as *Physics and Beyond*, 1971

on Felix Bloch's stating that space was the field of linear operations:

1 Nonsense. Space is blue and birds fly through it.

> Felix Bloch 'Heisenberg and the early days of quantum mechanics' in *Physics Today* December 1976

Joseph Heller 1923–

American novelist

2 There was only one catch and that was Catch-22, which specified that a concern for one's own safety in the face of dangers that were real and immediate was the process of a rational mind . . . Orr would be crazy to fly more missions and sane if he didn't, but if he was sane he had to fly them. If he flew them he was crazy and didn't have to; but if he didn't want to he was sane and had to.

> *Catch-22* (1961)

3 Some men are born mediocre, some men achieve mediocrity, and some men have mediocrity thrust upon them. With Major Major it had been all three.

> *Catch-22* (1961); see below

> Some men are born great, some achieve greatness, and some have greatness thrust upon them.
>
> William Shakespeare (1564–1616) *Twelfth Night* (1601)

4 Kissinger brought peace to Vietnam the same way Napoleon brought peace to Europe: by losing.

> *Good as Gold* (1979)

5 When I read something saying I've not done anything as good as *Catch-22* I'm tempted to reply, 'Who has?'

> in *The Times* 9 June 1993

Lillian Hellman 1905–84

American dramatist
on Hellman: see **McCarthy** 197:14

6 Cynicism is an unpleasant way of saying the truth.

> *The Little Foxes* (1939)

7 I cannot and will not cut my conscience to fit this year's fashions.

> letter to John S. Wood, 19 May 1952

Leona Helmsley c.1920–

American hotelier

8 Only the little people pay taxes.

> *comment made to her housekeeper in 1983, and reported at her trial for tax evasion*
>
> in *New York Times* 12 July 1989

Ernest Hemingway 1899–1961

American novelist
on Hemingway: see **Ross** 269:1, **Vidal** 317:5; *see also* **Fitzgerald** 112:18, **Stein** 296:6

9 Where do the noses go? I always wondered where the noses would go.

> *For Whom the Bell Tolls* (1940)

10 But did thee feel the earth move?

> *For Whom the Bell Tolls* (1940)

11 Cowardice, as distinguished from panic, is almost always simply a lack of ability to suspend the functioning of the imagination.

> *Men at War* (1942)

12 Paris is a movable feast.

> *A Movable Feast* (1964) epigraph

13 A man can be destroyed but not defeated.

> *The Old Man and the Sea* (1952)

14 The sun also rises.

> title of novel (1926)

15 Grace under pressure.

> *when asked what he meant by 'guts' in an interview with Dorothy* **Parker**
>
> in *New Yorker* 30 November 1929

16 I started out very quiet and I beat Mr Turgenev. Then I trained hard and I beat Mr de Maupassant. I've fought two draws with Mr Stendhal, and I think I had an edge in the last one. But nobody's going to get me in any ring with Mr Tolstoy unless I'm crazy or I keep getting better.

> in *New Yorker* 13 May 1950

17 The most essential gift for a good writer is a built-in, shock-proof shit detector. This is the writer's radar and all great writers have had it.

> in *Paris Review* Spring 1958

Arthur Henderson 1863–1935

Labour politician and from 1931 Party
Leader

*to critics in his own party, when as adviser on
labour matters he was made minister without
portfolio in* **Lloyd George***'s War Cabinet
(December* 1916*):*

1 I am not here either to please myself or
you; I am here to see the war through.
   in *Dictionary of National Biography* (1917–)

2 The first forty-eight hours decide whether
a Minister is going to run his office or
whether his office is going to run him.
   Susan Crosland *Tony Crosland* (1982)

Jimi Hendrix 1942–70

American rock musician

3 Purple haze is in my brain
Lately things don't seem the same.
   'Purple Haze' (1967 song)

4 A musician, if he's a messenger, is like a
child who hasn't been handled too many
times by man, hasn't had too many
fingerprints across his brain.
   in *Life Magazine* (1969)

Arthur W. D. Henley

5 Nobody loves a fairy when she's forty.
   title of song (1934)

Peter Hennessy 1947–

British historian and writer

6 The model of a modern Prime Minister
would be a kind of grotesque composite
freak—someone with the dedication to
duty of a Peel, the physical energy of a
Gladstone, the detachment of a Salisbury,
the brains of an Asquith, the balls of a
Lloyd George, the word-power of a
Churchill, the administrative gifts of an
Attlee, the style of a Macmillan, the
managerialism of a Heath, and the sleep
requirements of a Thatcher. Human
beings do not come like that.
   The Hidden Wiring (1995)

A. P. Herbert 1890–1971

English writer and humorist

7 Don't let's go to the dogs tonight,
For mother will be there.
   'Don't Let's Go to the Dogs Tonight' (1926)

8 The Farmer will never be happy again;
He carries his heart in his boots;
For either the rain is destroying his grain
Or the drought is destroying his roots.
   'The Farmer' (1922)

9 Not huffy, or stuffy, not tiny or tall,
But fluffy, just fluffy, with no brains at
all.
   'I Like them Fluffy' (1927)

10 Let's find out what everyone is doing,
And then stop everyone from doing it.
   'Let's Stop Somebody from Doing Something!'
   (1930)

11 As my poor father used to say
In 1863,
Once people start on all this Art
Goodbye, moralitee!
   'Lines for a Worthy Person' (1930)

12 Other people's babies—
That's my life!
Mother to dozens,
And nobody's wife.
   'Other People's Babies' (1930)

13 This high official, all allow,
Is grossly overpaid;
There wasn't any Board, and now
There isn't any Trade.
   'The President of the Board of Trade' (1922)

14 Nothing is wasted, nothing is in vain:
The seas roll over but the rocks remain.
   Tough at the Top (operetta c.1949)

15 Holy deadlock.
   title of novel (1934)

16 People must not do things for fun. We
are not here for fun. There is no reference
to fun in any Act of Parliament.
   Uncommon Law (1935) 'Is it a Free Country?'

17 The critical period in matrimony is
breakfast-time.
   Uncommon Law (1935) 'Is Marriage Lawful?'

18 'Was the cow crossed?'
'No, your worship, it was an open cow.'
   on an attempt to write a cheque on a cow
   Uncommon Law (1935) 'The Negotiable Cow'

Michael Heseltine 1933–
British Conservative politician

1 I knew that, 'He who wields the knife
never wears the crown.'
   in *New Society* 14 February 1986

2 The market has no morality.
   on *Panorama*, BBC1 TV, 27 June 1988

3 Polluted rivers, filthy streets, bodies
bedded down in doorways are no
advertisement for a prosperous or caring
society.
   speech at Conservative Party Conference 10
   October 1989

4 If I have to intervene to help British
companies . . . I'll intervene—before
breakfast, before lunch, before tea and
before dinner. And I'll get up the next
morning and I'll start all over again.
   of his role as President of the Board of Trade
   to the Conservative Party Conference, 7
   October 1992

Hermann Hesse 1877–1962
German novelist and poet

5 If you hate a person, you hate something
in him that is part of yourself. What isn't
part of ourselves doesn't disturb us.
   Demian (1919)

6 The bourgeois prefers comfort to
pleasure, convenience to liberty, and a
pleasant temperature to the deathly inner
consuming fire.
   Der Steppenwolf (1927) 'Tractat vom
   Steppenwolf'

Lord Hewart 1870–1943
British lawyer and politician

7 Justice should not only be done, but
should manifestly and undoubtedly be
seen to be done.
   Rex v. Sussex Justices, 9 November 1923

Robert Hewison 1943–
British historian

8 The turn of the century raises
expectations. The end of a millennium
promises apocalypse and revelation. But
at the close of the twentieth century the
golden age seems behind us, not ahead.
The end game of the 1990s promises
neither nirvana nor Armageddon, but
entropy.
   Future Tense (1990)

John Hewitt 1907–87
Northern Irish poet

9 We would be strangers in the Capitol;
this is our country also, no-where else;
and we shall not be outcast on the world.
   'The Colony' (1950)

10 I'm an Ulsterman, of planter stock. I was
born in the island of Ireland, so
secondarily I'm an Irishman. I was born
in the British archipelago and English is
my native tongue, so I am British. The
British archipelago consists of offshore
islands to the continent of Europe, so I'm
European. This is my hierarchy of values
and so far as I am concerned, anyone
who omits one step in that sequence of
values is falsifying the situation.
   in *The Irish Times* 4 July 1974

Reinhard Heydrich 1904–42
German Nazi leader

11 Now the rough work has been done we
begin the period of finer work. We need
to work in harmony with the civil
administration. We count on you
gentlemen as far as the final solution is
concerned.
   *on the planned mass murder of eleven million
   European Jews*
      speech in Wannsee, 20 January 1942; cf.
      Goering 129:12

Du Bose Heyward 1885–1940
and **Ira Gershwin** 1896–1983
American songwriters

12 It ain't necessarily so,
De t'ings dat yo' li'ble
To read in de Bible
It ain't necessarily so.
   'It ain't necessarily so' (1935 song)

1 Summer time an' the livin' is easy,
   Fish are jumpin' an' the cotton is high.
   'Summertime' (1935 song)

2 A woman is a sometime thing.
   title of song (1935)

J. R. Hicks 1904–

British economist

3 The best of all monopoly profits is a quiet
   life.
   Econometrica (1935) 'The Theory of Monopoly'

Seymour Hicks 1871–1949

English actor-manager and author

4 You will recognize, my boy, the first sign
   of old age: it is when you go out into the
   streets of London and realize for the first
   time how young the policemen look.
   C. R. D. Pulling *They Were Singing* (1952)

David Hilbert 1862–1943

German mathematician

5 The importance of a scientific work can
   be measured by the number of previous
   publications it makes it superfluous to
   read.
   attributed; Lewis Wolpert *The Unnatural Nature
   of Science* (1993)

Christopher Hill 1912–

British historian

6 Only very slowly and late have men
   come to realize that unless freedom is
   universal it is only extended privilege.
   Century of Revolution (1961)

7 Just as Oliver Cromwell aimed to bring
   about the kingdom of God on earth and
   founded the British Empire, so Bunyan
   wanted the millennium and got the
   novel.
   *A Turbulent, Seditious, and Factious People:
   John Bunyan and his Church, 1628-1688* (1988)

Damon Hill 1960–

English motor-racing driver

8 Winning is everything. The only ones
   who remember you when you come
   second are your wife and your dog.
   in *Sunday Times* 18 December 1994 'Quotes of
   the Year'

Geoffrey Hill 1932–

English poet

9   Poetry
   Unearths from among the speechless
   dead

   Lazarus mystified, common man
   Of death. The lily rears its gouged face
   From the provided loam.
   'History as Poetry' (1968)

10 She kept the siege. And every day
   We watched her brooding over death
   Like a strong bird above its prey.
   The room filled with the kettle's breath.

   Damp curtains glued against the pane
   Sealed time away. Her body froze
   As if to freeze us all, and chain
   Creation to a stunned repose.
   'In Memory of Jane Fraser' (1959)

11 I love my work and my children. God
   Is distant, difficult. Things happen.
   Too near the ancient troughs of blood
   Innocence is no earthly weapon.
   'Ovid in the Third Reich' (1968)

Joe Hill 1879–1915

American labour leader and songwriter
on Hill: see **Hayes** 143:2

12 Work and pray, live on hay,
   You'll get pie in the sky when you die.
   'Preacher and the Slave' (1911 song)

13 I will die like a true-blue rebel. Don't
   waste any time in mourning—organize.
   before his death by firing squad
      farewell telegram to Bill Haywood, 18
      November 1915

Pattie S. Hill 1868–1946

American educationist

14 Happy birthday to you.
   title of song (1935)

Edmund Hillary 1919–

New Zealand mountaineer

1 Well, we knocked the bastard off!
on conquering Mount Everest, 1953
Nothing Venture, Nothing Win (1975)

Fred Hillebrand 1893–

2 Home James, and don't spare the horses.
title of song (1934)

James Hilton 1900–54

English novelist

3 Nothing really wrong with him—only
anno domini, but that's the most fatal
complaint of all, in the end.
Goodbye, Mr Chips (1934)

Emperor Hirohito 1901–89

Emperor of Japan from 1926

4 The war situation has developed not
necessarily to Japan's advantage.
announcing Japan's surrender, in a broadcast to
his people after atom bombs had destroyed
Hiroshima and Nagasaki
on 15 August 1945

Damien Hirst 1965–

English artist

5 It's amazing what you can do with an E
in A-level art, twisted imagination and a
chainsaw.
after winning the 1995 Turner Prize
in *Observer* 3 December 1995 'Sayings of the
Week'

Ian Hislop 1960–

English satirical journalist

6 If this is justice, I am a banana.
on the libel damages awarded against Private Eye
to Sonia Sutcliffe, wife of the Yorkshire Ripper
comment, 24 May 1989

Alfred Hitchcock 1899–1980

British-born film director
on Hitchcock: see **Hedren** 144:10

7 Actors are cattle.
in *Saturday Evening Post* 22 May 1943

8 Television has brought back murder into
the home—where it belongs.
in *Observer* 19 December 1965

9 There is no terror in a bang, only in the
anticipation of it.
Leslie Halliwell (ed.) *Halliwell's Filmgoer's*
Companion (1984); attributed

Adolf Hitler 1889–1945

German dictator
on Hitler: see **Buchman** 48:2, **Chamberlain**
60:6

10 The night of the long knives.
referring to the massacre of Ernst Roehm and his
associates by Hitler on 29–30 June 1934
(subsequently associated with Harold
***Macmillan**'s Cabinet dismissals of 13 July 1962)*
S. H. Roberts *The House Hitler Built* (1937)

11 I go the way that Providence dictates
with the assurance of a sleepwalker.
speech in Munich, 15 March 1936

12 It is the last territorial claim which I have
to make in Europe.
on the Sudetenland
speech in Berlin, 26 September 1938

13 Is Paris burning?
on 5 August 1944; L. Collins and D. Lapierre *Is*
Paris Burning? (1965)

14 The broad mass of a nation . . . will more
easily fall victim to a big lie than to a
small one.
Mein Kampf (1925)

Eric Hobsbawm 1917–

British historian

15 For 80 per cent of humanity the Middle
Ages ended suddenly in the 1950s; or
perhaps better still, they were *felt* to end
in the 1960s.
Age of Extremes (1994)

1 This was the kind of war which existed in order to produce victory parades.
*of the **Falklands** War*
> in *Marxism Today* January 1983

David Hockney 1937–
British artist

2 All you can do with most ordinary photographs is stare at them—they stare back, blankly—and presently your concentration begins to fade. They stare you down. I mean, photography is all right if you don't mind looking at the world from the point of view of a paralysed cyclops—*for a split second.*
> as told to Lawrence Weschler, *Cameraworks* (1984)

3 All painting, no matter what you're painting, is abstract in that it's got to be organized.
> *David Hockney* (1976)

4 The thing with high-tech is that you always end up using scissors.
> in *Observer* 10 July 1994 'Sayings of the Week'

Ralph Hodgson 1871–1962
English poet

5 'Twould ring the bells of Heaven
The wildest peal for years,
If Parson lost his senses
And people came to theirs,
And he and they together
Knelt down with angry prayers
For tamed and shabby tigers
And dancing dogs and bears,
And wretched, blind, pit ponies,
And little hunted hares.
> 'Bells of Heaven' (1917)

Eric Hoffer 1902–83
American philosopher

6 When people are free to do as they please, they usually imitate each other. Originality is deliberate and forced, and partakes of the nature of a protest.
> *Passionate State of Mind* (1955)

Al Hoffman 1902–60
and Dick Manning 1912–

7 Takes two to tango.
> title of song (1952)

Gerard Hoffnung 1925–59
English humorist

8 Standing among savage scenery, the hotel offers stupendous revelations. There is a French widow in every bedroom, affording delightful prospects.
supposedly quoting a letter from a Tyrolean landlord
> in speech at the Oxford Union, 4 December 1958

Lancelot Hogben 1895–1975
English scientist

9 This is not the age of pamphleteers. It is the age of the engineers. The spark-gap is mightier than the pen.
> *Science for the Citizen* (1938) epilogue

Billie Holiday 1915–59
American singer

10 Mama may have, papa may have,
But God bless the child that's got his own!
> 'God Bless the Child' (1941 song, with Arthur Herzog Jnr)

11 Southern trees bear strange fruit,
Blood on the leaves and blood at the root,
Black bodies swinging in the Southern breeze,
Strange fruit hanging from the poplar trees.
> 'Strange Fruit' (1939)

12 You can be up to your boobies in white satin, with gardenias in your hair and no sugar cane for miles, but you can still be working on a plantation.
> *Lady Sings the Blues* (1956, with William Duffy)

13 In this country, don't forget, a habit is no damn private hell. There's no solitary

confinement outside of jail. A habit is hell for those you love.
of a drug habit
    Lady Sings the Blues (1956, with William Duffy)

John H. Holmes 1879–1964
American Unitarian minister

1 This, now, is the judgement of our scientific age—the third reaction of man upon the universe! This universe is not hostile, nor yet is it friendly. It is simply indifferent.
    The Sensible Man's View of Religion (1932)

Oliver Wendell Holmes Jr.
1841–1935
American lawyer

2 Certitude is not the test of certainty. We have been cocksure of many things that were not so.
    'Natural Law' (1918)

3 The most stringent protection of free speech would not protect a man falsely shouting fire in a theatre and causing a panic.
sometimes quoted as, 'shouting fire in a crowded theatre'
    in *Schenck v. United States* (1919)

4 The minute a phrase becomes current it becomes an apology for not thinking accurately to the end of the sentence.
    letter to Harold Laski, 2 July 1917

5 But I have long thought that if you knew a column of advertisements by heart, you could achieve unexpected felicities with them. You can get a happy quotation anywhere if you have the eye.
    letter to Harold Laski, 31 May 1923

Alec Douglas-Home, Lord Home 1903–95
British Conservative statesman; Prime Minister, 1963–4
on Home: see **Connolly** 74:16

6 When I have to read economic documents I have to have a box of matches and start moving them into

position to simplify and illustrate the points to myself.
    in *Observer* 16 September 1962

7 As far as the fourteenth earl is concerned, I suppose Mr Wilson, when you come to think of it, is the fourteenth Mr Wilson.
*replying to Harold **Wilson**'s remark (on Home's becoming leader of the Conservative party) that 'the whole [democratic] process has ground to a halt with a fourteenth Earl'*
    in *Daily Telegraph* 22 October 1963

Herbert Hoover 1874–1964
American Republican statesman, 31st President of the US, 1929–33

8 Our country has deliberately undertaken a great social and economic experiment, noble in motive and far-reaching in purpose.
on the Eighteenth Amendment enacting Prohibition
    letter to Senator W. H. Borah, 23 February 1928; Claudius O. Johnson *Borah of Idaho* (1936)

9 The American system of rugged individualism.
    speech, 22 October 1928

10 The slogan of progress is changing from the full dinner pail to the full garage.
sometimes paraphrased as, 'a car in every garage and a chicken in every pot'
    speech, 22 October 1928; see below

    I want there to be no peasant in my kingdom so poor that he is unable to have a chicken in his pot every Sunday.
    Henri IV, King of France (1553–1610) in Hardouin de Péréfixe *Histoire de Henry le Grand* (1681)

11 The grass will grow in the streets of a hundred cities, a thousand towns.
on proposals 'to reduce the protective tariff to a competitive tariff for revenue'
    speech, 31 October 1932

12 Older men declare war. But it is youth who must fight and die.
    speech at the Republican National Convention, Chicago, 27 June 1944

A. D. Hope 1907–

Australian poet

1 And her five cities, like teeming sores,
Each drains her: a vast parasite robber-
state
Where second-hand Europeans pullulate
Timidly on the edge of alien shores.
  'Australia' (1939)

Anthony Hope 1863–1933

English novelist
see also **Epitaphs** 105:9

2 Oh, for an hour of Herod!
  at the first night of Peter Pan in 1904
  D. Mackail Story of JMB (1941)

Bob Hope 1903–

American comedian

3 A bank is a place that will lend you
money if you can prove that you don't
need it.
  Alan Harrington Life in the Crystal Palace
  (1959) 'The Tyranny of Farms'

A. E. Housman 1859–1936

English poet
on Housman: see **Kingsmill** 172:16, 173:1;
see also **Last words** 182:15

4 The Grizzly Bear is huge and wild;
He has devoured the infant child.
The infant child is not aware
He has been eaten by the bear.
  'Infant Innocence' (1938)

5 And how am I to face the odds
Of man's bedevilment and God's?
I, a stranger and afraid
In a world I never made.
  Last Poems (1922) no. 12

6 The candles burn their sockets,
The blinds let through the day,
The young man feels his pockets
And wonders what's to pay.
  Last Poems (1922) no. 21

7 Their shoulders held the sky suspended;
They stood, and earth's foundations stay;
What God abandoned, these defended,

And saved the sum of things for pay.
  Last Poems (1922) no. 37 'Epitaph on an Army
  of Mercenaries'

8 For nature, heartless, witless nature,
Will neither care nor know
What stranger's feet may find the
  meadow
And trespass there and go,
Nor ask amid the dews of morning
If they are mine or no.
  Last Poems (1922) no. 40

9 Life, to be sure, is nothing much to lose;
But young men think it is, and we were
  young.
  More Poems (1936) no. 36

10 Experience has taught me, when I am
shaving of a morning, to keep watch
over my thoughts, because, if a line of
poetry strays into my memory, my skin
bristles so that the razor ceases to act . . .
The seat of this sensation is the pit of the
stomach.
  The Name and Nature of Poetry (1933)

11 Written English is now inert and
inorganic: not stem and leaf and flower,
not even trim and well-joined masonry,
but a daub of untempered mortar.
  in Cambridge Review 1917

12 Whence came the intrusive comma on p.
4? It did not fall from the sky.
  letter to the Richards Press, 3 July 1930

13 Cambridge has seen many strange sights.
It has seen Wordsworth drunk and
Porson sober. It is now destined to see
better a better scholar than Wordsworth
and a better poet than Porson betwixt
and between.
  speech at University College, London, 29
  March 1911, in R. W. Chambers Man's
  Unconquerable Mind (1939)

Geoffrey Howe 1926–

British Conservative politician
on Howe: see **Healey** 143:6

14 It is rather like sending your opening
batsmen to the crease only for them to
find the moment that the first balls are

bowled that their bats have been broken
before the game by the team captain.

*on the difficulties caused him as Foreign
Secretary by the Prime Mininster's anti-European
views*

> resignation speech as Deputy Prime Minister in
> the House of Commons 13 November 1990

1 The time has come for others to consider
their own response to the tragic conflict
of loyalties with which I have myself
wrestled for perhaps too long.

resignation speech

> in the House of Commons, 13 November 1990

Frankie Howerd 1922–92

British comedian

2 Such cruel glasses.

*of Robin **Day***

> *That Was The Week That Was* (BBC television
> series, from 1963)

3 It's television, you see. If you are not on
the thing every week, the public think
you are either dead or deported.

> attributed

Fred Hoyle 1915–

English astrophysicist

4 Space isn't remote at all. It's only an
hour's drive away if your car could go
straight upwards.

> in *Observer* 9 September 1979 'Sayings of the
> Week'

5 When I was young, the old regarded me
as an outrageous young fellow, and now
that I'm old the young regard me as an
outrageous old fellow.

> in *Scientific American* March 1995

6 There is a coherent plan to the universe,
though I don't know what it's a plan for.

> attributed

Elbert Hubbard 1859–1915

American writer

7 Life is just one damned thing after
another.

> in *Philistine* December 1909; often attributed
> to Frank Ward O'Malley; cf. **Millay** 214:15

Frank McKinney ('Kin') Hubbard 1868–1930

American humorist

8 Classic music is th'kind that we keep
thinkin'll turn into a tune.

> *Comments of Abe Martin and His Neighbors*
> (1923)

Howard Hughes Jr. 1905–76

American industrialist, aviator, and film
producer

9 That man's ears make him look like a
taxi-cab with both doors open.

of Clark Gable

> Charles Higham and Joel Greenberg *Celluloid
> Muse* (1969)

Jimmy Hughes and Frank Lake

10 Bless 'em all! Bless 'em all! The long and
the short and the tall.

> 'Bless 'Em All' (1940 song)

Langston Hughes 1902–67

American writer and poet

11 I, too, sing America.

I am the darker brother.
They send me to eat in the kitchen
When company comes.

> 'I, Too' (1925)

12 I've known rivers:
I've known rivers ancient as the world
   and older than the flow of human
   blood in human veins.

> 'The Negro Speaks of Rivers' (1921)

13 I bathed in the Euphrates when dawns
   were young.
I built my hut near the Congo and it
   lulled me to sleep.
I looked upon the Nile and raised the
   pyramids above it.
I heard the singing of the Mississippi
   when Abe Lincoln went down to New
   Orleans, and I've seen its muddy
   bosom turn all golden in the sunset.

> 'The Negro Speaks of Rivers' (1921)

14 'It's powerful,' he said.
'What?'

'That one drop of Negro blood—because just *one* drop of black blood makes a man coloured. *One* drop—you are a Negro!'
Simple Takes a Wife (1953)

Ted Hughes 1930–98
English poet

1 Daylong this tomcat lies stretched flat
As an old rough mat, no mouth and no eyes,
Continual wars and wives are what
Have tattered his ears and battered his head.
'Esther's Tomcat' (1960)

2 It took the whole of Creation
To produce my foot, my each feather:
Now I hold Creation in my foot.
'Hawk Roosting' (1960)

3   I saw the horses:
Huge in the dense grey—ten together—
Megalith-still.
'The Horses' (1957)

4 Adam ate the apple.
Eve ate Adam.
The serpent ate Eve.
This is the dark intestine.
'Theology' (1967)

5 Grape is my mulatto mother
In this frozen whited country.
'Wino' (1967)

6 Christianity deposes Mother Nature and begets, on her prostrate body, Science, which proceeds to destroy Nature.
in *Your Environment* Summer 1970

7 Imagination isn't merely a surplus mental department meant for entertainment, but the most essential piece of machinery we have if we are going to live the lives of human beings.
in *Children's Literature in Education* March 1970

Josephine Hull ?1886–1957
American actress

8 Shakespeare is so tiring. You never get a chance to sit down unless you're a king.
in *Time* 16 November 1953

Hubert Humphrey 1911–78
American Democratic politician

9 There are not enough jails, not enough policemen, not enough courts to enforce a law not supported by the people.
speech at Williamsburg, 1 May 1965

10 Here we are the way politics ought to be in America, the politics of happiness, the politics of purpose and the politics of joy.
speech in Washington, 27 April 1968

Lord Hunt of Tanworth 1919–
British civil servant; Secretary of the Cabinet 1973–9

of British Cabinet government, described as 'a shambles':
11 It has got to be, so far as possible, a democratic and accountable shambles.
at a seminar at the Institute of Historical Research, 20 October 1993

Robert Hunter 1941–

12 The word *Greenpeace* had a ring to it—it conjured images of Eden; it said ecology and antiwar in two syllables; it fit easily into even a one-column headline.
Warriors of the Rainbow (1979); cf. **Darnell** 83:5

Herman Hupfeld 1894–1951
American songwriter

13 You must remember this, a kiss is still a kiss,
A sigh is just a sigh;
The fundamental things apply,
As time goes by.
'As Time Goes By' (1931 song)

Douglas Hurd 1930–
British Conservative politician; Foreign Secretary

14 Lord Rothschild roamed like a condottiere through Whitehall, laying an ambush here, there breaching some crumbling fortress which had outlived its

usefulness . . . He respected persons
occasionally but rarely policies.
of Lord **Rothschild** *as first Director of the Central
Policy Review Staff*
    An End to Promises (1979)

1 One of the principal props which have
allowed Britain to punch above its weight
in the world.
of American support for Nato
    speech at Chatham House; in *Financial Times* 4
    February 1993

Saddam Hussein 1937–

Iraqi statesman, President since 1979

2 The mother of battles.
*popular interpretation of his description of the
approaching Gulf War; in* The Times *7 January
1991 it was reported that he was ready for the
'mother of all wars'*
    speech in Baghdad, 6 January 1991

Aldous Huxley 1894–1963

English novelist

3 The sexophones wailed like melodious
cats under the moon.
    Brave New World (1932)

4 That men do not learn very much from
the lessons of history is the most
important of all the lessons that history
has to teach.
    Collected Essays (1959) 'Case of Voluntary
    Ignorance'

5 The proper study of mankind is books.
    Crome Yellow (1921); see below

    The proper study of mankind is man.
    Alexander Pope (1688–1744) *An Essay on Man*
    (1733)

6 The end cannot justify the means, for the
simple and obvious reason that the
means employed determine the nature of
the ends produced.
    Ends and Means (1937)

7 So long as men worship the Caesars and
Napoleons, Caesars and Napoleons will
duly arise and make them miserable.
    Ends and Means (1937)

8 It is far easier to write ten passably
effective sonnets, good enough to take in
the not too enquiring critic, than one

effective advertisement that will take in a
few thousand of the uncritical buying
public.
    On the Margin (1923) 'Advertisement'

9 There is no substitute for talent. Industry
and all the virtues are of no avail.
    Point Counter Point (1928)

10 Those who believe that they are
exclusively in the right are generally
those who achieve something.
    Proper Studies (1927) 'Note on Dogma'

11 Facts do not cease to exist because they
are ignored.
    Proper Studies (1927) 'Note on Dogma'

12 Most human beings have an almost
infinite capacity for taking things for
granted.
    Themes and Variations (1950) 'Variations on a
    Philosopher'

13 A million million spermatozoa,
All of them alive:
Out of their cataclysm but one poor Noah
Dare hope to survive.

And among that billion minus one
Might have chanced to be
Shakespeare, another Newton, a new
    Donne—
But the One was Me.
    'Fifth Philosopher's Song' (1920); see below

    And a thousand thousand slimy things
    Lived on; and so did I.
    Samuel Taylor Coleridge (1772–1834) 'The
    Rime of the Ancient Mariner' (1798) pt. 1

14 Beauty for some provides escape,
Who gain a happiness in eyeing
The gorgeous buttocks of the ape
Or Autumn sunsets exquisitely dying.
    'Ninth Philosopher's Song' (1920)

15 Even if I could be Shakespeare, I think I
should still choose to be Faraday.
    in 1925, attributed; Walter M. Elsasser
    Memoirs of a Physicist in the Atomic Age
    (1978)

Julian Huxley 1887–1975

English biologist

16 Operationally, God is beginning to
resemble not a ruler but the last fading
smile of a cosmic Cheshire cat.
    Religion without Revelation (1957 ed.)

Nicholas Hytner 1956–

English theatre and film director

1 If you gave him a good script, actors and technicians, Mickey Mouse could direct a movie.

in an interview, *Daily Telegraph* 24 February 1994, prior to the UK release of his film *The Crucible*

Dolores Ibarruri ('La Pasionaria') 1895–1989

Spanish Communist leader

2 It is better to die on your feet than to live on your knees.

speech in Paris, 3 September 1936; also attributed to Emiliano **Zapata**

3 *No pasarán.*
They shall not pass.

radio broadcast, Madrid, 19 July 1936; cf. **Sayings** 278:20

Ice Cube 1970–

American rap musician

4 If I'm more of an influence to your son as a rapper than you are as a father . . . you got to look at yourself as a parent.

to Mike Sager in *Rolling Stone* 4 October 1990

Ice-T 1958–

American rap musician

5 When they call you articulate, that's another way of saying 'He talks good for a black guy'.

in *Independent* 30 December 1995 'Interviews of the Year'

Francis Iles 1893–1970

English crime writer

6 It was not until several weeks after he had decided to murder his wife that Dr Bickleigh took any active steps in the matter. Murder is a serious business.

Malice Aforethought (1931)

Ivan Illich 1926–

American sociologist

7 In a consumer society there are inevitably two kinds of slaves: the prisoners of addiction and the prisoners of envy.

Tools for Conviviality (1973)

Mick Imlah 1956–

British poet

8 Oh, foolish boys!
The English elephant
Never lies!

'Tusking' (1988)

Gary Indiana

American writer

9 We used to say: How can we live like this? And now the question really is: How can we die like this?
of Aids

Horse Crazy (1989)

Charles Inge 1868–1957

10 This very remarkable man
Commends a most practical plan:
You can do what you want
If you don't think you can't,
So don't think you can't think you can.

'On Monsieur Coué' (1928); cf. **Coué** 77:11

Dean Inge 1860–1954

English writer; Dean of St. Paul's, 1911–34

11 The enemies of Freedom do not argue; they shout and they shoot.

End of an Age (1948)

12 The effect of boredom on a large scale in history is underestimated. It is a main cause of revolutions, and would soon bring to an end all the static Utopias and the farmyard civilization of the Fabians.

End of an Age (1948)

13 It takes in reality only one to make a quarrel. It is useless for the sheep to pass resolutions in favour of vegetarianism,

while the wolf remains of a different opinion.

> *Outspoken Essays: First Series* (1919) 'Patriotism'

1 The nations which have put mankind and posterity most in their debt have been small states—Israel, Athens, Florence, Elizabethan England.

> *Outspoken Essays: Second Series* (1922) 'State, visible and invisible'

2 A man may build himself a throne of bayonets, but he cannot sit on it.

> *Philosophy of Plotinus* (1923); cf. **Yeltsin** 339:11

3 The aim of education is the knowledge not of facts but of values.

> 'The Training of the Reason' in A. C. Benson (ed.) *Cambridge Essays on Education* (1917)

4 Literature flourishes best when it is half a trade and half an art.

> *Victorian Age* (Rede Lecture delivered at Cambridge, 1922)

Bernard Ingham 1932–

British journalist and public relations specialist, Chief Press Secretary to the Prime Minister, 1979–90

5 Many journalists have fallen for the conspiracy theory of government. I do assure you that they would produce more accurate work if they adhered to the cock-up theory.

> in *Observer* 17 March 1985 'Sayings of the Week'

6 Blood sport is brought to its ultimate refinement in the gossip columns.

> speech, 5 February 1986

7 The media, I tell pedants in the Government, is like an oil painting. Close up, it looks like nothing on earth. Stand back and you get the drift.

> speech to the Parliamentary Press Gallery, February 1990

Richard Ingrams 1937–

English satirical journalist, editor of *Private Eye*

8 My motto is publish and be sued.

> on BBC Radio 4, 4 May 1977

Eugène Ionesco 1912–94

Romanian-born French dramatist

9 A civil servant doesn't make jokes.

> *The Killer* (1958)

10 Living is abnormal.

> *The Rhinoceros* (1959)

11 You can only predict things after they have happened.

> *The Rhinoceros* (1959)

Weldon J. Irvine

12 Young, gifted and black.

> title of song (1969); cf. **Hansberry** 138:6

Christopher Isherwood 1904–86

English novelist
see also **Auden** 16:4

13 The common cormorant (or shag)
Lays eggs inside a paper bag,
You follow the idea, no doubt?
It's to keep the lightning out.

But what these unobservant birds
Have never thought of, is that herds
Of wandering bears might come with buns
And steal the bags to hold the crumbs.

> 'The Common Cormorant' (written *c.*1925)

14 I am a camera with its shutter open, quite passive, recording, not thinking.

> *Goodbye to Berlin* (1939) 'Berlin Diary' Autumn 1930

Hastings Lionel ('Pug') Ismay 1887–1965

British general and Secretary to the Committee of Imperial Defence; first Secretary-General of Nato

15 NATO exists for three reasons—to keep the Russians out, the Americans in and the Germans down.

> *to a group of British Conservative backbenchers in* 1949
>
> Peter Hennessy *Never Again* (1992); oral tradition

Alec Issigonis

British engineer

1 A camel is a horse designed by a
committee.
on his dislike of working in teams
   in *Guardian* 14 January 1991 'Notes and
   Queries'; attributed

Charles Ives 1874–1954

American composer

2 Beauty in music is too often confused
with something that lets the ears lie back
in an easy chair.
   Joseph Machlis *Introduction to Contemporary
   Music* (1963)

Alija Izetbegović 1925–

Bosnian statesman; President of Bosnia and
Herzegovina since 1990

3 And to my people I say, this may not be a
just peace, but it is more just than a
continuation of war.
*after signing the Dayton accord with
representatives of Serbia and Croatia*
   in Dayton, Ohio, 21 November 1995

Jesse Jackson 1941–

American Democratic politician and
clergyman

4 When I look out at this convention, I see
the face of America, red, yellow, brown,
black, and white. We are all precious in
God's sight—the real rainbow coalition.
   speech at Democratic National Convention,
   Atlanta, 19 July 1988

Michael Jackson 1958–

American pop singer

5 Before you judge me, try hard to love me,
look within your heart
Then ask,—have you seen my
childhood?
   'Childhood' (1995 song)

Robert H. Jackson 1892–1954

American lawyer and judge

6 That four great nations, flushed with
victory and stung with injury, stay the
hands of vengeance and voluntarily
submit their captive enemies to the
judgement of the law, is one of the most
significant tributes that Power has ever
paid to Reason.
*opening statement for the prosecution at
Nuremberg*
   before the International Military Tribunal in
   Nuremberg, 21 November 1945

Joe Jacobs 1896–1940

American boxing manager

7 We was robbed!
*after Jack Sharkey beat Max Schmeling (of whom
Jacobs was manager) in the heavyweight title
fight, 21 June 1932*
   P. Heller *In This Corner* (1975)

8 I should of stood in bed.
*after leaving his sick-bed to attend the World
Baseball Series in Detroit, 1935, and betting on
the losers*
   J. Lardner *Strong Cigars* (1951)

Mick Jagger 1943–
and Keith Richards 1943–

English rock musicians

9 Get off of my cloud.
   title of song (1966)

10 And though she's not really ill,
There's a little yellow pill:
She goes running for the shelter
Of a mother's little helper.
   'Mother's Little Helper' (1966 song)

11 I can't get no satisfaction
I can't get no girl reaction.
   '(I Can't Get No) Satisfaction' (1965 song)

12 Ev'rywhere I hear the sound of
   marching, charging feet, boy,
'Cause summer's here and the time is
   right for fighting in the street, boy.
   'Street Fighting Man' (1968 song)

13 There's just no place for a street fighting
man!
   'Street Fighting Man' (1968 song)

Clive James 1939–

Australian critic and writer

1 Television is simultaneously blamed, often by the same people, for worsening the world and for being powerless to change it.
  Glued to the Box (1981)

Henry James 1843–1916

American novelist
on James: see **Guedalla** 135:4, **Maugham** 210:2, **Wells** 323:3

2 The ever-importunate murmur, 'Dramatize it, dramatize it!'
  The Altar of the Dead (1909 ed.) preface

3 The note I wanted; that of the strange and sinister embroidered on the very type of the normal and easy.
  The Altar of the Dead (1909 ed.) preface

4 The Story is just the spoiled child of art.
  The Ambassadors (1909 ed.) preface

5 The terrible *fluidity of self-revelation*.
  The Ambassadors (1909 ed.) preface

6 Live all you can; it's a mistake not to. It doesn't so much matter what you do in particular, so long as you have your life. If you haven't had that, what *have* you had?
  The Ambassadors (1903)

7 The deep well of unconscious cerebration.
  The American (1909 ed.) preface

8 The historian, essentially, wants more documents than he can really use; the dramatist only wants more liberties than he can really take.
  The Aspern Papers (1909 ed.) preface

9 The house of fiction has in short not one window, but a million . . . but they are, singly or together, as nothing without the posted presence of the watcher.
  The Portrait of a Lady (1908 ed.) preface

10 Life being all inclusion and confusion, and art being all discrimination and selection.
  The Spoils of Poynton (1909 ed.) preface

11 I could come back to America . . . to die—but never, never to live.
  letter to Mrs William James, 1 April 1913

12 The war has used up words.
  in *New York Times* 21 March 1915

13 Of course, of course.
  on hearing that Rupert **Brooke** *had died on a Greek island*
  C. Hassall *Rupert Brooke* (1964)

14 So here it is at last, the distinguished thing!
  on experiencing his first stroke
  Edith Wharton *A Backward Glance* (1934)

15 Summer afternoon—summer afternoon . . . the two most beautiful words in the English language.
  Edith Wharton *A Backward Glance* (1934)

P. D. James 1920–

English crime writer

16 What the detective story is about is not murder but the restoration of order.
  in *Face* December 1986

17 I believe that political correctness can be a form of linguistic fascism, and it sends shivers down the spine of my generation who went to war against fascism.
  in *Paris Review* 1995

Randall Jarrell 1914–65

American poet

18 In bombers named for girls, we burned
  The cities we had learned about in
    school—
  Till our lives wore out; our bodies lay
    among
  The people we had killed and never seen.
  When we lasted long enough they gave
    us medals;
  When we died they said, 'Our casualties
    were low.'
  'Losses' (1963)

19 To Americans, English manners are far more frightening than none at all.
  Pictures from an Institution (1954)

20 It is better to entertain an idea than to take it home to live with you for the rest of your life.
  Pictures from an Institution (1954)

1 One of the most obvious facts about grown-ups, to a child, is that they have forgotten what it is like to be a child.
   introduction to Christina Stead *The Man Who Loved Children* (1965)

Antony Jay

see **Lynn**

Douglas Jay 1907–96

British Labour politician
see also **Political slogans** 251:10

2 In the case of nutrition and health, just as in the case of education, the gentleman in Whitehall really does know better what is good for people than the people know themselves.
   The Socialist Case (1939)

3 He never used one syllable where none would do.
   of **Attlee**
   Peter Hennessy *Muddling Through* (1996)

Marianne Jean-Baptiste

British actress

4 The old men running the industry just have not got a clue . . . Britain is no longer totally a white place where people ride horses, wear long frocks and drink tea. The national dish is no longer fish and chips, it's curry.
   having been excluded from the group of actors invited to promote British talent at Cannes
   in *Observer* 18 May 1997 'Soundbites'

James Jeans 1877–1946

English astronomer, physicist, and mathematician

5 Taking a very gloomy view of the future of the human race, let us suppose that it can only expect to survive for two thousand million years longer, a period about equal to the past age of the earth. Then, regarded as a being destined to live for three-score years and ten, humanity, although it has been born in a house seventy years old, is itself only three days old.
   Eos (1928)

6 If we assume that the last breath of, say, Julius Caesar has by now become thoroughly scattered through the atmosphere, then the chances are that each of us inhales one molecule of it with every breath we take.
   now usually quoted as the 'dying breath of Socrates'
   An Introduction to the Kinetic Theory of Gases (1940)

7 Life exists in the universe only because the carbon atom possesses certain exceptional properties.
   The Mysterious Universe (1930)

8 From the intrinsic evidence of his creation, the Great Architect of the Universe now begins to appear as a pure mathematician.
   The Mysterious Universe (1930)

Patrick Jenkin 1926–

British Conservative politician

9 People can clean their teeth in the dark, use the top of the stove instead of the oven, all sorts of savings, but they must use less electricity.
   as Minister for Energy, asking the public to save electricity as a miners' strike reduced supplies; often summarized as, 'clean your teeth in the dark'
   radio broadcast, 15 January 1974

David Jenkins 1925–

English theologian; Bishop of Durham from 1984

10 The withdrawal of an imported, elderly American to leave a reconciling opportunity for some local product is surely neither dishonourable nor improper.
   referring to Ian **MacGregor**, *Chairman of the National Coal Board*
   in *The Times* 22 September 1984

11 I am not clear that God manoeuvres physical things . . . After all, a conjuring trick with bones only proves that it is as clever as a conjuring trick with bones.
   on the Resurrection
   in 'Poles Apart' (BBC radio, 4 October 1984)

Roy Jenkins 1920–

British politician; co-founder of the Social Democratic Party, 1981

1 There is nobody in politics I can remember and no case I can think of in history where a man combined such a powerful political personality with so little intelligence.
of James **Callaghan**
    Richard Crossman diary, 5 September 1969

2 He simply stopped the engine in its tracks, lifted it up, and put it back facing in the other direction.
of Ernest **Bevin** *changing the course of a Cabinet meeting*
    Roy Jenkins *Nine Men of Power* (1974)

3 The politics of the left and centre of this country are frozen in an out-of-date mould which is bad for the political and economic health of Britain and increasingly inhibiting for those who live within the mould. Can it be broken?
    speech to Parliamentary Press Gallery, 9 June 1980

4 A dead or dying beast lying across a railway line and preventing other trains from getting through.
of the Labour Party
    in *Guardian* 16 May 1987

5 A First Minister whose self-righteous stubbornness has not been equalled, save briefly by Neville Chamberlain, since Lord North.
of Margaret **Thatcher**
    in *Observer* 11 March 1990

6 A great lighthouse which stands there, flashing out beams of light, indifferent to the waves which beat against him.
of Edward **Heath**
    in *Independent* 22 September 1990

7 Nearly all Prime Ministers are dissatisfied with their successors, perhaps even more so if they come from their own party.
    Gladstone (1995)

Elizabeth Jennings 1926–

English poet

8 I hate a word like 'pets': it sounds so much

Like something with no living of its own.
    'My Animals' (1966)

Paul Jennings 1918–89

English writer

9 Resistentialism is concerned with what Things think about men.
    Even Oddlier (1952) 'Developments in Resistentialism'

C. E. M. Joad 1891–1953

English philosopher
see also **Catch-phrases** 58:13

10 It will be said of this generation that it found England a land of beauty and left it a land of 'beauty spots'.
    The Horrors of the Countryside (1931)

John XXIII 1881–1963

Italian cleric, Pope from 1958

11 If civil authorities legislate for or allow anything that is contrary to that order and therefore contrary to the will of God, neither the laws made or the authorizations granted can be binding on the consciences of the citizens, since God has more right to be obeyed than man.
    Pacem in Terris (1963)

12 The social progress, order, security and peace of each country are necessarily connected with the social progress, order, security and peace of all other countries.
    Pacem in Terris (1963)

13 Anybody can be pope; the proof of this is that I have become one.
    Henri Fesquet *Wit and Wisdom of Good Pope John* (1964)

14 I want to throw open the windows of the Church so that we can see out and the people can see in.
    attributed

15 Signora, do you believe my blessing cannot pass through plastic?
to a pilgrim who asked him to bless again some medals and rosaries which he had blessed before she had time to remove them from her purse, 1959
    Laureano López Rodó *Memorias* (1990)

Elton John 1947–
and Bernie Taupin 1950–

English pop singer and songwriter;
songwriter

1 It seems to me you lived your life
Like a candle in the wind.
Never knowing who to cling to
When the rain set in.
And I would have liked to have known
    you
But I was just a kid
The candle burned out long before
Your legend ever did.

Goodbye Norma Jean.
of Marilyn Monroe
    'Candle in the Wind' (song, 1973)

2 Even when you died
Oh the press still hounded you.
    'Candle in the Wind' (song, 1973)

3 Goodbye England's rose;
May you ever grow in our hearts.
*rewritten for and sung at the funeral of Diana,
Princess of Wales, 7 September 1997*
    'Candle in the Wind' (song, revised version,
    1997)

4 And it seems to me you lived your life
Like a candle in the wind:
Never fading with the sunset
When the rain set in.
And your footsteps will always fall here
On England's greenest hills;
Your candle's burned out long before
Your legend ever will.
    'Candle in the Wind' (song, revised version,
    1997)

5 Goodbye yellow brick road.
    title of song (1973); cf. **Harburg** 138:13

6 It's the only song I've ever written where
I get goose bumps every time I play it.
of 'Candle in the Wind'
    in *Daily Telegraph* 9 September 1997

John Paul II 1920–

Polish cleric, Pope since 1978

7 It would be simplistic to say that Divine
Providence caused the fall of
communism. It fell by itself as a
consequence of its own mistakes and
abuses. It fell by itself because of its own
inherent weaknesses.
*when asked by the Italian writer Vittorio Missori if
the fall of the USSR could be ascribed to God*
    Carl Bernstein and Marco Politi *His Holiness:
    John Paul II and the Hidden History of our Time*
    (1996)

Lyndon Baines Johnson
1908–73

American Democratic statesman, 36th
President of the US, 1963–9
on Johnson: see **Political slogans** 251:2,
251:11, **White** 326:10

*to a reporter who had queried his embracing
Richard Nixon on the vice-president's return from
a controversial tour of South America in 1958:*
8 Son, in politics you've got to learn that
overnight chicken shit can turn to
chicken salad.
    Fawn Brodie *Richard Nixon* (1983)

9 I am a free man, an American, a United
States Senator, and a Democrat, in that
order.
    in *Texas Quarterly* Winter 1958

10 I'll tell you what's at the bottom of it. If
you can convince the lowest white man
that he's better than the best coloured
man, he won't notice you're picking his
pocket. Hell, give him someone to look
down on and he'll empty his pockets for
you.
*during the 1960 Presidential campaign, to Bill
Moyers*
    Robert Dallek *Lone Star Rising* (1991)

11 All I have I would have given gladly not
to be standing here today.
following the assassination of J. F. Kennedy
    first speech to Congress as President, 27
    November 1963

12 We have talked long enough in this
country about equal rights. We have
talked for a hundred years or more. It is
time now to write the next chapter, and
to write it in the books of law.
    speech to Congress, 27 November 1963

13 We hope that the world will not narrow
into a neighbourhood before it has
broadened into a brotherhood.
    speech at the lighting of the Nation's
    Christmas Tree, 22 December 1963

1 This administration today, here and now declares unconditional war on poverty in America.

> State of the Union address to Congress, 8 January 1964

2 In your time we have the opportunity to move not only toward the rich society and the powerful society, but upward to the Great Society.

> speech at University of Michigan, 22 May 1964

3 We Americans know, although others appear to forget, the risks of spreading conflict. We still seek no wider war.

> speech on radio and television, 4 August 1964

4 We are not about to send American boys 9 or 10,000 miles away from home to do what Asian boys ought to be doing for themselves.

> speech at Akron University, 21 October 1964; cf. **Roosevelt** 267:12

5 Extremism in the pursuit of the Presidency is an unpardonable vice. Moderation in the affairs of the nation is the highest virtue.

> speech in New York, 31 October 1964

6 A President's hardest task is not to *do* what is right, but to *know* what is right.

> State of the Union address to Congress, 4 January 1965

7 Better to have him inside the tent pissing out, than outside pissing in.

> *of J. Edgar Hoover*
>> D. Halberstam *The Best and the Brightest* (1972)

8 Did you ever think that making a speech on economics is a lot like pissing down your leg? It seems hot to you, but it never does to anyone else.

> *to J. K. Galbraith*
>> J. K. Galbraith *A Life in Our Times* (1981)

9 I don't want loyalty. I want *loyalty*. I want him to kiss my ass in Macy's window at high noon and tell me it smells like roses. I want his pecker in my pocket.

> *discussing a prospective assistant*
>> D. Halberstam *The Best and the Brightest* (1972)

10 So dumb he can't fart and chew gum at the same time.

> *of Gerald* **Ford**
>> R. Reeves *A Ford, not a Lincoln* (1975)

Philander Chase Johnson
1866–1939
American journalist

11 Cheer up! the worst is yet to come!

> in *Everybody's Magazine* May 1920

Philip Johnson 1906–
American architect

12 Architecture is the art of how to waste space.

> in *New York Times* 27 December 1964

Hanns Johst 1890–1978
German dramatist

13 Whenever I hear the word culture . . . I release the safety-catch of my Browning!

> *often attributed to Hermann* **Goering**, *and quoted 'Whenever I hear the word culture, I reach for my pistol!'*
>> *Schlageter* (1933)

Al Jolson 1886–1950
American singer

14 You think that's noise—you ain't heard nuttin' yet!

> *first said in a café, competing with the din from a neighbouring building site, in 1906; subsequently an aside in the 1927 film* The Jazz Singer
>> M. Abramson *Real Story of Al Jolson* (1950); also the title of a Jolson song, 1919, 'You Ain't Heard Nothing Yet'

Steve Jones 1944–
English geneticist

15 Sex and taxes are in many ways the same. Tax does to cash what males do to genes. It dispenses assets among the population as a whole. Sex, not death, is the great leveller.

> speech to the Royal Society; in *Independent* 25 January 1997

Erica Jong 1942–

American writer

1 The zipless fuck is the purest thing there
is. And it is rarer than the unicorn. And I
have never had one.

  Fear of Flying (1973)

Janis Joplin 1943–70

American singer

2 Oh, Lord, won't you buy me a Mercedes
  Benz
My friends all drive Porsches,
I must make amends.

  'Mercedes Benz' (1970 song)

3 Fourteen heart attacks and he had to die
in my week. In MY week.

  *when ex-President **Eisenhower**'s death prevented
  her photograph appearing on the cover of
  Newsweek*

  in *New Musical Express* 12 April 1969

Jenny Joseph 1932–

English poet

4 When I am an old woman I shall wear
  purple
With a red hat which doesn't go, and
  doesn't suit me.
And I shall spend my pension on brandy
  and summer gloves
And satin sandals, and say we've got no
  money for butter.

  'Warning' (1974)

James Joyce 1882–1941

Irish novelist
*on Joyce: see **Forster** 116:2, **Lawrence**
184:15, **Woolf** 335:13*

5 His soul swooned slowly as he heard the
snow falling faintly through the universe
and faintly falling, like the descent of
their last end, upon all the living and the
dead.

  Dubliners (1914) 'The Dead'

6 riverrun, past Eve and Adam's, from
swerve of shore to bend of bay, brings us
by a commodious vicus of recirculation
back to Howth Castle and Environs.

  Finnegans Wake (1939)

7 That ideal reader suffering from an ideal
insomnia.

  Finnegans Wake (1939)

8 The flushpots of Euston and the hanging
garments of Marylebone.

  Finnegans Wake (1939)

9 All moanday, tearsday, wailsday,
thumpsday, frightday, shatterday till the
fear of the Law.

  Finnegans Wake (1939)

10 Three quarks for Muster Mark!

  Finnegans Wake (1939)

11 A portrait of the artist as a young man.

  title of novel, 1916

12 Once upon a time and a very good time it
was there was a moocow coming down
along the road and this moocow that was
down along the road met a nicens little
boy named baby tuckoo.

  A Portrait of the Artist as a Young Man (1916)

13 When the soul of a man is born in this
country, there are nets flung at it to hold
it back from flight. You talk to me of
nationality, language, religion. I shall try
to fly by those nets.

  A Portrait of the Artist as a Young Man (1916)

14 Ireland is the old sow that eats her
farrow.

  A Portrait of the Artist as a Young Man (1916)

15 Pity is the feeling which arrests the mind
in the presence of whatsoever is grave
and constant in human sufferings and
unites it with the human sufferer. Terror
is the feeling which arrests the mind in
the presence of whatsoever is grave and
constant in human sufferings and unites
it with the secret cause.

  A Portrait of the Artist as a Young Man (1916)

16 The artist, like the God of the creation,
remains within or behind or beyond or
above his handiwork, invisible, refined

out of existence, indifferent, paring his fingernails.

A Portrait of the Artist as a Young Man (1916)

1 I will not serve that in which I no longer believe whether it call itself my home, my fatherland or my church: and I will try to express myself in some mode of life or art as freely as I can and as wholly as I can, using for my defence the only arms I allow myself to use, silence, exile, and cunning.

A Portrait of the Artist as a Young Man (1916)

2 By an epiphany he meant a sudden spiritual manifestation, whether in vulgarity of speech or of gesture or in a memorable phase of the mind itself.

Stephen Hero (1944)

3 The snotgreen sea. The scrotumtightening sea.

Ulysses (1922)

4 It is a symbol of Irish art. The cracked lookingglass of a servant.

Ulysses (1922)

5 I fear those big words, Stephen said, which make us so unhappy.

Ulysses (1922)

6 History, Stephen said, is a nightmare from which I am trying to awake.

Ulysses (1922)

7 Lawn Tennyson, gentleman poet.

Ulysses (1922)

8 [He] saw the dark tangled curls of his bush floating, floating hair of the stream around the limp father of thousands.

Ulysses (1922)

9 Plenty to see and hear and feel yet. Feel live warm beings near you . . . Warm beds: warm full blooded life.

Ulysses (1922)

10 A man of genius makes no mistakes. His errors are volitional and are the portals of discovery.

Ulysses (1922)

11 Greater love than this, he said, no man hath that a man lay down his wife for his friend.

Ulysses (1922); see below

Greater love hath no man than this, that a man lay down his life for his friends.

Bible St John; cf. **Thorpe** 309:7

12 The heaventree of stars hung with humid nightblue fruit.

Ulysses (1922)

13 When a young man came up to him in Zurich and said, 'May I kiss the hand that wrote *Ulysses?*' Joyce replied, somewhat like King Lear, 'No, it did lots of other things too.'

Richard Ellmann *James Joyce* (1959); see below

GLOUCESTER: O! let me kiss that hand!
LEAR: Let me wipe it first; it smells of mortality.

William Shakespeare (1564–1616) *King Lear* (1605–6)

14 A writer should never write about the extraordinary. That is for the journalist.

letter to Djuna Barnes; Richard Ellman *James Joyce* (1959)

William Joyce (Lord Haw-Haw) 1906–46

wartime broadcaster from Nazi Germany, executed for treason

15 Germany calling! Germany calling!

habitual introduction to propaganda broadcasts to Britain during the Second World War

Juan Carlos I 1938–

King of Spain from 1975

16 The Crown, the symbol of the permanence and unity of Spain, cannot tolerate any actions by people attempting to disrupt by force the democratic process.

on the occasion of the attempted coup in 1981
television broadcast at 1.15 a.m., 24 February 1981

17 I will neither abdicate the Crown nor leave Spain. Whoever rebels will provoke a new civil war and will be responsible.

on the occasion of the attempted coup
television broadcast, 24 February 1981

Jack Judge 1878–1938 and Harry Williams 1874–1924

British songwriters

1 It's a long way to Tipperary,
It's a long way to go;
It's a long way to Tipperary,
To the sweetest girl I know!

'It's a Long Way to Tipperary' (1912 song)

Carl Gustav Jung 1875–1961

Swiss psychologist

2 A man who has not passed through the inferno of his passions has never overcome them.

Memories, Dreams, Reflections (1962)

3 As far as we can discern, the sole purpose of human existence is to kindle a light in the darkness of mere being.

Memories, Dreams, Reflections (1962)

4 Every form of addiction is bad, no matter whether the narcotic be alcohol or morphine or idealism.

Memories, Dreams, Reflections (1962)

5 The meeting of two personalities is like the contact of two chemical substances: if there is any reaction, both are transformed.

Modern Man in Search of a Soul (1933)

6 The afternoon of human life must also have a significance of its own and cannot be merely a pitiful appendage to life's morning.

The Stages of Life (1930)

7 Where love rules, there is no will to power, and where power predominates, love is lacking. The one is the shadow of the other.

'Über die Psychologie des Unbewussten' (1917)

8 If there is anything that we wish to change in the child, we should first examine it and see whether it is not something that could better be changed in ourselves.

'Vom Werden der Persönlichkeit' (1932)

9 I do not believe . . . I know.

L. van der Post *Jung and the Story of our Time* (1976)

John Junor 1919–97

British journalist and editor
see also **Catch-phrases** 59:4

10 Such a graceful exit. And then he had to go and do this on the doorstep.

on Harold **Wilson**'s *'Lavender List'* (the honours list he drew up on resigning the British premiership in 1976)

in *Observer* 23 January 1990

Donald Justice 1925–

American poet

11 Men at forty
Learn to close softly
The doors to rooms they will not be
Coming back to.

'Men at Forty' (1967)

Pauline Kael 1919–

American film critic

12 The words 'Kiss Kiss Bang Bang' which I saw on an Italian movie poster, are perhaps the briefest statement imaginable of the basic appeal of movies.

Kiss Kiss Bang Bang (1968) 'Note on the Title'

Franz Kafka 1883–1924

Czech novelist

13 When Gregor Samsa awoke one morning from uneasy dreams he found himself transformed in his bed into a gigantic insect.

The Metamorphosis (1915)

14 You may object that it is not a trial at all; you are quite right, for it is only a trial if I recognize it as such.

The Trial (1925)

15 It's often better to be in chains than to be free.

The Trial (1925)

Gus Kahn 1886–1941 and Raymond B. Egan 1890–1952

American songwriters

16 There's nothing surer,
The rich get rich and the poor get children.

In the meantime, in between time,
Ain't we got fun.
'Ain't We Got Fun' (1921 song)

George S. Kaufman
1889–1961
American dramatist
see also **Film lines** 110:16, **Hart** 141:11

1 Satire is what closes Saturday night.
Scott Meredith *George S. Kaufman and his Friends* (1974)

Gerald Kaufman 1930–
British Labour politician

2 The longest suicide note in history.
on the Labour Party manifesto New Hope for Britain *(1983)*
Denis Healey *The Time of My Life* (1989)

3 We would prefer to see the House run by a philistine with the requisite financial acumen than by the succession of opera and ballet lovers who have brought a great and valuable institution to its knees.
report of the Commons' Culture, Media and Sport select committee on Covent Garden, 3 December 1997

Paul Kaufman and Mike Anthony
American songwriters

4 Poetry in motion.
title of song (1960)

Kenneth Kaunda 1924–
Zambian statesman, President 1964–91

5 Westerners have aggressive problem-solving minds; Africans experience people.
attributed, 1990

Patrick Kavanagh 1904–67
Irish poet

6 Cassiopeia was over
Cassidy's hanging hill,

I looked and three whin bushes rode across
The horizon—the Three Wise Kings.
'A Christmas Childhood' (1947)

7 Clay is the word and clay is the flesh
Where the potato-gatherers like mechanized scarecrows move
Along the side-fall of the hill—Maguire and his men.
'The Great Hunger' (1947)

8 That was how his life happened.
No mad hooves galloping in the sky,
But the weak, washy way of true tragedy—
A sick horse nosing around the meadow for a clean place to die.
'The Great Hunger' (1947)

9 I hate what every poet hates in spite
Of all the solemn talk of contemplation.
Oh, Alexander Selkirk knew the plight
Of being king and government and nation.
A road, a mile of kingdom, I am king
Of banks and stones and every blooming thing.
'Inniskeen Road: July Evening' (1936); see below

I am monarch of all I survey . . .
Better dwell in the midst of alarms,
Than reign in this horrible place.
William Cowper (1731–1800) 'Verses Supposed to be Written by Alexander Selkirk' (1782)

Danny Kaye
see **Film lines** 111:13

Paul Keating 1944–
Australian Labor statesman, Prime Minister 1991–6

10 You look like an Easter Island statue with an arse full of razor blades.
in the Australian Parliament to the then Prime Minister, Malcolm Fraser, 1983
Michael Gordon *A Question of Leadership* (1993)

11 Even as it [Great Britain] walked out on you and joined the Common Market, you were still looking for your MBEs and your knighthoods, and all the rest of the

regalia that comes with it. You would take Australia right back down the time tunnel to the cultural cringe where you have always come from.

addressing Australian Conservative supporters of Great Britain

speech, House of Representatives (Australia) 27 February 1992; cf. **Phillips** 248:9

1 I'm a bastard. But I'm a bastard who gets the mail through. And they appreciate that.

in 1994, to a senior colleague

in *Sunday Telegraph* 20 November 1994

2 Leadership is not about being nice. It's about being right and being strong.

in *Time* 9 January 1995

John Keats 1920–

3 The automobile changed our dress, manners, social customs, vacation habits, the shape of our cities, consumer purchasing patterns, common tastes and positions in intercourse.

The Insolent Chariots (1958)

Garrison Keillor 1942–

American humorous writer and broadcaster

4 Years ago, manhood was an opportunity for achievement, and now it is a problem to be overcome.

The Book of Guys (1994)

5 Ronald Reagan, the President who never told bad news to the American people.

We Are Still Married (1989)

Helen Keller 1880–1968

American writer and social reformer

6 Science may have found a cure for most evils; but it has found no remedy for the worst of them all—the apathy of human beings.

My Religion (1927)

Jaan Kenbrovin and William Kellette

7 I'm forever blowing bubbles.

title of song (1919)

Florynce Kennedy 1916–

American lawyer

8 If men could get pregnant, abortion would be a sacrament.

in *Ms.* March 1973

James B. Kennedy and John W. Bratton

British songwriters

9 If you go down in the woods today
You're sure of a big surprise
If you go down in the woods today
You'd better go in disguise
For every Bear that ever there was
Will gather there for certain because,
Today's the day the Teddy Bears have their Picnic.

'Teddy Bear's Picnic' (1932 song)

Jimmy Kennedy 1902–84 and Michael Carr 1904–68

British songwriters

10 We're gonna hang out the washing on the Siegfried Line.

title of song (1939)

John Fitzgerald Kennedy 1917–63

American Democratic statesman, 35th President of the US, 1961–3; son of Joseph and Rose **Kennedy**, brother of Robert **Kennedy**, and first husband of Jacqueline Kennedy **Onassis**

on Kennedy: see **Bentsen** 32:7, **Kennedy** 170:1

11 Don't buy a single vote more than necessary. I'll be damned if I'm going to pay for a landslide.

telegraphed message from his father, read at a Gridiron dinner in Washington, 15 March 1958, and almost certainly JFK's invention; in J. F. Cutler *Honey Fitz* (1962)

1 We stand today on the edge of a new frontier.

> speech accepting the Democratic nomination, 15 July 1960

2 The torch has been passed to a new generation of Americans—born in this century, tempered by war, disciplined by a hard and bitter peace.

> inaugural address, 20 January 1961

3 We shall pay any price, bear any burden, meet any hardship, support any friend, oppose any foe to assure the survival and the success of liberty.

> inaugural address, 20 January 1961

4 If a free society cannot help the many who are poor, it cannot save the few who are rich.

> inaugural address, 20 January 1961

5 Let us never negotiate out of fear. But let us never fear to negotiate.

> inaugural address, 20 January 1961

6 All this will not be finished in the first 100 days. Nor will it be finished in the first 1,000 days, nor in the life of this Administration, nor even perhaps in our lifetime on this planet. But let us begin.

> inaugural address, 20 January 1961

7 And so, my fellow Americans: ask not what your country can do for you—ask what you can do for your country.

> inaugural address, 20 January 1961; cf. **Gibran** 127:10

8 I believe that this Nation should commit itself to achieving the goal, before this decade is out, of landing a man on the Moon and returning him safely to earth.

> Supplementary State of the Union message to Congress, 25 May 1961

9 Mankind must put an end to war or war will put an end to mankind.

> speech to United Nations General Assembly, 25 September 1961

10 Those who make peaceful revolution impossible will make violent revolution inevitable.

> speech at the White House, 13 March 1962

11 Probably the greatest concentration of talent and genius in this house except for perhaps those times when Thomas Jefferson ate alone.

> *of a dinner for Nobel Prizewinners at the White House*
>
> > in *New York Times* 30 April 1962

12 There are no 'white' or 'coloured' signs on the foxholes or graveyards of battle.

> *on proposed Civil Rights Bill*
>
> > message to Congress, 19 June 1963

13 *Ich bin ein Berliner.*

I am a Berliner.

> speech in West Berlin, 26 June 1963

14 When power leads man toward arrogance, poetry reminds him of his limitations. When power narrows the areas of man's concern, poetry reminds him of the richness and diversity of his existence. When power corrupts, poetry cleanses. For art establishes the basic human truths which must serve as the touchstone of our judgement.

> speech at Amherst College, Mass., 26 October 1963

15 In free society art is not a weapon . . . Artists are not engineers of the soul.

> speech at Amherst College, Mass., 26 October 1963; cf. **Gorky** 131:1

16 It was involuntary. They sank my boat.

> *on being asked how he became a war hero*
>
> > A. M. Schlesinger Jr. *A Thousand Days* (1965)

17 Washington is a city of southern efficiency and northern charm.

> Arthur M. Schlesinger Jr. *A Thousand Days* (1965)

Joseph P. Kennedy 1888–1969

American financier and diplomat; husband of Rose **Kennedy,** father of John Fitzgerald and Robert **Kennedy**
see also **Sayings and slogans** 279:14

18 This is a hell of a long way from East Boston.

> *to his wife Rose, on a visit to Windsor Castle two weeks after his arrival as Ambassador*
>
> > in *The Times* 24 January 1995 (obituary of Rose Kennedy)

1 We're going to sell Jack like soapflakes.

when his son John made his bid for the Presidency

John H. Davis *The Kennedy Clan* (1984)

Robert Kennedy 1925–68

American Democratic politician, son of Joseph and Rose **Kennedy**, brother of John Fitzgerald **Kennedy**

2 One-fifth of the people are against everything all the time.

speech, University of Pennsylvania, 6 May 1964

Rose Kennedy 1890–1995

wife of Joseph **Kennedy**, mother of John Fitzgerald and Robert **Kennedy**

3 It's our money, and we're free to spend it any way we please . . . If you have money you spend it, and win.

in response to criticism of overlavish funding of her son Robert's 1968 presidential campaign

in *Daily Telegraph* 24 January 1995 (obituary)

4 I would much rather be known as the mother of a great son than the author of a great book or the painter of a great masterpiece.

in *Daily Telegraph* 24 January 1995 (obituary); attributed

5 Now Teddy must run.

*to her daughter, on hearing of the assassination of Robert **Kennedy***

in *The Times* 24 January 1995 (obituary); attributed, perhaps apocryphal

Jomo Kenyatta 1891–1978

Kenyan statesman, Prime Minister of Kenya 1963 and President 1964–78

6 The African is conditioned, by the cultural and social institutions of centuries, to a freedom of which Europe has little conception, and it is not in his nature to accept serfdom forever. He realizes that he must fight unceasingly for his own emancipation; for without this he is doomed to remain the prey of rival imperialisms.

Facing Mount Kenya (1938); conclusion

Jack Kerouac 1922–69

Amerian novelist

*on Kerouac: see **Burroughs** 49:9*

7 The beat generation.

phrase coined in the course of a conversation; in *Playboy* June 1959

8 It is not my fault that certain so-called bohemian elements have found in my writings something to hang their peculiar beatnik theories on.

in *New York Journal-American* 8 December 1960

Jean Kerr 1923–

American writer

9 I feel about airplanes the way I feel about diets. It seems to me that they are wonderful things for other people to go on.

The Snake Has All the Lines (1958)

John Maynard Keynes
1883–1946

English economist

10 I work for a Government I despise for ends I think criminal.

letter to Duncan Grant, 15 December 1917

11 Lenin was right. There is no subtler, no surer means of overturning the existing basis of society than to debauch the currency.

Economic Consequences of the Peace (1919)

12 I do not know which makes a man more conservative—to know nothing but the present, or nothing but the past.

The End of Laissez-Faire (1926)

13 The important thing for Government is not to do things which individuals are doing already, and to do them a little better or a little worse; but to do those things which at present are not done at all.

The End of Laissez-Faire (1926)

14 This extraordinary figure of our time, this syren, this goat-footed bard, this half-human visitor to our age from the hag-ridden magic and enchanted woods of Celtic antiquity.

Essays in Biography (1933) 'Mr Lloyd George'

1 If the Treasury were to fill old bottles with banknotes, bury them at suitable depths in disused coalmines which are then filled up to the surface with town rubbish, and leave it to private enterprise on well-tried principles of *laissez-faire* to dig the notes up again . . . there need be no more unemployment and, with the help of the repercussions, the real income of the community, and its capital wealth also, would probably become a good deal greater than it actually is.

General Theory (1936)

2 Practical men, who believe themselves to be quite exempt from any intellectual influences, are usually the slaves of some defunct economist. Madmen in authority, who hear voices in the air, are distilling their frenzy from some academic scribbler of a few years back.

General Theory (1947 ed.)

3 *In the long run* we are all dead.

A Tract on Monetary Reform (1923)

4 I evidently knew more about economics than my examiners.

explaining why he performed badly in the Civil Service examinations

Roy Harrod *Life of John Maynard Keynes* (1951)

5 LADY VIOLET BONHAM-CARTER: What do you think happens to Mr Lloyd George when he is alone in the room?
KEYNES: When he is alone in the room there is nobody there.

Lady Violet Bonham-Carter *Impact of Personality in Politics* (Romanes Lecture, 1963)

6 We threw good housekeeping to the winds. But we saved ourselves and helped save the world.

of Britain in the Second World War

A. J. P. Taylor *English History, 1914–1945* (1965)

Ruhollah Khomeini 1900–89

Iranian Shiite Muslim leader

7 I would like to inform all the intrepid Muslims in the world that the author of the book entitled *The Satanic Verses*, which has been compiled, printed and

published in opposition to Islam, the Prophet and the Qur'an, as well as those publishers who were aware of its contents, have been declared *madhur el dam* [those whose blood must be shed]. I call on all zealous Muslims to execute them quickly, wherever they find them, so that no-one will dare to insult Islam again. Whoever is killed in this path will be regarded as a martyr.

fatwa against Salman **Rushdie**, *issued 14 February 1989; in Malise Ruthven A Satanic Affair (1990); cf.* **Wesker** *323:17*

Nikita Khrushchev 1894–1971

Soviet statesman; Premier, 1958–64
on Khrushchev: see **Epstein** *104:5*

8 If anyone believes that our smiles involve abandonment of the teaching of Marx, Engels and Lenin he deceives himself. Those who wait for that must wait until a shrimp learns to whistle.

speech in Moscow, 17 September 1955

9 Comrades! We must abolish the cult of the individual decisively, once and for all.

speech to secret session of 20th Congress of the Communist Party, 25 February 1956

10 If you don't like us, don't accept our invitations and don't invite us to come to see you. Whether you like it or not, history is on our side. We will bury you.

speech to Western diplomats in Moscow, 18 November 1956

11 If one cannot catch the bird of paradise, better take a wet hen.

in *Time* 6 January 1958

12 If you start throwing hedgehogs under me, I shall throw a couple of porcupines under you.

in *New York Times* 7 November 1963

Joyce Kilmer 1886–1918

American poet

13 I think that I shall never see
A poem lovely as a tree.

'Trees' (1914)

14 Poems are made by fools like me,
But only God can make a tree.

'Trees' (1914)

Lord Kilmuir (David Maxwell Fyfe) 1900–67

British Conservative politician and lawyer

1 Loyalty is the Tory's secret weapon.
   Anthony Sampson *Anatomy of Britain* (1962)

Martin Luther King 1929–68

American civil rights leader
see also: **Epitaphs** 105:3

2 I want to be the white man's brother, not his brother-in-law.
   in *New York Journal-American* 10 September 1962

3 Injustice anywhere is a threat to justice everywhere.
   letter from Birmingham Jail, Alabama, 16 April 1963

4 The Negro's great stumbling block in the stride toward freedom is not the White Citizens Councillor or the Ku Klux Klanner but the white moderate who is more devoted to order than to justice; who prefers a negative peace which is the absence of tension to a positive peace which is the presence of justice.
   letter from Birmingham Jail, Alabama, 16 April 1963

5 If a man hasn't discovered something he will die for, he isn't fit to live.
   speech in Detroit, 23 June 1963

6 I have a dream that one day on the red hills of Georgia the sons of former slaves and the sons of former slave owners will be able to sit down together at the table of brotherhood.
   speech at Civil Rights March in Washington, 28 August 1963

7 I have a dream that my four little children will one day live in a nation where they will not be judged by the colour of their skin but by the content of their character.
   speech at Civil Rights March in Washington, 28 August 1963

8 We must learn to live together as brothers or perish together as fools.
   speech at St Louis, 22 March 1964

9 I just want to do God's will. And he's allowed me to go up to the mountain. And I've looked over, and I've seen the promised land . . . So I'm happy tonight. I'm not worried about anything. I'm not fearing any man.
   on the day before his assassination
   speech in Memphis, 3 April 1968

10 Nothing in all the world is more dangerous than sincere ignorance and conscientious stupidity.
   Strength to Love (1963)

11 The means by which we live have outdistanced the ends for which we live. Our scientific power has outrun our spiritual power. We have guided missiles and misguided men.
   Strength to Love (1963)

12 A riot is at bottom the language of the unheard.
   Where Do We Go From Here? (1967)

Stephen King 1947–

American writer

13 Terror . . . often arises from a pervasive sense of disestablishment; that things are in the unmaking.
   Danse Macabre (1981)

William Lyon Mackenzie King 1874–1950

Canadian Liberal statesman, Prime Minister 1921–6, 1926–30, and 1935–48

14 If some countries have too much history, we have too much geography.
   speech, Canadian House of Commons, 18 June 1936

15 Not necessarily conscription, but conscription if necessary.
   speech, Canadian House of Commons, 7 July 1942

Hugh Kingsmill 1889–1949

English man of letters

16 What still alive at twenty-two,
   A clean upstanding chap like you?
   Sure, if your throat 'tis hard to slit,

Slit your girl's, and swing for it.
'Two Poems, after A. E. Housman' (1933) no. 1

1 But bacon's not the only thing
That's cured by hanging from a string.
'Two Poems, after A. E. Housman' (1933) no. 1

2 God's apology for relations.
of friends
Michael Holroyd *The Best of Hugh Kingsmill* (1970)

Miles Kington 1941–

English humorist

3 There are those who think that Britain is a class-ridden society, and those who think it doesn't matter either way as long as you know your place in the set-up.
Welcome to Kington (1989)

Neil Kinnock 1942–

British Labour politician

*during the Falklands War, replying to a heckler who said that Mrs **Thatcher** 'showed guts'*
4 It's a pity others had to leave theirs on the ground at Goose Green to prove it.
television interview, 6 June 1983

5 If Margaret Thatcher wins on Thursday, I warn you not to be ordinary, I warn you not to be young, I warn you not to fall ill, and I warn you not to grow old.
on the prospect of a Conservative re-election
speech at Bridgend, 7 June 1983

6 The grotesque chaos of a Labour council hiring taxis to scuttle round the city handing out redundancy notices to its own workers.
of the actions of the city council in Liverpool
speech at the Labour Party Conference, 1 October 1985

7 I would die for my country but I could never let my country die for me.
speech at Labour Party Conference, 30 September 1986

8 Why am I the first Kinnock in a thousand generations to be able to get to a university?
later plagiarized by the American politician Joe Biden
speech in party political broadcast, 21 May 1987

9 There are lots of ways to get socialism, but I think trying to fracture the Labour party by incessant contest cannot be one of them.
in *Guardian* 29 January 1988

Alfred Kinsey 1894–1956

American zoologist and sex researcher

10 The only unnatural sex act is that which you cannot perform.
in *Time* 21 January 1966

Rudyard Kipling 1865–1936

English writer and poet
*on Kipling: see **Orwell** 239:2; see also* **Epitaphs** 105:15; **Knox** 176:16

11 Foot—foot—foot—foot—sloggin' over Africa—
(Boots—boots—boots—boots—movin' up and down again!)
'Boots' (1903)

12 If any question why we died,
Tell them, because our fathers lied.
'Epitaphs of the War: Common Form' (1919)

13 I could not dig: I dared not rob:
Therefore I lied to please the mob.
Now all my lies are proved untrue
And I must face the men I slew.
What tale shall serve me here among
Mine angry and defrauded young?
'Epitaphs of the War: A Dead Statesman' (1919)

14 My son was killed while laughing at some jest. I would I knew
What it was, and it might serve me in a time when jests are few.
'Epitaphs of the War: A Son' (1919)

15 The female of the species is more deadly than the male.
'The Female of the Species' (1919)

16 For all we have and are,
For all our children's fate,
Stand up and take the war.
The Hun is at the gate!
For All We Have and Are (1914)

17 What stands if freedom fall?
Who dies if England live?
For All We Have and Are (1914)

18 The Garden called Gethsemane
In Picardy it was,

And there the people came to see
The English soldiers pass.
We used to pass—we used to pass
Or halt, as it may be
And ship our masks in case of gas
Beyond Gethsemane.
'Gethsemane' (1918)

1 The officer sat on the chair,
The men lay on the grass,
And all the time we halted there
I prayed my cup might pass.

It didn't pass—it didn't pass—
It didn't pass from me.
I drank it when we met the gas
Beyond Gethsemane!
'Gethsemane' (1918); see below

If it be possible, let this cup pass from
me
Bible St Matthew

2 Our England is a garden that is full of
stately views,
Of borders, beds and shrubberies and
lawns and avenues,
With statues on the terraces and
peacocks strutting by;
But the Glory of the Garden lies in more
than meets the eye.
'The Glory of the Garden' (1911)

3 Our England is a garden, and such
gardens are not made
By singing:—'Oh, how beautiful!' and
sitting in the shade,
While better men than we go out and
start their working lives
At grubbing weeds from gravel paths
with broken dinner-knives.
'The Glory of the Garden' (1911)

4 If you can keep your head when all about
you
Are losing theirs and blaming it on you.
'If—' (1910)

5 If you can meet with Triumph and
Disaster
And treat those two impostors just the
same.
'If—' (1910)

6 If you can talk with crowds and keep
your virtue,
Or walk with Kings—nor lose the
common touch . . .
If you can fill the unforgiving minute

With sixty seconds' worth of distance
run,
Yours is the Earth and everything that's
in it,
And—which is more—you'll be a Man,
my son!
'If—' (1910)

7 Then ye returned to your trinkets; then
ye contented your souls
With the flannelled fools at the wicket or
the muddied oafs at the goals.
'The Islanders' (1903)

8 They shall not return to us, the resolute,
the young,
The eager and whole-hearted whom we
gave:
But the men who left them thriftily to die
in their own dung,
Shall they come with years and honour
to the grave?
'Mesopotamia' (1917)

9 Shall we only threaten and be angry for
an hour?
When the storm is ended shall we find
How softly but how swiftly they have
sidled back to power
By the favour and contrivance of their
kind?

Even while they soothe us, while they
promise large amends,
Even while they make a show of fear,
Do they call upon their debtors, and take
counsel with their friends,
To confirm and re-establish each career?
'Mesopotamia' (1917)

10 Dawn off the Foreland—the young flood
making
Jumbled and short and steep—
Black in the hollows and bright where
it's breaking—
Awkward water to sweep.
'Mines reported in the fairway,
'Warn all traffic and detain.
' 'Sent up *Unity*, *Claribel*, *Assyrian*,
Stormcock, and *Golden Gain*.'
'Mine Sweepers' (1915)

11 'Have you news of my boy Jack?'
Not this tide.
'When d'you think that he'll come back?
Not with this wind blowing, and this tide.
'My Boy Jack' (1916)

1 Brothers and Sisters, I bid you beware
Of giving your heart to a dog to tear.
'The Power of the Dog' (1909)

2 Five and twenty ponies,
Trotting through the dark—
Brandy for the Parson,
'Baccy for the Clerk;
Laces for a lady, letters for a spy,
Watch the wall, my darling, while the
Gentlemen go by!
'A Smuggler's Song' (1906)

3 Of all the trees that grow so fair,
Old England to adorn,
Greater are none beneath the Sun,
Than Oak, and Ash, and Thorn.
'A Tree Song' (1906)

4 God gives all men all earth to love,
But since man's heart is small,
Ordains for each one spot shall prove
Belovèd over all.
Each to his choice, and I rejoice
The lot has fallen to me
In a fair ground—in a fair ground—
Yea, Sussex by the sea!
'Sussex' (1903)

5 The dark eleventh hour
Draws on and sees us sold
To every evil power
We fought against of old.
Rebellion, rapine, hate,
Oppression, wrong and greed
Are loosed to rule our fate
By England's act and deed.
'Ulster' (1912)

6 What answer from the North?
One Law, one Land, one Throne.
'Ulster' (1912)

7 They shut the road through the woods
Seventy years ago.
Weather and rain have undone it again,
And now you would never know
There was once a road through the
woods.
'The Way through the Woods' (1910)

8 It is always a temptation to a rich and
lazy nation,
To puff and look important and to say:—
'Though we know we should defeat you,
we have not the time to meet you,
We will therefore pay you cash to go
away.'

And that is called paying the Dane-geld;
But we've proved it again and again,
That if once you have paid him the Dane-
geld
You never get rid of the Dane.
'What Dane-geld means' (1911)

9 Human nature seldom walks up to the
word 'cancer'.
Debits and Credits (1926) 'The Wish House'

10 But the wildest of all the wild animals
was the Cat. He walked by himself, and
all places were alike to him.
Just So Stories (1902) 'The Cat that Walked by
Himself'

11 An Elephant's Child—who was full of
'satiable curtiosity.
Just So Stories (1902) 'The Elephant's Child'

12 Go to the banks of the great grey-green,
greasy Limpopo River, all set about with
fever-trees, and find out.
Just So Stories (1902) 'The Elephant's Child'

13 Little Friend of all the World.
Kim's nickname
Kim (1901)

14 The mad all are in God's keeping.
Kim (1901)

15 'Tisn't beauty, so to speak, nor good talk
necessarily. It's just It. Some women'll
stay in a man's memory if they once
walked down a street.
Traffics and Discoveries (1904) 'Mrs Bathurst'

16 Words are, of course, the most powerful
drug used by mankind.
speech, 14 February 1923

17 Power without responsibility: the
prerogative of the harlot throughout the
ages.
*summing up Lord **Beaverbrook**'s political
standpoint vis-à-vis the Daily Express, and
quoted by Stanley **Baldwin**, 18 March 1931*
in *Kipling Journal* December 1971

Henry Kissinger 1923–

American Republican politician and
diplomat

18 For [Woodrow] Wilson, the justification
of America's international role was
messianic: America had an obligation
not to the balance of power, but to

spread its principles throughout the world.

Diplomacy (1994)

1 The management of a balance of power is a permanent undertaking, not an exertion that has a foreseeable end.

White House Years (1979)

2 The conventional army loses if it does not win. The guerrilla wins if he does not lose.

in *Foreign Affairs* January 1969

3 There cannot be a crisis next week. My schedule is already full.

in *New York Times Magazine* 1 June 1969

4 Power is the great aphrodisiac.

in *New York Times* 19 January 1971

5 We are the President's men.

M. and B. Kalb *Kissinger* (1974)

6 The main advantage of being famous is that when you bore people at dinner parties they think it is their fault.

in *Spectator* 1 April 1995; attributed

7 For other nations, Utopia is a blessed past never to be recovered; for Americans it is just beyond the horizon.

attributed

Lord Kitchener 1850–1916

British soldier and politician
on Kitchener: see **Asquith** 14:10

8 Do your duty bravely. Fear God. Honour the King.

message to soldiers of the British Expeditionary Force (1914)
in *The Times* 19 August 1914

9 I don't mind your being killed, but I object to your being taken prisoner.

to the Prince of Wales during the First World War Journals and Letters of Viscount Esher (1938)
vol. 3, 18 December 1914

Paul Klee 1879–1940

Swiss painter

10 Art does not reproduce the visible; rather, it makes visible.

Inward Vision (1958) 'Creative Credo' (1920)

11 An active line on a walk, moving freely without a goal. A walk for walk's sake.

The agent is a point which moves around.

Pedagogical Sketchbook (1925)

12 Colour has taken hold of me; no longer do I have to chase after it. I know that it has hold of me for ever. That is the significance of this blessed moment.

on a visit to Tunis in 1914
Herbert Read *A Concise History of Modern Painting* (1968)

Charles Knight and Kenneth Lyle

British songwriters

13 When there's trouble brewing,
When there's something doing,
Are we downhearted?
No! Let 'em all come!

'Here we are! Here we are again!!' (1914 song)

Frank H. Knight 1885–1973

American economist

14 Costs merely register competing attractions.

Risk, Uncertainty and Profit (1921)

Ronald Knox 1888–1957

English writer and Roman Catholic priest

15 When suave politeness, tempering bigot zeal,
Corrected *I believe* to *One does feel*.

'Absolute and Abitofhell' (1913)

16 The tumult and the shouting dies,
The captains and the kings depart,
And we are left with large supplies
Of cold blancmange and rhubarb tart.

'After the Party' (1959); see below

The tumult and the shouting dies
The captains and the kings depart
Still stands Thine ancient Sacrifice,
An humble and a contrite heart.

Rudyard **Kipling** (1865–1936) 'Recessional' (1897)

17 There once was a man who said, 'God
Must think it exceedingly odd
If he finds that this tree
Continues to be

When there's no one about in the Quad.'
L. Reed *Complete Limerick Book* (1924), to
which came the anonymous reply:

Dear Sir,
Your astonishment's odd:
I am always about in the Quad.
And that's why the tree
Will continue to be,
Since observed by
Yours faithfully,
God.

1 It is stupid of modern civilization to have
given up believing in the devil, when he
is the only explanation of it.
Let Dons Delight (1939)

2 The baby doesn't understand English and
the Devil knows Latin.
on being asked to perform a baptism in English
Evelyn Waugh *Ronald Knox* (1959)

3 A loud noise at one end and no sense of
responsibility at the other.
definition of a baby
attributed

Ted Koehler

American songwriter

4 Stormy weather,
Since my man and I ain't together.
'Stormy Weather' (1933 song)

Arthur Koestler 1905–83

Hungarian-born writer

5 One may not regard the world as a sort of
metaphysical brothel for emotions.
Darkness at Noon (1940) 'The Second Hearing'

6 Behaviourism is indeed a kind of flat-
earth view of the mind . . . it has
substituted for the erstwhile
anthropomorphic view of the rat, a
ratomorphic view of man.
The Ghost in the Machine (1967)

7 God seems to have left the receiver off the
hook, and time is running out.
The Ghost in the Machine (1967)

8 The most persistent sound which
reverberates through man's history is the
beating of war drums.
Janus (1978)

9 Man can leave the earth and land on the
moon, but cannot cross from East to
West Berlin. Prometheus reaches for the
stars with an insane grin on his face and
a totem-symbol in his hand.
Janus (1978)

10 A writer's ambition should be . . . to
trade a hundred contemporary readers
for ten readers in ten years' time and for
one reader in a hundred years.
in *New York Times Book Review* 1 April 1951

Helmut Kohl 1930–

German statesman, Chancellor of West
Germany (1982–90) and first postwar
Chancellor of united Germany (1990–)

11 We Germans now have the historic
chance to realize the unity of our
fatherland.
on the reunification of Germany
in *Guardian* 15 February 1990

12 The policy of European integration is in
reality a question of war and peace in the
21st century.
speech at Louvain University, 2 February 1996

13 I am not a marketing manager for British
beef.
*asked whether he would 'trumpet the merits of
British beef' after lunching on it with John* **Major**
in *The Times* 30 April 1996

Karl Kraus 1874–1936

Austrian satirist

14 How is the world ruled and how do wars
start? Diplomats tell lies to journalists
and then believe what they read.
Aphorisms and More Aphorisms (1909)

15 There is no unhappier creature on earth
than a fetishist who yearns to embrace a
woman's shoe and has to embrace the
whole woman.
Aphorisms and More Aphorisms (1909)

16 What good is speed if the brain has oozed
out on the way?
in *Die Fackel* September 1909 'The Discovery of
the North Pole'

Charlie Kray c.1930–

English gangster

1 Even the most hardened criminal a few
years ago would help an old lady across
the road and give her a few quid if she
was skint.
    in *Observer* 28 December 1986

Jiddu Krishnamurti d. 1986

Indian spiritual philosopher

2 Religion is the frozen thought of men out
of which they build temples.
    in *Observer* 22 April 1928

3 Truth is a pathless land, and you cannot
approach it by any path whatsoever, by
any religion, by any sect.
    speech in Holland, 3 August 1929

4 Happiness is a state of which you are
unconscious, of which you are not
aware. The moment you are aware that
you are happy, you cease to be happy . . .
You want to be consciously happy; the
moment you are consciously happy,
happiness is gone.
    Penguin Krishnamurti Reader (1970)
    'Questions and Answers'

Kris Kristofferson 1936–

American actor

5 Freedom's just another word for nothin'
left to lose,
Nothin' ain't worth nothin', but it's free.
    'Me and Bobby McGee' (1969 song, with Fred
    Foster)

Joseph Wood Krutch

1893–1970

American critic and naturalist

6 The most serious charge which can be
brought against New England is not
Puritanism but February.
    The Twelve Seasons (1949)

7 Cats seem to go on the principle that it
never does any harm to ask for what you
want.
    Twelve Seasons (1949)

Stanley Kubrick 1928–

American film director

8 The great nations have always acted like
gangsters, and the small nations like
prostitutes.
    in *Guardian* 5 June 1963

Satish Kumar 1937–

Indian writer

9 Lead me from death to life, from
falsehood to truth.
Lead me from despair to hope, from fear
to trust.
Lead me from hate to love, from war to
peace.
Let peace fill our heart, our world, our
universe.
    'Prayer for Peace' (1981); adapted from the
    Upanishads

Milan Kundera 1929–

Czech novelist

10 The unbearable lightness of being.
    title of novel (1984)

Christian Lacroix 1951–

French couturier

11 Haute Couture should be fun, foolish and
almost unwearable.
    in *Observer* 27 December 1987 'Sayings of the
    Year'

Fiorello La Guardia

1882–1947

American politician

12 When I make a mistake, it's a beaut!
    *on the appointment of Herbert O'Brien as a judge
    in 1936*
        William Manners *Patience and Fortitude* (1976)

John Lahr 1941–

American critic

13 Society drives people crazy with lust and
calls it advertising.
    in *Guardian* 2 August 1989

1 Momentum was part of the exhilaration and the exhaustion of the twentieth century which Coward decoded for the British but borrowed wholesale from the Americans.
in *New Yorker* 9 September 1996

2 Terence Conran's vast Bluebird complex on the King's Road is to New Labour what the Crystal Palace was to High Victorianism.
in *Observer* 6 July 1997 'Soundbites'

R. D. Laing 1927–89
Scottish psychiatrist

3 The divided self.
title of book on schizophrenia, 1960

4 Schizophrenia cannot be understood without understanding despair.
The Divided Self (1960)

5 The brotherhood of man is evoked by particular men according to their circumstances. But it seldom extends to all men. In the name of our freedom and our brotherhood we are prepared to blow up the other half of mankind and to be blown up in turn.
The Politics of Experience (1967)

6 The experience and behaviour that gets labelled schizophrenic is a special strategy that a person invents in order to live in an unlivable situation.
Politics of Experience (1967)

7 Madness need not be all breakdown. It may also be break-through.
The Politics of Experience (1967)

8 True guilt is guilt at the obligation one owes to oneself to be oneself. False guilt is guilt felt at not being what other people feel one ought to be or assume that one is.
Self and Others (1961)

Constant Lambert 1905–51
English composer

9 The whole trouble with a folk song is that once you have played it through there is nothing much you can do except play it over again and play it rather louder.
Music Ho! (1934)

George Lamming 1927–
Barbados-born novelist and poet

10 In the castle of my skin.
title of novel (1953)

Norman Lamont 1942–
British Conservative politician
see also **Misquotations** 218:6

11 Rising unemployment and the recession have been the price that we've had to pay to get inflation down. [Labour shouts] That is a price well worth paying.
speech in the House of Commons, 16 May 1991

12 We give the impression of being in office but not in power.
as a backbencher
speech in the House of Commons, 9 June 1993

Giuseppe di Lampedusa 1896–1957
Italian writer

13 If we want things to stay as they are, things will have to change.
The Leopard (1957)

14 Love. Of course, love. Flames for a year, ashes for thirty.
The Leopard (1957)

Osbert Lancaster 1908–86
English writer and cartoonist

15 For self-revelation, whether it be a Tudor villa on the by-pass or a bomb-proof chalet at Berchtesgaden, there's no place like home.
Homes Sweet Homes (1939)

Fritz Lang 1890–1976
Austrian-born film director

16 Don't forget the Western is not only the history of this country, it is what the

Saga of the Nibelungen is for the
European.

Peter Bogdanovich *Fritz Lang in America* (1967)

Julia Lang

see **Catch-phrases** 57:5

Susanne Langer 1895–1985

American philosopher

1 Art is the objectification of feeling, and
the subjectification of nature.

Mind (1967) vol. 1

Philip Larkin 1922–85

English poet

2 Sexual intercourse began
In nineteen sixty-three
(Which was rather late for me)—
Between the end of the *Chatterley* ban
And the Beatles' first LP.

'Annus Mirabilis' (1974)

3 Time has transfigured them into
Untruth. The stone fidelity
They hardly meant has come to be
Their final blazon, and to prove
Our almost-instinct almost true:
What will survive of us is love.

'An Arundel Tomb' (1964)

4 Hatless, I take off
My cycle-clips in awkward reverence.

'Church Going' (1955)

5 Life is first boredom, then fear.
Whether or not we use it, it goes,
And leaves what something hidden from
us chose,
And age, and then the only end of age.

'Dockery & Son' (1964)

6 And that will be England gone,
The shadows, the meadows, the lanes,
The guildhalls, the carved choirs.
There'll be books; it will linger on
In galleries; but all that remains
For us will be concrete and tyres.

'Going, Going' (1974)

7 Next year we shall be living in a country
That brought its soldiers home for lack of
money.
The statues will be standing in the same
Tree-muffled squares, and look nearly the
same.
Our children will not know it's a different
country.
All we can hope to leave them now is
money.

'Homage to a Government' (1974)

8 Nothing, like something, happens
anywhere.

'I Remember, I Remember' (1955)

9 Never such innocence,
Never before or since,
As changed itself to past
Without a word—the men
Leaving the gardens tidy,
The thousands of marriages
Lasting a little while longer:
Never such innocence again.

'MCMXIV' (1964)

10 Perhaps being old is having lighted
rooms
Inside your head, and people in them,
acting.
People you know, yet can't quite name.

'The Old Fools' (1974)

11 Don't read too much now: the dude
Who lets the girl down before
The hero arrives, the chap
Who's yellow and keeps the store,
Seem far too familiar. Get stewed:
Books are a load of crap.

'Study of Reading Habits' (1964)

12 They fuck you up, your mum and dad.
They may not mean to, but they do.
They fill you with the faults they had
And add some extra, just for you.

'This Be The Verse' (1974)

13 Man hands on misery to man.
It deepens like a coastal shelf.
Get out as early as you can,
And don't have any kids yourself.

'This Be The Verse' (1974)

14 Why should I let the toad *work*
Squat on my life?
Can't I use my wit as a pitchfork

And drive the brute off?
'Toads' (1955)

1 Give me your arm, old toad;
Help me down Cemetery Road.
'Toads Revisited' (1964)

2 I thought of London spread out in the sun,
Its postal districts packed like squares of wheat.
'The Whitsun Weddings' (1964)

3 I listen to money singing. It's like looking down
From long french windows at a provincial town,
The slums, the canal, the churches ornate and mad
In the evening sun. It is intensely sad.
'Money' (1974)

4 Deprivation is for me what daffodils were for Wordsworth.
Required Writing (1983)

5 The notion of expressing sentiments in short lines having similar sounds at their ends seems as remote as mangoes on the moon.
letter to Barbara Pym, 22 January 1975

6 Far too many relied on the classic formula of a beginning, a muddle, and an end.
of the books entered for the 1977 Booker Prize
in *New Fiction* January 1978; see below

A whole is that which has a beginning, a middle, and an end.
Aristotle (384–322 BC) *Poetics*

Harold Laski 1893–1950

British Labour politician and writer
on Laski: see **Attlee** 15:6

7 I respect fidelity to colleagues even though they are fit for the hangman.
letter to Oliver Wendell **Holmes** Jr., 4 December 1926

8 It was like watching someone organize her own immortality. Every phrase and gesture was studied. Now and again, when she said something a little out of

the ordinary, she wrote it down herself in a notebook.
of Virginia **Woolf**
letter to Oliver Wendell **Holmes** Jr., 30 November 1930

■ Last words
see box overleaf

Harry Lauder 1870–1950

Scottish music-hall entertainer

9 Keep right on to the end of the road,
Keep right on to the end.
Tho' the way be long, let your heart be strong,
Keep right on round the bend.
'The End of the Road' (1924 song)

10 I love a lassie, a bonnie, bonnie lassie,
She's as pure as the lily in the dell.
She's as sweet as the heather, the bonnie bloomin' heather—
Mary, ma Scotch Bluebell.
'I Love a Lassie' (1905 song)

11 Roamin' in the gloamin'.
title of song (1911)

Stan Laurel 1890–1965

British-born American film comedian

12 Another nice mess you've gotten me into.
often 'another fine mess'
Another Fine Mess (1930 film) and many other Laurel and Hardy films; spoken by Oliver Hardy

13 Why don't you do something to *help* me?
Drivers' Licence Sketch (1947); spoken by Oliver Hardy

William L. Laurence 1888–1977

American journalist

14 At first it was a giant column that soon took the shape of a supramundane mushroom.
on the first atomic explosion in New Mexico, 16 July 1945, in *New York Times* 26 September 1945

Last words

1 Bugger Bognor.

King **George V** *(1865–1936) on his deathbed in 1936, when someone remarked 'Cheer up, your Majesty, you will soon be at Bognor again'; alternatively, a comment made in 1929, when it was proposed that the town be named Bognor Regis on account of the king's convalescence there after a serious illness*

K. Rose *King George V* (1983); cf. **Last words** 182:5

2 Come closer, boys. It will be easier for you.

Erskine **Childers** *(1870–1922) to the firing squad at his execution*

Burke Wilkinson *The Zeal of the Convert* (1976)

3 Farewell, my friends. I go to glory.

last words of Isadora Duncan (1878–1927) before her scarf caught in a car wheel, breaking her neck

Mary Desti *Isadora Duncan's End* (1929)

4 For God's sake look after our people.

Robert Falcon **Scott** *(1868–1912)*

last diary entry, 29 March 1912

5 How's the Empire?

said by King **George** *V (1865–1936) to his private secretary on the morning of his death*

K. Rose *King George V* (1983); cf. **Last words** 182:1

6 I am just going outside and may be some time.

last words of Captain Lawrence Oates (1880–1912)

Robert Falcon **Scott** diary entry, 16–17 March 1912; cf. **Epitaphs** 105:5

7 If this is dying, then I don't think much of it.

Lytton **Strachey** *(1880–1932) on his deathbed*

M. Holroyd *Lytton Strachey* (1968) vol. 2

8 In this life there's nothing new in dying,
But nor, of course, is living any newer.

the final poem of Sergei **Yesenin** *(1895–1925), written in his own blood the day before he hanged himself in his Leningrad hotel room*

'Goodbye, my Friend, Goodbye' (1925)

9 Let's do it!

Gary Gilmore (1941–77) to the firing squad at his execution; after his conviction for murder, Gilmore had refused to appeal, and petitioned the Supreme Court that the execution should be carried out

Norman Mailer *The Executioner's Song* (1979)

10 Lord take my soul, but the struggle continues.

Ken Saro-Wiwa (1941–95), just before he was hanged

in *Daily Telegraph* 13 November 1995

11 The love boat has crashed against the everyday. You and I, we are quits, and there is no point in listing mutual pains, sorrows, and hurts.

from an unfinished poem found among Vladimir **Mayakovsky**'s *papers, a variant of which he quoted in his suicide letter*

letter, 12 April 1930

12 Love? What is it? Most natural painkiller. What there is . . . LOVE.

final entry in the journal of William S. **Burroughs**, *1 August 1997, the day before he died*

in *New Yorker* 18 August 1997

13 Now I'll have eine kleine Pause.

last words of Kathleen Ferrier (1912–53)

Gerald Moore *Am I Too Loud?* (1962)

14 Tell them I've had a wonderful life.

Ludwig **Wittgenstein** *(1889–1951) to his doctor's wife, before losing consciousness, 28 April 1951*

Ray Monk *Ludwig Wittgenstein* (1990)

15 That is indeed very good. I shall have to repeat that on the Golden Floor!

said by A. E. **Housman** *(1859–1936) to his physician who had told him a risqué story*

attributed

▶

▶ **Last words** continued

1 We are putting passengers off in small boats . . . Engine room getting flooded . . . CQ.

CQD was the original SOS call for shipping

last signals sent from the *Titanic*, 15 April 1912

2 'What *is* the answer?' No answer came. She laughed and said, 'In that case what is the question?'

Gertrude **Stein** *(1874–1946)*

Donald Sutherland *Gertrude Stein, A Biography of her Work* (1951)

3 Why fear death? It is the most beautiful adventure in life.

the American theatrical manager Charles Frohman (1860–1915) before drowning in the Lusitania, *7 May 1915*

I. F. Marcosson and D. Frohman *Charles Frohman* (1916); cf. **Barrie** 23:12

4 Why not? Why not? Why not? Yeah.

Timothy **Leary** *(1920–96)*

in *Independent* 1 June 1996

D. H. Lawrence 1885–1930

English novelist and poet
on Lawrence: see **Griffith-Jones** 134:4, **Robinson** 265:11

5 To the Puritan all things are impure, as somebody says.
   Etruscan Places (1932) 'Cerveteri'; see below

   Unto the pure all things are pure.
   Bible Titus

6 It was in 1915 the old world ended.
   Kangaroo (1923)

7 Ours is essentially a tragic age, so we refuse to take it tragically.
   Lady Chatterley's Lover (1928)

8 John Thomas says good-night to Lady Jane, a little droopingly, but with a hopeful heart.
   Lady Chatterley's Lover (1928)

9 The English . . . are paralysed by fear. That is what thwarts and distorts the Anglo-Saxon existence . . . Nothing could be more lovely and fearless than Chaucer. But already Shakespeare is morbid with fear, fear of consequences. That is the strange phenomenon of the English Renaissance: this mystic terror of the consequences, the consequences of action.
   Phoenix (1936) 'An Introduction to these Paintings'

10 If you try to nail anything down in the novel, either it kills the novel, or the novel gets up and walks away with the nail.
   Phoenix (1936) 'Morality and the Novel'

11 Morality in the novel is the trembling instability of the balance. When the novelist puts his thumb in the scale, to pull down the balance to his own predilection, that is immorality.
   Phoenix (1936) 'Morality and the Novel'

12 Pornography is the attempt to insult sex, to do dirt on it.
   Phoenix (1936) 'Pornography and Obscenity'

13 In life . . . no new thing has ever arisen, or can arise, save out of the impulse of the male upon the female, the female upon the male. The interaction of the male and female spirit begot the wheel, the plough, and the first utterance that was made on the face of the earth.
   Phoenix (1936) 'Study of Thomas Hardy'

14 The novel is the one bright book of life.
   Phoenix (1936) 'Why the novel matters'

15 The bridge to the future is the phallus.
   Sex, Literature and Censorship (1955)

16 Never trust the artist. Trust the tale. The proper function of a critic is to save the tale from the artist who created it.
   Studies in Classic American Literature (1923)

17 Be a good animal, true to your instincts.
   The White Peacock (1911)

18 Don't you find it a beautiful clean thought, a world empty of people, just

uninterrupted grass, and a hare sitting up?

Women in Love (1920)

1 How beastly the bourgeois is
Especially the male of the species.
'How Beastly the Bourgeois Is' (1929)

2 While we have sex in the mind, we truly
have none in the body.
'Leave Sex Alone' (1929)

3 Men! The only animal in the world to
fear!
'Mountain Lion' (1923)

4 I never saw a wild thing
Sorry for itself.
'Self-Pity' (1929)

5 A snake came to my water-trough
On a hot, hot day, and I in pyjamas for
the heat,
To drink there.
'Snake' (1923)

6 And so, I missed my chance with one of
the lords
Of life.
And I have something to expiate:
A pettiness.
'Snake' (1923)

7 Not I, not I, but the wind that blows
through me!
'Song of a Man who has Come Through' (1917)

8 When I read Shakespeare I am struck
with wonder
That such trivial people should muse and
thunder
In such lovely language.
'When I Read Shakespeare' (1929)

9 Curse the blasted, jelly-boned swines, the
slimy, the belly-wriggling invertebrates,
the miserable sodding rotters, the flaming
sods, the snivelling, dribbling, dithering,
palsied, pulse-less lot that make up
England today. They've got white of egg
in their veins, and their spunk is that
watery it's a marvel they can breed. They
can nothing but frog-spawn—the
gibberers! God, how I hate them!
letter to Edward Garnett, 3 July 1912

10 Tragedy ought really to be a great kick at
misery.
letter to A. W. McLeod, 6 October 1912

11 I like to write when I feel spiteful; it's like
having a good sneeze.
letter to Lady Cynthia Asquith, *c.*25 November
1913

12 Australia has a marvellous sky and air
and blue clarity, and a hoary sort of land
beneath it, like a Sleeping Princess on
whom the dust of ages has settled.
letter to Jan Juta, 20 May 1922

13 The dead don't die. They look on and
help.
letter to J. Middleton Murry, 2 February 1923

14 I want to go south, where there is no
autumn, where the cold doesn't crouch
over one like a snow-leopard waiting to
pounce. The heart of the North is dead,
and the fingers of cold are corpse fingers.
letter to J. Middleton Murry, 3 October 1924

15 My God, what a clumsy *olla putrida* James
Joyce is! Nothing but old fags and
cabbage-stumps of quotations from the
Bible and the rest, stewed in the juice of
deliberate, journalistic dirty-mindedness.
letter to Aldous and Maria Huxley, 15 August
1928

T. E. Lawrence 1888–1935

English soldier and writer
on Lawrence: see **Berners** 33:15

16 Many men would take the death-
sentence without a whimper to escape
the life-sentence which fate carries in her
other hand.
The Mint (1955)

17 I loved you, so I drew these tides of men
into my hands and wrote my will
across the sky in stars.
To earn you freedom, the seven pillared
worthy house, that your eyes might be
shining for me
When we came.
Seven Pillars of Wisdom (1926) dedication

18 Poets hope too much, and their politics . . .
usually stink after twenty years.
letter to Cecil Day Lewis, November 1934

19 The trouble with Communism is that it
accepts too much of today's furniture. I
hate furniture.
letter to Cecil Day Lewis, 20 December 1934

1 Surely the sex business isn't worth all this damned fuss? I've met only a handful of people who cared a biscuit for it.

on reading Lady Chatterley's Lover
   Christopher Hassall *Edward Marsh* (1959)

Nigel Lawson 1932–

British Conservative politician

2 It represented the tip of a singularly ill-concealed iceberg, with all the destructive potential that icebergs possess.

*of an article by Alan Walters, Margaret **Thatcher**'s economic adviser, criticizing the Exchange Rate Mechanism*

   in the House of Commons following his resignation as Chancellor, 31 October 1989

Edmund Leach 1910–

English anthropologist

3 Far from being the basis of the good society, the family, with its narrow privacy and tawdry secrets, is the source of all our discontents.

   BBC Reith Lectures, 1967, in *Listener* 30 November 1967

Stephen Leacock 1869–1944

British-born Canadian humorist

4 When Rutherford was done with the atom all the solidity was pretty well knocked out of it.

   The Boy I Left Behind Me (1947)

5 The parent who could see his boy as he really is, would shake his head and say: 'Willie, is no good; I'll sell him.'

   Essays and Literary Studies (1916) 'Lot of a Schoolmaster'

6 Advertising may be described as the science of arresting human intelligence long enough to get money from it.

   Garden of Folly (1924) 'The Perfect Salesman'

7 A sportsman is a man who, every now and then, simply has to get out and kill something. Not that he's cruel. He wouldn't hurt a fly. It's not big enough.

   My Remarkable Uncle (1942)

8 Lord Ronald said nothing; he flung himself from the room, flung himself upon his horse and rode madly off in all directions.

   Nonsense Novels (1911) 'Gertrude the Governess'

Timothy Leary 1920–

American psychologist
on Leary: see **Epitaphs** 106:1; *see also* **Last words** 183:4

9 If you take the game of life seriously, if you take your nervous system seriously, if you take your sense organs seriously, if you take the energy process seriously, you must turn on, tune in and drop out.

   The Politics of Ecstasy (1968)

10 The PC is the LSD of the '90s.

   remark made in the early 1990s; in *Guardian* 1 June 1996

11 The key to dying well is for you to decide where, when, how and whom to invite to the last party.

   to a visitor, during the last days of his final illness
   in *Daily Telegraph* 3 May 1996

on abandoning his plan to have his head preserved by the cryonics movement:

12 They have no sense of humour. I was worried I would wake up in 50 years surrounded by people with clipboards.

   in *Daily Telegraph* 10 May 1996

F. R. Leavis 1895–1978

English literary critic
on Leavis: see **Lewis** 190:9

13 The common pursuit.

   title of book (1952)

14 The great tradition.

   title of book (1948)

15 It is well to start by distinguishing the few really great—the major novelists who count in the same way as the major poets, in the sense that they not only change the possibilities of the art for practitioners and readers, but that they are significant in terms of the human awareness they promote; awareness of the possibilities of life.

   The Great Tradition (1948)

1 He energized the Garden-Suburb ethos with a certain original talent and the vigour of a prolonged adolescence ... rather like Keats's vulgarity with a Public School accent.
*of Rupert **Brooke***
New Bearings in English Poetry (1932)

2 The Sitwells belong to the history of publicity rather than of poetry.
New Bearings in English Poetry (1932)

3 Self-contempt, well-grounded.
*on the foundation of T. S. **Eliot**'s work*
in *Times Literary Supplement* 21 October 1988

Fran Lebowitz 1946–
American humorist

4 Being a woman is of special interest only to aspiring male transsexuals. To actual women, it is merely a good excuse not to play football.
Metropolitan Life (1978)

5 Modern science was largely conceived of as an answer to the servant problem.
Metropolitan Life (1978)

6 If people don't want to listen to *you*, what makes you think they want to hear from your sweater?
on slogans on clothing
Metropolitan Life (1978)

7 The opposite of talking isn't listening. The opposite of talking is waiting.
Social Studies (1981)

8 Remember that as a teenager you are at the last stage in your life when you will be happy to hear that the phone is for you.
Social Studies (1981)

9 Wealth and power are much more likely to be the result of breeding than they are of reading.
on self-help books
Social Studies (1981)

10 The best fame is a writer's fame: it's enough to get a table at a good restaurant, but not enough that you get interrupted when you eat.
in *Observer* 30 May 1993 'Sayings of the Week'

Stanislaw Lec 1909–66
Polish writer

11 Is it progress if a cannibal uses knife and fork?
Unkempt Thoughts (1962)

12 One has to multiply thoughts to the point where there aren't enough policemen to control them.
Unkempt Thoughts (1962)

John le Carré 1931–
English thriller writer

13 The spy who came in from the cold.
title of novel (1963)

Le Corbusier 1887–1965
French architect

14 A house is a machine for living in.
Vers une architecture (1923)

15 This frightful word [function] was born under other skies than those I have loved—those where the sun reigns supreme.
Stephen Gardiner *Le Corbusier* (1974)

Gypsy Rose Lee 1914–70
American striptease artiste

16 God is love, but get it in writing.
attributed

Harper Lee 1926–
American novelist

17 Shoot all the bluejays you want, if you can hit 'em, but remember it's a sin to kill a mockingbird.
To Kill a Mockingbird (1960)

Tom Lehrer 1928–
American humorist

18 Plagiarize! Let no one else's work evade your eyes,
Remember why the good Lord made your eyes.
'Lobachevski' (1953 song)

1 It is sobering to consider that when
   Mozart was my age he had already been
   dead for a year.
     N. Shapiro (ed.) *An Encyclopedia of Quotations
     about Music* (1978)

2 In my youth there were words you
   couldn't say in front of a girl; now you
   can't say 'girl'.
     in *Sunday Telegraph* 10 March 1996

Vivien Leigh 1913–67
English actress

3 Shaw is like a train. One just speaks the
   words and sits in one's place. But
   Shakespeare is like bathing in the sea—
   one swims where one wants.
     letter from Harold Nicolson to Vita Sackville-
     West, 1 February 1956

Curtis E. LeMay 1906–90
American air-force officer

4 We're going to bomb them back into the
   Stone Age.
     on the North Vietnamese
     Mission with LeMay (1965)

John Le Mesurier
see **Epitaphs** 105:11

Lenin 1870–1924
Russian revolutionary

5 Imperialism is the monopoly stage of
   capitalism.
     Imperialism as the Last Stage of Capitalism
     (1916)

6 No, Democracy is *not* identical with
   majority rule. Democracy is a *State* which
   recognizes the subjection of the minority
   to the majority, that is, an organization
   for the systematic use of *force* by one class
   against the other, by one part of the
   population against another.
     State and Revolution (1919)

7 While the State exists, there can be no
   freedom. When there is freedom there
   will be no State.
     State and Revolution (1919)

8 What is to be done?
     title of pamphlet (1902); originally the title of a
     novel (1863) by N. G. Chernyshevsky

9 A good man fallen among Fabians.
     of George Bernard **Shaw**
       A. Ransome *Six Weeks in Russia in 1919* (1919)
       'Notes of Conversations with Lenin'

10 Communism is Soviet power plus the
   electrification of the whole country.
     report to 8th Congress, 1920

11 Who? Whom?
     *definition of political science, meaning 'Who will
     outstrip whom?'*
       in *Polnoe Sobranie Sochinenii* vol. 44 (1970) 17
       October 1921 and elsewhere

12 Liberty is precious—so precious that it
   must be rationed.
     Sidney and Beatrice Webb *Soviet Communism*
     (1936)

John Lennon 1940–80
English pop singer and songwriter
on Lennon: see **McCartney** 198:1; *see also*
Lennon and McCartney, Ono 236:7

13 Happiness is a warm gun.
     title of song (1968); cf. **Advertising slogans**
     3:21, **Ephron** 104:3, **Schulz** 280:13

14 Imagine there's no heaven,
   It's easy if you try,
   No hell below us,
   Above us only sky.
     'Imagine' (1971 song)

15 Will the people in the cheaper seats clap
   your hands? All the rest of you, if you'll
   just rattle your jewellery.
     at the Royal Variety Performance, 4 November
     1963; R. Colman *John Winston Lennon* (1984)

16 We're more popular than Jesus now; I
   don't know which will go first—rock 'n'
   roll or Christianity.
     of The Beatles
       interview in *Evening Standard* 4 March 1966;
       cf. **Chisholm** 64:12, **Gallagher** 124:2

John Lennon 1940–80
and Paul McCartney 1942–

English pop singers and songwriters
see also **Lennon, Macartney**

1 All you need is love.
   title of song (1967)

2 Back in the USSR.
   title of song (1968)

3 For I don't care too much for money,
   For money can't buy me love.
   'Can't Buy Me Love' (1964 song)

4 All the lonely people, where do they all
   come from?
   'Eleanor Rigby' (1966 song)

5 Give peace a chance.
   title of song (1969)

6 It's been a hard day's night,
   And I've been working like a dog.
   'A Hard Day's Night' (1964 song)

7 Strawberry fields forever.
   title of song (1967)

8 She's got a ticket to ride, but she don't
   care.
   'Ticket to Ride' (1965 song)

9 Will you still need me, will you still feed
   me,
   When I'm sixty four?
   'When I'm Sixty Four' (1967 song)

10 Oh I get by with a little help from my
   friends,
   Mm, I get high with a little help from my
   friends.
   'With a Little Help From My Friends' (1967
   song)

11 Yesterday, all my troubles seemed so far
   away,
   Now it looks as though they're here to
   stay.
   Oh I believe in yesterday.
   'Yesterday' (1965 song)

Alan Jay Lerner 1918–86

American songwriter

12 Don't let it be forgot
   That once there was a spot
   For one brief shining moment that was
   known

As Camelot.
*now particularly associated with the White House
of John Fitzgerald* **Kennedy**
   'Camelot' (1960 song)

13 I'm getting married in the morning,
   Ding! dong! the bells are gonna chime.
   Pull out the stopper;
   Let's have a whopper;
   But get me to the church on time!
   'Get Me to the Church on Time' (1956 song)

14 Why can't a woman be more like a man?
   Men are so honest, so thoroughly square;
   Eternally noble, historically fair.
   'A Hymn to Him' (1956)

15 We met at nine.
   We met at eight.
   I was on time.
   No, you were late.
   Ah yes! I remember it well.
   'I Remember it Well' (1958 song)

16 I've grown accustomed to the trace
   Of something in the air;
   Accustomed to her face.
   'I've Grown Accustomed to her Face' (1956
   song)

17 On a clear day (you can see forever).
   title of song (1965)

18 The rain in Spain stays mainly in the
   plain.
   'The Rain in Spain' (1956)

19 Thank heaven for little girls!
   For little girls get bigger every day.
   'Thank Heaven for Little Girls' (1958 song)

20 All I want is a room somewhere,
   Far away from the cold night air,
   With one enormous chair;
   Oh, wouldn't it be lovely?
   'Wouldn't it be Lovely' (1956 song)

21 Oozing charm from every pore,
   He oiled his way around the floor.
   'You Did It' (1956)

Doris Lessing 1919–

English writer

22 There's only one real sin, and that is to
   persuade oneself that the second-best is
   anything but the second-best.
   Golden Notebook (1962)

1 When old settlers say 'One has to understand the country,' what they mean is, 'You have to get used to our ideas about the native.'
  The Grass is Singing (1950)

2 What of October, that ambiguous month, the month of tension, the unendurable month?
  Martha Quest (1952)

3 What is charm then? . . . something extra, superfluous, unnecessary, essentially a power thrown away.
  Particularly Cats (1967)

Winifred Mary Letts
1882–1972
English writer

4 I saw the spires of Oxford
  As I was passing by,
  The grey spires of Oxford
  Against a pearl-grey sky;
  My heart was with the Oxford men
  Who went abroad to die.
  'The Spires of Oxford' (1916)

Oscar Levant 1906–72
American pianist

5 Underneath this flabby exterior is an enormous lack of character.
  Memoirs of an Amnesiac (1965)

6 Epigram: a wisecrack that played Carnegie Hall.
  in *Coronet* September 1958

Lord Leverhulme 1851–1925
English industrialist and philanthropist

7 Half the money I spend on advertising is wasted, and the trouble is I don't know which half.
  David Ogilvy *Confessions of an Advertising Man* (1963)

Primo Levi 1919–87
Italian novelist and poet

8 Our language lacks words to express this offence, the demolition of a man.
  of a year spent in Auschwitz
  If This is a Man (1958)

Bernard Levin 1928–
British journalist

9 The truth in these matters may be stated as a scientific law: 'The persistence of public officials varies inversely with the importance of the matter on which they are persisting.'
  In These Times (1986)

10 Paul Getty . . . had always been vastly, immeasurably wealthy, and yet went about looking like a man who cannot quite remember whether he remembered to turn the gas off before leaving home.
  The Pendulum Years (1970)

11 [Tony] Benn flung himself into the Sixties technology with the enthusiasm (not to say language) of a newly enrolled Boy Scout demonstrating knot-tying to his indulgent parents.
  The Pendulum Years (1970)

12 Between them, then, Walrus and Carpenter, they divided up the Sixties.
  of the Harolds, **Macmillan** *and* **Wilson**
  The Pendulum Years (1970)

13 The Stag at Bay with the mentality of a fox at large.
  of Harold **Macmillan**
  The Pendulum Years (1970)

14 I have heard tell of a Professor of Economics who has a sign on the wall of his study, reading 'the future is not what it was'. The sentiment was admirable; unfortunately, the past is not getting any better either.
  in *Sunday Times* 22 May 1977; cf. **Berra** 33:18

15 Whom the mad would destroy, they first make gods.
  of **Mao** *Zedong in 1967*
    Levin quoting himself in *The Times* 21 September 1987; see below

  Whom God would destroy He first sends mad.
    James Duport (1606–79) *Homeri Gnomologia* (1660), ultimately representing the scholastic annotation to Sophocles's *Antigone* 'Whenever God prepares evil for a man, He first damages his mind, with which he deliberates'

C. S. Lewis 1898–1963

English literary scholar

1 No one ever told me that grief felt so like
fear.
A Grief Observed (1961)

2 We have trained them [men] to think of
the Future as a promised land which
favoured heroes attain—not as
something which everyone reaches at the
rate of sixty minutes an hour, whatever
he does, whoever he is.
The Screwtape Letters (1942)

3 She's the sort of woman who lives for
others—you can always tell the others by
their hunted expression.
The Screwtape Letters (1942)

4 A young man who wishes to remain a
sound atheist cannot be too careful of his
reading.
Surprised by Joy (1955)

5 For twenty years I've stared my level best
To see if evening—any evening—would
suggest
A patient etherized upon a table;
In vain. I simply wasn't able.
on contemporary poetry
'A Confession' (1964); cf. **Eliot** 100:3

6 Often when I pray I wonder if I am not
posting letters to a non-existent address.
letter to Arthur Greeves, 24 December 1930

7 Courage is not simply *one* of the virtues
but the form of every virtue at the testing
point.
Cyril Connolly *The Unquiet Grave* (1944); cf.
Barrie 24:2

8 He that but looketh on a plate of ham
and eggs to lust after it, hath already
committed breakfast with it in his heart.
letter, 10 March 1954

9 Leavis demands moral earnestness; I
prefer morality . . . I mean I'd sooner live
among people who don't cheat at cards
than among people who are earnest
about not cheating at cards.
'Unreal Estates' in Kingsley Amis and Robert
Conquest (eds.) *Spectrum IV* (1965)

Sam M. Lewis 1885–1959 and Joe Young 1889–1939

American songwriters

10 How 'ya gonna keep 'em down on the
farm (after they've seen Paree)?
title of song (1919)

Sinclair Lewis 1885–1951

American novelist

11 Our American professors like their
literature clear and cold and pure and
very dead.
The American Fear of Literature (Nobel Prize
Address, 12 December 1930)

12 To George F. Babbitt, as to most
prosperous citizens of Zenith, his motor
car was poetry and tragedy, love and
heroism. The office was his pirate ship
but the car his perilous excursion ashore.
Babbitt (1922)

13 She did her work with the thoroughness
of a mind which reveres details and never
quite understands them.
Babbitt (1922)

Willmott Lewis 1877–1950

British journalist

14 I think it well to remember that, when
writing for the newspapers, we are
writing for an elderly lady in Hastings
who has two cats of which she is
passionately fond. Unless our stuff can
successfully compete for her interest with
those cats, it is no good.
Claud Cockburn *In Time of Trouble* (1957)

Wyndham Lewis 1882–1957

English novelist, painter, and critic

15 Gertrude Stein's prose-song is a cold,
black suet-pudding . . . Cut it at any
point, it is the same thing . . . all fat,
without nerve.
of Three Lives *(1909)*
Time and Western Man (1927)

16 Angels in jumpers.
*describing the figures in Stanley **Spencer's**
paintings*
attributed

Liberace 1919–87
American showman

1 I cry all the way to the bank.
on bad reviews (from the mid-1950s)
Autobiography (1973)

2 If I play Tchaikovsky I play his melodies and skip his spiritual struggles . . . If there's any time left over I fill in with a lot of runs up and down the keyboard.
Stuart Hall and Paddy Whannel (eds.) *The Popular Arts* (1964)

A. J. Liebling 1904–63
American writer

3 Freedom of the press is guaranteed only to those who own one.
'The Wayward Press: Do you belong in Journalism?' (1960)

J. A. Lindon

4 Points
Have no parts or joints
How then can they combine
To form a line?
M. Gardner *Wheels, Life and Other Mathematical Amusements* (1983)

Vachel Lindsay 1879–1931
American poet

5 Then I saw the Congo, creeping through the black,
Cutting through the forest with a golden track.
'The Congo' pt. 1 (1914)

6 Booth led boldly with his big bass drum—
(Are you washed in the blood of the Lamb?)
'General William Booth Enters into Heaven' (1913); see below

. . . Have washed their robes, and made them white in the blood of the Lamb.
Bible Revelation

7 Booth died blind and still by faith he trod,
Eyes still dazzled by the ways of God.
'General William Booth Enters into Heaven' (1913)

Gary Lineker 1960–
English footballer

8 The nice aspect about football is that, if things go wrong, it's the manager who gets the blame.
remark before his first match as captain of England
in *Independent* 12 September 1990

Eric Linklater 1899–1974
Scottish novelist

9 'There won't be any revolution in America,' said Isadore. Nikitin agreed. 'The people are all too clean. They spend all their time changing their shirts and washing themselves. You can't feel fierce and revolutionary in a bathroom.'
Juan In America (1931)

Walter Lippmann 1889–1974
American journalist

10 The final test of a leader is that he leaves behind him in other men the conviction and the will to carry on.
in *New York Herald Tribune* 14 April 1945

Joan Littlewood 1914–
British theatre director
and Charles Chilton 1914–

11 Oh what a lovely war.
title of stage show (1963)

Maxim Litvinov 1876–1951
Soviet diplomat

12 Peace is indivisible.
note to the Allies, 25 February 1920; A. U. Pope *Maxim Litvinoff* (1943)

Penelope Lively 1933–
English novelist

13 Language tethers us to the world; without it we spin like atoms.
Moon Tiger (1987)

14 We are walking lexicons. In a single sentence of idle chatter we preserve

Latin, Anglo-Saxon, Norse; we carry a museum inside our heads, each day we commemorate peoples of whom we have never heard.
Moon Tiger (1987)

Ken Livingstone 1945–
British Labour politician

1 If voting changed anything, they'd abolish it.
title of book, 1987

2 There are a lot of truly ghastly people gathered around Blair, like lice on the back of a hedgehog.
in *New Statesman* 10 October 1997

3 Politics is a marathon, not a sprint.
in *New Statesman* 10 October 1997

Richard Llewellyn 1907–83
Welsh novelist and dramatist

4 How green was my valley.
title of book (1939)

David Lloyd George
1863–1945
British Liberal statesman; Prime Minister, 1916–22
on Lloyd George: see **Anonymous** 10:11, **Asquith** 14:12, **Beaverbrook** 25:11, **Bennett** 31:8, **Clemenceau** 71:2, **Keynes** 170:14, 171:5

5 A mastiff? It is the Right Hon. Gentleman's poodle.
on the House of Lords and A. J. Balfour respectively
in the House of Commons, 26 June 1907

6 A fully-equipped duke costs as much to keep up as two Dreadnoughts; and dukes are just as great a terror and they last longer.
speech at Newcastle, 9 October 1909

7 The great peaks of honour we had forgotten—Duty, Patriotism, and—clad in glittering white—the great pinnacle of Sacrifice, pointing like a rugged finger to Heaven.
speech at Queen's Hall, London, 19 September 1914

8 At eleven o'clock this morning came to an end the cruellest and most terrible war that has ever scourged mankind. I hope we may say that thus, this fateful morning, came to an end all wars.
speech in the House of Commons, 11 November 1918

9 What is our task? To make Britain a fit country for heroes to live in.
speech at Wolverhampton, 23 November 1918

10 M. Clemenceau . . . is one of the greatest living orators, but he knows that the finest eloquence is that which gets things done and the worst is that which delays them.
speech at Paris Peace Conference, 18 January 1919

11 Unless I am mistaken, by the steps we have taken [in Ireland] we have murder by the throat.
speech at the Mansion House, 9 November 1920

*on being asked what place Arthur **Balfour** would have in history:*
12 He will be just like the scent on a pocket handkerchief.
Thomas Jones diary, 9 June 1922

13 If you want to succeed in politics, you must keep your conscience well under control.
Lord Riddell's diary, 23 April 1919

14 Death is the most convenient time to tax rich people.
Lord Riddell diary, 23 April 1919

15 The world is becoming like a lunatic asylum run by lunatics.
in *Observer* 8 January 1933; cf. **Rowland** 270:1

16 A politician was a person with whose politics you did not agree. When you did agree, he was a statesman.
speech at Central Hall, Westminster, 2 July 1935

17 Negotiating with de Valera . . . is like trying to pick up mercury with a fork.
to which de Valera replied, 'Why doesn't he use a spoon?'
M. J. MacManus *Eamon de Valera* (1944)

18 Sufficient conscience to bother him, but not sufficient to keep him straight.
*of Ramsay **MacDonald***
A. J. Sylvester *Life with Lloyd George* (1975)

David Lodge 1935–

English novelist

1 Literature is mostly about having sex and not much about having children. Life is the other way round.
The British Museum is Falling Down (1965)

2 Four times, under our educational rules, the human pack is shuffled and cut—at eleven-plus, sixteen-plus, eighteen-plus and twenty-plus—and happy is he who comes top of the deck on each occasion, but especially the last. This is called Finals, the very name of which implies that nothing of importance can happen after it.
Changing Places (1975)

Frank Loesser 1910–69

American songwriter

3 See what the boys in the back room will have
And tell them I'm having the same.
'Boys in the Back Room' (1939 song); cf. **Beaverbrook** 25:7

4 Isn't it grand! Isn't it fine! Look at the cut, the style, the line!
The suit of clothes is altogether, but altogether it's altogether
The most remarkable suit of clothes that I have ever seen.
'The King's New Clothes' (1952 song)

Frederick Loewe 1904–88

American composer

5 I don't like my music, but what is my opinion against that of millions of others.
Nat Shapiro (ed.) *An Encyclopedia of Quotations about Music* (1978)

Christopher Logue 1926–

English poet

6 Come to the edge.
We might fall.
Come to the edge.
It's too high!
COME TO THE EDGE!
And they came

and he pushed
and they flew . . .
on Apollinaire
'Come to the edge' (1969)

7 I, Christopher Logue, was baptized the year
Many thousands of Englishmen,
Fists clenched, their bellies empty,
Walked day and night on the capital city.
'The Song of Autobiography' (1996)

Jack London 1876–1916

American novelist

8 The call of the wild.
title of novel (1903)

Huey Long 1893–1935

American Democratic politician

9 For the present you can just call me the Kingfish.
Every Man a King (1933)

10 I can go Mr Wilson one better; I was born barefoot.
replying to the claim that an opponent had gone barefoot as a boy
T. Harry Williams *Huey Long* (1969); cf. **Bulmer-Thomas** 48:7

11 Oh hell, say that I am *sui generis* and let it go at that.
to journalists attempting to analyse his political personality
T. Harry Williams *Huey Long* (1969)

12 The time has come for all good men to rise above principle.
attributed

Lord Longford 1905–

British Labour politician and philanthropist

13 In 1969 I published a small book on Humility. It was a pioneering work which has not, to my knowledge, been superseded.
in *Tablet* 22 January 1994

Michael Longley 1939–

Irish poet

1 Astrologers or three wise men
Who may shortly be setting out
For a small house up the Shankill
Or the Falls, should pause on their way
To buy gifts at Jim Gibson's shop,
Dates and chestnuts and tangerines.
  'The Greengrocer' (1979)

2 I am travelling from one April to another.
It is the same train between the same
  embankments.
Gorse fires are smoking, but primroses
  burn
And celandines and white may and gorse
  flowers.
  'Gorse Fires' (1991)

Alice Roosevelt Longworth
1884–1980

daughter of Theodore **Roosevelt**
see also **Anonymous** 11:13

3 If you haven't got anything good to say
about anyone come and sit by me.
  maxim embroidered on a cushion in her home
    Michael Teague *Mrs L: Conversations with Alice
    Roosevelt Longworth* (1981)

Anita Loos 1893–1981

American writer

4 Gentlemen prefer blondes
  title of book (1925)

5 So this gentleman said a girl with brains
ought to do something with them besides
think.
  Gentlemen Prefer Blondes (1925)

6 She said she always believed in the old
addage, 'Leave them while you're
looking good.'
  Gentlemen Prefer Blondes (1925)

7 So I really think that American
gentlemen are the best after all, because
kissing your hand may make you feel
very very good but a diamond and safire
bracelet lasts forever.
  Gentlemen Prefer Blondes (1925); cf.
  Advertising slogans 3:12, **Robin** 265:6

8 Fun is fun but no girl wants to laugh all
of the time.
  Gentlemen Prefer Blondes (1925)

9 I'm furious about the women's
liberationists. They keep getting up on
soap boxes and proclaiming that women
are brighter than men. That's true, but it
should be kept very quiet or it ruins the
whole racket.
  attributed

Edward N. Lorenz 1917–

American meteorologist

10 Predictability: Does the flap of a
butterfly's wings in Brazil set off a
tornado in Texas?
  title of paper given to the American
  Association for the Advancement of Science,
  Washington, 29 December 1979; James Gleick
  Chaos (1988)

Konrad Lorenz 1903–89

Austrian zoologist

11 It is a good morning exercise for a
research scientist to discard a pet
hypothesis every day before breakfast.
  On Aggression (1966)

Joe Louis 1914–81

American boxer

12 He can run. But he can't hide.
  *of Billy Conn, his opponent, before a heavyweight
  title fight, 19 June 1946*
    Louis: My Life Story (1947)

Courtney Love 1965–

American rock singer, wife of Kurt **Cobain**

13 When . . . you're first famous and you're
flush with your influence and you say
something whimsical, at a party or
something to be cool, it gets reported for
real.
  interview in *Guardian* 28 February 1997

Bernard Lovell 1913–

British astronomer

14 The pursuit of the good and evil are now
linked in astronomy as in almost all

science . . . The fate of human civilization will depend on whether the rockets of the future carry the astronomer's telescope or a hydrogen bomb.
   The Individual and the Universe (1959)

1 Youth is vivid rather than happy, but memory always remembers the happy things.
   in *The Times* 20 August 1993

James Lovell 1928–

American astronaut

2 Houston, we've had a problem.
   on Apollo 13 space mission, 14 April 1970
   in *The Times* 15 April 1970

David Low 1891–1963

British political cartoonist

3 I have never met anyone who wasn't against war. Even Hitler and Mussolini were, according to themselves.
   in *New York Times Magazine* 10 February 1946

Amy Lowell 1874–1925

American poet

4 And the softness of my body will be
      guarded by embrace
   By each button, hook, and lace.
   For the man who should loose me is
      dead,
   Fighting with the Duke in Flanders,
   In a pattern called a war.
   Christ! What are patterns for?
   'Patterns' (1916)

5 All books are either dreams or swords,
   You can cut, or you can drug, with
      words.
   'Sword Blades and Poppy Seed' (1914); cf.
   Kipling 175:16

6 Do we want laurels for ourselves most,
   Or most that no one else shall have any?
   'La Ronde du Diable' (1925)

Robert Lowell 1917–77

American poet

7 Terrible that old life of decency
   without unseemly intimacy

or quarrels, when the unemancipated
   woman
still had her Freudian papa and maids!
   'During Fever' (1959)

8 The aquarium is gone. Everywhere,
   giant finned cars nose forward like fish;
   a savage servility
   slides by on grease.
   'For the Union Dead' (1964)

9 Their monument sticks like a fishbone
   in the city's throat.
   'For the Union Dead' (1964)

10 These are the tranquillized *Fifties*,
   and I am forty. Ought I to regret my
   seed-time?
   'Memories of West Street and Lepke' (1956)

11 At forty-five,
   What next, what next?
   At every corner,
   I meet my Father,
   my age, still alive.
   'Middle Age' (1964)

12   This is death.
   To die and know it. This is the Black
      Widow, death.
   'Mr Edwards and the Spider' (1950)

13 After fifty
   the clock can't stop,
   each saving breath
   takes something.
   'Our Afterlife I' (1977)

14 The Lord survives the rainbow of His
   will.
   'The Quaker Graveyard in Nantucket' (1950)

15 We feel the machine slipping from our
      hands
   As if someone else were steering;
   If we see light at the end of the tunnel,
   It's the light of the oncoming train.
   'Since 1939' (1977)

16 But I suppose even God was born
   too late to trust the old religion
   'Tenth Muse' (1964)

17 The present, yes,
   we are in it,
   it's the infection
   of things gone.
   'We Took Our Paradise' (1977)

L. S. Lowry 1887–1976

English painter

1 I'm a simple man, and I use simple materials.
    Mervyn Levy *Paintings of L. S. Lowry* (1975)

Malcolm Lowry 1909–57

English novelist

2 How alike are the groans of love to those of the dying.
    Under the Volcano (1947)

Mina Loy d. 1966

American poet

3 [Be] *Brave* and deny at the outset—that pathetic clap-trap war cry *Woman is the equal of man* for She is NOT! . . . Leave off looking to men to find out what you are *not*—Seek within yourselves to find out what you *are*.
    'Feminist Manifesto' (1914, unpublished) in Virginia M. Kovidis *Mina Loy* (1980)

Clare Booth Luce 1903–

American diplomat, politician, and writer

4 Much of . . . his global thinking is, no matter how you slice it, still globaloney.
    speech to the House of Representatives, February 1943

5 But if God had wanted us to think just with our wombs, why did He give us a brain?
    in *Life* 16 October 1970

Rosa Luxemburg 1871–1919

German revolutionary

6 Freedom is always and exclusively freedom for the one who thinks differently.
    Die Russische Revolution (1918)

Jonathan Lynn 1943– and Antony Jay 1930–

English writers

7 'We went in,' he said, 'to screw the French by splitting them off from the Germans. The French went in to protect their inefficient farmers from commercial competition. The Germans went in to cleanse themselves of genocide and apply for readmission to the human race.'
    of the European Community
        Yes Minister (1982) vol. 2

8 I think it will be a clash between the political will and the administrative won't.
    Yes Prime Minister (1987) vol. 2

Michael Lynton

English publisher

9 The book is the greatest interactive medium of all time. You can underline it, write in the margins, fold down a page, skip ahead. And you can take it anywhere.
    on taking over as head of Penguin Books
        in *Daily Telegraph* 19 August 1996

Mary McAleese 1951–

Irish stateswoman; President from 1997

10 Apart from the shamrock, the President should not wear emblems or symbols of any kind.
    deciding not to wear a poppy at her inauguration on 11 November 1997
        in *Guardian* 6 November 1997

11 I went back to the study hall where I met my husband at a debating competition and where, I am pleased to put it on record, I beat him.
    revisiting her old school
        in *Irish Times* 6 December 1997 'This Week They Said'

Alexander McArthur and H. Kingsley Long

12 Battles and sex are the only free diversions in slum life. Couple them with drink, which costs money, and you have the three principal outlets for that escape complex which is for ever working in the tenement dweller's subconscious mind.
    No Mean City (1935)

Douglas MacArthur
1880–1964

American general
on MacArthur: see **Perelman** 246:13,
Truman 313:7

1 I came through and I shall return.
*on reaching Australia, having broken through
Japanese lines en route from Corregidor*
    statement in Adelaide, 20 March 1942

2 In war, indeed, there can be no
substitute for victory.
    address to a Joint Meeting of Congress, 19
    April 1951

3 I still remember the refrain of one of the
most popular barracks ballads of that
day, which proclaimed most proudly that
old soldiers never die; they just fade
away. I now close my military career and
just fade away.
    address to a Joint Meeting of Congress, 19
    April 1951; cf. **Foley** 114:12

Rose Macaulay 1881–1958

English novelist

4 'Take my camel, dear,' said my aunt Dot,
as she climbed down from this animal on
her return from High Mass.
    The Towers of Trebizond (1956)

Anthony McAuliffe 1898–1975

American general

5 Nuts!
    replying to the German demand for surrender
    at Bastogne, Belgium, 22 December 1944

Eugene McCarthy 1916–

American Democratic politician

6 Being in politics is like being a football
coach. You have to be smart enough to
understand the game, and dumb enough
to think it's important.
    while campaigning for the presidency
    in an interview, 1968

Joseph McCarthy 1908–57

American politician and anti-Communist
agitator

7 I have here in my hand a list of two
hundred and five [people] that were
known to the Secretary of State as being
members of the Communist Party and
who nevertheless are still working and
shaping the policy of the State
Department.
    speech at Wheeling, West Virginia, 9 February
    1950

8 McCarthyism is Americanism with its
sleeves rolled.
    speech in Wisconsin, 1952; Richard Rovere
    Senator Joe McCarthy (1973)

Mary McCarthy 1912–89

American novelist

9 When an American heiress wants to buy
a man, she at once crosses the Atlantic.
The only really materialistic people I
have ever met have been Europeans.
    On the Contrary (1961) 'America the Beautiful'

10 The immense popularity of American
movies abroad demonstrates that Europe
is the unfinished negative of which
America is the proof.
    On the Contrary (1961) 'America the Beautiful'

11 If someone tells you he is going to make a
'realistic decision', you immediately
understand that he has resolved to do
something bad.
    On the Contrary (1961) 'American Realist
    Playwrights'

12 In violence, we forget who we are.
    On the Contrary (1961) 'Characters in Fiction'

13 There are no new truths, but only truths
that have not been recognized by those
who have perceived them without
noticing.
    On the Contrary (1961) 'Vita Activa'

14 Every word she writes is a lie, including
'and' and 'the'.
    on Lillian **Hellman**
    quoting herself, in *New York Times* 16 February
    1980

Paul McCartney 1942–

English pop singer and songwriter
see also **Lennon and McCartney**

1 He could be a manoeuvring swine, which
no one ever realized.
of John **Lennon**
Hunter Davies *The Beatles* (1985)

2 Ballads and babies. That's what
happened to me.
on reaching the age of fifty
in *Time* 8 June 1992

3 You cannot reheat a soufflé.
discounting rumours of a Beatles reunion
attributed; L. Botts *Loose Talk* (1980)

Ewen MacColl 1915–89

English folksinger and songwriter

4 I found my love by the gasworks crofts
Dreamed a dream by the old canal
Kissed my girl by the factory wall
Dirty old town, dirty old town.
'Dirty Old Town' (1950 song)

5 And I used to sleep standing on my feet
As we hunted for the shoals of herring.
'The Shoals of Herring' (1960 song, from the
BBC Radio broadcast *Singing the Fishing*)

David McCord 1897–

6 By and by
God caught his eye.
'Remainders' (1935); epitaph for a waiter

Horace McCoy 1897–1955

American novelist

7 They shoot horses don't they.
title of novel (1935)

John McCrae 1872–1918

Canadian poet and military physician

8 In Flanders fields the poppies blow
Between the crosses, row on row.
'In Flanders Fields' (1915)

Carson McCullers 1917–67

American writer

9 The heart is a lonely hunter.
title of novel (1940); see below

My heart is a lonely hunter that hunts
on a lonely hill.
Fiona McLeod (1855–1905) 'The Lonely Hunter'
(1896)

Derek McCulloch

see **Catch-phrases** 57:20

Hugh MacDiarmid 1892–1978

Scottish poet and nationalist

10 I'll ha'e nae hauf-way hoose, but aye be
whaur
Extremes meet—it's the only way I ken
To dodge the curst conceit o' bein' richt
That damns the vast majority o' men.
A Drunk Man Looks at the Thistle (1926)

11 He's no a man ava',
And lacks a proper pride,
Gin less than a' the world
Can ser' him for a bride!
A Drunk Man Looks at the Thistle (1926)

12 The rose of all the world is not for me.
I want for my part
Only the little white rose of Scotland
That smells sharp and sweet—and breaks
the heart.
'The Little White Rose' (1934)

13   I must be a Bolshevik
Before the Revolution, but I'll cease to be
one quick
When Communism comes to rule the
roost,
For real literature can exist only when
it's produced
By madmen, hermits, heretics,
Dreamers, rebels, sceptics,
—And such a door of utterance has been
given to me
As none may close whosoever they be.
'Talking with Five Thousand People in
Edinburgh' (1972)

14 Scotland small? Our multiform, our
infinite Scotland *small*?
Only as a patch of hillside may be a
cliché corner

To a fool who cries 'Nothing but
heather!' . . .
Direadh 1 (1974)

Dwight Macdonald 1906–82

American writer and film critic

1 Götterdämmerung without the gods.
of the use of atomic bombs against the Japanese
in *Politics* September 1945 'The Bomb'

Ramsay MacDonald
1866–1937

British Labour statesman; Prime Minister,
1924, 1931–5
on MacDonald: see **Churchill** 65:10, **Lloyd
George** 192:18

2 We hear war called murder. It is not: it is
suicide.
in *Observer* 4 May 1930

3 Tomorrow every Duchess in London will
be wanting to kiss me!
*after forming the National Government, 25 August
1931*
Viscount Snowden *An Autobiography* (1934)

Trevor McDonald 1939–

West Indian-born broadcaster

4 I am a West Indian peasant who has
drifted into this business and who has
survived. If I knew the secret, I would
bottle it and sell it.
in *Independent* 20 April 1996 'Quote Unquote'

John McEnroe 1959–

American tennis player

5 You cannot be serious!
said to tennis umpire at Wimbledon, early
1980s

Ian McEwan 1948–

English novelist

6 Shakespeare would have grasped wave
functions, Donne would have understood
complementarity and relative time. They
would have been excited. What richness!

They would have plundered this new
science for their imagery. And they
would have educated their audiences too.
But you 'arts' people, you're not only
ignorant of these magnificent things,
you're rather proud of knowing nothing.
The Child in Time (1987)

Patrick McGoohan 1928–

American actor,

George Markstein, and
David Tomblin

7 I am not a number, I am a free man!
Number Six, in *The Prisoner* (TV series
1967–68); additional title sequence from the
second episode onwards

Roger McGough 1937–

English poet

8 You will put on a dress of guilt
and shoes with broken high ideals.
'Comeclose and Sleepnow' (1967)

9 Let me die a youngman's death
Not a clean & in-between-
The-sheets, holy-water death.
'Let Me Die a Youngman's Death' (1967)

George McGovern 1922–

American Democratic politician, presidential
candidate in 1972

10 Sometimes, when they say you're ahead
of your time, it's just a polite way of
saying you have a real bad sense of
timing.
in *Observer* 18 March 1990 'Sayings of the
Week'

Ian MacGregor 1912–98

Scottish-born industrialist whose career
was developed in the US; Chairman of the
National Coal Board, 1983–6
on MacGregor: see **Jenkins** 160:10

11 People are now discovering the price of
insubordination and insurrection. And
boy, are we going to make it stick!
during the coal-miners' strike
in *Sunday Telegraph* 10 March 1985

Jimmie McGregor 1932–

Scottish singer and songwriter

1 Oh, he's football crazy, he's football mad
And the football it has robbed him o' the
wee bit sense he had.
And it would take a dozen skivvies, his
clothes to wash and scrub,
Since our Jock became a member of that
terrible football club.
'Football Crazy' (1960 song)

Lord McGregor 1921–

British sociologist

2 An odious exhibition of journalists
dabbling their fingers in the stuff of other
people's souls.
*on Press coverage of the marital difficulties of the
Prince and Princess of Wales, speaking as
Chairman of the Press Complaints Commission*
in *The Times* 9 June 1992

Dennis McHarrie

3 'He died who loved to live,' they'll say,
'Unselfishly so we might have today!'
Like hell! He fought because he had to
fight;
He died that's all. It was his unlucky
night.
'Luck' (1980); cf. **Epitaphs** 106:2

Compton Mackenzie
1883–1972

English novelist

4 Prostitution. Selling one's body to keep
one's soul: this is the meaning of the sins
that were forgiven to the woman because
she loved much: one might say of most
marriages that they were selling one's
soul to keep one's body.
The Adventures of Sylvia Scarlett (1918)

5 Women do not find it difficult nowadays
to behave like men, but they often find it
extremely difficult to behave like
gentlemen.
Literature in My Time (1933)

6 You are offered a piece of bread and
butter that feels like a damp handkerchief

and sometimes, when cucumber is added
to it, like a wet one.
Vestal Fire (1927)

7 Love makes the world go round? Not at
all. Whisky makes it go round twice as
fast.
Whisky Galore (1947)

Kelvin Mackenzie 1946–

British journalist and media executive

8 We are surfing food.
of cable television
in *Trouble at the Top* (BBC2) 12 February 1997,
a documentary on the launch of Live TV,
originally run by Janet **Street-Porter**

Alistair Maclean 1922–1987

Scottish thriller writer

9 Where eagles dare.
title of novel (1967)

Don McLean 1945–

American songwriter

10 Something touched me deep inside
The day the music died.
on the death of Buddy Holly
'American Pie' (1972 song)

11 So, bye, bye, Miss American Pie,
Drove my Chevy to the levee
But the levee was dry.
Them good old boys was drinkin'
whiskey and rye
Singin' 'This'll be the day that I die.'
'American Pie' (1972 song)

Archibald MacLeish
1892–1982

American poet, later public official

12 A poem should not mean
But be.
'Ars Poetica' (1926)

Iain Macleod 1913–70

British Conservative politician
on Macleod: see **Salisbury** 274:5

13 It is some measure of the tightness of the
magic circle on this occasion that neither

the Chancellor of the Exchequer nor the Leader of the House of Commons had any inkling of what was happening.

*of the 'evolvement' of Alec Douglas-**Home** as Conservative leader after the resignation of Harold **Macmillan***

in *The Spectator* 17 January 1964

1 The Conservative Party always in time forgives those who were wrong. Indeed often, in time, they forgive those who were right.

in *The Spectator* 21 February 1964

Marshall McLuhan 1911–80

Canadian communications scholar

2 The new electronic interdependence recreates the world in the image of a global village.

The Gutenberg Galaxy (1962); cf. **Debord** 86:3

3 Dewey in reacting against passive print culture was surf-boarding along the new electronic wave.

The Gutenberg Galaxy (1962)

4 One matter Englishmen don't think in the least funny is their happy consciousness of possessing a deep sense of humour.

Mechanical Bride (1951) 'The Ballet Luce'

5 When this circuit learns your job, what are you going to do?

The Medium is the Massage (1967)

6 If the nineteenth century was the age of the editorial chair, ours is the century of the psychiatrist's couch.

Understanding Media (1964)

7 The medium is the message.

Understanding Media (1964)

8 The name of a man is a numbing blow from which he never recovers.

Understanding Media (1964)

9 The car has become an article of dress without which we feel uncertain, unclad and incomplete in the urban compound.

Understanding Media (1964)

10 The car has become the carapace, the protective and aggressive shell, of urban and suburban man.

Understanding Media (1964)

11 People don't actually read newspapers. They get into them every morning, like a hot bath.

in 1965; attributed

12 Television brought the brutality of war into the comfort of the living room. Vietnam was lost in the living rooms of America—not the battlefields of Vietnam.

in *Montreal Gazette* 16 May 1975

13 Gutenberg made everybody a reader. Xerox makes everybody a publisher.

in *Guardian Weekly* 12 June 1977

Harold Macmillan 1894–1986

British Conservative statesman; Prime Minister, 1957–63
*on Macmillan: see **Levin** 189:12, 189:13, **Thorpe** 309:7; see also **Hitler** 149:10, **Misquotations** 218:13*

14 We . . . are Greeks in this American empire . . . We must run the Allied Forces HQ as the Greeks ran the operations of the Emperor Claudius

*to Richard **Crossman** in 1944*

in *Sunday Telegraph* 9 February 1964

15 There ain't gonna be no war.

following the Geneva summit

at a London press conference, 24 July 1955

16 Forever poised between a cliché and an indiscretion.

on the life of a Foreign Secretary

in *Newsweek* 30 April 1956

17 Let us be frank about it: most of our people have never had it so good.

'You Never Had It So Good' was the Democratic Party slogan during the 1952 US election campaign

speech at Bedford, 20 July 1957

18 I thought the best thing to do was to settle up these little local difficulties, and then turn to the wider vision of the Commonwealth.

on leaving for a Commonwealth tour, following the resignation of the Chancellor of the Exchequer and others

statement at London airport 7 January 1958

19 The wind of change is blowing through this continent, and, whether we like it or

not, this growth of [African] national consciousness is a political fact.

> speech at Cape Town, 3 February 1960; *Pointing the Way* (1972)

1 As usual the Liberals offer a mixture of sound and original ideas. Unfortunately none of the sound ideas is original and none of the original ideas is sound.

> speech to London Conservatives, 7 March 1961

2 He enjoys prophesying the imminent fall of the capitalist system and is prepared to play a part, any part, in its burial, except that of mute.

> *of Aneurin* **Bevan**
>
> Michael Foot *Aneurin Bevan* (1962)

3 I was determined that no British government should be brought down by the action of two tarts.

> *comment on the Profumo affair, July 1963*
>
> A. Sampson *Macmillan* (1967)

4 It is thinking about themselves that is really the curse of the younger generation—they appear to have no other subject which interests them at all.

> *the 'Tuesday memorandum', a draft of a letter to the Queen, advising on his successor but not sent, 1963*
>
> D. R. Thorpe *Alec Douglas-Home* (1996)

5 If people want a sense of purpose, they should get it from their archbishops. They should not hope to receive it from their politicians.

> to Henry Fairlie, 1963; H. Fairlie *The Life of Politics* (1968)

6 Power? It's like a Dead Sea fruit. When you achieve it, there is nothing there.

> Anthony Sampson *The New Anatomy of Britain* (1971)

7 There are three bodies no sensible man directly challenges: the Roman Catholic Church, the Brigade of Guards and the National Union of Mineworkers.

> in *Observer* 22 February 1981; cf. **Baldwin** 21:10

8 Events, dear boy. Events.

> *when asked what his biggest problem was*
>
> attributed

on the appointment of Michael Ramsey to succeed Geoffrey Fisher as Archbishop of Canterbury:

9 We have had enough of Martha and it is time for some Mary.

> attributed

Robert McNamara 1916–
American Democratic politician, Secretary of Defense during the Vietnam War

10 I don't object to it's being called 'McNamara's War' . . . It is a very important war and I am pleased to be identified with it and do whatever I can to win it.

> in *New York Times* 25 April 1964

11 We . . . acted according to what we thought were the principles and traditions of this nation. We were wrong. We were terribly wrong.

> *of the conduct of the Vietnam War by the* **Kennedy** *and* **Johnson** *administrations*
>
> speaking in Washington, just before the twentieth anniversary of the American withdrawal from Vietnam; in *Daily Telegraph* (electronic edition) 10 April 1995

12 Military force—especially when wielded by an outside power—cannot bring order in a country that cannot govern itself.

> in *Daily Telegraph* (electronic edition) 10 April 1995

Louis MacNeice 1907–63
British poet, born in Belfast

13 Better authentic mammon than a bogus god.

> *Autumn Journal* (1939)

14 It's no go the merrygoround, it's no go the rickshaw,
All we want is a limousine and a ticket for the peepshow.

> 'Bagpipe Music' (1938)

15 It's no go the picture palace, it's no go the stadium,
It's no go the country cot with a pot of pink geraniums,
It's no go the Government grants, it's no go the elections,
Sit on your arse for fifty years and hang your hat on a pension.

> 'Bagpipe Music' (1938)

1 The glass is falling hour by hour, the
glass will fall for ever,
But if you break the bloody glass you
won't hold up the weather.
'Bagpipe Music' (1938)

2 Crumbling between the fingers, under
the feet,
Crumbling behind the eyes,
Their world gives way and dies
And something twangs and breaks at the
end of the street.
'Débâcle' (1941)

3 So they were married—to be the more
together—
And found they were never again so
much together,
Divided by the morning tea,
By the evening paper,
By children and tradesmen's bills.
'Les Sylphides' (1941)

4 Time was away and somewhere else,
There were two glasses and two chairs
And two people with the one pulse.
'Meeting Point' (1941)

5 I am not yet born; O fill me
With strength against those who would
freeze my
humanity.
'Prayer Before Birth' (1944)

6 Let them not make me a stone and let
them not spill me,
Otherwise kill me.
'Prayer Before Birth' (1944)

7 World is crazier and more of it than we
think,
Incorrigibly plural. I peel and portion
A tangerine and spit the pips and feel
The drunkenness of things being various.
'Snow' (1935)

8 Down the road someone is practising
scales,
The notes like little fishes vanish with a
wink of tails,
Man's heart expands to tinker with his
car
For this is Sunday morning, Fate's great
bazaar.
'Sunday Morning' (1935)

9 The sunlight on the garden
Hardens and grows cold,
We cannot cage the minute

Within its net of gold.
'Sunlight on the Garden' (1938)

10 By a high star our course is set,
Our end is Life. Put out to sea.
'Thalassa' (1964)

Candia McWilliam 1955–

English novelist

11 With the birth of each child, you lose two
novels.
in *Guardian* 5 May 1993

Geoffrey Madan 1895–1947

English bibliophile

12 Conservative ideal of freedom and
progress: everyone to have an unfettered
opportunity of remaining exactly where
they are.
Geoffrey Madan's Notebooks (1981)

13 The dust of exploded beliefs may make a
fine sunset.
Livre sans nom: Twelve Reflections (privately
printed 1934)

Salvador de Madariaga
1886–1978

Spanish writer and diplomat

14 Since, in the main, it is not armaments
that cause wars but wars (or the fears
thereof) that cause armaments, it follows
that every nation will at every moment
strive to keep its armament in an efficient
state as required by its fear, otherwise
styled security.
Morning Without Noon (1974)

Madonna 1958–

American pop singer and actress

15 Many people see Eva Perón as either a
saint or the incarnation of Satan. That
means I can definitely identify with her.
on playing the starring role in the film Evita
in *Newsweek* 5 February 1996

John Gillespie Magee

1922–41

American airman, member of the Royal
Canadian Airforce

1 Oh! I have slipped the surly bonds of
earth
And danced the skies on laughter-
silvered wings.

*quoted by Ronald **Reagan** following the explosion
of the space shuttle* Challenger, *January 1986*
'High Flight' (1943); cf. **Reagan** 262:4

2 And, while with silent lifting mind I've
trod
The high, untrespassed sanctity of space,
Put out my hand and touched the face of
God.
'High Flight' (1943); cf. **Reagan** 262:4

Derek Mahon 1941–

Northern Irish poet

3 'I am just going outside and may be some
time.'
The others nod, pretending not to know.
At the heart of the ridiculous, the
sublime.
'Antarctica' (1985); cf. **Last words** 182:6

4 Somewhere beyond the scorched gable
end and the burnt-out buses
there is a poet indulging
his wretched rage for order.
'Rage for Order' (1978)

5 Even now there are places where a
thought might grow—
Peruvian mines, worked out and
abandoned
To a slow clock of condensation,
An echo trapped for ever, and a flutter
Of wildflowers in the lift-shaft . . .
And in a disused shed in Co. Wexford.
'A Disused Shed in Co. Wexford' (1978)

Margaret Mahy 1936–

New Zealand writer for children

6 Canadians are Americans with no
Disneyland.
The Changeover (1984)

Norman Mailer 1923–

American novelist and essayist

7 Sentimentality is the emotional
promiscuity of those who have no
sentiment.
Cannibals and Christians (1966)

8 The horror of the Twentieth Century was
the size of each event, and the paucity of
its reverberation.
A Fire on the Moon (1970)

9 So we think of Marilyn who was every
man's love affair with America, Marilyn
Monroe who was blonde and beautiful
and had a sweet little rinky-dink of a
voice and all the cleanliness of all the
clean American backyards.
Marilyn (1973)

10 Ultimately a hero is a man who would
argue with the Gods, and so awakens
devils to contest his vision.
The Presidential Papers (1976) Special Preface
to the 1st Berkeley Edition

11 Hip is the sophistication of the wise
primitive in a giant jungle.
Voices of Dissent (1959) 'The White Negro'

12 Once a newspaper touches a story, the
facts are lost forever, even to the
protagonists.
in *Esquire* June 1960

13 All the security around the American
president is just to make sure the man
who shoots him gets caught.
in *Sunday Telegraph* 4 March 1990

John Major 1943–

British Conservative statesman; Prime
Minister, 1990–7

14 If the policy isn't hurting, it isn't
working.
on controlling inflation
speech in Northampton, 27 October 1989; cf.
Political slogans 252:2

15 Society needs to condemn a little more
and understand a little less.
interview with *Mail on Sunday* 21 February
1993

16 Fifty years on from now, Britain will still
be the country of long shadows on

county [cricket] grounds, warm beer, invincible green suburbs, dog lovers, and—as George Orwell said—old maids bicycling to Holy Communion through the morning mist.

speech to the Conservative Group for Europe, 22 April 1993; cf. **Orwell** 238:5

1 It is time to get back to basics: to self-discipline and respect for the law, to consideration for others, to accepting responsibility for yourself and your family, and not shuffling it off on the state.

speech to the Conservative Party Conference, 8 October 1993

2 A thousand days of Labour could ditch a thousand years of British history.

*alluding to Tony **Blair**'s statement at the Labour Party Conference that he would have 1,000 days to prepare for the millennium*

speech in Mostyn, North Wales, 14 February 1997; cf. **Gaitskell** 122:14

3 So right. OK. We lost.

on election night

in *Guardian* 3 May 1997

4 When the final curtain comes down, it's time to get off the stage.

outside 10 Downing Street on 2 May, leaving office as Prime Minister and announcing that he would resign as Party Leader

in *Guardian* 3 May 1997

Bernard Malamud 1914–86

American novelist and short-story writer

5 The past exudes legend: one can't make pure clay of time's mud. There is no life that can be recaptured wholly; as it was. Which is to say that all biography is ultimately fiction.

Dubin's Lives (1979)

George Leigh Mallory
1886–1924

British mountaineer

6 Because it's there.

on being asked why he wanted to climb Mount Everest (Mallory was lost on Everest in the following year)

in *New York Times* 18 March 1923

André Malraux 1901–76

French novelist, essayist, and art critic

7 There are not fifty ways of fighting, there's only one, and that's to win. Neither revolution nor war consists in doing what one pleases.

L'Espoir (1937)

8 Man knows that the world is not made on a human scale; and he wishes that it were.

Les Noyers d'Altenburg (1945)

9 *L'art est un anti-destin.*
Art is a revolt against fate.

Les Voix du silence (1951)

Lord Mancroft 1914–87

British Conservative politician

10 Cricket—a game which the English, not being a spiritual people, have invented in order to give themselves some conception of eternity.

Bees in Some Bonnets (1979)

Nelson Mandela 1918–

South African statesman, President since 1994; former husband of Winnie **Mandela**

11 I have dedicated my life to this struggle of the African people. I have fought against white domination, and I have fought against black domination. I have cherished the ideal of a democratic and free society in which all persons live together in harmony with equal opportunities. It is an ideal which I hope to live for, and to see realized. But my lord, if needs be, it is an ideal for which I am prepared to die.

speech in Johannesburg, 20 April 1964, which he quoted on his release in Cape Town, 11 February 1990

12 I stand here before you not as a prophet but as a humble servant of you, the people. Your tireless and heroic sacrifices have made it possible for me to be here today. I therefore place the remaining years of my life in your hands.

speech in Cape Town 11 February 1990

13 Through its imperialist system Britain brought about untold suffering of

millions of people. And this is an historical fact. To be able to admit this would increase the respect, you know, which we have for British institutions.
in Guardian 2 April 1990

1 No one is born hating another person because of the colour of his skin, or his background, or his religion. People must learn to hate, and if they can learn to hate, they can be taught to love, for love comes more naturally to the human heart than its opposite.
Long Walk to Freedom (1994)

2 True reconciliation does not consist in merely forgetting the past.
speech, 7 January 1996

3 Ever since I came back from jail [in February 1990] not once has she ever entered my bedroom when I was awake.
*of his wife Winnie **Mandela** during the hearing of their divorce*
in Johannesburg, 18 March 1996; in Daily Telegraph 19 March 1996

Winnie Mandela 1934–
South African political activist; former wife of Nelson **Mandela**
*on Mandela: see **Mandela** 206:3*

4 With that stick of matches, with our necklace, we shall liberate this country.
speech in black townships, 14 April 1986

Peter Mandelson 1953–
British Labour politician

5 Few politicians are good at taking the high ground and throwing themselves off it.
*of Tony **Blair** and the revision of Clause Four; cf. **Blair** 38:12*
in New Yorker 5 February 1996

6 I can have a big say because I am the owner, the sole shareholder. I don't get involved in half measures.
on the £750 million Millennium Dome project
in Observer 6 July 1997 'Soundbites'

7 You'll say I'm in charge of a Mickey Mouse project.
refusing to be photographed holding a balloon at Disney World
in Daily Telegraph 5 January 1998

Nadezhda Mandelstam
d. 1980
wife of Osip **Mandelstam**

8 He was as helpless as everybody else, but at least he tried to do something for others.
of the Russian writer and journalist Ilya Ehrenburg (1891–1967)
Hope Abandoned (1974)

Osip Mandelstam 1892–1938
Russian poet; husband of Nadezhda **Mandelstam**

9 The age is rocking the wave
with human grief
to a golden beat, and an adder
is breathing in time with it in the grass.
'The Age' (1923)

10 Perhaps my whisper was already born before my lips.
'Poems Published Posthumously' (written 1934)

Herbie Mann 1930–
American jazz musician

11 If you're in jazz and more than ten people like you, you're labelled commercial.
Henry Pleasants Serious Music and all that Jazz! (1969)

Thomas Mann 1875–1955
German novelist

12 Death in Venice.
title of novella (1912)

13 Time has no divisions to mark its passage, there is never a thunderstorm or blare of trumpets to announce the beginning of a new month or year. Even when a new century begins it is only we mortals who ring bells and fire off pistols.
The Magic Mountain (1924)

14 We come out of the dark and go into the dark again, and in between lie the experiences of our life.
The Magic Mountain (1924)

1 A man's dying is more the survivors' affair than his own.
    The Magic Mountain (1924)

2 Speech is civilization itself. The word, even the most contradictory word, preserves contact—it is silence which isolates.
    The Magic Mountain (1924)

Katherine Mansfield
1888–1923

New Zealand-born short-story writer

3 E. M. Forster never gets any further than warming the teapot. He's a rare fine hand at that. Feel this teapot. Is it not beautifully warm? Yes, but there ain't going to be no tea.
    diary, May 1917

4 Whenever I prepare for a journey I prepare as though for death. Should I never return, all is in order.
    diary, 29 January 1922

Mao Zedong 1893–1976

Chinese statesman; chairman of the Communist Party of the Chinese People's Republic from 1949
on Mao: see **Levin** 189:15

5 Politics is war without bloodshed while war is politics with bloodshed.
    lecture, 1938; *Selected Works* (1965) vol. 2

6 Every Communist must grasp the truth, 'Political power grows out of the barrel of a gun'.
    speech, 6 November 1938

7 The atom bomb is a paper tiger which the United States reactionaries use to scare people. It looks terrible, but in fact it isn't . . . All reactionaries are paper tigers.
    interview, 1946; *Selected Works* (1961) vol. 4

8 Letting a hundred flowers blossom and a hundred schools of thought contend is the policy for promoting progress in the arts and the sciences and a flourishing socialist culture in our land.
    speech in Peking, 27 February 1957

Diego Maradona 1960–

Argentine football player

9 The goal was scored a little bit by the hand of God, another bit by head of Maradona.
    on his controversial goal against England in the 1986 World Cup
        in *Guardian* 1 July 1986

John Marchi 1948–

American Republican politician

10 We ought not to permit a cottage industry in the God business.
    on hearing that British scientists had successfully cloned a lamb (Dolly)
        in *Guardian* 28 February 1997

Princess Margaret 1930–

British princess, sister of **Elizabeth II**

11 My children are not royal, they just happen to have the Queen as their aunt.
    Elizabeth Longford (ed.) *The Oxford Book of Royal Anecdotes* (1989)

Miriam Margolyes 1941–

English actress

12 Life, if you're fat, is a minefield—you have to pick your way, otherwise you blow up.
    in *Observer* 9 June 1991

Lynn Margulis 1938–

American biologist

13 Gaia is a tough bitch. People think the earth is going to die and they have to save it, that's ridiculous . . . There's no doubt that Gaia can compensate for our output of greenhouse gases, but the environment that's left will not be happy for any people.
    in *New York Times Biographical Service* January 1996

Johnny Marks 1909–85

American songwriter

14 Rudolph, the Red-Nosed Reindeer
    Had a very shiny nose,

And if you ever saw it,
You would even say it glows.

> 'Rudolph, the Red-Nosed Reindeer' (1949 song)

Bob Marley 1945–81

Jamaican reggae musician and songwriter

1 Get up, stand up
Stand up for your rights
Get up, stand up
Never give up the fight.

> 'Get up, Stand up' (1973 song)

2 I shot the sheriff
But I swear it was in self-defence
I shot the sheriff
And they say it is a capital offence.

> 'I Shot the Sheriff' (1974 song)

Don Marquis 1878–1937

American poet and journalist

3 procrastination is the
art of keeping
up with yesterday.

> *archy and mehitabel* (1927) 'certain maxims of archy'

4 an optimist is a guy
that has never had
much experience.

> *archy and mehitabel* (1927) 'certain maxims of archy'

5 it s cheerio
my deario that
pulls a lady through.

> *archy and mehitabel* (1927) 'cheerio, my deario'

6 I have got you out here
in the great open spaces
where cats are cats.

> *archy and mehitabel* (1927) 'mehitabel has an adventure'

7 but wotthehell archy wotthehell
jamais triste archy jamais triste
that is my motto.

> *archy and mehitabel* (1927) 'mehitabel sees paris'

8 boss there is always
a comforting thought
in time of trouble when
it is not our trouble.

> *archy does his part* (1935) 'comforting thoughts'

9 did you ever
notice that when
a politician
does get an idea
he usually
gets it all wrong.

> *archys life of mehitabel* (1933) 'archygrams'

10 now and then
there is a person born
who is so unlucky
that he runs into accidents
which started to happen
to somebody else.

> *archys life of mehitabel* (1933) 'archy says'

11 Prohibition makes you want to cry into
your beer and denies you the beer to cry
into.

> *Sun Dial Time* (1936)

12 The art of newspaper paragraphing is to
stroke a platitude until it purrs like an
epigram.

> E. Anthony *O Rare Don Marquis* (1962)

13 Writing a book of poetry is like dropping
a rose petal down the Grand Canyon and
waiting for the echo.

> E. Anthony *O Rare Don Marquis* (1962)

Anthony Marriott 1931–
and Alistair Foot

14 No sex please—we're British.

> title of play (1971)

Arthur Marshall 1910–89

British journalist and former schoolmaster

15 What, knocked a tooth out? Never mind,
dear, laugh it off, laugh it off; it's all part
of life's rich pageant.

> *The Games Mistress* (recorded monologue, 1937)

Thomas R. Marshall

1854–1925

American politician

1 What this country needs is a really good 5-cent cigar.

in *New York Tribune* 4 January 1920

Dean Martin 1917–95

American singer and actor

2 You're not drunk if you can lie on the floor without holding on.

Paul Dickson *Official Rules* (1978)

Holt Marvell 1901–69

English songwriter

3 These foolish things remind me of you.

title of song (1935)

4 A cigarette that bears a lipstick's traces, An airline ticket to romantic places.

'These Foolish Things Remind Me of You' (1935 song)

Chico Marx 1891–1961

American film comedian

5 I wasn't kissing her, I was just whispering in her mouth.

on being discovered by his wife with a chorus girl
Groucho Marx and Richard J. Anobile *Marx Brothers Scrapbook* (1973)

Groucho Marx 1895–1977

American film comedian
see also **Epitaphs** 105:6, **Film lines** 110:3, 110:12, 110:16, 111:14, 112:2

6 PLEASE ACCEPT MY RESIGNATION. I DON'T WANT TO BELONG TO ANY CLUB THAT WILL ACCEPT ME AS A MEMBER.

Groucho and Me (1959)

7 I never forget a face, but in your case I'll be glad to make an exception.

Leo Rosten *People I have Loved, Known or Admired* (1970) 'Groucho'

8 I've been around so long, I knew Doris Day before she was a virgin.

Max Wilk *The Wit and Wisdom of Hollywood* (1972)

Queen Mary 1867–1953

Queen Consort of **George V**

9 Well, Mr Baldwin! *this* is a pretty kettle of fish!

*after **Edward VIII** had told her he was prepared to give up the throne to marry Mrs Simpson*
said on 17 November 1936; James Pope-Hennessy *Life of Queen Mary* (1959)

10 All *this* thrown away for *that*.

*on returning home to Marlborough House, London after the abdication of her son, King **Edward VIII**, December 1936*
David Duff *George and Elizabeth* (1983)

11 I do not think you have ever realised the shock, which the attitude you took up caused your family and the whole nation. It seemed inconceivable to those who had made such sacrifices during the war that you, as their King, refused a lesser sacrifice.

letter to the Duke of Windsor (formerly **Edward VIII**), July 1938; James Pope-Hennessy *Queen Mary* (1959)

12 So *that's* what hay looks like.

said at Badminton House, where she was evacuated during the Second World War
James Pope-Hennessy *Life of Queen Mary* (1959)

Eric Maschwitz 1901–69

13 A nightingale sang in Berkeley Square.

title of song (1940)

Donald Mason 1913–

American naval officer

14 Sighted sub, sank same.

on sinking a Japanese submarine in the Atlantic region (the first US naval success in the war)
radio message, 28 January 1942; in *New York Times* 27 February 1942

Leonard Matlovich d. 1988

American Air Force Sergeant

15 When I was in the military, they gave me a medal for killing two men and a discharge for loving one.

attributed

W. Somerset Maugham

1874–1965

English novelist

1 From the earliest times the old have rubbed it into the young that they are wiser than they, and before the young had discovered what nonsense this was they were old too, and it profited them to carry on the imposture.

Cakes and Ale (1930)

2 Poor Henry [James], he's spending eternity wandering round and round a stately park and the fence is just too high for him to peep over and they're having tea just too far away for him to hear what the countess is saying.

Cakes and Ale (1930)

3 You can't learn too soon that the most useful thing about a principle is that it can always be sacrificed to expediency.

The Circle (1921)

4 It is not true that suffering ennobles the character; happiness does that sometimes, but suffering, for the most part, makes men petty and vindictive.

The Moon and Sixpence (1919)

5 A woman can forgive a man for the harm he does her, but she can never forgive him for the sacrifices he makes on her account.

The Moon and Sixpence (1919)

6 Like all weak men he laid an exaggerated stress on not changing one's mind.

Of Human Bondage (1915)

7 People ask you for criticism, but they only want praise.

Of Human Bondage (1915)

8 Money is like a sixth sense without which you cannot make a complete use of the other five.

Of Human Bondage (1915)

9 I [Death] was astonished to see him in Baghdad, for I had an appointment with him tonight in Samarra.

Sheppey (1933)

10 A novelist must preserve a childlike belief in the importance of things which

common sense considers of no great consequence.

A Writer's Notebook (1949) written in 1933

11 There is no need for the writer to eat a whole sheep to be able to tell you what mutton tastes like. It is enough if he eats a cutlet. But he should do that.

A Writer's Notebook (1949) written in 1941

12 I am told that today rather more than 60 per cent of the men who go to the universities go on a Government grant. This is a new class that has entered upon the scene . . . They are scum.

in *Sunday Times* 25 December 1955

13 Dying is a very dull, dreary affair. And my advice to you is to have nothing whatever to do with it.

to his nephew Robin, in 1965

Robin Maugham *Conversations with Willie* (1978)

Bill Mauldin 1921–

American cartoonist

14 I feel like a fugitive from th' law of averages.

cartoon caption in *Up Front* (1945)

André Maurois 1885–1967

French writer

15 Growing old is no more than a bad habit which a busy man has no time to form.

The Art of Living (1940)

16 Wells, in part of Europe and in the United States, will for some years have wielded an intellectual dominion comparable to that won and held by Voltaire in the eighteenth century.

André Maurois *Poets and Prophets* (1936)

James Maxton 1885–1946

British Labour politician

17 All I say is, if you cannot ride two horses you have no right in the circus.

opposing disaffiliation of the Scottish Independent Labour Party from the Labour Party; usually quoted as, '. . . no right in the bloody circus'

in *Daily Herald* 12 January 1931

Glyn Maxwell 1962–

English poet

1 May his anorak grow big with jotters,
   Noting the numbers of trains he saw.
   'Curse on a Child' (1995)

Vladimir Mayakovsky
1893–1930

Russian poet
see also **Last words** 182:11

2 If you wish—
   . . . I'll be irreproachably tender;
   not a man, but—a cloud in trousers!
   'The Cloud in Trousers' (1915)

3 Not a sound. The universe sleeps, resting
   a huge ear on its paw with mites of stars.
   'The Cloud in Trousers' (1915)

4 In our language rhyme is a barrel. A
   barrel of dynamite. The line is a fuse. The
   line smoulders to the end and explodes;
   and the town is blown sky-high in a
   stanza.
   'Conversation with an Inspector of Taxes about
   Poetry' (1926)

5 The poet is always indebted to the
   universe, paying interest and fines on
   sorrow.
   'Conversation with an Inspector of Taxes about
   Poetry' (1926)

6 Oh for just
   one
   more conference
   regarding the eradication of all
       conferences!
   'In Re Conferences'; Herbert Marshall (ed.)
   Mayakovsky (1965)

7 To us love says humming that the heart's
   stalled motor has begun working again.
   'Letter from Paris to Comrade Kostorov on the
   Nature of Love' (1928)

8 Ours is the land.
   The air—ours.
   Ours the diamond mines of stars.
   And we will never,
   never!
   Allow anyone,
   anyone!
   To ravage our land with shells,

to tear our air with sharpened spear
points.
'Revolution: a Poet's Chronicle' (1917)

Percy Mayfield 1920–84

9 Hit the road, Jack.
   title of song (1961)

Charles H. Mayo 1865–1939

10 The definition of a specialist as one who
   'knows more and more about less and
   less' is good and true.
   in *Modern Hospital* September 1938

Margaret Mead 1901–78

American anthropologist

11 The knowledge that the personalities of
   the two sexes are socially produced is
   congenial to every programme that looks
   forward towards a planned order of
   society. It is a two-edged sword.
   *Sex and Temperament in Three Primitive
   Societies* (1935)

12 Women want mediocre men, and men
   are working hard to be as mediocre as
   possible.
   in *Quote Magazine* 15 June 1958

Shepherd Mead 1914–

American advertising executive

13 How to succeed in business without
   really trying.
   title of book (1952)

Hughes Mearns 1875–1965

American writer

14 As I was walking up the stair
   I met a man who wasn't there.
   He wasn't there again today.
   I wish, I wish he'd stay away.
   lines written for an amateur play *The Psycho-
   ed* (1910) and set to music in 1939 as 'The
   Little Man Who Wasn't There'

Peter Medawar 1915–87
English immunologist and author

1 A bishop wrote gravely to the *Times* inviting all nations to destroy 'the formula' of the atomic bomb. There is no simple remedy for ignorance so abysmal.
   The Hope of Progress (1972)

2 If a scientist were to cut his ear off, no one would take it as evidence of a heightened sensibility.
   'J. B. S.' (1968)

3 If it were an innocent, passive gullibility it would be excusable; but all too clearly, alas, it is an active willingness to be deceived.
   review of **Teilhard de Chardin**'s *The Phenomenon of Man* in *Mind* 1961 vol. 70

4 If politics is the art of the possible, research is surely the art of the soluble. Both are immensely practical-minded affairs.
   in *New Statesman* 19 June 1964; cf. **Butler** 50:10, **Galbraith** 123:14

5 During the 1950s, the first great age of molecular biology, the English Schools of Oxford and particularly of Cambridge produced more than a score of graduates of quite outstanding ability—much more brilliant, inventive, articulate and dialectically skilful than most young scientists; right up in the Watson class. But Watson had one towering advantage over all of them: in addition to being extremely clever he had something important to be clever *about*.
   review of James D. **Watson**'s *The Double Helix* in *New York Review of Books* 28 March 1968

6 Like all good memoirs it has not been emasculated by considerations of good taste.
   review of James D. **Watson**'s *The Double Helix* in *New York Review of Books* 28 March 1968

Golda Meir 1898–1978
Israeli stateswoman, Prime Minister 1969–74

7 Women's Liberation is just a lot of foolishness. It's the men who are discriminated against. They can't bear

children. And no-one's likely to do anything about that.
   in *Newsweek* 23 October 1972

Nellie Melba 1861–1931
Australian operatic soprano

8 Sing 'em muck! It's all they can understand!
   advice to Dame Clara Butt, prior to her departure for Australia
   W. H. Ponder *Clara Butt* (1928)

David Mellor 1949–
British Conservative politician

9 I do believe the popular press is drinking in the last chance saloon.
   interview on *Hard News* (Channel 4), 21 December 1989

H. L. Mencken 1880–1956
American journalist and literary critic

10 When women kiss it always reminds one of prize-fighters shaking hands.
   Chrestomathy (1949)

11 Love is the delusion that one woman differs from another.
   Chrestomathy (1949)

12 Puritanism. The haunting fear that someone, somewhere, may be happy.
   Chrestomathy (1949)

13 Democracy is the theory that the common people know what they want, and deserve to get it good and hard.
   A Little Book in C major (1916)

14 Conscience: the inner voice which warns us that someone may be looking.
   A Little Book in C major (1916)

15 It is now quite lawful for a Catholic woman to avoid pregnancy by a resort to mathematics, though she is still forbidden to resort to physics and chemistry.
   Notebooks (1956) 'Minority Report'

16 All successful newspapers are ceaselessly querulous and bellicose. They never

defend any one or anything if they can help it; if the job is forced upon them, they tackle it by denouncing some one or something else.

   Prejudices (1919) 1st series

1 Injustice is relatively easy to bear; what stings is justice.

   Prejudices (1922) 3rd series

2 No one in this world, so far as I know— and I have searched the records for years, and employed agents to help me—has ever lost money by underestimating the intelligence of the great masses of the plain people.

   in *Chicago Tribune* 19 September 1926

3 The saddest life is that of a political aspirant under democracy. His failure is ignominious and his success is disgraceful.

   in *Baltimore Evening Sun* 9 December 1929

4 He slept more than any other President, whether by day or by night. Nero fiddled, but Coolidge only snored.

   of Calvin **Coolidge**

   in *American Mercury* April 1933

5 If there had been any formidable body of cannibals in the country he would have promised to provide them with free missionaries fattened at the taxpayer's expense.

   of Harry **Truman** *in the* 1948 *presidential campaign*

   in *Baltimore Sun* 7 November 1948

Yehudi Menuhin 1916–

American-born British violinist

6 Whenever I see a newspaper I think of the poor trees. As trees they provide beauty, shade and shelter. But as paper all they provide is rubbish.

   attributed, 1982

7 It is only in our advanced and synthetic civilization that mothers no longer sing to the babies they are carrying.

   in *Observer* 4 January 1987

Robert Gordon Menzies
1894–1978
Australian Liberal statesman, Prime Minister 1939–41 and 1949–66

8 What Great Britain calls the Far East is to us the near north.

   in *Sydney Morning Herald* 27 April 1939

David Mercer 1928–80
English dramatist

9 A suitable case for treatment.

   title of television play (1962); later filmed as *Morgan–A Suitable Case for Treatment* (1966)

Johnny Mercer 1909–76
American songwriter

10 You've got to ac-cent-tchu-ate the positive
Elim-my-nate the negative
Latch on to the affirmative
Don't mess with Mister In-between.

   'Ac-cent-tchu-ate the Positive' (1944 song)

11 Jeepers Creepers—where you get them peepers?

   'Jeepers Creepers' (1938 song)

12 We're drinking my friend,
To the end of a brief episode,
Make it one for my baby
And one more for the road.

   'One For My Baby' (1943 song)

13 That old black magic.

   title of song (1942)

Bob Merrill 1921–98
American songwriter and composer

14 How much is that doggie in the window?

   title of song (1953)

15 People who need people are the luckiest people in the world.

   'People who Need People' (1964 song)

Anthony Meyer 1920–

British Conservative politician

1 I question the right of that great Moloch, national sovereignty, to burn its children to save its pride.
speaking against the Falklands War, 1982
in *Listener* 27 September 1990

Viola Meynell 1886–1956

English poet

2 The dust comes secretly day after day,
Lies on my ledge and dulls my shining things.
But O this dust that I shall drive away
Is flowers and Kings,
Is Solomon's temple, poets, Nineveh.
'Dusting' (1919)

Princess Michael of Kent 1945–

Austrian-born British princess

3 I don't enjoy my public obligations. I was not made to cut ribbons and kiss babies.
in *Life* November 1986

George Mikes 1912–

Hungarian-born writer

4 On the Continent people have good food; in England people have good table manners.
How to be an Alien (1946)

5 Continental people have sex life; the English have hot-water bottles.
How to be an Alien (1946)

6 An Englishman, even if he is alone, forms an orderly queue of one.
How to be an Alien (1946)

Edna St Vincent Millay 1892–1950

American poet

7 Childhood is the kingdom where nobody dies.
Nobody that matters, that is.
'Childhood is the Kingdom where Nobody dies' (1934)

8 Down, down, down into the darkness of the grave
Gently they go, the beautiful, the tender, the kind;
Quietly they go, the intelligent, the witty, the brave.
I know. But I do not approve. And I am not resigned.
'Dirge Without Music' (1928)

9 My candle burns at both ends;
It will not last the night;
But ah, my foes, and oh, my friends—
It gives a lovely light.
A Few Figs From Thistles (1920) 'First Fig'

10 Euclid alone
Has looked on Beauty bare. Fortunate they
Who, though once only and then but far away,
Have heard her massive sandal set on stone.
The Harp-Weaver and Other Poems (1923) sonnet 22

11 Justice denied in Massachusetts.
*relating to the trial of Sacco and **Vanzetti** and their execution on 22 August 1927*
title of poem (1928)

12 The sun that warmed our stooping backs and withered the weeds uprooted—
We shall not feel it again.
We shall die in darkness, and be buried in the rain.
'Justice Denied in Massachusetts' (1928)

13 Death devours all lovely things;
Lesbia with her sparrow
Shares the darkness—presently
Every bed is narrow.
'Passer Mortuus Est' (1921)

14 After all, my erstwhile dear,
My no longer cherished,
Need we say it was not love,
Now that love is perished?
'Passer Mortuus Est' (1921)

15 It's not true that life is one damn thing after another—it's one damn thing over and over.
letter to Arthur Davison Ficke, 24 October 1930; cf. **Hubbard** 153:7

Alice Duer Miller 1874–1942

American writer

1 I am American bred,
I have seen much to hate here—much to forgive,
But in a world where England is finished and dead,
I do not wish to live.
The White Cliffs (1940)

Arthur Miller 1915–

American dramatist
on Miller: see **Newspaper headlines** 231:4

2 A suicide kills two people, Maggie, that's what it's for!
After the Fall (1964)

3 Death of a salesman
title of play (1949)

4 The world is an oyster, but you don't crack it open on a mattress.
Death of a Salesman (1949)

5 Willy Loman never made a lot of money. His name was never in the paper. He's not the finest character that ever lived. But he's a human being, and a terrible thing is happening to him. So attention must be paid.
Death of a Salesman (1949)

6 For a salesman, there is no rock bottom to the life. He don't put a bolt to a nut, he don't tell you the law or give you medicine. He's a man way out there in the blue, riding on a smile and a shoeshine. And when they start not smiling back—that's an earthquake . . . A salesman is got to dream, boy. It comes with the territory.
Death of a Salesman (1949) 'Requiem'

7 The car, the furniture, the wife, the children—everything has to be disposable. Because you see the main thing today is—shopping.
The Price (1968)

8 This is Red Hook, not Sicily . . . This is the gullet of New York swallowing the tonnage of the world.
A View from the Bridge (1955)

9 The structure of a play is always the story of how the birds came home to roost.
'Shadows of the Gods' in *Harper's Magazine* August 1958

10 A good newspaper, I suppose, is a nation talking to itself.
in *Observer* 26 November 1961

11 A theatre where no-one is allowed to walk out and everyone is forced to applause.
describing Eastern Europe
Omnibus (BBC TV) 30 October 1987; in *Independent* 31 October 1987

Henry Miller 1891–1980

American novelist

12 Even before the music begins there is that bored look on people's faces. A polite form of self-imposed torture, the concert.
Tropic of Cancer (1934)

13 Every man with a bellyful of the classics is an enemy to the human race.
Tropic of Cancer (1934)

Jonathan Miller 1934–

English writer and director

14 I'm not really a *Jew*. Just Jew-*ish*. Not the whole hog, you know.
Beyond the Fringe (1960 revue) 'Real Class'

15 I successfully don't think about it for most of my life because I'm in that sunlit part of the landscape where I don't hear the cries of the tormented. It's the way things are.
when asked how he dealt with the atrocities of this century
in *Observer* 10 March 1996

16 A sort of cognitive equivalent of a condom—it's a layer of contraceptive rubber between the direct experience and the cognitive system.
of reading text from a computer screen
in *Independent on Sunday* 14 January 1996 'Quotes of the Week'

Spike Milligan 1918–

British comedian and writer
see also **Catch-phrases** 58:6, 59:18, 59:20

1 Money couldn't buy friends but you got a better class of enemy.
   Puckoon (1963)

A. J. Mills, Fred Godfrey, and Bennett Scott

British songwriters

2 Take me back to dear old Blighty.
   title of song (1916)

Irving Mills 1894–1985

3 It don't mean a thing
   If it ain't got that swing.
   'It Don't Mean a Thing' (1932 song; music by Duke Ellington)

A. A. Milne 1882–1956

English writer for children
on Milne: see **Parker** 243:11

4 The more it snows
   (Tiddely pom),
   The more it goes
   (Tiddely pom),
   The more it goes
   (Tiddely pom)
   On snowing.
   House at Pooh Corner (1928)

5 The more he looked inside the more Piglet wasn't there.
   The House at Pooh Corner (1928)

6 When you are a Bear of Very Little Brain, and you Think of Things, you find sometimes that a Thing which seemed very Thingish inside you is quite different when it gets out into the open and has other people looking at it.
   The House at Pooh Corner (1928)

7 I am a Bear of Very Little Brain, and long words Bother me.
   Winnie-the-Pooh (1926)

8 Time for a little something.
   Winnie-the-Pooh (1926)

9 My spelling is Wobbly. It's good spelling but it Wobbles, and the letters get in the wrong places.
   Winnie-the-Pooh (1926)

10 Owl hasn't exactly got Brain, but he Knows Things.
   Winnie-the-Pooh (1926)

11 They're changing guard at Buckingham Palace—
   Christopher Robin went down with Alice.
   Alice is marrying one of the guard.
   'A soldier's life is terrible hard,'
   Says Alice.
   'Buckingham Palace' (1924)

12 James James
   Morrison Morrison
   Weatherby George Dupree
   Took great
   Care of his Mother,
   Though he was only three.
   James James
   Said to his Mother,
   'Mother,' he said, said he;
   'You must never go down to the end of the town, if you don't go down with me.'
   'Disobedience' (1924)

13 There once was a Dormouse who lived in a bed
   Of delphiniums (blue) and geraniums (red),
   And all the day long he'd a wonderful view
   Of geraniums (red) and delphiniums (blue).
   'The Dormouse and the Doctor' (1924)

14 King John was not a good man—
   He had his little ways.
   And sometimes no one spoke to him
   For days and days and days.
   'King John's Christmas' (1927)

15 The King asked
   The Queen, and
   The Queen asked
   The Dairymaid:
   'Could we have some butter for
   The Royal slice of bread?'
   'The King's Breakfast' (1924)

16 *What* is the matter with Mary Jane?
   She's perfectly well and she hasn't a pain,

And it's lovely rice pudding for dinner again!
What *is* the matter with Mary Jane?
'Rice Pudding' (1924)

1 Hush! Hush! Whisper who dares!
Christopher Robin is saying his prayers.
'Vespers' (1924); cf. **Morton** 223:7

Helen Mirren 1945–

English actress

2 When you do Shakespeare they think
you must be intelligent because they
think you understand what you're
saying.
interviewed on *Ruby Wax Meets . . .* ; in *Mail
on Sunday* 16 February 1997 'Night and Day'

■ Misquotations

see box overleaf

Adrian Mitchell 1932–

English poet, novelist, and dramatist

3 Most people ignore most poetry
because
most poetry ignores most people.
Poems (1964) p. 8

Joni Mitchell 1945–

Canadian singer and songwriter

4 They paved paradise
And put up a parking lot.
'Big Yellow Taxi' (1970 song)

5 I've looked at life from both sides now,
From win and lose and still somehow
It's life's illusions I recall;
I really don't know life at all.
'Both Sides Now' (1967 song)

6 We are stardust,
We are golden,
And we got to get ourselves
Back to the garden.
'Woodstock' (1969 song)

Margaret Mitchell 1900–49

American novelist

7 Death and taxes and childbirth! There's
never any convenient time for any of
them.

Gone with the Wind (1936)

8 I wish I could care what you do or where
you go but I can't . . . My dear, I don't
give a damn.
Gone with the Wind (1936); cf. **Film lines** 110:6

9 After all, tomorrow is another day.
Gone with the Wind (1936), closing lines

Nancy Mitford 1904–73

English writer

10 An aristocracy in a republic is like a
chicken whose head has been cut off: it
may run about in a lively way, but in
fact it is dead.
Noblesse Oblige (1956) 'The English
Aristocracy'

11 Wooing, so tiring.
The Pursuit of Love (1945)

12 I have only ever read one book in my life,
and that is *White Fang*. It's so frightfully
good I've never bothered to read another.
The Pursuit of Love (1945)

13 Abroad is unutterably bloody and
foreigners are fiends.
The Pursuit of Love (1945); cf. **George VI**
126:13

François Mitterrand 1916–

French socialist statesman; President of
France 1981–95

14 She has the eyes of Caligula, but the
mouth of Marilyn Monroe.
of Margaret **Thatcher***, briefing his new European
Minister Roland Dumas*
in *Observer* 25 November 1990

Wilson Mizner 1876–1933

American dramatist

15 Be nice to people on your way up
because you'll meet 'em on your way
down.
A. Johnston *The Legendary Mizners* (1953)

▶▶

Misquotations

1 Beam me up, Scotty.
supposedly the form in which Captain Kirk
habitually requested to be returned from a
planet to the Starship *Enterprise*; in fact the
nearest equivalent found is

Beam us up, Mr Scott.
Gene Roddenberry *Star Trek* (1966 onwards)
'Gamesters of Triskelion'

2 Come with me to the Casbah.
*often attributed to Charles Boyer (1898–1978) in
the film* Algiers *(1938), but the line does not in
fact occur*
L. Swindell *Charles Boyer* (1983)

3 Crisis? What crisis?
in *Sun* headline, 11 January 1979;
summarizing James **Callaghan**'s remark

I don't think other people in the
world would share the view there is
mounting chaos.
interview at London Airport, 10 January 1979

4 Dreams are the royal road to the
unconscious.
summary of **Freud**'s view; see **Freud** 118:13

5 Elementary, my dear Watson,
elementary.
*remark attributed to Sherlock Holmes, but not
found in this form in any book by Arthur Conan
Doyle, first found in P.G. Wodehouse* Psmith
Journalist *(1915)*
attributed

6 The green shoots of recovery.
popular misquotation of the Chancellor's
upbeat assessment of the economic
situation

The green shoots of economic spring
are appearing once again.
Norman Lamont, speech at Conservative
Party Conference, 9 October 1991

7 I paint with my prick.
attributed to Pierre Auguste Renoir
(1841–1919); possibly an inversion of

It's with my brush I make love.
A. André *Renoir* (1919)

8 Licensed to kill.
popular description of the status of Secret
Service agent James Bond, 007, in the novels
of Ian **Fleming**

The licence to kill for the Secret
Service, the double-o prefix, was a
great honour.
Dr No (1958)

when asked what jazz is:
9 Man, if you gotta ask you'll never
know.
frequently quoted version of Louis
Armstrong's response

If you still have to ask . . . shame on
you.
Max Jones et al. *Salute to Satchmo* (1970)

10 Me Tarzan, you Jane.
*Johnny Weissmuller summing up his role in
Tarzan, the Ape Man (1932 film); the words
occur neither in the film nor the original, by
Edgar Rice Burroughs*
in *Photoplay Magazine* June 1932

11 My lips are sealed.
misquotation from Stanley **Baldwin**'s speech
on the Abyssinian crisis

I shall be but a short time tonight. I
have seldom spoken with greater
regret, for my lips are not yet
unsealed. Were these troubles over I
would make a case, and I guarantee
that not a man would go into the
lobby against us.
speech in the House of Commons, 10
December 1935

12 Play it again, Sam.
in the film Casablanca, *written by Julius J.
Epstein et al., Humphrey Bogart says, 'If she
can stand it, I can. Play it!'; earlier in the film
Ingrid Bergman says, 'Play it, Sam. Play* As Time
Goes By.*'*
Casablanca (1942 film); cf. **Film lines** 110:11

13 Selling off the family silver.
summary of Harold **Macmillan**'s attack on
privatization

First of all the Georgian silver goes,
and then all that nice furniture that
used to be in the saloon. Then the
Canalettos go.
speech to the Tory Reform Group, 8
November 1985

▶

> **Misquotations** continued

1 The soft under-belly of Europe.
popular version of Winston **Churchill**'s
phrase

We make this wide encircling
movement in the Mediterranean,
having for its primary object the
recovery of the command of that vital
sea, but also having for its object the
exposure of the under-belly of the
Axis, especially Italy, to heavy
attack.
speech in the House of Commons, 11
November 1942

2 Something must be done.
popular summary of King **Edward VIII**'s
words at the derelict Dowlais Iron and Steel
Works, 18 November 1936

These works brought all these people
here. Something should be done to
get them at work again.
in *Western Mail* 19 November 1936

3 We are the masters now.
*from Hartley **Shawcross**'s assertion of Labour's
strength after winning the 1945 election, "'But,"
said Alice, "the question is whether you can
make a word mean different things." "Not so,"
said Humpty-Dumpty, "the question is which is
to be master. That's all." We are the masters at
the moment, and not only at the moment, but
for a very long time to come.'*
in the House of Commons, 2 April 1946; see
below; cf. **Blair** 39:3

'When *I* use a word,' Humpty
Dumpty said in a rather scornful
tone, 'it means just what I choose it
to mean—neither more nor less.'
Lewis Carroll (1832–98) *Through the Looking-
Glass* (1872)

4 The white heat of technology.
phrase deriving from Harold **Wilson**'s speech

The Britain that is going to be forged
in the white heat of this revolution
will be no place for restrictive
practices or for outdated methods on
either side of industry.
speech at the Labour Party Conference, 1
October 1963

5 Why don't you come up and see me
sometime?
alteration of Mae **West**'s invitation

Why don't you come up sometime,
and see me?
She Done Him Wrong (1933 film)

6 You dirty rat!
*associated with James Cagney (1899–1986), but
not used by him in any film; in a speech at the
American Film Institute banquet, 13 March 1974,
Cagney said, 'I never said "Mmm, you dirty
rat!"'*
Cagney by Cagney (1976)

►► **Wilson Mizner** continued

7 If you steal from one author, it's
plagiarism; if you steal from many, it's
research.
A. Johnston *The Legendary Mizners* (1953)

8 A trip through a sewer in a glass-
bottomed boat.
of Hollywood
A. Johnston *The Legendary Mizners* (1953)

Ariane Mnouchkine

French theatre director

9 A cultural Chernobyl.
of Euro Disney
in *Harper's Magazine* July 1992; cf. **Ballard**
22:3

Emilio Mola 1887–1937

Spanish nationalist general

10 Fifth column.
*an extra body of supporters claimed by General
Mola in a broadcast as being within Madrid when
he besieged the city with four columns of
Nationalist forces*
in *New York Times* 16 and 17 October 1936

Walter Mondale 1928–

American Democratic politician

11 When I hear your new ideas I'm
reminded of that ad, 'Where's the beef?'
in a televised debate with Gary Hart, 11 March
1984; cf. **Advertising slogans** 4:29

Piet Mondrian 1872–1944

Dutch painter

1 The essence of painting has actually always been to make it [the universal] plastically perceptible through colour and line.
   'Natural Reality and Abstract Reality' (written 1919)

2 In order to approach the spiritual in art, one employs reality as little as possible . . . This explains logically why primary forms are employed. Since these forms are abstract, an abstract art comes into being.
   Sketchbook II (1914)

Jean Monnet 1888–1979

French economist and diplomat; founder of the European Community

3 Europe has never existed. It is not the addition of national sovereignties in a conclave which creates an entity. One must genuinely *create* Europe.
   Anthony Sampson *The New Europeans* (1968)

4 The common market is a process, not a product.
   Anthony Sampson *The New Europeans* (1968)

5 I did not understand the politics of Versailles, only the economics.
   of the Treaty of Versailles
   in an interview in 1971; François Duchêne *Jean Monnet* (1994)

6 We should not create a nation Europe instead of a nation France.
   François Duchêne *Jean Monnet* (1994)

Marilyn Monroe 1926–62

American actress
on Monroe: see **Curtis** 82:8, **John** 162:1, **Mailer** 204:9, **Newspaper headlines** 231:4, **Wilder** 328:13; *see also* **Mitterrand** 217:14

when asked if she really had nothing on in a calendar photograph:
7 I had the radio on.
   in *Time* 11 August 1952

on being asked what she wore in bed:
8 Chanel No. 5.
   Pete Martin *Marilyn Monroe* (1956)

Charles Edward Montague 1867–1928

English writer and journalist

9 War hath no fury like a non-combatant.
   Disenchantment (1922)

John Montague 1929–

Irish poet and writer

10   To grow
   a second tongue, as
   harsh a humiliation
   as twice to be born.
   'A Grafted Tongue' (1972)

11 Like dolmens round my childhood, the old people.
   'Like Dolmens Round my Childhood' (1972)

Lord Montgomery of Alamein 1887–1976

British field marshal
on Montgomery: see **Churchill** 68:2

12 *Here* we will stand and fight; there will be no further withdrawal. I have ordered that all plans and instructions dealing with further withdrawal are to be burnt, and at once. We will stand and fight *here*. If we can't stay here alive, then let us stay here dead.
   speech in Cairo, 13 August 1942

13 Rule 1, on page 1 of the book of war, is: 'Do not march on Moscow' . . . [Rule 2] is: 'Do not go fighting with your land armies in China.'
   speech in the House of Lords, 30 May 1962

14 I have heard some say . . . [homosexual] practices are allowed in France and in other NATO countries. We are not French, and we are not other nationals. We are British, thank God!
   on the 2nd reading of the Sexual Offences Bill
   speech in the House of Lords, 24 May 1965

Monty Python's Flying Circus 1969–74

BBC TV programme, written by Graham Chapman (1941–89), John **Cleese** (1939–), Terry Gilliam (1940–), Eric Idle (1943–), Terry Jones (1942–), and Michael Palin (1943–)
see also **Catch-phrases** 57:2

1 Your wife interested in . . . *photographs?* Eh? Know what I mean—*photographs?* He asked him knowingly . . . nudge nudge, snap snap, grin grin, wink wink, say no more.
   Monty Python's Flying Circus (1969)

2 It's *not* pining—it's passed on! This parrot is no more! It has ceased to be! It's expired and gone to meet its maker! This is a late parrot! It's a stiff! Bereft of life it rests in peace—if you hadn't nailed it to the perch it would be pushing up the daisies! It's rung down the curtain and joined the choir invisible! THIS IS AN EX–PARROT!
   Monty Python's Flying Circus (1969)

3 Nobody expects the Spanish Inquisition!
   Monty Python's Flying Circus (1970)

Henry Moore 1898–1986

English sculptor and draughtsman

4 The first hole made through a piece of stone is a revelation.
   in *Listener* 18 August 1937

Marianne Moore 1887–1972

American poet

5   O to be a dragon,
a symbol of the power of Heaven—of silkworm
size or immense; at times invisible.
Felicitous phenomenon!
   'O To Be a Dragon' (1959)

6 I, too, dislike it: there are things that are important beyond all this fiddle.
Reading it, however, with a perfect contempt for it, one discovers in it, after all, a place for the genuine.
   'Poetry' (1935)

7 Nor till the poets among us can be 'literalists of

the imagination'—above insolence and triviality and can present for inspection, imaginary gardens with real toads in them, shall we have it.
   'Poetry' (1935)

8 My father used to say,
   'Superior people never make long visits, have to be shown Longfellow's grave or the glass flowers at Harvard.'
   'Silence' (1935)

Oscar Moore 1960–96

English journalist

9 Would someone turn the lights back on please? I can hear the splash and swish of car tyres on wet tarmac outside my window, and I can hear rain rapping like fingernails on the glass, but I cannot see across the room, let alone outside, into the street.
   on his blindness in the final stages of Aids
   in *Guardian* 10 August 1996

Jeanne Moreau 1928–

French actress

10 The rhythm hammers us, hits us and possesses us, making us prisoners of noise. It's like a drug.
   of popular music
   in *Guardian* 13 August 1997

Larry Morey 1905–71

11 Heigh-ho, heigh-ho,
   It's off to work we go.
   'Heigh-Ho' (1937 song)

12 Whistle while you work.
   title of song (1937)

Robin Morgan 1941–

American feminist

13 Sisterhood is powerful.
   title of book (1970)

Christopher Morley
1890–1957
American writer

1 Life is a foreign language: all men mispronounce it.
Thunder on the Left (1925)

Countess Morphy fl. 1930–50

2 The tragedy of English cooking is that 'plain' cooking cannot be entrusted to 'plain' cooks.
English Recipes (1935)

Desmond Morris 1928–
English anthropologist

3 The city is not a concrete jungle, it is a human zoo.
The Human Zoo (1969) introduction

4 There are one hundred and ninety-three living species of monkeys and apes. One hundred and ninety-two of them are covered with hair. The exception is a naked ape self-named *Homo sapiens*.
The Naked Ape (1967) introduction

Blake Morrison 1950–
British poet and critic

5 Only a culture without hope cannot forgive—a culture that doesn't believe in progress or redemption. Have we so little faith in ourselves we can't accept the possibility of maturation, change, cure?
on the killing of James Bulger
As If (1997)

Herbert Morrison 1888–1965
British Labour politician

6 Work is the call. Work at war speed. Good-night—and go to it.
broadcast as Minister of Supply, 22 May 1940

Jim Morrison 1943–71
American rock singer and songwriter

7 C'mon, baby, light my fire.
'Light My Fire' (1967 song, with Robby Krieger)

8 We want the world and we want it now!
'When the Music's Over' (1967 song)

9 When you make your peace with authority, you become an authority.
Andrew Doe and John Tobler *In Their Own Words: The Doors* (1988)

Van Morrison 1945–
Irish singer, songwriter, and musician

10 Music is spiritual. The music business is not.
in *The Times* 6 July 1990

Dwight Morrow 1873–1931
American lawyer, banker, and diplomat

11 The world is divided into people who do things and people who get the credit. Try, if you can, to belong to the first class. There's far less competition.
letter to his son, in Harold Nicolson *Dwight Morrow* (1935)

Owen Morshead 1893–
English librarian

12 The House of Hanover, like ducks, produce bad parents—they trample on their young.
as Royal Librarian, in conversation with Harold Nicolson, biographer of George V
Harold Nicolson, letter to Vita Sackville-West, 7 January 1949

John Mortimer 1923–
English novelist, barrister, and dramatist

13 No power on earth, however, can abolish the merciless class distinction between those who are physically desirable and the lonely, pallid, spotted, silent, unfancied majority.
Clinging to the Wreckage (1982)

1 What obsesses a writer starting out on a
lifetime's work is the panic-stricken
search for a voice of his own.
  Clinging to the Wreckage (1982)

2 They do you a decent death on the
hunting-field.
  Paradise Postponed (1985)

3 At school I never minded the lessons. I
just resented having to work terribly
hard at playing.
  A Voyage Round My Father (1971)

4 No brilliance is needed in the law.
Nothing but common sense, and
relatively clean fingernails.
  A Voyage Round My Father (1971)

5 The virtue of much literature is that it is
dangerous and may do you extreme
harm.
  foreword to C. H. Rolph *Books in the Dock*
  (1969)

6 The worst fault of the working classes is
telling their children they're not going to
succeed, saying: 'There is life, but it's not
for you.'
  in *Daily Mail* 31 May 1988

J. B. Morton
('Beachcomber') 1893–1975

British journalist

7 Hush, hush,
Nobody cares!
Christopher Robin
Has
Fallen
Down-
Stairs.
  By the Way (1931); cf. **Milne** 217:1

8 The Doctor is said also to have invented
an extraordinary weapon which will
make war less brutal. It is described as a
very powerful liquid which rots braces at
a distance of a mile.
  Gallimaufry (1936) 'Bracerot'

9 Dr Strabismus (Whom God Preserve) of
Utrecht has patented a new invention. It
is an illuminated trouser-clip for bicyclists
who are using main roads at night.
  Morton's Folly (1933)

Jelly Roll Morton 1885–1941

American jazz pianist, composer, and
bandleader

10 Jazz music is to be played sweet, soft,
plenty rhythm.
  Mister Jelly Roll (1950)

Rogers Morton 1914–79

American public relations officer

11 I'm not going to rearrange the furniture
on the deck of the Titanic.
  *having lost five of the last six primaries as
  President Ford's campaign manager*
  in *Washington Post* 16 May 1976

Edwin Moses 1955–

American athlete

12 I don't really see the hurdles. I sense
them like a memory.
  attributed

Oswald Mosley 1896–1980

British politician and Fascist leader

13 I am not, and never have been, a man of
the right. My position was on the left and
is now in the centre of politics.
  letter to *The Times* 26 April 1968

Andrew Motion 1952–

English poet

14 Each sudden gust of light explains itself
as flames, but neither they, nor even

bombs redoubled on the hills tonight
can quite include me in their fear.
What does remains invisible, is lost
in curt societies whose deaths become

revenge by morning, and whose homes
are nothing more than all they pity most.
  'Leaving Belfast' (1978)

15 Beside the river, swerving under ground.
your future tracked you, snapping at
    your heels:
Diana, breathless, hunted by your own
    quick hounds.
  'Mythology' (1997)

Earl Mountbatten of Burma
1900–79
British sailor, soldier, and statesman
on Mountbatten: see **Ziegler** 341:5

1 Right, now I understand people think you're the Forgotten Army on the Forgotten Front. I've come here to tell you you're quite wrong. You're not the Forgotten Army on the Forgotten Front. No, make no mistake about it. Nobody's ever *heard* of you.
encouragement to troops when taking over as Supreme Allied Commander South-East Asia in late 1943
R. Hough *Mountbatten* (1980)

2 The nuclear arms race has no military purpose. Wars cannot be fought with nuclear weapons. Their existence only adds to our perils.
speech at Strasbourg, 11 May 1979; P. Ziegler *Mountbatten* (1985)

3 I can't think of a more wonderful thanksgiving for the life I have had than that everyone should be jolly at my funeral.
Richard Hough *Mountbatten* (1980)

Daniel P. Moynihan 1927–
American Democratic politician

4 Welfare became a term of opprobrium—a contentious, often vindictive area of political conflict in which liberals and conservatives clashed and children were lost sight of.
in *The Washington Post* 25 November 1994

5 There have been seven directors, or acting directors, in six years. That's not an organization. That's an institutional collapse.
on the CIA
in *Independent on Sunday* 23 March 1997

Lord Moynihan 1865–1936
British surgeon

6 Lord Dawson of Penn
Has killed lots of men.
So that's why we sing
God save the King.
Kenneth Rose *King George V* (1983)

Robert Mugabe 1924–
African statesman; Prime Minister of Zimbabwe, 1980–7, President since 1987

7 Cricket civilizes people and creates good gentlemen. I want everyone to play cricket in Zimbabwe; I want ours to be a nation of gentlemen.
in *Sunday Times* 26 February 1984

Kitty Muggeridge
wife of Malcolm **Muggeridge**

8 David Frost has risen without trace.
said c.1965 to Malcolm Muggeridge

Malcolm Muggeridge
1903–90
British journalist; husband of Kitty **Muggeridge**

9 To succeed pre-eminently in English public life it is necessary to conform either to the popular image of a bookie or of a clergyman; Churchill being a perfect example of the former, Halifax of the latter.
The Infernal Grove (1973)

10 Working for [C. P.] Scott was like waltzing with some sedate old dowager at a mayoral reception in Manchester; for Beaverbrook, like taking the floor in a night-club in the early hours of the morning, when everyone is more or less drunk.
The Infernal Grove (1975)

11 Something beautiful for God.
title of book (1971); see **Teresa** 304:6

12 The orgasm has replaced the Cross as the focus of longing and the image of fulfilment.
Tread Softly (1966)

13 He was not only a bore; he bored for England.
of Anthony **Eden**
Tread Softly (1966)

14 Good taste and humour . . . are a contradiction in terms, like a chaste whore.
in *Time* 14 September 1953

1 On television I feel like a man playing a piano in a brothel; every now and again he solaces himself by playing 'Abide with Me' in the hope of edifying both the clients and the inmates.
> interview on *Parkinson*, BBC1 TV, 23 September 1972

Edwin Muir 1887–1959
Scottish poet

2 And without fear the lawless roads Ran wrong through all the land.
> 'Hölderlin's Journey' (1937)

3 Barely a twelvemonth after
The seven days war that put the world to sleep,
Late in the evening the strange horses came.
> 'The Horses' (1956)

Frank Muir 1920–98
English writer and broadcaster

4 The thinking man's crumpet.
> *of Joan* **Bakewell**
> attributed

Paul Muldoon 1951–
Irish poet

5 I thought of you tonight, *a leanbh*, lying there in your long barrow,
colder and dumber than a fish by Francisco de Herrera.
> 'Incantata' (1994)

6 The Volkswagen parked in the gap,
But gently ticking over.
You wonder if it's lovers
And not men hurrying back
Across two fields and a river.
> 'Ireland' (1980)

H. J. Muller 1890–1967
American geneticist

7 To say, for example, that a man is made up of certain chemical elements is a satisfactory description only for those who intend to use him as a fertilizer.
> *Science and Criticism* (1943)

Herbert J. Muller 1905–
American writer

8 Few have heard of Fra Luca Pacioli, the inventor of double-entry book-keeping; but he has probably had much more influence on human life than has Dante or Michelangelo.
> *Uses of the Past* (1957)

Lewis Mumford 1895–
American sociologist

9 Every generation revolts against its fathers and makes friends with its grandfathers.
> *The Brown Decades* (1931)

10 Our national flower is the concrete cloverleaf.
> in *Quote Magazine* 8 October 1961

Iris Murdoch 1919–
English novelist
on Murdoch: see **Bayley** 25:3

11 Dora Greenfield left her husband because she was afraid of him. She decided six months later to return to him for the same reason.
> *The Bell* (1958)

12 The chief requirement of the good life, is to live without any image of oneself.
> *The Bell* (1958) (said by James Tayper Payce)

13 Only in our virtues are we original, because virtue is difficult . . . Vices are general, virtues are particular.
> *Nuns and Soldiers* (1980)

14 One doesn't have to get anywhere in a marriage. It's not a public conveyance.
> *A Severed Head* (1961)

15 Love is the extremely difficult realisation that something other than oneself is real. Love, and so art and morals, is the discovery of reality.
> 'The Sublime and the Good' in *Chicago Review* 13 (1959)

16 Anything that consoles is fake.
> R. Harries *Prayer and the Pursuit of Happiness* (1985)

1 I'm just wandering, I think of things and then they go away for ever.

in September 1996 on her inability to write; the following February it was announced that she was suffering from Alzheimer's disease

in *Times* 5 February 1997

Rupert Murdoch 1931–

Australian-born American publisher and media entrepreneur

asked why he had allowed Page 3 to develop:
2 I don't know. The editor did it when I was away.

in *Guardian* 25 February 1994

3 I'd say our newspapers paid far too much for them.

of buying paparazzi pictures

in *Daily Telegraph* 8 October 1997

Ed Murrow 1908–65

American broadcaster and journalist

4 No one can terrorize a whole nation, unless we are all his accomplices.

of Joseph McCarthy

'See It Now', broadcast, 7 March 1954

5 He mobilized the English language and sent it into battle to steady his fellow countrymen and hearten those Europeans upon whom the long dark night of tyranny had descended.

of Winston Churchill

broadcast, 30 November 1954; *In Search of Light* (1967)

6 When the politicians complain that TV turns their proceedings into a circus, it should be made plain that the circus was already there, and that TV has merely demonstrated that not all the performers are well trained.

in *Observer* 27 December 1959

7 Anyone who isn't confused doesn't really understand the situation.

on the Vietnam War

Walter Bryan *The Improbable Irish* (1969)

Benito Mussolini 1883–1945

Italian Fascist dictator
on Mussolini: see **Taylor** 303:14

8 We must leave exactly on time . . . From now on everything must function to perfection.

to a station-master

Giorgio Pini *Mussolini* (1939); cf. Infanta Eulalia of Spain *Courts and Countries after the War* (1925): 'The first benefit of Benito Mussolini's direction in Italy begins to be felt when one crosses the Italian Frontier and hears "*Il treno arriva all'orario* [the train is arriving on time]" '

A. J. Muste 1885–1967

American pacifist

9 If I can't love Hitler, I can't love at all.

at a Quaker meeting 1940; in *New York Times* 12 February 1967

10 There is no way to peace. Peace is the way.

in *New York Times* 16 November 1967

Vladimir Nabokov 1899–1977

Russian novelist

11 Curiously enough, one cannot *read* a book: one can only reread it. A good reader, a major reader, an active and creative reader is a rereader.

Lectures on Literature (1980) 'Good Readers and Good Writers'

12 Her exotic daydreams do not prevent her from being small-town bourgeois at heart, clinging to conventional ideas or committing this or that conventional violation of the conventional, adultery being a most conventional way to rise above the conventional.

Lectures on Literature (1980) 'Madame Bovary'

13 Lolita, light of my life, fire of my loins. My sin, my soul. Lo-lee-ta: the tip of the tongue taking a trip of three steps down the palate to tap, at three, on the teeth. Lo. Lee. Ta.

Lolita (1955)

14 You can always count on a murderer for a fancy prose style.

Lolita (1955)

1 Life is a great surprise. I do not see why
   death should not be an even greater one.
   Pale Fire (1962)

2 The cradle rocks above an abyss, and
   common sense tells us that our existence
   is but a brief crack of light between two
   eternities of darkness.
   Speak, Memory (1951)

3 That life-quickening atmosphere of a big
   railway station where everything is
   something trembling on the brink of
   something else.
   Spring in Fialta and other stories (1956)
   'Spring in Fialta'

4 I think like a genius, I write like a
   distinguished author, and I speak like a
   child.
   Strong Opinions (1973)

5 A work of art has no importance
   whatever to society. It is only important
   to the individual, and only the individual
   reader is important to me.
   Strong Opinions (1973)

Ralph Nader 1934–

American consumer protectionist

6 Unsafe at any speed.
   title of book (1965)

Sarojini Naidu 1879–1949

Indian politician

7 If only Bapu knew the cost of setting him
   up in poverty!
   of Gandhi
   A. Campbell-Johnson *Mission with
   Mountbatten* (1951)

V. S. Naipaul 1932–

Trinidadian novelist and travel writer

8 I am the kind of writer that people think
   other people are reading.
   in *Radio Times* 14 March 1979

Fridtjof Nansen 1861–1930

Norwegian polar explorer

9 Never stop because you are afraid—you
   are never so likely to be wrong. Never

keep a line of retreat: it is a wretched
invention. The difficult is what takes a
little time; the impossible is what takes a
little longer.
   in *Listener* 14 December 1939; cf. **Sayings**
   278:11

Ogden Nash 1902–71

American humorist

10 The turtle lives 'twixt plated decks
   Which practically conceal its sex.
   I think it clever of the turtle
   In such a fix to be so fertile.
   'Autres Bêtes, Autres Moeurs' (1931)

11 A bit of talcum
   Is always walcum.
   'The Baby' (1931)

12 Oh, what a tangled web do parents
      weave
   When they think that their children are
      naive.
   'Baby, What Makes the Sky Blue' (1940); see
   below

   O what a tangled web we weave,
   When first we practise to deceive!
   Sir Walter Scott (1771–1832) *Marmion* (1808)

13 The cow is of the bovine ilk;
   One end is moo, the other, milk.
   'The Cow' (1931)

14 A door is what a dog is perpetually on
   the wrong side of.
   'A Dog's Best Friend is his Illiteracy' (1953)

15 Let us pause to consider the English,
   Who when they pause to consider
      themselves they get all reticently
      thrilled and tinglish,
   Because every Englishman is convinced
      of one thing, viz.:
   That to be an Englishman is to belong to
      the most exclusive club there is.
   'England Expects' (1938)

16 One would be in less danger
   From the wiles of the stranger
   If one's own kin and kith
   Were more fun to be with.
   'Family Court' (1931)

17 Women would rather be right than be
   reasonable.
   'Frailty, Thy Name is a Misnomer' (1942)

1 Parsley
Is gharsley.
'Further Reflections on Parsley' (1942)

2 I believe a little incompatibility is the
spice of life, particularly if he has income
and she is pattable.
'I Do, I Will, I Have' (1949)

3 Professional men, they have no cares;
Whatever happens, they get theirs.
'I Yield to My Learned Brother' (1935)

4 The trouble with a kitten is
THAT
Eventually it becomes a
CAT.
'The Kitten' (1940)

5 Beneath this slab
John Brown is stowed.
He watched the ads,
And not the road.
'Lather as You Go' (1942)

6 Do you think my mind is maturing late,
Or simply rotted early?
'Lines on Facing Forty' (1942)

7 Good wine needs no bush,
And perhaps products that people really
want need no hard-sell or soft-sell TV
push.
Why not?
Look at pot.
'Most Doctors Recommend or Yours For Fast,
Fast, Fast Relief' (1972)

8 Children aren't happy with nothing to
ignore,
And that's what parents were created
for.
'The Parent' (1933)

9 He tells you when you've got on too
much lipstick,
And helps you with your girdle when
your hips stick.
'The Perfect Husband' (1949)

10 Any kiddie in school can love like a fool,
But hating, my boy, is an art.
'Plea for Less Malice Toward None' (1933)

11 Candy
Is dandy
But liquor
Is quicker.
'Reflections on Ice-breaking' (1931)

12 I test my bath before I sit,
And I'm always moved to wonderment
That what chills the finger not a bit
Is so frigid upon the fundament.
'Samson Agonistes' (1942)

13 I think that I shall never see
A billboard lovely as a tree.
Perhaps, unless the billboards fall,
I'll never see a tree at all.
'Song of the Open Road' (1933); cf. **Kilmer**
171:13

14 Sure, deck your lower limbs in pants;
Yours are the limbs, my sweeting.
You look divine as you advance—
Have you seen yourself retreating?
'What's the Use?' (1940)

15 Life is not having been told that the man
has just waxed the floor.
'You and Me and P. B. Shelley' (1942)

Terry Nation
see **Catch-phrases** 57:17

James Ball Naylor 1860–1945

16 King David and King Solomon
Led merry, merry lives,
With many, many lady friends,
And many, many wives;
But when old age crept over them—
With many, many qualms!—
King Solomon wrote the Proverbs
And King David wrote the Psalms.
'King David and King Solomon' (1935)

Jawaharlal Nehru 1889–1964

Indian statesman, Prime Minister 1947–64
on Nehru: see **Patil** 245:10

17 There is no easy walk-over to freedom
anywhere, and many of us will have to
pass through the valley of the shadow
again and again before we reach the
mountain-tops of our desire.
'From Lucknow to Tripuri' (1939)

18 At the stroke of the midnight hour, while
the world sleeps, India will awake to life
and freedom.
immediately prior to Independence
speech to the Indian Constituent Assembly, 14
August 1947

1 The light has gone out of our lives and there is darkness everywhere.
following Gandhi's assassination
    broadcast, 30 January 1948

2 I may lose many things including my temper, but I do not lose my nerve.
    at a press conference in Delhi, 4 June 1958

3 Democracy and socialism are means to an end, not the end itself.
    'Basic Approach'; written for private circulation and reprinted in Vincent Shean *Nehru: the Years of Power* (1960)

4 Normally speaking, it may be said that the forces of a capitalist society, if left unchecked, tend to make the rich richer and the poor poorer and thus increase the gap between them.
    'Basic Approach' in Vincent Shean *Nehru . . .* (1960)

5 After every other Viceroy has been forgotten, Curzon will be remembered because he restored all that was beautiful in India.
    in conversation with Lord Swinton
    Kenneth Rose *Superior Person* (1969)

6 I shall be the last Englishman to rule in India.
    J. K. Galbraith *A Life in Our Times* (1981)

A. S. Neill 1883–1973
Scottish teacher and educationist

7 If we have to have an exam at 11, let us make it one for humour, sincerity, imagination, character—and where is the examiner who could test such qualities.
    letter to *Daily Telegraph* 1957; in *Daily Telegraph* 25 September 1973

Howard Nemerov 1920–91
American poet and novelist

8 praise without end the go-ahead zeal of whoever it was invented the wheel; but never a word for the poor soul's sake that thought ahead, and invented the brake.
    'To the Congress of the United States, Entering Its Third Century' 26 February 1989

Pablo Neruda 1904–73
Chilean poet

9 I have gone marking the blank atlas of your body
with crosses of fire.
My mouth went across: a spider, trying to hide.
In you, behind you, timid, driven by thirst.
    'I Have Gone Marking' (1924), translated 1969 by W. S. Merwin

10 The typewriter separated me from a deeper intimacy with poetry, and my hand brought me closer to that intimacy again.
    in *Writers at Work* (5th series, 1981)

Edith Nesbit 1858–1924
English novelist and children's writer

11 The affection you get back from children is sixpence given as change for a sovereign.
    Julia Briggs *A Woman of Passion* (1987)

John von Neumann 1903–57
Hungarian-born American mathematician and computer pioneer

12 In mathematics you don't understand things. You just get used to them.
    Gary Zukav *The Dancing Wu Li Masters* (1979)

Allan Nevins 1890–1971
American historian

13 The former Allies had blundered in the past by offering Germany too little, and offering even that too late.
    in *Current History* (New York) May 1935

Anthony Newley 1931–
English singer, songwriter, and actor
and Leslie Bricusse 1931–
English songwriter and composer

14 Stop the world, I want to get off.
    title of musical (1961)

■ Newspaper headlines and leaders

see box opposite
see also **Cockburn** 72:2

Huey Newton 1942–

American political activist

1 I suggested [in 1966] that we use the panther as our symbol and call our political vehicle the Black Panther Party. The panther is a fierce animal, but he will not attack until he is backed into a corner; then he will strike out.
  Revolutionary Suicide (1973)

Trevor Newton

Managing Director of Yorkshire Water

2 I personally haven't had a bath or shower now for three months, and no-one has noticed.
  appealing to customers to stop bathing to reduce consumption
  in *The Times* 20 September 1995

Nancy Nicholson d. 1977

daughter of English artist William Nicholson

3 God is a man, so it must be all rot.
  reading the marriage service for the first time, on the morning of her wedding to Robert **Graves**
  R. Graves *Goodbye to All That* (1929)

Vivian Nicholson 1936–

4 I want to spend, and spend, and spend.
  said to reporters on arriving to collect her husband's football pools winnings of £152,000
  in *Daily Herald* 28 September 1961

Harold Nicolson 1886–1968

English diplomat, politician, and writer; husband of Vita **Sackville-West** and father of Nigel **Nicolson**

5 Chamberlain (who has the mind and manner of a clothes-brush) aims only at assuring temporary peace at the price of ultimate defeat.
  diary, 6 June 1938

6 We shall have to walk and live a Woolworth life hereafter.
  anticipating the aftermath of the Second World War
  diary, 4 June 1941

7 To be a good diarist one must have a little snouty, sneaky mind.
  diary, 9 November 1947

8 Attlee is a charming and intelligent man, but as a public speaker he is, compared to Winston [Churchill], like a village fiddler after Paganini.
  diary, 10 November 1947

9 I do not think it is quite fair to say that the British businessman has trampled on the faces of the poor. But he has sometimes not been very careful where he put his feet.
  replying to a heckler in the North Croydon by-election, 1948
  Nigel Nicolson (ed.) *Diaries and Letters of Harold Nicolson 1945–1962* vol. 3 (1968)

10 For seventeen years he did nothing at all but kill animals and stick in stamps.
  of King **George V**
  diary, 17 August 1949

11 Suez—a smash and grab raid that was all smash and no grab.
  in conversation with Antony Jay, November 1956; see also letter to Vita Sackville-West, 8 November 1956, 'Our smash-and-grab raid got stuck at the smash'

Nigel Nicolson 1917–

British Conservative politician and writer; son of Harold **Nicolson**

12 One final tip to rebels: always have a second profession in reserve.
  on the Maastricht Treaty vote in the House of Commons, having lost his own seat after abstaining on the Suez Crisis in 1956
  in *The Spectator* 7 November 1992

Reinhold Niebuhr 1892–1971

American theologian

13 Man's capacity for justice makes democracy possible, but man's inclination to injustice makes democracy necessary.
  Children of Light and Children of Darkness (1944)

▶▶

Newspaper headlines and leaders

1 Believe it or not.
title of syndicated newspaper feature (from 1918), written by Robert L. Ripley (1893–1949)

2 Crisis? What Crisis?
*summarizing an interview with James **Callaghan***
headline in *Sun*, 11 January 1979; cf. **Misquotations** 218:3

3 Dewey defeats Truman.
*anticipating the result of the Presidential election, which **Truman** won against expectation*
in *Chicago Tribune* 3 November 1948

4 Egghead weds hourglass.
*on the marriage of Arthur **Miller** and Marilyn **Monroe***
headline in *Variety* 1956; attributed

5 Freddie Starr ate my hamster.
headline in *Sun* 13 March 1986

6 GOTCHA!
on the sinking of the General Belgrano
headline in *Sun* 4 May 1982

7 It *is* a moral issue.
leader following the resignation of Profumo
in *The Times* 11 June 1963; cf. **Hailsham** 136:4, **Macmillan** 202:3

8 It's that man again . . . ! At the head of a cavalcade of seven black motor cars Hitler swept out of his Berlin Chancellery last night on a mystery journey.
*the acronym ITMA became the title of a BBC radio show, from September 1939 (cf. individual entries at **Catch-phrases**)*
headline in *Daily Express* 2 May 1939

9 It's The Sun Wot Won It.
following the 1992 general election
headline in *Sun* 11 April 1992

10 King's Moll Reno'd in Wolsey's Home Town.
on Wallis Simpson's divorce proceedings in Ipswich
US newspaper headline; F. Donaldson *Edward VIII* (1974)

11 Sticks nix hick pix.
on the lack of enthusiasm for farm dramas among rural populations
headline in *Variety* 17 July 1935

12 Wall St. lays an egg.
on the Wall St. crash
headline in *Variety* 30 October 1929

13 Who breaks a butterfly on a wheel?
*defending Mick **Jagger** after his arrest for cannabis possession*
leader in *The Times* 1 June 1967, written by William Rees-Mogg; see below

Who breaks a butterfly upon a wheel?
Alexander Pope (1688–1744) 'An Epistle to Dr Arbuthnot' (1735)

14 Whose finger do you want on the trigger?
referring to the atom bomb
in *Daily Mirror* 21 September 1951

15 Winter of discontent.
headline in *Sun* 30 April 1979; see below; cf. **Callaghan** 51:10

Now is the winter of our discontent
Made glorious summer by this sun of York.
William Shakespeare (1564–1616) *Richard III* (1591)

▶▶ **Reinhold Niebuhr** continued

16 Our gadget-filled paradise suspended in a hell of international insecurity.
Pious and Secular America (1957)

17 God, give us the serenity to accept what cannot be changed;
Give us the courage to change what should be changed;

Give us the wisdom to distinguish one from the other.
prayer said to have been first published in 1951
Richard Wightman Fox *Reinhold Niebuhr* (1985)

Martin Niemöller 1892–1984
German theologian

18 Ask the first man you meet what he means by defending freedom, and he'll tell you privately he means defending the standard of living.

address at Augsburg, January 1958; James Bentley *Martin Niemöller* (1984)

1 When Hitler attacked the Jews I was not a Jew, therefore, I was not concerned. And when Hitler attacked the Catholics, I was not a Catholic, and therefore, I was not concerned. And when Hitler attacked the unions and the industrialists, I was not a member of the unions and I was not concerned. Then, Hitler attacked me and the Protestant church—and there was nobody left to be concerned.

in *Congressional Record* 14 October 1968

Richard Nixon 1913–94

American Republican statesman, 37th President of the US, 1969–74
on Nixon: see **Abzug** 1:4, **Political slogans** 251:13, **Stevenson** 298:6, 298:9, **Ziegler** 341:6

2 But as I leave you I want you to know— just think how much you're going to be missing. You won't have Nixon to kick around any more because, gentlemen, this is my last press conference.

after losing the election for Governor of California to the press, 5 November 1962

3 This is the greatest week in the history of the world since the Creation.

welcoming the return of the first men to land on the moon
speech 24 July 1969

4 The great silent majority.

broadcast, 3 November 1969

5 Let us understand: North Vietnam cannot defeat or humiliate the United States. Only Americans can do that.

broadcast, 3 November 1969

6 There can be no whitewash at the White House.

on Watergate
television speech 30 April 1973

7 People have got to know whether or not their President is a crook. Well, I'm not a crook.

speech, 17 November 1973

8 I brought myself down. I gave them a sword. And they stuck it in.

television interview, 19 May 1977; David Frost *I Gave Them a Sword* (1978)

9 When the President does it, that means that it is not illegal.

David Frost *I Gave Them a Sword* (1978)

Kwame Nkrumah 1900–72

Ghanaian statesman, Prime Minister 1957–60, President 1960–6

10 Freedom is not something that one people can bestow on another as a gift. They claim it as their own and none can keep it from them.

speech in Accra, 10 July 1953

11 We face neither East nor West: we face forward.

conference speech, Accra, 7 April 1960; *Axioms of Kwame Nkrumah* (1967)

Christopher Nolan 1965–

Irish writer

12 My real motive is to describe how my brain-damaged life is as normal for me as my friends' able-bodied life is to them. My mind is just like a spin-dryer at full speed; my thoughts fly around my skull while millions of beautiful words cascade down into my lap. Images gunfire across my consciousness and while trying to discipline them I jump in awe at the soulfilled bounty of my mind's expanse. Try then to imagine how frustrating it is to give expression to that avalanche in efforts of one great nod after the other.

of his reasons for writing The Eye of the Clock
in *Observer* 8 November 1987

Steven Norris 1945–

British Conservative politician

13 You have your own company, your own temperature control, your own music— and don't have to put up with dreadful human beings sitting alongside you.

on cars compared to public transport
comment to Commons Environment Select Committee, in *Daily Telegraph* 9 February 1995

Lord Northcliffe 1865–1922

British newspaper proprietor

1 The power of the press is very great, but not so great as the power of suppress.

  office message, *Daily Mail* 1918; R. Rose and G. Harmsworth *Northcliffe* (1959)

2 When I want a peerage, I shall buy it like an honest man.

  Tom Driberg *Swaff* (1974)

Lord Nuffield 1877–1963

British motor manufacturer and philanthropist

on seeing the Morris Minor prototype in 1945:

3 It looks like a poached egg—we can't make that.

  attributed

Sam Nunn

American Democratic politician

4 Don't ask, don't tell.

  summary of the **Clinton** administration's compromise policy on homosexuals serving in the armed forces, in *New York Times* 12 May 1993

Julius Nyerere 1922–

Tanzanian statesman, President of Tanganyika 1962–4 and of Tanzania 1964–85

5 Should we really let our people starve so we can pay our debts?

  in *Guardian* 21 March 1985

6 We are a poor country and we opted for socialist policies, but to build a socialist society you have to have a developed society.

  in *Observer* 28 July 1985 'Sayings of the Week'

Lawrence Oates

see **Last words** 182:6

Conor Cruise O'Brien 1917–

Irish politician, writer, and journalist

7 The strength of these men was that each of them could look a Pearsean ghost in the eye . . . Each of them, in their youth, had done the thing the ghost asked them to do, in 1916 or 1919—21 or both. That was it; from now on they would do what seemed reasonable to themselves in the interests of the actual people inhabiting the island of Ireland and not of a personified abstraction, or of a disembodied voice, or of a ghost.

  of Sean Lemass (1899–1971) and other senior Irish politicians in the 1960s; cf. **Pearse** 246:5

  Ancestral Voices (1994)

8 If I saw Mr Haughey buried at midnight at a crossroads, with a stake driven through his heart—politically speaking—I should continue to wear a clove of garlic round my neck, just in case.

  in *Observer* 10 October 1982

Edna O'Brien 1936–

Irish novelist and short-story writer

9 August is a wicked month.

  title of novel (1965)

Flann O'Brien 1911–66

Irish novelist and journalist

10 The conclusion of your syllogism, I said lightly, is fallacious, being based upon licensed premises.

  At Swim-Two-Birds (1939)

11 The play was consumed in wholesome fashion by large masses in places of public resort; the novel was self-administered in private.

  At Swim-Two-Birds (1939)

12 A pint of plain is your only man.

  At Swim-Two-Birds (1939)

13 Waiting for the German verb is surely the ultimate thrill.

  The Hair of the Dogma (1977)

14 It is not that I half knew my mother. I knew half of her: the lower half—her lap, legs, feet, her hands and wrists as she bent forward.

  The Hard Life (1961)

Sean O'Casey 1880–1964

Irish dramatist

1 I killin' meself workin', an' he sthruttin'
about from mornin' till night like a
paycock!
Juno and the Paycock (1925)

2 He's an oul' butty o' mine—oh, he's a
darlin' man, a daarlin' man.
Juno and the Paycock (1925)

3 The whole worl's in a state o' chassis!
Juno and the Paycock (1925)

4 There's no reason to bring religion into
it. I think we ought to have as great a
regard for religion as we can, so as to
keep it out of as many things as possible.
The Plough and the Stars (1926)

5 It's my rule never to lose me temper till it
would be dethrimental to keep it.
The Plough and the Stars (1926)

6 English literature's performing flea.
of P. G. Wodehouse
P. G. Wodehouse *Performing Flea* (1953)

7 When one has reached 81 . . . one likes
to sit back and let the world turn by
itself, without trying to push it.
in *New York Times* 25 September 1960

Bernard O'Donoghue 1945–

Irish poet and academic

8 We were terribly lucky to catch
The Ceauşescus' execution, being
By sheer chance that Christmas Day
In the only house for twenty miles
With satellite TV. We sat,
Cradling brandies, by the fire
Watching those two small, cranky
    autocrats
Lying in snow against a blood-spattered
    wall,
Hardly able to believe our good fortune.
'Carolling' (1995)

9 The reporter told us how
The cross woman's peasant origins
Came out at the last, shouting
At her executioners 'I have been
A mother to you and this is how
You thank me for it.'
'Carolling' (1995)

Denise O'Donoghue

10 They [men] are happier with women
who make their coffee than make their
programmes.
G. Kinnock and F. Miller (eds.) *By Faith and
Daring* (1993)

■ Official advice

see box opposite

David Ogilvy 1911–

British-born advertising executive

11 The consumer isn't a moron; she is your
wife.
Confessions of an Advertising Man (1963)

John O'Hara 1905–70

American writer

12 George [Gershwin] died on July 11,
1937, but I don't have to believe that if I
don't want to.
in *Newsweek* 15 July 1940

13 An artist is his own fault.
The Portable F. Scott Fitzgerald (1945)
introduction

Abraham Okpik

Canadian Inuit spokesman

14 I am proud to be an Eskimo, but I think
we can improve on the igloo as a
permanent dwelling.
in *Northern Affairs Bulletin* March 1960

15 There are very few Eskimos, but millions
of Whites, just like mosquitoes. It is
something very special and wonderful to
be an Eskimo—they are like the snow
geese. If an Eskimo forgets his language
and Eskimo ways, he will be nothing but
just another mosquito.
attributed, 1966

Bruce Oldfield 1950–

English fashion designer

16 Fashion is more usually a gentle
progression of revisited ideas.
in *Independent* 9 September 1989

Official advice

1 Careless talk costs lives.
  wartime security slogan, 1940s

2 Clunk, click, every trip.
  road safety campaign promoting the use of
  seat-belts, 1971

3 Coughs and sneezes spread diseases.
  Trap the germs in your handkerchief.
  Second World War health slogan, 1942

4 Dig for victory.
  radio broadcast by Reginald Dorman-Smith
  (1899–1977), Minister for Agriculture, 3
  October 1939

5 Don't ask a man to drink and drive.
  UK road safety slogan, from 1964

6 Don't die of ignorance.
  Aids publicity campaign, 1987

7 Is your journey *really* necessary?
  slogan coined to discourage Civil Servants
  from going home for Christmas, 1939

8 Keep Britain tidy.
  issued by the Central Office of Information,
  1950s

9 Make do and mend.
  wartime slogan, 1940s

10 Slip, slop, slap.
  sun protection slogan, meaning slip *on a
  T-shirt,* slop *on some suncream,* slap *on a hat*
  Australian health education programme,
  1980s

11 Smoking can seriously damage your
  health.
  *government health warning now required by
  British law to be printed on cigarette packets*
  from early 1970s, in form 'Smoking can
  damage your health'

12 Stop-look-and-listen.
  road safety slogan, current in the US from
  1912

13 *Taisez-vous! Méfiez-vous! Les oreilles
  ennemies vous écoutent.*
  Keep your mouth shut! Be on your
  guard! Enemy ears are listening to you.
  official notice in France, 1915

14 Tradition dictates that we have a
  lawn—but do we really need one? Why
  not increase the size of your borders or
  replace lawned areas with paving
  stones or gravel?
  Severn Trent Water 'The Gardener's Water
  Code' (1996)

Laurence Olivier 1907–89

English actor and director

15 The tragedy of a man who could not
  make up his mind.
  introduction to his 1948 screen adaptation of
  Hamlet

16 Shakespeare—the nearest thing in
  incarnation to the eye of God.
  in *Kenneth Harris Talking To* (1971) 'Sir
  Laurence Olivier'

17 Acting is a masochistic form of
  exhibitionism. It is not quite the
  occupation of an adult.
  in *Time* 3 July 1978

18 Can a muse of fire exist under a ceiling of
  commerce?
  *appealing on behalf of the Rose Theatre remains
  in The Times 12 July 1989; see below*

O! for a Muse of fire.
Shakespeare *Henry V* (1599) chorus

Jacqueline Kennedy Onassis
1929–94

wife of John Fitzgerald **Kennedy,** First Lady
of the US 1961–3

19 If you bungle raising your children I
  don't think whatever else you do well
  matters very much.
  Theodore C. Sorenson *Kennedy* (1965)

20 The one thing I do not want to be called
  is First Lady. It sounds like a saddle
  horse.
  Peter Collier and David Horowitz *The Kennedys*
  (1984)

Eugene O'Neill 1888–1953

American dramatist

1 For de little stealin' dey gits you in jail soon or late. For de big stealin' dey makes you Emperor and puts you in de Hall o' Fame when you croaks.
  The Emperor Jones (1921)

2 The iceman cometh.
  title of play (1946)

3 A long day's journey into night.
  title of play (written 1940–1)

4 Mourning becomes Electra
  title of play (1931)

5 The sea hates a coward!
  Mourning becomes Electra (1931)

6 What beastly incidents our memories insist on cherishing! . . . the ugly and disgusting . . . the beautiful things we have to keep diaries to remember!
  Strange Interlude (1928)

Yoko Ono 1933–

Japanese poet and songwriter

7 Woman is the nigger of the world.
  interview for *Nova* magazine (1968); adopted by her husband John **Lennon** as song title (1972)

J. Robert Oppenheimer 1904–67

American physicist

8 I remembered the line from the Hindu scripture, the *Bhagavad Gita* . . . 'I am become death, the destroyer of worlds.'
  on the explosion of the first atomic bomb near Alamogordo, New Mexico, 16 July 1945
    Len Giovannitti and Fred Freed *The Decision to Drop the Bomb* (1965)

9 The physicists have known sin; and this is a knowledge which they cannot lose.
  lecture at Massachusetts Institute of Technology, 25 November 1947

10 When you see something that is technically sweet, you go ahead and do it and you argue about what to do about it only after you have had your technical

success. That is the way it was with the atomic bomb.
  in *In the Matter of J. Robert Oppenheimer, USAEC Transcript of Hearing Before Personnel Security Board* (1954)

Susie Orbach 1946–

American psychotherapist

11 Fat is a feminist issue.
  title of book (1978)

Roy Orbison 1936–88

American singer and songwriter

and Joe Melsom

12 Only the lonely (know the way I feel).
  title of song (1960)

P. J. O'Rourke 1947–

American humorous writer

13 You can't put your VISA bill on your American Express card.
  The Bachelor Home Companion (1987)

14 Not only is this the first live televised war, it's also the first war ever covered by sober journalists.
  of the Gulf War
    Give War a Chance (1992)

15 That happy sense of purpose people have when they are standing up for a principle they haven't really been knocked down for yet.
  Give War a Chance (1992)

16 Liberals have invented whole college majors—psychology, sociology, women's studies— to prove that nothing is anybody's fault.
  Give War a Chance (1992)

17 You can't shame or humiliate modern celebrities. What used to be called shame and humiliation is now called publicity.
  Give War a Chance (1992)

18 Every government is a parliament of whores. The trouble is, in a democracy the whores are us.
  Parliament of Whores (1991)

19 Whatever it is that the government does, sensible Americans would prefer that the

government does it to somebody else. This is the idea behind foreign policy.

Parliament of Whores (1991)

1 Whose woods are whose everybody knows exactly, and everybody knows who got them rezoned for a shopping mall and who couldn't get the financing to begin construction and why it was he couldn't get it.

on a traditional New England community

Parliament of Whores (1991); cf. **Frost** 120:2

José Ortega y Gasset
1883–1955

Spanish writer and philosopher

2 I am I plus my surroundings, and if I do not preserve the latter I do not preserve myself.

Meditaciones del Quijote (1914)

3 Civilization is nothing more than the effort to reduce the use of force to the last resort.

La Rebelión de las Masas (1930)

Joe Orton 1933–67

English dramatist

4 I'd the upbringing a nun would envy and that's the truth. Until I was fifteen I was more familiar with Africa than my own body.

Entertaining Mr Sloane (1964)

5 KATH: Can he be present at the birth of his child? . . .
ED: It's all any reasonable child can expect if the dad is present at the conception.

Entertaining Mr Sloane (1964)

6 Every luxury was lavished on you— atheism, breast-feeding, circumcision.

Loot (1967)

7 Reading isn't an occupation we encourage among police officers. We try to keep the paper work down to a minimum.

Loot (1967)

8 You were born with your legs apart. They'll send you to the grave in a Y-shaped coffin.

What the Butler Saw (1969)

9 The kind of people who always go on about whether a thing is in good taste invariably have very bad taste.

in *Transatlantic Review* Spring 1967

George Orwell 1903–50

English novelist
on Orwell: see **Connolly** 75:2

10 Man is the only creature that consumes without producing.

Animal Farm (1945)

11 Four legs good, two legs bad.

Animal Farm (1945)

12 All animals are equal but some animals are more equal than others.

Animal Farm (1945)

13 Good prose is like a window-pane.

Collected Essays (1968) vol. 1 'Why I Write'

14 I'm fat, but I'm thin inside. Has it ever struck you that there's a thin man inside every fat man, just as they say there's a statue inside every block of stone?

Coming up For Air (1939); cf. **Connolly** 74:17

15 Roast beef and Yorkshire, or roast pork and apple sauce, followed up by suet pudding and driven home, as it were, by a cup of mahogany-brown tea, have put you in just the right mood . . . In these blissful circumstances, what is it that you want to read about?
  Naturally, about a murder.

Decline of the English Murder and other essays (1965) title essay, written 1946

16 Down and out in Paris and London

title of book (1933)

17 He was an embittered atheist (the sort of atheist who does not so much disbelieve in God as personally dislike Him), and took a sort of pleasure in thinking that human affairs would never improve.

Down and Out in Paris and London (1933)

18 There was much in it that I did not understand, in some ways I did not even

like it, but I recognized it immediately as a state of affairs worth fighting for.

Homage to Catalonia (1938)

1 Down here it was still the England I had known in my childhood: the railway cuttings smothered in wild flowers . . . the red buses, the blue policemen—all sleeping the deep, deep sleep of England, from which I sometimes fear that we shall never wake till we are jerked out of it by the roar of bombs.

Homage to Catalonia (1938)

2 Most revolutionaries are potential Tories, because they imagine that everything can be put right by altering the *shape* of society; once that change is effected, as it sometimes is, they see no need for any other.

Inside the Whale (1940) 'Charles Dickens'

3 Keep the aspidistra flying.

title of novel (1936)

4 England is not the jewelled isle of Shakespeare's much-quoted passage, nor is it the inferno depicted by Dr Goebbels. More than either it resembles a family, a rather stuffy Victorian family, with not many black sheep in it but with all its cupboards bursting with skeletons . . . A family with the wrong members in control.

The Lion and the Unicorn (1941) pt. 1 'England Your England'

5 Old maids biking to Holy Communion through the mists of the autumn mornings . . . these are not only fragments, but *characteristic* fragments, of the English scene.

The Lion and the Unicorn (1941) pt. 1 'England Your England'; cf. **Major** 204:16

6 Probably the battle of Waterloo *was* won on the playing-fields of Eton, but the opening battles of all subsequent wars have been lost there.

The Lion and the Unicorn (1941) pt. 1 'England Your England'; see below

The battle of Waterloo was won on the playing fields of Eton.

Duke of Wellington (1769–1852) oral tradition, but not found in this form of words

7 It was a bright cold day in April, and the clocks were striking thirteen.

Nineteen Eighty-Four (1949)

8 BIG BROTHER IS WATCHING YOU.

Nineteen Eighty-Four (1949)

9 War is peace. Freedom is slavery. Ignorance is strength.

Nineteen Eighty-Four (1949)

10 Who controls the past controls the future: who controls the present controls the past.

Nineteen Eighty-Four (1949)

11 Freedom is the freedom to say that two plus two make four. If that is granted, all else follows.

Nineteen Eighty-Four (1949)

12 The Lottery, with its weekly pay-out of enormous prizes, was the one public event to which the proles paid serious attention . . . It was their delight, their folly, their anodyne, their intellectual stimulant . . . the prizes were largely imaginary. Only small sums were actually paid out, the winners of the big prizes being non-existent persons.

Nineteen Eighty-Four (1949)

13 *Doublethink* means the power of holding two contradictory beliefs in one's mind simultaneously, and accepting both of them.

Nineteen Eighty-Four (1949)

14 Power is not a means, it is an end. One does not establish a dictatorship in order to safeguard a revolution; one makes the revolution in order to establish the dictatorship.

Nineteen Eighty-Four (1949)

15 If you want a picture of the future, imagine a boot stamping on a human face—for ever.

Nineteen Eighty-Four (1949)

16 The road to Wigan Pier.

title of book (1937)

17 It is only because miners sweat their guts out that superior persons can remain superior.

The Road to Wigan Pier (1937)

18 A person of bourgeois origin goes through life with some expectation of

getting what he wants, within reasonable limits. Hence the fact that in times of stress 'educated' people tend to come to the front.

The Road to Wigan Pier (1937)

1 To the ordinary working man, the sort you would meet in any pub on Saturday night, Socialism does not mean much more than better wages and shorter hours and nobody bossing you about.

The Road to Wigan Pier (1937)

2 The high-water mark, so to speak, of Socialist literature is W. H. Auden, a sort of gutless Kipling.

The Road to Wigan Pier (1937)

3 We of the sinking middle class . . . may sink without further struggles into the working class where we belong, and probably when we get there it will not be so dreadful as we feared, for, after all, we have nothing to lose but our aitches.

The Road to Wigan Pier (1937)

4 Serious sport has nothing to do with fair play. It is bound up with hatred, jealousy, boastfulness, and disregard of all the rules.

Shooting an Elephant (1950) 'I Write as I Please'

5 The great enemy of clear language is insincerity. When there is a gap between one's real and one's declared aims, one turns as it were instinctively to long words and exhausted idioms, like a cuttlefish squirting out ink.

Shooting an Elephant (1950) 'Politics and the English Language'

6 Political language . . . is designed to make lies sound truthful and murder respectable, and to give an appearance of solidity to pure wind.

Shooting an Elephant (1950) 'Politics and the English Language'

7 Saints should always be judged guilty until they are proved innocent.

Shooting an Elephant (1950) 'Reflections on Gandhi'

8 [Serious sport] is war minus the shooting.

Shooting an Elephant (1950) 'The Sporting Spirit'

9 Whatever is funny is subversive, every joke is ultimately a custard pie . . . A dirty joke is a sort of mental rebellion.

in *Horizon* September 1941 'The Art of Donald McGill'

10 [Clement] Attlee reminds me of nothing so much as a recently dead fish, before it has had time to stiffen.

diary, 19 May 1942

11 The Catholic and the Communist are alike in assuming that an opponent cannot be both honest and intelligent.

in *Polemic* January 1946 'The Prevention of Literature'

12 The quickest way of ending a war is to lose it.

in *Polemic* May 1946 'Second Thoughts on James Burnham'

13 At 50, everyone has the face he deserves.

last words in his notebook, 17 April 1949; *Collected Essays, Journalism and Letters* . . . (1968)

14 Advertising is the rattling of a stick inside a swill bucket.

attributed

John Osborne 1929–94

English dramatist; former husband of Jill **Bennett**
on Osborne: see **Bennett** 31:14

15 Don't clap too hard—it's a very old building.

The Entertainer (1957)

16 Thank God we're normal,
Yes, this is our finest shower!

The Entertainer (1957)

17 But I have a go, lady, don't I? I 'ave a go. I do.

The Entertainer (1957)

18 Look back in anger.

title of play (1956)

19 Oh heavens, how I long for a little ordinary human enthusiasm. Just enthusiasm—that's all. I want to hear a warm, thrilling voice cry out Hallelujah! Hallelujah! I'm alive!

Look Back in Anger (1956)

20 His knowledge of life and ordinary human beings is so hazy, he really

deserves some sort of decoration for it—a medal inscribed 'For Vaguery in the Field'.

Look Back in Anger (1956)

1 Slamming their doors, stamping their high heels, banging their irons and saucepans—the eternal flaming racket of the female.

Look Back in Anger (1956)

2 I don't think one 'comes down' from Jimmy's university. According to him, it's not even red brick, but white tile.

Look Back in Anger (1956)

3 Reason and Progress, the old firm, is selling out!

Look Back in Anger (1956)

4 They spend their time mostly looking forward to the past.

Look Back in Anger (1956)

5 There aren't any good, brave causes left. If the big bang does come, and we all get killed off, it won't be in aid of the old-fashioned, grand design. It'll just be for the Brave New-nothing-very-much-thank-you. About as pointless and inglorious as stepping in front of a bus.

Look Back in Anger (1956)

6 She's like the old line about justice—not only must be done, but must be seen to be done.

Time Present (1968)

7 Royalty is the gold filling in a mouthful of decay.

'They call it cricket' in T. Maschler (ed.) *Declaration* (1957)

8 This is a letter of hate. It is for you my countrymen, I mean those men of my country who have defiled it. The men with manic fingers leading the sightless, feeble, betrayed body of my country to its death . . . damn you England.

in *Tribune* 18 August 1961

9 The schoolteacher is certainly underpaid as a childminder, but ludicrously overpaid as an educator.

in *Observer* 21 July 1985 'Sayings of the Week'

David Owen 1938–

British Social Democratic politician

10 The price of championing human rights is a little inconsistency at times.

speech, House of Commons, 30 March 1977

11 We are fed up with fudging and mudging, with mush and slush. We need courage, conviction, and hard work.

speech to his supporters at Labour Party Conference in Blackpool, 2 October 1980

Wilfred Owen 1893–1918

English poet

12 My subject is War, and the pity of War. The Poetry is in the pity.

Poems (1963) preface (written 1918)

13 All a poet can do today is warn.

Poems (1963) preface (written 1918)

14 What passing-bells for these who die as cattle?
Only the monstrous anger of the guns.

'Anthem for Doomed Youth' (written 1917)

15 The shrill, demented choirs of wailing shells;
And bugles calling for them from sad shires.

'Anthem for Doomed Youth' (written 1917)

16 The pallor of girls' brows shall be their pall;
Their flowers the tenderness of patient minds,
And each slow dusk a drawing-down of blinds.

'Anthem for Doomed Youth' (written 1917)

17 If you could hear, at every jolt, the blood
Come gargling from the froth-corrupted lungs,
Obscene as cancer, bitter as the cud
Of vile, incurable sores on innocent tongues,—
My friend, you would not tell with such high zest
To children ardent for some desperate glory,

The old Lie: Dulce et decorum est
Pro patria mori.

   'Dulce et Decorum Est' (1963 ed.); see below

Dulce et decorum est pro patria mori.

Lovely and honourable it is to die for
one's country.

   Horace (65–8 BC) *Odes*; cf. **Pound** 254:1

1 Was it for this the clay grew tall?
—O what made fatuous sunbeams toil
To break earth's sleep at all?

   'Futility' (written 1918)

2 Red lips are not so red
As the stained stones kissed by the
   English dead.

   'Greater Love' (written 1917)

3 It seemed that out of battle I escaped
Down some profound dull tunnel, long
   since scooped
Through granites which titanic wars had
   groined.

   'Strange Meeting' (written 1918)

4 'Strange friend,' I said, 'here is no cause
   to mourn.'
'None,' said that other, 'save the undone
   years,
The hopelessness. Whatever hope is
   yours,
Was my life also.'

   'Strange Meeting' (written 1918)

5 Courage was mine, and I had mystery,
Wisdom was mine, and I had mastery.

   'Strange Meeting' (written 1918)

6 I am the enemy you killed, my friend.
I knew you in this dark.

   'Strange Meeting' (written 1918)

7 Let us sleep now.

   'Strange Meeting' (written 1918)

Vance Packard 1914–

American writer and journalist

8 The hidden persuaders.

   title of a study of the advertising industry
   (1957)

Ignacy Jan Paderewski
1860–1941

Polish pianist, composer, and statesman

9 What a terrible revenge by the culture of
the Negroes on that of the whites!

   of jazz

   Nat Shapiro (ed.) *An Encyclopedia of
   Quotations about Music* (1978)

Reginald Paget 1908–90

British Labour politician

10 There is no disguise or camouflage about
the Prime Minister. He is the original
banana man, yellow outside and a softer
yellow inside.

   *of Anthony **Eden***

   in a House of Commons debate, 14 September
   1956

11 When self-indulgence has reduced a man
to the shape of Lord Hailsham, sexual
continence requires no more than a sense
of the ridiculous.

   speech in the House of Commons during the
   Profumo affair, 17 June 1963

12 I know of no book which has been a
source of brutality and sadistic conduct,
both public and private, that can
compare with the Bible.

   in *Observer* 28 June 1964 'Sayings of the Week'

Camille Paglia 1947–

American author and critic

13 Modern body building is ritual, religion,
sport, art, and science, awash in Western
chemistry and mathematics. Defying
nature, it surpasses it.

   Sex, Art, and American Culture (1992)

14 If civilization had been left in female
hands, we would still be living in grass
huts.

   Sexual Personae (1990)

15 Television is actually closer to reality
than anything in books. The madness of
TV is the madness of human life.

   in *Harper's Magazine* March 1991

16 There is no female Mozart because there
is no female Jack the Ripper.

   in *International Herald Tribune* 26 April 1991

Marcel Pagnol 1895–1974

French dramatist and film-maker

1 Honour is like a match, you can only use it once.
   Marius (1946)

2 It's better to choose the culprits than to seek them out.
   Topaze (1930)

Leroy ('Satchel') Paige

1906–82

American baseball player

3 Don't look back. Something may be gaining on you.
   in *Collier's* 13 June 1953

Ian Paisley 1926–

Presbyterian minister and Northern Irish politician

4 I would rather be British than just.
   remark to Bernadette Devlin, October 1969, reported by *Sunday Times* Insight Team in *Ulster* (1972)

Christabel Pankhurst

1880–1958

English suffragette; daughter of Emmeline Pankhurst
see also **Political slogans** 251:23

5 Never lose your temper with the Press or the public is a major rule of political life.
   Unshackled (1959)

6 We are here to claim our right as women, not only to be free, but to fight for freedom. That it is our right as well as our duty.
   speech in London, 23 March 1911

Emmeline Pankhurst

1858–1928

English suffragette leader; founder of the Women's Social and Political Union, 1903
see also **Political slogans** 251:23

7 There is something that Governments care far more for than human life, and that is the security of property, and so it is through property that we shall strike the enemy . . . I say to the Government: You have not dared to take the leaders of Ulster for their incitement to rebellion. Take me if you dare.
   speech at Albert Hall, 17 October 1912

8 The argument of the broken window pane is the most valuable argument in modern politics.
   G. Dangerfield *The Strange Death of Liberal England* (1936)

Anna Paquin 1982–

New Zealand actress

9 Acting is pretending to be someone else.
   in *Guardian* 24 January 1997

Mitchell Parish

10 When the deep purple falls over sleepy garden walls.
   'Deep Purple' (1939 song)

Charlie Parker 1920–55

American jazz saxophonist

11 Music is your own experience, your thoughts, your wisdom. If you don't live it, it won't come out of your horn.
   Nat Shapiro and Nat Hentoff *Hear Me Talkin' to Ya* (1955)

Dorothy Parker 1893–1967

American critic and humorist
on Parker: see **Benchley** 29:6, **Woollcott** 335:18; see also **Epitaphs** 105:2, **Telegrams** 305:3

12 Scratch a lover, and find a foe.
   'Ballade of a Great Weariness' (1937)

13 Oh, life is a glorious cycle of song,
   A medley of extemporanea;
   And love is a thing that can never go wrong;
   And I am Marie of Roumania.
   'Comment' (1937)

14 Four be the things I'd been better without:
   Love, curiosity, freckles, and doubt.
   'Inventory' (1937)

1 Men seldom make passes
  At girls who wear glasses.
  'News Item' (1937)

2 Why is it no one ever sent me yet
  One perfect limousine, do you suppose?
  Ah no, it's always just my luck to get
  One perfect rose.
  'One Perfect Rose' (1937)

3 Whose love is given over-well
  Shall look on Helen's face in hell
  Whilst they whose love is thin and wise
  Shall see John Knox in Paradise.
  'Partial Comfort' (1937)

4 If, with the literate, I am
  Impelled to try an epigram,
  I never seek to take the credit;
  We all assume that Oscar said it.
  'A Pig's-Eye View of Literature' (1937)

5 Guns aren't lawful;
  Nooses give;
  Gas smells awful;
  You might as well live.
  'Résumé' (1937)

6 Where's the man could ease a heart like
  a satin gown?
  'The Satin Dress' (1937)

7 By the time you say you're his,
  Shivering and sighing
  And he vows his passion is
  Infinite, undying—
  Lady, make a note of this:
  One of you is lying.
  'Unfortunate Coincidence' (1937)

8 Sorrow is tranquillity remembered in
  emotion.
  Here Lies (1939) 'Sentiment'; see below

  Poetry . . . takes its origin from
  emotion recollected in tranquillity.
  William Wordsworth (1770–1850) Lyrical
  Ballads (2nd ed., 1802)

9 Brevity is the soul of lingerie, as the
  Petticoat said to the Chemise.
  caption written for Vogue (1916); John Keats
  You Might as well Live (1970); see below

  Brevity is the soul of wit.
  William Shakespeare (1564–1616) Hamlet
  (1601)

10 The affair between Margot Asquith and
   Margot Asquith will live as one of the
   prettiest love stories in all literature.
   review of Margot Asquith's Lay Sermons in
   New Yorker 22 October 1927

11 And it is that word 'hummy', my
   darlings, that marks the first place in
   'The House at Pooh Corner' at which
   Tonstant Weader fwowed up.
   in New Yorker 20 October 1928 (review by
   Dorothy Parker as 'Constant Reader')

12 House Beautiful is play lousy.
   New Yorker review (1933); P. Hartnoll Plays and
   Players (1984)

13 She ran the whole gamut of the emotions
   from A to B.
   of Katharine Hepburn at a Broadway first night,
   1933
   attributed

14 That woman speaks eighteen languages,
   and can't say No in any of them.
   Alexander Woollcott While Rome Burns (1934)
   'Our Mrs Parker'

15 And there was that wholesale libel on a
   Yale prom. If all the girls attending it
   were laid end to end, Mrs Parker said,
   she wouldn't be at all surprised.
   Alexander Woollcott While Rome Burns (1934)
   'Our Mrs Parker'

16 There's a hell of a distance between wise-
   cracking and wit. Wit has truth in it;
   wise-cracking is simply callisthenics with
   words.
   in Paris Review Summer 1956

17 How do they know?
   on being told that Calvin **Coolidge** had died
   M. Cowley Writers at Work 1st Series (1958)

18 As artists they're rot, but as providers
   they're oil wells; they gush.
   on lady novelists
   Malcolm Cowley Writers at Work 1st Series
   (1958)

19 Hollywood money isn't money. It's
   congealed snow, melts in your hand, and
   there you are.
   Malcolm Cowley Writers at Work 1st Series
   (1958)

20 It serves me right for putting all my eggs
   in one bastard.
   on her abortion
   J. Keats You Might as well Live (1970)

1 One more drink and I'd have been under the host.

> Howard Teichmann *George S. Kaufman* (1972)

2 You can lead a horticulture, but you can't make her think.

> J. Keats *You Might as well Live* (1970)

Ross Parker 1914–74
and Hugh Charles 1907–

British songwriters

3 There'll always be an England
While there's a country lane,
Wherever there's a cottage small
Beside a field of grain.

> 'There'll always be an England' (1939 song)

4 We'll meet again, don't know where,
Don't know when,
But I know we'll meet again some sunny day.

> 'We'll Meet Again' (1939 song)

C. Northcote Parkinson
1909–93

English writer

5 Expenditure rises to meet income.

> *The Law and the Profits* (1960)

6 Work expands so as to fill the time available for its completion.

> *Parkinson's Law* (1958)

7 Time spent on any item of the agenda will be in inverse proportion to the sum involved.

> *Parkinson's Law* (1958)

8 Perfection of planned layout is achieved only by institutions on the point of collapse.

> *Parkinson's Law* (1958)

9 The man who is denied the opportunity of taking decisions of importance begins to regard as important the decisions he is allowed to take.

> *Parkinson's Law* (1958)

10 Men enter local politics solely as a result of being unhappily married.

> *Parkinson's Law* (1958)

Rosa Parks 1913–

American civil rights activist

11 Our mistreatment was just not right, and I was tired of it.

> *of her refusal, in December 1955, to surrender her seat on a segregated bus in Alabama to a white man*
> *Quiet Strength* (1994)

Matthew Parris 1949–

British journalist and former politician

> *of Lady **Thatcher** in the House of Lords:*

12 A big cat detained briefly in a poodle parlour, sharpening her claws on the velvet.

> *Look Behind You!* (1993)

13 Nice guys, when we turn nasty, can make a terrible mess of it, usually because we've had so little practice, and have bottled it up for too long.

> in *The Spectator* 27 February 1993

14 Being an MP feeds your vanity and starves your self-respect.

> in *The Times* 9 February 1994

15 Why waste it on some vanilla-flavoured pixie. Bring on the fruitcakes, we want a fruitcake for an unlosable seat. They enliven the Commons.

> *the day before the Kensington and Chelsea association chose Alan **Clark** as their parliamentary candidate*
> in *Mail on Sunday* 26 January 1997

Tony Parsons 1953–

English critic and writer

16 I never saw a beggar yet who would recognise guilt if it bit him on his unwashed ass.

> *Dispatches from the Front Line of Popular Culture* (1994)

Frances Partridge 1900–

English writer and diarist

1 Thirty years is a very long time to live alone and life doesn't get any nicer.
on widowhood, at the age of 92
G. Kinnock and F. Miller (eds.) *By Faith and Daring* (1993)

Boris Pasternak 1890–1960

Russian novelist and poet

2 Man is born to live, not to prepare for life.
Doctor Zhivago (1958)

3 Most people experience love, without noticing that there is anything remarkable about it.
Doctor Zhivago (1958)

4 I don't like people who have never fallen or stumbled. Their virtue is lifeless and it isn't of much value. Life hasn't revealed its beauty to them.
Doctor Zhivago (1958)

5 The whole human way of life has been destroyed and ruined. All that's left is the bare, shivering human soul, stripped to the last shred, the naked force of the human psyche for which nothing has changed because it was always cold and shivering and reaching out to its nearest neighbour, as cold and lonely as itself.
Doctor Zhivago (1958)

6 Art always serves beauty, and beauty is the joy of possessing form, and form is the key to organic life since no living thing can exist without it.
Doctor Zhivago (1958)

7 Yet the order of the acts is planned
And the end of the way inescapable.
I am alone; all drowns in the Pharisees' hypocrisy.
To live your life is not as simple as to cross a field.
Doctor Zhivago (1958) 'Hamlet'

8 Work seethes in the hands of spring,
That strapping dairymaid.
Doctor Zhivago (1958) 'March'

9 In time to come, I tell them, we'll be equal
to any living now. If cripples, then

no matter; we shall just have been run over
by 'New Man' in the wagon of his 'Plan'.
'When I Grow Weary' (1932)

Sadashiv Kanoji Patil

Indian politician

10 The Prime Minister is like the great banyan tree. Thousands shelter beneath it, but nothing grows.
when asked in an interview who would be **Nehru**'s *successor*
J. K. Galbraith *A Life in Our Times* (1981)

Alan Paton 1903–

South African writer

11 Cry, the beloved country.
title of novel (1948)

Leslie Paul 1905–85

Irish writer

12 Angry young man.
title of book (1951); the phrase subsequently associated with John **Osborne**'s play *Look Back in Anger* (1956)

Wolfgang Pauli 1900–58

Austrian-born American physicist who worked chiefly in Switzerland
on Pauli: see **Weisskopf** 322:7

13 I don't mind your thinking slowly: I mind your publishing faster than you think.
attributed

Tom Paulin 1949–

English poet and critic

14 That stretch of water, it's always
There for you to cross over
To the other shore, observing
The light of cities on blackness.
'States' (1977)

15 Now dream
of that sweet
equal republic
where the juniper

talks to the oak,
the thistle,
the bandaged elm,
and the jolly jolly chestnut.
  'The Book of Juniper' (1983)

1 The owl of Minerva in a hired car.
  'Desertmartin' (1983)

Jeremy Paxman 1950–
British journalist and broadcaster

2 It's like turning news into a sausage
factory.
*on the BBC's proposed changes to radio and
television news broadcasting*
  in *Guardian* 18 September 1997

Norman Vincent Peale 1898–
American religious broadcaster and writer

3 The power of positive thinking.
  title of book (1952)

Patrick Pearse 1879–1916
Irish nationalist leader; executed after the
Easter Rising

4 The fools, the fools, the fools, they have
left us our Fenian dead, and while
Ireland holds these graves Ireland unfree
shall never be at peace.
  oration over the grave of the Fenian Jeremiah
  O'Donovan Rossa, 1 August 1915

5 Here be ghosts that I have raised this
Christmastide, ghosts of dead men that
have bequeathed a trust to us living men.
Ghosts are troublesome things in a house
or in a family, as we knew even before
Ibsen taught us. There is only one way to
appease a ghost. You must do the thing it
asks you. The ghosts of a nation
sometimes ask very big things and they
must be appeased, whatever the cost.
  on Christmas Day, 1915; Conor Cruise O'Brien
  Ancestral Voices (1994); cf. **O'Brien** 233:7

Hesketh Pearson 1887–1964
English actor and biographer

6 Misquotation is, in fact, the pride and
privilege of the learned. A widely-read
man never quotes accurately, for the

rather obvious reason that he has read
too widely.
  Common Misquotations (1934)

7 There is no stronger craving in the world
than that of the rich for titles, except
perhaps that of the titled for riches.
  The Pilgrim Daughters (1961)

Lester Pearson 1897–1972
Canadian diplomat and Liberal statesman,
Prime Minister 1963–8

8 The grim fact is that we prepare for war
like precocious giants and for peace like
retarded pygmies.
  speech in Toronto, 14 March 1955

Pelé 1940–
Brazilian footballer

9 Football? It's the beautiful game.
  attributed

Vladimir Peniakoff 1897–1951
Belgian soldier and writer

10 A message came on the wireless for me.
It said: 'SPREAD ALARM AND
DESPONDENCY' . . . The date was, I think,
May 18th, 1942.
  *'reports calculated to create unnecessary alarm or
  despondency' derives from the Army Act of 1879*
    Private Army (1950)

Roger Penrose 1931–
British mathematician and theoretical
physicist

11 Consciousness . . . is the phenomenon
whereby the universe's very existence is
made known.
  The Emperor's New Mind (1989)

S. J. Perelman 1904–79
American humorist

12 Crazy like a fox.
  title of book (1944)

13 God, whom you doubtless remember as
that quaint old subordinate of General
Douglas MacArthur.
  letter to Mel Elliott, 24 April 1951

Shimon Peres 1923–
Israeli statesman

1 Television has made dictatorship impossible, but democracy unbearable.
   at a Davos meeting, in *Financial Times* 31 January 1995

Anthony Perkins 1932–92
American actor

2 I have learned more about love, selflessness and human understanding in this great adventure in the world of Aids than I ever did in the cut-throat, competitive world in which I spent my life.
   posthumous statement, in *Independent on Sunday* 20 September 1992

Eva Perón 1919–52
wife of Juan **Perón**
on Perón: see **Epitaphs** 105:10, **Madonna** 203:15

3 Keeping books on charity is capitalist nonsense! I just use the money for the poor. I can't stop to count it.
   Fleur Cowles *Bloody Precedent: the Peron Story* (1952)

Juan Perón 1895–1974
Argentine soldier and statesman, President 1946–55 and 1973–4; husband of Eva **Perón**

4 If I had not been born Perón, I would have liked to be Perón.
   in *Observer* 21 February 1960

H. Ross Perot 1930–
American businessman; independent presidential candidate in the 1992 election

5 An activist is the guy who cleans the river, not the guy who concludes it's dirty.
   a favourite saying; Ken Gross *Ross Perot* (1992)

6 I don't have any experience in running up a $4 trillion debt.
   after George **Bush** *had laid stress on the value of experience in presidential candidates*
   in *Newsweek* 19 October 1992

Jimmy Perry
British songwriter

7 Who do you think you are kidding, Mister Hitler?
   theme song of *Dad's Army*, BBC television (1968–77)

Ted Persons

8 Things ain't what they used to be.
   title of song (1941)

Max Perutz 1914–
Austrian-born scientist

9 The priest persuades humble people to endure their hard lot; the politician urges them to rebel against it; and the scientist thinks of a method that does away with the hard lot altogether.
   Is Science Necessary (1989)

Marshal Pétain 1856–1951
French soldier and statesman
see also **Sayings** 278:10

10 To write one's memoirs is to speak ill of everybody except oneself.
   in *Observer* 26 May 1946

Laurence J. Peter 1919–90
Canadian writer

11 In a hierarchy every employee tends to rise to his level of incompetence.
   The Peter Principle (1969)

12 Competence, like truth, beauty and contact lenses, is in the eye of the beholder.
   The Peter Principle (1969)

Mike Peters
American cartoonist

13 When I go into the voting booth, do I vote for the person who is the best President? Or the slime bucket who will make my life as a cartoonist wonderful?
   in *Wall Street Journal* 20 January 1993

Michelle Pfeiffer 1959–
American actress

1 You can have it all, but you can't do it all.

> attributed; in *Guardian* 4 January 1996

Kim Philby 1912–88
British intelligence officer and Soviet spy

2 To betray, you must first belong.

> in *Sunday Times* 17 December 1967

Prince Philip, Duke of Edinburgh 1921–
husband of **Elizabeth II**

3 Gentlemen, I think it is about time we 'pulled our fingers out' . . . If we want to be more prosperous we've simply got to get down to it and work for it. The rest of the world does not owe us a living.

> speech in London, 17 October 1961

4 It is very much better to go out in a bowler and speaking Spanish than in a sombrero and speaking English.

> in *Observer* 15 April 1962

5 I never see any home cooking. All I get is fancy stuff.

> in *Observer* 28 October 1962

6 If you stay here much longer you'll all be slitty-eyed.

> remark to Edinburgh University students in Peking, 16 October 1986

7 I don't think doing it [killing animals] for money makes it any more moral. I don't think a prostitute is more moral than a wife, but they are doing the same thing.

> *comparing participation in blood sports to selling slaughtered meat*
> speech in London, 6 December 1988

8 Tolerance is the one essential ingredient . . . You can take it from me that the Queen has the quality of tolerance in abundance.

> *his recipe for a successful marriage, during celebrations for their golden wedding anniversary*
> in *The Times* 20 November 1997

Arthur Angell Phillips 1900–85
Australian critic and editor

9 Above our writers—and other artists— looms the intimidating mass of Anglo-Saxon culture. Such a situation almost inevitably produces the characteristic Australian Cultural Cringe—appearing either as the Cringe Direct, or as the Cringe Inverted, in the attitude of the Blatant Blatherskite, the God's-Own-Country and I'm-a-better-man-than-you-are Australian bore.

> *Meanjin* (1950) 'The Cultural Cringe'; cf. **Keating** 167:11

Morgan Phillips 1902–63
British Labour politician

10 The Labour Party owes more to Methodism than to Marxism.

> James Callaghan *Time and Chance* (1987)

Eden Phillpotts 1862–1960
English writer

11 A little dreamin', a little dyin',
A little lew corner of airth to lie in.

> 'Gaffer's Song' (1942)

Pablo Picasso 1881–1973
Spanish painter

12 The fact that for a long time Cubism has not been understood and that even today there are people who cannot see anything in it, means nothing. I do not read English, an English book is a blank book to me. This does not mean that the English language does not exist.

> interview with Marius de Zayas, 1923; Herschel B. Chipp *Theories of Modern Art* (1968)

13 There is nothing more dangerous than justice in the hands of judges, and a paintbrush in the hands of a painter. Just think of the danger to society! But today we haven't the heart to expel the painters and poets from society because we refuse to admit to ourselves that there

is any danger in keeping them in our midst.

conversation, 1935; Herschel B. Chipp *Theories of Modern Art* (1968)

1 No, painting is not made to decorate apartments. It's an offensive and defensive weapon against the enemy.

interview with Simone Téry, 24 March 1945, in Alfred H. Barr *Picasso* (1946)

2 When I was the age of these children I could draw like Raphael: it took me many years to learn how to draw like these children.

*to Herbert **Read**, when visiting an exhibition of children's drawings*

quoted in letter from Read to *The Times* 27 October 1956

3 I paint objects as I think them, not as I see them.

John Golding *Cubism* (1959)

4 God is really only another artist. He invented the giraffe, the elephant, and the cat. He has no real style. He just goes on trying other things.

F. Gilot and C. Lake *Life With Picasso* (1964)

5 Every positive value has its price in negative terms . . . The genius of Einstein leads to Hiroshima.

F. Gilot and C. Lake *Life With Picasso* (1964)

6 We all know that Art is not truth. Art is a lie that makes us realize truth.

Dore Ashton *Picasso on Art* (1972) 'Two statements by Picasso'

Ben Pimlott 1945–

English historian and royal biographer

7 If you have a Royal Family you have to make the best of whatever personalities the genetic lottery comes up with.

in *Independent* 13 September 1997 'Quote Unquote'

Harold Pinter 1930–

English dramatist

8 I can't drink Guinness from a thick mug. I only like it out of a thin glass.

The Caretaker (1960)

9 If only I could get down to Sidcup! I've been waiting for the weather to break.

He's got my papers, this man I left them with, it's got it all down there, I could prove everything.

The Caretaker (1960)

10 Apart from the known and the unknown, what else is there?

The Homecoming (1965)

11 The weasel under the cocktail cabinet.

on being asked what his plays were about
J. Russell Taylor *Anger and After* (1962)

Luigi Pirandello 1867–1936

Italian dramatist and novelist

12 Six characters in search of an author.

title of play (1921)

Armand J. Piron

13 I wish I could shimmy like my sister Kate,
She shivers like the jelly on a plate.

'Shimmy like Kate' (1919 song)

Robert M. Pirsig 1928–

American writer

14 Zen and the art of motorcycle maintenance.

title of book (1974)

15 That's the classical mind at work, runs fine inside but looks dingy on the surface.

Zen and the Art of Motorcycle Maintenance (1974)

Walter B. Pitkin 1878–1953

16 Life begins at forty.

title of book (1932)

Pius XII 1876–1958

Italian cleric; Pope from 1939

17 One Galileo in two thousand years is enough.

*on being asked to proscribe the works of **Teilhard de Chardin***

attributed; Stafford Beer *Platform for Change* (1975)

Max Planck 1858–1947

German physicist

1 A new scientific truth does not triumph
by convincing its opponents and making
them see the light, but rather because its
opponents eventually die, and a new
generation grows up that is familiar with
it.
A Scientific Autobiography (1949)

Sylvia Plath 1932–63

American poet

2 Is there no way out of the mind?
'Apprehensions' (1971)

3 Every woman adores a Fascist,
The boot in the face, the brute
Brute heart of a brute like you.
'Daddy' (1963)

4 Dying,
Is an art, like everything else.
'Lady Lazarus' (1963)

5 Love set you going like a fat gold watch.
'Morning Song' (1965)

6 Widow. The word consumes itself.
'Widow' (1971)

William Plomer 1903–73

British poet

7 Out of that bungled, unwise war
An alp of unforgiveness grew.
'The Boer War' (1960)

8 A family portrait not too stale to record
Of a pleasant old buffer, nephew to a
lord,
Who believed that the bank was mightier
than the sword,
And that an umbrella might pacify
barbarians abroad:
Just like an old liberal
Between the wars.
'Father and Son: 1939' (1945)

9 With first-rate sherry flowing into
second-rate whores,
And third-rate conversation without one
single pause:
Just like a young couple
Between the wars.
'Father and Son: 1939' (1945)

10 On a sofa upholstered in panther skin
Mona did researches in original sin.
'Mews Flat Mona' (1960)

■ Political slogans

see box opposite

Harry Pollitt 1890–1960

British Communist politician

*on being asked by Stephen **Spender** in the 1930s
how best a poet could serve the Communist
cause:*

11 Go to Spain and get killed. The
movement needs a Byron.
attributed, perhaps apocryphal

Jackson Pollock 1912–56

American painter

12 There was a reviewer a while back who
wrote that my pictures didn't have any
beginning or any end. He didn't mean it
as a compliment, but it was. It was a fine
compliment.
Francis V. O'Connor *Jackson Pollock* (1967)

Georges Pompidou 1911–74

French statesman; President of France from
1969

13 A statesman is a politician who places
himself at the service of the nation. A
politician is a statesman who places the
nation at his service.
in *Observer* 30 December 1973 'Sayings of the
Year'

Karl Popper 1902–94

Austrian-born British philosopher

14 I shall certainly admit a system as
empirical or scientific only if it is capable
of being *tested* by experience. These
considerations suggest that not the
verifiability but the *falsifiability* of a system
is to be taken as a criterion of
demarcation . . . *It must be possible for an
empirical scientific system to be refuted by
experience.*
The Logic of Scientific Discovery (1934)

▶▶

Political slogans

1 All power to the Soviets.
workers in Petrograd, 1917

2 All the way with LBJ.
US Democratic Party campaign slogan, 1960

3 Ban the bomb.
US anti-nuclear slogan, adopted by the
Campaign for Nuclear Disarmament, 1953
onwards

4 A bayonet is a weapon with a worker
at each end.
British pacifist slogan, 1940

5 Better red than dead.
slogan of nuclear disarmament campaigners,
late 1950s

6 Black is beautiful.
slogan of American civil rights campaigners,
mid-1960s

7 Can't pay, won't pay.
anti-Poll Tax slogan, c.1990; cf. **Fo** 114:9

8 Burn, baby, burn.
black extremist slogan, Los Angeles riots,
August 1965

9 *Ein Reich, ein Volk, ein Führer.*
One realm, one people, one leader.
Nazi Party slogan, early 1930s

10 Fair shares for all, is Labour's call.
slogan for the North Battersea by-election,
1946, coined by Douglas Jay
Douglas Jay *Change and Fortune* (1980)

11 Hey, hey, LBJ, how many kids did you
kill today?
anti-Vietnam marching slogan, 1960s

12 I like Ike.
*used when General **Eisenhower** was first seen*
as a potential presidential nominee
US button badge, 1947; coined by Henry D.
Spalding (d. 1990)

13 It'll play in Peoria.
catch-phrase of the **Nixon** administration
(early 1970s) meaning 'it will be acceptable
to middle America', but originating in a
standard music hall joke of the 1930s

14 It's morning again in America.
Ronald **Reagan**'s 1984 election campaign
slogan; coined by Hal Riney (1932–)

15 It's the economy, stupid.
on a sign put up at the 1992 **Clinton**
presidential campaign headquarters by
campaign manager James Carville

16 *Kraft durch Freude.*
Strength through joy.
German Labour Front slogan, from 1933;
coined by Robert Ley (1890–1945)

17 Labour isn't working.
on poster showing a long queue outside an
unemployment office
Conservative Party slogan 1978–9

18 Labour's double whammy.
Conservative Party election slogan 1992

19 Life's better with the Conservatives.
Don't let Labour ruin it.
Conservative Party election slogan, 1959

20 New Labour, new danger.
Conservative slogan, 1996

21 Power to the people.
slogan of the Black Panther movement, from
c.1968; cf. **Newton** 230:1

22 Thirteen years of Tory misrule.
unofficial Labour party election slogan, also
in the form 'Thirteen wasted years', 1964

23 Votes for women.
adopted when it proved impossible to use a
banner with the longer slogan 'Will the Liberal
Party Give Votes for Women?' made by
*Emmeline **Pankhurst** (1858–1928), Christabel*
***Pankhurst** (1880–1958),and Annie Kenney*
(1879–1953)
slogan of the women's suffrage movement,
from 13 October 1905; Emmeline Pankhurst
My Own Story (1914)

24 War will cease when men refuse to
fight.
pacifist slogan, often quoted 'Wars will
cease . . . ', from c.1936

▶

> ▶ **Political slogans** continued

1 Would you buy a used car from this man?

campaign slogan directed against Richard **Nixon**, 1968

2 Yes it hurt, yes it worked.

Conservative Party slogan, 1996; cf. **Major** 204:14

3 Yesterday's men (they failed before!).

Labour Party slogan, referring to the Conservatives, 1970; coined by David Kingsley, Dennis Lyons, and Peter Lovell-Davis

---

▶▶ **Karl Popper** continued

4 We may become the makers of our fate when we have ceased to pose as its prophets.

The Open Society and its Enemies (1945)

5 We should therefore claim, in the name of tolerance, the right not to tolerate the intolerant.

The Open Society and Its Enemies (1945)

6 There is no history of mankind, there are only many histories of all kinds of aspects of human life. And one of these is the history of political power. This is elevated into the history of the world.

The Open Society and its Enemies (1945)

7 Science must begin with myths, and with the criticism of myths.

'The Philosophy of Science' in C. A. Mace (ed.) *British Philosophy in the Mid-Century* (1957)

8 For this, indeed, is the true source of our ignorance—the fact that our knowledge can only be finite, while our ignorance must necessarily be infinite.

lecture to British Academy, 20 January 1960

Cole Porter 1891–1964

American songwriter

9 But I'm always true to you, darlin', in my fashion.
Yes I'm always true to you, darlin', in my way.

'Always True to You in my Fashion' (1949 song)

10 In olden days a glimpse of stocking
Was looked on as something shocking

Now, heaven knows,
Anything goes.

'Anything Goes' song (1934)

11 When they begin the Beguine
It brings back the sound of music so tender,
It brings back a night of tropical splendour,
It brings back a memory ever green.

'Begin the Beguine' (1935 song)

12 Oh, give me land, lots of land
Under starry skies above
DON'T FENCE ME IN.

'Don't Fence Me In' (1934 song)

13 There's no love song finer,
But how strange the change from major to minor
Every time we say goodbye.

'Every Time We Say Goodbye' (1944 song)

14 I get no kick from champagne,
Mere alcohol doesn't thrill me at all.

'I Get a Kick Out of You' song (1934)

15 I've got you under my skin.

title of song (1936)

16 Night and day, you are the one,
Only you beneath the moon and under the sun.

'Night and Day' (1932 song)

17 So goodbye dear, and Amen,
Here's hoping we meet now and then,
It was great fun,
But it was just one of those things.

'Just One of Those Things' (1935 song)

18 Birds do it, bees do it,
Even educated fleas do it.

Let's do it, let's fall in love.

'Let's Do It' (1954 song; words added to the 1928 original)

1 Miss Otis regrets (she's unable to lunch today).

title of song (1934)

2 My heart belongs to Daddy.

title of song (1938)

3 SHE: Have you heard it's in the stars,
Next July we collide with Mars?
HE: WELL, DID YOU EVAH! What a swell
party this is.

'Well, Did You Evah?' (1956 song)

4 Who wants to be a millionaire?

title of song (1956)

Dennis Potter 1935–94

English television dramatist

5 Below my window . . . the blossom is out
in full now . . . I *see* it is the whitest,
frothiest, blossomiest blossom that there
ever could be, and I can see it. Things are
both more trivial than they ever were,
and more important than they ever were,
and the difference between the trivial and
the important doesn't seem to matter.
But the nowness of everything is
absolutely wondrous.

*on his heightened awareness of things, in the
face of his imminent death*

interview with Melvyn Bragg on Channel 4,
March 1994, in *Seeing the Blossom* (1994)

6 Religion to me has always been the
wound, not the bandage.

interview with Melvyn Bragg on Channel 4,
March 1994, in *Seeing the Blossom* (1994)

7 But the cigarette, well, I love stroking
this lovely tube of delight.

interview with Melvyn Bragg on Channel 4,
March 1994, in *Seeing the Blossom* (1994)

Stephen Potter 1900–69

British writer

8 A good general rule is to state that the
bouquet is better than the taste, and vice
versa.

on wine-tasting

One-Upmanship (1952)

9 *How to be one up*—how to make the other
man feel that something has gone
wrong, however slightly.

Lifemanship (1950)

10 'Yes, but not in the South', with slight
adjustments, will do for any argument
about any place, if not about any person.

Lifemanship (1950)

11 The theory and practice of
gamesmanship or The art of winning
games without actually cheating.

title of book (1947)

Ezra Pound 1885–1972

American poet
on Pound: see **Stein** 296:7

12 Winter is icummen in,
Lhude sing Goddamm,
Raineth drop and staineth slop,
And how the wind doth ramm!
Sing: Goddamm.

'Ancient Music' (1917); see below

Sumer is icumen in,
Lhude sing cuccu!
Groweth sed, and bloweth med,
And springeth the wude nu.

Anonymous 'Cuckoo Song' (*c*.1250)

13 With usura hath no man a house of good
stone
each block cut smooth and well fitting.

Cantos (1954) no. 45

14 Tching prayed on the mountain and
wrote MAKE IT NEW
on his bath tub.

Cantos (1954) no. 53

15 Bah! I have sung women in three cities,
But it is all the same;
And I will sing of the sun.

'Cino' (1908)

16 And even I can remember
A day when the historians left blanks in
their writings,
I mean for things they didn't know.

Draft of XXX Cantos (1930) no. 13

17 Christ follows Dionysus,
Phallic and ambrosial
Made way for macerations;
Caliban casts out Ariel.

Hugh Selwyn Mauberley (1920) 'E. P. *Ode* . . . '
pt. 3

1 Died some, pro patria,
non 'dulce' non 'et decor' . . .
walked eye-deep in hell
believing in old men's lies, the
   unbelieving
came home, home to a lie.
   Hugh Selwyn Mauberley (1920) 'E. P. *Ode* . . . '
   pt. 4; see below

   Dulce et decorum est pro patria mori.
   Lovely and honourable it is to die for
   one's country.
   Horace (65–8 BC) *Odes*; cf. **Owen** 240:17

2 There died a myriad,
And of the best, among them,
For an old bitch gone in the teeth,
For a botched civilization.
   Hugh Selwyn Mauberley (1920) 'E. P. *Ode* . . . '
   pt. 5

3 The tip's a good one, as for literature
It gives no man a sinecure.

   And no one knows, at sight, a
      masterpiece.
   And give up verse, my boy,
   There's nothing in it.
   Hugh Selwyn Mauberley (1920) 'Mr Nixon'

4 The apparition of these faces in the
   crowd;
Petals on a wet, black bough.
   'In a Station of the Metro' (1916)

5 The ant's a centaur in his dragon world.
   Pisan Cantos (1948) no. 81

6 Pull down thy vanity
Thou art a beaten dog beneath the hail,
A swollen magpie in a fitful sun,
Half black half white
Nor knowst'ou wing from tail.
   Pisan Cantos (1948) no. 81

7 I had over-prepared the event,
that much was ominous.
With middle-ageing care
I had laid out just the right books.
I had almost turned down the pages.
   'Villanelle: the psychological hour' (1916)

8 Music begins to atrophy when it departs
too far from the dance . . . poetry begins
to atrophy when it gets too far from
music.
   The ABC of Reading (1934) 'Warning'

9 Any general statement is like a cheque
drawn on a bank. Its value depends on
what is there to meet it.
   The ABC of Reading (1934)

10 One of the pleasures of middle age is to
find out that one WAS right, and that one
was much righter than one knew at say
17 or 23.
   ABC of Reading (1934)

11 Literature is news that STAYS news.
   The ABC of Reading (1934)

12 Real education must ultimately be limited
to one who INSISTS on knowing, the rest
is mere sheep-herding.
   The ABC of Reading (1934)

13 Great literature is simply language
charged with meaning to the utmost
possible degree.
   How To Read (1931)

14 Artists are the antennae of the race, but
the bullet-headed many will never learn
to trust their great artists.
   Literary Essays (1954) 'Henry James'

15 Poetry must be *as well written as prose*.
   letter to Harriet Monroe, January 1915

Anthony Powell 1905–
English novelist

16 He fell in love with himself at first sight
and it is a passion to which he has
always remained faithful.
   The Acceptance World (1955)

17 Dinner at the Huntercombes' possessed
'only two dramatic features—the wine
was a farce and the food a tragedy'.
   The Acceptance World (1955)

18 Books do furnish a room.
   title of novel (1971)

19 Parents—especially step-parents—are
sometimes a bit of a disappointment to
their children. They don't fufil the
promise of their early years.
   A Buyer's Market (1952)

20 A dance to the music of time.
   title of novel sequence (1951–75), after *Le 4
   stagioni che ballano al suono del tempo* (title
   given by Giovanni Pietro Bellori to a painting
   by Nicolas Poussin)

1 He's so wet you could shoot snipe off
him.
   A Question of Upbringing (1951)

2 Growing old is like being increasingly
penalized for a crime you haven't
committed.
   Temporary Kings (1973)

Colin Powell 1937–

American general

3 First, we are going to cut it off, and then,
we are going to kill it.
   *strategy for dealing with the Iraqi Army in the Gulf
War*
      at a press conference, 23 January 1991

4 My philosophy in all this is rather simple:
match political expectations to military
means in a wholly realistic way. Don't
slide in, don't mislead yourself.
   *speech at the National Press Club luncheon, 28
September 1993*
      in *The National Interest* Spring 1994

Dilys Powell 1902–95

English critic and writer

5 You come out of *Gone With the Wind*
feeling that history isn't so disturbing
after all. One can always make a dress
out of a curtain.
   in *Independent on Sunday* 29 April 1990

Enoch Powell 1912–98

British Conservative politician

6 History is littered with the wars which
everybody knew would never happen.
   speech to Conservative Party Conference, 19
October 1967

7 Those whom the gods wish to destroy,
they first make mad. We must be mad,
literally mad, as a nation to be permitting
the annual inflow of some 50,000
dependents, who are for the most part
the material of the future growth of the
immigrant descended population. It is
like watching a nation busily engaged in
heaping up its own funeral pyre.
   speech at Annual Meeting of West Midlands
Area Conservative Political Centre,
Birmingham, 20 April 1968

8 As I look ahead, I am filled with
foreboding. Like the Roman, I seem to see
'the River Tiber foaming with much
blood'.
   speech at Birmingham, 20 April 1968; see
below
   I see wars, horrible wars, and the Tiber
   foaming with much blood.
   Virgil (70–19 BC) *Aeneid*

9 Judas was paid! I am sacrificing my
whole political life.
   *response to a heckler's call of 'Judas', having
advised Conservatives to vote Labour at the
coming general election*
      speech at Bull Ring, Birmingham, 23 February
1974

10 Office before honour was the password of
Conservative government.
   of the 1970–4 Conservative administration
      in *Spectator* 15 October 1977

11 To write a diary every day is like
returning to one's own vomit.
   interview in *Sunday Times* 6 November 1977

12 For a politician to complain about the
press is like a ship's captain complaining
about the sea.
   in *Guardian* 3 December 1984

13 ANNE BROWN: How would you like to be
remembered?
ENOCH POWELL: I should like to have been
killed in the war.
   in a radio interview, 13 April 1986

14 To be and to remain a member of the
House of Commons was the overriding
and undiscussable motivation of my life
as a politician.
   'Theory and Practice' 1990

15 What is history except a nation's
collective memory?
   on BBC Radio 4 10 February 1991

16 All political lives, unless they are cut off
in midstream at a happy juncture, end in
failure, because that is the nature of
politics and of human affairs.
   Joseph Chamberlain (1977)

Vince Powell and Harry Driver

17 Never mind the quality, feel the width.
   title of ITV comedy series, 1967–9

Terry Pratchett 1948–

English science fiction writer

1 Most modern fantasy just rearranges the furniture in Tolkien's attic.

> Stan Nicholls (ed.) *Wordsmiths of Wonder* (1993)

John Prescott 1938–

British Labour politician

2 People like me were branded, pigeon-holed, a ceiling put on our ambitions.

on failing his 11-plus

> speech at Ruskin College, Oxford, 13 June 1996; in *Guardian* 14 June 1996

3 We did it! Let's wallow in our victory!

*on Tony **Blair**'s warning that the Labour Party should not be triumphalist in victory*

> speech to the Labour Party Conference, 29 September 1997

Keith Preston 1884–1927

American poet

4 Of all the literary scenes
Saddest this sight to me:
The graves of little magazines
Who died to make verse free.

> 'The Liberators'

Jacques Prévert 1900–77

French poet and screenwriter

5 *C'est tellement simple, l'amour.*
It's so simple, love.

> *Les Enfants du Paradis* (1945 film)

Anthony Price 1928–

English thriller writer and editor

6 The Devil himself had probably redesigned Hell in the light of information he had gained from observing airport layouts.

> *The Memory Trap* (1989)

Gerald Priestland 1927–91

English writer and journalist

7 Journalists belong in the gutter because that is where the ruling classes throw their guilty secrets.

> on Radio London 19 May 1988; in *Observer* 22 May 1988

J. B. Priestley 1894–1984

English novelist, dramatist, and critic

8 I never read the life of any important person without discovering that he knew more and could do more than I could ever hope to know or to do in half a dozen lifetimes.

> *Apes and Angels* (1928)

9 The first fall of snow is not only an event, but it is a magical event. You go to bed in one kind of world and wake up to find yourself in another quite different, and if this is not enchantment, then where is it to be found?

> *Apes and Angels* (1928) 'First Snow'

10 To say that these men paid their shillings to watch twenty-two hirelings kick a ball is merely to say that a violin is wood and catgut, that *Hamlet* is so much paper and ink. For a shilling the Bruddersford United AFC offered you Conflict and Art.

> *Good Companions* (1929)

11 First you take their faces from 'em by calling 'em the masses and then you accuse 'em of not having any faces.

> *Saturn Over the Water* (1961)

12 Our great-grand-children, when they learn how we began this war by snatching glory out of defeat, and then swept on to victory, may also learn how the little holiday steamers made an excursion to hell and came back glorious.

on the evacuation of Dunkirk

> radio broadcast, 5 June 1940

13 It is hard to tell where the MCC ends and the Church of England begins.

> in *New Statesman* 20 July 1962

14 God can stand being told by Professor Ayer and Marghanita Laski that He doesn't exist.

> in *Listener* 1 July 1965

1 The weakness of American civilization,
and perhaps the chief reason why it
creates so much discontent, is that it is so
curiously abstract. It is a bloodless
extrapolation of a satisfying life . . . You
dine off the advertiser's 'sizzling' and not
the meat of the steak.
  in *New Statesman* 10 December 1971

V. S. Pritchett 1900–97

English writer and critic

2 The principle of procrastinated rape is
said to be the ruling one in all the great
best-sellers.
  The Living Novel (1946) 'Clarissa'

3 What Chekhov saw in our failure to
communicate was something positive
and precious: the private silence in
which we live, and which enables us to
endure our own solitude. We live, as his
characters do, beyond any tale we
happen to enact.
  Myth Makers (1979) 'Chekhov, a doctor'

4 The detective novel is the art-for-art's-
sake of our yawning Philistinism, the
classic example of a specialized form of
art removed from contact with the life it
pretends to build on.
  in *New Statesman* 16 June 1951 'Books in
  General'

Marcel Proust 1871–1922

French novelist

5 *A la recherche du temps perdu.*
  In search of lost time.
  translated by C. K. Scott-Moncrieff and S. Hudson,
  1922–31, as Remembrance of things past
    title of novel (1913–27); see below

      When to the sessions of sweet silent
        thought
      I summon up remembrance of things
        past.
    William Shakespeare (1564–1616) sonnet 30

6 I have a horror of sunsets, they're so
romantic, so operatic.
  Cities of the Plain (1922)

7 Everything we think of as great has come
to us from neurotics. It is they and they
alone who found religions and create

great works of art. The world will never
realise how much it owes to them and
what they have suffered in order to
bestow their gifts on it.
  Guermantes Way (1921)

8 An artist has no need to express his
thought directly in his work for the latter
to reflect its quality; it has even been said
that the highest praise of God consists in
the denial of Him by the atheist who
finds creation so perfect that it can
dispense with a creator.
  Guermantes Way (1921)

9 And suddenly the memory revealed itself.
The taste was that of the little piece of
madeleine which . . . my aunt Léonie
used to give me, dipping it first in her
own cup of tea or tisane.
  Swann's Way (1913)

10 The true paradises are the paradises that
we have lost.
  Time Regained (1926)

11 For if unhappiness develops the forces of
the mind, happiness alone is salutary to
the body.
  Time Regained (1926)

12 One becomes moral as soon as one is
unhappy.
  Within a Budding Grove (1918)

John Pudney 1909–77

English poet and writer

13 Do not despair
  For Johnny-head-in-air;
  He sleeps as sound
  As Johnny underground.
    'For Johnny' (1942)

14 And keep your tears
  For him in after years.

  Better by far
  For Johnny-the-bright-star,
  To keep your head,
  And see his children fed.
    'For Johnny' (1942)

Sarah-Louise Puntan-Galeo

British student representative

1 There are now two classes of student—
those who have enough money not to
bother about the issues and those who
are so skint they have to work in Tesco
every afternoon, so haven't the time.
on student protest
   in Daily Telegraph 21 January 1997

Al Purdy 1918–

Canadian poet and writer

2 Look here
You've never seen this country
it's not the way you thought it was
Look again.
of Canada
   'The Country of the Young' (1976)

Mario Puzo 1920–

American novelist

3 I'll make him an offer he can't refuse.
   The Godfather (1969)

4 A lawyer with his briefcase can steal
more than a hundred men with guns.
   The Godfather (1969)

Barbara Pym 1913–80

English novelist

5 She experienced all the cosiness and
irritation which can come from living
with thoroughly nice people with whom
one has nothing in common.
   Less than Angels (1955)

Mary Quant 1934–

English fashion designer

6 It was she who established the fact that
this latter half of the twentieth century
belongs to Youth.
of her invention, the Chelsea Girl
   Quant by Quant (1966)

7 Having money is rather like being a
blonde. It is more fun but not vital.
   in Observer 2 November 1986

8 Being young is greatly overestimated . . .
Any failure seems so total. Later on you
realize you can have another go.
   interview in Observer 5 May 1996

Dan Quayle 1947–

American Republican politician
on Quayle: see **Bentsen** 32:7

9 Space is almost infinite. As a matter of
fact, we think it is infinite.
   in Daily Telegraph 8 March 1989

10 What a waste it is to lose one's mind, or
not to have a mind. How true that is.
   speech to the United Negro College Fund,
   whose slogan is 'a mind is a terrible thing to
   waste'; *in The Times* 26 May 1989

Peter Quennell 1905–93

English writer

11 An elderly fallen angel travelling
incognito.
of André **Gide**
   The Sign of the Fish (1960)

Arthur Quiller-Couch

1863–1944

English writer and academic

12 All the old statues of Victory have wings:
but Grief has no wings. She is the
unwelcome lodger that squats on the
hearthstone between us and the fire and
will not move or be dislodged.
   Armistice Day anniversary sermon, Cambridge,
   November 1923

W. V. O. Quine 1908–

American philosopher

13 On the doctrinal side, I do not see that we
are farther along today than where
[David] Hume left us. The Humean
predicament is the human predicament.
   Ontological Relativity and Other Essays (1969)

14 It is the tension between the scientist's
laws and his own attempted breaches of
them that powers the engines of science
and makes it forge ahead.
   Quiddities (1987)

1 Students of the heavens are separable into astronomers and astrologers as readily as are the minor domestic ruminants into sheep and goats, but the separation of philosophers into sages and cranks seems to be more sensitive to frames of reference.
   Theories and Things (1981)

2 Different persons growing up in the same language are like different bushes trimmed and trained to take the shape of identical elephants. The anatomical details of twigs and branches will fulfill the elephantine shape differently from bush to bush, but the overall outward results are alike.
   Word and Object (1960)

Yitzhak Rabin 1922–95

Israeli statesman and military leader, Prime Minister 1974–7 and 1992–5

3 We say to you today in a loud and a clear voice: enough of blood and tears. Enough.
   to the Palestinians, at the signing of the Israel–Palestine Declaration
   in Washington, 13 September, 1993

Lord Radcliffe 1899–1977

British lawyer and public servant

4 Society has become used to the standing armies of power—the permanent Civil Service, the police force, the tax-gatherer—organized on a scale which was unknown to earlier centuries.
   Power and the State (BBC Reith Lectures, 1951)

5 Governments always tend to want not really a free press but a managed or well-conducted one.
   in 1967; Peter Hennessy *What the Papers Never Said* (1985)

James Rado 1939– and Gerome Ragni 1942–

American songwriters

6 When the moon is in the seventh house, And Jupiter aligns with Mars, Then peace will guide the planets, And love will steer the stars; This is the dawning of the age of Aquarius.
   'Aquarius' (1967 song)

John Rae 1931–

English writer

7 War is, after all, the universal perversion. We are all tainted: if we cannot experience our perversion at first hand we spend our time reading war stories, the pornography of war; or seeing war films, the blue films of war; or titillating our senses with the imagination of great deeds, the masturbation of war.
   The Custard Boys (1960)

Craig Raine 1944–

English poet

8 In homes, a haunted apparatus sleeps, that snores when you pick it up.

   If the ghost cries, they carry it to their lips and soothe it to sleep

   with sounds. And yet, they wake it up deliberately, but tickling it with a finger.
   'A Martian sends a Postcard Home' (1979)

Claude Rains

see **Film lines** 111:3

Walter Raleigh 1861–1922

English lecturer and critic

9 In examinations those who do not wish to know ask questions of those who cannot tell.
   Laughter from a Cloud (1923) 'Some Thoughts on Examinations'

10 I wish I loved the Human Race;
   I wish I loved its silly face;
   I wish I liked the way it walks;
   I wish I liked the way it talks;
   And when I'm introduced to one
   I wish I thought *What Jolly Fun!*
   'Wishes of an Elderly Man' (1923)

11 An anthology is like all the plums and orange peel picked out of a cake.
   letter to Mrs Robert Bridges, 15 January 1915

Srinivasa Ramanujan
1887–1920

Indian mathematician

replying to G. H. Hardy's suggestion that the number of a taxi-cab (1729) was 'dull':

1 No, it is a very interesting number; it is the smallest number expressible as a sum of two cubes in two different ways.
  the two ways being 1^3+12^3 and 9^3+10^3

  in *Proceedings of the London Mathematical Society* 26 May 1921

John Crowe Ransom
1888–1974

American poet and critic

2 Two evils, monstrous either one apart,
Possessed me, and were long and loath at going:
A cry of Absence, Absence, in the heart,
And in the wood the furious winter blowing.
  'Winter Remembered' (1945)

Arthur Ransome

see **Telegrams** 305:2

Frederic Raphael 1931–

British novelist and screenwriter

3 Your idea of fidelity is not having more than one man in bed at the same time.
  Darling (1965)

4 'So this is the city of dreaming spires,' Sheila said. 'Theoretically speaking that's Oxford,' Adam said. 'This is the city of perspiring dreams.'
  of Cambridge
  The Glittering Prizes (1976); see below

  And that sweet City with her dreaming spires.
  Matthew Arnold (1822–88) 'Thyrsis' (1866)

5 I come from suburbia . . . and I don't ever want to go back. It's the one place in the world that's further away than anywhere else.
  The Glittering Prizes (1976) 'A Sex Life'

Gerald Ratner 1949–

English businessman

6 We even sell a pair of earrings for under £1, which is cheaper than a prawn sandwich from Marks & Spencers. But I have to say the earrings probably won't last as long.
  speech to the Institute of Directors, Albert Hall, 23 April 1991

Terence Rattigan 1911–77

English dramatist

7 Let us invent a character, a nice respectable, middle-class, middle-aged, maiden lady, with time on her hands and the money to help her pass it. She enjoys pictures, books, music, and the theatre and though to none of these arts (or rather, for consistency's sake, to none of these three arts and the one craft) does she bring much knowledge or discernment, at least, as she is apt to tell her cronies, she 'does know what she likes'. Let us call her Aunt Edna . . . Aunt Edna is universal, and to those who may feel that all the problems of the modern theatre might be solved by her liquidation, let me add that I have no doubt at all that she is also immortal.
  Collected Plays (1953) vol. 2, preface

8 French without tears
  title of play (1937)

9 Do you know what 'le vice Anglais'—the English vice—really is? Not flagellation, not pederasty—whatever the French believe it to be. It's our refusal to admit our emotions. We think they demean us, I suppose.
  In Praise of Love (1973)

10 You can be in the Horseguards and still be common, dear.
  Separate Tables (1954) 'Table Number Seven'

Irina Ratushinskaya 1954–

Russian poet

11 Russian literature saved my soul. When I was a young girl in school and I asked

what is good and what is evil, no one in that corrupt system could show me.

> in *Observer* 15 October 1989 'Sayings of the Week'

Gwen Raverat 1885–1957

English wood-engraver

1 Ladies were ladies in those days; they did not do things themselves.
> *Period Piece* (1952)

Derek Raymond 1931–94

English thriller writer

2 The psychopath is the furnace that gives no heat.
> *The Hidden Files* (1992)

Claire Rayner 1931–

English journalist

3 I always say I don't think everyone has the right to happiness or to be loved. Even the Americans have written into their constitution that you have the right to the 'pursuit of happiness'. You have the right to try but that is all.
> G. Kinnock and F. Miller (eds.) *By Faith and Daring* (1993)

Herbert Read 1893–1968

English art historian

4 Do not judge this movement kindly. It is not just another amusing stunt. It is defiant—the desperate act of men too profoundly convinced of the rottenness of our civilization to want to save a shred of its respectability.
> International Surrealist Exhibition Catalogue, New Burlington Galleries, London, 11 June–4 July 1936, introduction

5 Art is . . . pattern informed by sensibility.
> *The Meaning of Art* (1955)

6 Lorca was killed, singing,
and Fox who was my friend.
The rhythm returns: the song
which has no end.
> 'The Heart Conscripted' (1938)

7 I saw him stab
And stab again

A well-killed Boche.
This is the happy warrior,
This is he . . .
> *Naked Warriors* (1919) 'The Scene of War, 4. The Happy Warrior'

Piers Paul Read 1941–

English novelist

8 Sins become more subtle as you grow older. You commit sins of despair rather than lust.
> in *Daily Telegraph* 3 October 1990

Peter Reading 1946–

English critic

9 If you want art to be like ovaltine, then clearly some art is not for you.
> in *Critics' Forum*, Radio 3, 22 November 1986; attributed

Nancy Reagan 1923–

American actress and wife of Ronald **Reagan,** First Lady of the US, 1981–9

10 A woman is like a teabag—only in hot water do you realize how strong she is.
> in *Observer* 29 March 1981

11 If the President has a bully pulpit, then the First Lady has a white glove pulpit . . . more refined, restricted, ceremonial, but it's a pulpit all the same.
> in *New York Times* 10 March 1988; cf. **Roosevelt** 268:8

Ronald Reagan 1911–

American Republican statesman; 40th President of the US, 1981–9; husband of Nancy **Reagan**
on Reagan: see **Keillor** 168:5, **Schroeder** 280:12, **Vidal** 317:12, **Warner** 319:10; see also **Dempsey** 88:1, **Gipp** 128:9, **Magee** 204:1, 204:2

12 Politics is supposed to be the second oldest profession. I have come to realize that it bears a very close resemblance to the first.
> at a conference in Los Angeles, 2 March 1977; Bill Adler *Reagan Wit* (1981)

1 You can tell a lot about a fellow's character by his way of eating jellybeans.

   in *New York Times* 15 January 1981

2 My fellow Americans, I am pleased to tell you I just signed legislation which outlaws Russia forever. The bombing begins in five minutes.

   said during radio microphone test, 11 August 1984

3 We are especially not going to tolerate these attacks from outlaw states run by the strangest collection of misfits, Looney Tunes, and squalid criminals since the advent of the Third Reich.

   following the hijack of a US plane

   speech, 8 July 1985

4 We will never forget them, nor the last time we saw them this morning, as they prepared for the journey and waved goodbye and 'slipped the surly bonds of earth' to 'touch the face of God.'

   after the loss of the space shuttle Challenger *with all its crew*

   broadcast from the Oval Office, 28 January 1986; cf. **Magee** 204:1, 204:2

5 This mad dog of the Middle East.

   of Colonel Gadaffi of Libya

   speech at press conference, 9 April 1986

6 To grasp and hold a vision, that is the very essence of successful leadership— not only on the movie set where I learned it, but everywhere.

   in *The Wilson Quarterly* Winter 1994; attributed

7 I now begin the journey that will lead me into the sunset of my life.

   statement to the American people revealing that he had Alzheimer's disease

   in *Daily Telegraph* 5 January 1995

John Redmond 1856–1918

Irish politician and nationalist leader

in the spring of 1914 Redmond was asked by a friend, a priest from Tipperary, if anything could now rob them of Home Rule:

8 A European war might do it.

   in *Dictionary of National Biography* (1917–)

Henry Reed 1914–86

English poet and dramatist

9 Today we have naming of parts. Yesterday,
   We had daily cleaning. And tomorrow morning,
   We shall have what to do after firing. But today,
   Today we have naming of parts.

   'Lessons of the War: 1, Naming of Parts' (1946)

10 They call it easing the Spring: it is perfectly easy
   If you have any strength in your thumb: like the bolt,
   And the breech, and the cocking-piece, and the point of balance,
   Which in our case we have not got.

   'Lessons of the War: 1, Naming of Parts' (1946)

11 And the sooner the tea's out of the way, the sooner we can get out the gin, eh?

   Private Life of Hilda Tablet (1954 radio play)

12 Modest? My word, no . . . He was an all-the-lights-on man.

   A Very Great Man Indeed (1953 radio play)

13 I have known her pass the whole evening without mentioning a single book, or *in fact anything unpleasant*, at all.

   A Very Great Man Indeed (1953 radio play)

John Reed 1887–1920

American journalist and revolutionary

14 Ten days that shook the world.

   title of book (1919)

Keith Reid 1946–

English pop singer and songwriter

15 Her face, at first . . . just ghostly
   Turned a whiter shade of pale.

   'A Whiter Shade of Pale' (1967 song)

Lord Reith 1889–1971

British administrator and politician, first general manager (1922–7) and first director-general (1927–8) of the BBC

16 By the time the civil service has finished drafting a document to give effect to a

principle, there may be little of the principle left.
Into the Wind (1949)

1 When people feel deeply, impartiality is bias.
Into the Wind (1949)

Erich Maria Remarque
1898–1970
German novelist

2 All quiet on the western front.
English title of *Im Westen nichts Neues* (1929 novel)

Montague John Rendall
1862–1950
Member of the first BBC Board of Governors

3 Nation shall speak peace unto nation.
motto of the BBC (1927); see below

Nation shall not lift up sword against nation.
Bible Isaiah

Jean Renoir 1894–1979
French film director

4 Is it possible to succeed without any act of betrayal?
My Life and My Films (1974) 'Nana'

5 Don't think that this is a letter. It is only a small eruption of a disease called friendship.
letter to Janine Bazin, 12 June 1974

Pierre Auguste Renoir
see **Misquotations** 218:7

David Reuben 1933–
American psychiatrist

6 Everything you always wanted to know about sex, but were afraid to ask.
title of book (1969)

Walter Reuther 1907–70
American labour leader

7 If it looks like a duck, walks like a duck and quacks like a duck, then it just may be a duck.
as a test, during the **McCarthy** era, of Communist affiliations
attributed

Malvina Reynolds 1900–78
American songwriter

8 Little boxes on the hillside,
Little boxes made of ticky-tacky,
Little boxes on the hillside,
Little boxes all the same.
on the tract houses in the hills to the south of San Francisco
'Little Boxes' (1962 song)

Jean Rhys c.1890–1979
British novelist and short-story writer

9 We can't all be happy, we can't all be rich, we can't all be lucky—and it would be so much less fun if we were . . . Some must cry so that others may be able to laugh the more heartily.
Good Morning, Midnight (1939)

10 The perpetual hunger to be beautiful and that thirst to be loved which is the real curse of Eve.
The Left Bank (1927) 'Illusion'

11 The feeling of Sunday is the same everywhere, heavy, melancholy, standing still. Like when they say 'As it was in the beginning, is now, and ever shall be, world without end.'
Voyage in the Dark (1934)

12 A doormat in a world of boots.
describing herself
in *Guardian* 6 December 1990

Grantland Rice 1880–1954
American sports writer

13 For when the One Great Scorer comes to mark against your name,
He writes—not that you won or lost—but how you played the Game.
'Alumnus Football' (1941)

1 All wars are planned by old men
In council rooms apart.
'The Two Sides of War' (1955)

2 Outlined against a blue-grey October sky,
the Four Horsemen rode again. In
dramatic lore they were known as
Famine, Pestilence, Destruction, and
Death. These are only aliases. Their real
names are Stuhldreher, Miller, Crowley,
and Layden. They formed the crest of the
South Bend cyclone before which
another fighting Army football team was
swept over the precipice.
report of football match between US Military
Academy at West Point NY and University of
Notre Dame, in *New York Tribune* 19 October
1924

Tim Rice 1944–

English songwriter

3 Don't cry for me Argentina.
title of song (1976) from the musical *Evita*,
based on the life of Eva **Perón**

4 Prove to me that you're no fool
Walk across my swimming pool.
Jesus Christ Superstar (1970) 'Herod's Song'

Mandy Rice-Davies 1944–

English model and showgirl

5 He would, wouldn't he?
*on hearing that Lord Astor denied her allegations,
concerning himself and his house parties at
Cliveden*
at the trial of Stephen Ward, 29 June 1963

Ann Richards 1933–

American Democratic politician

6 That dog won't hunt.
of Republican policies
keynote speech at the Democratic convention,
1988; Wallace O. Chariton *This Dog'll Hunt*
(1989)

7 Poor George, he can't help it—he was
born with a silver foot in his mouth.
of George **Bush**
keynote speech at the Democratic convention,
1988; in *Independent* 20 July 1988

I. A. Richards 1893–1979

English literary critic

8 We believe a scientist because he can
substantiate his remarks, not because he
is eloquent and forcible in his
enunciation. In fact, we distrust him
when he seems to be influencing us by
his manner.
Science and Poetry (1926)

9 It [poetry] is capable of saving us; it is a
perfectly possible means of overcoming
chaos.
Science and Poetry (1926)

Keith Richards 1943–

English rock musician
see also **Jagger**

10 Sure thing, man. I used to be a
laboratory myself once.
*on being asked to autograph a fan's school
chemistry book*
in *Independent on Sunday* 7 August 1994

Justin Richardson 1900–75

British poet

11 People who have three daughters try
once more
And then it's fifty-fifty they'll have four.
Those with a son or sons will let things
be.
Hence all these surplus women. Q.E.D.
'Note for the Scientist' (1959)

12 For years a secret shame destroyed my
peace—
I'd not read Eliot, Auden or MacNeice.
But then I had a thought that brought
me hope—
Neither had Chaucer, Shakespeare,
Milton, Pope.
'Take Heart, Illiterates' (1966)

Ralph Richardson 1902–83

English actor

13 Acting is merely the art of keeping a
large group of people from coughing.
in *New York Herald Tribune* 19 May 1946

Nicholas Ridley 1929–93

British Conservative politician

of the European community:
1 This is all a German racket, designed to take over the whole of Europe.

in *Spectator* 14 July 1990

Rainer Maria Rilke 1875–1926

German poet

2 We live our lives, for ever taking leave.

Duineser Elegien (1948) no. 8

César Ritz 1850–1918

Swiss hotel proprietor

3 *Le client n'a jamais tort.*
The customer is never wrong.

R. Nevill and C. E. Jerningham *Piccadilly to Pall Mall* (1908)

Joan Riviere b. 1883

4 Civilization and its discontents.

title given to her translation of Sigmund Freud's *Das Unbehagen in der Kultur* (1930)

Lord Robbins 1898–1984

British economist

5 Economics is the science which studies human behaviour as a relationship between ends and scarce means which have alternative uses.

Essay on the Nature and Significance of Economic Science (1932)

Leo Robin 1900–

American songwriter

6 A kiss on the hand may be quite continental,
But diamonds are a girl's best friend.

'Diamonds are a Girl's Best Friend' (1949 song); from the film *Gentlemen Prefer Blondes*; cf. **Loos** 194:7

7 Thanks for the memory.

title of song (with Ralph Rainger, 1937)

Edwin Arlington Robinson 1869–1935

American poet

8 I shall have more to say when I am dead.

'John Brown' (1920)

9 The world is not a 'prison house', but a kind of kindergarten, where millions of bewildered infants are trying to spell God with the wrong blocks.

Literature in the Making (1917)

John Robinson 1919–83

English theologian; Bishop of Woolwich, 1959–69

10 Honest to God.

title of book (1963)

11 I think Lawrence tried to portray this [sex] relation as in a real sense an act of holy communion. For him flesh was sacramental of the spirit.

as defence witness in the case against Penguin Books for publishing Lady Chatterley's Lover

comment, 27 October 1960; cf. **Griffith-Jones** 134:4

Mary Robinson 1944–

Irish Labour stateswoman; President 1990–97

12 Instead of rocking the cradle, they rocked the system.

in her victory speech, paying tribute to the women of Ireland

in *The Times* 10 November 1990

Sugar Ray Robinson 1920–89

American boxer

when asked by the coroner if he had intended to 'get Doyle in trouble':
13 Mister, it's my *business* to get him in trouble.

following the death of Jimmy Doyle from his injuries after fighting Robinson, 24 June 1947

Sugar Ray Robinson with Dave Anderson *Sugar Ray* (1970)

Gene Roddenberry 1921–91

American film producer
see also **Misquotations** 218:1

1 These are the voyages of the starship
Enterprise. Its five-year mission . . . to
boldly go where no man has gone before.
Star Trek (television series, from 1966)

Anita Roddick 1942–

English businesswoman

2 How do you ennoble the spirit when you
are selling something as inconsequential
as a cosmetic cream?
Body and Soul (1991)

3 I think that business practices would
improve immeasurably if they were
guided by 'feminine' principles—qualities
like love and care and intuition.
Body and Soul (1991)

Sue Rodriguez 1951–94

Canadian activist for the legalization of
assisted suicide

4 If I cannot give consent to my own
death, then whose body is this? Who
owns my life?
*appealing to a subcomittee of the Canadian
Commons, November 1992, as the victim of a
terminal illness*
in *Globe and Mail* 5 December 1992

Theodore Roethke 1908–63

American poet

5 Thought does not crush to stone.
The great sledge drops in vain.
Truth never is undone;
Its shafts remain.
'The Adamant' (1941)

6 I have known the inexorable sadness of
pencils,
Neat in their boxes, dolour of pad and
paper-weight,
All the misery of manilla folders and
mucilage,
Desolation in immaculate public places.
'Dolour' (1948)

7 The body and the soul know how to play
In that dark world where gods have lost
their way.
'Four for Sir John Davies' (1953) no. 2

8   O who can be
Both moth and flame? The weak moth
blundering by.
Whom do we love? I thought I knew the
truth;
Of grief I died, but no one knew my
death.
'The Sequel' (1964)

9 I wake to sleep, and take my waking
slow.
I feel my fate in what I cannot fear.
I learn by going where I have to go.
The Waking (1953)

Will Rogers 1879–1935

American actor and humorist

10 There is only one thing that can kill the
movies, and that is education.
Autobiography of Will Rogers (1949)

11 Income Tax has made more Liars out of
the American people than Golf.
The Illiterate Digest (1924) 'Helping the Girls
with their Income Taxes'

12 Everything is funny as long as it is
happening to Somebody Else.
The Illiterate Digest (1924) 'Warning to Jokers:
lay off the prince'

13 Well, all I know is what I read in the
papers.
in *New York Times* 30 September 1923

14 You know everybody is ignorant, only on
different subjects.
in *New York Times* 31 August 1924

15 Heroing is one of the shortest-lived
professions there is.
newspaper article, 15 February 1925, in Paula
McSpadden Grove *The Will Rogers Book* (1961)

16 Communism is like prohibition, it's a
good idea but it won't work.
Weekly Articles (1981); first published 1927

17 You can't say civilization don't advance,
however, for in every war they kill you in
a new way.
in *New York Times* 23 December 1929

1 Half our life is spent trying to find something to do with the time we have rushed through life trying to save.

> letter in *New York Times* 29 April 1930

Mies van der Rohe 1886–1969

German-born architect and designer

2 Less is more.

> P. Johnson *Mies van der Rohe* (1947); cf. **Venturi** 317:1

3 God is in the details.

> in *New York Times* 19 August 1969

Eleanor Roosevelt 1884–1962

American humanitarian and diplomat; wife of Franklin **Roosevelt**
on Roosevelt: see **Stevenson** 298:8

4 No one can make you feel inferior without your consent.

> in *Catholic Digest* August 1960

Franklin D. Roosevelt

1882–1945

American Democratic statesman, 32nd President of the US, 1933–45; husband of Eleanor **Roosevelt**

5 These unhappy times call for the building of plans that . . . build from the bottom up and not from the top down, that put their faith once more in the forgotten man at the bottom of the economic pyramid.

> radio address, 7 April 1932

6 I pledge you, I pledge myself, to a new deal for the American people.

> speech to the Democratic Convention in Chicago, 2 July 1932, accepting the presidential nomination

7 The only thing we have to fear is fear itself.

> inaugural address, 4 March 1933

8 In the field of world policy I would dedicate this Nation to the policy of the good neighbour.

> inaugural address, 4 March 1933

9 I have seen war. I have seen war on land and sea. I have seen blood running from the wounded. I have seen men coughing out their gassed lungs. I have seen the dead in the mud. I have seen cities destroyed. I have seen 200 limping, exhausted men come out of line—the survivors of a regiment of 1,000 that went forward 48 hours before. I have seen children starving. I have seen the agony of mothers and wives. I hate war.

> speech at Chautauqua, NY, 14 August 1936

10 I see one-third of a nation ill-housed, ill-clad, ill-nourished.

> second inaugural address, 20 January 1937

11 I am reminded of four definitions: A Radical is a man with both feet firmly planted—in the air. A Conservative is a man with two perfectly good legs who, however, has never learned to walk forward. A Reactionary is a somnambulist walking backwards. A Liberal is a man who uses his legs and his hands at the behest—at the command—of his head.

> radio address to *New York Herald Tribune* Forum, 26 October 1939

12 I have said this before, but I shall say it again and again and again: Your boys are not going to be sent into any foreign wars.

> speech in Boston, 30 October 1940; cf. **Johnson** 163:4

13 We must be the great arsenal of democracy.

> broadcast, 29 December 1940

14 We look forward to a world founded upon four essential human freedoms. The first is freedom of speech and expression—everywhere in the world. The second is freedom of every person to worship God in his own way— everywhere in the world. The third is freedom from want . . . The fourth is freedom from fear.

> message to Congress, 6 January 1941

15 Yesterday, December 7, 1941—a date which will live in infamy—the United States of America was suddenly and deliberately attacked by naval and air forces of the Empire of Japan.

> address to Congress, 8 December 1941

16 Books can not be killed by fire. People die, but books never die. No man and no

force can abolish memory. No man and no force can put thought in a concentration camp forever. No man and no force can take from the world the books that embody man's eternal fight against tyranny of every kind. In this war, we know, books are weapons. And it is a part of your dedication always to make them weapons for man's freedom.

'Message to the Booksellers of America' 6 May 1942

1 It is fun to be in the same decade with you.

acknowledging congratulations on his 60th birthday

cabled reply to Winston **Churchill**, in W. S. Churchill *The Hinge of Fate* (1950)

2 The work, my friend, is peace. More than an end of this war—an end to the beginnings of all wars.

undelivered address for Jefferson Day, 13 April 1945 (the day after Roosevelt died)

Theodore Roosevelt
1858–1919

American Republican statesman, 26th President of the US, 1901–9

3 Speak softly and carry a big stick; you will go far.

quoting an 'old adage'

speech in Chicago, 3 April 1903

4 A man who is good enough to shed his blood for the country is good enough to be given a square deal afterwards.

speech at the Lincoln Monument, Springfield, Illinois, 4 June 1903

5 The men with the muck-rakes are often indispensable to the well-being of society; but only if they know when to stop raking the muck.

speech in Washington, 14 April 1906

6 There is no room in this country for hyphenated Americanism.

speech in New York, 12 October 1915

7 One of our defects as a nation is a tendency to use what have been called 'weasel words'. When a weasel sucks eggs the meat is sucked out of the egg. If you use a 'weasel word' after another, there is nothing left of the other.

speech in St Louis, 31 May 1916

8 I have got such a bully pulpit!

his personal view of the presidency

in *Outlook* (New York) 27 February 1909; cf. **Reagan** 261:11

9 Foolish fanatics . . . the men who form the lunatic fringe in all reform movements.

Autobiography (1913)

Lord Rootes 1894–1964

English motor-car manufacturer

10 No other man-made device since the shields and lances of ancient knights fulfils a man's ego like an automobile.

attributed, 1958

Billy Rose 1899–1966 and Marty Bloom

11 Does the spearmint lose its flavour on the bedpost overnight?

revived in 1959 by Lonnie Donegan with the title 'Does your chewing-gum lose its flavour on the bedpost overnight?'

title of song (1924)

Ethel Rosenberg 1916–53 and Julius Rosenberg 1918–53

American couple convicted of spying for the Russians, and executed for espionage

12 We are innocent, as we have proclaimed and maintained from the time of our arrest. This is the whole truth. To forsake this truth is to pay too high a price even for the priceless gift of life—for life thus purchased we could not live out in dignity and self-respect.

petition for executive clemency, filed 9 January 1953

13 Ethel wants it made known that we are the first victims of American Fascism.

letter from Julius to Emanuel Bloch before the execution, 19 June 1953

Harold Ross 1892–1951

American journalist and editor

1 I understand the hero keeps getting in bed with women, and the war wasn't fought that way.
   *of **Hemingway**'s A Farewell to Arms*
      James Thurber *The Years with Ross* (1959)

2 The *New Yorker* will be the magazine which is not edited for the old lady in Dubuque.
      James Thurber *The Years with Ross* (1959)

3 Who he?
   frequent comment on manuscripts and proofs
      Dale Kramer *Ross and The New Yorker* (1952)

Jean Rostand 1894–1977

French biologist

4 The biologist passes, the frog remains.
   sometimes quoted as 'Theories pass. The frog remains'
      Inquiétudes d'un Biologiste (1967)

5 To be adult is to be alone.
      Pensées d'un biologiste (1954)

6 Kill a man, and you are an assassin. Kill millions of men, and you are a conqueror. Kill everyone, and you are a god.
      Pensées d'un biologiste (1939)

Leo Rosten 1908–97

American writer and social scientist

7 Any man who hates dogs and babies can't be all bad.
   *of W. C. **Fields**, and often attributed to him*
      speech at Masquers' Club dinner, 16 February 1939; letter in *Times Literary Supplement* 24 January 1975

Philip Roth 1933–

American novelist

8 A Jewish man with parents alive is a fifteen-year-old boy, and will remain a fifteen-year-old boy until *they die!*
      Portnoy's Complaint (1967)

9 Doctor, my doctor, what do you say, LET'S PUT THE ID BACK IN YID!
      Portnoy's Complaint (1967)

Lord Rothschild 1910–90

British administrator and scientist
*on Rothschild: see **Hurd** 154:14*

10 Politicians often believe that their world is the real one. Officials sometimes take a different view.
   on resigning as Director of the Central Policy Review Staff
      in *The Times* 13 October 1974

11 The promises and panaceas that gleam like false teeth in the party manifestoes.
      Meditations of a Broomstick (1977)

Matthew Rowbottom, Richard Stannard, and The Spice Girls

(Melanie Brown, Victoria Adams, Geri Halliwell, Emma Bunton, and Melanie Chisholm)

English songwriters and English pop singers
*see also **Chisholm***

12 Yo I'll tell you what I want, what I really
      really want
   so tell me what you want, what you
      really really want.
      'Wannabe' (1996 song)

Helen Rowland 1875–1950

American writer

13 A husband is what is left of a lover, after the nerve has been extracted.
      A Guide to Men (1922)

14 Somehow a bachelor never quite gets over the idea that he is a thing of beauty and a boy forever.
      A Guide to Men (1922); see below

   A thing of beauty is a joy for ever.
      John Keats (1795–1821) *Endymion* (1818)

15 The follies which a man regrets most, in his life, are those which he didn't commit when he had the opportunity.
      A Guide to Men (1922)

Richard Rowland c.1881–1947

American film producer

1 The lunatics have taken charge of the asylum.
*on the take-over of United Artists by Charles **Chaplin** and others*
> T. Ramsaye *A Million and One Nights* (1926)

Maude Royden 1876–1956

English religious writer

2 The Church [of England] should go forward along the path of progress and be no longer satisfied only to represent the Conservative Party at prayer.
> in *The Times* 17 July 1917

Mike Royko 1932–97

American journalist

3 No self-respecting fish would be wrapped in a Murdoch newspaper.
resigning from the Chicago Sun-Times *in 1984 when the paper was sold to Rupert **Murdoch***
> Karl E. Meyer (ed.) *Pundits, Poets, and Wits* (1990)

Paul Alfred Rubens

1875–1917

English songwriter

4 Oh! we don't want to lose you but we think you ought to go
For your King and your Country both need you so.
> 'Your King and Country Want You' (1914 song)

Robert Runcie 1921–

English Protestant clergyman; Archbishop of Canterbury
*on Runcie: see **Field** 108:4*

5 People are mourning on both sides of this conflict. In our prayers we shall quite rightly remember those who are bereaved in our own country and the relations of the young Argentinian soldiers who were killed. Common sorrow could do something to reunite those who were engaged in this struggle.

A shared anguish can be a bridge of reconciliation. Our neighbours are indeed like us.
> service of thanksgiving at the end of the Falklands war, St. Paul's Cathedral, London, 26 July 1982

6 In the middle ages people were tourists because of their religion, whereas now they are tourists because tourism is their religion.
> speech in London, 6 December 1988

7 I have done my best to die before this book is published. It now seems possible that I may not succeed.
> letter to Humphrey Carpenter, July 1996, in H. Carpenter *Robert Runcie* (1996)

Damon Runyon 1884–1946

American writer

8 'My boy,' he says, 'always try to rub up against money, for if you rub up against money long enough, some of it may rub off on you.'
> in *Cosmopolitan* August 1929, 'A Very Honourable Guy'

9 I do see her in tough joints more than somewhat.
> in *Collier's* 22 May 1930, 'Social Error'

10 I long ago come to the conclusion that all life is 6 to 5 against.
> in *Collier's* 8 September 1934, 'A Nice Price'

Salman Rushdie 1947–

Indian-born British novelist

11 What is freedom of expression? Without the freedom to offend, it ceases to exist.
> in *Weekend Guardian* 10 February 1990

12 One of the things a writer is for is to say the unsayable, speak the unspeakable and ask difficult questions.
> in *Independent on Sunday* 10 September 1995 'Quotes of the Week'

Willie Rushton 1937–96

British humorist and cartoonist

13 Bollocks the butler speaking. What splendid news about mad cow disease.

That explains the last 20 years and I thought I was the one who was barmy. Please leave a spring-like message after the moo . . . Moooooooooo!
recorded message on his answering machine
  in *The Times* 12 December 1996

Dean Rusk 1909–94

American politician; Secretary of State, 1961–9

1 We're eyeball to eyeball, and I think the other fellow just blinked.
on the Cuban missile crisis
  24 October 1962; in *Saturday Evening Post* 8 December 1962

2 Scratch any American and underneath you'll find an isolationist.
  to the British Foreign Secretary, George Brown; Tony Benn, diary, 12 January 1968

Bertrand Russell 1872–1970

British philosopher and mathematician

3 Three passions, simple but overwhelmingly strong, have governed my life: the longing for love, the search for knowledge, and unbearable pity for the suffering of mankind.
Autobiography (1967)

4 I was told that the Chinese said they would bury me by the Western Lake and build a shrine to my memory. I have some slight regret that this did not happen as I might have become a god, which would have been very *chic* for an atheist.
Autobiography (1968)

5 Men who are unhappy, like men who sleep badly, are always proud of the fact.
The Conquest of Happiness (1930)

6 Boredom is . . . a vital problem for the moralist, since half the sins of mankind are caused by the fear of it.
The Conquest of Happiness (1930)

7 One of the symptoms of approaching nervous breakdown is the belief that one's work is terribly important, and that to take a holiday would bring all kinds of disaster.
The Conquest of Happiness (1930)

8 One should as a rule respect public opinion in so far as is necessary to avoid starvation and to keep out of prison, but anything that goes beyond this is voluntary submission to an unnecessary tyranny.
The Conquest of Happiness (1930)

9 A sense of duty is useful in work, but offensive in personal relations. People wish to be liked, not to be endured with patient resignation.
The Conquest of Happiness (1930)

10 Of all forms of caution, caution in love is perhaps the most fatal to true happiness.
The Conquest of Happiness (1930)

11 To be able to fill leisure intelligently is the last product of civilization.
The Conquest of Happiness (1930)

12 Aristotle maintained that women have fewer teeth than men; although he was twice married, it never occurred to him to verify this statement by examining his wives' mouths.
Impact of Science on Society (1952)

13 Work is of two kinds: first, altering the position of matter at or near the earth's surface relatively to other such matter; second, telling other people to do so. The first kind is unpleasant and ill paid; the second is pleasant and highly paid.
In Praise of Idleness and Other Essays (1986) title essay (1932)

14 The fact that an opinion has been widely held is no evidence whatever that it is not utterly absurd; indeed in view of the silliness of the majority of mankind, a widespread belief is more likely to be foolish than sensible.
Marriage and Morals (1929)

15 Mathematics may be defined as the subject in which we never know what we are talking about, nor whether what we are saying is true.
Mysticism and Logic (1918)

16 Mathematics, rightly viewed, possesses not only truth, but supreme beauty—a beauty cold and austere, like that of sculpture.
Philosophical Essays (1910)

17 The man who has fed the chicken every day throughout its life at last wrings its

neck instead, showing that a more refined view as to the uniformity of nature would have been useful to the chicken.

The Problems of Philosophy (1912)

1 Every man, wherever he goes, is encompassed by a cloud of comforting convictions, which move with him like flies on a summer day.

Sceptical Essays (1928) 'Dreams and Facts'

2 We have, in fact, two kinds of morality side by side: one which we preach but do not practise, and another which we practise but seldom preach.

Sceptical Essays (1928) 'Eastern and Western Ideals of Happiness'

3 The fundamental defect of fathers, in our competitive society, is that they want their children to be a credit to them.

Sceptical Essays (1928) 'Freedom versus Authority in Education'

4 Machines are worshipped because they are beautiful, and valued because they confer power; they are hated because they are hideous, and loathed because they impose slavery.

Sceptical Essays (1928) 'Machines and Emotions'

5 The infliction of cruelty with a good conscience is a delight to moralists. That is why they invented Hell.

Sceptical Essays (1928) 'On the Value of Scepticism'

6 It is obvious that 'obscenity' is not a term capable of exact legal definition; in the practice of the Courts, it means 'anything that shocks the magistrate'.

Sceptical Essays (1928) 'The Recrudescence of Puritanism'

7 Man is a credulous animal, and must believe *something*; in the absence of good grounds for belief, he will be satisfied with bad ones.

Unpopular Essays (1950) 'Outline of Intellectual Rubbish'

8 Fear is the main source of superstition, and one of the main sources of cruelty.

Unpopular Essays (1950) 'An Outline of Intellectual Rubbish'

9 'Change' is scientific, 'progress' is ethical; change is indubitable, whereas progress is a matter of controversy.

Unpopular Essays (1950) 'Philosophy and Politics'

10 The linguistic philosophy, which cares only about language, and not about the world, is like the boy who preferred the clock without the pendulum because, although it no longer told the time, it went more easily than before and at a more exhilarating pace.

foreword to Ernest Gellner *Words and Things* (1959)

Dora Russell 1894–1986

English feminist

11 We want better reasons for having children than not knowing how to prevent them.

Hypatia (1925)

Ernest Rutherford 1871–1937

New Zealand physicist
on Rutherford: see **Bullard** 48:5, **Leacock** 185:4

12 All science is either physics or stamp collecting.

J. B. Birks *Rutherford at Manchester* (1962)

13 If your experiment needs statistics, you ought to have done a better experiment.

Norman T. J. Bailey *The Mathematical Approach to Biology and Medicine* (1967)

14 It was quite the most incredible event that has ever happened to me in my life. It was almost as incredible as if you fired a 15-inch shell at a piece of tissue paper and it came back and hit you.

on the back-scattering effect of metal foil on alpha-particles

E. N. da C. Andrade *Rutherford and the Nature of the Atom* (1964)

15 We haven't got the money, so we've got to think!

in *Bulletin of the Institute of Physics* (1962) vol. 13

Gilbert Ryle 1900–76

English philosopher

1 A myth is, of course, not a fairy story. It is the presentation of facts belonging to one category in the idioms appropriate to another. To explode a myth is accordingly not to deny the facts but to re-allocate them.
The Concept of Mind (1949)

2 Philosophy is the replacement of category-habits by category-disciplines.
The Concept of Mind (1949)

3 The dogma of the Ghost in the Machine.
the mind viewed as distinct from the body
The Concept of Mind (1949)

Vita Sackville-West
1892–1962

English writer and gardener; wife of Harold **Nicolson**

4 The greater cats with golden eyes Stare out between the bars.
The King's Daughter (1929)

Anwar al-Sadat 1918–81

Egyptian statesman, President 1970–81

5 Peace is much more precious than a piece of land.
speech in Cairo, 8 March 1978

Françoise Sagan 1935–

French novelist

6 To jealousy, nothing is more frightful than laughter.
La Chamade (1965)

Antoine de Saint-Exupéry
1900–44

French writer and aviator

7 Grown-ups never understand anything for themselves, and it is tiresome for children to be always and forever explaining things to them.
Le Petit Prince (1943)

8 Experience shows us that love does not consist in gazing at each other but in looking together in the same direction.
Wind, Sand and Stars (1939)

Lord St John of Fawsley
1929–

British Conservative politician and author

9 The monarchy has become our only truly popular institution at a time when the House of Commons has declined in public esteem and the Lords is a matter of controversy. The monarchy is, in a real sense, underpinning the other two estates of the realm.
in *The Times* 1 February 1982

Yves Saint Laurent 1936–

French couturier

10 I don't really like knees.
in *Observer* 3 August 1958

Andrei Sakharov 1921–89

Russian nuclear physicist

11 Every day I saw the huge material, intellectual and nervous resources of thousands of people being poured into the creation of a means of total destruction, something capable of annihilating all human civilization. I noticed that the control levers were in the hands of people who, though talented in their own ways, were cynical.
Sakharov Speaks (1974)

Saki 1870–1916

British writer

12 Waldo is one of those people who would be enormously improved by death.
Beasts and Super-Beasts (1914) 'The Feast of Nemesis'

13 The people of Crete unfortunately make more history than they can consume locally.
Chronicles of Clovis (1911) 'The Jesting of Arlington Stringham'

1 The cook was a good cook, as cooks go;
and as good cooks go, she went.
   Reginald (1904) 'Reginald on Besetting Sins'

J. D. Salinger 1919–
American novelist and short-story writer

2 The catcher in the rye.
   title of novel (1951)

3 What really knocks me out is a book
that, when you're all done reading it,
you wish the author that wrote it was a
terrific friend of yours and you could call
him up on the phone whenever you felt
like it.
   The Catcher in the Rye (1951)

4 Sex is something I really don't
understand too hot. You never know
where the hell you are. I keep making up
these sex rules for myself, and then I
break them right away.
   The Catcher in the Rye (1951)

Lord Salisbury 1893–1972
British Conservative politician

5 Too clever by half.
   *of Iain **Macleod**, Colonial Secretary; the term 'too
clever by half' had been applied by an earlier
Lord Salisbury (1830–1903) to Disraeli's
amendment on Disestablishment, 30 March 1868*
   in the House of Lords, 7 March 1961

Anthony Sampson 1926–
British author and journalist

6 A secret tome of *The Great and the Good* is
kept, listing everyone who has the right,
safe qualifications of worthiness,
soundness and discretion; and from this
tome came the stage army of committee
people.
   Anatomy of Britain Today (1965)

7 Of all the legacies of empire, the most
dangerous is surely an immobile
bureaucracy which can perpetuate its
own interests and values, like those
ancient hierarchies which presided over
declining civilizations . . . As the British
mandarins reinforce their defences,
awarding each other old imperial

honours, do they hear any echoes from
Castile or Byzantium?
   The Changing Anatomy of Britain (1982)

Lord Samuel 1870–1963
British Liberal politician

8 A library is thought in cold storage.
   A Book of Quotations (1947)

Paul A. Samuelson 1915–
American economist

9 The consumer, so it is said, is the
king . . . each is a voter who uses his
money as votes to get the things done
that he wants done.
   Economics (8th ed., 1970)

Carl Sandburg 1878–1967
American poet

10 Hog Butcher for the World,
Tool Maker, Stacker of Wheat,
Player with Railroads and the Nation's
   Freight Handler;
Stormy, husky, brawling,
City of the Big Shoulders.
   'Chicago' (1916)

11 When Abraham Lincoln was shovelled
   into the tombs,
he forgot the copperheads and the
   assassin . . .
in the dust, in the cool tombs.
   'Cool Tombs' (1918)

12 The fog comes
on little cat feet.

It sits looking
over harbour and city
on silent haunches
and then moves on.
   'Fog' (1916)

13 Pile the bodies high at Austerlitz and
   Waterloo.
Shovel them under and let me work—
I am the grass; I cover all.
   'Grass' (1918)

14 Why is there always a secret singing
When a lawyer cashes in?
Why does a hearse horse snicker

Hauling a lawyer away?
'The Lawyers Know Too Much' (1920)

1 I tell you the past is a bucket of ashes.
'Prairie' (1918)

2 I am an idealist. I don't know where I'm
going but I'm on the way.
Incidentals (1907)

3 Little girl . . . Sometime they'll give a war
and nobody will come.
The People, Yes (1936); 'Suppose They Gave a
War and No One Came?' was the title of a
piece by Charlotte Keyes in *McCall's* October
1966; 'Suppose They Gave a War and Nobody
Came?' was the title of a 1970 film; cf.
Ginsberg 128:6

4 Poetry is the achievement of the
synthesis of hyacinths and biscuits.
in *Atlantic Monthly* March 1923 'Poetry
Considered'

5 Slang is a language that rolls up its
sleeves, spits on its hands and goes to
work.
in *New York Times* 13 February 1959

Henry 'Red' Sanders 1905–58

6 Sure, winning isn't everything. It's the
only thing.
in *Sports Illustrated* 26 December 1955; often
attributed to Vince Lombardi

George Santayana 1863–1952

Spanish-born philosopher and critic

7 The young man who has not wept is a
savage, and the old man who will not
laugh is a fool.
Dialogues in Limbo (1925)

8 Fanaticism consists in redoubling your
effort when you have forgotten your aim.
The Life of Reason (1905)

9 Those who cannot remember the past are
condemned to repeat it.
The Life of Reason (1905)

10 Fashion is something barbarous, for it
produces innovation without reason and
imitation without benefit.
The Life of Reason (1905)

11 The cry was for vacant freedom and
indeterminate progress: *Vorwärts! Avanti!
Onwards! Full speed ahead!*, without
asking whether directly before you was
not a bottomless pit.
My Host the World (1953)

12 There is no cure for birth and death save
to enjoy the interval.
Soliloquies in England (1922) 'War Shrines'

13 It is a great advantage for a system of
philosophy to be substantially true.
The Unknowable (1923)

14 For an idea ever to be fashionable is
ominous, since it must afterwards be
always old-fashioned.
Winds of Doctrine (1913)

John Singer Sargent
1856–1925

American painter

15 Every time I paint a portrait I lose a
friend.
N. Bentley and E. Esar *Treasury of Humorous
Quotations* (1951)

Leslie Sarony 1897–1985

British songwriter

16 Ain't it grand to be blooming well dead?
title of song (1932)

Ken Saro-Wiwa

see **Last words** 182:10

Nathalie Sarraute 1902–

French novelist

17 Radio and television, to which we devote
so many of the leisure hours once spent
listening to parlour chatter and parlour
music, have succeeded in lifting the
manufacture of banality out of the sphere

of handicraft and placed it in that of a major industry.

in *Times Literary Supplement* 10 June 1960

Jean-Paul Sartre 1905–80

French philosopher, novelist, dramatist, and critic
on Sartre: see **de Gaulle** 87:10

1 When the rich wage war it's the poor who die.

Le Diable et le bon Dieu (1951)

2 Nothingness haunts being.

L'Être et le néant (1943)

3 I am condemned to be free.

L'Être et le néant (1943)

4 Man is a useless passion.

L'Être et le néant (1943)

5 Hell is other people.

Huis Clos (1944)

6 Like all dreamers, I mistook disenchantment for truth.

Les Mots (1964) 'Écrire'

7 I confused things with their names: that is belief.

Les Mots (1964) 'Écrire'

8 There is no good father, that's the rule. Don't lay the blame on men but on the bond of paternity, which is rotten. To beget children, nothing better; to *have* them, what iniquity!

Les Mots (1964) 'Lire'

9 The poor don't know that their function in life is to exercise our generosity.

Les Mots (1964) 'Lire'

10 She believed in nothing; only her scepticism kept her from being an atheist.

Les Mots (1964) 'Lire'

11 Human life begins on the far side of despair.

Les Mouches (1943)

12 Three o'clock is always too late or too early for anything you want to do.

La Nausée (Nausea, 1938) 'Vendredi'

13 I hate victims who respect their executioners.

Les Séquestrés d'Altona (1960)

14 A writer must refuse, therefore, to allow himself to be transformed into an institution.

refusing the Nobel Prize
declaration read at Stockholm, 22 October 1964

15 The whole question boils down to knowing whether one is interested in talking about the flight of butterflies or the condition of the Jews.

attributed

Siegfried Sassoon 1886–1967

English poet

16 If I were fierce, and bald, and short of breath,
I'd live with scarlet Majors at the Base,
And speed glum heroes up the line to death.

'Base Details' (1918)

17 Does it matter?—losing your sight? . . .
There's such splendid work for the blind;
And people will always be kind,
As you sit on the terrace remembering
And turning your face to the light.

'Does it Matter?' (1918)

18 Soldiers are citizens of death's grey land,
Drawing no dividend from time's tomorrows.

'Dreamers' (1918)

19 You are too young to fall asleep for ever;
And when you sleep you remind me of the dead.

'The Dug-Out' (1919)

20 Everyone suddenly burst out singing;
And I was filled with such delight
As prisoned birds must find in freedom.

'Everyone Sang' (1919)

21 The song was wordless; the singing will never be done.

'Everyone Sang' (1919)

22 'He's a cheery old card,' grunted Harry to Jack

As they slogged up to Arras with rifle and pack.

But he did for them both by his plan of attack.

'The General' (1918)

1 Here was the world's worst wound. And here with pride
'Their name liveth for ever' the Gateway claims.
Was ever an immolation so belied
As these intolerably nameless names?

'On Passing the New Menin Gate' (1928); cf. **Epitaphs** 105:15

2 Who will remember, passing through this Gate,
The unheroic Dead who fed the guns?

'On Passing the New Menin Gate' (1928)

3 I am making this statement as an act of wilful defiance of military authority, because I believe that the War is being deliberately prolonged by those who have the power to end it.

'A Soldier's Declaration' addressed to his commanding officer and sent to the *Bradford Pioneer* July 1917; Stanley Jackson *The Sassoons* (1968)

Dorothy L. Sayers 1893–1957

English writer of detective fiction

4 A society in which consumption has to be artificially stimulated in order to keep production going is a society founded on trash and waste, and such a society is a house built upon sand.

Creed or Chaos? (1947)

5 I admit it is better fun to punt than to be punted, and that a desire to have all the fun is nine-tenths of the law of chivalry.

Gaudy Night (1935)

6 I always have a quotation for everything—it saves original thinking.

Have His Carcase (1932)

7 As I grow older and older,
And totter towards the tomb,
I find that I care less and less
Who goes to bed with whom.

'That's Why I Never Read Modern Novels', in Janet Hitchman *Such a Strange Lady* (1975)

8 Those who prefer their English sloppy have only themselves to thank if the advertisement writer uses his mastery of vocabulary and syntax to mislead their weak minds . . . The moral of all this . . . is that we have the kind of advertising we deserve.

in *Spectator* 19 November 1937 'The Psychology of Advertising'

9 Perhaps it is no wonder that women were first at the Cradle and the Cross. They had never known a man like this man—there has never been such another . . . who never made jokes about them, never treated them either as 'The women, God help us', or 'The ladies, God bless them!'

J. Morley and H. Ward (eds.) *Celebrating Women* (1986); attributed

■ **Sayings and slogans**

see box overleaf
see also **Advertising slogans, Official advice, Political slogans**

Gerald Scarfe 1936–

English caricaturist

10 I find a particular delight in taking the caricature as far as I can. It satisfies me to stretch the human frame about and recreate it and yet keep a likeness.

Scarfe by Scarfe (1986)

Arthur Scargill 1938–

British trades-union leader

11 Parliament itself would not exist in its present form had people not defied the law.

evidence to House of Commons Select Committee on Employment, 2 April 1980

Sayings and slogans

1 Action this day.

annotation as used by Winston Churchill at the Admiralty in 1940

2 Are we downhearted? No!

expression much taken up by British soldiers during the First World War

3 Been there, done that, got the T-shirt.

'been there, done that' recorded from 1980s, expanded form from 1990s

4 Burn your bra.

feminist slogan, 1970s

5 Business is like a car: it will not run by itself except downhill.

American saying

6 Children: one is one, two is fun, three is a houseful.

American

7 A committee is a group of the unwilling, chosen from the unfit, to do the unnecessary.

various attributions (origin unknown)

8 Crime doesn't pay.

a slogan of the FBI and the cartoon detective Dick Tracy

9 Daddy, what did you do in the Great War?

daughter to father in First World War recruiting poster

10 [Death is] nature's way of telling you to slow down.

life insurance proverb; in *Newsweek* 25 April 1960

11 The difficult we do immediately, the impossible takes a little longer.

US Armed Forces slogan

12 Do not fold, spindle or mutilate.

instruction on punched cards (1950s, and in differing forms from the 1930s)

13 The family that prays together stays together.

motto devised by Al Scalpone for the Roman Catholic Family Rosary Crusade, 1947

14 Fifty million Frenchmen can't be wrong.

saying popular with American servicemen during the First World War; later associated with Mae **West** and Texas Guinan (1884–1933), it was also the title of a 1927 song by Billy Rose and Willie Raskin

15 Garbage in, garbage out.

in computing, incorrect or faulty input will always cause poor output; origin of the acronym GIGO

16 Go to jail. Go directly to jail. Do not pass go. Do not collect £200.

instructions on 'Community Chest' card in the game 'Monopoly'; invented by Charles Brace Darrow (1889–1967) in 1931

17 If it ain't broke, don't fix it.

Bert Lance (1931–), in *Nation's Business* May 1977

18 If it moves, salute it; if it doesn't move, pick it up; and if you can't pick it up, paint it.

1940s saying; P. Dickson *The Official Rules* (1978)

19 If you pay peanuts, you get monkeys.

recorded from the mid 1960s, and most commonly associated with pay negotiations

20 *Ils ne passeront pas.*

They shall not pass.

slogan of the French army at the defence of Verdun 1916; variously attributed to Marshal **Pétain** and to General Robert Nivelle, and taken up by the Republicans in the Spanish Civil War; cf. **Ibarruri** 156:3

21 I'm backing Britain.

slogan coined by workers at the Colt factory, Surbiton, Surrey and subsequently used in a national campaign, in *The Times* 1 January 1968

22 It takes 40 dumb animals to make a fur coat, but only one to wear it.

slogan of an anti-fur campaign poster, 1980s; sometimes attributed to David **Bailey**

▶

► **Sayings and slogans** continued

1 Lions led by donkeys.

associated with British soldiers during the First World War

attributed to Max Hoffman (1869–1927) in Alan Clark *The Donkeys* (1961); this attribution has not been traced elsewhere, and the phrase was well-known by the 1870s

2 Lousy but loyal.

London East End slogan at **George V**'s Jubilee (1935)

3 Make love not war.

student slogan, 1960s

4 The opera ain't over 'til the fat lady sings.

Dan Cook, in *Washington Post* 3 June 1978

5 Pile it high, sell it cheap.

slogan coined by John Cohen (1898–1979), founder of Tesco

6 Save the whale.

environmental slogan associated with alarm over the rapidly declining whale population which led in 1985 to a moratorium on commercial whaling

7 There is one thing stronger than all the armies in the world; and that is an idea whose time has come.

in *Nation* 15 April 1943

8 There's no such thing as a free lunch.

colloquial axiom in US economics from the 1960s, much associated with Milton **Friedman**; recorded in form 'there ain't no such thing as a free lunch' from 1938, which gave rise to the acronym TANSTAAFL in Robert Heinlein's *The Moon is a Harsh Mistress* (1966)

9 Think globally, act locally.

Friends of the Earth slogan, *c.*1985

10 To err is human but to really foul things up requires a computer.

Farmers' Almanac for 1978 'Capsules of Wisdom'; see below

To err is human; to forgive, divine.

Alexander Pope (1688–1744) *An Essay on Criticism* (1711)

11 We shall not be moved.

title of labour and civil rights song (1931) adapted from an earlier gospel hymn

12 We shall overcome.

title of song, originating from before the American Civil War, adapted as a Baptist hymn ('I'll Overcome Some Day', 1901) by C. A. Tindley; revived in 1946 as a protest song by tobacco workers, and in 1963 during the Civil Rights Campaign

13 What you see is what you get.

often shortened to the acronym *wysiwyg*, especially in Computing

14 When the going gets tough, the tough get going.

attributed to Joseph P. **Kennedy** (1888–1969), and also to Knute Rockne

15 Who dares wins.

motto of the British Special Air Service regiment, from 1942

16 Your King and Country need you.

recruitment slogan for First World War, coined by Eric Field; *Advertising* (1959)

Lord Scarman 1911–

British judge

17 The people as a source of sovereign power are in truth only occasional partners in the constitutional minuet danced for most of the time by Parliament and the political party in power.

The Shape of Things to Come (1989)

18 A government above the law is a menace to be defeated.

Why Britain Needs a Written Constitution (1992)

Barry Scheck

American lawyer

1 It is not a question of how skilfully we played our cards but of whether we were given a fair deck.

appealing against the conviction of Louise Woodward for second-degree murder, asserting that photographic evidence had not been made available to the defence at an early enough stage

in Cambridge, Massachusetts, 4 November 1997

Arthur M. Schlesinger Jr.

1917–

American historian

2 The answer to the runaway Presidency is not the messenger-boy Presidency. The American democracy must discover a middle way between making the President a czar and making him a puppet.

The Imperial Presidency (1973); preface

3 Suppose . . . that Lenin had died of typhus in Siberia in 1895 and Hitler had been killed on the western front in 1916. What would the twentieth century have looked like now?

The Cycles of American History (1986)

Moritz Schlick 1882–1936

German philosopher

4 The meaning of a proposition is the method of its verification.

in *Philosophical Review* (1936) vol. 45

Artur Schnabel 1882–1951

Austrian-born pianist

5 Children are given Mozart because of the small *quantity* of the notes; grown-ups avoid Mozart because of the great *quality* of the notes.

My Life and Music (1961)

6 I know two kinds of audiences only—one coughing, and one not coughing.

My Life and Music (1961)

7 Applause is a receipt, not a note of demand.

in *Saturday Review of Literature* 29 September 1951

8 The notes I handle no better than many pianists. But the pauses between the notes—ah, that is where the art resides!

in *Chicago Daily News* 11 June 1958

9 Too easy for children, and too difficult for artists.

of Mozart's sonatas

Nat Shapiro (ed.) *Encyclopaedia of Quotations about Music* (1978

Arnold Schoenberg

1874–1951

Austrian-born American composer and musical theorist

10 If it is art, it is not for the masses. 'If it is for the masses it is not art' is a topic which is rather similar to a word of yourself.

letter to W. S. Schlamm, 1 July 1945

11 I am delighted to add another unplayable work to the repertoire. I want the Concerto to be difficult and I want the little finger to become longer. I can wait.

of his Violin Concerto

Joseph Machlis *Introduction to Contemporary Music* (1963)

Patricia Schroeder 1940–

American Democratic politician

12 Ronald Reagan . . . is attempting a great breakthrough in political technology—he has been perfecting the Teflon-coated Presidency. He sees to it that nothing sticks to him.

speech in the US House of Representatives, 2 August 1983

Charles Monroe Schulz

1922–

American cartoonist

13 Happiness is a warm puppy.

title of book (1962); cf. **Advertising slogans** 3:21, **Ephron** 104:3, **Lennon** 187:13

E. F. Schumacher 1911–77

German-born economist

1 It was not the power of the Spaniards that destroyed the Aztec Empire but the disbelief of the Aztecs in themselves.
Roots of Economic Growth (1962)

2 Small is beautiful. A study of economics as if people mattered.
title of book (1973)

3 Call a thing immoral or ugly, soul-destroying or a degradation of man, a peril to the peace of the world or to the well-being of future generations: as long as you have not shown it to be 'uneconomic' you have not really questioned its right to exist, grow, and prosper.
Small is Beautiful (1973)

4 The most striking thing about modern industry is that it requires so much and accomplishes so little. Modern industry seems to be inefficient to a degree that surpasses one's ordinary powers of imagination. Its inefficiency therefore remains unnoticed.
Small is Beautiful (1973)

5 It is of little use trying to suppress terrorism if the production of deadly devices continues to be deemed a legitimate employment of man's creative powers.
Small is Beautiful (1973)

J. A. Schumpeter 1883–1950

American economist

6 The cold metal of economic theory is in Marx's pages immersed in such a wealth of steaming phrases as to acquire a temperature not naturally its own.
Capitalism, Socialism and Democracy (1942)

7 One servant is worth a thousand gadgets.
J. K. Galbraith *A Life in our Times* (1981)

Albert Schweitzer 1875–1965

Franco-German missionary

8 'Hullo! friend,' I call out, 'Won't you lend us a hand?' 'I am an intellectual and don't drag wood about,' came the answer. 'You're lucky,' I reply. 'I too wanted to become an intellectual, but I didn't succeed.'
More from the Primeval Forest (1931)

9 Late on the third day, at the very moment when, at sunset, we were making our way through a herd of hippopotamuses, there flashed upon my mind, unforeseen and unsought, the phrase, 'Reverence for Life'.
My Life and Thought (1933)

Kurt Schwitters 1887–1948

German painter

10 I am a painter and I nail my pictures together.
R. Hausmann *Am Anfang war Dada* (1972)

C. P. Scott 1846–1932

British journalist; editor of the *Manchester Guardian*, 1872–1929
on Scott: see **Muggeridge** 224:10

11 Comment is free, but facts are sacred.
in *Manchester Guardian* 5 May 1921; cf. **Stoppard** 299:3

12 *Television?* The word is half Greek, half Latin. No good can come of it.
Asa Briggs *The BBC: the First Fifty Years* (1985)

Robert Falcon Scott
1868–1912

English polar explorer
see also **Last words** 182:4

13 Great God! this is an awful place.
of the South Pole
diary, 17 January 1912

14 We took risks, we knew we took them; things have come out against us, and therefore we have no cause for complaint.
'The Last Message' in *Scott's Last Expedition* (1913)

Alan Seeger 1888–1916

American poet

1 I have a rendezvous with Death
At some disputed barricade.
'I Have a Rendezvous with Death' (1916)

Pete Seeger 1919–

American folk singer and songwriter

2 Where have all the flowers gone?
title of song (1961)

3 Education is when you read the fine
print; experience is what you get when
you don't.
L. Botts *Loose Talk* (1980)

Erich Segal 1937–

American novelist

4 Love means not ever having to say
you're sorry.
Love Story (1970)

Rony Seikaly

American basketball player

5 The NBA players are smart enough to
know you get the virus from unprotected
sex, and we're not going to have
unprotected sex on the basketball court.
*on the return of Earvin 'Magic' Johnson, who is
HIV-positive*
in *San Francisco Chronicle* 8 February 1996

Arthur Seldon 1916–

British economist

6 Government of the busy by the bossy for
the bully.
on over-government
Capitalism (1990)

Will Self 1961–

English novelist and journalist

7 So I was smacked out on the Prime
Minister's jet, big deal.
having been dismissed as a columnist by the
Observer *after taking heroin on John **Major**'s
plane during the election campaign*
in *Independent on Sunday* 20 April 1997

W. C. Sellar 1898–1951
and R. J. Yeatman 1898–1968

British writers

8 1066 and all that.
title of book (1930)

9 History is not what you thought. *It is
what you can remember.*
1066 and All That (1930) 'Compulsory Preface'

10 The Roman Conquest was, however, a
Good Thing, since the Britons were only
natives at the time.
1066 and All That (1930)

11 The Cavaliers (Wrong but Wromantic)
and the Roundheads (Right but
Repulsive).
1066 and All That (1930)

12 The National Debt is a very Good Thing
and it would be dangerous to pay it off,
for fear of Political Economy.
1066 and All That (1930)

13 [Gladstone] spent his declining years
trying to guess the answer to the Irish
Question; unfortunately whenever he
was getting warm, the Irish secretly
changed the Question.
1066 and All That (1930)

14 AMERICA was thus clearly top nation, and
History came to a .
1066 and All That (1930)

15 Do not on any account attempt to write
on both sides of the paper at once.
1066 and All That (1930) 'Test Paper 5'

Gitta Sereny 1923–

Hungarian-born British writer and journalist

*to Albert Speer, who having always denied
knowledge of the Holocaust had said that he was
at fault in having 'looked away':*
16 You cannot look away from something
you don't know. If you looked away,
then you knew.
recalled on BBC2 *Reputations*, 2 May 1996

Robert W. Service 1874–1958

Canadian poet

17 A promise made is a debt unpaid, and the
trail has its own stern code.
'The Cremation of Sam McGee' (1907)

1 Ah! the clock is always slow;
It is later than you think.
'It Is Later Than You Think' (1921)

2 This is the law of the Yukon, that only
the Strong shall thrive;
That surely the Weak shall perish, and
only the Fit survive.
'The Law of the Yukon' (1907)

3 When we, the Workers, all demand:
'What are WE fighting for?' . . .
Then, then we'll end that stupid crime,
that devil's madness—War.
'Michael' (1921)

4 Back of the bar, in a solo game, sat
Dangerous Dan McGrew,
And watching his luck was his light-
o'-love, the lady that's known as Lou.
'The Shooting of Dan McGrew' (1907)

Anne Sexton 1928–74

American poet

5 God owns heaven
but He craves the earth.
'The Earth' (1975)

6 In a dream you are never eighty.
'Old' (1962)

Peter Shaffer 1926–

English dramatist

7 The Normal is the good smile in a child's
eyes—all right. It is also the dead stare in
a million adults. It both sustains and
kills—like a God. It is the Ordinary made
beautiful; it is also the Average made
lethal.
Equus (1983 ed.)

8 That's the main trouble with the two
nations: bad Brits are snobs, bad
Americans are slobs.
Whom Do I Have the Honour of Addressing?
(1990)

Bill Shankly 1914–81

Scottish footballer and club manager

9 Some people think football is a matter of
life and death . . . I can assure them it is
much more serious than that.
in Sunday Times 4 October 1981

Robert Shapiro 1942–

American lawyer

10 Not only did we play the race card, we
played it from the bottom of the deck.
on the defence team's change of strategy at the
trial of O. J. Simpson
in The Times 5 October 1995

George Bernard Shaw

1856–1950

Irish dramatist and writer
on Shaw: see **Agate** 2:8, **Leigh** 187:3, **Lenin**
187:9, **Taylor** 303:12; see also **Catch-
phrases** 57:3

11 You see things; and you say 'Why?' But I
dream things that never were; and I say
'Why not?'
Back to Methuselah (1921)

12 I enjoy convalescence. It is the part that
makes illness worth while.
Back to Methuselah (1921)

13 The worst sin towards our fellow
creatures is not to hate them, but to be
indifferent to them: that's the essence of
inhumanity.
The Devil's Disciple (1901)

14 Martyrdom . . . the only way in which a
man can become famous without ability.
The Devil's Disciple (1901)

15 The British soldier can stand up to
anything except the British War Office.
The Devil's Disciple (1901)

16 There is at bottom only one genuinely
scientific treatment for all diseases, and
that is to stimulate the phagocytes.
The Doctor's Dilemma (1911)

17 All professions are conspiracies against
the laity.
The Doctor's Dilemma (1911)

18 Parentage is a very important profession,
but no test of fitness for it is ever imposed
in the interest of the children.
Everybody's Political What's What? (1944)

19 A government which robs Peter to pay
Paul can always depend on the support
of Paul.
Everybody's Political What's What? (1944)

1 The one point on which all women are in furious secret rebellion against the existing law is the saddling of the right to a child with the obligation to become the servant of a man.
Getting Married (1911) preface 'The Right to Motherhood'

2 The natural term of the affection of the human animal for its offspring is six years.
Heartbreak House (1919)

3 The captain is in his bunk, drinking bottled ditch-water; and the crew is gambling in the forecastle. She will strike and sink and split. Do you think the laws of God will be suspended in favour of England because you were born in it?
Heartbreak House (1919)

4 What really flatters a man is that you think him worth flattering.
John Bull's Other Island (1907)

5 The greatest of evils and the worst of crimes is poverty.
Major Barbara (1907) preface

6 I am a Millionaire. That is my religion.
Major Barbara (1907)

7 I can't talk religion to a man with bodily hunger in his eyes.
Major Barbara (1907)

8 Wot prawce Selvytion nah?
Major Barbara (1907)

9 Alcohol is a very necessary article . . . It enables Parliament to do things at eleven at night that no sane person would do at eleven in the morning.
Major Barbara (1907)

10 He knows nothing; and he thinks he knows everything. That points clearly to a political career.
Major Barbara (1907)

11 Nothing is ever done in this world until men are prepared to kill one another if it is not done.
Major Barbara (1907)

12 But a lifetime of happiness! No man alive could bear it: it would be hell on earth.
Man and Superman (1903)

13 Of all human struggles there is none so treacherous and remorseless as the struggle between the artist man and the mother woman.
Man and Superman (1903)

14 Hell is full of musical amateurs: music is the brandy of the damned.
Man and Superman (1903)

15 Englishmen never will be slaves: they are free to do whatever the Government and public opinion allow them to do.
Man and Superman (1903)

16 An Englishman thinks he is moral when he is only uncomfortable.
Man and Superman (1903)

17 In the arts of peace Man is a bungler.
Man and Superman (1903)

18 When the military man approaches, the world locks up its spoons and packs off its womankind.
Man and Superman (1903)

19 Beauty is all very well at first sight; but who ever looks at it when it has been in the house three days?
Man and Superman (1903)

20 There are two tragedies in life. One is not to get your heart's desire. The other is to get it.
Man and Superman (1903)

21 Do not do unto others as you would that they should do unto you. Their tastes may not be the same.
Man and Superman (1903) 'Maxims for Revolutionists: The Golden Rule'

22 The golden rule is that there are no golden rules.
Man and Superman (1903) 'Maxims for Revolutionists: The Golden Rule'

23 The art of government is the organization of idolatry.
Man and Superman (1903) 'Maxims: Idolatry'

24 Democracy substitutes election by the incompetent many for appointment by the corrupt few.
Man and Superman (1903) 'Maxims: Democracy'

1 Liberty means responsibility. That is why most men dread it.

Man and Superman (1903) 'Maxims: Liberty and Equality'

2 He who can, does. He who cannot, teaches.

Man and Superman (1903) 'Maxims: Education'

3 Marriage is popular because it combines the maximum of temptation with the maximum of opportunity.

Man and Superman (1903) 'Maxims: Marriage'

4 If you strike a child take care that you strike it in anger, even at the risk of maiming it for life. A blow in cold blood neither can nor should be forgiven.

Man and Superman (1903) 'Maxims: How to Beat Children'

5 Beware of the man whose god is in the skies.

Man and Superman (1903) 'Maxims: Religion'

6 Self-denial is not a virtue: it is only the effect of prudence on rascality.

Man and Superman (1903) 'Maxims: Virtues and Vice'

7 The reasonable man adapts himself to the world: the unreasonable one persists in trying to adapt the world to himself. Therefore all progress depends on the unreasonable man.

Man and Superman (1903) 'Maxims: Reason'

8 Decency is Indecency's conspiracy of silence.

Man and Superman (1903) 'Maxims: Decency'

9 Home is the girl's prison and the woman's workhouse.

Man and Superman (1903) 'Maxims: Women in the Home'

10 Youth, which is forgiven everything, forgives itself nothing: age, which forgives itself everything, is forgiven nothing.

Man and Superman (1903) 'Maxims: Stray Sayings'

11 Take care to get what you like or you will be forced to like what you get.

Man and Superman (1903) 'Maxims: Stray Sayings'

12 Beware of the man who does not return your blow: he neither forgives you nor allows you to forgive yourself.

Man and Superman (1903) 'Maxims: Stray Sayings'

13 Anarchism is a game at which the police can beat you.

Misalliance (1914)

14 You'll never have a quiet world till you knock the patriotism out of the human race.

O'Flaherty V.C. (1919)

15 A perpetual holiday is a good working definition of hell.

Parents and Children (1914) 'Children's Happiness'

16 It is impossible for an Englishman to open his mouth without making some other Englishman hate or despise him.

Pygmalion (1916) preface

17 Remember that you are a human being with a soul and the divine gift of articulate speech: that your native language is the language of Shakespeare and Milton and The Bible; and don't sit there crooning like a bilious pigeon.

Pygmalion (1916)

18 I don't want to talk grammar, I want to talk like a lady.

Pygmalion (1916)

19 I'm one of the undeserving poor . . . up agen middle-class morality all the time . . . What is middle-class morality? Just an excuse for never giving me anything.

Pygmalion (1916)

20 Gin was mother's milk to her.

Pygmalion (1916)

21 Walk! Not bloody likely.

Pygmalion (1916)

22 No Englishman is ever fairly beaten.

Saint Joan (1924)

23 Must then a Christ perish in torment in every age to save those that have no imagination?

Saint Joan (1924)

1 Assassination is the extreme form of censorship.

> *The Showing-Up of Blanco Posnet* (1911) 'Limits to Toleration'

2 The photographer is like the cod which produces a million eggs in order that one may reach maturity.

> introduction to the catalogue for Alvin Langdon Coburn's exhibition at the Royal Photographic Society, 1906; Bill Jay and Margaret Moore *Bernard Shaw and Photography* (1989)

3 We must use the war to give the coup-de-grace to medieval diplomacy, medieval autocracy, and anarchic export of capital, and make its conclusion convince the world that Democracy is invincible, and Militarism a rusty sword that breaks in the hand.

> in *Current History* December 1914 'Common Sense about the War'

4 The trouble, Mr Goldwyn, is that you are only interested in art and I am only interested in money.

> *telegraphed version of the outcome of a conversation between Shaw and Sam **Goldwyn***
>
> A. Johnson *The Great Goldwyn* (1937)

replying to a lady's proposal 'You have the greatest brain in the world, and I have the most beautiful body; so we ought to produce the most perfect child':

5 What if the child inherits my body and your brains?

> Hesketh Pearson *Bernard Shaw* (1942)

6 [Dancing is] a perpendicular expression of a horizontal desire.

> in *New Statesman* 23 March 1962; attributed

7 England and America are two countries divided by a common language.

> attributed in this and other forms, but not found in Shaw's published writings

Hartley Shawcross 1902–

British Labour politician and lawyer
see also **Misquotations** 219:3

8 I don't think it was right. It was victors' justice.

> *of the Nuremberg trials, at which he appeared for the prosecution*
>
> interviewed on his 95th birthday, in *Daily Telegraph* 10 February 1997

Patrick Shaw-Stewart
1888–1917
English poet

9 I saw a man this morning
Who did not wish to die;
I ask and cannot answer
If otherwise wish I.

> written 1916; M. Baring *Have You Anything to Declare?* (1936)

10 Stand in the trench, Achilles,
Flame-capped, and shout for me.

> written 1916; M. Baring *Have You Anything to Declare?* (1936)

11 I continue to believe that the luck of my generation must change . . . nowadays we who are alive have the sense of being old, old survivors.

> letter from Gallipoli, where he was killed; Brian Gardner (ed.) *Up the Line to Death* (rev. ed., 1976)

Burt Shevelove 1915–82
and Larry Gelbart ?1928–

12 A funny thing happened on the way to the Forum.

> title of musical (1962)

Emanuel Shinwell 1884–1986

British Labour politician

13 We know that the organized workers of the country are our friends. As for the rest, they don't matter a tinker's cuss.

> speech to the Electrical Trades Union conference at Margate, 7 May 1947

Mikhail Sholokhov 1905–84

Russian novelist

14 And quiet flows the Don.

> title of novel (1934)

Clare Short 1946–

British Labour politician

contrasting political advisers with elected politicians:

15 I sometimes call them the people who live in the dark. Everything they do is in

hiding . . . Everything we do is in the light. They live in the dark.
in New Statesman 9 August 1996

1 It will be golden elephants next.
suggesting that the government of Montserrat was 'talking mad money' in claiming assistance for evacuating the island
in Observer 24 August 1997

Jean Sibelius 1865–1957

Finnish composer

2 Remember, a statue has never been set up in honour of a critic!
Bengt de Törne Sibelius: A Close-Up (1937)

Maurice Sigler 1901–61 and Al Hoffman 1902–60

American songwriters

3 Little man, you've had a busy day.
title of song (1934)

Alan Sillitoe 1928–

English writer

4 The loneliness of the long-distance runner.
title of novel (1959)

Frank Silver 1892–1960 and Irving Cohn 1898–1961

5 Yes! we have no bananas,
We have no bananas today.
'Yes! We Have No Bananas' (1923 song)

Georges Simenon 1903–89

Belgian novelist

6 Writing is not a profession but a vocation of unhappiness.
interview in Paris Review Summer 1955

Neil Simon 1927–

American dramatist

7 I *love* living. I have some problems with my *life*, but living is the best thing they've come up with so far.
Last of the Red Hot Lovers (1970)

Paul Simon 1942–

American singer and songwriter

8 Like a bridge over troubled water
I will lay me down.
'Bridge over Troubled Water' (1970 song)

9 And here's to you, Mrs Robinson
Jesus loves you more than you will know.
'Mrs Robinson' (1967 song, from the film The Graduate)

10 People talking without speaking
People hearing without listening . . .
'Fools,' said I, 'You do not know
Silence like a cancer grows.'
'Sound of Silence' (1964 song)

11 Improvisation is too good to leave to chance.
in International Herald Tribune 12 October 1990

John Simpson 1944–

British journalist

12 I'm sick to death of the 'I'm going to tell you everything about me and what I think' school of journalism. You don't watch the BBC for polemic.
interview in Radio Times 9 August 1997

13 You might get bigger audiences for 'Noble Rover, the labrador, who saved beautiful baby in fire', but that ain't news—just an insidious form of patronising propaganda.
on the desirability of promoting 'good news' stories
interview in Radio Times 9 August 1997

Kirke Simpson 1881–1972

American journalist

14 [Warren] Harding of Ohio was chosen by a group of men in a smoke-filled room early today as Republican candidate for President.
often attributed to Harry Daugherty, one of Harding's supporters, who appears merely to have concurred with this version of events, when pressed for comment by Simpson
news report, filed 12 June 1920; W. Safire New Language of Politics (1968)

C. H. Sisson 1914–

English poet

1 Here lies a civil servant. He was civil
To everyone, and servant to the devil.
The London Zoo (1961)

Edith Sitwell 1887–1964

English poet and critic
on Sitwell: see **Bowen** 42:15, **Coward** 79:4,
Leavis 186:2

2 Jane, Jane,
Tall as a crane,
The morning light creaks down again.
Façade (1923) 'Aubade'

3 The fire was furry as a bear.
Façade (1923) 'Dark Song'

4 Still falls the Rain—
Dark as the world of man, black as our
loss—
Blind as the nineteen hundred and forty
nails
Upon the Cross.
'Still Falls the Rain' (1942)

5 I enjoyed talking to her, but thought
nothing of her writing. I considered her 'a
beautiful little knitter'.
of Virginia **Woolf**
letter to Geoffrey Singleton, 11 July 1955

Osbert Sitwell 1892–1969

English writer
on Sitwell: see **Coward** 79:4, **Leavis** 186:2

6 The British Bourgeoise
Is not born,
And does not die,
But, if it is ill,
It has a frightened look in its eyes.
At the House of Mrs Kinfoot (1921)

7 On the coast of Coromandel
Dance they to the tunes of Handel.
'On the Coast of Coromandel' (1943)

8 *Educ*: during the holidays from Eton.
entry in *Who's Who* (1929)

'Red' Skelton 1913–

American comedian

9 Well, it only proves what they always
say—give the public something they
want to see, and they'll come out for it.
on crowds attending the funeral of Harry Cohn
comment, on 2 March 1958; Bob Thomas *King
Cohn* (1967)

B. F. Skinner 1904–90

American psychologist

10 The real question is not whether
machines think but whether men do.
Contingencies of Reinforcement (1969)

11 Education is what survives when what
has been learned has been forgotten.
in *New Scientist* 21 May 1964

Gillian Slovo 1952–

South African writer

12 In most families it is the children who
leave home. In mine it was the parents.
*of her anti-apartheid activist parents, Joe Slovo
and Ruth First*
Every Secret Thing (1997)

Alfred Emanuel Smith
1873–1944

American politician

13 All the ills of democracy can be cured by
more democracy.
speech in Albany, 27 June 1933

14 No sane local official who has hung up
an empty stocking over the municipal
fireplace, is going to shoot Santa Claus
just before a hard Christmas.
on the New Deal
in *New Outlook* December 1933

Delia Smith

English cookery expert

15 Football and cookery are the two most
important subjects in the country.
*having been appointed a director of Norwich City
football club*
in *Observer* 23 February 1997 'Said and Done'

Dodie Smith 1896–1990

English novelist and dramatist

1 The family—that dear octopus from
whose tentacles we never quite escape.
   Dear Octopus (1938)

F. E. Smith, Lord Birkenhead
1872–1930

British Conservative politician and lawyer
on Smith: see **Chesterton** 61:16

2 The world continues to offer glittering
prizes to those who have stout hearts and
sharp swords.
   Rectorial Address, Glasgow University, 7
   November 1923

3 JUDGE: You are extremely offensive,
young man.
SMITH: As a matter of fact, we both are,
and the only difference between us is that
I am trying to be, and you can't help it.
   2nd Earl of Birkenhead *Earl of Birkenhead*
   (1933)

4 JUDGE DARLING: And who is George
Robey?
SMITH: Mr George Robey is the Darling of
the music halls, m'lud.
   A. E. Wilson *The Prime Minister of Mirth* (1956)

Godfrey Smith 1926–

English journalist and columnist

5 In a world full of audio visual marvels,
may words matter to you and be full of
magic.
   letter to a new grandchild, in *Sunday Times* 5
   July 1987

Ian Smith 1919–

Rhodesian statesman; Prime Minister,
1964–79

6 I don't believe in black majority rule in
Rhodesia—not in a thousand years.
   broadcast speech, 20 March 1976

Logan Pearsall Smith
1865–1946

American-born man of letters

7 What music is more enchanting than the
voices of young people, when you can't
hear what they say?
   Afterthoughts (1931) 'Age and Death'

8 The denunciation of the young is a
necessary part of the hygiene of older
people, and greatly assists the circulation
of their blood.
   Afterthoughts (1931) 'Age and Death'

9 A best-seller is the gilded tomb of a
mediocre talent.
   Afterthoughts (1931) 'Art and Letters'

10 People say that life is the thing, but I
prefer reading.
   Afterthoughts (1931) 'Myself'

11 Thank heavens, the sun has gone in, and
I don't have to go out and enjoy it.
   Afterthoughts (1931) 'Myself'

12 When they come downstairs from their
Ivory Towers, Idealists are very apt to
walk straight into the gutter.
   Afterthoughts (1931) 'Other People'

13 All Reformers, however strict their social
conscience, live in houses just as big as
they can pay for.
   Afterthoughts (1931) 'Other People'

Stevie Smith 1902–71

English poet and novelist

14 Oh I am a cat that likes to
Gallop about doing good.
   'The Galloping Cat' (1972)

15 Why does my Muse only speak when she
is unhappy?
She does not, I only listen when I am
unhappy
When I am happy I live and despise
writing
For my Muse this cannot but be
· dispiriting.
   'My Muse' (1964)

1 I was much too far out all my life
   And not waving but drowning.
   'Not Waving but Drowning' (1957)

2 People who are always praising the past
   And especially the times of faith as best
   Ought to go and live in the Middle Ages
   And be burnt at the stake as witches and
   sages.
   'The Past' (1957)

3 Private Means is dead
   God rest his soul, officers and fellow-
   rankers said.
   'Private Means is Dead' (1962)

4 This Englishwoman is so refined
   She has no bosom and no behind.
   'This Englishwoman' (1937)

5 I long for the Person from Porlock
   To bring my thoughts to an end,
   I am growing impatient to see him
   I think of him as a friend.
   'Thoughts about the "Person from Porlock" '
   (1962); see below

   At this moment he was unfortunately
   called out by a person on business
   from Porlock.
   Samuel Taylor Coleridge (1772–1834) 'Kubla
   Khan' (1816) preliminary note

6 A good time was had by all.
   title of book (1937)

7 If there wasn't death, I think you
   couldn't go on.
   in Observer 9 November 1969

Jan Christiaan Smuts

1870–1950

South African soldier and statesman, Prime
Minister 1919–24 and 1939–48

8 Mankind is once more on the move. The
   very foundations have been shaken and
   loosened, and things are again fluid. The
   tents have been struck, and the great
   caravan of humanity is once more on the
   march.
   on the setting up of the League of Nations, in the
   wake of the First World War
   W. K. Hancock Smuts (1968)

John Snagge 1904–96

English sports commentator

9 I can't see who's in the lead but it's
   either Oxford or Cambridge.
   commentary on the 1949 Boat Race
   C. Dodd Oxford and Cambridge Boat Race
   (1983)

C. P. Snow 1905–80

English novelist and scientist

10 The official world, the corridors of power.
    Homecomings (1956)

11 The two cultures and the scientific
    revolution.
    title of The Rede Lecture (1959)

Alexander Solzhenitsyn
1918–

Russian novelist

12 If decade after decade the truth cannot be
    told, each person's mind begins to roam
    irretrievably. One's fellow countrymen
    become harder to understand than
    Martians.
    Cancer Ward (1968)

13 You only have power over people as long
    as you don't take *everything* away from
    them. But when you've robbed a man of
    everything he's no longer in your
    power—he's free again.
    The First Circle (1968)

14 The Gulag archipelago.
    title of book (1973–5)

15 Work was like a stick. It had two ends.
    When you worked for the knowing you
    gave them quality; when you worked for
    a fool you simply gave him eye-wash.
    One Day in the Life of Ivan Denisovich (1962)

16 How can you expect a man who's warm
    to understand one who's cold?
    One Day in the Life of Ivan Denisovich (1962)

17 The thoughts of a prisoner—they're not
    free either. They keep returning to the
    same things.
    One Day in the Life of Ivan Denisovich (1962)

1 In our country the lie has become not just a moral category but a pillar of the State.

> 1974 interview, printed in appendix to *The Oak and the Calf* (1975)

2 After the suffering of decades of violence and oppression, the human soul longs for higher things, warmer and purer than those offered by today's mass living habits, introduced as by a calling card by the revolting invasion of commercial advertising, by TV stupor and by intolerable music.

> speech in Cambridge, Massachusetts, 8 June 1978

3 Yes, we are still the prisoners of communism, and yet, for us in Russia, communism is a dead dog, while for many people in the West it is still a living lion.

> broadcast on BBC Russian Service, in *Listener* 15 February 1979

4 The clock of communism has stopped striking. But its concrete building has not yet come crashing down. For that reason, instead of freeing ourselves, we must try to save ourselves being crushed by the rubble.

> in *Komsomolskaya Pravda* 18 September 1990

5 The Iron Curtain did not reach the ground and under it flowed liquid manure from the West.

> speaking at Far Eastern Technical University, Vladivostok, 30 May 1994; cf. **Churchill** 67:9

Anastasio Somoza 1925–80

Nicaraguan dictator

6 You won the elections, but I won the count.

> *replying to an accusation of ballot-rigging*
> in *Guardian* 17 June 1977

Stephen Sondheim 1930–

American songwriter

7 I like to be in America!
OK by me in America!
Ev'rything free in America
For a small fee in America!

> 'America' (1957 song)

8 Everything's coming up roses.

> title of song (1959)

9 A toast to that invincible bunch
The dinosaurs surviving the crunch
Let's hear it for the ladies who lunch.

> 'The Ladies who Lunch' (1970)

10 Send in the clowns

> title of song (1973)

11 Isn't it rich?
Are we a pair?
Me here at last on the ground, you in mid-air.

> 'Send in the Clowns' (1973 song)

Susan Sontag 1933–

American writer

12 Societies need to have one illness which becomes identified with evil, and attaches blame to its 'victims'.

> *AIDS and its Metaphors* (1989)

13 Interpretation is the revenge of the intellect upon art.

> in *Evergreen Review* December 1964

14 What pornography is really about, ultimately, isn't sex but death.

> in *Partisan Review* Spring 1967

15 The truth is that Mozart, Pascal, Boolean algebra, Shakespeare, parliamentary government, baroque churches, Newton, the emancipation of women, Kant, Marx, Balanchine ballet *et al.*, don't redeem what this particular civilization has wrought upon the world. The white race *is* the cancer of human history, it is the white race, and it alone—its ideologies and inventions—which eradicates autonomous civilizations wherever it spreads, which has upset the ecological balance of the planet, which now threatens the very existence of life itself.

> in *Partisan Review* Winter 1967

16 The camera makes everyone a tourist in other people's reality, and eventually in one's own.

> in *New York Review of Books* 18 April 1974

17 Illness is the night-side of life, a more onerous citizenship. Everyone who is born holds dual citizenship, in the

kingdom of the well and in the kingdom of the sick.

in *New York Review of Books* 26 January 1978

Charles Hamilton Sorley

1895–1915

English poet

1 We swing ungirded hips,
And lightened are our eyes,
The rain is on our lips,
We do not run for prize.

'Song of the Ungirt Runners' (1916)

2 When you see millions of the mouthless dead
Across your dreams in pale battalions go,
Say not soft things as other men have said,
That you'll remember. For you need not so.
Give them not praise. For, deaf, how should they know
It is not curses heaped on each gashed head?

'A Sonnet' (1916)

3 I do wish people would not deceive themselves by talk of a just war. There is no such thing as a just war. What we are doing is casting out Satan by Satan.

letter to his mother from Aldershot, March 1915

John Philip Sousa 1854–1932

American composer and conductor

4 Jazz will endure, just as long as people hear it through their feet instead of their brains.

Nat Shapiro (ed.) *An Encyclopedia of Quotations about Music* (1978)

Muriel Spark 1918–

British novelist

5 From my experience of life I believe my personal motto should be 'Beware of men bearing flowers.'

Curriculum Vitae (1992)

6 I am a hoarder of two things: documents and trusted friends.

Curriculum Vitae (1992)

7 I used to think it a pity that her mother rather than she had not thought of birth control.

of Marie **Stopes**
Curriculum Vitae (1992)

8 Parents learn a lot from their children about coping with life.

The Comforters (1957)

9 I am putting old heads on your young shoulders . . . all my pupils are the crème de la crème.

The Prime of Miss Jean Brodie (1961)

10 Give me a girl at an impressionable age, and she is mine for life.

The Prime of Miss Jean Brodie (1961)

11 One's prime is elusive. You little girls, when you grow up, must be on the alert to recognise your prime at whatever time of your life it may occur.

The Prime of Miss Jean Brodie (1961)

12 If you're going to do a thing, you should do it thoroughly. If you're going to be a Christian, you may as well be a Catholic.

in *Independent* 2 August 1989

John Sparrow 1906–92

English barrister and academic, Warden of All Souls College, Oxford, 1952–77
see also **Epitaphs** 106:3

13 That indefatigable and unsavoury engine of pollution, the dog.

letter to *The Times* 30 September 1975

Phil Spector 1940–

American record producer and songwriter

14 I'm dealing in rock'n'roll. I'm, like, I'm not a bona fide human being.

attributed

Lord Spencer 1964–

English peer

15 I always believed the press would kill her in the end. But not even I could believe they would take such a direct hand in her death as seems to be the case . . .
Every proprietor and editor of every publication that has paid for intrusive

and exploitative photographs of her . . . has blood on their hands today.

*on the death of his sister, **Diana**, Princess of Wales, in a car crash while being pursued by photographers, 31 August 1997*

in *Daily Telegraph* 1 September 1997

1 She needed no royal title to continue to generate her particular brand of magic.

*tribute at the funeral of his sister, **Diana**, Princess of Wales, 7 September 1997*

in *Guardian* 8 September 1997

2 A girl given the name of the ancient goddess of hunting was, in the end, the most hunted person of the modern age.

funeral tribute, 7 September 1997

in *Guardian* 8 September 1997

3 We, your blood family, will do all we can to continue the imaginative way in which you were steering these two exceptional young men so that their souls are not simply immersed by duty and tradition but can sing openly as you planned.

referring to his nephews, Prince William and Prince Harry; funeral tribute, 7 September 1997

in *Guardian* 8 September 1997

Raine, Countess Spencer
1929–

4 Alas, for our towns and cities. Monstrous carbuncles of concrete have erupted in gentle Georgian Squares.

The Spencers on Spas (1983); cf. **Charles** 61:13

Stanley Spencer 1891–1959

English painter
on Spencer: see **Lewis** 190:16

5 Painting is saying 'Ta' to God.

letter from Spencer's daughter Shirin, in *Observer* 7 February 1988

Stephen Spender 1909–95

English poet
on Spender: see **Waugh** 321:14; *see also* **Pollitt** 250:11

6 After the first powerful plain manifesto
The black statement of pistons, without more fuss

But gliding like a queen, she leaves the station.

'The Express' (1933)

7 I think continually of those who were truly great.

'I think continually of those who were truly great' (1933)

8 Born of the sun they travelled a short while towards the sun,
And left the vivid air signed with their honour.

'I think continually of those who were truly great' (1933)

9 My parents kept me from children who were rough
And who threw words like stones and who wore torn clothes.

'My parents kept me from children who were rough' (1933)

10 Never being, but always at the edge of Being.

title of poem (1933)

11   Their collected
Hearts wound up with love, like little watch springs.

'The Past Values' (1939)

12 Pylons, those pillars
Bare like nude, giant girls that have no secret.

'The Pylons' (1933)

13 But far above and far as sight endures
Like whips of anger
With lightning's danger
There runs the quick perspective of the future.

'The Pylons' (1933)

14 Consider: only one bullet in ten thousand kills a man.
Ask: was so much expenditure justified
On the death of one so young and so silly
Stretched under the olive trees, Oh, world, Oh, death?

'Regum Ultimo Ratio' (1939)

15 What I had not foreseen
Was the gradual day
Weakening the will

Leaking the brightness away.
'What I expected, was' (1933)

1 Who live under the shadow of a war,
What can I do that matters?
'Who live under the shadow of a war' (1933)

2 People sometimes divide others into those
you laugh at and those you laugh with.
The young Auden was someone you
could laugh-at-with.
W. H. Auden (address delivered at Auden's
memorial service in Oxford, 27 October 1973)

3 The nineties is a good time to die.
Joseph Brodsky *On Grief and Reason* (1996)

Oswald Spengler 1880–1936

German philosopher

4 Socialism is nothing but the capitalism of
the lower classes.
The Hour of Decision (1933)

Spice Girls

see **Chisholm, Rowbottom**

Benjamin Spock 1903–

American paediatrician and writer

5 You know more than you think you do.
Common Sense Book of Baby and Child Care
(1946) [later *Baby and Child Care*], opening
words

6 To win in Vietnam, we will have to
exterminate a nation.
Dr Spock on Vietnam (1968)

William Archibald Spooner
1844–1930

English clergyman and scholar; Warden of
New College, Oxford, 1903–24

7 Her late husband, you know, a very sad
death—eaten by missionaries—poor
soul!
William Hayter *Spooner* (1977)

8 Our queer old dean.
toast said to have been proposed by Spooner
Oxford University What's What (1948); William
Hayter in *Spooner* (1977) maintains this saying
is apocryphal

9 You have tasted your worm, you have
hissed my mystery lectures, and you
must leave by the first town drain.
to an undergraduate
Oxford University What's What (1948); William
Hayter in *Spooner* (1977) maintains this saying
is apocryphal

10 You will find as you grow older that the
weight of rages will press harder and
harder upon the employer.
William Hayter *Spooner* (1977)

Cecil Spring-Rice 1859–1918

British diplomat; Ambassador to
Washington from 1912

11 I vow to thee, my country—all earthly
things above—
Entire and whole and perfect, the service
of my love,
The love that asks no question: the love
that stands the test,
That lays upon the altar the dearest and
the best:
The love that never falters, the love that
pays the price,
The love that makes undaunted the final
sacrifice.
'I Vow to Thee, My Country' (written on the eve
of his departure from Washington, 12 January
1918)

Bruce Springsteen 1949–

American rock singer and songwriter

12 Born in the USA.
title of song (1984)

13 Born down in a dead man's town
The first kick I took was when I hit the
ground.
'Born in the USA' (1984 song)

14 We gotta get out while we're young,
'Cause tramps like us, baby, we were
born to run.
'Born to Run' (1974 song)

J. C. Squire 1884–1958

English man of letters

1 I'm not so think as you drunk I am.

'Ballade of Soporific Absorption' (1931)

2 It did not last: the Devil howling 'Ho!
Let Einstein be!' restored the status quo.

'In continuation of Pope on Newton' (1926);
see below

Nature, and Nature's laws lay hid in
night.
God said, *Let Newton be!* and all was
light.

Alexander Pope (1688–1744) 'Epitaph:
Intended for Sir Isaac Newton' (1730)

3 God heard the embattled nations sing
and shout
'Gott strafe England!' and 'God save the
King!'
God this, God that, and God the other
thing—
'Good God!' said God, 'I've got my work
cut out.'

'The Dilemma' (1916); cf. **Funke** 122:6

Joseph Stalin 1879–1953

Soviet dictator

4 The State is an instrument in the hands
of the ruling class, used to break the
resistance of the adversaries of that class.

Foundations of Leninism (1924)

5 There are various forms of production:
artillery, automobiles, lorries. You also
produce 'commodities', 'works',
'products'. Such things are highly
necessary. Engineering things. For
people's souls. 'Products' are highly
necessary too. 'Products' are very
important for people's souls. You are
engineers of human souls.

speech to writers at **Gorky**'s house, 26 October
1932; A. Kemp-Welch *Stalin and the Literary
Intelligentsia, 1928–39* (1991); cf. **Gorky** 131:1

6 The Pope! How many divisions has *he*
got?

*on being asked to encourage Catholicism in
Russia by way of conciliating the Pope, 13 May
1935*

W. S. Churchill *The Gathering Storm* (1948)

7 One death is a tragedy, a million deaths a
statistic.

attributed

Charles E. Stanton 1859–1933

American soldier

8 *Lafayette, nous voilà!*
Lafayette, we are here.

at the tomb of Lafayette in Paris, 4 July 1917

Freya Stark 1893–1993

English writer and traveller

9 The great and almost only comfort about
being a woman is that one can always
pretend to be more stupid than one is and
no one is surprised.

The Valleys of the Assassins (1934)

Enid Starkie 1897–1970

English academic

10 Unhurt people are not much good in the
world.

letter, 18 June 1943; Joanna Richardson *Enid
Starkie* (1973); cf. **Hart** 141:5

Christina Stead 1902–83

Australian novelist

11 If all the rich people in the world divided
up their money among themselves there
wouldn't be enough to go round.

House of All Nations (1938)

12 A self-made man is one who believes in
luck and sends his son to Oxford.

House of All Nations (1938)

David Steel 1938–

British Liberal politician; Leader of the
Liberal Party 1976–88

13 I have the good fortune to be the first
Liberal leader for over half a century who
is able to say to you at the end of our
annual assembly: go back to your
constituencies and prepare for
government.

speech to the Liberal Party Assembly, 18
September 1981

Lincoln Steffens 1866–1936

American journalist

1 I have seen the future; and it works.
following a visit to the Soviet Union in 1919
    letter to Marie Howe, 3 April 1919

Gertrude Stein 1874–1946

American writer
on Stein: see **Anonymous** 9:16, **Fadiman**
106:7, **Lewis** 190:16; *see also* **Last words**
183:2

2 Remarks are not literature.
Autobiography of Alice B. Toklas (1933)

3 In the United States there is more space
where nobody is than where anybody is.
That is what makes America what it is.
The Geographical History of America (1936)

4 Disillusionment in living is the finding
out nobody agrees with you not those
that are and were fighting with you.
Disillusionment in living is the finding
out nobody agrees with you not those
that are fighting for you. Complete
disillusionment is when you realise that
no one can for they can't change.
Making of Americans (1934)

5 Rose is a rose is a rose is a rose, is a rose.
Sacred Emily (1913)

6 You are all a lost generation.
of the young who served in the First World War
    subsequently taken by Ernest **Hemingway** as
    epigraph to *The Sun Also Rises* (1926)

7 A village explainer, excellent if you were
a village, but if you were not, not.
of Ezra **Pound**
    Janet Hobhouse *Everyone who was Anybody*
    (1975)

John Steinbeck 1902–68

American novelist

8 Man, unlike any other thing organic or
inorganic in the universe, grows beyond
his work, walks up the stairs of his
concepts, emerges ahead of his
accomplishments.
The Grapes of Wrath (1939)

9 I know this—a man got to do what he
got to do.
The Grapes of Wrath (1939)

10 Okie use' ta mean you was from
Oklahoma. Now it means you're a dirty
son-of-a-bitch. Okie means you're scum.
Don't mean nothing itself, it's the way
they say it.
The Grapes of Wrath (1939)

Gloria Steinem 1934–

American journalist

11 We are becoming the men we wanted to
marry.
    in *Ms* July/August 1982

12 A woman without a man is like a fish
without a bicycle.
    attributed

George Steiner 1926–

American French-born critic and writer

13 Nothing is more symptomatic of the
enervation, of the decompression of the
Western imagination, than our
incapacity to respond to the landings on
the Moon. Not a single great poem,
picture, metaphor has come of this
breathtaking act, of Prometheus' rescue
of Icarus or of Phaeton in flight towards
the stars.
    'Modernity, Mythology and Magic', lecture at
    the 1994 Salzburg Festival; in *Guardian* 6
    August 1994

Casey Stengel 1891–1975

American baseball player and manager

14 All you have to do is keep the five players
who hate your guts away from the five
who are undecided.
    John Samuel (ed.) *The Guardian Book of Sports
    Quotes* (1985)

James Stephens 1882–1950

Irish poet and writer

15 Finality is death. Perfection is finality.
Nothing is perfect. There are lumps in it.
The Crock of Gold (1912)

1 I hear a sudden cry of pain!
There is a rabbit in a snare:
Now I hear the cry again,
But I cannot tell from where . . .
Little one! Oh, little one!
I am searching everywhere.
'The Snare' (1915)

Anthony Stevens

2 Whereas nature turns girls into women,
society has to make boys into men.
Archetype (1982)

Brooks Stevens 1911–

American industrial designer

3 Our whole economy is based on planned
obsolescence.
V. Packard *The Waste Makers* (1960)

Wallace Stevens 1879–1955

American poet

4 The poet is the priest of the invisible.
'Adagia' (1957)

5 Chieftain Iffucan of Azcan in caftan
Of tan with henna hackles, halt!
'Bantams in Pine Woods' (1923)

6 Call the roller of big cigars,
The muscular one, and bid him whip
In kitchen cups concupiscent curds.
'The Emperor of Ice-Cream' (1923)

7 Let be be finale of seem.
The only emperor is the emperor of ice-
cream.
'The Emperor of Ice-Cream' (1923)

8 Frogs eat butterflies. Snakes eat frogs.
Hogs eat snakes. Men eat hogs.
title of poem (1923)

9 Poetry is the supreme fiction, madame.
'A High-Toned old Christian Woman' (1923)

10 They said, 'You have a blue guitar,
You do not play things as they are.'

The man replied, 'Things as they are
Are changed upon the blue guitar.'
'The Man with the Blue Guitar' (1937)

11 Twenty men crossing a bridge,
Into a village,
Are twenty men crossing twenty bridges,
Into twenty villages,
Or one man
Crossing a single bridge into a village.
'Metaphors of a Magnifico' (1923)

12 The inconceivable idea of the sun.

You must become an ignorant man
again
And see the sun again with an ignorant
eye
And see it clearly in the idea of it.
Notes Toward a Supreme Fiction (1947) 'It Must
Be Abstract' no. 1

13 They will get it straight one day at the
Sorbonne.
We shall return at twilight from the
lecture
Pleased that the irrational is rational.
Notes Toward a Supreme Fiction (1947) 'It Must
Give Pleasure' no. 10

14 Music is feeling, then, not sound.
'Peter Quince at the Clavier' (1923)

15 Beauty is momentary in the mind—
The fitful tracing of a portal;
But in the flesh it is immortal.
The body dies; the body's beauty lives.
'Peter Quince at the Clavier' (1923)

16 Complacencies of the peignoir, and late
Coffee and oranges in a sunny chair,
And the green freedom of a cockatoo
Upon a rug mingle to dissipate
The holy hush of ancient sacrifice.
'Sunday Morning' (1923)

17 I do not know which to prefer,
The beauty of inflections
Or the beauty of innuendoes,
The blackbird whistling
Or just after.
'Thirteen Ways of Looking at a Blackbird'
(1923)

Adlai Stevenson 1900–65

American Democratic politician

18 I suppose flattery hurts no one, that is, if
he doesn't inhale.
television broadcast, 30 March 1952

19 If they [the Republicans] will stop telling
lies about the Democrats, we will stop
telling the truth about them.
speech during 1952 Presidential campaign; J.
B. Martin *Adlai Stevenson and Illinois* (1976)

1 Let's talk sense to the American people. Let's tell them the truth, that there are no gains without pains.

> speech of acceptance at the Democratic National Convention, 26 July 1952

2 A hungry man is not a free man.

> speech at Kasson, Minnesota, 6 September 1952

3 There is no evil in the atom; only in men's souls.

> speech at Hartford, Connecticut, 18 September 1952

4 In America any boy may become President and I suppose it's just one of the risks he takes!

> speech in Indianapolis, 26 September 1952

5 A free society is a society where it is safe to be unpopular.

> speech in Detroit, 7 October 1952

6 The young man [Richard Nixon] who asks you to set him one heart-beat from the Presidency of the United States.

> commonly quoted as 'just a heart-beat away . . . '
> speech at Cleveland, Ohio, 23 October 1952

7 We hear the Secretary of State boasting of his brinkmanship—the art of bringing us to the edge of the abyss.

> speech in Hartford, Connecticut, 25 February 1956; cf. **Dulles** 92:9

8 She would rather light a candle than curse the darkness, and her glow has warmed the world.

> on learning of Eleanor **Roosevelt**'s death
> in New York Times 8 November 1962

9 The kind of politician who would cut down a redwood tree, and then mount the stump and make a speech on conservation.

> of Richard **Nixon**
> Fawn M. Brodie Richard Nixon (1983)

Anne Stevenson 1933–

English poet

10 Blackbirds are the cellos of the deep farms.

> 'Green Mountain, Black Mountain' (1982)

Sting 1951–

English rock singer, songwriter, and actor

11 If I were a Brazilian without land or money or the means to feed my children, I would be burning the rain forest too.

> in International Herald Tribune 14 April 1989

Mervyn Stockwood 1913–95

English Anglican clergyman, Bishop of Southwark 1959–80

12 A psychiatrist is a man who goes to the Folies-Bergère and looks at the audience.

> in Observer 15 October 1961

Leopold Stokowski 1882–1977

Polish-born American conductor

13 On matters of intonation and technicalities I am more than a martinet—I am a martinetissimo!

> Nat Shapiro (ed.) An Encyclopedia of Quotations about Music (1978)

Marie Stopes 1880–1958

Scottish pioneer of birth-control clinics
on Stopes: see **Spark** 292:7

14 An impersonal and scientific knowledge of the structure of our bodies is the surest safeguard against prurient curiosity and lascivious gloating.

> Married Love (1918)

Tom Stoppard 1937–

Czechoslovakian-born British dramatist

15 It's not the voting that's democracy, it's the counting.

> Jumpers (1972)

16 My problem is that I am not frightfully interested in anything, except myself. And of all forms of fiction autobiography is the most gratuitous.

> Lord Malquist and Mr Moon (1966)

17 The House of Lords, an illusion to which I have never been able to subscribe—responsibility without power, the

prerogative of the eunuch throughout the ages.
> *Lord Malquist and Mr Moon* (1966); cf. **Kipling** 175:17

1 The media. It sounds like a convention of spiritualists.
> *Night and Day* (1978)

2 I'm with you on the free press. It's the newspapers I can't stand.
> *Night and Day* (1978)

3 Comment is free but facts are on expenses.
> *Night and Day* (1978); cf. **Scott** 281:11

4 Save the gerund and screw the whale.
> *The Real Thing* (1982); cf. **Sayings and slogans** 279:6

5 We do on stage things that are supposed to happen off. Which is a kind of integrity, if you look on every exit as being an entrance somewhere else.
> *Rosencrantz and Guildenstern Are Dead* (1967)

6 I can do you blood and love without the rhetoric, and I can do you blood and rhetoric without the love, and I can do you all three concurrent or consecutive, but I can't do you love and rhetoric without the blood. Blood is compulsory—they're all blood, you see.
> *Rosencrantz and Guildenstern are Dead* (1967)

7 We're *actors*—we're the opposite of people! . . . Think, in your head, *now*, think of the most . . . *private* . . . *secret* . . . *intimate* thing you have ever done secure in the knowledge of its privacy . . . Are you thinking of it? . . . *Well, I saw you do it!*
> *Rosencrantz and Guildenstern Are Dead* (1967)

8 Eternity's a terrible thought. I mean, where's it all going to end?
> *Rosencrantz and Guildenstern are Dead* (1967)

9 The bad end unhappily, the good unluckily. That is what tragedy means.
> *Rosencrantz and Guildenstern are Dead* (1967)

10 Life is a gamble at terrible odds—if it was a bet, you wouldn't take it.
> *Rosencrantz and Guildenstern are Dead* (1967)

11 War is capitalism with the gloves off and many who go to war know it but they go

to war because they don't want to be a hero.
> *Travesties* (1975)

12 Childhood is Last Chance Gulch for happiness. After that, you know too much.
> *Where Are They Now?* (1973)

13 Maturity is a high price to pay for growing up.
> *Where Are They Now?* (1973)

14 I doubt that art needed Ruskin any more than a moving train needs one of its passengers to shove it.
> in *Times Literary Supplement* 3 June 1977

15 I don't think I can be expected to take seriously any game which takes less than three days to reach its conclusion.
> *a cricket enthusiast on baseball*
> in *Guardian* 24 December 1984 'Sports Quotes of the Year'

Lytton Strachey 1880–1932
English biographer
see also **Last words** 182:7

16 Ignorance is the first requisite of the historian—ignorance, which simplifies and clarifies, which selects and omits, with a placid perfection unattainable by the highest art.
> *Eminent Victorians* (1918) preface

17 CHAIRMAN OF MILITARY TRIBUNAL: What would you do if you saw a German soldier trying to violate your sister?
STRACHEY: I would try to get between them.
> *otherwise rendered as, 'I should interpose my body'*
> Robert Graves *Good-bye to All That* (1929)

18 Discretion is not the better part of biography.
> M. Holroyd *Lytton Strachey* (1967) vol. 1

William L. Strauss and A. J. E. Cave

19 Notwithstanding, if he could be reincarnated and placed in a New York subway—provided that he were bathed, shaved, and dressed in modern clothing—it is doubtful whether he would attract any more attention than some of its other denizens.

of Neanderthal man

in *Quarterly Review of Biology* Winter 1957

Igor Stravinsky 1882–1971

Russian composer

1 Tradition is entirely different from habit, even from an excellent habit, since habit is by definition an unconscious acquisition and tends to become mechanical, whereas tradition results from a conscious and deliberate acceptance . . . Tradition presupposes the reality of what endures.

Poetics of Music (1947)

2 Conductors' careers are made for the most part with 'romantic' music. 'Classic' music eliminates the conductor; we do not remember him in it.

Robert Craft *Conversations with Stravinsky* (1958)

3 My music is best understood by children and animals.

in *Observer* 8 October 1961

4 Academism results when the reasons for the rule change, but not the rule.

attributed

5 Music is, by its very nature, essentially powerless to *express* anything at all . . . music expresses itself.

in *Esquire* December 1972

John Whitaker ('Jack') Straw 1946–

British Labour politician

6 It's not because ageing wrinklies have tried to stop people having fun. It's because . . . these so-called soft drugs are potentially very dangerous.

asserting his opposition to the legalization of cannabis

on *Breakfast with Frost*, BBC1 TV, 4 January 1998

Janet Street-Porter 1946–

English broadcaster and programme-maker

7 A terminal blight has hit the TV industry nipping fun in the bud and stunting our growth. This blight is management—the dreaded Four M's: male, middle class, middle-aged and mediocre.

MacTaggart Lecture, Edinburgh Television Festival, 25 August 1995

Roy Strong 1935–

English art historian

8 You've got to have two out of death, sex and jewels.

the ingredients for a successful exhibition

in *Sunday Times* 23 January 1994

Randall E. Stross

9 American anti-intellectualism will never again be the same because of Bill Gates. Gates embodies what was supposed to be impossible—the practical intellectual.

The Microsoft Way (1996)

Simeon Strunsky 1879–1948

10 People who want to understand democracy should spend less time in the library with Aristotle and more time on the buses and in the subway.

No Mean City (1944)

11 Famous remarks are very seldom quoted correctly.

No Mean City (1944)

Jan Struther 1901–53

English-born novelist and hymn-writer

12 Lord of all hopefulness, Lord of all joy,
Whose trust, ever childlike, no cares
    could destroy,
Be there at our waking, and give us, we
    pray,
Your bliss in our hearts, Lord, at the
    break of the day.

'All Day Hymn' (1931)

G. A. Studdert Kennedy
1883–1929

British poet

1 When Jesus came to Birmingham they
  simply passed Him by,
  They never hurt a hair of Him, they only
  let Him die.
    'Indifference' (1921)

2 Waste of Blood, and waste of Tears,
  Waste of youth's most precious years,
  Waste of ways the saints have trod,
  Waste of Glory, waste of God,
  War!
    'Waste' (1919)

Andrew Sullivan 1963–

British journalist

3 Faces you had got used to seeing in the
  gym kept turning up on the obit pages.
    in *Independent on Sunday* 16 February 1997

J. W. N. Sullivan 1886–1937

4 It is much easier to make measurements
  than to know exactly what you are
  measuring.
    comment, 1928; R. L. Weber *More Random
    Walks in Science* (1982)

Louis Henri Sullivan
1856–1924

American architect

5 Form follows function.
    The Tall Office Building Artistically Considered
    (1896)

Arthur Hays Sulzberger
1891–1968

American newspaper proprietor

6 We tell the public which way the cat is
  jumping. The public will take care of the
  cat.
    on journalism
    in *Time* 8 May 1950

Edith Summerskill 1901–80

British Labour politician

7 Nagging is the repetition of unpalatable
  truths.
    speech to the Married Women's Association, 14
    July 1960

Jacqueline Susann 1921–74

American novelist

8 Valley of the dolls.
    title of novel (1966)

David Sutton 1944–

English poet

9 Sorrow in all lands, and grievous omens.
  Great anger in the dragon of the hills,
  And silent now the earth's green oracles
  That will not speak again of innocence.
    'Geomancies' (1991)

Hannen Swaffer 1879–1962

English journalist and critic

10 Freedom of the press in Britain means
   freedom to print such of the proprietor's
   prejudices as the advertisers don't object
   to.
    Tom Driberg *Swaff* (1974)

Gloria Swanson 1899–1983

American actress

11 There's a man here whose eyes are
   hurting me. Throw him out.
    of John **Grierson**
    Forsyth Hardy *John Grierson* (1979)

Herbert Bayard Swope
1882–1958

American journalist and editor
see also **Baruch** 24:9

12 The First Duty of a newspaper is to be
   Accurate. If it is Accurate, it follows that
   it is Fair.
    letter to *New York Herald Tribune* 16 March
    1958

1 He [Swope] enunciated no rules for success, but offered a sure formula for failure: *Just try to please everyone.*
  E. J. Kahn Jr. *World of Swope* (1965)

Thomas Szasz 1920–
Hungarian-born psychiatrist

2 A child becomes an adult when he realizes that he has a right not only to be right but also to be wrong.
  The Second Sin (1973) 'Childhood'

3 A teacher should have maximal authority and minimal power.
  The Second Sin (1973) 'Education'

4 Happiness is an imaginary condition, formerly often attributed by the living to the dead, now usually attributed by adults to children, and by children to adults.
  The Second Sin (1973) 'Emotions'

5 The stupid neither forgive nor forget; the naive forgive and forget; the wise forgive but do not forget.
  The Second Sin (1973) 'Personal Conduct'

6 If you talk to God, you are praying; if God talks to you, you have schizophrenia. If the dead talk to you, you are a spiritualist; if God talks to you, you are a schizophrenic.
  The Second Sin (1973) 'Schizophrenia'

7 Formerly, when religion was strong and science weak, men mistook magic for medicine; now, when science is strong and religion weak, men mistake medicine for magic.
  The Second Sin (1973) 'Science and Scientism'

8 Traditionally, sex has been a very private, secretive activity. Herein perhaps lies its powerful force for uniting people in a strong bond. As we make sex less secretive, we may rob it of its power to hold men and women together.
  The Second Sin (1973) 'Sex'

9 Two wrongs don't make a right, but they make a good excuse.
  The Second Sin (1973) 'Social Relations'

George Szell 1897–1970
American conductor

10 Conductors must give unmistakable and suggestive signals to the orchestra—not choreography to the audience.
  in *Newsweek* 28 January 1963

Albert von Szent-Györgyi 1893–1986
Hungarian-born biochemist

11 Discovery consists of seeing what everybody has seen and thinking what nobody has thought.
  I. Good (ed.) *The Scientist Speculates* (1962)

12 Water is life's *mater* and *matrix*, mother and medium. There is no life without water.
  in *Perspectives in Biology and Medicine* Winter 1971

Rabindranath Tagore 1861–1941
Bengali poet and philosopher

13 Bigotry tries to keep truth safe in its hand With a grip that kills it.
  Fireflies (1928)

14 Man goes into the noisy crowd to drown his own clamour of silence.
  'Stray Birds' (1916)

Nellie Talbot

15 Jesus wants me for a sunbeam.
  title of hymn (1921)

Derek Tangye 1912–96
English writer

16 The twentieth century decorates life like a Christmas cake, but it still cannot do anything about the basic ingredients.
  A Gull on the Roof (1961)

Sony Labou Tansi 1947–95
African writer

17 What good is an ounce of justice in an ocean of shit?
  The Antipeople (1983)

Bernie Taupin

see Elton **John** and Bernie Taupin

R. H. Tawney 1880–1962

British economic historian

1 Militarism . . . is fetish worship. It is the prostration of men's souls and the laceration of their bodies to appease an idol.
  The Acquisitive Society (1921)

2 Those who dread a dead-level of income or wealth . . . do not dread, it seems, a dead-level of law and order, and of security for life and property.
  Equality (4th ed., 1931)

3 Private property is a necessary institution, at least in a fallen world; men work more and dispute less when goods are private than when they are common. But it is to be tolerated as a concession to human frailty, not applauded as desirable in itself.
  Religion and the Rise of Capitalism (1926)

4 To take usury is contrary to Scripture; it is contrary to Aristotle; it is contrary to nature, for it is to live without labour; it is to sell time, which belongs to God, for the advantage of wicked men.
  Religion and the Rise of Capitalism (1926)

5 What harm have I ever done to the Labour Party?
  declining the offer of a peerage
  in *Evening Standard* 18 January 1962

A. J. P. Taylor 1906–90

English historian

6 History gets thicker as it approaches recent times.
  English History 1914–45 (1965) bibliography

7 The First World War had begun— imposed on the statesmen of Europe by railway timetables.
  The First World War (1963)

8 A racing tipster who only reached Hitler's level of accuracy would not do well for his clients.
  Origins of the Second World War (1962)

9 If men are to respect each other for what they are, they must cease to respect each other for what they own.
  Politicians, Socialism and Historians (1980)

10 Crimea: the war that would not boil.
  Rumours of Wars (1952)

11 The glories of his revolutionary triumph pale before the nobility of his later defeats.
  on **Trotsky**
  in *New Statesman and Nation* 20 February 1954

12 The magic of Shaw's words may still bewitch posterity . . . but it will find that he has nothing to say.
  in *Observer* 22 July 1956

13 Like most of those who study history, he [Napoleon III] learned from the mistakes of the past how to make new ones.
  in *Listener* 6 June 1963 'Mistaken Lessons from the Past'

14 A great showman whose technique improved as the real situation deteriorated.
  of **Mussolini**
  in *Observer* 28 February 1982

Ron Taylor

Scottish headteacher

15 Evil visited us yesterday. We don't know why.
  following the murder of sixteen children and their teacher at Dunblane primary school
  in *Daily Telegraph* 15 March 1996

Norman Tebbit 1931–

British Conservative politician
on Tebbit: see **Foot** 115:2

16 I grew up in the Thirties with our unemployed father. He did not riot, he got on his bike and looked for work.
  speech, 15 October 1981

17 The trigger of today's outburst of crime and violence . . . lies in the era and attitudes of postwar funk which gave birth to the 'permissive society'.
  in *Guardian* 4 November 1985

18 The cricket test—which side do they cheer for? . . . Are you still looking back

to where you came from or where you are?

on the loyalties of Britain's immigrant population
    interview in *Los Angeles Times*, reported in
    Daily Telegraph 20 April 1990

Pierre Teilhard de Chardin
1881–1955

French Jesuit philosopher and
palaeontologist
on Teilhard de Chardin: see **Pius XII** 249:17;
see also **Medawar** 212:3

1 The history of the living world can be
summarised as the elaboration of ever
more perfect eyes within a cosmos in
which there is always something more to
be seen.
    The Phenomenon of Man (1959)

■ Telegrams
see box opposite

William Temple 1881–1944

English theologian; Archbishop of
Canterbury from 1942

2 In place of the conception of the power-
state we are led to that of the welfare-
state.
    Citizen and Churchman (1941)

3 Christianity is the most materialistic of all
great religions.
    Readings in St John's Gospel (1939) vol. 1

4 Personally, I have always looked on
cricket as organized loafing.
    attributed

Mother Teresa 1910–97

Roman Catholic nun and missionary, born in
what is now Macedonia of Albanian
parentage

5 We ourselves feel that what we are doing
is just a drop in the ocean. But if that
drop was not in the ocean, I think the
ocean would be less because of that
missing drop. I do not agree with the big
way of doing things.
    A Gift for God (1975)

6 Now let us do something beautiful for
God.
    letter to Malcolm Muggeridge before making a
    BBC TV programme about the Missionaries of
    Charity, 1971; cf. **Muggeridge** 224:11

7 The biggest disease today is not leprosy
or tuberculosis, but rather the feeling of
being unwanted, uncared for and
deserted by everybody.
    in *The Observer* 3 October 1971

A. S. J. Tessimond 1902–62

8 Cats, no less liquid than their shadows,
Offer no angles to the wind.
    Cats (1934)

Margaret Thatcher 1925–

British Conservative stateswoman; Prime
Minister, 1979–90
on Thatcher: see **Anonymous** 10:3,
Callaghan 52:1, **Carrington** 54:4, **Critchley**
80:7, **Healey** 143:7, **Healey** 143:8, **Jenkins**
161:5, **Kinnock** 173:5, **Mitterand** 217:14,
Parris 244:12, **West** 325:6

9 No woman in my time will be Prime
Minister or Chancellor or Foreign
Secretary—not the top jobs. Anyway I
wouldn't want to be Prime Minister. You
have to give yourself 100%.
    *on her appointment as Shadow Education
    Spokesman*
    in *Sunday Telegraph* 26 October 1969

10 In politics if you want anything said, ask
a man. If you want anything done, ask a
woman.
    in *People* (New York) 15 September 1975

11 I stand before you tonight in my red
chiffon evening gown, my face softly
made up, my fair hair gently waved . . .
the Iron Lady of the Western World! Me?
A cold war warrior? Well, yes—if that is
how they wish to interpret my defence of
values and freedoms fundamental to our
way of life.
    speech at Finchley, 31 January 1976; cf.
    Anonymous 10:3

▶▶

Telegrams

1 AM IN MARKET HARBOROUGH. WHERE OUGHT I TO BE?

sent by G. K. Chesterton to his wife in London

G. K. Chesterton *Autobiography* (1936)

2 BETTER DROWNED THAN DUFFERS IF NOT DUFFERS WONT DROWN.

Arthur Ransome *Swallows and Amazons* (1930)

3 GOOD WORK, MARY. WE ALL KNEW YOU HAD IT IN YOU.

from Dorothy Parker to Mrs Sherwood on the arrival of her baby

Alexander Woollcott *While Rome Burns* (1934) 'Our Mrs Parker'

4 HOW DARE YOU BECOME PRIME MINISTER WHEN I'M AWAY GREAT LOVE CONSTANT THOUGHT VIOLET.

from Violet Bonham Carter (1887–1969) to her father, H. H. Asquith, 7 April 1908

Mark Bonham Carter and Mark Pottle (eds.) *Lantern Slides* (1996)

in response to a telegraphic enquiry, HOW OLD CARY GRANT?:

5 OLD CARY GRANT FINE. HOW YOU?

from Cary Grant (1904–86)

R. Schickel *Cary Grant* (1983)

6 STREETS FLOODED. PLEASE ADVISE.

message sent by Robert Benchley on arriving in Venice

R. E. Drennan (ed.) *Wits End* (1973)

▶▶ **Margaret Thatcher** continued

7 Where there is discord may we bring harmony.
Where there is error may we bring truth.
Where there is doubt may we bring faith.
Where there is despair may we bring hope.

Downing Street, London, 4 May 1979; see below

Lord, make me an instrument of Your peace!
Where there is hatred let me sow love;
Where there is injury, pardon;
Where there is doubt, faith;
Where there is despair, hope.

St Francis of Assisi (1181–1226) 'Prayer of St Francis' (attributed)

8 Pennies don't fall from heaven. They have to be earned on earth.

in *Observer* 18 November 1979 'Sayings of the Week'; cf. **Burke** 49:6

9 No one would remember the Good Samaritan if he'd only had good intentions. He had money as well.

television interview, 6 January 1980

10 I don't mind how much my Ministers talk, as long as they do what I say.

in *Observer* 27 January 1980

11 We have to get our production and our earnings in balance. There's no easy popularity in what we are proposing, but it is fundamentally sound. Yet I believe people accept there is no real alternative.

popularly encapsulated in the acronym TINA

speech at Conservative Women's Conference, 21 May 1980

12 To those waiting with bated breath for that favourite media catch-phrase, the U-turn, I have only this to say. 'You turn if you want; the lady's not for turning.'

speech at Conservative Party Conference in Brighton, 10 October 1980; cf. **Fry** 121:9

13 Economics are the method; the object is to change the soul.

in *Sunday Times* 3 May 1981

14 Just rejoice at that news and congratulate our armed forces and the Marines. Rejoice!

on the recapture of South Georgia, usually quoted as, 'Rejoice, rejoice!'

to newsmen outside 10 Downing Street, 25 April 1982

15 It is exciting to have a real crisis on your hands, when you have spent half your political life dealing with humdrum issues like the environment.

on the Falklands campaign, 1982

   speech to Scottish Conservative Party conference, 14 May 1982; Hugo Young *One of Us* (1990)

1 We have to see that the spirit of the South Atlantic—the real spirit of Britain—is kindled not only by war but can now be fired by peace. We have the first prerequisite. We know that we can do it—we haven't lost the ability. That is the Falklands Factor.

   speech in Cheltenham, 3 July 1982

2 Let me make one thing absolutely clear. The National Health Service is safe with us.

   speech at Conservative Party Conference, 8 October 1982

3 I was asked whether I was trying to restore Victorian values. I said straight out I was. And I am.

   speech to the British Jewish Community, 21 July 1983, referring to an interview with Brian Walden on 17 January 1983

4 Now it must be business as usual.

   on the steps of Brighton police station a few hours after the bombing of the Grand Hotel, Brighton; often quoted as 'We shall carry on as usual'

   in *The Times* 13 October 1984

5 In church on Sunday morning—it was a lovely morning and we haven't had many lovely days—the sun was coming through a stained glass window and falling on some flowers, falling right across the church. It just occurred to me that this was the day I was meant not to see.

   after the Brighton bombing

   television interview, 15 October 1984

6 We can do business together.

   *of Mikhail **Gorbachev***

   in *The Times* 18 December 1984

7 We must try to find ways to starve the terrorist and the hijacker of the oxygen of publicity on which they depend.

   speech, 15 July 1985

8 There is no such thing as Society. There are individual men and women, and there are families.

   in *Woman's Own* 31 October 1987

9 We have not successfully rolled back the frontiers of the State in Britain only to see them reimposed at European level, with a European super-State exercising a new dominance from Brussels.

   speech in Bruges, 20 September 1988

10 We have become a grandmother.

   in *The Times* 4 March 1989

11 I am extraordinarily patient, provided I get my own way in the end.

   in *Observer* 4 April 1989

12 Advisers advise and ministers decide.

   *on the respective roles of her personal economic adviser, Alan Walters, and her Chancellor, Nigel **Lawson** (who resigned the following day)*

   in the House of Commons, 26 October 1989

13 I am naturally very sorry to see you go, but understand . . . your wish to be able to spend more time with your family.

   *reply to Norman **Fowler's** resignation letter*

   in *Guardian* 4 January 1990; cf. **Fowler** 117:6

14 No! No! No!

   making clear her opposition to a single European currency, and more centralized controls from Brussels

   in the House of Commons, 30 October 1990

15 I fight on, I fight to win.

   having failed to win outright in the first ballot for party leader

   comment, 21 November 1990

16 It's a funny old world.

   on withdrawing from the contest for leadership of the Conservative party

   comment, 22 November 1990; cf. **Film lines** 110:15

17 I shan't be pulling the levers there but I shall be a very good back-seat driver.

   after leaving office as Prime Minister

   in *Independent* 27 November 1990

18 Home is where you come to when you have nothing better to do.

   in *Vanity Fair* May 1991

of the poll tax:

19 Given time, it would have been seen as one of the most far-reaching and beneficial reforms ever made in the working of local government.

   The Downing Street Years (1993)

20 I think sometimes the Prime Minister should be intimidating. There's not much

point being a weak, floppy thing in the chair, is there?

on 'The Thatcher Years' (BBC 1), 21 October 1993

Dylan Thomas 1914–53

Welsh poet

1 Though lovers be lost love shall not;
And death shall have no dominion.

'And death shall have no dominion' (1936); see below

Christ being raised from the dead dieth no more; death hath no more dominion over him.

Bible Romans

2 Do not go gentle into that good night,
Old age should burn and rave at close of day;
Rage, rage against the dying of the light.

'Do Not Go Gentle into that Good Night' (1952)

3 Now as I was young and easy under the apple boughs
About the lilting house and happy as the grass was green.

'Fern Hill' (1946)

4 The force that through the green fuse drives the flower
Drives my green age.

'The force that through the green fuse' (1934)

5 The hand that signed the paper felled a city;
Five sovereign fingers taxed the breath,
Doubled the globe of dead and halved a country;
These five kings did a king to death.

'The hand that signed the paper felled a city' (1936)

6 The hand that signed the treaty bred a fever,
And famine grew, and locusts came;
Great is the hand that holds dominion over
Man by a scribbled name.

'The hand that signed the paper felled a city' (1936)

7 Light breaks where no sun shines;
Where no sea runs, the waters of the heart
Push in their tides.

'Light breaks where no sun shines' (1934)

8 It was my thirtieth year to heaven.

'Poem in October' (1946)

9 There could I marvel
My birthday
Away but the weather turned around.

'Poem in October' (1946)

10 After the first death, there is no other.

'A Refusal to Mourn the Death, by Fire, of a Child in London' (1946)

11 I can never remember whether it snowed for six days and six nights when I was twelve or whether it snowed for twelve days and twelve nights when I was six.

A Child's Christmas in Wales (1954)

12 Books that told me everything about the wasp, except why.

A Child's Christmas in Wales (1954)

13 Too many of the artists of Wales spend too much time talking about the position of the artists of Wales. There is only one position for an artist anywhere: and that is, upright.

Quite Early One Morning (1954)

14 To begin at the beginning: It is spring, moonless night in the small town, starless and bible-black.

Under Milk Wood (1954)

15 Chasing the naughty couples down the grassgreen gooseberried double bed of the wood.

Under Milk Wood (1954)

16 Before you let the sun in, mind it wipes its shoes.

Under Milk Wood (1954)

17 Oh, isn't life a terrible thing, thank God?

Under Milk Wood (1954)

18 The land of my fathers. My fathers can have it.

of Wales

in *Adam* December 1953

19 A man you don't like who drinks as much as you do.

definition of an alcoholic

Constantine Fitzgibbon *Life of Dylan Thomas* (1965)

20 Poetry is not the most important thing in life . . . I'd much rather lie in a hot bath reading Agatha Christie and sucking sweets.

Joan Wyndham *Love is Blue* (1986) 6 July 1943

Edward Thomas 1878–1917

English poet

1 Yes; I remember Adlestrop—
The name, because one afternoon
Of heat the express-train drew up there
Unwontedly. It was late June.
'Adlestrop' (1917)

2 The past is the only dead thing that
smells sweet.
'Early one morning in May I set out' (1917)

3 If I should ever by chance grow rich
I'll buy Codham, Cockridden, and
Childerditch,
Roses, Pyrgo, and Lapwater,
And let them all to my elder daughter.
'Household Poems: Bronwen' (1917)

4 I have come to the borders of sleep,
The unfathomable deep
Forest where all must lose
Their way.
'Lights Out' (1917)

5   I see and hear nothing;
Yet seem, too, to be listening, lying in
wait
For what I should, yet never can,
remember.
'Old Man' (1917)

6 Out in the dark over the snow
The fallow fawns invisible go.
'Out in the dark' (1917)

7 As well as any bloom upon a flower
I like the dust on the nettles, never lost
Except to prove the sweetness of a
shower.
'Tall Nettles' (1917)

Gwyn Thomas 1913–81

Welsh novelist and dramatist

8 I wanted a play that would paint the full
face of sensuality, rebellion and
revivalism. In South Wales these three
phenomena have played second fiddle
only to Rugby Union which is a
distillation of all three.
introduction to Jackie the Jumper (1962)

9 There are still parts of Wales where the
only concession to gaiety is a striped
shroud.
in Punch 18 June 1958

Irene Thomas

British writer and broadcaster

10 Protestant women may take the pill.
Roman Catholic women must keep
taking The Tablet.
in Guardian 28 December 1990

R. S. Thomas 1913–

Welsh poet and clergyman

11   Doctors in verse
Being scarce now, most poets
Are their own patients.
'The Cure' (1958)

12 There is no love
For such, only a willed
gentleness.
'They' (1968)

13 There is no present in Wales,
And no future;
There is only the past,
Brittle with relics . . .
And an impotent people,
Sick with inbreeding,
Worrying the carcase of an old song.
'Welsh Landscape' (1955)

Emma Thompson 1959–

English actress

of Jane Austen:
14 I hope she knows how big she is in
Uruguay.
accepting an Oscar for the screenplay of Sense
and Sensibility (1995 film)
in Los Angeles, 26 March 1996

E. P. Thompson 1924–

British social historian

15 Humankind must at last grow up. We
must recognize that the Other is
ourselves.
Beyond the Cold War (1982)

16 This 'going into Europe' will not turn out
to be the thrilling mutual exchange
supposed. It is more like nine middle-aged
couples with failing marriages meeting in

a darkened bedroom in a Brussels hotel for a Group Grope.

in *Sunday Times* 27 April 1975

Hunter S. Thompson 1939–

American writer

1 Fear and loathing in Las Vegas.

title of two articles in *Rolling Stone* 11 and 25 November 1971 (under the pseudonym 'Raoul Duke')

Julian Thompson 1934–

British soldier, second-in-command of the land forces during the Falklands campaign.

2 You don't mind dying for Queen and country, but you certainly don't want to die for politicians.

'The Falklands War— the Untold Story' (Yorkshire Television) 1 April 1987; cf. **France** 117:11, **Graham** 131:6

David Thomson 1941–

film critic

3 [*Gandhi*] looms over the real world like an abandoned space station—eternal, expensive and forsaken.

A Biographical Dictionary of Film (1994)

4 There is nothing funnier than a huge man trying to inspire order in the world.

of John **Cleese**

A Biographical Dictionary of Film (1994)

5 Fiction is the great virus waiting to do away with fact—that is one of the most ominous meanings of the film.

of Citizen Kane

Rosebud: the Story of Orson Welles (1996)

Roy Thomson 1894–1976

Canadian-born British newspaper proprietor

6 Like having your own licence to print money.

on the profitability of commercial television in Britain

R. Braddon *Roy Thomson* (1965)

Jeremy Thorpe 1929–

British Liberal politician

7 Greater love hath no man than this, that he lay down his friends for his life.

on Harold **Macmillan***'s sacking seven of his Cabinet on 13 July 1962*

D. E. Butler and A. King *General Election of 1964* (1965); see below

Greater love hath no man than this, that a man lay down his life for his friends.

Bible St John

James Thurber 1894–1961

American humorist

8 I suppose that the high-water mark of my youth in Columbus, Ohio, was the night the bed fell on my father.

My Life and Hard Times (1933)

9 Her own mother lived the latter years of her life in the horrible suspicion that electricity was dripping invisibly all over the house.

My Life and Hard Times (1933)

10 All right, have it your own way—you heard a seal bark!

cartoon caption in *New Yorker* 30 January 1932

11 The war between men and women.

cartoon series title in *New Yorker* 20 January–28 April 1934

12 It's a naive domestic Burgundy without any breeding, but I think you'll be amused by its presumption.

cartoon caption in *New Yorker* 27 March 1937

13 Well, if I called the wrong number, why did you answer the phone?

cartoon caption in *New Yorker* 5 June 1937

14 Early to rise and early to bed makes a male healthy and wealthy and dead.

'The Shrike and the Chipmunks' in *New Yorker* 18 February 1939

15 Then, with that faint fleeting smile playing about his lips, he faced the firing squad; erect and motionless, proud and disdainful, Walter Mitty, the undefeated, inscrutable to the last.

in *New Yorker* 18 March 1939 'The Secret Life of Walter Mitty'

1 Humour is emotional chaos remembered in tranquillity.
   in *New York Post* 29 February 1960; see below

   Poetry . . . takes its origin from emotion recollected in tranquillity.
   William Wordsworth (1770–1850) *Lyrical Ballads* (2nd ed., 1802)

Anthony Thwaite 1930–
English writer

2 The name is history.
         The thick Miljacka flows
   Under its bridges through a canyon's breadth
   Fretted with minarets and plump with domes,
   Cupped in its mountains, caught on a drawn breath.
   'Sarajevo: I' (1973)

Lionel Tiger 1937–
American anthropologist

3 Male bonding.
   Men in Groups (1969)

Paul Tillich 1886–1965
German-born Protestant theologian

4 Neurosis is the way of avoiding non-being by avoiding being.
   The Courage To Be (1952)

Alvin Toffler 1928–
American writer

5 Future shock.
   defined by Toffler as 'the dizzying disorientation brought on by the premature arrival of the future' in Horizon *Summer 1965*
   title of book (1970)

J. R. R. Tolkien 1892–1973
British philologist and writer
on Tolkien: see **Pratchett 256:1**

6 In a hole in the ground there lived a hobbit.
   The Hobbit (1937)

7 Never laugh at live dragons.
   The Hobbit (1937)

8 One Ring to rule them all, One Ring to find them
   One Ring to bring them all and in the darkness bind them.
   The Lord of the Rings pt. 1 *The Fellowship of the Ring* (1954) epigraph

9 Do not meddle in the affairs of Wizards, for they are subtle and quick to anger.
   The Lord of the Rings pt. 1 *The Fellowship of the Ring* (1954)

10 Bingo Bolger-Baggins a bad name. Let Bingo = Frodo.
   on the first draft of The Lord of the Rings
   note, *c.*1938; Humphrey Carpenter *J. R. R. Tolkien* (1977)

Michael Torke 1961–

11 Why waste money on psychotherapy when you can listen to the B Minor Mass?
   in *Observer* 23 September 1990 'Sayings of the Week'

Arturo Toscanini 1867–1957
Italian conductor

12 I smoked my first cigarette and kissed my first woman on the same day. I have never had time for tobacco since.
   in *Observer* 30 June 1946

Sue Townsend 1946–
English writer

13 The secret diary of Adrian Mole aged $13\frac{3}{4}$.
   title of book (1982)

Pete Townshend 1945–
British rock musician and songwriter

14 Hope I die before I get old.
   'My Generation' (1965 song)

Arnold Toynbee 1889–1975
English historian

15 The twentieth century will be remembered chiefly, not as an age of political conflicts and technical inventions, but as an age in which

human society dared to think of the health of the whole human race as a practical objective.

attributed

Polly Toynbee 1946–

English journalist

1 Feminism is the most revolutionary idea there has ever been. Equality for women demands a change in the human psyche more profound than anything Marx dreamed of. It means valuing parenthood as much as we value banking.

in *Guardian* 19 January 1987

of daytime television:
2 It is Stupidvision—where most of the presenters look like they have to pretend to be stupid because they think their audience is . . . It patronises. It talks to the vacuum cleaner and the washing machine and the microwave without much contact with the human brain.

in *Radio Times* 11 May 1996

Merle Travis 1917–83

American country singer

3 Sixteen tons, what do you get?
Another day older and deeper in debt.
Say brother, don't you call me 'cause I
   can't go
I owe my soul to the company store.

'Sixteen Tons' (1947 song)

Herbert Beerbohm Tree 1852–1917

English actor–manager

4 Ladies, just a little more virginity, if you don't mind.

to a motley collection of females, assembled to play ladies-in-waiting to a queen
   Alexander Woollcott *Shouts and Murmurs* (1923)

5 Sirs, I have tested your machine. It adds a new terror to life and makes death a long-felt want.

when pressed by a gramophone company for a written testimonial
   Hesketh Pearson *Beerbohm Tree* (1956)

Lord Trend 1914–87

British civil servant; Cabinet Secretary 1963–73

6 The acid test of any political decision is, 'What is the alternative?'

attributed, 1975

G. M. Trevelyan 1876–1962

English historian

7 Disinterested intellectual curiosity is the life-blood of real civilization.

English Social History (1942)

8 If the French noblesse had been capable of playing cricket with their peasants, their chateaux would never have been burnt.

English Social History (1942)

9 [Education] has produced a vast population able to read but unable to distinguish what is worth reading, an easy prey to sensations and cheap appeals.

English Social History (1942)

John Trevelyan

British film censor

10 We are paid to have dirty minds.

in *Observer* 15 November 1959 'Sayings of the Week'

William Trevor 1928–

Anglo-Irish novelist and short story writer

11 A disease in the family that is never mentioned.

of the troubles in Northern Ireland
in *Observer* 18 November 1990

Calvin Trillin 1935–

American journalist and writer

12 The shelf life of the modern hardback writer is somewhere between the milk and the yoghurt.

in *Sunday Times* 9 June 1991; attributed

David Trimble 1944–

Northern Irish politician, leader of the Ulster Unionists

1 We are not here to negotiate with them, but to confront them.

on entering the Mitchell talks on Northern Ireland with Sinn Fein

in *Guardian* 18 September 1997

Tommy Trinder 1909–89

British comedian

2 Overpaid, overfed, oversexed, and over here.

of American troops in Britain during the Second World War

associated with Trinder, but probably not original

Leon Trotsky 1879–1940

Russian revolutionary
on Trotsky: see **Taylor** 303:11

3 Civilization has made the peasantry its pack animal. The bourgeoisie in the long run only changed the form of the pack.

History of the Russian Revolution (1933)

4 You [the Mensheviks] are pitiful isolated individuals; you are bankrupts; your role is played out. Go where you belong from now on—into the dustbin of history!

History of the Russian Revolution (1933)

5 Where force is necessary, there it must be applied boldly, decisively and completely. But one must know the limitations of force; one must know when to blend force with a manoeuvre, a blow with an agreement.

What Next? (1932)

6 It was the supreme expression of the mediocrity of the apparatus that Stalin himself rose to his position.

My Life (1930)

7 Old age is the most unexpected of all things that happen to a man.

diary, 8 May 1935

8 Not believing in force is the same thing as not believing in gravitation.

G. Maximov *The Guillotine at Work* (1940)

Pierre Trudeau 1919–

Canadian Liberal statesman, Prime Minister, 1968–79 and 1980–4

9 The state has no place in the nation's bedrooms.

interview, Ottawa, 22 December 1967

10 The twentieth century really belongs to those who will build it. The future can be promised to no one.

in 1968; see below

The nineteenth century was the century of the United States. I think we can claim that it is Canada that shall fill the twentieth century.

Wilfrid Laurier (1841–1919) speech, Ottawa, 18 January 1904

11 Living next to you is in some ways like sleeping with an elephant. No matter how friendly and even-tempered the beast, one is affected by every twitch and grunt.

on relations between Canada and the US

speech at National Press Club, Washington D. C., 25 March 1969

François Truffaut 1932–84

French film director

12 I've always had the impression that real militants are like cleaning women, doing a thankless, daily but necessary job.

letter to Jean-Luc Godard, May-June 1973

Harry S. Truman 1884–1972

American Democratic statesman, 33rd President of the US, 1945–53
on Truman: see **Mencken** 213:5*; see also* **Newspaper headlines** 231:3

13 All the President is, is a glorified public relations man who spends his time flattering, kissing and kicking people to get them to do what they are supposed to do anyway.

letter to his sister, 14 November 1947

14 Those who want the Government to regulate matters of the mind and spirit are like men who are so afraid of being

murdered that they commit suicide to avoid assassination.

> address at the National Archives, Washington, D.C., 15 December 1952

1 I never give them [the public] hell. I just tell the truth, and they think it is hell.

> in *Look* 3 April 1956

2 A statesman is a politician who's been dead 10 or 15 years.

> in *New York World Telegram and Sun* 12 April 1958

3 It's a recession when your neighbour loses his job; it's a depression when you lose yours.

> in *Observer* 13 April 1958

4 Wherever you have an efficient government you have a dictatorship.

> lecture at Columbia University, 28 April 1959

5 Always be sincere, even if you don't mean it.

> attributed

6 The buck stops here.

> unattributed motto on Truman's desk

7 I didn't fire him [General MacArthur] because he was a dumb son of a bitch, although he was, but that's not against the law for generals. If it was, half to three-quarters of them would be in jail.

> Merle Miller *Plain Speaking* (1974)

8 If you can't stand the heat, get out of the kitchen.

> *attributed by Truman himself to Harry Vaughan, his 'military jester'*
> in *Time* 28 April 1952

Donald Trump 1946–

American businessman

9 Deals are my art form. Other people paint beautifully on canvas or write wonderful poetry. I like making deals, preferably big deals. That's how I get my kicks.

> Donald Trump and Tony Schwartz *The Art of the Deal* (1987)

Marina Tsvetaeva 1892–1941

Russian poet

10 In this
most Christian of worlds all poets

are Jews.

> 'Poem of the End' (1924)

Barbara W. Tuchman 1912–89

American historian and writer

11 Dead battles, like dead generals, hold the military mind in their dead grip and Germans, no less than other peoples, prepare for the last war.

> *August 1914* (1962)

12 For one August in its history Paris was French—and silent.

> *August 1914* (1962)

Sophie Tucker 1884–1966

Russian-born American vaudeville artiste

13 From birth to 18 a girl needs good parents. From 18 to 35, she needs good looks. From 35 to 55, good personality. From 55 on, she needs good cash.

> M. Freedland *Sophie* (1978)

14 I've been rich and I've been poor: rich is better.

> attributed

Alan Turing 1912–54

English mathematician and codebreaker

15 We are not interested in the fact that the brain has the consistency of cold porridge.

> A. P. Hodges *Alan Turing: the Enigma* (1983)

Sherry Turkle 1948–

American sociologist

16 Like the anthropologist returning home from a foreign culture, the voyager in virtuality can return home to a real world better equipped to understand its artifices.

> *Life on the Screen: Identity in the Age of the Internet* (1995)

Walter James Redfern Turner 1889–1946

British writer and critic

17 When I was but thirteen or so
I went into a golden land,

Chimborazo, Cotopaxi
Took me by the hand.
'Romance' (1916)

John Tusa 1936–

British broadcaster and radio journalist

1 Management that wants to change an
institution must first show it loves that
institution.
in *Observer* 27 February 1994 'Sayings of the
Week'

Jill Tweedie 1936–93

British journalist

2 My boredom threshold is low at the best
of times but I have spent more time being
slowly and excruciatingly bored by
children than any other section of the
human race.
It's Only Me (1980)

3 I blame the women's movement for ten
years in a boiler suit.
attributed, 1989

Twiggy 1949–

English model and actress

4 It always makes me laugh when people
ask why anyone would want to do a
sitcom in America. If it runs five years,
you never have to work again.
in *Independent* 4 October 1997 'Quote
Unquote'

Kenneth Tynan 1927–80

English theatre critic

5 Forty years ago he was Slightly in *Peter
Pan*, and you might say that he has been
wholly in *Peter Pan* ever since.
of Noel **Coward**
Curtains (1961)

6 What, when drunk, one sees in other
women, one sees in Garbo sober.
Curtains (1961)

7 He walks top-heavily, like a salmon
standing on its tail.
Profiles (ed. Kathleen Tynan, 1989) 'Charles
Laughton'

8 A good drama critic is one who perceives
what is happening in the theatre of his
time. A great drama critic also perceives
what is *not* happening.
Tynan Right and Left (1967)

9 A critic is a man who knows the way but
can't drive the car.
in *New York Times Magazine* 9 January 1966

10 'Sergeant Pepper'—a decisive moment in
the history of Western Civilization.
in 1967; Howard Elson *McCartney* (1986)

11 A neurosis is a secret you don't know
you're keeping.
Kathleen Tynan *Life of Kenneth Tynan* (1987)

Miguel de Unamuno
1864–1937

Spanish philosopher and writer

12 *La vida es duda,*
y la fe sin la duda es sólo muerte.
Life is doubt,
And faith without doubt is nothing but
death.
'Salmo II' (1907)

John Updike 1932–

American novelist and short-story writer

13 A healthy male adult bore consumes *each
year* one and a half times his own weight
in other people's patience.
Assorted Prose (1965) 'Confessions of a Wild
Bore'

14 The heart *prefers* to move against the
grain of circumstance; perversity is the
soul's very life.
Assorted Prose (1965) 'More Love in the
Western World'

15 A soggy little island huffing and puffing
to keep up with Western Europe.
of England
Picked Up Pieces (1976) 'London Life' (written
1969)

16 America is a land whose centre is
nowhere; England one whose centre is
everywhere.
Picked Up Pieces (1976) 'London Life' (written
1969)

1 America is a vast conspiracy to make you happy.

> *Problems* (1980) 'How to love America and Leave it at the Same Time'

2 Celebrity is a mask that eats into the face.

> *Self-Consciousness: Memoirs* (1989)

3 Neutrinos, they are very small
They have no charge and have no mass
And do not interact at all.

> 'Cosmic Gall' (1964)

4 The artist brings something into the world that didn't exist before, and . . . he does it without destroying something else.

> George Plimpton (ed.) *Writers at Work* (4th series, 1977)

5 I've never much enjoyed going to plays . . . The unreality of painted people standing on a platform saying things they've said to each other for months is more than I can overlook.

> George Plimpton (ed.) *Writers at Work* 4th Series (1977)

Peter Ustinov 1921–
Russian-born actor, director, and writer

6 Laughter . . . the most civilized music in the world.

> *Dear Me* (1977)

7 I do not believe that friends are necessarily the people you like best, they are merely the people who got there first.

> *Dear Me* (1977)

8 At the age of four with paper hats and wooden swords we're all Generals. Only some of us never grow out of it.

> *Romanoff and Juliet* (1956)

9 A diplomat these days is nothing but a head-waiter who's allowed to sit down occasionally.

> *Romanoff and Juliet* (1956)

10 Laughter would be bereaved if snobbery died.

> in *Observer* 13 March 1955

11 If Botticelli were alive today he'd be working for *Vogue*.

> in *Observer* 21 October 1962 'Sayings of the Week'

12 Pavarotti is not vain, but conscious of being unique.

> in *Independent on Sunday* 12 September 1993

Paul Valéry 1871–1945
French poet, critic, and man of letters

13 A poem is never finished; it's always an accident that puts a stop to it—that is to say, gives it to the public.

> *Littérature* (1930)

14 Science means simply the aggregate of all the recipes that are always successful. The rest is literature.

> *Moralités* (1932)

15 God created man and, finding him not sufficiently alone, gave him a companion to make him feel his solitude more keenly.

> *Tel Quel 1* (1941) 'Moralités'

16 Politics is the art of preventing people from taking part in affairs which properly concern them.

> *Tel Quel 2* (1943) 'Rhumbs'

Paul Vance and Lee Pockriss
American singer and American songwriter

17 Itsy bitsy teenie weenie, yellow polkadot bikini.

> title of song (1960)

Vivian van Damm c.1889–1960
British theatre manager

18 We never closed.

> of the Windmill Theatre, London, during the Second World War
> *Tonight and Every Night* (1952)

Laurens van der Post
1906–96
South African explorer and writer

19 Human beings are perhaps never more frightening than when they are convinced beyond doubt that they are right.

> *Lost World of the Kalahari* (1958)

1 I don't think a man who has watched the sun going down could walk away and commit a murder.

in *Daily Telegraph* 17 December 1996; obituary

Henry Van Dyke 1852–1933

American Presbyterian minister and writer

2 Time is
Too slow for those who wait,
Too swift for those who fear,
Too long for those who grieve,
Too short for those who rejoice;
But for those who love,
Time is eternity.

'Time is too slow for those who wait' (1905), read at the funeral of **Diana**, Princess of Wales; Nigel Rees in 'Quote . . . Unquote' October 1997 notes that the original form of the last line is 'Time is not'

Raoul Vaneigem 1934–

Belgian philosopher

3 Never before has a civilization reached such a degree of a contempt for life; never before has a generation, drowned in mortification, felt such a rage to live.

of the 1960s

The Revolution of Everyday Life (1967)

4 The same people who are murdered slowly in the mechanized slaughterhouses of work are also arguing, singing, drinking, dancing, making love, holding the streets, picking up weapons and inventing a new poetry.

The Revolution of Everyday Life (1967)

5 Work to survive, survive by consuming, survive to consume: the hellish cycle is complete.

The Revolution of Everyday Life (1967)

Bartolomeo Vanzetti 1888–1927

American anarchist, born in Italy
see also **Millay** 214:11, 214:12

6 Sacco's name will live in the hearts of the people and in their gratitude when Katzmann's and yours bones will be dispersed by time, when your name, his name, your laws, institutions, and your

false god are but a deem rememoring of a cursed past in which man was wolf to the man.

statement disallowed at his trial, with Nicola Sacco, for murder and robbery,; M. D. Frankfurter and G. Jackson *Letters of Sacco and Vanzetti* (1928); see below

A man is a wolf rather than a man to another man, when he hasn't yet found out what he's like.

Plautus (*c.*250–184 BC) *Asinaria*; often quoted as 'A man is a wolf to another man'

7 If it had not been for these thing, I might have live out my life talking at street corners to scorning men. I might have die, unmarked, unknown, a failure. Now we are not a failure. This is our career and our triumph. Never in our full life could we hope to do such work for tolerance, for joostice, for man's onderstanding of man as now we do by accident.

statement after being sentenced to death, 9 April 1927

Janet-Maria Vaughan 1899–1993

English scientist

8 I am here—trying to do science in hell.

working as a doctor in Belsen at the end of the war

letter to a friend, 12 May 1945; P. A. Adams (ed.) *Janet-Maria Vaughan* (1993)

Ralph Vaughan Williams 1872–1958

English composer

9 I don't know whether I like it, but it's what I meant.

on his 4th symphony

Christopher Headington *Bodley Head History of Western Music* (1974)

on being asked by a reporter, 'What do you think about music?':

10 It's a Rum Go!

Leslie Ayr *The Wit of Music* (1966)

Robert Venturi 1925–

American architect

1 Less is a bore.
Complexity and Contradiction in Architecture
(1966); cf. **Rohe** 267:2

Gianni Versace 1949–96

Italian designer

2 I like to dress egos. If you haven't got an
ego today, you can forget it.
in *Guardian* 16 July 1997; obituary

Hendrik Frensch Verwoerd
1901–66

South African statesman; Prime Minister
from 1958

3 Up till now he [the Bantu] has been
subjected to a school system which drew
him away from his own community and
practically misled him by showing him
the green pastures of the European but
still did not allow him to graze
there . . . It is abundantly clear that
unplanned education creates many
problems, disrupts the communal life of
the Bantu and endangers the communal
life of the European.
speech in South African Senate, 7 June 1954

Sid Vicious 1957–79

British rock musician

4 You just pick a chord, go twang, and
you've got music.
attributed

Gore Vidal 1925–

American novelist and critic

5 What other culture could have produced
someone like Hemingway and *not* seen
the joke?
Pink Triangle and Yellow Star (1982)

6 American writers want to be not good
but great; and so are neither.
Two Sisters (1970)

7 It is the spirit of the age to believe that
any fact, no matter how suspect, is
superior to any imaginative exercise, no
matter how true.
in *Encounter* December 1967, 'French Letters:
Theories of the New Novel'

8 I'm all for bringing back the birch, but
only between consenting adults.
in *Sunday Times Magazine* 16 September 1973

9 Whenever a friend succeeds, a little
something in me dies.
in *Sunday Times Magazine* 16 September 1973

10 [Commercialism is] doing well that which
should not be done at all.
in *Listener* 7 August 1975

11 It is not enough to succeed. Others must
fail.
G. Irvine *Antipanegyric for Tom Driberg* 8
December 1976

12 A triumph of the embalmer's art.
*of Ronald **Reagan***
in *Observer* 26 April 1981

*on being asked what would have happened in
1963, had **Khrushchev** and not **Kennedy** been
assassinated:*
13 With history one can never be certain,
but I think I can safely say that Aristotle
Onassis would not have married Mrs
Khrushchev.
in *Sunday Times* 4 June 1989

14 A genius with the IQ of a moron.
*of Andy **Warhol***
in *Observer* 18 June 1989

*of Truman **Capote**'s death:*
15 Good career move.
attributed

16 He will lie even when it is inconvenient:
the sign of the true artist.
attributed

José Antonio Viera Gallo
1943–

Chilean politician

17 Socialism can only arrive by bicycle.
Ivan Illich *Energy and Equity* (1974) epigraph

John Wain 1925–94

English poet and novelist

1 Poetry is to prose as dancing is to
  walking.
    BBC radio broadcast, 13 January 1976

Derek Walcott 1930–

West Indian poet and dramatist

2 I who have cursed
  The drunken officer of British rule, how
    choose
  Between this Africa and the English
    tongue I love?
    'A Far Cry From Africa' (1962)

3 Famine sighs like scythe
  across the field of statistics and the desert
  is a moving mouth.
    'The Fortunate Traveller' (1981)

4 I come from a backward place: your duty
  is supplied by life around you. One guy
  plants bananas; another plants cocoa;
  I'm a writer, I plant lines. There's the
  same clarity of occupation, and the sense
  of devotion.
    in Guardian 12 July 1997

William Waldegrave 1946–

British Conservative politician

5 In exceptional circumstances it is
  necessary to say something that is untrue
  in the House of Commons.
    in Guardian 9 March 1994

Lech Wałęsa 1943–

Polish trade unionist and statesman,
President since 1990

6 You have riches and freedom here but I
  feel no sense of faith or direction. You
  have so many computers, why don't you
  use them in the search for love?
    in Paris, on his first journey outside the Soviet
    area, in Daily Telegraph 14 December 1988

Arthur Waley 1889–1966

English orientalist and poet

7 What is hard today is to censor one's
  own thoughts—

To sit by and see the blind man
On the sightless horse, riding into the
  bottomless abyss.
    Censorship

Alice Walker 1944–

American poet

8 Did this happen to your mother? Did
  your sister throw up a lot?
    title of poem, 1979

9 Expect nothing. Live frugally
  on surprise.
    'Expect nothing' (1973)

10 The quietly pacifist peaceful
   always die
   to make room for men
   who shout.
    'The QPP' (1973)

11 We have a beautiful
   mother
   Her green lap
   immense
   Her brown embrace
   eternal
   Her blue body
   everything
   we know.
    'We Have a Beautiful Mother' (1991)

12 I think it pisses God off if you walk by the
   colour purple in a field somewhere and
   don't notice it.
    The Colour Purple (1982)

Edgar Wallace 1875–1932

English thriller writer

13 What is a highbrow? He is a man who
   has found something more interesting
   than women.
    in New York Times 24 January 1932

George Wallace 1919–

American Democratic politician

14 Segregation now, segregation tomorrow
   and segregation forever!
    inaugural speech as Governor of Alabama,
    January 1963

Henry Wallace 1888–1965

American Democratic politician

1 The century on which we are entering—the century which will come out of this war—can be and must be the century of the common man.

speech, 8 May 1942

Graham Wallas 1858–1932

British politicial scientist

2 The little girl had the making of a poet in her who, being told to be sure of her meaning before she spoke, said, 'How can I know what I think till I see what I say?'

The Art of Thought (1926)

Barbara Ward 1914–81

British author and educator

3 We cannot cheat on DNA. We cannot get round photosynthesis. We cannot say I am not going to give a damn about phytoplankton. All these tiny mechanisms provide the preconditions of our planetary life. To say we do not care is to say in the most literal sense that 'we choose death'.

Only One Earth (1972)

Andy Warhol 1927–87

American artist
on Warhol: see **Vidal** 317:14

4 In the future everybody will be world famous for fifteen minutes.

Andy Warhol (1968)

5 Being good in business is the most fascinating kind of art.

Philosophy of Andy Warhol (From A to B and Back Again) (1975)

6 Buying is much more American than thinking and I'm as American as they come.

Philosophy of Andy Warhol (From A to B and Back Again) (1975)

7 An artist is someone who produces things that people don't need to have but that he—for *some reason*—thinks it would be a good idea to give them.

Philosophy of Andy Warhol (From A to B and Back Again) (1975)

8 Isn't life a series of images that change as they repeat themselves?

Victor Bokris *Andy Warhol* (1989)

9 The things I want to show are mechanical. Machines have less problems.

Mike Wrenn *Andy Warhol: In His Own Words* (1991)

Jack Warner 1892–1978

American film producer

*on hearing that Ronald **Reagan** was seeking nomination as Governor of California:*

10 No, *no. Jimmy Stewart* for governor—Reagan for his best friend.

Max Wilk *The Wit and Wisdom of Hollywood* (1972)

Sylvia Townsend Warner
1893–1978

English writer

11 I discovered that dinners follow the order of creation—fish first, then entrées, then joints, lastly the apple as dessert. The soup is chaos.

diary, 26 May 1929

12 One need not write in a diary what one is to remember for ever.

diary, 22 October 1930

13 An old teapot, used daily, can tell me more of my past than anything I recorded of it. Continuity . . . continuity . . . it is that which we cannot write down, it is that we cannot compass, record or control.

letter to Alyse Gregory, 26 May 1953

14 One cannot overestimate the power of a good rancorous hatred on the part of the *stupid*. The stupid have so much more industry and energy to expend on hating. They build it up like coral insects.

diary, 26 September 1954

15 Total grief is like a minefield. No knowing when one will touch the tripwire.

diary, 11 December 1969

1 The present civilization is riddled by the do-ers and the done-by. Do you know what George Sand said as she lay dying? *Laissez verdurer. Idiots* suppose that she was giving directions about her grave.
   letter, 21 February 1972

Frank Warren

British boxing promoter

2 I have lost half a stone. The Lead Plan Diet I call it.
   after recovering from being shot in the chest
   attributed, 1989

Robert Penn Warren

1905–1989

American poet, novelist, and critic

3 Long ago in Kentucky, I, a boy, stood
   By a dirt road, in first dark, and heard
   The great geese hoot northward.
   Audubon (1969) 'Tell Me a Story'

Ned Washington 1901–76

American songwriter

4 Hi diddle dee dee (an actor's life for me).
   title of song from the film *Pinocchio* (1940)

5 The night is like a lovely tune,
   Beware my foolish heart!
   How white the ever-constant moon,
   Take care, my foolish heart!
   'My Foolish Heart' (1949 song)

Keith Waterhouse 1929–

English novelist, dramatist, and screenwriter

6 Jeffery Bernard is unwell.
   from the Spectator's *habitual explanation for the non-appearance of Jeffery* **Bernard**'s *column*
   title of play (1989)

James D. Watson 1928–

American biologist
see also **Crick and Watson**

7 No *good* model ever accounted for *all* the facts, since some data was bound to be misleading if not plain wrong.
   Francis Crick *Some Mad Pursuit* (1988)

8 Some day a child is going to sue its parents for being born. They will say, my life is so awful with these terrible genetic defects and you just callously didn't find out.
   on the question of genetic screening of foetuses
   interview in *Sunday Telegraph* 16 February 1997

Thomas Watson Snr.

1874–1956

American businessman; Chairman of IBM 1914–52

9 Clothes don't make the man . . . but they go a long way toward making a businessman.
   Robert Sobel *IBM: Colossus in Transition* (1981)

10 You cannot be a success in any business without believing that it is the greatest business in the world . . . You have to put your heart in the business and the business in your heart.
   Robert Sobel *IBM: Colossus in Transition* (1981)

Evelyn Waugh 1903–66

English novelist

11 I am not I: thou art not he or she: they are not they.
   Brideshead Revisited (1945) 'Author's Note'

12 Charm is the great English blight. It does not exist outside these damp islands. It spots and kills anything it touches. It kills love, it kills art.
   Brideshead Revisited (1945)

13 The sound of English county families baying for broken glass.
   Decline and Fall (1928); cf. **Belloc** 28:4

14 I expect you'll be becoming a schoolmaster, sir. That's what most of the gentlemen does, sir, that gets sent down for indecent behaviour.
   Decline and Fall (1928)

15 'I often think,' he continued, 'that we can trace almost all the disasters of English history to the influence of Wales!'
   Decline and Fall (1928)

1 There is a species of person called a 'Modern Churchman' who draws the full salary of a beneficed clergyman and need not commit himself to any religious belief.
> *Decline and Fall* (1928)

2 Any one who has been to an English public school will always feel comparatively at home in prison. It is the people brought up in the gay intimacy of the slums, Paul learned, who find prison so soul-destroying.
> *Decline and Fall* (1928)

3 Only when one has lost all curiosity about the future has one reached the age to write an autobiography.
> *A Little Learning* (1964)

4 You never find an Englishman among the underdogs—except in England, of course.
> *The Loved One* (1948)

5 In the dying world I come from quotation is a national vice. No one would think of making an after-dinner speech without the help of poetry. It used to be the classics, now it's lyric verse.
> *The Loved One* (1948)

6 He abhorred plastics, Picasso, sunbathing and jazz—everything in fact that had happened in his own lifetime.
> *The Ordeal of Gilbert Pinfold* (1957)

7 *The Beast* stands for strong mutually antagonistic governments everywhere . . . Self-sufficiency at home, self-assertion abroad.
> *Scoop* (1938)

8 Up to a point, Lord Copper.
> *Scoop* (1938)

9 Feather-footed through the plashy fen passes the questing vole.
> *Scoop* (1938)

10 News is what a chap who doesn't care much about anything wants to read. And it's only news until he's read it. After that it's dead.
> *Scoop* (1938)

11 I will not stand for being called a woman in my own house.
> *Scoop* (1938)

12 Other nations use 'force'; we Britons alone use 'Might'.
> *Scoop* (1938)

13 All this fuss about sleeping together. For physical pleasure I'd sooner go to my dentist any day.
> *Vile Bodies* (1930)

14 To see him fumbling with our rich and delicate language is to experience all the horror of seeing a Sèvres vase in the hands of a chimpanzee.
> *of Stephen* **Spender**
> in *The Tablet* 5 May 1951

15 Impotence and sodomy are socially O.K. but birth control is flagrantly middle-class.
> 'An Open Letter' in Nancy Mitford (ed.)
> *Noblesse Oblige* (1956)

16 Punctuality is the virtue of the bored.
> diary, 26 March 1962

17 Manners are especially the need of the plain. The pretty can get away with anything.
> in *Observer* 15 April 1962

18 A typical triumph of modern science to find the only part of Randolph that was not malignant and remove it.
> *on hearing that Randolph Churchill's lung, when removed, proved non-malignant*
> diary, March 1964

19 You have no idea how much nastier I would be if I was not a Catholic. Without supernatural aid I would hardly be a human being.
> Noel Annan *Our Age* (1990)

Frederick Weatherly
1848–1929

English songwriter

20 Roses are flowering in Picardy,
But there's never a rose like you.
> 'Roses of Picardy' (1916 song)

Beatrice Webb 1858–1943

English socialist

21 I never visualised labour as separate men and women of different sorts and

kinds . . . labour was an abstraction, which seemed to denote an arithmetically calculable mass of human beings, each individual a repetition of the other.
My Apprenticeship (1926)

1 If I ever felt inclined to be timid as I was going into a room full of people, I would say to myself, 'You're the cleverest member of one of the cleverest families in the cleverest class of the cleverest nation in the world, why should you be frightened?'
Bertrand Russell *Autobiography* (1967)

Sidney Webb 1859–1947
English socialist

2 The inevitability of gradualness.
Presidential address to the annual conference of the Labour Party, 26 June 1923

3 Marriage is the waste-paper basket of the emotions.
Bertrand Russell *Autobiography* (1967)

Simone Weil 1909–43
French essayist and philosopher

4 An obligation which goes unrecognized by anybody loses none of the full force of its existence. A right which goes unrecognized by anybody is not worth very much.
L'Enracinement (1949) 'Les Besoins de l'âme'

5 All sins are attempts to fill voids.
La Pesanteur et la grâce (1948)

6 What a country calls its vital economic interests are not the things which enable its citizens to live, but the things which enable it to make war.
W. H. Auden *A Certain World* (1971)

Victor Weisskopf 1908–
American physicist

7 It was absolutely marvellous working for Pauli. You could ask him anything. There was no worry that he would think a particular question was stupid, since he thought *all* questions were stupid.
in *American Journal of Physics* 1977

Johnny Weissmuller
see **Misquotations** 218:10

Chaim Weizmann 1874–1952
Russian-born Israeli statesman, President 1949–52

8 Something had been done for us which, after two thousand years of hope and yearning, would at last give us a resting-place in this terrible world.
of the Balfour declaration
speech in Jerusalem, 25 November 1936

Fay Weldon 1931–
British novelist and scriptwriter
see also **Advertising slogans** 3:19

9 Natalie had left the wives and joined the women.
Heart of the Country (1987)

10 The life and loves of a she-devil.
title of novel (1984)

11 Reading about sex in yesterday's novels is like watching people smoke in old films.
in *Guardian* 1 December 1989

12 Every time you open your wardrobe, you look at your clothes and you wonder what you are going to wear. What you are really saying is 'Who am I going to be today?'
in *New Yorker* 26 June 1995

Colin Welland 1934–
English actor and scriptwriter

13 The British are coming.
speech accepting an Oscar for his *Chariots of Fire* screenplay, 30 March 1982

Orson Welles 1915–85
American actor and film director
see also **Film lines** 110:14

14 The biggest electric train set any boy ever had!
of the RKO studios
Peter Noble *The Fabulous Orson Welles* (1956)

1 I hate television. I hate it as much as peanuts. But I can't stop eating peanuts.
  in New York Herald Tribune 12 October 1956

2 There are only two emotions in a plane: boredom and terror.
  interview to celebrate his 70th birthday, in *The Times* 6 May 1985

H. G. Wells 1866–1946

English novelist and political writer
on Wells: see **Maurois** 210:16; *see also* **Epitaphs** 105:4

3 It is leviathan retrieving pebbles. It is a magnificent but painful hippopotamus resolved at any cost, even at the cost of its dignity, upon picking up a pea which has got into a corner of its den.
  of Henry **James**
  Boon (1915)

4 He had read Shakespeare and found him weak in chemistry.
  Complete Short Stories (1927) 'Lord of the Dynamos'

5 'Sesquippledan,' he would say. 'Sesquippledan verboojuice.'
  The History of Mr Polly (1909)

6 'I'm a Norfan, both sides,' he would explain, with the air of one who had seen trouble.
  Kipps (1905)

7 I was thinking jest what a Rum Go everything is.
  Kipps (1905)

8 The Social Contract is nothing more or less than a vast conspiracy of human beings to lie to and humbug themselves and one another for the general Good. Lies are the mortar that bind the savage individual man into the social masonry.
  Love and Mr Lewisham (1900)

9 Human history becomes more and more a race between education and catastrophe.
  The Outline of History (1920)

10 The shape of things to come.
  title of book (1933)

11 The war that will end war.
  title of book (1914); cf. **Lloyd George** 192:8

12 Moral indignation is jealousy with a halo.
  The Wife of Sir Isaac Harman (1914)

13 In England we have come to rely upon a comfortable time-lag of fifty years or a century intervening between the perception that something ought to be done and a serious attempt to do it.
  The Work, Wealth and Happiness of Mankind (1931)

14 If Max [Beaverbrook] gets to Heaven he won't last long. He will be chucked out for trying to pull off a merger between Heaven and Hell . . . after having secured a controlling interest in key subsidiary companies in both places, of course.
  A. J. P. Taylor *Beaverbrook* (1972)

Irvine Welsh 1957–

Scottish novelist

15 It's nae good blamin' it oan the English fir colonising us. Ah don't hate the English. They're just wankers. We can't even pick a decent vibrant, healthy culture to be colonised by.
  Trainspotting (1994)

Arnold Wesker 1932–

English dramatist

16 Chips with every damn thing. You breed babies and you eat chips with everything.
  Chips with Everything (1962)

17 The Khomeini cry for the execution of Rushdie is an infantile cry. From the beginning of time we have seen that. To murder the thinker does not murder the thought.
  in *Weekend Guardian* 3 June 1989; cf. **Khomeini** 171:7

Mary Wesley 1912–

English novelist

18 When people discussed tonics, pick-me-ups after a severe illness, she kept to herself the prescription of a quick dip in bed with someone you liked but were not in love with. A shock of sexual

astonishment which could make you feel astonishingly well and high spirited.
  Not That Sort of Girl (1987)

1 In my day, I would only have sex with a man if I found him extremely attractive. These days, girls seem to choose them in much the same way as they might choose to suck on a boiled sweet.
  in *Independent* 18 October 1997 'Quote Unquote'

Mae West 1892–1980

American film actress
see also **Misquotations** 219:5, **Sayings and slogans** 278:14

2 It's better to be looked over than overlooked.
  Belle of the Nineties (1934 film)

3 A man in the house is worth two in the street.
  Belle of the Nineties (1934 film)

4 I always say, keep a diary and some day it'll keep you.
  Every Day's a Holiday (1937 film)

5 Beulah, peel me a grape.
  I'm No Angel (1933 film)

6 I've been things and seen places.
  I'm No Angel (1933 film)

7 When I'm good, I'm very, very good, but when I'm bad, I'm better.
  I'm No Angel (1933 film)

8 It's not the men in my life that counts— it's the life in my men.
  I'm No Angel (1933 film)

9 Give a man a free hand and he'll try to put it all over you.
  Klondike Annie (1936 film)

10 Between two evils, I always pick the one I never tried before.
  Klondike Annie (1936 film)

11 'Goodness, what beautiful diamonds!' 'Goodness had nothing to do with it.'
  Night After Night (1932 film)

12 I've been in *Who's Who*, and I know what's what, but it'll be the first time I ever made the dictionary.
  letter to the RAF, early 1940s, on having an inflatable life jacket named after her
  Fergus Cashin *Mae West* (1981)

13 Is that a gun in your pocket, or are you just glad to see me?
  usually quoted as, 'Is that a pistol in your pocket . . . '
  J. Weintraub *Peel Me a Grape* (1975)

14 I used to be Snow White . . . but I drifted.
  Joseph Weintraub *Peel Me a Grape* (1975)

15 A hard man is good to find.
  attributed

16 It's not what I do, but the way I do it. It's not what I say, but the way I say it.
  G. Eells and S. Musgrove *Mae West* (1989)

Rebecca West 1892–1983

English novelist and journalist

17 Having watched the form of our traitors for a number of years, I cannot think that espionage can be recommended as a technique for building an impressive civilization. It's a lout's game.
  The Meaning of Treason (1982 ed.)

18 She was not so much a person as an implication of dreary poverty, like an open door in a mean house that lets out the smell of cooking cabbage and the screams of children.
  The Return of the Soldier (1918)

19 The point is that nobody likes having salt rubbed into their wounds, even if it is the salt of the earth.
  The Salt of the Earth (1935)

20 God forbid that any book should be banned. The practice is as indefensible as infanticide.
  The Strange Necessity (1928) 'The Tosh Horse'

21 It is queer how it is always one's virtues and not one's vices that precipitate one into disaster.
  There is No Conversation (1935)

22 I myself have never been able to find out precisely what feminism is: I only know that people call me a feminist whenever I

express sentiments that differentiate me from a doormat or a prostitute.

in *The Clarion* 14 November 1913

1 It was in dealing with the early feminist that the Government acquired the tact and skilfulness with which it is now handling Ireland.

in *Daily News* 7 August 1916

2 Just how difficult it is to write biography can be reckoned by anybody who sits down and considers just how many people know the truth about his or her love affairs.

in *Vogue* 1 November 1952

3 Journalism—an ability to meet the challenge of filling the space.

in *New York Herald Tribune* 22 April 1956

4 There is, of course, no reason for the existence of the male sex except that sometimes one needs help with moving the piano.

in *Sunday Telegraph* 28 June 1970

5 Any writer worth his salt knows that only a small proportion of literature does more than partly compensate people for the damage they have suffered in learning to read.

Peter Vansittart *Path from a White Horse* (1985), author's note

6 Whatever happens, never forget that people would rather be led to *perdition* by a man, than to *victory* by a woman.

in conversation in 1979, just before Margaret **Thatcher***'s first election victory*

in *Sunday Telegraph* 17 January 1988

7 Every other inch a gentleman.

of Michael Arlen; the phrase is also attributed to Arlen himself

Victoria Glendinning *Rebecca West* (1987)

Loelia, Duchess of Westminster 1902–93

English aristocrat

8 Anybody seen in a bus over the age of thirty has been a failure in life.

Cocktails and Laughter (1983); habitual remark

R. P. Weston 1878–1936
and Bert Lee 1880–1947

British songwriters

9 Good-bye-ee!—Good-bye-ee!
Wipe the tear, baby dear, from your eye-ee.
Tho' it's hard to part, I know,
I'll be tickled to death to go.
Don't cry-ee—don't sigh-ee!
There's a silver lining in the sky-ee!
Bonsoir, old thing! cheerio! chin-chin!
Nahpoo! Toodle-oo! Good-bye-ee!

'Good-bye-ee!' (*c*.1915 song)

Alan Wharton 1923–

English cricketer

10 It's a well-known fact that, when I'm on 99, I'm the best judge of a run in all the bloody world.

to Cyril Washbrook; Freddie Trueman *You Nearly Had Me That Time* (1978)

Edith Wharton 1862–1937

American novelist

11 An unalterable and unquestioned law of the musical world required that the German text of French operas sung by Swedish artists should be translated into Italian for the clearer understanding of English-speaking audiences.

The Age of Innocence (1920)

12 If he paid for each day's comfort with the small change of his illusions, he grew daily to value the comfort more and set less store upon the coin.

The Descent of Man (1904) 'The Other Two'

13 Another unsettling element in modern art is that common symptom of immaturity, the dread of doing what has been done before.

The Writing of Fiction (1925)

14 Mrs Ballinger is one of the ladies who pursue Culture in bands, as though it were dangerous to meet it alone.

Xingu and Other Stories (1916) 'Xingu'

15 To your generation, I must represent the literary equivalent of tufted furniture and gas chandeliers.

letter to F. Scott Fitzgerald, 8 June 1925

E. B. White 1899–1985
American humorist

1 MOTHER: It's broccoli, dear.
CHILD: I say it's spinach, and I say the hell with it.
cartoon caption in *New Yorker* 8 December 1928

2 The so-called science of poll-taking is not a science at all but a mere necromancy. People are unpredictable by nature, and although you can take a nation's pulse, you can't be sure that the nation hasn't just run up a flight of stairs.
in *New Yorker* 13 November 1948

3 Commuter—one who spends his life
In riding to and from his wife;
A man who shaves and takes a train,
And then rides back to shave again.
'The Commuter' (1982)

Edmund White 1940–
American writer and critic

4 The Aids epidemic has rolled back a big rotting log and revealed all the squirming life underneath it, since it involves, all at once, the main themes of our existence: sex, death, power, money, love, hate, disease and panic. No American phenomenon has been so compelling since the Vietnam War.
States of Desire: Travels in Gay America (afterword to 1986 edition)

Patrick White 1912–90
Australian novelist

5 Conversation is imperative if gaps are to be filled, and old age, it is the last gap but one.
The Tree of Man (1955)

6 In all directions stretched the great Australian Emptiness, in which the mind is the least of possessions.
The Vital Decade (1968) 'The Prodigal Son'

7 [The average Australian practises] that hateful religion of *ordinariness*.
letter to Ben Huebsch, 20 January 1960

T. H. White 1906–64
English novelist

8 The once and future king.
taken from Sir Thomas Malory Le Morte d'Arthur: 'Hic iacet Arthurus, rex quondam rexque futurus'
title of novel (1958)

Theodore H. White 1915–86
American writer and journalist

9 America is a nation created by all the hopeful wanderers of Europe, not out of geography and genetics, but out of purpose.
The Making of the President (1960)

10 Johnson's instinct for power is as primordial as a salmon's going upstream to spawn.
*of Lyndon **Johnson***
The Making of the President (1964)

11 The flood of money that gushes into politics today is a pollution of democracy.
in *Time* 19 November 1984

Alfred North Whitehead 1861–1947
English philosopher and mathematician

12 Life is an offensive, directed against the repetitive mechanism of the Universe.
Adventures of Ideas (1933)

13 It is more important that a proposition be interesting than that it be true. This statement is almost a tautology. For the energy of operation of a proposition in an occasion of experience is its interest, and is its importance. But of course a true proposition is more apt to be interesting than a false one.
Adventures of Ideas (1933)

14 There are no whole truths; all truths are half-truths. It is trying to treat them as whole truths that plays the devil.
Dialogues (1954) prologue

15 Intelligence is quickness to apprehend as distinct from ability, which is capacity to act wisely on the thing apprehended.
Dialogues (1954) 15 December 1939

16 What is morality in any given time or place? It is what the majority then and

there happen to like, and immorality is what they dislike.
Dialogues (1954) 30 August 1941

1 Art is the imposing of a pattern on experience, and our aesthetic enjoyment is recognition of the pattern.
Dialogues (1954) 10 June 1943

2 Civilization advances by extending the number of important operations which we can perform without thinking about them.
Introduction to Mathematics (1911)

3 No more impressive warning can be given to those who would confine knowledge and research to what is apparently useful, than the reflection that conic sections were studied for eighteen hundred years merely as an abstract science, without regard to any utility other than to satisfy the craving for knowledge on the part of mathematicians, and that then at the end of this long period of abstract study, they were found to be the necessary key with which to attain the knowledge of the most important laws of nature.
Introduction to Mathematics (1911)

4 The safest general characterization of the European philosophical tradition is that it consists of a series of footnotes to Plato.
Process and Reality (1929)

Katharine Whitehorn 1928–
English journalist

5 Children and zip fasteners do not respond to force . . . Except occasionally.
Observations (1970)

6 In our society mothers take the place elsewhere occupied by the Fates, the System, Negroes, Communism or Reactionary Imperialist Plots; mothers go on getting blamed until they're eighty, but shouldn't take it personally.
Observations (1970)

7 Being young is not having any money; being young is not minding not having any money.
Observations (1970)

8 Like a monkey scratching for the wrong fleas, every age assiduously seeks out in itself those vices which it does not in fact have, while ignoring the large, red, beady-eyed crawlers who scuttle around unimpeded.
Observations (1970)

9 An office party is not, as is sometimes supposed, the Managing Director's chance to kiss the tea-girl. It is the tea-girl's chance to kiss the Managing Director.
Roundabout (1962) 'The Office Party'

10 I wouldn't say when you've seen one Western you've seen the lot; but when you've seen the lot you get the feeling you've seen one.
Sunday Best (1976) 'Decoding the West'

Gough Whitlam 1916–
Australian Labor statesman, Prime Minister 1972–5

11 Well may he say 'God Save the Queen'. But after this nothing will save the Governor-General.
having been dismissed from office by the Governor-General
speech in Canberra, 11 November 1975

Ben Whittaker 1934–

12 We can no more hope to end drug abuse by eliminating heroin and cocaine than we could alter the suicide rate by outlawing high buildings or the sale of rope.
The Global Fix (1987)

Charlotte Whitton 1896–1975
Canadian writer and politician

13 Whatever women do they must do twice as well as men to be thought half as good.
in *Canada Month* June 1963

William H. Whyte 1917–
American writer

14 This book is about the organization man . . . I can think of no other way to describe the people I am talking about.

They are not the workers, nor are they the white-collar people in the usual, clerk sense of the word. These people only work for the Organization. The ones I am talking about *belong* to it as well.

The Organization Man (1956)

Ann Widdecombe 1947–

British Conservative politician

1 He has something of the night in him.

of Michael Howard as a contender for the Conservative leadership

in *Sunday Times* 11 May 1997 (electronic edition)

Elie Wiesel 1928–

Romanian-born American writer and Nobel Prize winner; Auschwitz survivor

2 Take sides. Neutrality helps the oppressor, never the victim. Silence encourages the tormentor, never the tormented.

accepting the Nobel Peace Prize

in *New York Times* 11 December 1986

3 Remember the nocturnal processions of children and more children and more children, frightened, quiet, so quiet and so beautiful.

at an unofficial ceremony at Auschwitz on 26 January 1995, commemorating the 50th anniversary of its liberation

in *Independent* 27 January 1995

4 God of forgiveness, do not forgive those murderers of Jewish children here.

at Auschwitz

in *The Times* 27 January 1995

Richard Wilbur 1921–

American poet

5 Spare us all word of the weapons, their force and range,
The long numbers that rocket the mind.

'Advice to a Prophet' (1961)

6 We milk the cow of the world, and as we do
We whisper in her ear, 'You are not true.'

'Epistemology' (1950)

7 Mind in its purest play is like some bat
That beats about in caverns all alone,
Contriving by a kind of senseless wit
Not to conclude against a wall of stone.

'Mind' (1956)

8 The good grey guardians of art
Patrol the halls on spongy shoes.

'Museum Piece' (1950)

Toyah Wilcox

British television presenter, actress, and singer

9 Sex has never been an act of freedom for me. Robert and I climb into the bath together, but we tend to talk about quantum physics.

in *Independent on Sunday* 29 December 1996 'Comment'

Billy Wilder 1906–

American screenwriter and director
see also **Film lines** 111:16, 112:4

10 It used to be that we in films were the lowest form of art. Now we have something to look down on.

of television

A. Madsen *Billy Wilder* (1968)

11 What they [critics] call dirty in our pictures, they call lusty in foreign films.

A. Madsen *Billy Wilder* (1968)

12 Hindsight is always twenty-twenty.

J. R. Columbo *Wit and Wisdom of the Moviemakers* (1979)

on Marilyn **Monroe***'s unpunctuality:*

13 My Aunt Minnie would always be punctual and never hold up production, but who would pay to see my Aunt Minnie?

P. F. Boller and R. L. Davis *Hollywood Anecdotes* (1988)

Thornton Wilder 1897–1975

American novelist and dramatist

14 Marriage is a bribe to make a housekeeper think she's a householder.

The Merchant of Yonkers (1939)

15 Literature is the orchestration of platitudes.

in *Time* 12 January 1953

Robert Wilensky 1951–

American academic

1 We've all heard that a million monkeys banging on a million typewriters will eventually reproduce the entire works of Shakespeare. Now, thanks to the Internet, we know this is not true.

> in *Mail on Sunday* 16 February 1997 'Quotes of the Week'; cf. **Eddington** 95:2

Geoffrey Willans 1911–58 and Ronald Searle 1920–

English humorous writers

2 As any fule kno.

> *Down with Skool!* (1953)

3 History started badly and hav been geting steadily worse.

> *Down with Skool!* (1953)

4 There is no better xsample of a goody-goody than fotherington-tomas in the world in space. You kno he is the one who sa Hullo Clouds Hullo Sky and skip about like a girly.

> *How To Be Topp* (1954)

5 Still xmas is a good time with all those presents and good food and i hope it will never die out or at any rate not until i am grown up and hav to pay for it all.

> *How To Be Topp* (1954)

David Willcocks 1919–

British musician

6 It's the building. That acoustic would make a fart sound like a sevenfold Amen.

> *on King's College Chapel*
> in *Ned Sherrin in his Anecdotage* (1993)

Heathcote Williams 1941–

British dramatist and poet

7 Whales play, in an amniotic paradise.
Their light minds shaped by buoyancy,
   unrestricted by gravity,
Somersaulting.
Like angels, or birds;
Like our own lives, in the womb.

> *Whale Nation* (1988)

Kenneth Williams 1926–88

English actor

8 The nice thing about quotes is that they give us a nodding acquaintance with the originator which is often socially impressive.

> *Acid Drops* (1980)

R. J. P. Williams 1926–

English chemist

9 Biology is the search for the chemistry that works.

> lecture in Oxford, June 1996

Shirley Williams 1930–

British Labour and Social Democrat politician

10 No test tube can breed love and affection. No frozen packet of semen ever read a story to a sleepy child.

> in *Daily Mirror* 2 March 1978

11 The Catholic Church has never really come to terms with women. What I object to is being treated either as Madonnas or Mary Magdalenes.

> in *Observer* 22 March 1981

Tennessee Williams 1911–83

American dramatist

12 We're all of us guinea pigs in the laboratory of God. Humanity is just a work in progress.

> *Camino Real* (1953)

13 What is the victory of a cat on a hot tin roof?—I wish I knew . . . Just staying on it, I guess, as long as she can.

> *Cat on a Hot Tin Roof* (1955)

14 BRICK: Well, they say nature hates a vacuum, Big Daddy.
BIG DADDY: That's what they say, but sometimes I think that a vacuum is a hell of a lot better than some of the stuff that nature replaces it with.

> *Cat on a Hot Tin Roof* (1955)

1 Mendacity is a system that we live in. Liquor is one way out an' death's the other.
Cat on a Hot Tin Roof (1955)

2 I didn't go to the moon, I went much further—for time is the longest distance between two places.
The Glass Menagerie (1945)

3 We're all of us sentenced to solitary confinement inside our own skins, for life!
Orpheus Descending (1958)

4 Turn that off! I won't be looked at in this merciless glare!
A Streetcar Named Desire (1947)

5 BLANCHE: I don't want realism.
MITCH: Naw, I guess not.
BLANCHE: I'll tell you what I want. Magic!
A Streetcar Named Desire (1947)

6 I have always depended on the kindness of strangers.
A Streetcar Named Desire (1947)

William Carlos Williams
1883–1963
American poet

7 Minds like beds always made up,
(more stony than a shore)
unwilling or unable.
Paterson (1946)

8 so much depends
upon

a red wheel
barrow

glazed with rain
water

beside the white
chickens.
'The Red Wheelbarrow' (1923)

9 Is it any better in Heaven, my friend Ford,
Than you found it in Provence?
'To Ford Madox Ford in Heaven' (1944)

Marianne Williamson 1953–
American writer and philanthropist

10 Our deepest fear is not that we are inadequate. Our deepest fear is that we are powerful beyond measure. It is our light, not our darkness, that most frightens us.
A Return to Love (1992)

Roy Williamson 1936–90
Scottish folksinger and musician

11 O flower of Scotland, when will we see
   your like again,
that fought and died for your bit hill and
   glen
and stood against him, proud Edward's
   army,
and sent him homeward tae think again.
unofficial Scottish Nationalist anthem
'O Flower of Scotland' (1968)

Wendell Willkie 1892–1944
American lawyer and politician

12 The constitution does not provide for first and second class citizens.
An American Programme (1944)

Angus Wilson 1913–91
English novelist and short-story writer

13 Once a Catholic always a Catholic.
The Wrong Set (1949)

Charles E. Wilson 1890–1961
American industrialist; President of General Motors, 1941–53
on Wilson: see **Anonymous** 9:5

14 For years I thought what was good for our country was good for General Motors and vice versa.
testimony to the Senate Armed Services Committee on his proposed nomination for Secretary of Defence, 15 January 1953

Edward O. Wilson 1929–
sociobiologist

15 Every human brain is born not as a blank tablet (a *tabula rasa*) waiting to be filled in

by experience but as 'an exposed negative waiting to be slipped into developer fluid'.

on the nature v. nurture debate

attributed; Tom Wolfe in *Independent on Sunday* 2 February 1997

Harold Wilson 1916–

British Labour statesman; Prime Minister, 1964–70, 1974–6
on Wilson: see **Benn** 29:15, **Bulmer-Thomas** 48:7, **Crosland** 80:13, **Home** 151:7, **Junor** 166:10, **Levin** 189:12; *see also* **Misquotations** 219:4

1 All these financiers, all the little gnomes in Zurich.

speech, House of Commons, 12 November 1956

2 I myself have always deprecated . . . in crisis after crisis, appeals to the Dunkirk spirit as an answer to our problems.

in the House of Commons, 26 July 1961

3 This party is a moral crusade or it is nothing.

speech at the Labour Party Conference, 1 October 1962

4 If I had the choice between smoked salmon and tinned salmon, I'd have it tinned. With vinegar.

in *Observer* 11 November 1962

5 The university of the air.

an early term for the Open University

In *Glasgow Herald* 9 September 1963

6 A week is a long time in politics.

probably first said at the time of the 1964 sterling crisis

Nigel Rees *Sayings of the Century* (1984)

7 [Labour is] the natural party of government.

in 1965; Anthony Sampson *The Changing Anatomy of Britain*

8 From now the pound abroad is worth 14 per cent or so less in terms of other currencies. It does not mean, of course, that the pound here in Britain, in your

pocket or purse or in your bank, has been devalued.

often quoted as 'the pound in your pocket'

ministerial broadcast, 19 November 1967

9 Get your tanks off my lawn, Hughie.

*to the trade union leader Hugh **Scanlon**, at Chequers in June 1969*

Peter Jenkins *The Battle of Downing Street* (1970); cf. **Clarke** 70:8

10 The Monarchy is a labour-intensive industry.

in *Observer* 13 February 1977

11 This party is a bit like an old stagecoach. If you drive along at a rapid rate, everyone aboard is either so exhilarated or so seasick that you don't have a lot of difficulty.

of the Labour Party

Anthony Sampson *The Changing Anatomy of Britain* (1982)

12 Whichever party is in office, the Treasury is in power.

while in opposition

Anthony Sampson *The Changing Anatomy of Britain* (1982)

13 I'm at my best in a messy, middle-of-the-road muddle.

remark in Cabinet, 21 January 1975; Philip Ziegler *Wilson* (1993)

Sandy Wilson 1924–

English songwriter

14 We've got to have
We plot to have
For it's so dreary not to have
That certain thing called the Boy Friend.

The Boyfriend (1954) title song

Woodrow Wilson 1856–1924

American Democratic statesman, 28th President of the US, 1913–21
on Wilson: see **Clemenceau** 71:2, **Kissinger** 175:18

15 The future is not for parties 'playing politics', but for measures conceived in the largest spirit, pushed by parties whose leaders are statesmen, not demagogues, who love, not their offices, but their duty and their opportunity for service

> speech at Trenton, New Jersey, 5 September 1910

1 It is like writing history with lightning. And my only regret is that it is all so terribly true.
on seeing D. W. Griffith's film The Birth of a Nation
> at the White House, 18 February 1915

2 No nation is fit to sit in judgement upon any other nation.
> speech in New York, 20 April 1915

3 There is such a thing as a man being too proud to fight.
> speech in Philadelphia, 10 May 1915

4 We have stood apart, studiously neutral.
> speech to Congress, 7 December 1915

5 It must be a peace without victory . . . Only a peace between equals can last.
> speech to US Senate, 22 January 1917

6 Armed neutrality is ineffectual enough at best.
> speech to Congress, 2 April 1917

7 The world must be made safe for democracy.
> speech to Congress, 2 April 1917

8 Once lead this people into war and they will forget there ever was such a thing as tolerance.
> John Dos Passos *Mr Wilson's War* (1917)

9 Open covenants of peace, openly arrived at.
first of Fourteen Points
> speech to Congress, 8 January 1918

10 America is the only idealistic nation in the world.
> speech at Sioux Falls, South Dakota, 8 September 1919

Duchess of Windsor (Wallis Simpson) 1896–1986

wife of the former **Edward VIII**
see also **Anonymous** 9:14

11 You can never be too rich or too thin.
> attributed

Duke of Windsor

see **Edward VIII**

Jeanette Winterson 1959–

English novelist and critic

12 [Roger Fry] gave us the term 'Post-Impressionist', without realising that the late twentieth century would soon be entirely fenced in with posts.
> *Art Objects* (1995)

13 No one working in the English language now comes close to my exuberance, my passion, my fidelity to words.
on being asked to name the best living author writing in English
> in *Sunday Times* 13 March 1994

Ludwig Wittgenstein 1889–1951

Austrian-born philosopher
see also **Last words** 182:14

14 Philosophy is a battle against the bewitchment of our intelligence by means of language.
> *Philosophische Untersuchungen* (1953)

15 What is your aim in philosophy?—To show the fly the way out of the fly-bottle.
> *Philosophische Untersuchungen* (1953)

16 What can be said at all can be said clearly; and whereof one cannot speak thereof one must be silent.
> *Tractatus Logico-Philosophicus* (1922)

17 The world is everything that is the case.
> *Tractatus Logico-Philosophicus* (1922)

18 The limits of my language mean the limits of my world.
> *Tractatus Logico-Philosophicus* (1922)

P. G. Wodehouse 1881–1975

English writer; an American citizen from 1955
on Wodehouse: see **O'Casey** 234:6

19 Chumps always make the best husbands . . . All the unhappy marriages come from the husbands having brains.
> *The Adventures of Sally* (1920)

1 It is never difficult to distinguish between a Scotsman with a grievance and a ray of sunshine.

> *Blandings Castle and Elsewhere* (1935) 'The Custody of the Pumpkin'

2 There was another ring at the front door. Jeeves shimmered out and came back with a telegram.

> *Carry On, Jeeves!* (1925) 'Jeeves Takes Charge'

3 He spoke with a certain what-is-it in his voice, and I could see that, if not actually disgruntled, he was far from being gruntled.

> *The Code of the Woosters* (1938)

4 Slice him where you like, a hellhound is always a hellhound.

> *The Code of the Woosters* (1938)

5 It is no use telling me that there are bad aunts and good aunts. At the core, they are all alike. Sooner or later, out pops the cloven hoof.

> *The Code of the Woosters* (1938)

6 Roderick Spode? Big chap with a small moustache and the sort of eye that can open an oyster at sixty paces?

> *The Code of the Woosters* (1938)

7 To my daughter Leonora without whose never-failing sympathy and encouragement this book would have been finished in half the time.

> *The Heart of a Goof* (1926) dedication

8 I turned to Aunt Agatha, whose demeanour was now rather like that of one who, picking daisies on the railway, has just caught the down express in the small of the back.

> *The Inimitable Jeeves* (1923)

9 When Aunt is calling to Aunt like mastodons bellowing across primeval swamps.

> *The Inimitable Jeeves* (1923)

10 It was my Uncle George who discovered that alcohol was a food well in advance of medical thought.

> *The Inimitable Jeeves* (1923)

11 It is a good rule in life never to apologize. The right sort of people do not want apologies, and the wrong sort take a mean advantage of them.

> *The Man Upstairs* (1914)

12 He trusted neither of them as far as he could spit, and he was a poor spitter, lacking both distance and control.

> *Money in the Bank* (1946)

13 She fitted into my biggest armchair as if it had been built round her by someone who knew they were wearing armchairs tight about the hips that season.

> *My Man Jeeves* (1919) 'Jeeves and the Unbidden Guest'

14 Ice formed on the butler's upper slopes.

> *Pigs Have Wings* (1952)

15 The Right Hon. was a tubby little chap who looked as if he had been poured into his clothes and had forgotten to say 'When!'

> *Very Good, Jeeves* (1930) 'Jeeves and the Impending Doom'

Terry Wogan 1938–

Irish broadcaster

16 Television contracts the imagination and radio expands it.

> in *Observer* 30 December 1984 'Sayings of the Year'

Naomi Wolf 1962–

17 To ask women to become unnaturally thin is to ask them to relinquish their sexuality.

> *The Beauty Myth* (1990)

Humbert Wolfe 1886–1940

British poet

18 You cannot hope
to bribe or twist,
thank God! the
British journalist.

But, seeing what
the man will do
unbribed, there's
no occasion to.

> 'Over the Fire' (1930)

Thomas Wolfe 1900–38

American novelist

1 Most of the time we think we're sick, it's all in the mind.
   Look Homeward, Angel (1929)

2 'Where they got you stationed now, Luke?' . . . 'In Norfolk at the Navy base,' Luke answered, 'm-m-making the world safe for hypocrisy.'
   Look Homeward, Angel (1929); cf. **Wilson** 332:7

Tom Wolfe 1931–

American writer

3 The bonfire of the vanities.
   title of novel (1987); deriving from Savonarola's 'burning of the vanities' in Florence, 1497

4 A liberal is a conservative who has been arrested.
   The Bonfire of the Vanities (1987)

5 Electric Kool-Aid Acid test.
   title of novel on hippy culture (1968)

6 By day, Structuralists constructed the structure of meaning and pondered the meaning of structure. By night, Deconstructionists pulled the cortical edifice down. And the next day the Structuralists started in again.
   From Bauhaus to Our House (1981)

7 We are now in the Me Decade—seeing the upward roll of . . . the third great religious wave in American history . . . and this one has the mightiest, holiest roll of all, the beat that goes . . . *Me* . . . *Me* . . . *Me* . . . *Me.*
   Mauve Gloves and Madmen (1976) 'The Me Decade'

8 Radical Chic . . . is only radical in Style; in its heart it is part of Society and its tradition—Politics, like Rock, Pop, and Camp, has its uses.
   in *New York* 8 June 1970

Lewis Wolpert 1929–

English biologist

9 If Watson and Crick had not discovered the nature of DNA, one can be virtually certain that other scientists would eventually have determined it. With art—whether painting, music or literature—it is quite different. If Shakespeare had not written *Hamlet,* no other playwright would have done so.
   The Unnatural Nature of Science (1993)

Kenneth Wolstenholme

English sports commentator

10 They think it's all over—it is now.
   television commentary in closing moments of the World Cup Final, 30 July 1966

Tiger Woods

American golfer

11 Growing up, I came up with this name: I'm a Cablinasian.
   explaining his rejection of 'African-American' as the term to describe his Caucasian, Afro-American, Native American, Thai, and Chinese ancestry
   interviewed by Oprah Winfrey, 21 April 1997

George Woodcock 1912–95

Canadian writer

12 Canadians do not like heroes, and so they do not have them.
   Canada and the Canadians (1970)

Thomas Woodrooffe 1899–1978

British naval officer

13 The whole Fleet's lit up. When I say 'lit up', I mean lit up by fairy lamps.
   live outside broadcast, Spithead Review, 20 May 1937
   Asa Briggs *History of Broadcasting in the UK* (1965) vol. 2

Harry Woods

14 Oh we ain't got a barrel of money,
   Maybe we're ragged and funny,
   But we'll travel along
   Singin' a song,
   Side by side.
   'Side by Side' (1927 song)

Virginia Woolf 1882–1941

English novelist
on Woolf: see **Laski** 181:8, **Sitwell** 288:5

1 Life is not a series of gig lamps symmetrically arranged; life is a luminous halo, a semi-transparent envelope surrounding us from the beginning of consciousness to the end.
The Common Reader (1925) 'Modern Fiction'

2 Each had his past shut in him like the leaves of a book known to him by heart; and his friends could only read the title.
Jacob's Room (1922)

3 On or about December 1910 human nature changed . . . All human relations have shifted—those between masters and servants, husbands and wives, parents and children. And when human relations change there is at the same time a change in religion, conduct, politics, and literature.
'Mr Bennett and Mrs Brown' (1924)

4 A woman must have money and a room of her own if she is to write fiction.
A Room of One's Own (1929)

5 Women have served all these centuries as looking-glasses possessing the magic and delicious power of reflecting the figure of a man at twice its natural size.
A Room of One's Own (1929)

6 Literature is strewn with the wreckage of men who have minded beyond reason the opinions of others.
A Room of One's Own (1929)

7 This is an important book, the critic assumes, because it deals with war. This is an insignificant book because it deals with the feelings of women in a drawing room.
A Room of One's Own (1929)

8 So that is marriage, Lily thought, a man and a woman looking at a girl throwing a ball.
To the Lighthouse (1927)

9 I have lost friends, some by death . . . others through sheer inability to cross the street.
The Waves (1931)

10 The vast events now shaping across the Channel are towering over us too closely and too tremendously to be worked into fiction without a painful jolt in the perspective.
in *Times Literary Supplement* 1 March 1917

11 What sort of diary should I like mine to be? . . . I should like it to resemble some deep old desk, or capacious hold-all, in which one flings a mass of odds and ends without looking them through.
diary, 20 April 1919

12 One likes people much better when they're battered down by a prodigious siege of misfortune than when they triumph.
diary, 13 August 1921

13 The scratching of pimples on the body of the bootboy at Claridges.
of James **Joyce**'s *Ulysses*
letter to Lytton Strachey, 24 April 1922

14 I enjoy almost everything. Yet I have some restless searcher in me. Why is there not a discovery in life? Something one can lay one's hands on and say "This is it"?
diary, 27 February 1926

15 As an experience, madness is terrific . . . and in its lava I still find most of the things I write about.
letter to Ethel Smyth, 22 June 1930

16 And now with some pleasure I find that it's seven; and must cook dinner. Haddock and sausage meat. I think it is true that one gains a certain hold on sausage and haddock by writing them down.
diary, 8 March 1941

Alexander Woollcott
1887–1943

American writer

17 She was like a sinking ship firing on the rescuers.
of Mrs Patrick **Campbell**
While Rome Burns (1944) 'The First Mrs Tanqueray'

18 She is so odd a blend of Little Nell and Lady Macbeth. It is not so much the familiar phenomenon of a hand of steel

in a velvet glove as a lacy sleeve with a bottle of vitriol concealed in its folds.
*of Dorothy **Parker***
While Rome Burns (1934) 'Our Mrs Parker'

1 A broker is a man who takes your fortune and runs it into a shoestring.
S. Hopkins Adams *Alexander Woollcott* (1945)

2 All the things I really like to do are either illegal, immoral, or fattening.
R. E. Drennan *Wit's End* (1973)

Terry Worrall
spokesman for British Rail

3 It was the wrong kind of snow.
explaining disruption on British Rail
in *The Independent* 16 February 1991

Neville Wran 1926–
Australian politician

4 The average footslogger in the New South Wales Right . . . generally speaking carries a dagger in one hand and a Bible in the other and doesn't put either to really elegant use.
in 1973; Michael Gordon *A Question of Leadership* (1993)

Frank Lloyd Wright
1867–1959
American architect

5 The necessities were going by default to save the luxuries until I hardly knew which were necessities and which luxuries.
Autobiography (1945)

6 The physician can bury his mistakes, but the architect can only advise his client to plant vines—so they should go as far as possible from home to build their first buildings.
in *New York Times* 4 October 1953

7 The modern city is a place for banking and prostitution and very little else.
Robert C. Twombly *Frank Lloyd Wright* (1973)

Harry Wu
Chinese-born American political activist

8 I want to see the word *laogai* in every dictionary in every language in the world. I want to see the laogai ended. Before 1974, the word 'gulag' did not appear in any dictionary. Today, this single word conveys the meaning of Soviet political violence and its labour camp system. 'Laogai' also deserves a place in our dictionaries.
the laogai *are Chinese labour camps*
in *Washington Post* 26 May 1996

Tammy Wynette 1942–98 and Billy Sherrill c.1938–

9 Stand by your man.
title of song (1968)

John Yates 1925–
English theologian; Bishop of Gloucester from 1975

10 There is a lot to be said in the Decade of Evangelism for believing more and more in less and less.
in *Gloucester Diocesan Gazette* August 1991

W. B. Yeats 1865–1939
Irish poet
*on Yeats: see **Auden** 16:10*

11 O body swayed to music, O brightening glance
How can we know the dancer from the dance?
'Among School Children' (1928)

12 Only God, my dear,
Could love you for yourself alone
And not your yellow hair.
'Anne Gregory' (1932)

13 The unpurged images of day recede;
The Emperor's drunken soldiery are abed.
'Byzantium' (1933)

14 A starlit or a moonlit dome disdains
All that man is;
All mere complexities,
The fury and the mire of human veins.
'Byzantium' (1933)

1 Those images that yet
Fresh images beget,
That dolphin-torn, that gong-tormented
   sea.
   'Byzantium' (1933)

2 Now that my ladder's gone
I must lie down where all ladders start
In the foul rag and bone shop of the
   heart.
   'The Circus Animals' Desertion' (1939)

3 We were the last romantics—chose for
   theme
Traditional sanctity and loveliness.
   'Coole Park and Ballylee, 1931' (1933)

4 The intellect of man is forced to choose
Perfection of the life, or of the work,
And if it take the second must refuse
A heavenly mansion, raging in the dark.
   'The Choice' (1933)

5 A woman can be proud and stiff
When on love intent;
But Love has pitched his mansion in
The place of excrement;
For nothing can be sole or whole
That has not been rent.
   'Crazy Jane Talks with the Bishop' (1932)

6 Nor dread nor hope attend
A dying animal;
A man awaits his end
Dreading and hoping all.
   'Death' (1933)

7 He knows death to the bone—
Man has created death.
   'Death' (1933)

8 All changed, changed utterly:
A terrible beauty is born.
   'Easter, 1916' (1921)

9 Too long a sacrifice
Can make a stone of the heart.
   'Easter, 1916' (1921)

10 I write it out in a verse—
MacDonagh and MacBride
And Connolly and Pearse
Now and in time to be,
Wherever green is worn,
Are changed, changed utterly:
A terrible beauty is born.
   'Easter, 1916' (1921)

11 The rhetorician would deceive his
   neighbours,

The sentimentalist himself; while art
Is but a vision of reality.
   'Ego Dominus Tuus' (1917)

12 The fascination of what's difficult
Has dried the sap out of my veins, and
   rent
Spontaneous joy and natural content
Out of my heart.
   'The Fascination of What's Difficult' (1910)

13 The friends that have it I do wrong
When ever I remake a song,
Should know what issue is at stake:
It is myself that I remake.
   'The friends that have it I do wrong' (1908)

14 Never to have lived is best, ancient
   writers say;
Never to have drawn the breath of life,
   never to have looked into the eye of
   day;
The second best's a gay goodnight and
   quickly turn away.
   'From *Oedipus at Colonus*' (1928); see below

   Not to be born is, past all prizing, best.
   Sophocles (c.496–406 BC) Oedipus Coloneus

15 The ghost of Roger Casement
Is beating on the door.
   'The Ghost of Roger Casement' (1939)

16 The innocent and the beautiful
Have no enemy but time.
   'In Memory of Eva Gore Booth and Con
   Markiewicz' (1933)

17 My country is Kiltartan Cross;
My countrymen Kiltartan's poor!
   'An Irish Airman Foresees his Death' (1919)

18 Nor law, nor duty bade me fight,
Nor public men, nor cheering crowds.
   'An Irish Airman Foresees his Death' (1919)

19 The years to come seemed waste of
   breath,
A waste of breath the years behind
In balance with this life, this death.
   'An Irish Airman Foresees his Death' (1919)

20 A shudder in the loins engenders there
The broken wall, the burning roof and
   tower
And Agamemnon dead.
   'Leda and the Swan' (1928)

1 Like a long-legged fly upon the stream
His mind moves upon silence.
'Long-Legged Fly' (1939)

2 Did that play of mine send out
Certain men the English shot?
'The Man and the Echo' (1939)

3 We had fed the heart on fantasies,
The heart's grown brutal from the fare.
'Meditations in Time of Civil War' no. 6 'The
Stare's Nest by my Window' (1928)

4 Think where man's glory most begins
and ends
And say my glory was I had such friends.
'The Municipal Gallery Re-visited' (1939)

5 I think it better that at times like these
We poets keep our mouths shut, for in
truth
We have no gift to set a statesman right;
He's had enough of meddling who can
please
A young girl in the indolence of her
youth
Or an old man upon a winter's night.
'On being asked for a War Poem' (1919)

6 Where, where but here have Pride and
Truth,
That long to give themselves for wage,
To shake their wicked sides at youth
Restraining reckless middle age?
'On hearing that the Students of our New
University have joined the Agitation against
Immoral Literature' (1910)

7 An intellectual hatred is the worst,
So let her think opinions are accursed.
'A Prayer for My Daughter' (1920)

8 Out of Ireland have we come.
Great hatred, little room,
Maimed us at the start.
'Remorse for Intemperate Speech' (1933)

9 That is no country for old men. The
young
In one another's arms, birds in the
trees—
Those dying generations—at their song.
'Sailing to Byzantium' (1928)

10 An aged man is but a paltry thing,
A tattered coat upon a stick, unless

Soul clap its hands and sing, and louder
sing
For every tatter in its mortal dress.
'Sailing to Byzantium' (1928)

11 And therefore I have sailed the seas and
come
To the holy city of Byzantium.
'Sailing to Byzantium' (1928)

12 All shuffle there; all cough in ink;
All wear the carpet with their shoes;
All think what other people think;
All know the man their neighbour
knows.
Lord, what would they say
Did their Catullus walk that way?
'The Scholars' (1919)

13 Things fall apart; the centre cannot hold;
Mere anarchy is loosed upon the world,
The blood-dimmed tide is loosed, and
everywhere
The ceremony of innocence is drowned;
The best lack all conviction, while the
worst
Are full of passionate intensity.
'The Second Coming' (1921)

14 And what rough beast, its hour come
round at last,
Slouches towards Bethlehem to be born?
'The Second Coming' (1921)

15 Romantic Ireland's dead and gone,
It's with O'Leary in the grave.
'September, 1913' (1914)

16 Oh, who could have foretold
That the heart grows old?
'A Song' (1919)

17 You think it horrible that lust and rage
Should dance attendance upon my old
age;
They were not such a plague when I was
young;
What else have I to spur me into song?
'The Spur' (1939)

18 Swift has sailed into his rest;
Savage indignation there
Cannot lacerate his breast.
'Swift's Epitaph' (1933); see below

Ubi saeva indignatio ulterius cor lacerare nequit.

Where fierce indignation can no longer tear his heart.

Jonathan Swift (1667–1745) epitaph

1 But was there ever dog that praised his fleas?

'To a Poet, Who would have Me Praise certain bad Poets, Imitators of His and of Mine' (1910)

2 Michaelangelo left a proof
On the Sistine Chapel roof,
Where but half-awakened Adam
Can disturb globe-trotting Madam.

'Under Ben Bulben' (1939)

3 Irish poets, learn your trade,
Sing whatever is well made.

'Under Ben Bulben' (1939)

4 Cast your mind on other days
That we in coming days may be
Still the indomitable Irishry.

'Under Ben Bulben' (1939)

5 Cast a cold eye
On life, on death.
Horseman, pass by!

'Under Ben Bulben' (1939)

6 We make out of the quarrel with others, rhetoric, but of the quarrel with ourselves, poetry.

Essays (1924) 'Anima Hominis'

7 Even when the poet seems most himself . . . he is never the bundle of accident and incoherence that sits down to breakfast; he has been reborn as an idea, something intended, complete.

Essays and Introductions (1961) 'A General Introduction for my Work'

8 In dreams begins responsibility.

Responsibilities (1914) epigraph

of the Anglo-Irish:
9 We . . . are no petty people. We are one of the great stocks of Europe. We are the people of Burke; we are the people of Swift, the people of Emmet, the people of Parnell. We have created most of the modern literature of this country. We have created the best of its political intelligence.

speech in the Irish Senate, 11 June 1925, in the debate on divorce

10 Think like a wise man but express yourself like the common people.

letter to Dorothy Wellesley, 21 December 1935; see below

He that will write well in any tongue, must follow this counsel of Aristotle, to speak as the common people do, to think as wise men do; and so should every man understand him, and the judgement of wise men allow him.

Roger Ascham (1515–68) *Toxophilus* (1545)

Boris Yeltsin 1931–

Russian statesman, President of the Russian Federation since 1991

11 You can make a throne of bayonets, but you can't sit on it for long.

from the top of a tank, during the attempted military coup against **Gorbachev**

in *Independent* 24 August 1991; cf. **Inge** 157:2

12 Europe is in danger of plunging into a cold peace.

at the summit meeting of the Conference on Security and Co-operation in Europe

in *Newsweek* 19 December 1994; cf. **Baruch** 24:9

13 Today is the last day of an era past.

at a Berlin ceremony to end the Soviet military presence

in *Guardian* 1 September 1994

Sergei Yesenin 1895–1925

Russian poet
see also **Last words** 182:8

14 It's always the good feel rotten.
Pleasure's for those who are bad.

'Pleasure's for the Bad' (1923)

Yevgeny Yevtushenko 1933–

Russian poet

15 Over Babiy Yar
There are no memorials.
The steep hillside like a rough inscription.

'Babiy Yar' (1961)

16 So on and on
we walked without thinking of rest

passing craters, passing fire,
under the rocking sky of '41
tottering crazy on its smoking columns.
'The Companion' (1954)

1 Life is a rainbow which also includes
black.
in *Guardian* 11 August 1987

Shoichi Yokoi 1915–97
Japanese soldier

2 It is a terrible shame for me—I came
back, still alive, without having won the
war.
*on returning to Japan after surviving for 28 years
in the jungles of Guam before surrendering to the
Americans in 1972*
in *Independent* 26 September 1997

Sarah, Duchess of York
1959–

3 I think it's a fresh, clean page. I think I
go onwards and upwards.
the day before her divorce was made absolute
in an interview on *Sky News* 29 May 1996; in
Daily Telegraph 30 May 1996

Andrew Young 1932–
American clergyman and diplomat

4 Nothing is illegal if one hundred well-
placed business men decide to do it.
Morris K. Udall *Too Funny to be President*
(1988)

G. M. Young 1882–1959
English historian

5 Being published by the Oxford University
Press is rather like being married to a
duchess: the honour is almost greater
than the pleasure.
Rupert Hart-Davis, letter to George Lyttelton,
29 April 1956

Neil Young 1945–
and Jeff Blackburn
Canadian singer and songwriter

6 It's better to burn out
Than to fade away.
*quoted by Kurt **Cobain** in his suicide note, 8 April
1994*
'My My, Hey Hey (Out of the Blue)' (1978 song)

Yevgeny Zamyatin 1884–1937
Russian writer

7 Heretics are the only bitter remedy
against the entropy of human thought.
'Literature, Revolution and Entropy' quoted in
The Dragon and other Stories (1967)
introduction

8 Yesterday there was a tsar and there
were slaves; today there is no tsar, but
the slaves remain; tomorrow there will
be only tsars . . . We have lived through
the epoch of suppression of the masses;
we are living in an epoch of suppression
of the individual in the name of the
masses; tomorrow will bring the
liberation of the individual—in the name
of man.
'Tomorrow' (1919) in *A Soviet Heretic* (1970)

Israel Zangwill 1864–1926
Jewish spokesman and writer

9 America is God's Crucible, the great
Melting-Pot where all the races of Europe
are melting and re-forming!
The Melting Pot (1908)

Emiliano Zapata 1879–1919
Mexican revolutionary
*see also **Ibarruri** 156:2*

10 Many of them, so as to curry favour with
tyrants, for a fistful of coins, or through
bribery or corruption, are shedding the
blood of their brothers.
*on the maderistas who, in Zapata's view, had
betrayed the revolutionary cause*
Plan de Ayala 28 November 1911

Frank Zappa 1940–93

American rock musician and songwriter

1 A drug is neither moral or immoral—it's a chemical compound. The compound itself is not a menace to society until a human being treats it as if consumption bestowed a temporary licence to act like an asshole.

The Real Frank Zappa Book (1989)

2 Rock journalism is people who can't write interviewing people who can't talk for people who can't read.

L. Botts *Loose Talk* (1980)

Benjamin Zephaniah 1958–

British poet

3 I think poetry should be alive. You should be able to dance it.

in *Sunday Times* 23 August 1987

Mikhail Zhvanetsky 1934–

Russian writer

4 We enjoyed . . . his slyness. He mastered the art of walking backward into the future. He would say 'After me'. And some people went ahead, and some went behind, and he would go backward.

*of Mikhail **Gorbachev***

in *Time* 12 September 1994; attributed

Philip Ziegler 1929–

British historian

5 Remember. In Spite of Everything, He Was A Great Man.

*notice kept on his desk while working on his biography of **Mountbatten** (published 1985)*

Andrew Roberts *Eminent Churchillians* (1994)

Ronald L. Ziegler 1939–

American government spokesman

6 [Mr Nixon's latest statement] is the Operative White House Position . . . and all previous statements are inoperative.

at the time of the Watergate Affair

in *Boston Globe* 18 April 1973

Grigori Zinoviev 1883–1936

Soviet politician

7 Armed warfare must be preceded by a struggle against the inclinations to compromise which are embedded among the majority of British workmen, against the ideas of evolution and peaceful extermination of capitalism. Only then will it be possible to count upon complete success of an armed insurrection.

letter to the British Communist Party, 15 September 1924; the 'Zinoviev Letter', said by some to be a forgery

Hiller B. Zobel

American judge

8 Asking the ignorant to use the incomprehensible to decide the unknowable.

'The Jury on Trial' in *American Heritage* July–August 1995

9 Judges must follow their oaths and do their duty, heedless of editorials, letters, telegrams, threats, petitions, panellists and talk shows.
   In this country, we do not administer justice by plebiscite. A judge . . . is a public servant who must follow his conscience, whether or not he counters the manifest wishes of those he serves; whether or not his decision seems a surrender to prevalent demands.

judicial ruling reducing the conviction of Louise Woodward from murder to manslaughter, 10 November 1997·

Selective Thematic Index

Buying more American than thinking

WARH 319:6

cheaper than a prawn sandwich RATN 260:6
crazy with lust, calls it advertising LAHR 178:13
Deals are my art form TRUM 313:9
Do you sincerely want to be rich? CORN 77:3
good for General Motors WILS 330:14
Greed is all right BOES 40:6
green shoots of recovery MISQ 218:6
guided by 'feminine' principles RODD 266:3
ideals of nation by advertisements DOUG 91:7
market has no morality HESE 147:2
merger between Heaven and Hell WELL 323:14
not run by itself except downhill SAYI 278:5
Only the paranoid survive GROV 134:12
put your heart in the business WATS 320:10
really want to make a million ANON 10:2
riding on a smile and a shoeshine MILL 215:6
romantic sleeping under the desk GATE 125:5
salary of the chief executive GALB 123:9
Virgin is the possibility BRAN 43:5
vital economic interests WEIL 322:6

Education

able to read but unable to TREV 311:9
ceiling put on our ambitions PRES 256:2
crème de la crème SPAR 292:9
destroy every grammar school CROS 80:11
dread of games BETJ 35:16
during the holidays from Eton SITW 288:8
exam for humour, sincerity NEIL 229:7
gained in the university of life BOTT 42:5
Headmasters have powers CHUR 68:7
He who cannot, teaches SHAW 285:2
Ignorance is an evil weed BEVE 37:2
knew more than examiners KEYN 171:4
knowledge not of facts but of values

INGE 157:3

More will mean worse AMIS 8:2
No more Latin, no more French ANON 10:14
not even red brick but white tile OSBO 240:2
read Shakespeare and shoot dice BANK 22:12
Technology is just a tool GATE 125:6

Environment

billboard lovely as a tree NASH 228:13
Green how I love you GARC 125:2
Greenpeace said ecology and antiwar

HUNT 154:12

humdrum issues like the environment

THAT 305:15

I am the grass; I cover all SAND 274:13
I would be burning the rain forest STIN 298:11
left it a land of 'beauty spots' JOAD 161:10
Little boxes all the same REYN 263:8
Make it a *green* peace DARN 83:5
Polluted rivers, filthy streets HESE 147:3
remains will be concrete and tyres LARK 180:6
replace lawns with paving stones OFFI 235:14
silent spring CARS 54:7
Spaceship Earth FULL 122:3
Switzerland lacks: manure GIDE 128:1
They paved paradise MITC 217:4
Think globally, act locally SAYI 279:9

Fashion

Amusing little seams and witty pleats

BAIL 20:2

Clothes are our weapons CART 54:8
ease a heart like a satin gown PARK 243:6
gentle progression of revisited ideas

OLDF 234:16

get ahead, get a hat ADVE 3:25
had often heard shoes described HALS 137:4
Haute Couture should be fun LACR 178:11
I don't really like knees SAIN 273:10
I like to dress egos VERS 317:2
trick of wearing mink BALM 22:6
well dressed in cheap shoes AMIE 7:6
Who am I going to be today WELD 322:12

Film

biggest electric train set WELL 322:14
cinema is truth 24 times per second

GODA 129:5

images of life and death BERG 32:8
Kiss Kiss Bang Bang KAEL 166:12
lie down in clean postures FOWL 117:4
lunatics taken charge of the asylum

ROWL 270:1

messages delivered by Western Union

GOLD 130:11

Mickey Mouse could direct a movie HYTN 156:1
park, a policeman and a pretty girl CHAP 61:9
pictures that got small FILM 112:4
seen one Western you've seen them all

WHIT 327:10

shoot me through linoleum BANK 22:13
Sticks nix hick pix NEWS 231:11
Western is the Saga of the Nibelungen

LANG 179:16

writing history with lightning WILS 332:1

poetry makes nothing happen   AUDE 16:11
principle of procrastinated rape   PRIT 257:2
school of Snobbery with Violence   BENN 31:1
shelf life of the modern hardback writer
                                          TRIL 311:12
shock-proof shit detector   HEMI 145:17
way of taking life by the throat   FROS 121:5
What was the message of your play   BEHA 27:3
wish your wife or servants to read   GRIF 134:4
world full of audio visual marvels   SMIT 289:5

Love

All you need is love   LENN 188:1
Birds do it, bees do it   PORT 252:18
consisted in discussing if it existed
                                          GUNN 135:10
enough to give him diamonds back
                                          GABO 122:9
Games people play   BERN 33:14
Love is a universal migraine   GRAV 131:12
love is of man's life a thing apart   AMIS 7:11
money can't buy me love   LENN 188:3
most natural painkiller   LAST 182:12
my North, my South, my East and West
                                          AUDE 16:8
Night and day, you are the one   PORT 252:16
not ever having to say you're sorry   SEGA 282:4
outer life of telegrams and anger   FORS 116:8
pour nous, c'est l'amour   BOUS 42:7
someone to call you darling after sex
                                          BARN 23:8
whatever that may mean   CHAR 61:12

Marriage and the Family

Being a husband is a whole-time job
                                          BENN 31:11
Bigamy is having one husband too many
                                          ANON 9:4
deep peace of the double-bed   CAMP 52:4
father was frightened of his mother
                                          GEOR 126:11
fundamental defect of fathers   RUSS 272:3
get anywhere in a marriage   MURD 225:14
Get me to the church on time   LERN 188:13
having two children you are a referee
                                          FROS 119:14
I'd hire the other two   HALL 137:1
If Miss means respectably unmarried
                                          CART 54:10
If you bungle raising your children
                                          ONAS 235:19
I married beneath me, all women do
                                          ASTO 14:16

isn't a word . . . it's a sentence   FILM 111:6
man who hates his mother   BENN 31:14
maximum of temptation   SHAW 285:3
never again so much together   MACN 203:3
No test tube can breed love   WILL 329:10
not getting married today. I'm in bed
                                          GALL 123:16
not that adults produce children   DE V 88:14
old maid like death by drowning   FERB 107:12
source of all our discontents   LEAC 185:3
tangled web do parents weave   NASH 227:12
They fuck you up, your mum and dad
                                          LARK 180:12
three of us in this marriage   DIAN 89:8
two is fun, three is a houseful   SAYI 278:6
waste-paper basket of the emotions
                                          WEBB 322:3

Media and Communication

all that an interviewer allows you to say
                                          BENN 30:7
convention of spiritualists   STOP 299:1
Internet is an élite organization   CHOM 64:14
It is Stupidvision   TOYN 311:2
licence to print money   THOM 309:6
lifting the manufacture of banality
                                          SARR 275:17
like an oil painting   INGH 157:7
madness of TV is madness of life   PAGL 241:15
male, middle class, middle-aged   STRE 300:7
manifesto written by Dr Mori   BENN 30:2
medium is the message   MCLU 201:7
monkeys banging on typewriters   WILE 329:1
No good can come of it   SCOT 281:12
no plain women on television   FORD 115:3
no such thing as bad publicity   BEHA 27:4
One picture worth ten thousand words
                                          BARN 23:3
PC is the LSD of the '90s   LEAR 185:10
playing a piano in a brothel   MUGG 225:1
so much chewing gum for the eyes   ANON 11:8
talking about surfing the Net   ELIZ 103:2
Television contracts the imagination
                                          WOGA 333:16
Television is for appearing on   COWA 79:2
Television thrives on unreason   DAY 84:14
turning news into a sausage factory
                                          PAXM 246:2
ultimate sanction of switching off   EYRE 106:5
voyager in virtuality can return   TURK 313:16
We are surfing food   MACK 200:8
when people write every other day   DOUG 91:8
When seagulls follow a trawler   CANT 53:8
Xerox makes everybody a publisher
                                          MCLU 201:13

Men and Women

....

all men are rapists	FREN 118:9
become the servant of a man	SHAW 284:1
becoming the men we wanted to marry	
	STEI 296:11
desire to have all the fun	SAYE 277:5
difficult to behave like gentlemen	MACK 200:5
doormat or a prostitute	WEST 324:22
do twice as well as men	WHIT 327:13
Every woman adores a Fascist	PLAT 250:3
food, sports and last, relationships	FISH 109:3
good excuse not to play football	LEBO 186:4
help with moving the piano	WEST 325:4
If men had to have babies	DIAN 89:5
juggle work, love, home and children	
	FRIE 119:5
like a fish without a bicycle	STEI 296:12
little idea of how much men hate them	
	GREE 133:2
Making contact with this Wild Man	BLY 40:2
manhood was an opportunity for	
achievement	KEIL 168:4
they don't have to sew buttons	BROU 46:8
Toughness not in a pinstripe suit	FEIN 107:6
wanted us to think with our wombs	
	LUCE 196:5
We are lads	GALL 123:17
we would still be living in grass huts	
	PAGL 241:14
who does the dishes	FREN 118:10
Why can't a woman be more like a man	
	LERN 188:14
woman has only the right to spring	
	FOND 114:13
Women have no wilderness in them	
	BOGA 40:7
Women want mediocre men	MEAD 211:12

Music

....

brandy of the damned	SHAW 284:14
en famille angels play Mozart	BART 24:7
French operas sung by Swedish artists	
	WHAR 325:11
guy gets stabbed in the back	GARD 125:3
hear it through their feet	SOUS 292:4
how potent cheap music is	COWA 78:16
if you gotta ask you'll never know	MISQ 218:9
it's what I meant	VAUG 316:9
it won't come out of your horn	PARK 242:11
jazz the sound of surprise	BALL 22:5
just pick a chord, go twang	VICI 317:4

Let's face the music and dance	BERL 32:12
lets the ears lie back in an easy chair	
	IVES 158:2
like scrabble with the vowels missing	
	ELLI 103:8
little finger to become longer	SCHO 280:11
making us prisoners of noise	MORE 221:10
Music is feeling, then, not sound	STEV 297:14
not a bona fide human being	SPEC 292:14
pauses between the notes	SCHN 280:8
revenge by the culture of the Negroes	
	PADE 241:9
start together and finish together	BEEC 26:17
sweet, soft, plenty rhythm	MORT 223:10
to get laid, to get fame	GELD 125:9
too good to leave to chance	SIMO 287:11

Politics

....

argument of the broken window pane	
	PANK 242:8
Art of the Possible	BUTL 50:10
blame Marx for what was done	BENN 30:1
can take a nation's pulse	WHIT 326:2
done very well out of the war	BALD 21:2
dumb enough to think it's important	
	MCCA 197:6
election by the incompetent many	
	SHAW 284:24
executive expression of human immaturity	
	BRIT 44:9
feeds your vanity, starves your self-respect	
	PARR 244:14
future refusing to be born	BEVA 36:15
government by discussion	ATTL 15:10
Great Britain has lost an empire	ACHE 1:8
Instead of rocking the cradle	ROBI 265:12
iron curtain has descended	CHUR 67:9
it's a good idea but it won't work	ROGE 266:16
job all working-class parents want	ABBO 1:1
most people vote against somebody	ADAM 1:14
not the voting that's democracy	STOP 298:15
only safe pleasure	CRIT 80:6
owes more to Methodism than to Marxism	
	PHIL 248:10
places the nation at his service	POMP 250:13
prerogative of the eunuch	STOP 298:17
Safe is spelled D-U-L-L	CLAR 69:16
second oldest profession	REAG 261:12
socialism would not lose its human face	
	DUBČ 92:5
taking money from poor people	BAUE 25:1
they are lower than vermin	BEVA 36:5
Through talk, we tamed kings	BENN 29:16

Popular Culture

Religion

Royalty

Science and Technology

means of total destruction   SAKH 273:11
most incomprehensible fact   EINS 97:1
not be content to manufacture life   BERN 33:9
one small step for a man   ARMS 13:4
physicists have known sin   OPPE 236:9
scientist says that something is possible
                                                CLAR 70:5
set a limit to infinite error   BREC 43:12
shocked by this subject   BOHR 40:10
spark-gap is mightier than the pen   HOGB 150:9
technology indistinguishable from magic
                                                CLAR 70:4
There is no democracy in physics   ALVA 7:2
thought ahead, and invented the brake
                                                NEME 229:8
to really foul things up   SAYI 279:10
when I don't know what I'm doing   BRAU 43:9
white heat of technology   MISQ 219:4
you always end up using scissors   HOCK 150:4

Sex

act of holy communion   ROBI 265:11
ask somebody older than me   BLAK 39:6
composer and *not* homosexual   DIAG 89:4
did thee feel the earth move   HEMI 145:10
Give a man a free hand   WEST 324:9
He said it was artificial respiration   BURG 49:3
If men could get pregnant   KENN 168:8
in the street and frighten the horses   CAMP 52:5
Is that a pistol in your pocket   WEST 324:13
It's just It   KIPL 175:15
make passes at girls who wear glasses
                                                PARK 243:1
most fun I ever had without laughing   ALLE 6:7
not got your niche in creation   HALL 137:3
only if I found him attractive   WESL 324:1
only unnatural sex act   KINS 173:10
orgasm has replaced the Cross   MUGG 224:12
rapist bothers to buy a bottle of wine
                                                DWOR 94:2
Sexual intercourse began in 1963   LARK 180:2
something I really don't understand   SALI 274:4
sooner go to my dentist   WAUG 321:13
We are British, thank God   MONT 220:14
zipless fuck is the purest thing   JONG 164:1

Society

as long as you know your place   KING 173:3
cannot help the many who are poor
                                                KENN 169:4
condemn a little more and understand
                                                MAJO 204:15

culture without hope cannot forgive
                                                MORR 222:5
no such thing as Society   THAT 306:8
prisoners of addiction and envy   ILLI 156:7
to build a socialist society   NYER 233:6
To give employment to the artisan   BELL 28:3
twelve-year-olds having babies   GING 128:4
When Hitler attacked the Jews   NIEM 232:1
where it is safe to be unpopular   STEV 298:5

Sport

by the hand of God   MARA 207:9
don't really see the hurdles   MOSE 223:12
flannelled fools at the wicket   KIPL 174:7
Football an art central to our culture
                                                GREE 133:6
football is a matter of life and death
                                                SHAN 283:9
Football? It's the beautiful game   PELÉ 246:9
game is about glory   BLAN 39:9
game which takes less than three days
                                                STOP 299:15
get to shake a bat at a white man   GREG 133:10
I'm the greatest   ALI 6:1
manager who gets the blame   LINE 191:8
my *business* to get him in trouble   ROBI 265:13
Nice guys finish last   DURO 93:8
not as fast as the world record   COLE 72:13
nothing to do with fair play   ORWE 239:4
offered you Conflict and Art   PRIE 256:10
show business with blood   BRUN 47:4
Spill your guts at Wimbledon   CONN 75:4
swearing is very much part of it   GREA 132:2
war minus the shooting   ORWE 239:8
Winning is everything   HILL 148:8

Transport

any colour so long as it is black   FORD 115:7
automobile changed our dress, manners
                                                KEAT 168:3
car crash as a sexual event   BALL 22:2
car has become an article of dress   MCLU 201:9
Commuter—one who spends his life
                                                WHIT 326:3
dreadful human beings alongside   NORR 232:13
equivalent of the great Gothic cathedrals
                                                BART 24:8
lances of ancient knights   ROOT 268:10
looks like a poached egg   NUFF 233:3
Night Mail crossing the Border   AUDE 17:4
only two emotions in a plane   WELL 323:2

redesigned Hell from airport layouts   PRIC 256:6
seen in a bus over the age of 30   WEST 325:8
slipped the surly bonds of earth   MAGE 204:1
steel canisters hurtling about   CASS 55:11
Take my camel, dear   MACA 197:4
the car his perilous excursion ashore
LEWI 190:12

Travel and Exploration

Abroad is bloody   GEOR 126:13
'abroad' to be Catholic and sensual   CHAN 61:4
Been there, done that   SAYI 278:3
landing a man on the Moon   KENN 169:8
São Paulo is like Reading   FLEM 114:7
this is an awful place   SCOT 281:13
tourism is their religion   RUNC 270:6
travel broadens the mind; but   CHES 63:18

Twentieth Century

belongs to those who will build it   TRUD 312:10
century of the common man   WALL 319:1
December 1910 human nature changed
WOOL 335:3
decorates life like a Christmas cake
TANG 302:16
degree of contempt for life   VANE 316:3
don't hear the cries of the tormented
MILL 215:15
Everything is becoming science fiction
BALL 22:1
exhilaration and exhaustion   LAHR 179:1
gadget-filled paradise   NIEB 231:16
image worthy of it   BURC 48:13
in 1915 the old world ended   LAWR 183:6
Middle Ages ended suddenly in the 1950s
HOBS 149:15
neither nirvana nor Armageddon   HEWI 147:8
Ours is the age of substitutes   BENT 32:6
paying the price for the Eighties   AUST 18:20
plastics, Picasso, sunbathing   WAUG 321:6
problem is that *man is dead*   FROM 119:13
problem of the colour line   DU B 92:6
seen the future and it works   STEF 296:1
size of each event   MAIL 204:8
Suppose Lenin had died of typhus   SCHL 280:3
the long week-end   FORS 116:3
thought of modern civilization   GAND 124:13
twentieth century belongs to Youth
QUAN 258:6
We are now in the Me Decade   WOLF 334:7
world is changing almost too fast   ELIZ 102:14

War

blood, toil, tears and sweat   CHUR 66:2
bomber will always get through   BALD 21:7
bomb them back into the Stone Age
LEMA 187:4
capitalism with the gloves off   STOP 299:11
casting out Satan by Satan   SORL 292:3
counted them all back   HANR 138:5
destroy the town in order to save it   ANON 10:4
fight for its King and Country   GRAH 131:6
first live televised war   O'RO 236:14
Forgotten Army   MOUN 224:1
for these who die as cattle   OWEN 240:14
give a war and nobody will come   SAND 275:3
Götterdämmerung without the gods
MACD 199:1
guerrilla wins if he does not lose   KISS 176:2
In bombers named for girls   JARR 159:18
In Flanders fields, the poppies blow   MCCR 198:8
just for a scrap of paper   BETH 34:10
lost in the living rooms of America
MCLU 201:12
no allies to be polite to   GEOR 126:12
Patriotism is not enough   CAVE 56:8
Peace is indivisible   LITV 191:12
rather have butter or guns   GOER 129:11
Rule 1, on page 1 of the book of war
MONT 220:13
smell of napalm in the morning   FILM 110:13
Somme is like the Holocaust   BARK 23:1
so much owed by so many to so few   CHUR 66:7
steamers made an excursion to hell
PRIE 256:12
survival is all there is   FULL 122:5
there can be no substitute for victory
MACA 197:2
this may not be a just peace   IZET 158:3
This was their finest hour   CHUR 66:6
war has used up words   JAME 159:12
wave a red flag myself sooner   GEOR 126:10
way to win an atomic war   BRAD 43:1
Who has matched us with His hour
BROO 45:14
will cease when men refuse to fight
POLI 251:24

Youth

Any failure seems so total   QUAN 258:8
At eighteen our convictions are hills   FITZ 113:1
curse of younger generation   MACM 202:4
door opens and lets the future in   GREE 132:13
forgotten what it is like   JARR 160:1

Keyword Index

adventure (*cont.*):

awfully big a.	BARR 23:12
most beautiful a. in life	LAST 183:3
pass out into a.	FORS 116:4

adventurer greatest a. — BUTL 50:7

advertise a. food to hungry — GALB 123:8

advertisement no a. for — HESE 147:3

one effective a. — HUXL 155:8

advertisements ideals by its a. — DOUG 91:7

knew a column of a. — HOLM 151:5

advertiser a.'s 'sizzling' — PRIE 257:1

advertisers a. don't object to — SWAF 301:10

advertising A. is the rattling — ORWE 239:14

A. may be described — LEAC 185:6

a. we deserve — SAYE 277:8

invasion of a. — SOLZ 291:2

lust and calls it a. — LAHR 178:13

money I spend on a. — LEVE 189:7

advise Advisers a. — THAT 306:12

A. the prince — ELIO 100:9

PLEASE A. — TELE 305:6

advisers political a. — SHOR 286:15

aeroplanes it wasn't the a. — FILM 111:12

aesthetic a. enjoyment — WHIT 327:1

a. experiment — GRIE 134:3

degree of my a. emotion — BELL 27:6

affair a. between Margot Asquith — PARK 243:10

affairs his or her love a. — WEST 325:2

taking part in a. — VALÉ 315:16

affection a. of the human animal — SHAW 284:2

a. you get back — NESB 229:11

affluence A. was a question — DRAB 92:2

affluent a. society — GALB 123:2

so-called a. society — BEVA 36:13

afraid a. of the big bad wolf — CHUR 65:3

a. of Virginia Woolf — ALBE 5:8

because she was a. of him — MURD 225:11

I, a stranger and a. — HOUS 152:5

in short, I was a. — ELIO 100:8

not a. to die — ALLE 6:12

to be a. — FAUL 107:2

were a. to ask — REUB 263:6

Africa A. than my own body — ORTO 237:4

choose between this A. — WALC 318:2

deported A. — GENE 126:3

sloggin' over A. — KIPL 173:11

Till China and A. meet — AUDE 15:15

African A. is conditioned — KENY 170:6

A. national consciousness — MACM 201:19

struggle of the A. people — MAND 205:11

Africans A. experience people — KAUN 167:5

after A. the first death — THOM 307:10

A. you, Claude — CATC 57:1

one damned thing a. another — HUBB 153:7

Or just a. — STEV 297:17

afternoon a. of human life — JUNG 166:6

At five in the a. — GARC 125:1

Christ coming this a. — CART 55:2

lose the war in an a. — CHUR 68:16

summer a. — JAME 159:15

again déjà vu all over a. — BERR 34:2

I'll see you a. — COWA 78:5

against a. everything — KENN 170:2

always vote *a.* — FIEL 108:12

anyone who wasn't a. war — LOW 195:3

He was a. it — COOL 76:5

life is 6 to 5 a. — RUNY 270:10

vote a. somebody — ADAM 1:14

Agamemnon And A. dead — YEAT 337:20

When A. cried aloud — ELIO 101:5

age a. is rocking the wave — MAND 206:9

a. shall not weary them — BINY 37:13

a., which forgives itself — SHAW 285:10

dawning of the a. of Aquarius — RADO 259:6

every a. seeks out in itself — WHIT 327:8

I meet my Father, my a. — LOWE 195:11

old a. always fifteen years — BARU 24:10

Old a. is the most unexpected — TROT 312:7

Old a. should burn — THOM 307:2

only end of a. — LARK 180:5

that men call a. — BROO 45:7

when Mozart was my a. — LEHR 187:1

With leaden a. o'ercargoed — FLEC 114:3

aged a. man is but a paltry thing — YEAT 338:10

learn how to be a. — BLYT 40:4

agenda any item of the a. — PARK 244:7

agnosticism all a. means — DARR 83:6

agony it was a., Ivy — CATC 57:13

most extreme a. — BETT 36:3

agreement blow with an a. — TROT 312:5

agrees nobody a. with you — STEI 296:4

ahea say you're a. of your time — MCGO 199:10

ahead get a., get a hat — ADVE 3:25

aid Foreign a. is a system — BAUE 25:1

aids adventure in the world of A. — PERK 247:2

A. epidemic has rolled — WHIT 326:4

[A. was] an illness — GUIB 135:7

box of A. — DOTY 91:2

seventeen-year-olds dying of A. — GING 128:4

stop them catching A. — CURR 82:7

aim forgotten your a. — SANT 275:8

ain't a. necessarily so — HEYW 147:12

air death of a. — ELIO 99:7

lands hatless from the a. — BETJ 35:1

university of the a. — WILS 331:5

air conditioning respectability and a.

BARA 22:14

airline a. ticket to romantic — MARV 209:4

airplanes feel about a. — KERR 170:9

airport observing a. layouts — PRIC 256:6

aitches lose but our a. — ORWE 239:3

Alamein Before A. we never had — CHUR 68:15

alarm SPREAD A. AND DESPONDENCY — PENI 246:10

alas A. but cannot pardon — AUDE 17:17

Albert Went there with young A.   EDGA 95:10
alcohol A. a necessary article   SHAW 284:9
  A. didn't cause   BOAZ 40:5
  a. doesn't thrill me   PORT 252:14
  a. or morphine   JUNG 166:4
  a. was a food   WODE 333:10
  taken more out of a.   CHUR 68:1
Aldershot burnish'd by A. sun   BETJ 35:13
alibi always has an a.   ELIO 100:15
Alice Pass the sick bag, A.   CATC 59:4
  went down with A.   MILN 216:11
alien a. people clutching   ELIO 100:2
  damned if I'm an a.   GEOR 126:9
alike all places were a. to him   KIPL 175:10
  human beings are more a.   ANGE 8:11
alive a. and well   ANON 10:5
  a. and working on   ANON 9:13
  came back, still a.   YOKO 340:2
  gets out of it a.   FILM 110:15
  Half dead and half a.   BETJ 34:14
  Hallelujah! I'm a.   OSBO 239:19
  If we can't stay here a.   MONT 220:12
  Not while I'm a.   BEVI 37:10
  poetry should be a.   ZEPH 341:3
  still a. at twenty-two   KING 172:16
  ways of being a.   DAWK 84:6
all 1066 and a. that   SELL 282:8
  a. shall be well   ELIO 99:12
  Evening, a.   CATC 57:14
  You can have it a.   PFEI 248:1
allegiance Any victim demands a.   GREE 132:9
  you have pledged a.   BALD 20:13
alley rats' a.   ELIO 101:11
allies no a. to be polite to   GEOR 126:12
alone adult is to be a.   ROST 269:5
  a. against smiling enemies   BOWE 42:13
  dangerous to meet it a.   WHAR 325:14
  I want to be a.   GARB 124:14
  long time to live a.   PART 245:1
  never a. with a Strand   ADVE 4:30
  not sufficiently a.   VALÉ 315:15
  When he is a. in the room   KEYN 171:5
  You'll never walk a.   HAMM 137:18
alp a. of unforgiveness   PLOM 250:7
altar high a. on the move   BOWE 42:15
  lays upon the a.   SPRI 294:11
alternative Considering the a.   CHEV 64:8
  no real a.   THAT 305:11
  What is the a.   TREN 311:6
alternatives decide between a.   BONH 41:6
  exhausted other a.   EBAN 94:16
altogether A. elsewhere   AUDE 16:7
always a. be an England   PARK 244:3
Alzheimer from A.'s disease   BAYL 25:3
  he had A.'s disease   REAG 262:7
  on A.'s disease   MURD 226:1
amateur a. is a man who can't   AGAT 2:10

amateurs Hell full of musical a.   SHAW 284:14
  rule by a.   ATTL 15:11
ambiguity Seven types of a.   EMPS 104:2
ambition Routine a sign of a.   AUDE 18:10
ambitions ceiling put on our a.   PRES 256:2
ambrosial Phallic and a.   POUN 253:17
amen sound like a sevenfold A.   WILL 329:6
America A. is a land whose   UPDI 314:16
  A. is a nation   WHIT 326:9
  A. is a vast conspiracy   UPDI 315:1
  A. is gigantic   FREU 119:2
  A. is God's Crucible   ZANG 340:9
  A. is the proof   MCCA 197:10
  A. only idealistic nation   WILS 332:10
  A.'s international role   KISS 175:18
  A. thus top nation   SELL 282:14
  back to A. . . . to die   JAME 159:11
  do a sitcom in A.   TWIG 314:4
  England and A. divided   SHAW 286:7
  God bless A.   BERL 32:11
  I like to be in A.   SOND 291:7
  impresses me about A.   EDWA 96:1
  in the living rooms of A.   MCLU 201:12
  I, too, sing A.   HUGH 153:11
  love affair with A.   MAIL 204:9
  makes A. what it is   STEI 296:3
  morning again in A.   POLI 251:14
  next to god a.   CUMM 81:9
American A. as cherry pie   BROW 46:13
  A. culture   COLO 73:5
  A. daydream   BROD 44:11
  A. Express   ADVE 3:4
  A. white man to find   BALD 20:10
  A. writers want to be   VIDA 317:6
  bad news to the A. people   KEIL 168:5
  business of the A. people   COOL 76:3
  Buying is much more A.   WARH 319:6
  controlling A. soil   DYLA 94:13
  free man, an A.   JOHN 162:9
  Greeks in this A. empire   MACM 201:14
  I am A. bred   MILL 215:1
  imported, elderly A.   JENK 160:10
  in love with A. names   BENÉ 29:8
  justice and the A. way   ANON 9:12
  knocking the A. system   CAPO 53:10
  Miss A. Pie   MCLE 200:11
  process whereby A. girls   HAMP 138:2
  Scratch any A.   RUSK 271:2
  second acts in A. lives   FITZ 113:10
  send A. boys   JOHN 163:4
  tenth A. muse   BRON 45:6
  weakness of A. civilization   PRIE 257:1
American Express VISA bill on A.   O'RO 236:13
Americanism A. with its sleeves   MCCA 197:8
  hyphenated A.   ROOS 268:6
Americans A. with no Disneyland   MAHY 204:6
  bad A. are slobs   SHAF 283:8

Americans (*cont.*):
borrowed from the A. LAHR 179:1
for A. it is just beyond KISS 176:7
keep the A. in ISMA 157:15
my fellow A. KENN 169:7
new generation of A. KENN 169:2
Only A. can do that NIXO 232:5
Amis cocoa for Kingsley A. COPE 76:12
ammunition pass the a. FORG 115:12
amniotic in an a. paradise WILL 329:7
amour *c'est l'a.* BOUS 42:7
amuse talent to a. COWA 78:4
amused a. by its presumption THUR 309:12
analogies A. decide nothing FREU 118:15
analysts A. already know BELL 28:13
anarchism A. is a game SHAW 285:13
anarchist run a trace of the a. CROS 80:12
anarchy Mere a. is loosed YEAT 338:13
anatomy A. is destiny FREU 118:12
ancient rivers a. as the world HUGH 153:12
and including 'a.' MCCA 197:14
Andromache kissed his sad A. CORN 77:5
angel elderly fallen a. QUEN 258:11
angelheaded a. hipsters burning GINS 128:7
angels A. can fly because CHES 63:16
a. go about their task BART 24:7
A. in jumpers LEWI 190:16
Blake saw a treefull of a. BENÉ 29:11
herald a. sing ANON 9:14
anger a. of men who have no CHES 63:6
Frozen a. FREU 119:1
Great a. in the dragon SUTT 301:9
life of telegrams and a. FORS 116:8
Look back in a. OSBO 239:18
monstrous a. of the guns OWEN 240:14
strike it in a. SHAW 285:4
angles Offer no a. TESS 304:8
Anglo-Irishman He was an A. BEHA 27:1
Anglo Saxon White-A.-Protestant BALT 22:7
angry A. young man PAUL 245:12
anguish going to be howls of a. HEAL 143:4
animal attend a dying a. YEAT 337:6
Be a good a. LAWR 183:17
only a. in the world to fear LAWR 184:3
animals All a. are equal ORWE 237:12
not over-fond of a. ATTE 15:3
soft little a. pottering CASS 55:11
takes 40 dumb a. SAYI 278:22
annals War's a. will cloud HARD 140:2
annihilating a. all civilization SAKH 273:11
annihilation by my own a. GUNN 135:9
anno domini only a. HILT 149:3
annoy a. with what you write AMIS 8:3
annus a. horribilis ELIZ 102:12
anorak a. grow big with jotters MAXW 211:1
another a. fine mess LAUR 181:12
answer a. is blowin' in the wind DYLA 94:3

a. the phone THUR 309:13
a. to the Irish Question SELL 282:13
way to a pertinent a. BRON 45:4
What *is* the a. LAST 183:2
answered no one a. DE L 87:17
answers Science offers best a. DAWK 84:10
ant a.'s a centaur POUN 254:5
like an a. which has foreseen BART 24:6
antennae a. of the race POUN 254:14
anthology a. is like all RALE 259:11
anthropomorphic a. view of rat KOES 177:6
anti-Christ a. of Communism BUCH 48:2
anticipation only in the a. of it HITC 149:9
antiwar ecology and a. HUNT 154:12
anybody Is there a. there DE L 87:16
anything A. goes PORT 252:10
A. you can do BERL 32:9
believe in a. CHES 64:7
nobody tells me a. GALS 124:5
anywhere get a. in a marriage MURD 225:14
apart a., studiously neutral WILS 332:4
man's life a thing a. AMIS 7:11
apathy a. of human beings KELL 168:6
ape gorgeous buttocks of the a. HUXL 155:14
naked a. MORR 222:4
aphorists A. can be wrong FENT 107:11
aphrodisiac Power is the great a. KISS 176:4
Apollo young A., golden-haired CORN 77:7
apologies do not want a. WODE 333:11
apologize good rule never to a. WODE 333:11
Never a. FISH 109:7
apology God's a. for relations KING 173:2
apparatus haunted a. sleeps RAIN 259:8
mediocrity of the a. TROT 312:6
appearing Television is for a. on COWA 79:2
applause A. is a receipt SCHN 280:7
everyone is forced to a. MILL 215:11
apple a. falling towards England AUDE 17:5
under the a. boughs THOM 307:3
apples moon-washed a. of wonder DRIN 92:4
appointment a. at the end DINE 90:2
a. by the corrupt few SHAW 284:24
a. with him tonight MAUG 210:9
apprenticeship a. for freedom BARA 22:16
April A. is the cruellest month ELIO 101:6
bright cold day in A. ORWE 238:7
from one A. to another LONG 194:2
aquarium a. is gone LOWE 195:8
Aquarius dawning of the age of A. RADO 259:6
Arabia spell of far A. DE L 87:13
Arbeit A. *macht frei* ANON 9:2
arch triumphant a. COMM 73:7
archbishop a. had come to see me BURG 49:2
archbishops get it from their a. MACM 202:5
arches Underneath the A. FLAN 113:12
archipelago Gulag a. SOLZ 290:14
architect a. can only advise WRIG 336:6

A. of the Universe	JEAN 160:8
architecture A. acts most slowly	DIMN 90:1
A. is the art	JOHN 163:12
fall of English a.	BETJ 36:2
Argentina Don't cry for me A.	RICE 264:3
Argentinian young A. soldiers	RUNC 270:5
argument a. of the broken window	PANK 242:8
once in the use of an a.	BENN 31:8
This is a rotten a.	ANON 11:12
arguments attract the worst a.	FISH 109:11
arias Clear a. of light	DAY- 85:4
Ariel Caliban casts out A.	POUN 253:17
aristocracy a. in a republic	MITF 217:10
a. means government by	CHES 64:6
Aristotle A. maintained that	RUSS 271:12
arm did not put your a. around it	BLAC 38:9
Armageddon County Road or A.	DYLA 94:12
armaments not a. that cause wars	
	MADA 203:14
armchairs a. tight about the hips	WODE 333:13
armed a. conflict	EDEN 95:7
A. neutrality	WILS 332:6
A. warfare must be preceded	ZINO 341:7
Armenteers Mademoiselle from A.	ANON 10:12
armful very nearly an a.	GALT 124:6
armies standing a. of power	RADC 259:4
armistice a. for twenty years	FOCH 114:11
armoured a. cars of dreams	BISH 38:7
arms a. not spending money alone	EISE 97:12
in my a. till break of day	AUDE 16:17
pair of a. around you	DIAN 89:6
army contemptible little a.	ANON 9:11
Forgotten A.	MOUN 224:1
little ships brought the A.	GUED 135:2
aroma a. of performing seals	HART 141:7
arrange French a.	CATH 56:3
arrested conservative been a.	WOLF 334:4
arrive a. where we started	ELIO 99:9
arrived a. and to prove it	CATC 58:15
arrow time's a.	EDDI 95:1
arse a. full of razor blades	KEAT 167:10
politician is an a. upon	CUMM 81:12
Sit on your a. for fifty years	MACN 202:15
arsenal great a. of democracy	ROOS 267:13
arses Massing of A.	CONN 74:19
art A. always serves beauty	PAST 245:6
A. and Religion are two roads	BELL 27:5
A. a revolt against fate	MALR 205:9
A. for art's sake	DIET 89:14
A. is born of humiliation	AUDE 18:12
a. is but a vision of reality	YEAT 337:11
A. is meant to disturb	BRAQ 43:6
A. is not a *brassière*	BARN 23:5
A. is not a mirror	GRIE 134:2
a. is not a weapon	KENN 169:15
A. is not truth	PICA 249:6
A. is pattern informed by	READ 261:5

A. is significant deformity	FRY 121:14
A. is the imposing of pattern	WHIT 327:1
A. is the objectification	LANG 180:1
a. is the only thing	BOWE 42:10
A. is vice	DEGA 86:7
a. needed Ruskin	STOP 299:14
A. not reproduce the visible	KLEE 176:10
a. of the impossible	HAVE 142:6
a. of the soluble	MEDA 212:4
Deals are my a. form	TRUM 313:9
Dying is an a.	PLAT 250:4
E in A-level a.	HIRS 149:5
element in modern a.	WHAR 325:13
enemy of good a.	CONN 74:14
example of modern a.	CHUR 69:3
fascinating kind of a.	WARH 319:5
films the lowest form of a.	WILD 328:10
Football is an a. central	GREE 133:6
good grey guardians of a.	WILB 328:8
great religious a.	CLAR 70:2
half a trade and half an a.	INGE 157:4
it is not a.	SCHO 280:10
novel is a.-for-art's-sake	PRIT 257:4
offered you Conflict and A.	PRIE 256:10
only interested in a.	SHAW 286:4
people start on all this A.	HERB 146:11
responsibility is to his a.	FAUL 107:4
revenge of intellect upon a.	SONT 291:13
stick to murder and leave a.	EPST 104:5
Story the spoiled child of a.	JAME 159:4
symbol of Irish a.	JOYC 165:4
want a. to be like ovaltine	READ 261:9
where the a. resides	SCHN 280:8
work of a. has no importance	NABO 227:5
articulate When they call you a.	ICE- 156:5
artificial a. respiration	BURG 49:3
artisan give employment to the a.	BELL 28:3
artist a. brings something into	UPDI 315:4
a. has no need to	PROU 257:8
a. is his own fault	O'HA 234:13
a. is someone who	WARH 319:7
a. man and mother woman	SHAW 284:13
a. remains within	JOYC 164:16
a. will be judged	CONN 74:20
God only another a.	PICA 249:4
Never trust the a.	LAWR 183:16
portrait of the a.	JOYC 164:11
sign of a true a.	VIDA 317:16
artists A. are not engineers	KENN 169:15
a. are the antennae	POUN 254:14
As a. they're rot	PARK 243:18
position of the a.	THOM 307:13
too difficult for a.	SCHN 280:9
arts interested in the a.	AYCK 19:4
you 'a.' people	MCEW 199:6
ash a. on an old man's sleeve	ELIO 99:6
empty a. can	CRAN 79:7

ash (*cont.*):

Oak, and A., and Thorn KIPL 175:3
ashen Your a. hair Shulamith CELA 56:10
ashes a. for thirty LAMP 179:14
past is a bucket of a. SAND 275:1
Asia not in A. ARDR 12:12
Asian A. boys ought to be JOHN 163:4
ask a. and cannot answer SHAW 286:9
a. not what your country KENN 169:7
could a. him anything WEIS 322:7
Don't a., don't tell NUNN 233:4
Don't let's a. for the moon FILM 110:2
if you gotta a. MISQ 218:9
never does any harm to a. KRUT 178:7
To a. the hard question AUDE 17:18
were afraid to a. REUB 263:6
Would this man a. why AUDE 16:5
asking a. is not always easy COMP 74:3
mere a. of a question FORS 116:14
asleep Half a. as they stalk HARD 140:1
asphalt only monument the a. road
ELIO 101:1
aspidistra biggest a. HARP 140:16
Keep the a. flying ORWE 238:3
leaf of the a. GREE 132:17
aspirin a. for a brain tumour CHAN 60:9
Asquith affair between Margot A. PARK 243:10
ass kiss my a. in Macy's window JOHN 163:9
on his unwashed a. PARS 244:16
assassin copperheads and the a. SAND 274:11
you are an a. ROST 269:6
assassination A. is extreme form SHAW 286:1
suicide to avoid a. TRUM 312:14
assurance low on whom a. sits ELIO 101:17
astonish A. me DIAG 89:3
astonished rightly a. by events BART 24:6
astonishment Your a.'s odd KNOX 176:17
astounded merely a. by them ATTE 15:3
astrologers A. or three wise men LONG 194:1
astronomers and a. QUIN 259:1
astronomers a. and astrologers QUIN 259:1
astronomy linked in a. LOVE 194:14
asylum lunatic a. run by lunatics LLOY 192:15
taken charge of the a. ROWL 270:1
ate Freddie Starr a. my hamster NEWS 231:5
atheism a., breast-feeding ORTO 237:6
atheist a. is a man BUCH 47:13
chic for an a. RUSS 271:4
denial of Him by the a. PROU 257:8
from being an a. SART 276:10
I am still an a. BUÑU 48:11
remain a sound a. LEWI 190:4
sort of a. ORWE 237:17
village a. brooding CHES 64:1
atheists no a. in the foxholes CUMM 82:4
atlas blank a. of your body NERU 229:9
atom a. has changed everything EINS 97:3

carbon a. possesses JEAN 160:7
done with the a. LEAC 185:4
grasped mystery of the a. BRAD 43:2
leads through the a. EDDI 95:5
no evil in the a. STEV 298:3
atomic win an a. war BRAD 43:1
atoms motions of a. in my brain HALD 136:10
attack by his plan of a. SASS 276:22
attacking I am a. FOCH 114:10
attendant a. lord ELIO 100:9
attention a. must be paid MILL 215:5
attic furniture in Tolkien's a. PRAT 256:1
attractions register competing a. KNIG 176:14
audacity tactful in a. COCT 72:5
Auden Just a smack at A. EMPS 103:14
audience looks at the a. STOC 298:12
audiences English-speaking a. WHAR 325:11
two kinds of a. SCHN 280:6
audio visual full of a. marvels SMIT 289:5
august A. is a wicked month O'BR 233:9
corny as Kansas in A. HAMM 137:17
aunt Aunt is calling to A. WODE 333:9
have the Queen as their a. MARG 207:11
pay to see my a. Minnie WILD 328:13
aunts bad a. and good aunts WODE 333:5
Auschwitz saved one Jew from A. AUDE 18:16
write a poem after A. ADOR 2:5
year spent in A. LEVI 189:8
Austerlitz A. and Waterloo SAND 274:13
Australia A. has a marvellous sky
LAWR 184:12
take A. right back down KEAT 167:11
Australian average A. practises WHIT 326:7
great A. Emptiness WHIT 326:6
Australians A. wouldn't give ADVE 3:6
Austria Don John of A. is going CHES 62:9
author a. made a mistake DIRA 90:5
a. of *The Satanic Verses* KHOM 171:7
in search of an a. PIRA 249:12
wish the a. was a friend SALI 274:3
authority A. doesn't work DE G 87:6
make your peace with a. MORR 222:9
solely on a. AYER 19:5
teacher have maximal a. SZAS 302:3
autobiography age to write an a. WAUG 321:3
a. is an obituary CRIS 80:4
A. is now as common GRIG 134:6
a. most gratuitous STOP 298:16
automatic with a. hand ELIO 101:18
automobile a. changed our dress KEAT 168:3
like an a. ROOT 268:10
autumn a. arrives BOWE 42:8
mists of the a. mornings ORWE 238:5
average a. guy who could carry EPIT 105:8
A. made lethal SHAF 283:7
averages from th' law of a. MAUL 210:14
avoiding a. being TILL 310:4

barricade some disputed b.   SEEG 282:1
barrow there in your long b.   MULD 225:5
baseball B. is very big   GREG 133:10
  cricket enthusiast on b.   STOP 299:15
basics time to get back to b.   MAJO 205:1
basketball sex on the b. court   SEIK 282:5
bastard all my eggs in one b.   PARK 243:20
  b. who gets the mail   KEAT 168:1
  we knocked the b. off   HILL 149:1
Bastille Voltaire in the B.   DE G 87:10
bat couldn't b. for the length of time
          COMP 73:8
  purest play is like some b.   WILB 328:7
  shake a b. at a white man   GREG 133:10
bath climb into the b. together   WILC 328:9
  haven't had a b. or shower   NEWT 230:2
  rather lie in a hot b.   THOM 307:20
  test my b. before I sit   NASH 228:12
bathroom revolutionary in a b.   LINK 191:9
bats b. have been broken   HOWE 152:14
batsmen opening b. to the crease
          HOWE 152:14
battalions in pale b. go   SORL 292:2
battle B. of Britain   CHUR 66:6
  France has lost a b.   DE G 86:8
  out of b. I escaped   OWEN 241:3
battles B. and sex   MCAR 196:12
  b. of subsequent wars   ORWE 238:6
  Dead b., like dead generals   TUCH 313:11
  mother of all b.   HUSS 155:2
bayonet b. is a weapon with   POLI 251:4
bayonets throne of b.   INGE 157:2
  throne of b.   YELT 339:11
bazaar Fate's great b.   MACN 203:8
BBC don't watch B. for polemic   SIMP 287:12
be Let b. be finale of seem   STEV 297:7
  poem should not mean but b.   MACL 200:12
beach On the b.   CHES 63:7
beaches fight on the b.   CHUR 66:5
beam B. me up, Scotty   MISQ 218:1
beans B. meanz Heinz   ADVE 3:7
bear B. of Very Little Brain   MILN 216:7
  Cannot b. very much reality   ELIO 98:11
  embrace the Russian b.   CHAN 61:8
  fire was furry as a b.   SITW 288:3
  Grizzly B. is huge and wild   HOUS 152:4
  so b. ourselves that   CHUR 66:6
bears b. might come with buns   ISHE 157:13
  b. the marks of the last person who
          HAIG 135:13
  dancing dogs and b.   HODG 150:5
  Teddy B. have their Picnic   KENN 168:9
beast Beauty killed the B.   FILM 111:12
  dead or dying b.   JENK 161:4
  fit night out for man or b.   FIEL 108:11
  What rough b.   YEAT 338:14
beastly b. the bourgeois is   LAWR 184:1

  b. to the Germans   COWA 78:3
beat b. generation   KERO 170:7
  I b. him   MCAL 196:11
beaten No Englishman is fairly b.
          SHAW 285:22
beatings dread of b.   BETJ 35:16
Beatles B.' first LP   LARK 180:2
beatnik peculiar b. theories   KERO 170:8
beats b. as it sweeps   ADVE 3:27
beautiful b. and damned   FITZ 112:19
  b. game   PELÉ 246:9
  Black is b.   POLI 251:6
  entirely b.   AUDE 16:17
  hunger to be b.   RHYS 263:10
  innocent and the b.   YEAT 337:16
  singing:—'Oh, how b.'   KIPL 174:3
  Small is b.   SCHU 281:2
  Something b. for God   MUGG 224:11
  something b. for God   TERE 304:6
  what a b. mornin'   HAMM 137:12
beauty B. at first sight   SHAW 284:19
  b. cold and austere   RUSS 271:16
  B. for some provides   HUXL 155:14
  B. in music   IVES 158:2
  B. killed the Beast   FILM 111:12
  B. momentary in the mind   STEV 297:15
  b. of inflections   STEV 297:17
  b. the joy of possessing   PAST 245:6
  B. vanishes   DE L 87:14
  b. without vanity   DUNC 92:11
  body's b. lives   STEV 297:15
  have b. in one's equations   DIRA 90:4
  land of 'b. spots'   JOAD 161:10
  looked on B. bare   MILL 214:10
  terrible b. is born   YEAT 337:8
  thing of b.   ROWL 269:14
  Where B. was   GALS 124:3
Beaverbrook mind of Lord B.   ATTL 15:5
because B. I do not hope to turn   ELIO 98:2
  B. it's there   MALL 205:6
  B. We're here   ANON 11:16
bed b. fell on my father   THUR 309:8
  b. people of below-stairs   CLAR 70:1
  getting in b. with women   ROSS 269:1
  gooseberried double b.   THOM 307:15
  I'm in b.   GALL 123:16
  love to remain in b.   BERL 32:13
  Lying in b. would be   CHES 63:19
  mind is not a b.   AGAT 2:9
  more than one man in b.   RAPH 260:3
  no need to get out of b.   AMIS 7:13
  on the lawn I lie in b.   AUDE 17:7
  prescription of a quick dip in b.   WESL 323:18
  should of stood in b.   JACO 158:8
  Who goes to b. with whom   SAYE 277:7
  wore in b.   MONR 220:8
bedpost on the b. overnight   ROSE 268:11

bedroom French widow in every b.		
	HOFF	150:8
not entered my b.	MAND	206:3
take care of the b. bit	HALL	137:1
unless with b. eyes	AUDE	17:8
what you do in the b.	CAMP	52:5
bedrooms in the nation's b.	TRUD	312:9
beds Minds like b. always made up	WILL	330:7
bee sting like a b.	ALI	6:2
beef love British b.	BAKE	20:7
manager for British b.	KOHL	177:13
Where's the b.	ADVE	4:29
Where's the b.	MOND	219:11
beefy b. ATS without their hats	BETJ	35:2
been B. there, done that	SAYI	278:3
b. things and seen places	WEST	324:6
beer b. of a man in Klondike	CHES	63:1
denies you the b. to cry into	MARQ	208:11
only here for the b.	ADVE	3:26
warm b., invincible suburbs	MAJO	204:16
beers other b. cannot reach	ADVE	3:23
bees b. do it	PORT	252:18
bees-winged was it his b. eyes	BETJ	34:11
Beethoven B.'s Fifth Symphony	FORS	116:5
Roll over, B.	BERR	34:4
beetles special preference for b.	HALD	136:12
before Broad b. and broad behind	BETJ	36:1
what has been done b.	WHAR	325:13
beggar b. would recognise guilt	PARS	244:16
begin b. at the beginning	THOM	307:14
b. the Beguine	PORT	252:11
But let us b.	KENN	169:6
Then I'll b.	CATC	57:5
beginning b., a muddle	LARK	181:6
b. is often the end	ELIO	99:10
end of the b.	CHUR	67:4
In my b. is my end	ELIO	98:14
Movies should have a b.	GODA	129:7
pictures didn't have b.	POLL	250:12
venture is a new b.	ELIO	99:1
begins glory most b. and ends	YEAT	338:4
Beguine begin the B.	PORT	252:11
behave all b. quite differently	COWA	78:14
b. like gentlemen	MACK	200:5
behaviour studies human b.	ROBB	265:5
behaviourism B. a flat-earth view	KOES	177:6
B. works	AUDE	18:2
behind no bosom and no b.	SMIT	290:4
being at the edge of B.	SPEN	293:10
avoiding b.	TILL	310:4
darkness of mere b.	JUNG	166:3
may not be worried into b.	FROS	121:4
Nothingness haunts b.	SART	276:2
unbearable lightness of b.	KUND	178:10
Belbroughton B. Road is bonny	BETJ	35:8
belief that is b.	SART	276:7
widespread b. more likely	RUSS	271:14

beliefs dust of exploded b.	MADA	203:13
believe b. in life	DU B	92:7
b. in the life to come	BECK	25:14
b. is not necessarily true	BELL	27:7
B. it or not	NEWS	231:1
b. what isn't happening	COLE	72:12
Corrected I b.	KNOX	176:15
don't b. in fairies	BARR	23:11
don't have to b. that	O'HA	234:12
even if you don't b.	BOHR	40:9
he couldn't b. it	CUMM	81:13
I b. in yesterday	LENN	188:11
I do not b. . . . I know	JUNG	166:9
If you b., clap your hands	BARR	23:13
must b. *something*	RUSS	272:7
really b. in themselves	CHES	63:11
We b. a scientist	RICH	264:8
believes never b. what he says	DE G	87:3
believing b. more and more	YATE	336:10
Not b. in force	TROT	312:8
stop b. in God	CHES	64:7
bellies their b. empty	LOGU	193:7
bells b. of Hell go ting-a-ling	ANON	10:17
floating many b. down	CUMM	81:8
ring the b. of Heaven	HODG	150:5
belong b. to it as well	WHYT	327:14
betray, you must first b.	PHIL	248:2
don't want to b. to any club	MARX	209:6
I b. to Glasgow	FYFF	122:7
they b. to you	GIBR	127:11
where we really b.	GREE	132:8
belongs moon b. to everyone	DE S	88:12
twentieth century b.	TRUD	312:10
beloved Cry, the b. country	PATO	245:11
below-stairs people of b. class	CLAR	70:1
belt b. without hitting below it	ASQU	14:12
bend right on round the b.	LAUD	181:9
beneath married b. me	ASTO	14:16
benediction clouds in b.	DAY-	85:4
bereaved b. if snobbery died	USTI	315:10
Berkeley sang in B. Square	MASC	209:13
Berlin cross from East to West B.	KOES	177:9
Berliner *Ich bin ein B.*	KENN	169:13
Bernard Jeffery B. is unwell	WATE	320:6
Bertie Burlington B.	HARG	140:12
best bad in the b. of us	ANON	11:9
b. lack all conviction	YEAT	338:13
b. of all possible worlds	CABE	50:13
b. Prime Minister we have	BUTL	50:8
b. things in life are free	DE S	88:12
b. way out is always through	FROS	120:19
we will do our b.	CHUR	66:12
best-seller b. is the gilded tomb	SMIT	289:9
best-sellers all the great b.	PRIT	257:2
bet You b. your sweet bippy	CATC	59:15
Bethlehem Slouches towards B.	YEAT	338:14
Betjemanless We are now B.	EWAR	104:10

betray b., you must first belong   PHIL 248:2
   guts to b. my country   FORS 116:19
betrayal any act of b.   RENO 263:4
   ecstasy of b.   GENE 126:4
better b. to be looked over   WEST 324:2
   Every day, I am getting b.   COUÉ 77:11
   Fail b.   BECK 26:9
   go b. with Coke   ADVE 4:23
   I can do b.   BERL 32:9
   If way to the B. there be   HARD 139:12
   nothing b. to do   THAT 306:18
   when I'm bad, I'm b.   WEST 324:7
between B. the idea   ELIO 99:18
   try to get b. them   STRA 299:17
beware B. my foolish heart   WASH 320:5
   B. of men bearing flowers   SPAR 292:5
   B. of rudely crossing it   AUDE 17:8
   bid you b.   KIPL 175:1
bewildered bothered, and b.   HART 141:6
   to the utterly b.   CAPP 53:12
bewitched B., bothered   HART 141:6
bewrapt B. past knowing   HARD 140:5
beyond But is there anything b.   BROO 45:9
bias impartiality is b.   REIT 263:1
biases critic is a bundle of b.   BALL 22:4
bible compare with the B.   PAGE 241:12
   dagger in one hand and a B.   WRAN 336:4
   read in de B.   HEYW 147:12
bible-black starless and b.   THOM 307:14
bicker safely afford to b.   BALF 21:14
bicycle arrive by b.   VIER 317:17
   fish without a b.   STEI 296:12
   so is a b. repair kit   CONN 74:10
bicycle-pump b. the human heart   AMIS 7:11
bicycling old maids b.   MAJO 204:16
bicyclists trouser-clip for b.   MORT 223:9
big b. enough to take away   FORD 115:6
   b. she is in Uruguay   THOM 308:14
   b. spender   FIEL 108:5
   b. way of doing things   TERE 304:5
   fall victim to a b. lie   HITL 149:14
   I am b.   FILM 112:4
bigamy B. is one husband too many   ANON 9:4
biggest b. electric train set   WELL 322:14
bigotry B. the anger of men who   CHES 63:6
   B. tries to keep truth   TAGO 302:13
bike got on his b.   TEBB 303:16
   Mind my b.   CATC 59:1
bikini yellow polkadot b.   VANC 315:17
billboard b. lovely as a tree   NASH 228:13
bills children and tradesmen's b.   MACN 203:3
bingo Let B. = Frodo   TOLK 310:10
biographers muck-raking b.   BENN 31:7
   picklocks of b.   BENÉ 29:10
biography better part of b.   STRA 299:18
   B. is about Chaps   BENT 32:2
   B. should be written by   BALF 21:13

   b. ultimately fiction   MALA 205:5
   forthcoming b.   BELL 28:15
   to write b.   WEST 325:2
biologist b. passes   ROST 269:4
biology B. is the search for   WILL 329:9
bippy You bet your sweet b.   CATC 59:15
birch bringing back the b.   VIDA 317:8
bird catch the b. of paradise   KHRU 171:11
   It's a b.   ANON 9:12
birds b., and Prime Ministers   BALD 21:4
   b. fly throught it   HEIS 145:1
   b. got to fly   HAMM 137:7
   b. trying to communicate   AUDE 18:14
   prisoned b. must find   SASS 276:20
Birmingham B. by way of Beachy Head
     CHES 62:11
   B. Six released   DENN 88:10
   When Jesus came to B.   STUD 301:1
birth B., and copulation   ELIO 101:2
   b. of each child   MCWI 203:11
   by the accident of b.   CHES 63:14
   no cure for b. and death   SANT 275:12
   present at the b.   ORTO 237:5
   seen b. and death   ELIO 100:1
birth control b. is middle-class   WAUG 321:15
   had not thought of b.   SPAR 292:7
birthday Happy b. to you   HILL 148:14
   marvel my b. away   THOM 307:9
   my eighty-first b.   BURG 49:2
biscuit cared a b. for it   LAWR 185:1
biscuits hyacinths and b.   SAND 275:4
bisexuality b. doubles your chances   ALLE 6:17
bishop make a b. kick a hole   CHAN 60:7
bitch Gaia a tough b.   MARG 207:13
   old b. gone in the teeth   POUN 254:2
bits swallowed their b.   BETJ 35:4
black b. against may   BUNT 48:9
   b. as our loss   SITW 288:4
   B. is beautiful   POLI 251:6
   b. majority rule   SMIT 289:6
   B. Panther Party   NEWT 230:1
   B. Power   HAMI 54:1
   but b. and grey   GREE 132:12
   growth of b. consciousness   BIKO 37:11
   old b. magic   MERC 213:13
   one drop of b. blood   HUGH 153:14
   rainbow which includes b.   YEVT 340:1
   so long as it is b.   FORD 115:7
   talks good for a b. guy   ICE- 156:5
   young, gifted and b.   HANS 138:6
   Young, gifted and b.   IRVI 157:12
blackbird B. has spoken   FARJ 106:8
   b. whistling   STEV 297:17
blackbirds B. are the cellos   STEV 298:10
black holes will be b. one day   BERN 33:13
Blackpool seaside place called B.   EDGA 95:10
black widow This is the B., death   LOWE 195:12

Blake B. saw a treefull of angels — BENÉ 29:11
blame Bad women never take the b. — BROO 46:1
  b. Marx for what was done — BENN 30:1
  manager who gets the b. — LINE 191:8
blamed mothers go on getting b. — WHIT 327:6
blaming b. it on you — KIPL 174:4
  b. on his boots — BECK 26:2
blancmange cold b. and rhubarb — KNOX 176:16
bland bland lead the b. — GALB 123:4
blanket with the b. over his head — BABE 19:12
blankets rough male kiss of b. — BROO 45:8
blast In b.-beruffled plume — HARD 139:10
blatherskite Blatant B. — PHIL 248:9
blazer make them wear a b. — BAIL 20:3
bleeding instead of b., he sings — GARD 125:3
Blenheim still fighting B. — BEVA 36:7
bless B. 'em all — HUGH 153:10
blessing b. cannot pass through — JOHN 161:15
blight great English b. — WAUG 320:12
Blighty back to dear old B. — MILL 216:2
blind b. side of the heart — CHES 62:2
  b. watchmaker — DAWK 84:5
  Booth died b. — LIND 191:7
  see the b. man — WALE 318:7
  splendid work for the b. — SASS 276:17
  without science is b. — EINS 96:6
blinds drawing-down of b. — OWEN 240:16
blinked other fellow just b. — RUSK 271:1
bliss promise of pneumatic b. — ELIO 101:20
  Your b. in our hearts — STRU 300:12
blitz b. of a boy — CAUS 56:5
block each b. cut smooth — POUN 253:13
blonde b. to make a bishop kick — CHAN 60:7
  having money like being b. — QUAN 258:7
blondes Gentlemen prefer b. — LOOS 194:4
blood ancient troughs of b. — HILL 148:11
  b. and love without — STOP 299:6
  b. come gargling — OWEN 240:17
  b. on their hands — SPEN 292:15
  B. sport brought to — INGH 157:6
  b., toil, tears and sweat — CHUR 66:2
  enough of b. and tears — RABI 259:3
  flow of human b. — HUGH 153:12
  foaming with much b. — POWE 255:8
  for cooling the b. — FLAN 113:14
  In the b. of the socialist — CROS 80:12
  one drop of black b. — HUGH 153:14
  rather have b. on my hands — GREE 132:3
  show business with b. — BRUN 47:4
  washed in the b. of the Lamb — LIND 191:6
  We, your b. family — SPEN 293:3
blood-dimmed b. tide is loosed — YEAT 338:13
bloodshed war without b. — MAO 207:5
bloody Abroad is b. — GEOR 126:13
  b. curtain — ELIS 102:9
  B. men like bloody buses — COPE 76:10

Not b. likely — SHAW 285:21
  sang within the b. wood — ELIO 101:5
  Sunday, b. Sunday — FILM 112:15
bloom sort of b. on a woman — BARR 23:14
blooming grand to be b. well dead — SARO 275:16
blossom frothiest, blossomiest b. — POTT 253:5
  hundred flowers b. — MAO 207:8
blow B. out, you bugles — BROO 45:7
  b. up the other half — LAIN 179:5
  b. with an agreement — TROT 312:5
  not return your b. — SHAW 285:12
blowing answer is b. in the wind — DYLA 94:3
  I'm forever b. bubbles — KENB 168:7
blue b. guitar — STEV 297:10
  b. of the night — CROS 80:9
  Her b. body — WALK 318:11
  Space is b. — HEIS 145:1
bluebell Mary, ma Scotch B. — LAUD 181:10
bluebirds There'll be b. over — BURT 49:14
blunder so grotesque a b. — BENT 32:3
board There wasn't any B. — HERB 146:13
boat sank my b. — KENN 169:16
  sewer in a glass-bottomed b. — MIZN 219:8
boats b. against the current — FITZ 113:4
  passengers off in small b. — LAST 183:1
Boche well-killed B. — READ 261:7
bodies Pile the b. high — SAND 274:13
  structure of our b. — STOP 298:14
  well-developed b. — FORS 115:14
body Africa than my own b. — ORTO 237:4
  b. and the soul know — ROET 266:7
  b. building is ritual — PAGL 241:13
  b. his body around — FRY 121:10
  b.'s beauty lives — STEV 297:15
  b. swayed to music — YEAT 336:11
  i like my b. — CUMM 82:2
  interpose my b. — STRA 299:17
  my b. and your brains — SHAW 286:5
  none in the b. — LAWR 184:2
  salutary to the b. — PROU 257:11
  to keep one's b. — MACK 200:4
  whose b. is this — RODR 266:4
Bognor Bugger B. — LAST 182:1
bogus than a b. god — MACN 202:13
bohemian so-called b. elements — KERO 170:8
boil war that would not b. — TAYL 303:10
boiler ten years in a b. suit — TWEE 314:3
boldly to b. go — RODD 266:1
Bolshevik I must be a B. — MACD 198:13
bolt b., and the breech — REED 262:10
bomb atom b. is a paper tiger — MAO 207:7
  Ban the b. — POLI 251:3
  b. them back into Stone Age — LEMA 187:4
  defence against the atom b. — ANON 9:3
  'formula' of the atomic b. — MEDA 212:1
bombed glad we've been b. — ELIZ 103:3

bomber b. will always get through   BALD 21:7
bombers b. named for girls   JARR 159:18
bombing b. begins in five minutes   REAG 262:2
bombs b. redoubled on the hills   MOTI 223:14
  Come, friendly b.   BETJ 35:12
bonding male b.   TIGE 310:3
bonds surly b. of earth   MAGE 204:1
  surly b. of earth   REAG 262:4
bone knows death to the b.   YEAT 337:7
boneless b. wonder   CHUR 65:10
bones b. of one British Grenadier   HARR 141:1
  conjuring trick with b.   JENK 160:11
  dead men lost their b.   ELIO 101:11
bonfire b. of the vanities   WOLF 334:3
bonjour B. tristesse   ÉLUA 103:13
bonkers stark, raving b.   HAIL 136:5
bonny Belbroughton Road is b.   BETJ 35:8
book before this b. is published   RUNC 270:7
  b. known to him by heart   WOOL 335:2
  b. should be banned   WEST 324:20
  b. the greatest interactive   LYNT 196:9
  b. would have been finished   WODE 333:7
  b. you would wish your wife   GRIF 134:4
  insignificant b. because   WOOL 335:7
  knocks me out is a b.   SALI 274:3
  mentioning a single b.   REED 262:13
  read one b. in my life   MITF 217:12
  review a bad b.   AUDE 18:8
bookie b. or a clergyman   MUGG 224:9
book-keeping double-entry b.   MULL 225:8
books B. are a load of crap   LARK 180:11
  b. are either dreams   LOWE 195:5
  b. are weapons   ROOS 267:16
  B. do furnish a room   POWE 254:18
  B. from Boots'   BETJ 35:6
  B. say: she did this because   BARN 23:6
  b. undeservedly forgotten   AUDE 18:7
  his b. were read   BELL 28:7
  If my b. had been any worse   CHAN 60:11
  Keeping b. on charity   PERÓ 247:3
  laid out just the right b.   POUN 254:7
  made the b. and he died   FAUL 107:1
  read any good b. lately   CATC 58:1
  study of mankind is b.   HUXL 155:5
  You remember b.   CROS 81:1
boot b. in the face   PLAT 250:3
  b. stamping on a human face   ORWE 238:15
bootboy b. at Claridges   WOOL 335:13
Booth B. led boldly   LIND 191:6
boots blaming on his b.   BECK 26:2
  Books from B.'   BETJ 35:6
  b. are made for walkin'   HAZL 143:3
  boots—b.—movin'   KIPL 173:11
  doormat in a world of b.   RHYS 263:12
  on a pedestal in bronze b.   GRIG 134:7
  went to school without any b.   BULM 48:7
booze fool with b. until he's 50   FAUL 107:5

boozes tell a man who "b."   BURT 49:12
bop Playing 'B.'   ELLI 103:8
border Night Mail crossing the B.   AUDE 17:4
borders b. of sleep   THOM 308:4
bore b. people at dinner parties   KISS 176:6
  b. you to death for hours   COPE 76:14
  healthy male adult b.   UPDI 314:13
  Less is a b.   VENT 317:1
bored b. by children   TWEE 314:2
  b. for England   MUGG 224:13
  Ever to confess you're b.   BERR 34:7
  I'd get b. and fall over   COMP 73:8
  virtue of the b.   WAUG 321:16
  works and is not b.   CASA 55:8
boredom b. and terror   WELL 323:2
  B. is a vital problem   RUSS 271:6
  b. on a large scale   INGE 156:12
  b. stays   CHAN 61:1
  first b., then fear   LARK 180:5
  perish of despair and b.   FRAN 117:9
Borgias In Italy under the B.   FILM 110:14
boring b. kind of guy   BUSH 50:3
  Life, friends, is b.   BERR 34:7
born already b. before my lips   MAND 206:10
  because you were b. in it   SHAW 284:3
  B. in the USA   SPRI 294:12
  B. of the sun   SPEN 293:8
  b. three thousand years old   DELA 87:21
  b. to run   SPRI 294:14
  b. with your legs apart   ORTO 237:8
  British Bourgeoise is not b.   SITW 288:6
  for being b.   WATS 320:8
  future refusing to be b.   BEVA 36:15
  human beings are b. free   ANON 8:15
  I am not yet b.   MACN 203:5
  I was b. barefoot   LONG 193:10
  Man is b. to live   PAST 245:2
  not to be b. is best   AUDE 16:3
  One is not b. a woman   DE B 85:11
  Then surely I was b.   CHES 62:4
bosom no b. and no behind   SMIT 290:4
boss b. there is always   MARQ 208:8
bossing nobody b. you   ORWE 239:1
bossy by the b. for the bully   SELD 282:6
Boston long way from East B.   KENN 169:18
botanist I'd be a b.   FERM 107:13
botch I make a b.   BELL 28:6
bother conscience to b. him   LLOY 192:18
  long words B. me   MILN 216:7
  young whom I hope to b.   AUDE 17:12
bothered Bewitched, b.   HART 141:6
Botticelli If B. were alive   USTI 315:11
bottle bothers to buy a b.   DWOR 94:2
  b. it and sell it   MCDO 199:4
  way out of the fly-b.   WITT 332:15
bottles old b. with banknotes   KEYN 171:1
bottom at the b. of our garden   FYLE 122:8

forgotten man at the b.   ROOS 267:5
from the b. of the deck   SHAP 283:10
bough Petals on a wet, black b.   POUN 254:4
bouquet b. better than the taste   POTT 253:8
bourgeois beastly the b. is   LAWR 184:1
b. prefers comfort   HESS 147:6
person of b. origin   ORWE 238:18
bourgeoise British B. is not born   SITW 288:6
bourgeoisie b. in the long run   TROT 312:3
charm of the b.   FILM 112:7
Bovril B. prevents   ADVE 3:8
bower b. we shrined to Tennyson   HARD 139:5
bowler go out in a b.   PHIL 248:4
box B. of AIDS   DOTY 91:2
life like a b. of chocolates   FILM 111:9
boxes Little b. on the hillside   REYN 263:8
boxing B.'s just showbusiness with blood
    BRUN 47:4
boy and a b. forever   ROWL 269:14
any b. may become President   STEV 298:4
b. brought in the white sheet   GARC 125:1
b. will ruin himself   GEOR 126:8
Mad about the b.   COWA 78:7
remain a fifteen-year-old b.   ROTH 269:8
sat the journeying b.   HARD 140:5
You silly twisted b.   CATC 59:20
boy friend thing called the B.   WILS 331:14
boyhood b. of Judas   Æ 2:6
boys b. in the back room   LOES 193:3
b. in the back rooms   BEAV 25:7
b. not going to be sent   ROOS 267:12
see if the b. are still there   BARU 24:12
send American b.   JOHN 163:4
Till the b. come home   FORD 115:11
bra Burn your b.   SAYI 278:4
braces liquid which rots b.   MORT 223:8
bracket date slides into the b.   EWAR 104:10
Bradford on a B. millionaire   ELIO 101:17
Bradshaw vocabulary of 'B.'   DOYL 91:13
brain Bear of Very Little B.   MILN 216:7
b. has the consistency   TURI 313:15
b.? my second favourite   ALLE 6:10
dry b. in a dry season   ELIO 99:15
fingerprints across his b.   HEND 146:4
hasn't exactly got B.   MILN 216:10
if the b. has oozed out   KRAU 177:16
motions of atoms in my b.   HALD 136:10
why did He give us a b.   LUCE 196:5
brains b. of a Minerva   BARR 24:3
feet instead of their b.   SOUS 292:4
girl with b. ought to   LOOS 194:5
my body and your b.   SHAW 286:5
brainwashing It is called b.   GREE 133:4
brake invented the b.   NEME 229:8
brandy B. for the parson   KIPL 175:2
b. of the damned   SHAW 284:14
brassière Art is not a b.   BARN 23:5

Brazilian If I were a B.   STIN 298:11
bread eat dusty b.   BOGA 40:7
piece of b. and butter   MACK 200:6
Royal slice of b.   MILN 216:15
break at the b. of the day   STRU 300:12
Can it be b.   JENK 161:3
give a sucker an even b.   FIEL 108:10
Have a b.   ADVE 3:22
if you b. the bloody glass   MACN 203:1
breakdown approaching nervous b.
    RUSS 271:7
Madness need not be b.   LAIN 179:7
breakers b. cliffward leaping   CRAN 79:6
breakfast bad review may spoil b.   AMIS 8:4
committed b. with it   LEWI 190:8
critical period is b.   HERB 146:17
intervene—before b.   HESE 147:4
that sits down to b.   YEAT 339:7
breaks be there when it b.   CAMP 52:6
something twangs and b.   MACN 203:2
breath drawn the b. of life   YEAT 337:14
each saving b.   LOWE 195:13
last b. of Julius Caesar   JEAN 160:6
seemed waste of b.   YEAT 337:19
taxed the b.   THOM 307:5
breeding result of b.   LEBO 186:9
without any b.   THUR 309:12
brevity B. the soul of lingerie   PARK 243:9
brew b. that is true   FILM 111:13
bribe cannot hope to b. or twist   WOLF 333:18
Marriage is a b.   WILD 328:14
bribes open to b.   GREE 132:5
brick Follow the yellow b. road   HARB 138:13
Goodbye yellow b. road   JOHN 162:5
threw it a b. at a time   HARG 140:13
bride ser' him for a b.   MACD 198:11
bridge b. over troubled water   SIMO 287:8
b. to the future   LAWR 183:15
Every good poem is a b.   DAY- 85:6
going a b. too far   BROW 47:1
Twenty men crossing a b.   STEV 297:11
Women, and Champagne, and B.   BELL 28:5
bright young lady named B.   BULL 48:6
brighter women are b. than men   LOOS 194:9
brightness leaking the b. away   SPEN 293:15
brink trembling on the b.   NABO 227:3
walked to the b.   DULL 92:9
brinkmanship boasting of his b.   STEV 298:7
bristles my skin b.   HOUS 152:10
Britain Battle of B.   CHUR 66:6
B. a fit country   LLOY 192:9
B. will be honoured   HARL 140:14
B. will still be   MAJO 204:16
further you got from B.   CALL 52:1
I'm backing B.   SAYI 278:21
Keep B. tidy   OFFI 235:8
speak for B.   BOOT 41:8

Britain (*cont.*):
  Without B., Europe   ERHA 104:6
British bones of one B. Grenadier HARR 141:1
  B. are coming   WELL 322:13
  B. journalist   WOLF 333:18
  B. nation is unique   CHUR 66:11
  drunken officer of B. rule   WALC 318:2
  for b. institutions   MAND 205:13
  No sex please—we're B.   MARR 208:14
  rather be B. than just   PAIS 242:4
  We are B., thank God   MONT 220:14
Britons B. alone use 'Might'   WAUG 321:12
Brits bad B. are snobs   SHAF 283:8
broad B. of Church   BETJ 36:1
broadens travel b. the mind; but CHES 63:18
broccoli b., dear   WHIT 326:1
broke If it ain't b.   SAYI 278:17
broken bats have been b.   HOWE 152:14
  Morning has b.   FARJ 106:8
  taken up the b. blade   DE G 86:10
broker b. a man who takes fortune   WOOL 336:1
bronze noontide was b.   CHUR 68:4
brothel b. for the emotions   KOES 177:5
  playing a piano in a b.   MUGG 225:1
brother be the white man's b.   KING 172:2
  BIG B. IS WATCHING YOU   ORWE 238:8
  B. can you spare a dime   HARB 138:8
brotherhood broadened into a b. JOHN 162:13
  freedom and our b.   LAIN 179:5
  table of b.   KING 172:6
brother-in-law brother, not b.   KING 172:2
brothers live together as b.   KING 172:8
  two b. and eight cousins   HALD 136:13
brow meet my Maker b. to brow CORN 77:4
brown Her b. embrace   WALK 318:11
  river Is a strong b. god   ELIO 99:3
Browning safety-catch of my B. JOHS 163:13
brows pallor of girls' b.   OWEN 240:16
Bruce made Adam and B.   BRYA 47:6
brutal heart's grown b.   YEAT 338:3
brutality source of b.   PAGE 241:12
brute heart of a b. like you   PLAT 250:3
BSE B. holds no terror   BAKE 20:7
bubbles I'm forever blowing b. KENB 168:7
buck bigger bang for a b.   ANON 9:5
  b. stops here   TRUM 313:6
bucket past is a b. of ashes   SAND 275:1
  stick inside a swill b.   ORWE 239:14
Buckingham Palace guard at B. MILN 216:11
bugger B. Bognor   LAST 182:1
bugles Blow out, you b.   BROO 45:7
  b. calling from sad shires   OWEN 240:15
building very old b.   OSBO 239:15
builds Office b. up a man only if BENN 29:15
built not what they b.   FENT 107:8
  Who b. Thebes   BREC 44:4

bulimia on b.   DIAN 89:6
  yuppie version of b.   EHRE 96:2
bull Dance tiptoe, b.   BUNT 48:9
bullet Faster than a speeding b. ANON 9:12
  one b. in ten thousand   SPEN 293:14
bullet-headed b. many will never   POUN 254:14
bully by the bossy for the b.   SELD 282:6
  such a b. pulpit   ROOS 268:8
bum Indicat Motorem B.   GODL 129:8
bumpy going to be a b. night   FILM 110:5
bundle never the b. of accident YEAT 339:7
bungler Man is a b.   SHAW 284:17
bunk Exercise is b.   FORD 115:10
  History more or less b.   FORD 115:8
bunkers gloomy b. were built   ESHE 104:9
buns bears might come with b. ISHE 157:13
Bunyan B. wanted the millennium HILL 148:7
burden bear any b.   KENN 169:3
  carry the heavy b.   EDWA 95:11
bureaucracy immobile b.   SAMP 274:7
bureaucrats Guidelines for b. BORE 41:10
burgled We have b. houses   GALL 123:17
burgundy naive domestic B.   THUR 309:12
buried b. at midnight   O'BR 233:8
  b. in the rain   MILL 214:12
Burlington B. Bertie   HARG 140:12
burn better to b. out   YOUN 340:6
  B., baby, burn   POLI 251:8
  b. its children to save   MEYE 214:1
  B. your bra   SAYI 278:4
  Old age should b.   THOM 307:2
burning b. of the leaves   BINY 38:1
  b. roof and tower   YEAT 337:20
  b. the rain forest   STIN 298:11
  by b. him   CEAU 56:9
  Is Paris b.   HITL 149:13
  Keep the Home-fires b.   FORD 115:11
  lady's not for b.   FRY 121:9
burnished Furnish'd and b.   BETJ 35:13
burns candle b. at both ends MILL 214:9
burnt b. at the stake as witches SMIT 290:2
  if all this was b. cork   GREG 133:9
burnt-out b. ends of smoky days ELIO 100:16
bury B. my heart at Wounded Knee BENÉ 29:9
  physician can b.   WRIG 336:6
  We will b. you   KHRU 171:10
bus Anybody seen in a b.   WEST 325:8
  Can it be a Motor B.   GODL 129:8
  missed the b.   CHAM 60:6
  run over by a b.   CARR 54:4
  stepping in front of a b.   OSBO 240:5
buses Bloody men are like bloody b.   COPE 76:10
  more time on the b.   STRU 300:10
bushes like different b. trimmed QUIN 259:2

business Being good in b.   WARH 319:5
  b. as usual   THAT 306:4
  B. carried on as usual   CHUR 65:6
  B. is like a car   SAYI 278:5
  b. of the American people   COOL 76:3
  b. practices improve   RODD 266:3
  b. to get him in trouble   ROBI 265:13
  do b. together   THAT 306:6
  heart in the b.   WATS 320:10
  How to succeed in b.   MEAD 211:13
  Liberty is unfinished b.   ANON 10:9
  music b. is not   MORR 222:10
  no b. like show business   BERL 33:1
businessman b. has trampled on   NICO 230:9
  toward making a b.   WATS 320:9
businessmen message to the b.   CURR 82:7
  well-placed b. decide   YOUN 340:4
bust dance it b. to bust   GREN 133:12
  Uncorseted, her friendly b.   ELIO 101:20
busting June is b. out all over   HAMM 137:9
busy b. man has no time   MAUR 210:15
  Government of the b.   SELD 282:6
  had a b. day   SIGL 287:3
but If and Perhaps and B.   ELIO 98:8
butcher Hog B. for the World   SAND 274:10
  Prime Minister to be a b.   BUTL 50:9
butler b. did it   CATC 57:6
  on the b.'s upper slopes   WODE 333:14
butter b. for the Royal slice   MILN 216:15
  guns not with b.   GOEB 129:9
  no money for b.   JOSE 164:4
  rather have b. or guns   GOER 129:11
  Stork from b.   ADVE 3:10
butterflies flight of b.   SART 276:15
  Frogs eat b.   STEV 297:8
butterfly breaks a b. on a wheel   NEWS 231:13
  flap of a b.'s wings   LORE 194:10
  float like a b.   ALI 6:2
buttocks gorgeous b. of the ape   HUXL 155:14
button each b., hook, and lace   LOWE 195:4
  job of sewing on a b.   BROU 46:8
butty oul' b. o' mine   O'CA 234:2
buy b. a used car   POLI 252:1
  b. Codham, Cockridden   THOM 308:3
  b. it like an honest man   NORT 233:2
  b. me a Mercedes Benz   JOPL 164:2
  client will beg to b.   BURR 49:10
  Don't b. a single vote more   KENN 168:11
  money can't b. me love   LENN 188:3
  Stop me and b. one   ADVE 4:21
buying B. is much more American

                       WARH 319:6

by B. and by   MCCO 198:6
Byron movement needs a B.   POLL 250:11
Byronic think all poets were B.   COPE 76:15
Byzantium holy city of B.   YEAT 338:11

cabbage smell of cooking c.   WEST 324:18
cabinet another to mislead the C.   ASQU 14:8
  c. minister on a pedestal   GRIG 134:7
  group of C. Ministers   CURZ 82:10
cable little c. cars climb   CROS 81:3
  of c. television   MACK 200:8
Cablinasian I'm a C.   WOOD 334:11
cad Cocoa is a c. and coward   CHES 62:14
Caesars worship the C.   HUXL 155:7
café in ev'ry street c.   HAMM 137:10
caff ace c. with a nice museum   ADVE 3:2
caftan Iffucan of Azcan in c.   STEV 297:5
cage cannot c. the minute   MACN 203:9
cake life like a Christmas c.   TANG 302:16
  picked out of a c.   RALE 259:11
calamity Oh, c.   CATC 59:3
calculating desiccated c. machine   BEVA 36:12
Caliban C. casts out Ariel   POUN 253:17
California C. is a fine place to live   ALLE 6:4
  From C. to   GUTH 135:12
Caligula eyes of C.   MITT 217:14
call c. it a day   COMD 73:6
  c. of the wild   LOND 193:8
  how you c. to me   HARD 140:6
  May I c. you 338   COWA 78:18
calling Germany c.   JOYC 165:15
callisthenics c. with words   PARK 243:16
calls If anybody c. Say   BENT 32:5
Cambridge C. ladies who live   CUMM 82:3
  C. people rarely smile   BROO 45:12
  either Oxford or C.   SNAG 290:9
came I c. through   MACA 197:1
  Tell them I c.   DE L 87:17
camel c. is a horse   ISSI 158:1
  Take my c., dear   MACA 197:4
Camelot known as C.   LERN 188:12
camera c. makes everyone   SONT 291:16
  I am a c.   ISHE 157:14
campaign c. in poetry   CUOM 82:5
  In a c., first put up   GING 128:5
can *c.* nothing but frog-spawn   LAWR 184:9
  He who c., does   SHAW 285:2
  know a man who c.   ADVE 3:9
  think you c.   INGE 156:10
Canada C. could have enjoyed   COLO 73:5
  I see C.   DAVI 83:10
Canadian definition of a C.   BERT 34:9
Canadians C. are Americans with   MAHY 204:6
  C. do not like heroes   WOOD 334:12
cancer c. close to the Presidency   DEAN 85:7
  Obscene as c.   OWEN 240:17
  Silence like a c. grows   SIMO 287:10
  up to the word 'c.'   KIPL 175:9
  white race *is* the c.   SONT 291:15
candle c. burns at both ends   MILL 214:9
  c. in that great turnip   CHUR 67:12
  c. in the wind   JOHN 162:1

candle (*cont.*):
c. in the wind JOHN 162:4
rather light a c. STEV 298:8
candles c. burn their sockets HOUS 152:6
candour combines force with c. CHUR 69:3
candy C. is dandy NASH 228:11
canisters steel c. hurtling about CASS 55:11
cannibal c. uses knife and fork LEC 186:11
cannibals formidable body of c. MENC 213:5
cannon loose c. like her ANON 11:15
canoe make love in a c. BERT 34:9
can't I c. go on BECK 25:15
cantos c. of unvanquished space CRAN 79:5
capitalism c. is a necessary FRIE 119:7
C. is using its money CAST 56:2
c. of lower classes SPEN 294:4
c. with the gloves off STOP 299:11
definition of c. HAMP 138:2
extermination of c. ZINO 341:7
monopoly stage of c. LENI 187:5
unacceptable face of c. HEAT 144:6
capitalist fall of the c. system MACM 202:2
forces of a c. society NEHR 229:4
slave of c. society CONN 75:3
Capitol strangers in the C. HEWI 147:9
captain broken by the team c. HOWE 152:14
c. is in his bunk SHAW 284:3
ship's c. complaining POWE 255:12
captains c. and the kings depart KNOX 176:16
Star c. glow FLEC 113:17
car Business is like a c. SAYI 278:5
buy a used c. POLI 252:1
can't drive the c. TYNA 314:9
c. could go straight upwards HOYL 153:4
c. crash as a sexual event BALL 22:2
c. has become an article of dress MCLU 201:9
c. has become the carapace MCLU 201:10
c. in every garage HOOV 151:10
motor c. was poetry LEWI 190:12
owl of Minerva in a hired c. PAUL 246:1
to tinker with his c. MACN 203:8
caravan great c. of humanity SMUT 290:8
carbon c. atom possesses JEAN 160:7
carbuncle monstrous c. CHAR 61:13
carbuncles Monstrous c. SPEN 293:4
carcase c. of an old song THOM 308:13
carcinoma sing of rectal c. HALD 136:11
card play the race c. SHAP 283:10
card-indexes memories are c. CONN 74:18
cards buy a pack of c. COLE 72:16
c. with a man called Doc ALGR 5:14
don't cheat at c. LEWI 190:9
played our c. SCHE 280:1
care better c. of myself BLAK 39:7
c. less and less SAYE 277:7
don't c. too much for money LENN 188:3
full of c. DAVI 84:2

she don't c. LENN 188:8
Teach us to c. ELIO 98:3
Took great C. of his Mother MILN 216:12
To say we do not c. WARD 319:3
career close my military c. MACA 197:3
Good c. move VIDA 317:15
loyal to his own c. DALT 83:3
our c. and our triumph VANZ 316:7
re-establish each c. KIPL 174:9
careful be c. out there CATC 58:20
careless C. talk costs lives OFFI 235:1
They were c. people FITZ 113:3
carelessness carefullest c. BETJ 35:14
cares Nobody c. MORT 223:7
caricature c. as far as I can SCAR 277:10
caring prosperous or c. society HESE 147:3
carollings little cause for c. HARD 139:11
carpenter I said to the c. CART 55:4
Walrus and C. LEVI 189:12
carry c. a big stick ROOS 268:3
cars c. the great Gothic cathedrals BART 24:8
cartoonist life as a c. wonderful PETE 247:13
casbah Come with me to the C. MISQ 218:2
case everything that is the c. WITT 332:17
in our c. we have not got REED 262:10
would have passed in any c. BECK 26:7
casement ghost of Roger C. YEAT 337:15
cash needs good c. TUCK 313:13
Cassidy C.'s hanging hill KAVA 167:6
Cassiopeia C. was over KAVA 167:6
cast C. a cold eye YEAT 339:5
castle c. of my skin LAMM 179:10
casualties c. were low JARR 159:18
cat big c. in a poodle parlour PARR 244:12
c. on a hot tin roof WILL 329:13
c. that likes to gallop SMIT 289:14
C. walked by himself KIPL 175:10
Eventually it becomes a c. NASH 228:4
if a c. is black or white DENG 88:3
Like a powerful graceful c. CHUR 68:3
smile of a cosmic Cheshire c. HUXL 155:16
which way the c. is jumping SULZ 301:6
catalogue c. of human crime CHUR 66:3
catamite in bed with my c. BURG 49:2
catastrophe education and c. WELL 323:9
unparalleled c. EINS 97:3
Catch-22 anything as good as C. HELL 145:5
C., which specified HELL 145:2
catcher c. in the rye SALI 274:2
category replacement of c.-habits RYLE 273:2
cathedral C. time ANON 9:7
cathedrals cars the great Gothic c. BART 24:8
Catherine child of Karl Marx and C. ATTL 15:9
catholic C. and the Communist ORWE 239:11
C. Church has never come WILL 329:11
if I was not a C. WAUG 321:19

lawful for a C. woman	MENC 212:15
may as well be a C.	SPAR 292:12
Once a C.	WILS 330:13
Roman C. Church	MACM 202:7
Roman C. women must	THOM 308:10
to be C. and sensual	CHAN 61:4
Catholics C. and Communists	GREE 132:3
Hitler attacked the C.	NIEM 232:1
cats C. go on the principle	KRUT 178:7
C. look down on us	CHUR 69:1
C., no less liquid	TESS 304:8
elderly lady who has two c.	LEWI 190:14
greater c. with golden eyes	SACK 273:4
where c. are cats	MARQ 208:6
cattle Actors are c.	HITC 149:7
Catullus Did their C. walk that way	
	YEAT 338:12
caught man who shoots him gets c.	
	MAIL 204:13
cause c. may be inconvenient	BENN 31:10
little c. for carollings	HARD 139:11
Rebel without a c.	FILM 112:14
causes aren't any good, brave c.	OSBO 240:5
best c. tend to attract	FISH 109:11
Tough on the c. of crime	BLAI 38:10
caution c. in love	RUSS 271:10
cavaliers C. (Wrong but)	SELL 282:11
caverns beats about in c.	WILB 328:7
caves c. in which we hide	FITZ 113:1
Ceauşescus C.' execution	O'DO 234:8
Cecilia Blessed C., appear	AUDE 15:14
ceiling draw on the c.	CHES 63:19
celebrity C. is a mask	UPDI 315:2
c. is a person	ALLE 6:5
celibate happy undersexed c.	COFF 72:8
cell tight hot c. of their hearts	BOGA 40:7
cello of the c.	CASA 55:7
cellos c. of the deep farms	STEV 298:10
cells little grey c.	CHRI 65:1
vast assembly of nerve c.	CRIC 79:13
Celtic woods of C. antiquity	KEYN 170:14
cemetery Help me down C. Road	LARK 181:1
censor c. one's own thoughts	WALE 318:7
censorship extreme form of c.	SHAW 286:1
cent did with every c.	FROS 120:9
centaur ant's a c.	POUN 254:5
centre c. cannot hold	YEAT 338:13
c. is everywhere	UPDI 314:16
centuries Through what wild c.	DE L 87:12
century c. of psychiatrist's couch	MCLU 201:6
c. of the common man	WALL 319:1
c.'s cool nursery	AKHM 5:5
sad, glittering c.	BURC 48:13
So the 20th C.	CRAN 79:9
when a new c. begins	MANN 206:13
cerebration unconscious c.	JAME 159:7
ceremony c. of innocence	YEAT 338:13

certainty not the test of c.	HOLM 151:2
chains better to be in c.	KAFK 166:15
chainsaw imagination and a c.	HIRS 149:5
chaise-longue hurly-burly of c.	CAMP 52:4
chalice c. from the palace	FILM 111:13
champagne get no kick from c.	PORT 252:14
like c. or high heels	BENN 31:10
some c.	DEAN 85:8
Women, and C., and Bridge	BELL 28:5
chance C. has appointed her	BUNT 48:8
Give peace a c.	LENN 188:5
I missed my c.	LAWR 184:6
institutions by c.	HAIL 136:8
in the last c. saloon	MELL 212:9
too good to leave to c.	SIMO 287:11
chandeliers gas c.	WHAR 325:15
Chanel C. No. 5	MONR 220:8
change 'C.' is scientific	RUSS 272:9
c. the people who teach	BYAT 50:12
c. we think we see	FROS 120:1
Management that wants to c.	TUSA 314:1
things will have to c.	LAMP 179:13
time for a c.	DEWE 89:2
torrent of c.	CHES 63:15
try to c. things	BOLD 41:3
wind of c. is blowing	MACM 201:19
wish to c. in the child	JUNG 166:8
changed accept what cannot be c.	
	NIEB 231:17
changed, c. utterly	YEAT 337:8
changed, c. utterly	YEAT 337:10
c. upon the blue guitar	STEV 297:10
human nature c.	WOOL 335:3
If voting c. anything	LIVI 192:1
changing fixed point in a c. age	DOYL 91:12
not c. one's mind	MAUG 210:6
times they are a-c.	DYLA 94:14
world is c.	ELIZ 102:14
channel Fog in C.	BROC 44:10
open c. to the soul	BELL 28:14
chaos Humour is emotional c.	THUR 310:1
means of overcoming c.	RICH 264:9
chaps Biography is about C.	BENT 32:2
chapter write the next c.	JOHN 162:12
character about a fellow's c.	REAG 262:1
content of their c.	KING 172:7
enormous lack of c.	LEVA 189:5
characters Six c. in search	PIRA 249:12
charge I'm in c.	CATC 58:11
charging marching, c. feet	JAGG 158:12
charity Keeping books on c.	PERÓ 247:3
charm C. a sort of bloom	BARR 23:14
c. of the bourgeoisie	FILM 112:7
C. the great English blight	WAUG 320:12
Completing the c.	ELIO 98:7
northern c.	KENN 169:17
Oozing c. from every pore	LERN 188:21

charm (*cont.*):
what c. is   CAMU 52:12
What is c.   LESS 189:3
chase have to c. after it   KLEE 176:12
chassis worl's in a state o' c.   O'CA 234:3
Chattanooga C. Choo-choo   GORD 130:17
Chatterley end of the C. ban   LARK 180:2
cheap how potent c. music is   COWA 78:16
in c. shoes   AMIE 7:6
sell it c.   SAYI 279:5
Words are c.   CHAP 61:10
cheaper c. than a prawn sandwich
                                                RATN 260:6
in the c. seats   LENN 187:15
cheat cannot c. on DNA   WARD 319:3
don't c. at cards   LEWI 190:9
cheated Old men who never c.   BETJ 35:1
cheek dancing c.-to-cheek   BERL 32:10
cheer which side do they c. for   TEBB 303:18
cheerful It's being so c.   CATC 58:14
cheeriness Chintzy, Chintzy c.   BETJ 34:14
cheerio c. my deario   MARQ 208:5
cheerioh 'c.' or 'cheeri-bye'   BETJ 35:2
cheers Two c. for Democracy   FORS 116:20
cheese like some valley c.   AUDE 17:13
of c.   FADI 106:6
varieties of c.   DE G 87:2
chemical made up of c. elements   MULL 225:7
two c. substances   JUNG 166:5
chemistry c. that works   WILL 329:9
weak in c.   WELL 323:4
cheque statement is like a c.   POUN 254:9
cherished My no longer c.   MILL 214:14
Chernobyl cultural C.   MNOU 219:9
cherries just a bowl of c.   BROW 46:14
cherry American as c. pie   BROW 46:13
Cheshire smile of a cosmic C. cat   HUXL 155:16
Chesterton dared attack my C.   BELL 28:2
Chevy Drove my C. to the levee   MCLE 200:11
chew can't fart and c. gum   JOHN 163:10
chewing gum c. for the eyes   ANON 11:8
chic c. for an atheist   RUSS 271:4
Radical C.   WOLF 334:8
chicken c. in every pot   HOOV 151:10
c. shit can turn   JOHN 162:8
c. whose head has been cut off   MITF 217:10
fed the c. every day   RUSS 271:17
Some c.! Some neck   CHUR 67:1
chickens beside the white c.   WILL 330:8
chieftain C. Iffucan of Azcan   STEV 297:5
child birth of each c.   MCWI 203:11
c. becomes an adult   SZAS 302:2
c. inherits my body   SHAW 286:5
God bless the c.   HOLI 150:10
has devoured the infant c.   HOUS 152:4
I am to have his c.   BURG 49:3
If you strike a c.   SHAW 285:4

like a c. in a forest   BART 24:6
one c. makes you a parent   FROS 119:14
right to a c.   SHAW 284:1
speak like a c.   NABO 227:4
what it is like to be a c.   JARR 160:1
wish to change in the c.   JUNG 166:8
childbirth Death and taxes and c.   MITC 217:7
childhood C. is Last Chance Gulch
                                                STOP 299:12
C. is the kingdom   MILL 214:7
dolmens round my c.   MONT 220:11
have you seen my c.   JACK 158:5
one moment in c.   GREE 132:13
childminder underpaid as a c.   OSBO 240:9
children bored by c.   TWEE 314:2
burn its c. to save   MEYE 214:1
by c. to adults   SZAS 302:4
c. and tradesmen's bills   MACN 203:3
C. and zip fasteners   WHIT 327:5
C. are dumb to say   GRAV 131:8
c. are naive   NASH 227:12
c. are not your children   GIBR 127:11
C. aren't happy with   NASH 228:8
c. died in the streets   AUDE 16:6
C. have never been very good   BALD 20:8
C.: one is one   SAYI 278:6
c. produce adults   DE V 88:14
c. to be a credit   RUSS 272:3
c. were lost sight of   MOYN 224:4
c. who leave home   SLOV 288:12
c. who were rough   SPEN 293:9
draw like these c.   PICA 249:2
first class, and with c.   BENC 29:3
get back from c.   NESB 229:11
Goodnight, c.   CATC 57:20
interest of the c.   SHAW 283:18
made c. laugh   AWDR 19:2
music understood by c.   STRA 300:3
my c. are frightened of me   GEOR 126:11
nocturnal processions of c.   WIES 328:3
not much about having c.   LODG 193:1
other people's c.   CLIN 71:8
Parents learn from c.   SPAR 292:8
poor get c.   KAHN 166:16
raising your c.   ONAS 235:19
reasons for having c.   RUSS 272:11
screams of c.   WEST 324:18
see his c. fed   PUDN 257:14
sleepless c.'s hearts   BETJ 34:12
their unborn c. did   DURC 93:6
tiresome for c.   SAIN 273:7
To beget c.   SART 276:8
Too easy for c.   SCHN 280:9
violations committed by c.   BOWE 42:11
We are c.   FORS 116:12
Chile Small earthquake in C.   COCK 72:2
Chimborazo C., Cotopaxi   TURN 313:17

chimpanzee vase in the hands of a c.
                                        WAUG 321:14
China Hong Kong's return to C.   DENG 88:4
  land armies in C.   MONT 220:13
  Till C. and Africa meet   AUDE 15:15
  wall of C. was finished   BREC 44:4
Chinese went to a C. dinner   FLEM 114:8
chintzy Chintzy, C. cheeriness   BETJ 34:14
chips c. with everything   WESK 323:16
chivalry law of c.   SAYE 277:5
chocolates life like a box of c.   FILM 111:9
choices sum of all the c.   DIDI 89:13
choirs c. of wailing shells   OWEN 240:15
choo-choo Chattanooga C.   GORD 130:17
choose better to c. the culprits   PAGN 242:2
  forced to c.   YEAT 337:4
  I do not c. to run   COOL 76:4
  wisdom to c. correctly   ALLE 6:13
chord just pick a c.   VICI 317:4
choreography c. to the audience   SZEL 302:10
Christ C. coming this afternoon   CART 55:2
  C. follows Dionysus   POUN 253:17
  C. perish in torment   SHAW 285:23
Christian C. ideal not been tried   CHES 64:2
  going to be a C.   SPAR 292:12
  most C. of worlds   TSVE 313:10
  persuades me to be a C.   FRY 121:15
Christianity C. deposes Nature   HUGH 154:6
  C. most materialistic   TEMP 304:3
  C., of course   BALF 21:12
  Disneyfication of C.   CUPI 82:6
  local thing called C.   HARD 140:11
  rock 'n' roll or C.   LENN 187:16
Christmas child on C. Eve   BART 24:6
  c. is a good time   WILL 329:5
  C. is the Disneyfication   CUPI 82:6
  C.-morning bells say 'Come!'   BETJ 34:12
  dreaming of a white C.   BERL 33:3
  just before a hard C.   SMIT 288:14
  Let them know it's C.   GELD 125:10
  turkeys vote for C.   CALL 51:11
Christopher Robin C. has fallen   MORT 223:7
  C. is saying   MILN 217:1
chuck C. it, Smith   CHES 61:17
chumps C. make the best husbands
                                        WODE 332:19
church Broad of C.   BETJ 36:1
  C. is 'one generation'   CARE 53:15
  C. [of England] should   ROYD 270:2
  C.'s Restoration   BETJ 35:5
  Get me to the c. on time   LERN 188:13
  MCC ends and the C.   PRIE 256:13
  open the windows of the C.   JOHN 161:14
  Stands the C. clock   BROO 45:13
Churchill voice was that of Mr C.   ATTL 15:5
churchman called a 'Modern C.'   WAUG 321:1
CIA on the C.   MOYN 224:5

cigar c. called Hamlet   ADVE 3:21
  really good 5-cent c.   MARS 209:1
cigarette But the c., well   POTT 253:7
  c. that bears   MARV 209:4
  smoked my first c.   TOSC 310:12
cigars roller of big c.   STEV 297:6
cinema c. is truth 24 times   GODA 129:5
circle Round and round the c.   ELIO 98:7
  tightness of the magic c.   MACL 200:13
circuit c. learns your job   MCLU 201:5
circumcision breast-feeding, c.   ORTO 237:6
circus no right in the c.   MAXT 210:17
  proceedings into a c.   MURR 226:6
cistern loud the c.   BENN 31:4
cities c., like teeming sores   HOPE 152:1
  c. we had learned about   JARR 159:18
  in the streets of a hundred c.   HOOV 151:11
  lousy skin scabbed by c.   BUNT 48:8
  shape of our c.   KEAT 168:3
citizen c. or the police   AUDE 17:10
citizens c. of death's grey land   SASS 276:18
  first and second class c.   WILL 330:12
city big hard-boiled c.   CHAN 60:8
  c. is not a concrete jungle   MORR 222:3
  c. of perspiring dreams   RAPH 260:4
  C. of the Big Shoulders   SAND 274:10
  modern c. is a place   WRIG 336:7
  paper felled a c.   THOM 307:5
civil c. to everyone   SISS 288:1
civilization annihilating all c.   SAKH 273:11
  C. advances by   WHIT 327:2
  C. and discontents   RIVI 265:4
  C. and profits   COOL 76:2
  c. has from time   ELLI 103:12
  C. has made peasantry   TROT 312:3
  c. left in female   PAGL 241:14
  C. nothing more than   ORTE 237:3
  For a botched c.   POUN 254:2
  history of Western C.   TYNA 314:10
  last product of c.   RUSS 271:11
  life-blood of c.   TREV 311:7
  rottenness of our c.   READ 261:4
  say c. don't advance   ROGE 266:17
  soft resort-style c.   BAUD 24:14
  Speech is c.   MANN 207:2
  stupid of modern c.   KNOX 177:1
  thought of modern c.   GAND 124:13
civilizes Cricket c. people   MUGA 224:7
civil servant c. doesn't make   IONE 157:9
  Here lies a c.   SISS 288:1
civil servants conviction c., no   BANC 22:8
  gifted c.   CLAR 70:3
  of c.   BRID 44:8
Civil Service business of the C.   ARMS 13:6
  c. has finished   REIT 262:16
  C. is deferential   CROS 81:5
claim last territorial c.   HITL 149:12

clamour c. of silence   TAGO 302:14
clap c. your hands   LENN 187:15
    Don't c. too hard   OSBO 239:15
    If you believe, c. your hands   BARR 23:13
    Soul c. its hands and sing   YEAT 338:10
clapped-out c., post-imperial   DRAB 92:1
class c.-ridden society   KING 173:3
    could have had c.   FILM 110:10
    first and second c. citizens   WILL 330:12
    hands of the ruling c.   STAL 295:4
    merciless c. distinction   MORT 222:13
    solvent of c. distinction   BENN 30:10
    use of *force* by one c.   LENI 187:6
    While there is a lower c.   DEBS 86:6
classes capitalism of lower c.   SPEN 294:4
    Clashing of C.   CONN 74:19
    lower c. had such white   CURZ 82:12
    two c. of travel   BENC 29:3
classic 'c.' music eliminates   STRA 300:2
    C. music is th'kind   HUBB 153:8
    loathe C. FM   BENN 31:6
classical c. mind at work   PIRS 249:15
classics bellyful of the c.   MILL 215:13
classify Germans c.   CATH 56:3
Claus ain't no Sanity C.   FILM 110:16
claws pair of ragged c.   ELIO 100:7
clay c. grew tall   OWEN 241:1
    C. is the word   KAVA 167:7
    pure c. of time's mud   MALA 205:5
clean c. American backyards   MAIL 204:9
    c. place to die   KAVA 167:8
    c. the sky   ELIO 100:14
    lie down in c. postures   FOWL 117:4
    Not a c. & in-between   MCGO 199:9
    one more thing to keep c.   FRY 121:11
    tragedy is c.   ANOU 12:4
cleaning militants like c. women   TRUF 312:12
cleanliness What c. everywhere   GIDE 128:1
cleanness into c. leaping   BROO 45:14
cleans guy who c. the river   PERO 247:5
    sweeps as it c.   ADVE 3:27
clear On a c. day   LERN 188:17
clercs *trahison des c.*   BEND 29:7
clergyman bookie or a c.   MUGG 224:9
clever all the c. people round   CAMP 52:8
    c. enough to get all that   CHES 64:4
    important to be c. *about*   MEDA 212:5
    Too c. by half   SALI 274:5
cleverest c. member   WEBB 322:1
cliché c. and an indiscretion   MACM 201:16
    used every c. except   CHUR 66:9
clichés new c.   GOLD 130:10
click Clunk, c., every trip   OFFI 235:2
client c. will crawl through   BURR 49:10
cliffs chalk c. of Dover   BALD 21:8
    white c. of Dover   BURT 49:14
climate lived in a warm, sunny c.   COWA 78:14

    whole c. of opinion   AUDE 16:9
climax works its way up to a c.   GOLD 130:12
climb C. ev'ry mountain   HAMM 137:8
climbing c. clear up to the sky   HAMM 137:11
clinging c. to their crosses   CHES 61:16
clipboards people with c.   LEAR 185:12
clock After fifty the c. can't   LOWE 195:13
    c. is always slow   SERV 283:1
    c. of communism has stopped   SOLZ 291:4
    c. without the pendulum   RUSS 272:10
    rock around the c.   DE K 87:11
    Stands the Church c.   BROO 45:13
clocks c. were striking thirteen   ORWE 238:7
clockwork c. orange   BURG 49:1
clods harrowing c.   HARD 140:1
cloned successfully c. a lamb   MARC 207:10
Clonmacnoise monks at C.   HEAN 143:14
close C. encounters   FILM 112:6
    c. your eyes before   AYCK 19:3
    peacefully towards its c.   DAWS 84:13
closed it was c.   FIEL 108:15
    We never c.   VAN 315:18
closer Come c., boys   LAST 182:2
closest c. friends won't tell you   ADVE 3:17
closing c. time in the gardens   CONN 74:20
cloth trick of wearing a c. coat   BALM 22:6
clothes C. are our weapons   CART 54:8
    C. by a man who doesn't   CHAN 60:14
    C. don't make the man   WATS 320:9
    poured into his c.   WODE 333:15
    remarkable suit of c.   LOES 193:4
clothes-brush manner of a c.   NICO 230:5
clothing sheep in sheep's c.   CHUR 69:6
cloud c. in trousers   MAYA 211:2
    each c. contains pennies   BURK 49:6
    Get off my c.   JAGG 158:9
clouds Hullo C. Hullo Sky   WILL 329:4
    slow movement of c.   DAY- 85:4
cloven out pops the c. hoof   WODE 333:5
cloverleaf concrete c.   MUMF 225:10
clowns Send in the c.   SOND 291:10
club don't want to belong to any c.   MARX 209:6
    most exclusive c.   NASH 227:15
    that terrible football c.   MCGR 200:1
clunk C., click, every trip   OFFI 235:2
clutching c. their gods   ELIO 100:2
Clyde poems should be C.-built   DUNN 93:3
coal island made mainly of c.   BEVA 36:4
    like miners' c. dust   BOOT 41:9
coalition real rainbow c.   JACK 158:4
coals No more c. to Newcastle   GEOR 126:7
coast c. of Coromandel   SITW 288:7
coat eternal Footman hold my c.   ELIO 100:8
    tattered c. upon a stick   YEAT 338:10
Coca-Cola blue jeans and C.   GREE 133:3
cocaine C. habit-forming   BANK 22:9

cock c. crowing on its own dunghill ALDI 5:9
  Our c. won't fight BEAV 25:5
cockatoo green freedom of a c. STEV 297:16
cocksure c. of many things HOLM 151:2
cocktail weasel under c. cabinet PINT 249:11
cock-up adhered to the c. theory INGH 157:5
cocoa c. for Kingsley Amis COPE 76:12
  C. is a cad and coward CHES 62:14
coconuts loverly bunch of c. HEAT 144:7
cod photographer is like the c. SHAW 286:2
code trail has its own stern c. SERV 282:17
coffee put poison in your c. CHUR 69:2
  with c. spoons ELIO 100:6
  women who make their c. O'DO 234:10
coffin in a Y-shaped c. ORTO 237:8
cognitive c. equivalent of condom MILL 215:16
coin less store upon the c. WHAR 325:12
coins for a fistful of c. ZAPA 340:10
coke go better with C. ADVE 4:23
cold Cast a c. eye YEAT 339:5
  c. and lonely PAST 245:5
  c. coming we had of it ELIO 99:20
  c. metal of economic theory SCHU 281:6
  C. on Monday HART 141:12
  C. the seat BENN 31:4
  c. war BARU 24:9
  c. war warrior THAT 304:11
  fingers of c. are corpse LAWR 184:14
  past the common c. AYRE 19:9
  plunging into a c. peace YELT 339:12
  spy who came in from the c. LE C 186:13
  understand one who's c. SOLZ 290:16
colder c. and dumber than a fish MULD 225:5
colleagues respect fidelity to c. LASK 181:7
colonized culture to be c. by WELS 323:15
colony fuzzy wuzzy c. CAIR 51:5
colour any c. that he wants FORD 115:7
  by the c. of their skin KING 172:7
  C. has taken hold of me KLEE 176:12
  c. purple WALK 318:12
  I know the c. rose ABSE 1:3
  perceptible through c. MOND 220:1
  problem of the c. line DU B 92:6
coloured best c. man JOHN 162:10
  no 'white' or 'c.' signs KENN 169:12
colourless C. green ideas CHOM 64:13
colours map-makers' c. BISH 38:6
  nailing his c. FIEL 108:4
Columbus youth in C., Ohio THUR 309:8
column Fifth c. MOLA 219:10
columns crazy on its smoking c. YEVT 339:16
comb two bald men over a c. BORG 42:4
come believe in the life to c. BECK 25:14
  C. to the edge LOGU 193:6
  c. up and see me sometime MISQ 219:5
  don't want to c. out BERR 34:1
  I go—I c. back CATC 58:8

nobody will c. SAND 275:3
shape of things to c. WELL 323:10
they'll c. out for it SKEL 288:9
where do they all c. from LENN 188:4
comeback c. kid CLIN 71:10
comedy All I need to make a c. CHAP 61:9
  C. is tragedy that happens CART 54:9
comes Nothing happens, nobody c. BECK 26:5
comfort bourgeois prefers c. HESS 147:6
  c. cruel men CHES 62:8
  gives you a feeling of c. DIAN 89:6
  naught for your c. CHES 61:18
  value the c. more WHAR 325:12
comfortably Are you sitting c. CATC 57:5
comforting always a c. thought MARQ 208:8
  cloud of c. convictions RUSS 272:1
comforts recapture the c. BRYS 47:8
comical Beautiful c. things HARV 142:1
coming British are c. WELL 322:13
  cold c. we had of it ELIO 99:20
  c. for us that night BALD 21:1
  Everything's c. up roses SOND 291:8
  I was c. to that GRAV 131:13
  Yanks are c. COHA 72:9
comma intrusive c. on p. 4 HOUS 152:12
comment C. is free SCOT 281:11
  C. is free STOP 299:3
  couldn't possibly c. CATC 59:16
commerce under a ceiling of c. OLIV 235:18
commercial you're labelled c. MANN 206:11
commercialism [C. is] doing well VIDA 317:10
commissions royal c. FRAN 118:4
committed c. breakfast with it LEWI 190:8
committee C.—a group of men who ALLE 6:6
  c. a group of unwilling SAYI 278:7
  horse designed by a c. ISSI 158:1
common age of the c. man COWA 78:19
  and still be c. RATT 260:10
  century of the c. man WALL 319:1
  c. pursuit LEAV 185:13
  like the c. people YEAT 339:10
  nor lose the c. touch KIPL 174:6
  nothing in c. PYM 258:5
commoner persistent c. BENN 29:12
commons C. has declined in esteem ST J 273:9
  libraries of the C. CHAN 61:6
  member of the House of C. POWE 255:14
  untrue in the House of C. WALD 318:5
common sense c. considers of no MAUG 210:10
  C. is nothing more EINS 97:5
  Nothing but c. MORT 223:4
communicate birds trying to c. AUDE 18:14
  our failure to c. PRIT 257:3
communicated C. monthly BETJ 35:1
Communism C. is like prohibition ROGE 266:16
communism anti-Christ of C. BUCH 48:2
  caused the fall of c. JOHN 162:7

communism (*cont.*):
  clock of c. has stopped   SOLZ 291:4
  c. is a dead dog   SOLZ 291:3
  C. is Soviet power   LENI 187:10
  C. the illegitimate child   ATTL 15:9
  trouble with C.   LAWR 184:19
communist call me a c.   CAMA 52:2
  Catholic and the C.   ORWE 239:11
  members of the C. Party   MCCA 197:7
  Picasso is a C.   DALI 83:2
communists Catholics and C.   GREE 132:3
commuter C.—one who spends   WHIT 326:3
companion gave him a c.   VALÉ 315:15
company c. he chooses   BURT 49:12
  soul to the c. store   TRAV 311:3
compassion c. of the healer's art   ELIO 98:18
  feel c. for fellow men   ANNA 8:13
compensates c. for the misery   DRAB 92:3
compete need to show off and c.   COPE 76:14
competence C., like truth, beauty   PETE 247:12
competing register c. attractions   KNIG 176:14
competition rigour of c.   ANON 9:8
complacencies C. of the peignoir   STEV 297:16
complaint fatal c. of all   HILT 149:3
  no cause for c.   SCOT 281:14
complete become c. yourself   FRIE 119:4
complexion schoolgirl c.   ADVE 4:5
complexities All mere c.   YEAT 336:14
compliance c. with my wishes   CHUR 68:14
complicity Our tribe's c.   HEAN 143:11
composer c. and *not* homosexual   DIAG 89:4
composing C.'s not voluntary   BIRT 38:4
compound it's a chemical c.   ZAPP 341:1
comprehensible universe is c.   EINS 97:1
compris *Je vous ai c.*   DE G 86:11
computer modern c. hovers   BREN 44:6
  reading from a c. screen   MILL 215:16
  requires a c.   SAYI 279:10
  work of an eyeless c.   BETJ 35:10
computers C. are anti-Faraday   CORN 77:2
  C. are composed of   AUGA 18:17
  so many c.   WAŁĘ 318:6
  to be left to c.   BUCH 48:3
conceit curst c. o' bein' richt   MACD 198:10
conception present at the c.   ORTO 237:5
concepts up the stairs of his c.   STEI 296:8
concerned nobody left to be c.   NIEM 232:1
concert At the c. I make them play   BEEC 26:15
  self-imposed, the c.   MILL 215:12
concerto C. to be difficult   SCHO 280:11
concrete city is not a c. jungle   MORR 222:3
  c. and tyres   LARK 180:6
  c. cloverleaf   MUMF 225:10
concupiscent c. curds   STEV 297:6
condemn c. a little more   MAJO 204:15
condemned c. to be free   SART 276:3
condition c. for freedom   FRIE 119:7

condom cognitive equivalent of c.   MILL 215:16
condottiere roamed like a c.   HURD 154:14
conductor music eliminates the c.   STRA 300:2
conductors C. must give signals   SZEL 302:10
cones eat the c. under his pines   FROS 120:12
conference ever born in a c.   FITZ 113:8
  naked into the c. chamber   BEVA 36:11
conferences eradication of c.   MAYA 211:6
confinement solitary c. inside our own skins
                                          WILL 330:3
conflict armed c.   EDEN 95:7
  field of human c.   CHUR 66:7
  offered you C. and Art   PRIE 256:10
  tragic c. of loyalties   HOWE 153:1
conforms industry applies, man c.   ANON 11:4
confront to c. them   TRIM 312:1
confused anyone who isn't c.   MURR 226:7
confusion in our sea of c.   GAMO 124:7
Congo C., creeping through   LIND 191:5
conic c. sections were studied   WHIT 327:3
conjuring c. trick with bones   JENK 160:11
conked c. out on November 15th   EPIT 105:11
connect Only c.   FORS 116:9
conquered They c. continents   DUNN 93:4
conqueror you are a c.   ROST 269:6
conscience C.: the inner voice   MENC 212:14
  c. to bother him   LLOY 192:18
  c. under control   LLOY 192:13
  cruelty with a good c.   RUSS 272:5
  strict their social c.   SMIT 289:13
  taking your c. round   BEVI 37:6
  will not cut my c.   HELL 145:7
consciences binding on the c.   JOHN 161:11
consciousness c.-expanding drug   CLAR 70:7
  C. the phenomenon   PENR 246:11
  tragic c.   FUEN 121:16
conscription Not necessarily c.   KING 172:15
consensus c. breaking up   CROS 81:6
consent without your c.   ROOS 267:4
consenting only between c. adults   VIDA 317:8
consequences terror of the c.   LAWR 183:9
conservation make a speech on c.   STEV 298:9
conservatism c. is based upon   CHES 63:15
conservative become a c.   AREN 13:1
  c. been arrested   WOLF 334:4
  C. ideal of freedom   MADA 203:12
  C. is a man   ROOS 267:11
  C. Party always   MACL 201:1
  C. Party at prayer   ROYD 270:2
  make me c. when old   FROS 120:14
  makes a man more c.   KEYN 170:12
  most c. man   BEVI 37:5
Conservatives better with the C.   POLI 251:19
  C. do not believe   HAIL 136:2
consoles Anything that c. is fake
                                          MURD 225:16
conspicuous Vega c. overhead   AUDE 17:7

conspiracies c. against the laity   SHAW 283:17
conspiracy c. theory of government
                                             INGH 157:5
  c. to make you happy   UPDI 315:1
  Indecency's c.   SHAW 285:8
constituencies go back to your c.   STEE 295:13
constitution c. does not provide   WILL 330:12
  establishment of C.   CARD 53:13
constitutional c. minuet   SCAR 279:17
consume more history than they can c.
                                             SAKI 273:13
consumer c. isn't a moron   OGIL 234:11
  c. is the king   SAMU 274:9
  c. society   ILLI 156:7
consumes c. without producing   ORWE 237:10
consuming survive by c.   VANE 316:5
consumption c. to be artificially   SAYE 277:4
contact c. with this Wild Man   BLY 40:2
  word preserves c.   MANN 207:2
contemplation Has left for c.   BETJ 35:5
contemptible c. little army   ANON 9:11
contender could have been a c.   FILM 110:10
content joy and natural c.   YEAT 337:12
contest not the victory but the c.   COUB 77:10
continent Africa, drifting c.   GENE 126:3
  C. isolated   BROC 44:10
continental may be quite c.   ROBI 265:6
continually think c. of those   SPEN 293:7
continuity C. . . . . continuity   WARN 319:13
contraception c. and abortion   BURC 48:12
  oral c.   ALLE 6:14
contract Social C. nothing more   WELL 323:8
  verbal c. isn't worth   GOLD 130:4
contradict Never c.   FISH 109:7
contrast enjoyment from a c.   FREU 118:11
control Ground c. to Major Tom   BOWI 42:16
  kept rigidly under c.   BENN 30:17
  wrong members in c.   ORWE 238:4
controls Who c. the past   ORWE 238:10
controversial what is c. from   EPHR 104:4
convalescence enjoy c.   SHAW 283:12
convenience prefers c. to liberty   HESS 147:6
convent C. of the Sacred Heart   ELIO 101:5
conventional c. wisdom   GALB 123:3
  most c. way   NABO 226:12
conversation C. is imperative   WHIT 326:5
  his c., so nicely   ELIO 98:8
  third-rate c.   PLOM 250:9
conviction best lack all c.   YEAT 338:13
  C. politicians   BANC 22:8
convictions cloud of comforting c.   RUSS 272:1
  c. are hills   FITZ 113:1
convinces man who c. the world   DARW 83:9
cook c. in the kitchen   HALL 137:1
  good c., as cooks go   SAKI 274:1
cooked c. a few meals   CONR 75:11
cookery Football and c.   SMIT 288:15

cookies baked c. and had teas   CLIN 71:7
cooking never see any home c.   PHIL 248:5
  'plain' c.   MORP 222:2
cool c. as a mountain stream   ADVE 3:11
  c. web of language   GRAV 131:9
  rather be dead than c.   COBA 71:12
  something to be c.   LOVE 194:13
Coolidge admiration for Mr C.   ANON 11:13
cooling for c. the blood   FLAN 113:14
cooperation partnership and c.   ANON 9:8
copperheads c. and the assassin   SAND 274:11
cops C. are like a doctor   CHAN 60:9
copulating Two skeletons c.   BEEC 26:19
copulation Birth, and c.   ELIO 101:2
coral like c. insects   WARN 319:14
core c. of a world's culture   BOLD 41:1
cork c. out of my lunch   FIEL 108:9
  if all this was burnt c.   GREG 133:9
corkscrews crooked as c.   AUDE 16:3
cormorant common c. (or shag)   ISHE 157:13
corn c. is as high   HAMM 137:11
corner At every c., I meet   LOWE 195:11
  c. of a foreign field   BROO 45:15
  in a c., some untidy spot   AUDE 17:2
  just around the c.   COWA 78:13
  mutters away in a c.   CARE 53:14
corny c. as Kansas in August   HAMM 137:17
Coromandel coast of C.   SITW 288:7
coronation King's C. depends   BLUN 40:1
corpse carry one's father's c.   APOL 12:9
correctness political c. can be   JAME 159:17
correlative objective c.   ELIO 102:1
corridors c. of power   SNOW 290:10
corrupted c. by sentiment   GREE 132:5
cosiness Classic FM for its c.   BENN 31:6
  c. and irritation   PYM 258:5
cosmetic selling c. cream   RODD 266:2
cost But at what c.   BECK 25:13
  c. of setting him up   NAID 227:7
costs C. merely register   KNIG 176:14
Cotopaxi Chimborazo, C.   TURN 313:17
cotton c. is high   HEYW 148:1
cough all c. in ink   YEAT 338:12
coughing keeping people from c.   RICH 264:13
  one c., and one not   SCHN 280:6
coughs C. and sneezes spread   OFFI 235:3
council chaos of a Labour c.   KINN 173:6
count c. everything   CORN 77:2
  if you can c. your money   GETT 127:7
  I won the c.   SOMO 291:6
counted c. them all out   HANR 138:5
counterpoint Too much c.   BEEC 26:18
counting it's the c.   STOP 298:15
country ask not what your c.   KENN 169:7
  betraying my c.   FORS 116:19
  Britain a fit c.   LLOY 192:9
  Cry, the beloved c.   PATO 245:11

country (*cont.*):

died to save their c.	CHES 62:6
dying for Queen and c.	THOM 309:2
dying for your c.	FRAN 117:11
England, this c. of ours	AUDE 18:11
everyday story of c. folk	CATC 57:16
fight for its King and C.	GRAH 131:6
How can you govern a c.	DE G 87:2
In this frozen whited c.	HUGH 154:5
King and c. need you	SAYI 279:16
love to serve my c.	GIBR 127:10
My c. is Kiltartan Cross	YEAT 337:17
never let my c. die for me	KINN 173:7
no c. for old men	YEAT 338:9
past is a foreign c.	HART 141:13
peace of each c.	JOHN 161:12
put party before c.	CREW 79:12
quarrel in a far away c.	CHAM 60:3
understand the c.	LESS 189:1
vow to thee, my c.	SPRI 294:11
what was good for our c.	WILS 330:14
While there's a c. lane	PARK 244:3
your King and your C.	RUBE 270:4
You've never seen this c.	PURD 258:2

countryman c. must have praise	BLYT 40:3
county English c. families	WAUG 320:13
couple young c. between the wars	PLOM 250:9
couples chasing the naughty c.	THOM 307:15
courage C. is the thing	BARR 24:2
C. not simply *one*	LEWI 190:7
c. to change	NIEB 231:17
C. was mine	OWEN 241:5
Pathos, piety, c.	FORS 116:15
course Of c., of course	JAME 159:13
courting Are yer c.	CATC 57:4
courtmartialled c. in my absence	BEHA 27:2
cousins two brothers and eight c.	HALD 136:13
couture Haute C. should be fun	LACR 178:11
covenants Open c. of peace	WILS 332:9
Covent Garden on C.	KAUF 167:3
cover I c. all	SAND 274:13
cow c. is of the bovine ilk	NASH 227:13
grass to graze a c.	BETJ 35:12
milk the c. of the world	WILB 328:6
news about mad c. disease	RUSH 270:13
Two wise acres and a c.	COWA 79:4
Was the c. crossed	HERB 146:18
coward sea hates a c.	O'NE 236:5
cowardice C., a lack of ability	HEMI 145:11
cows contented—for the c.	CHAN 61:2
cowslip C. and shad-blow	CRAN 79:6
crack C. and sometimes break	ELIO 98:13
c. in the tea-cup opens	AUDE 16:1
cracking c. sound	CROS 81:6
cradle c. rocks above an abyss	NABO 227:2
from the c. to the grave	CHUR 67:5
rocking the c.	ROBI 265:12

craftsmen work not of c.	CLAR 70:3
cramped won't lie too c.	CELA 56:10
crane tall as a c.	SITW 288:2
cranks into sages and c.	QUIN 259:1
crap Books are a load of c.	LARK 180:11
crash car c. as a sexual event	BALL 22:2
craters passing c., passing fire	YEVT 339:16
crazed c. with the spell	DE L 87:13
crazy C. like a fox	PERE 246:12
c. to fly more missions	HELL 145:2
he's football c.	MCGR 200:1
two c. people together	HART 141:9
creaks morning light c. down	SITW 288:2
create genuinely c. Europe	MONN 220:3
What I cannot c.	FEYN 108:3
creation before you think c.'s	FORS 116:18
finds c. so perfect	PROU 257:8
follow the order of c.	WARN 319:11
I hold C. in my foot	HUGH 154:2
world since the C.	NIXO 232:3
your niche in c.	HALL 137:3
creative man's c. powers	SCHU 281:5
creator can dispense with a c.	PROU 257:8
feel at times like the C.	BELL 27:9
credit children to be a c.	RUSS 272:3
people who get the c.	MORR 222:11
To c. marvels	HEAN 143:13
credulous Man is a c. animal	RUSS 272:7
crème c. de la crème	SPAR 292:9
Crete people of c. unfortunately	SAKI 273:13
crevasse like a scream from a c.	GREE 132:10
cricket C.—a game which	MANC 205:10
c. as organized loafing	TEMP 304:4
C. civilizes people	MUGA 224:7
c. enthusiast on baseball	STOP 299:15
c. test	TEBB 303:18
c. with their peasants	TREV 311:8
everything lost but c.	CARD 53:13
cried when he c.	AUDE 16:6
crime catalogue of human c.	CHUR 66:3
C. doesn't pay	SAYI 278:8
c. rates of the '20s	BOAZ 40:5
c. you haven't committed	POWE 255:2
Tough on c.	BLAI 38:10
crimes worst of c.	SHAW 284:5
criminal ends I think c.	KEYN 170:10
most hardened c.	KRAY 178:1
while there is a c.	DEBS 86:6
criminals squalid c.	REAG 262:3
cringe Australian Cultural C.	PHIL 248:9
cultural c. where you have	KEAT 167:11
cripples If c., then no matter	PAST 245:9
crises age has consisted of c.	ATKI 15:2
crisis cannot be a c. next week	KISS 176:3
C.? What crisis	MISQ 218:3
C.? What Crisis	NEWS 231:2
drama out of a c.	ADVE 4:28

cuss don't matter a tinker's c.   SHIN 286:13
customer c. is never wrong   RITZ 265:3
cut c. his ear off   MEDA 212:2
   we are going to c. it off   POWE 255:3
   will not c. my conscience   HELL 145:7
cutlet if he eats a c.   MAUG 210:11
cutting hand is the c. edge   BRON 45:3
cuttlefish like a c.   ORWE 239:5
cycle-clips take off my c.   LARK 180:4
cyclone South Bend c.   RICE 264:2
cyclops view of a paralysed c.   HOCK 150:2
cynicism C. is an unpleasant way   HELL 145:6
Cyprus rings black C.   FLEC 114:3
Cyril Nice one, C.   ADVE 4:13

dabbling d. their fingers   MCGR 200:2
dad fuck you up, your mum and d.   LARK 180:12
   girls in slacks remember D.   BETJ 34:12
   if the d. is present   ORTO 237:5
dada mama of d.   FADI 106:7
daddy D., what did you do   SAYI 278:9
   heart belongs to d.   PORT 253:2
daffodils d. were for Wordsworth   LARK 181:4
dagger d. in one hand and a Bible   WRAN 336:4
daintily have things d. served   BETJ 35:3
dairymaid Queen asked the D.   MILN 216:15
   strapping d.   PAST 245:8
damage d. they have suffered   WEST 325:5
   seriously d. your health   OFFI 235:11
damaged D. people are dangerous   HART 141:5
dame nothin' like a d.   HAMM 137:16
damn d. you England   OSBO 240:8
   don't give a d.   FILM 110:6
   don't give a d.   MITC 217:8
   one d. thing over and over   MILL 214:15
damnation From sleep and from d.   CHES 62:8
damned beautiful and d.   FITZ 112:19
   brandy of the d.   SHAW 284:14
damp d. souls of housemaids   ELIO 100:11
Dan Dangerous D. McGrew   SERV 283:4
dance d., dance, little lady   COWA 78:2
   d. round in a ring   FROS 120:17
   d. to the music of time   POWE 254:20
   know the dancer from the d.   YEAT 336:11
   Let's face the music and d.   BERL 32:12
   Lord of the D.   CART 55:5
   should be able to d. it   ZEPH 341:3
   too far from the d.   POUN 254:8
danced d. his did   CUMM 81:8
   d. with the Prince of Wales   FARJ 106:9
dancer know the d. from the dance   YEAT 336:11
dancers d. are all gone   ELIO 98:16
dances Slightly bald. Also d.   ANON 9:6
dancing [D.] a perpendicular   SHAW 286:6

d. cheek-to-cheek   BERL 32:10
d. is to walking   WAIN 318:1
Dane never get rid of the D.   KIPL 175:8
Dane-geld paying the D.   KIPL 175:8
danger less d. from the wiles   NASH 227:16
   New Labour, new d.   POLI 251:20
dangerous Damaged people are d.   HART 141:5
   d. to meet it alone   WHAR 325:14
   many a d. thing   BISH 38:7
   more d. than an idea   ALAI 5:7
   more d. than justice   PICA 248:13
   much literature d.   MORT 223:5
dare It wouldn't d.   CARR 54:4
   Take me if you d.   PANK 242:7
dares Who d. wins   SAYI 279:15
dark clean your teeth in the d.   JENK 160:9
   come out of the d.   MANN 206:14
   D. as the world of man   SITW 288:4
   d. is light enough   FRY 121:8
   d. night of the soul   FITZ 113:7
   d. world where gods   ROET 266:7
   I knew you in the d.   OWEN 241:6
   In the nightmare of the d.   AUDE 16:13
   O d. dark dark   ELIO 98:17
   Out in the d.   THOM 308:6
   people who live in the d.   SHOR 286:15
   raging in the d.   YEAT 337:4
darker d. days   CHUR 66:13
   I am the d. brother   HUGH 153:11
darkness curse the d.   STEV 298:8
   Go out into the d.   HASK 142:2
   in the d. bind them   TOLK 310:8
   light in the d. of mere being   JUNG 166:3
   there is d. everywhere   NEHR 229:1
   two eternities of d.   NABO 227:2
darling call you d. after sex   BARN 23:8
   d. man, a daarlin' man   O'CA 234:2
   D. of the music halls   SMIT 289:4
data some d. was bound to be   WATS 320:7
date d. which will live in infamy   ROOS 267:15
   doubles your chances for a d.   ALLE 6:17
   last d. slides   EWAR 104:10
   Standards are always out of d.   BENN 30:15
daughter put your d. on the stage   COWA 78:9
   to my elder d.   THOM 308:3
daughters have three d.   RICH 264:11
David D. wrote the Psalms   NAYL 228:16
Davy Sir Humphrey D. Abominated   BENT 32:4
dawn took you away at d.   AKHM 5:4
dawning d. of the age of Aquarius   RADO 259:6
day Action this D.   SAYI 278:1
   d. I was meant not to see   THAT 306:5
   d. that I die   MCLE 200:11
   d. the music died   MCLE 200:10
   d. war broke out   CATC 57:9
   Doris D. before she was   MARX 209:8
   gold of the d.   CROS 80:9

death (*cont.*):

no one knew my d.	ROET 266:8
nothing but d.	UNAM 314:12
Oh, world, Oh, d.	SPEN 293:14
one fear, D.'s shadow	BLUN 39:11
On life, on d.	YEAT 339:5
prepare as though for d.	MANS 207:4
reaction to her d.	ELIZ 102:13
rendezvous with D.	SEEG 282:1
seen birth and d.	ELIO 100:1
stars of d.	AKHM 5:3
suicide 25 years after his d.	BEAV 25:9
Swarm over, D.	BETJ 35:12
This is the Black Widow, d.	LOWE 195:12
thoughts so crowded with d.	GUNN 135:9
up the line to d.	SASS 276:16
what d. makes us think	DE G 87:8
While there is d.	CROS 81:4
Why fear d.	LAST 183:3

deaths million d. a statistic — STAL 295:7

death sentence d. without a whimper

LAWR 184:16

debating d. competition	MCAL 196:11
debt deeper in d.	TRAV 311:3
National D. a very Good Thing	SELL 282:12
promise made is a d. unpaid	SERV 282:17
running up a $4 trillion d.	PERO 247:6
debts so we can pay our d.	NYER 233:5
decade in the same d. with you	ROOS 268:1
Me D.	WOLF 334:7
decay D. with imprecision	ELIO 98:13
deceived willingness to be d.	MEDA 212:3
deceiving nearly d. your friends	CORN 77:9
December May to D.	ANDE 8:8
roses in D.	BARR 24:1
decency D. Indecency's conspiracy	

SHAW 285:8

old life of d.	LOWE 195:7
decide ministers d.	THAT 306:12
decision losses from a delayed d.	GALB 123:12
make a 'realistic d.'	MCCA 197:11
monologue is not a d.	ATTL 15:4
test of any political d.	TREN 311:6
decisions d. allowed to take	PARK 244:9
deck from the bottom of the d.	SHAP 283:10
given a fair d.	SCHE 280:1
decline management of d.	ARMS 13:6
decoded Coward d. for the British	LAHR 179:1
deconstructionists D. pulled down	WOLF 334:6
decorate painting not made to d.	PICA 249:1
decorum Dulce et d. est	OWEN 240:17
deduction d. from the smallest	EINS 97:6
deed right d. for the wrong	ELIO 100:13
deep d. sleep of England	ORWE 238:1
deepens d. like a coastal shelf	LARK 180:13
defeat d. is an orphan	CIAN 69:10
In d.: defiance	CHUR 68:10

In d. unbeatable	CHUR 68:2
North Vietnam cannot d.	NIXO 232:5
price of ultimate d.	NICO 230:5
defeated destroyed but not d.	HEMI 145:13
history to the d.	AUDE 17:17
defeats Dewey d. Truman	NEWS 231:3
nobility of his later d.	TAYL 303:11
defence d. against the atom bomb	ANON 9:3
only d. is in offence	BALD 21:7
think of the d. of England	BALD 21:8
defend never d. any one	MENC 212:16
defended God abandoned, these d.	

HOUS 152:7

defending means by d. freedom	NIEM 231:18
defiance In defeat: d.	CHUR 68:10
wilful d. of military	SASS 277:3
definite d. maybe	GOLD 130:9
definition working d. of hell	SHAW 285:15
deformity Art is significant d.	FRY 121:14
déjà d. vu all over again	BERR 34:2
delay Nothing lost by d.	GREE 132:4
delayed losses from a d. decision	GALB 123:12
delegate When in trouble, d.	BORE 41:10
deleted Expletive d.	ANON 9:10
deliberately d. tries to hurt	BAIN 20:4
delight lovely tube of d.	POTT 253:7
deliver d. us, good Lord	CHES 62:8
delphiniums d. (blue)	MILN 216:13
demand not a note of d.	SCHN 280:7
democracy cured by more d.	SMIT 288:13
D. and socialism	NEHR 229:3
D. is the theory	MENC 212:13
D. is the worst form	CHUR 67:10
d. means government	ATTL 15:10
D. means government by	CHES 64:6
D. *not* identical	LENI 187:6
d. of the dead	CHES 63:13
D. resumed her reign	BELL 28:5
D. substitutes election	SHAW 284:24
d. unbearable	PERE 247:1
five hundred years of d.	FILM 110:14
great arsenal of d.	ROOS 267:13
justice makes d. possible	NIEB 230:13
less d. to save	ATKI 15:1
made safe for d.	WILS 332:7
no d. can afford	BEVE 37:2
no d. in physics	ALVA 7:2
not voting that's d.	STOP 298:15
political aspirant under d.	MENC 213:3
pollution of d.	WHIT 326:11
Russia an empire or d.	BRZE 47:9
Two cheers for D.	FORS 116:20
want to understand d.	STRU 300:10
democrat Senator, and a D.	JOHN 162:9
democratic d. and accountable	HUNT 154:11
get on with the d. process	BENN 30:8
democratically d. governed	HAIL 136:3

democrats D. object to men being   CHES 63:14
demolition d. of a man   LEVI 189:8
denial d. of Him by the atheist   PROU 257:8
denied Justice d.   MILL 214:11
denizen spider is sole d.   HARD 139:5
denouncing by d. some one   MENC 212:16
dentist sooner go to my d.   WAUG 321:13
denunciation d. of the young   SMIT 289:8
depends d. what you mean by   CATC 58:13
    so much d.   WILL 330:8
deported think you are dead or d.   HOWE 153:3
deportment adapt her methods and d.
    CRAN 79:8
depression d. when you lose yours
    TRUM 313:3
deprivation D. is for me   LARK 181:4
Derry oak would sprout in D.   HEAN 144:2
desert d. is a moving mouth   WALC 318:3
    d. sighs in the bed   AUDE 16:1
    my own d. places   FROS 120:5
deserting d. friends conciliates   ASQU 14:9
deserve d. to get it   MENC 212:13
    only d. it   CHUR 66:8
    somehow haven't to d.   FROS 120:4
deserves gets what he d.   ANON 10:6
desiccated d. calculating machine   BEVA 36:12
designs Official d.   BETJ 35:10
desirable physically d.   MORT 222:13
desire get your heart's d.   SHAW 284:20
desired You who d. so much   CRAN 79:11
desires d. of the heart   AUDE 16:3
desk sleeping under the d.   GATE 125:5
    subservience to the d.   FRAN 118:3
    Turn upward from the d.   ELIO 101:15
desolation D. in immaculate   ROET 266:6
despair D. is the price   GREE 132:6
    Do not d.   PUDN 257:13
    far side of d.   SART 276:11
    one path leads to d.   ALLE 6:13
    sins of d.   READ 261:8
    Where there is d.   THAT 305:7
    without understanding d.   LAIN 179:4
despise Government I d.   KEYN 170:10
despondency SPREAD ALARM AND D.
    PENI 246:10
destiny Anatomy is d.   FREU 118:12
    walking with d.   CHUR 68:11
destroy d. the town   ANON 10:4
    determined to d. himself   CUMM 81:16
    gods wish to d.   CONN 74:13
    Whom the mad would d.   LEVI 189:15
destroyed d. but not defeated   HEMI 145:13
destroyer d. of worlds   OPPE 236:8
destroying without d. something   UPDI 315:4
destruction mad d. is wrought   GAND 124:9
    means of total d.   SAKH 273:11
details God is in the d.   ROHE 267:3

    mind which reveres d.   LEWI 190:13
detective d. novel   PRIT 257:4
    d. story is about   JAME 159:16
detector shock-proof shit d.   HEMI 145:17
de Valera Negotiating with d.   LLOY 192:17
developed fairly d. minds   FORS 115:14
    have a d. society   NYER 233:6
developer slipped into d.   WILS 330:15
devil believing in the d.   KNOX 177:1
    D. howling 'Ho'   SQUI 295:2
    D. knows Latin   KNOX 177:2
    d.'s madness—War   SERV 283:3
    d.'s walking parody   CHES 62:4
    Old D. Moon in your eyes   HARB 138:10
    reference to the d.   CHUR 68:13
devils so awakens d.   MAIL 204:10
dialect purify the d.   ELIO 99:8
diamond d. and safire bracelet   LOOS 194:7
    d. is forever   ADVE 3:12
diamonds d. a girl's best friend   ROBI 265:6
    to give him d. back   GABO 122:9
    what beautiful d.   WEST 324:11
Diana D., breathless, hunted   MOTI 223:15
diaries keep d. to remember   O'NE 236:6
diarist To be a good d.   NICO 230:7
diary discreet d.   CHAN 61:5
    keep a d. and some day   WEST 324:4
    living for one's d.   AGAT 2:11
    secret d. of Adrian Mole   TOWN 310:13
    What sort of d.   WOOL 335:11
    write a d. every day   POWE 255:11
    write in a d.   WARN 319:12
dice God does not play d.   EINS 96:9
dictates still d. to us   ALLI 6:20
dictation told at d. speed   AMIS 7:9
dictators D. ride to and fro   CHUR 65:12
    weed d. may cultivate   BEVE 37:2
dictatorship d. impossible   PERE 247:1
    elective d.   HAIL 136:7
    establish a d.   ORWE 238:14
    have a d.   TRUM 313:4
    inefficiencies of d.   GALB 123:13
dictionary ever made the d.   WEST 324:12
    search for a d.   GLEN 129:3
did danced his d.   CUMM 81:8
die back to America . . . to d.   JAME 159:11
    better to d. on your feet   IBAR 156:2
    clean place to d.   KAVA 167:8
    day that I d.   MCLE 200:11
    did not wish to d.   SHAW 286:9
    d. before book is published   RUNC 270:7
    d. for politicians   THOM 309:2
    d. for the industrialists   FRAN 117:11
    d. in my week   JOPL 164:3
    d. like a true-blue rebel   HILL 148:13
    Don't d. of ignorance   OFFI 235:6
    faith is something you d. for   BENN 30:3

die (*cont.*):

gave its victims time to d.	GUIB 135:7
Hope I d. before	TOWN 310:14
How can we d. like this	INDI 156:9
I did not d.	ANON 9:9
If I should d.	ANON 10:1
If I should d.	BROO 45:15
I'll d. young	BRUC 47:3
Let me d. a youngman's death	MCGO 199:9
Live and let d.	FLEM 114:6
love one another or d.	AUDE 17:10
never let my country d. for me	KINN 173:7
nineties is a good time to d.	SPEN 294:3
not afraid to d.	ALLE 6:12
Old soldiers never d.	FOLE 114:12
only let Him d.	STUD 301:1
pie in the sky when you d.	HILL 148:12
something he will d. for	KING 172:5
these who d. as cattle	OWEN 240:14
To d. and know it	LOWE 195:12
To d. will be an awfully big	BARR 23:12
where myths Go when they d.	FENT 107:10

died D. some, pro patria

	POUN 254:1
d. to save their country	CHES 62:6
He d. that's all	MCHA 200:3
'I never d.,' says he	HAYE 143:2
made the books and he d.	FAUL 107:1
Mother d. today	CAMU 53:4
question why we d.	KIPL 173:12

dies kingdom where nobody d.

	MILL 214:7
something in me d.	VIDA 317:9
Who d. if England lives	KIPL 173:17

diesel d.-engined — FLAN 113:16

diet Lead Plan D. — WARR 320:2

dietetics first law of d. — ASIM 14:3

diets feel about d. — KERR 170:9

difference d. within the sexes — COMP 74:7

has made all the d.	FROS 120:16
What d. does it make	GAND 124:9

differences against small d. — FREU 118:14

different on d. subjects — ROGE 266:14

rich are d.	FITZ 112:18
something completely d.	CATC 57:2
thought they were d.	ELIO 100:1

differently do things d. there — HART 141:13

one who thinks d.	LUXE 196:6

difficult d.; and left untried — CHES 64:2

d. takes a little time	NANS 227:9
d. we do immediately	SAYI 278:11
fascination of what's d.	YEAT 337:12
Poets must be *d.*	ELIO 102:7
too d. for artists	SCHN 280:9

difficulties little local d. — MACM 201:18

dig D. for victory — OFFI 235:4

I could not d.	KIPL 173:13
I'll d. with it	HEAN 143:12

dignity d. which His Majesty — BALD 21:9

dilly-dally Don't d. on the way — COLL 73:2

dime Brother can you spare a d. — HARB 138:8

dinner asking it to d. — HALS 137:5

best number for a d. party	GULB 135:8
hungry for d. at eight	HART 141:8
went to a Chinese d.	FLEM 114:8

dinner-knives with broken d. — KIPL 174:3

dinners d. follow the creation — WARN 319:11

diplomacy D. is to do and say — GOLD 129:13

diplomas d. they can't read — GING 128:4

diplomat d. these days — USTI 315:9

diplomats D. tell lies — KRAU 177:14

direct could d. a movie — HYTN 156:1

direction in which d. to point — AUDE 18:9

directions madly off in all d. — LEAC 185:8

directors seven d. in six years — MOYN 224:5

way with these d.	GOLD 130:6

dirt crossness and d. succeed — FORS 116:2

d. doesn't get any worse	CRIS 80:3
thicker will be the d.	GALB 123:7

dirty call d. in our pictures — WILD 328:11

d. old town	MACC 198:4
give pornography a d. name	BARN 23:4
Is sex d.	ALLE 6:9
'Jug Jug' to d. ears	ELIO 101:10
paid to have d. minds	TREV 311:10
You d. rat	MISQ 219:6

dirty-mindedness journalistic d. — LAWR 184:15

disappointed you have d. us — BELL 27:13

disappointing least d. — BARU 24:11

disappointment d. to children — POWE 254:19

disaster precipitate one into d. — WEST 324:21

Triumph and D.	KIPL 174:5

disasters d. of English history — WAUG 320:15

disastrous d. and the unpalatable — GALB 123:14

discharge d. for loving one — MATL 209:15

discipline d. of public service — GRIE 134:3

disciplines by category-d. — RYLE 273:2

discontent winter of d. — CALL 51:10

Winter of d.	NEWS 231:15

discontents Civilization and d. — RIVI 265:4

source of all our d.	LEAC 185:3

discovered d. the nature of DNA — WOLP 334:9

discovery D. consists of seeing — SZEN 302:11

Medicinal d.	AYRE 19:9
not a d. in life	WOOL 335:14

discreet d. charm — FILM 112:7

d. diary	CHAN 61:5

discretion D. not the better part — STRA 299:18

discriminated men who are d. — MEIR 212:7

discussing In d. if it existed — GUNN 135:10

discussion after reasonable d. — CHUR 68:14

government by d.	ATTL 15:10

disease biggest d. today — TERE 304:7

d. called friendship	RENO 263:5
D., Ignorance, Squalor	BEVE 37:3
d. in the family	TREV 311:11

Life a sexually transmitted d.   ANON 10:10
no Cure for this D.   BELL 27:11
Progress is a comfortable d.   CUMM 81:14
diseases sneezes spread d.   OFFI 235:3
disenchantment d. for truth   SART 276:6
disestablishment sense of d.   KING 172:13
disgrace Intellectual d. Stares   AUDE 16:13
disgruntled if not actually d.   WODE 333:3
disguise better go in d.   KENN 168:9
this identical d.   BROO 46:5
dishes who does the d.   FREN 118:10
disillusionment D. is finding out   STEI 296:4
disinterested D. curiosity   TREV 311:7
dislike I, too, d. it   MOOR 221:6
Disney of Euro D.   BALL 22:3
Disneyfication D. of Christianity   CUPI 82:6
Disneyland Americans with no D.   MAHY 204:6
disorder put back in d.   CONN 74:18
there to preserve d.   DALE 83:1
disposable to be d.   MILL 215:7
Disraeli D. school of Prime Ministers   BLAI 39:5
disregard Atones for later d.   FROS 120:15
dissolution lingering d.   BECK 25:12
dissolve d. the people   BREC 44:5
distance longest d. between   WILL 330:2
prestige without d.   DE G 87:6
distempered questions the d. part   ELIO 98:18
distinguished d. thing   JAME 159:14
diver Don't forget the d.   CATC 57:11
divided d. by a common language   SHAW 286:7
D. by the morning tea   MACN 203:3
d. self   LAIN 179:3
dividend Drawing no d.   SASS 276:18
divine say that D. providence   JOHN 162:7
divisions How many d. has *he* got STAL 295:6
DNA cannot cheat on D.   WARD 319:3
discovered the nature of D.   WOLP 334:9
do as long as they d. what I say   THAT 305:10
because we know how to d. them   FOX 117:7
Can I d. you now, sir   CATC 57:7
did not d. things themselves   RAVE 261:1
d. a girl in   ELIO 101:3
D. not do unto others   SHAW 284:21
d. those things which   KEYN 170:13
d. what had to be done   HAVE 142:3
D. what thou wilt   CROW 81:7
Let's d. it   LAST 182:9
Let's d. it   PORT 252:18
man got to d.   STEI 296:9
people who d. things   MORR 222:11
supposed to d. anyway   TRUM 312:13
time now to d.   BLAI 39:2
way I d. it   WEST 324:16
doc cards with a man called D.   ALGR 5:14
What's up, D.   CATC 59:13
doctors D. in verse   THOM 308:11
d. know a hopeless case   CUMM 81:15

doctrinal On the d. side   QUIN 258:13
doctrine d. something you kill for BENN 30:3
documents d. and friends   SPAR 292:6
do-ers d. and the done-by   WARN 320:1
does D. she or doesn't she   ADVE 3:13
dog communism is a dead d.   SOLZ 291:3
door is what a d.   NASH 227:14
drover's d. could lead   HAYD 143:1
engine of pollution, the d.   SPAR 292:13
heart to a d. to tear   KIPL 175:1
jumps over the lazy d.   ANON 11:2
lost d. somewhere   ANOU 12:6
mad d. of the Middle East   REAG 262:5
man bites a d.   BOGA 40:8
That d. won't hunt   RICH 264:6
was there ever d.   YEAT 339:1
working like a d.   MCCA 188:6
your wife and your d.   HILL 148:8
doggie How much is that d.   MERR 213:14
dogma Any stigma to beat a d.   GUED 135:1
dogs d. go on with their doggy life AUDE 17:2
D. look up to us   CHUR 69:1
d. of Europe bark   AUDE 16:13
go to the d. tonight   HERB 146:7
hates d. and babies   ROST 269:7
keep parrots or puppy d.   CAMP 52:11
Mad d. and Englishmen   COWA 78:8
paparazzi d. of war   DENE 88:2
doing stop everyone from d. it   HERB 146:10
dolls Valley of the d.   SUSA 301:8
dolmens d. round my childhood   MONT 220:11
dolour d. of pad and paper-weight   ROET 266:6
dolphin-torn That d.   YEAT 337:1
dome Millennium D.   MAND 206:6
starlit or a moonlit d.   YEAT 336:14
domes plump with d.   THWA 310:2
domestic respectable d. establishment
                                        BENN 30:13

domination against white d.   MAND 205:11
dominion death shall have no d.   THOM 307:1
domino 'falling d.' principle   EISE 97:13
don D. John of Austria is going   CHES 62:9
quiet flows the D.   SHOL 286:14
Remote and ineffectual D.   BELL 28:2
done Been there, d. that   SAYI 278:3
be seen to be d.   OSBO 240:6
decide that d. can be done   ALLE 6:6
d. very well out of the war   BALD 21:2
If you want anything d.   THAT 304:10
Nothing to be d.   BECK 26:1
should not be d. at all   VIDA 317:10
Something must be d.   MISQ 219:2
that which gets things d.   LLOY 192:10
What is to be d.   LENI 187:8
donkeys Lions led by d.   SAYI 279:1
Donne another Newton, a new D.   HUXL 155:13
don't George—d. do that   GREN 133:11

door beating on the d.	YEAT 337:15	salesman is got to d.	MILL 215:6
Death's shadow at the d.	BLUN 39:11	till you find your d.	HAMM 137:8
d. is what a dog	NASH 227:14	**dreamed** d. I saw Joe Hill	HAYE 143:2
d. opens and lets the future	GREE 132:13	**dreaming** d. of a white Christmas	BERL 33:3
d. we never opened	ELIO 98:10	d. on the verge of strife	CORN 77:7
through the d. with a gun	CHAN 60:13	little d.	PHIL 248:11
wrong side of the d.	CHES 62:2	**dreams** armoured cars of d.	BISH 38:7
doormat d. in a world of boots	RHYS 263:12	city of perspiring d.	RAPH 260:4
d. or a prostitute	WEST 324:22	D. are the royal road	MISQ 218:4
doors close softly the d.	JUST 166:11	either d. or swords	LOWE 195:5
with both d. open	HUGH 153:9	In d. begins responsibility	YEAT 339:8
doorstep do this on the d.	JUNO 166:10	interpretation of d.	FREU 118:13
dorma Nessun d.	ADAM 1:10	scream for help in d.	CANE 53:7
double joke with a d. meaning	BARK 23:2	**dreamt** d. I went to Manderley	DU M 92:10
Labour's d. whammy	POLI 251:18	**dress** automobile changed our d.	KEAT 168:3
double-bed peace of the d.	CAMP 52:4	I like to d. egos	VERS 317:2
doubles d. your chances for a date	ALLE 6:17	make a d. out of a curtain	POWE 255:5
doublethink D. means the power	ORWE 238:13	put on a d. of guilt	MCGO 199:8
doubt curiosity, freckles, and d.	PARK 242:14	**dressed** all d. up	BURT 49:13
d. and good taste	BROD 45:2	d. in modern clothing	STRA 299:19
Life is d.	UNAM 314:12	impossible to be well d.	AMIE 7:6
Dover white cliffs of D.	BURT 49:14	**drift** adamant for d.	CHUR 65:11
dowager sedate old d.	MUGG 224:10	**drifted** but I d.	WEST 324:14
down born with D.'s syndrome	DE G 87:9	**drink** d. and drive	OFFI 235:5
D. and out in Paris	ORWE 237:16	One more d.	PARK 244:1
d. express in the back	WODE 333:8	reason I don't d.	ASTO 14:15
d. into the darkness	MILL 214:8	your husband I would d. it	CHUR 69:2
meet 'em on your way d.	MIZN 217:15	**drinka** D. Pinta Milka Day	ADVE 3:16
downhearted Are we d.	KNIG 176:13	**drinks** d. as much as you	THOM 307:19
Are we d.	SAYI 278:2	**dripping** electricity was d.	THUR 309:9
downhill run by itself except d.	SAYI 278:5	**drive** can't d. the car	TYNA 314:9
dozens Mother to d.	HERB 146:12	drink and d.	OFFI 235:5
drag don't d. wood about	SCHW 281:8	**driver** in the d.'s seat	BEAV 25:11
dragon d.-green, the luminous	FLEC 114:1	very good back-seat d.	THAT 306:17
d. of the hills	SUTT 301:9	**droopingly** d., but with a hopeful	LAWR 183:8
O to be a d.	MOOR 221:5	**drop** d. in the ocean	TERE 304:5
dragons laugh at live d.	TOLK 310:7	one d. of black blood	HUGH 153:14
drain leave by the first town d.	SPOO 294:9	turn on, tune in and d. out	LEAR 185:9
drains comes to unblock your d.	GLEN 129:4	**drops** d. on gate-bars hang	HARD 140:8
drama d. out of a crisis	ADVE 4:28	**drought** d. destroying his roots	HERB 146:8
great d. critic	TYNA 314:8	**drover** d.'s dog could lead	HAYD 143:1
dramatist d. want more liberties	JAME 159:8	**drowned** BETTER D. THAN DUFFERS	TELE 305:2
dramatize D. it, dramatize it	JAME 159:2	**drowning** like death by d.	FERB 107:12
draw d. like these children	PICA 249:2	not waving but d.	SMIT 290:1
drawing room through my d.	EDEN 95:9	**drug** consciousness-expanding d.	CLAR 70:7
women in a d.	WOOL 335:7	d. neither moral nor immoral	ZAPP 341:1
dread d. of beatings	BETJ 35:16	like a d.	MORE 221:10
Nor d. nor hope attend	YEAT 337:6	no more hope to end d. abuse	WHIT 327:12
dreadful d. human beings sitting	NORR 232:13	Words the most powerful d.	KIPL 175:16
dreadnoughts keep up as two D.	LLOY 192:6	you can d., with words	LOWE 195:5
dream d. I am dreaming	COWA 78:11	**drugs** D. don't cause crime rates	BOAZ 40:5
d. my dreams away	FLAN 113:12	D. is like having a cup	GALL 124:1
D. the impossible	DARI 83:4	Sex and d. and rock and roll	DURY 94:1
d. things that never were	SHAW 283:11	so-called soft d.	STRA 300:6
I have a d.	KING 172:6	**drum** big bass d.	LIND 191:6
I have a d.	KING 172:7	still the most effective d.	GIRA 128:10
In a d. you are never 80	SEXT 283:6	**drums** beating of war d.	KOES 177:8

drunk d., one sees in other women — TYNA 314:6
everyone is more or less d. — MUGG 224:10
not d. if you can lie on — MART 209:2
not so think as you d. — SQUI 295:1
Winston, you're d. — CHUR 69:9
Wordsworth d. — HOUS 152:13
drunkenness d. of things being — MACN 203:7
dry d. brain in a dry season — ELIO 99:15
into a d. Martini — FILM 111:1
old man in a d. month — ELIO 99:13
Dubuque for the old lady in D. — ROSS 269:2
duchess every D. in London — MACD 199:3
married to a d. — YOUN 340:5
duck just forgot to d. — DEMP 88:1
looks like a d. — REUT 263:7
ducks d., produce bad parents — MORS 222:12
I turn to d. — HARV 142:1
duffers BETTER DROWNED THAN D. — TELE 305:2
dugs old man with wrinkled d. — ELIO 101:16
duke fully-equipped d. — LLOY 192:6
dukes drawing room of d. — AUDE 18:6
dulce D. et decorum est — OWEN 240:17
dull Heaven would be too d. — EPIT 106:3
very d., dreary affair — MAUG 210:13
dumb Children are d. to say — GRAV 131:8
d. son of a bitch — TRUM 313:7
So d. he can't — JOHN 163:10
takes 40 d. animals — SAYI 278:22
dump What a d. — FILM 112:1
dung die in their own d. — KIPL 174:8
dunghill cock crowing on its own d. — ALDI 5:9
Dunkirk appeals to the D. spirit — WILS 331:2
duration not only dead for the d. — ASQU 14:4
dusk each slow d. — OWEN 240:16
dust d. comes secretly — MEYN 214:2
d. of ages has settled — LAWR 184:12
d. of exploded beliefs — MADA 203:13
d. on the nettles — THOM 308:7
D. yourself off — FIEL 108:8
Excuse My D. — EPIT 105:2
fear in a handful of d. — ELIO 101:8
in the d., in the cool tombs — SAND 274:11
rich earth a richer d. — BROO 45:15
dustbin d. of history — TROT 312:4
duty as much a d. as cooperation — GAND 124:12
Nor law, nor d. — YEAT 337:18
sense of d. useful — RUSS 271:9
dying achieve it through not d. — ALLE 6:18
attend a d. animal — YEAT 337:6
dead or d. beast — JENK 161:4
D. a very dull, dreary — MAUG 210:13
d. breath of Socrates — JEAN 160:6
d., has made us gifts — BROO 45:7
D. is an art — PLAT 250:4
d. is nothing — ANOU 12:5
d. of the light — THOM 307:2
If this is d. — LAST 182:7

key to d. well — LEAR 185:11
little d. — PHIL 248:11
love to those of the d. — LOWR 196:2
man's d. is more — MANN 207:1
nothing new in d. — LAST 182:8
sunsets exquisitely d. — HUXL 155:14
Those d. generations — YEAT 338:9
dynamite barrel of d. — MAYA 211:4
dynamo starry d. — GINS 128:7

e E = mc² — EINS 96:7
eagle E. has landed — ARMS 13:4
Fate is not an e. — BOWE 42:12
eagles Where e. dare — MACL 200:9
ear cut his e. off — MEDA 212:2
penetrates the e. with facility — BEEC 26:13
earl e. and a knight — ATTL 15:8
fourteenth e. — HOME 151:7
earlier Here's one I made e. — CATC 58:4
early E. to rise — THUR 309:14
too late or too e. — SART 276:12
earned e. on earth — THAT 305:8
earnestness demans moral e. — LEWI 190:9
earrings e. for under £1 — RATN 260:6
ears Enemy e. are listening — OFFI 235:13
lets the e. lie back — IVES 158:2
That man's e. — HUGH 153:9
earth all e. to love — KIPL 175:4
call this planet E. — CLAR 70:6
earned on e. — THAT 305:8
E., receive an honoured guest — AUDE 16:12
E.'s the right place — FROS 119:15
feel the e. move — HEMI 145:10
he craves the e. — SEXT 283:5
rich e. a richer dust — BROO 45:15
Spaceship E. — FULL 122:3
surly bonds of e. — MAGE 204:1
surly bonds of e. — REAG 262:4
Yours is the E. — KIPL 174:6
earthquake Small e. in Chile — COCK 72:2
starts with an e. — GOLD 130:12
easier e. job like publishing — AYER 19:7
easing e. the Spring — REED 262:10
east Britain calls the Far E. — MENZ 213:8
face neither E. nor West — NKRU 232:11
East End look the E. in the face — ELIZ 103:3
Easter E. island statue — KEAT 167:10
eastern E. promise — ADVE 3:18
easy normal and e. — JAME 159:3
Too e. for children — SCHN 280:9
eat e. at a place called Mom's — ALGR 5:14
E. my shorts — CATC 57:12
eaten e. by missionaries — SPOO 294:7
He has been e. by the bear — HOUS 152:4
we've already e. — BENN 29:14
eating E. people is wrong — FLAN 113:15

Ebenezer Pale E. thought it wrong   BELL 28:8
ecclesiologist keen e.   BETJ 36:1
echo e. of a pistol-shot   DURR 93:9
Footfalls e. in the memory   ELIO 98:10
waiting for the e.   MARQ 208:13
ecological upset the e. balance   SONT 291:15
ecology e. and antiwar   HUNT 154:12
economic cold metal of e. theory   SCHU 281:6
vital e. interests   WEIL 322:6
when I read e. documents   HOME 151:6
economical e. with the *actualité*   CLAR 69:14
e. with the truth   ARMS 13:5
economics E. are the method   THAT 305:13
E. is the science   ROBB 265:5
knew more about e.   KEYN 171:4
making a speech on e.   JOHN 163:8
only the e.   MONN 220:5
study of e.   SCHU 281:2
economist slaves of defunct e.   KEYN 171:2
economy fear of Political E.   SELL 282:12
It's the e., stupid   POLI 251:15
Stakeholder E.   BLAI 38:13
ecstasy e. of betrayal   GENE 126:4
ecstatic such e. sound   HARD 139:11
Eden attempt a picnic in E.   BOWE 42:14
edge at the e. of Being   SPEN 293:10
Come to the e.   LOGU 193:6
editor e. did it when I was away   MURD 226:2
editorial age of the e. chair   MCLU 201:6
Edna Aunt E. is universal   RATT 260:7
educated 'e.' people come   ORWE 238:18
government by badly e.   CHES 64:6
education aim of e.   INGE 157:3
best kind of e.   BUCH 47:11
e. and catastrophe   WELL 323:9
e., education, education   BLAI 39:1
[E.] has produced   TREV 311:9
E. is what survives   SKIN 288:11
E. is when you read   SEEG 282:3
liberal e.   BANK 22:12
poor e. I have received   BOTT 42:5
Real e. must ultimately   POUN 254:12
that is e.   ROGE 266:10
unplanned e. creates   VERW 317:3
educator overpaid as an e.   OSBO 240:9
effective one e. advertisement   HUXL 155:8
efficiencies e. of freedom   GALB 123:13
efficiency southern e.   KENN 169:17
efficient have an e. government   TRUM 313:4
effort all wasted e.   AYER 19:6
e. nor the failure tires   EMPS 104:1
redoubling your e.   SANT 275:8
effusive don't be too e.   ELIZ 103:1
egg Go to work on an e.   ADVE 3:19
hand that lays the golden e.   GOLD 130:6
looks like a poached e.   NUFF 233:3
Wall St. lays an e.   NEWS 231:12

egghead E. weds hourglass   NEWS 231:4
eggs all my e. in one bastard   PARK 243:20
Lays e. inside a paper bag   ISHE 157:13
ego fulfils a man's e.   ROOT 268:10
egos I like to dress e.   VERS 317:2
eighteen before you reach e.   EINS 97:5
eighty dream you are never e.   SEXT 283:6
live beyond e.   CALL 51:7
ein *E. Reich, ein Volk*   POLI 251:9
Einstein Let E. be   SQUI 295:2
elderly e. lady, who mutters away   CARE 53:14
imported, e. American   JENK 160:10
elect dissolve the people and e.   BREC 44:5
election e. by incompetent many   SHAW 284:24
elections e. are won   ADAM 1:14
You won the e.   SOMO 291:6
elective e. dictatorship   HAIL 136:7
Electra Mourning becomes E.   O'NE 236:4
electric biggest e. train set   WELL 322:14
E. Kool-Aid Acid test   WOLF 334:5
tried to mend the E. Light   BELL 28:3
electricity e. was dripping   THUR 309:9
must use less e.   JENK 160:9
electrification power plus e.   LENI 187:10
electronic new e. interdependence   MCLU 201:2
elegant Most intelligent, very e.   BUCK 48:4
so e. So intelligent   ELIO 101:12
elementary E., my dear Watson   MISQ 218:5
elephant as high as an e.'s eye   HAMM 137:11
can say is 'e.'   CHAP 61:10
E.'s Child   KIPL 175:11
English e. *Never* lies   IMLA 156:8
fit the profile of an e.   GAMO 124:8
herd of e. pacing   DINE 90:2
sleeping with an e.   TRUD 312:11
elephants golden e. next   SHOR 287:1
shape of identical e.   QUIN 259:2
eleven-plus on failing his e.   PRES 256:2
eleventh dark e. hour   KIPL 175:5
eliminate does not e. evil   HAVE 142:5
Eliot unpleasant to meet Mr E.   ELIO 98:8
eloquence finest e. is that   LLOY 192:10
else does it to somebody e.   O'RO 236:19
happening to Somebody E.   ROGE 266:12
elsewhere Altogether e.   AUDE 16:7
life happens e.   BENN 31:3
Elysium Keep alive our lost E.   BETJ 35:9
embalmer triumph of the e.'s art   VIDA 317:12
embarrassment in our place is e.   BENN 30:10
emergencies prepared for all e.   FORS 116:7
emergency one e. following   FISH 109:4
Emily E., hear   CRAN 79:11
emotion degree of my aesthetic e.   BELL 27:6
escape from e.   ELIO 102:4
remembered in e.   PARK 243:8
emotional e. promiscuity   MAIL 204:7
Gluttony an e. escape   DE V 88:13

emotions brothel for the e.   KOES 177:5
  e. were riveted   FOOT 114:14
  gamut of the e.   PARK 243:13
  only two e. in a plane   WELL 323:2
  refusal to admit our e.   RATT 260:9
  Television strikes at e.   DAY 84:14
  waste-paper basket of e.   WEBB 322:3
  world of the e.   COLE 72:14
emperor dey makes you E.   O'NE 236:1
  e. of ice-cream   STEV 297:7
  E.'s drunken soldiery   YEAT 336:13
emperors E. can do nothing   BREC 43:14
empire E. strikes back   FILM 112:8
  e. walking very slowly   FITZ 113:5
  founded the British E.   HILL 148:7
  Greeks in this American e.   MACM 201:14
  How's the E.   LAST 182:5
  liquidation of British E.   CHUR 67:3
  lost an e.   ACHE 1:8
  meaning of E. Day   CHES 63:1
  Russia an e. or democracy   BRZE 47:9
  way she disposed of an e.   HARL 140:14
empires e. of the future   CHUR 67:7
empirical *e. scientific system*   POPP 250:14
employee In a hierarchy every e.   PETE 247:11
employer harder upon the e.   SPOO 294:10
employers e. of past generations   BALD 21:6
employment give e. to the artisan   BELL 28:3
  seek gainful e.   ACHE 1:7
emptiness e. The human lack   BOLD 41:1
  great Australian E.   WHIT 326:6
  kind of e.   DE B 85:9
empty Bring on the e. horses   CURT 82:9
enchanted Some e. evening   HAMM 137:14
encounters Close e.   FILM 112:6
end any beginning or any e.   POLL 250:12
  at the e. of the world   DINE 90:2
  came to an e. all wars   LLOY 192:8
  e. cannot justify the means   HUXL 155:6
  e. is where we start from   ELIO 99:10
  e. of a thousand years   GAIT 122:14
  e. of history   FUKU 121:17
  e. of the beginning   CHUR 67:4
  e. of the way inescapable   PAST 245:7
  e. to beginnings of all wars   ROOS 268:2
  evokes the e. of the world   BAUD 24:14
  have the power to e. it   SASS 277:3
  In my beginning is my e.   ELIO 98:14
  muddle, and an e.   LARK 181:6
  only e. of age   LARK 180:5
  on to the e. of the road   LAUD 181:9
  Our e. is Life   MACN 203:10
  Waiting for the e.   EMPS 103:15
  war that will e. war   WELL 323:11
  where's it all going to e.   STOP 299:8
  world will e. in fire   FROS 120:6
endeavours all my e. are unlucky   DOUG 91:3

ended in 1915 the old world e.   LAWR 183:6
ending way of e. a war   ORWE 239:12
ends between e. and scarce means   ROBB 265:5
  similar sounds at their e.   LARK 181:5
endure props to help him e.   FAUL 107:3
endured e. with resignation   RUSS 271:9
enemies alone against smiling e.   BOWE 42:13
  conciliates e.   ASQU 14:9
  e. of Freedom do not argue   INGE 156:11
enemy better class of e.   MILL 216:1
  e. of good art   CONN 74:14
  e. to the human race   MILL 215:13
  I am the e. you killed   OWEN 241:6
  no e. but time   YEAT 337:16
  quieten your e. by talking   CEAU 56:9
  Sir, no man's e.   AUDE 17:14
  sometimes his own worst e.   BEVI 37:10
  written by an acute e.   BALF 21:13
energy important source of e.   EINS 97:2
engine be a Really Useful E.   AWDR 19:1
  e. of pollution, the dog   SPAR 292:13
  human e. waits   ELIO 101:15
  stopped the e.   JENK 161:2
engineers age of the e.   HOGB 150:9
  e. of human souls   STAL 295:5
  e. of the soul   GORK 131:1
  not e. of the soul   KENN 169:15
England always be an E.   PARK 244:3
  apple falling towards E.   AUDE 17:5
  bored for E.   MUGG 224:13
  damn you E.   OSBO 240:8
  deep sleep of E.   ORWE 238:1
  E. and America divided   SHAW 286:7
  E. is a garden   KIPL 174:3
  E. not the jewelled isle   ORWE 238:4
  E. one whose centre   UPDI 314:16
  E.'s act and deed   KIPL 175:5
  E.'s native people   BURN 49:8
  E.'s not a bad country   DRAB 92:1
  E.'s the one land   BROO 45:11
  E. will have her neck   CHUR 67:1
  found E. a land of beauty   JOAD 161:10
  Goodbye, E.'s rose   JOHN 162:3
  Gott strafe E.   FUNK 122:6
  History is now and E.   ELIO 99:11
  in E. people have   MIKE 214:4
  lot that make up E. today   LAWR 184:9
  Speak for E.   AMER 7:4
  suspended in favour of E.   SHAW 284:3
  That is for ever E.   BROO 45:15
  that will be E. gone   LARK 180:6
  think of the defence of E.   BALD 21:8
  Wake up, E.   GEOR 126:5
  we are the people of E.   CHES 62:13
  What do you think about E.   AUDE 18:11
  Who dies if E. lives   KIPL 173:17

ex-parrot THIS IS AN E.   MONT 221:2
expect E. nothing   WALK 318:9
expectations match political e.   POWE 255:4
    rising e.   CLEV 71:6
    talents and our e.   DE B 86:2
expects Nobody e.   MONT 221:3
expediency be sacrificed to e.   MAUG 210:3
expedition abandoning the e.   DOUG 91:3
expenditure E. rises to meet   PARK 244:5
expenses facts are on e.   STOP 299:3
expensive e. and forsaken   THOM 309:3
    how e. it is to be poor   BALD 20:9
experience e. has taught me   EDEN 95:8
    e. in runnning up   PERO 247:6
    e. is what you get   SEEG 282:3
    had the e. but missed   ELIO 99:4
    man of no e.   CURZ 82:11
    never had much e.   MARQ 208:4
    one year's e. 30 times   CARR 54:3
    refuted by e.   POPP 250:14
    to be filled in by e.   WILS 330:15
    we need not e. it   FRIS 119:11
experiences e. of our life   MANN 206:14
experiment e. needs statistics   RUTH 272:13
    have them fit e.   DIRA 90:4
    social and economic e.   HOOV 151:8
expert e. is someone who knows   HEIS 144:12
    e. knows more and more   BUTL 50:6
experts 'e.' make worst Ministers   ATTL 15:11
expiate something to e.   LAWR 184:6
explain e. why it didn't happen   CHUR 68:17
    Never e.   FISH 109:7
explainer village e.   STEI 296:7
explaining forever e. things   SAIN 273:7
expletive E. deleted   ANON 9:10
explodes line smoulders and e.   MAYA 211:4
exploitation forms of mutual e.   AUDE 18:5
explorers unlucky e.   DOUG 91:3
exploring end of all our e.   ELIO 99:9
express down e. in the back   WODE 333:8
    e. yourself like   YEAT 339:10
expresses music e. itself   STRA 300:5
expressing worth e. in music   DELI 87:22
exterior this flabby e.   LEVA 189:5
exterminate e. a nation   SPOC 294:6
    Exterminate! E.   CATC 57:17
extermination e. of capitalism   ZINO 341:7
extinction leads to total e.   ALLE 6:13
    one generation from e.   CARE 53:15
extra add some e., just for you   LARK 180:12
extraordinary write about the e.   JOYC 165:14
extremes E. meet   MACD 198:10
extremism E. in pursuit   JOHN 163:5
    e. in the defence   GOLD 130:2
eye Cast a cold e.   YEAT 339:5
    close one e.   DOUG 91:6
    e. that can open an oyster   WODE 333:6

    if you have the e.   HOLM 151:5
    less in this than meets the e.   BANK 22:10
    looked into the e. of day   YEAT 337:14
    My tiny watching e.   DE L 87:20
    to the e. of God   OLIV 235:16
eyeball e. to eyeball   RUSK 271:1
eyeless work of an e. computer   BETJ 35:10
eyes bodily hunger in his e.   SHAW 284:7
    chewing gum for the e.   ANON 11:8
    close your e. before   AYCK 19:3
    Crumbling behind the e.   MACN 203:2
    ever more perfect e.   TEIL 304:1
    e. are hurting me   SWAN 301:11
    e. as wide as football-pool   CAUS 56:5
    e. of Caligula   MITT 217:14
    E. still dazzled   LIND 191:7
    frightened look in its e.   SITW 288:6
    good Lord made your e.   LEHR 186:18
    Smoke gets in your e.   HARB 138:7
    Stars scribble on our e.   CRAN 79:5
    was it his bees-winged e.   BETJ 34:11

Fabians good man fallen among F.   LENI 187:9
façade first you put up the f.   GING 128:5
face Accustomed to her f.   LERN 188:16
    f. looks like a weddding-cake   AUDE 18:15
    f. neither East nor West   NKRU 232:11
    f. of a Venus   BARR 24:3
    f. of 'evil'   BURR 49:11
    has the f. he deserves   ORWE 239:13
    I am the family f.   HARD 139:14
    keep your f.   CART 55:6
    lose its human f.   DUBČ 92:5
    mask that eats into the f.   UPDI 315:2
    never forget a f.   MARX 209:7
    rabbit has a charming f.   ANON 11:3
    stamping on a human f.   ORWE 238:15
    touched the f. of God   MAGE 204:2
    unacceptable f.   HEAT 144:6
    whole life shows in your f.   BACA 19:14
faces f. in the crowd   POUN 254:4
    F. you had got used to   SULL 301:3
    not having any f.   PRIE 256:11
    Private f. in public places   AUDE 17:6
fact f., no matter how suspect   VIDA 317:7
    waiting to do away with f.   THOM 309:5
factor Falklands F.   THAT 306:1
facts accounted for *all* the f.   WATS 320:7
    f. are lost forever   MAIL 204:12
    f. are on expenses   STOP 299:3
    f. are sacred   SCOT 281:11
    F. do not cease to exist   HUXL 155:11
    give you all the f.   AUDE 17:11
    not of f. but of values   INGE 157:3
    not to deny the f.   RYLE 273:1
    number of empirical f.   EINS 97:6

That's all the f.	FLIO 101:2
fade just f. away	MACA 197:3
Than to f. away	YOUN 340:6
They simply f. away	FOLE 114:12
fail F. better	BECK 26:9
Others must f.	VIDA 317:11
shall not flag or f.	CHUR 66:5
failed they f. before	POLI 252:3
failure Any f. seems so total	QUAN 258:8
different kind of f.	ELIO 99:2
effort nor the f. tires	EMPS 104:1
f. in life	WEST 325:8
f. is ignominious	MENC 213:3
f.'s no success at all	DYLA 94:9
formula for f.	SWOP 302:1
Now we are not a f.	VANZ 316:7
political lives end in f.	POWE 255:16
success only a delayed f.	GREE 132:15
fair F. shares for all	POLI 251:10
follows that it is F.	SWOP 301:12
fairies beginning of f.	BARR 23:10
don't believe in f.	BARR 23:11
Do you believe in f.	BARR 23:13
f. at the bottom	FYLE 122:8
fairy f. when she's forty	HENL 146:5
myth not a f. story	RYLE 273:1
faith f. and fire within us	HARD 140:4
f. is something you die for	BENN 30:3
f. of those in the pulpit	AUST 18:20
f. without doubt	UNAM 314:12
World, you have kept f.	HARD 139:13
faithless Human on my f. arm	AUDE 16:16
fake Anything that consoles is f.	MURD 225:16
Falklands F. Factor	THAT 306:1
F. thing was a fight	BORG 42:4
fall Life is a horizontal f.	COCT 72:3
Things f. apart	YEAT 338:13
fallen Christopher Robin has f.	MORT 223:7
good man f. among Fabians	LENI 187:9
people who have never f.	PAST 245:4
falling apple f. towards England	AUDE 17:5
'f. domino' principle	EISE 97:13
f. from stair to stair	BAYL 25:3
falls F. the Shadow	ELIO 99:18
falsifiability *f.* of a system	POPP 250:14
falters love that never f.	SPRI 294:11
fame best f. is a writer's fame	LEBO 186:10
Physicians of the Utmost F.	BELL 27:11
families rooks in f. homeward go	HARD 140:8
there are f.	THAT 306:8
family disease in the f.	TREV 311:11
f. firm	GEOR 126:14
f.—that dear octopus	SMIT 289:1
f. that prays together	SAYI 278:13
f., with its narrow privacy	LEAC 185:3
f. with the wrong members	ORWE 238:4
I am the f. face	HARD 139:14

I have a young f.	FOWL 117:6
Selling off the f. silver	MISQ 218:13
spend more time with f.	THAT 306:13
We, your blood f.	SPEN 293:3
famine F. sighs like scythe	WALC 318:3
famous advantage of being f.	KISS 176:6
by that time I was too f.	BENC 29:5
f. for fifteen minutes	WARH 319:4
F. remarks are very seldom	STRU 300:11
f. without ability	SHAW 283:14
When you're first f.	LOVE 194:13
fanatic f. a great leader	BROU 46:11
fanaticism f. consists in	SANT 275:8
fancy All I see is f. stuff	PHIL 248:5
fantasies fed the heart on f.	YEAT 338:3
fantasy Most modern f.	PRAT 256:1
far f. side of despair	SART 276:11
going a bridge too f.	BROW 47:1
how f. one can go too far	COCT 72:5
much too f. out all my life	SMIT 290:1
quarrel in a f. away country	CHAM 60:3
Faraday anti-F. machines	CORN 77:2
still choose to be F.	HUXL 155:15
farce second time as f.	BARN 23:7
wine was a f.	POWE 254:17
farewell F., my friends	LAST 182:3
So f. then	CATC 59:7
farm down on the f.	LEWI 190:10
farmer F. will never be happy	HERB 146:8
farmers inefficient f.	LYNN 196:7
farms cellos of the deep f.	STEV 298:10
farrow old sow that eats her f.	JOYC 164:14
fart can't f. and chew gum	JOHN 163:10
f. sound like sevenfold Amen	WILL 329:6
farther only much f. away	FLEM 114:7
fascination f. of what's difficult	YEAT 337:12
fascism F. not a new order	BEVA 36:15
form of linguistic f.	JAME 159:17
victims of American F.	ROSE 268:13
Fascist Every woman adores a F.	PLAT 250:3
fashion f. in these things	FRAN 118:4
F. is more usually	OLDF 234:16
F. is something barbarous	SANT 275:10
in my f.	PORT 252:9
never cared for f.	BAIL 20:2
fashionable idea ever to be f.	SANT 275:14
fashions fit this year's f.	HELL 145:7
fast as f. as the world record	COLE 72:13
fasten F. your seat-belts	FILM 110:5
faster F. than a speeding bullet	ANON 9:12
fat addicted to f.	BAKE 20:7
Butter merely makes us f.	GOER 129:11
F. is a feminist issue	ORBA 236:11
f. lady sings	SAYI 279:4
f. white woman	CORN 77:6
in every f. man	CONN 74:17
Life, if you're f.	MARG 207:12

fat (*cont.*):
  outside every f. man   AMIS 7:10
  thin man inside every f. man   ORWE 237:14
fatal most f. complaint of all   HILT 149:3
fate Art a revolt against f.   MALR 205:9
  decide the f. of the world   DE G 86:12
  F. is not an eagle   BOWE 42:12
  F.'s great bazaar   MACN 203:8
  I feel my f.   ROET 266:9
  makers of our f.   POPP 252:4
father bed fell on my f.   THUR 309:8
  carry one's f.'s corpse   APOL 12:9
  I meet my F., my age   LOWE 195:11
  limp f. of thousands   JOYC 165:8
  Lloyd George knew my f.   ANON 10:11
  no good f.   SART 276:8
  than you are as a f.   ICE 156:4
fatherhood mirrors and f.   BORG 42:3
fatherland unity of our f.   KOHL 177:11
fathers because our f. lied   KIPL 173:12
  fundamental defect of f.   RUSS 272:3
  My f. can have it   THOM 307:18
  not the sins of the f.   FREN 118:8
  revolts against its f.   MUMF 225:9
  Victory has a hundred f.   CIAN 69:10
fatigue under the weight of f.   CAMU 52:15
fattening illegal, immoral, or f.   WOOL 336:2
fault artist is his own f.   O'HA 234:13
  nothing is anybody's f.   O'RO 236:16
  think it is their f.   BROO 46:1
faults f. of his feet   BECK 26:2
  fill you with the f.   LARK 180:12
favour being in and out of f.   FROS 120:1
  f. and contrivance   KIPL 174:9
favourite My second f. organ   ALLE 6:10
fawns fallow f. invisible   THOM 308:6
fear English are paralysed by f.   LAWR 183:9
  F. and loathing   THOM 309:1
  F. God. Honour the King   KITC 176:8
  f. in a handful of dust   ELIO 101:8
  F. is the main source   RUSS 272:8
  f. of finding something worse   BELL 27:12
  f. of the Law   JOYC 164:9
  f. those big words   JOYC 165:5
  f. to negotiate   KENN 169:5
  first boredom, then f.   LARK 180:5
  fourth is freedom from f.   ROOS 267:14
  grief felt so like f.   LEWI 190:1
  in the direction of our f.   BERR 34:6
  in what I cannot f.   ROET 266:9
  one f., Death's shadow   BLUN 39:11
  only thing we have to f.   ROOS 267:7
  Our deepest f. is not   WILL 330:10
  too much joy or too much f.   GRAV 131:9
  without f. the lawless roads   MUIR 225:2
feast Paris is a movable f.   HEMI 145:12
feather my each f.   HUGH 154:2

feather-footed f. through   WAUG 321:9
February not Puritanism but F.   KRUT 178:6
fed f. the chicken every day   RUSS 271:17
fee For a small f. in America   SOND 291:7
feed F. the world   GELD 125:10
  will you still f. me   LENN 188:9
feel don't f. worse   FRAY 118:6
  to *One does f.*   KNOX 176:15
feeling f. of Sunday is the same   RHYS 263:11
  mess of imprecision of f.   ELIO 99:1
  Music is f., then   STEV 297:14
  objectification of f.   LANG 180:1
fees as they took their F.   BELL 27:11
feet better to die on your f.   IBAR 156:2
  both f. firmly planted   ROOS 267:11
  careful where he put his f.   NICO 230:9
  faults of his f.   BECK 26:2
  fog comes on little cat f.   SAND 274:12
  hear it through their f.   SOUS 292:4
  marching, charging f.   JAGG 158:12
  palms before my f.   CHES 62:5
  stranger's f. may find   HOUS 152:8
fell It f. by itself   JOHN 162:7
female F. Eunuch   GREE 133:3
  f. of the species   KIPL 173:15
  f. principle   CLAR 70:2
  f. worker is the slave   CONN 75:3
  left in f. hands   PAGL 241:14
  male upon the f.   LAWR 183:13
  no f. Mozart   PAGL 241:16
  racket of the f.   OSBO 240:1
feminine 'f.' principles   RODD 266:3
feminism discussions of f.   FREN 118:10
feminist call me a f.   WEST 324:22
  dealing with the early f.   WEST 325:1
  Fat is a f. issue   ORBA 236:11
fen through the plashy f.   WAUG 321:9
fence colours to the f.   FIEL 108:4
  DON'T F. ME IN   PORT 252:12
  f. is just too high   MAUG 210:2
fences Good f. make   FROS 120:12
Fenian left us our F. dead   PEAR 246:4
Fermanagh dreary steeples of F.   CHUR 65:7
ferocious press is f.   DIAN 89:11
fertile In such a fix to be so f.   NASH 227:10
fertilizer use him as a f.   MULL 225:7
fester limbs that f.   ABSE 1:3
fetish Militarism . . . is f. worship   TAWN 303:1
fetishist f. who yearns   KRAU 177:15
fever enigma of the f. chart   ELIO 98:18
  treaty bred a f.   THOM 307:6
few owed by so many to so f.   CHUR 66:7
fiction F. is the great virus   THOM 309:5
  form of continuous f.   BEVA 36:14
  house of f.   JAME 159:9
  if she is to write f.   WOOL 335:4
  of all forms of f.   STOP 298:16

Poetry is the supreme f.   STEV 297:9
Reality beats f.   CONR 75:7
worked into f.   WOOL 335:10
fiddle beyond all this f.   MOOR 221:6
fiddler village f. after Paganini   NICO 230:8
fidelity respect f. to colleagues   LASK 181:7
stone f.   LARK 180:3
Your idea of f.   RAPH 260:3
field corner of a foreign f.   BROO 45:15
not as simple as to cross a f.   PAST 245:7
Vaguery in the F.   OSBO 239:20
fifteen always f. years older   BARU 24:10
famous for f. minutes   WARH 319:4
fifth F. column   MOLA 219:10
fifties tranquillized F.   LOWE 195:10
fifty After f. the clock can't   LOWE 195:13
At f., everyone has   ORWE 239:13
booze until he's f.   FAUL 107:5
until I was nearly f.   HEAN 143:13
fight f. and fight again   GAIT 122:13
f. between two bald men   BORG 42:4
f. for freedom   PANK 242:6
f. for its King and Country   GRAH 131:6
f. on the beaches   CHUR 66:5
he is dead, who will not f.   GREN 133:13
I f. on   THAT 306:15
must f. to the end   HAIG 136:1
Never give up the f.   MARL 208:1
nor duty bade me f.   YEAT 337:18
those who bade me f.   EWER 104:12
thought it wrong to f.   BELL 28:8
too proud to f.   WILS 332:3
when men refuse to f.   POLI 251:24
fighting f. for this woman's honour
                                            FILM 111:14
In f. to the death   DAYA 85:1
not fifty ways of f.   MALR 205:7
state of affairs worth f. for   ORWE 237:18
still f. Blenheim   BEVA 36:7
street f. man   JAGG 158:13
What are WE f. for   SERV 283:3
who dies f. has increase   GREN 133:13
figure f. a poem makes   FROS 121:2
f. is unbelievable   CONR 75:11
losing her f. or her face   CART 55:6
fill O f. me   MACN 203:5
trying to f. them   CIOR 69:12
filling f. the space   WEST 325:3
films call lusty in foreign f.   WILD 328:11
f. the lowest form of art   WILD 328:10
seldom go to f.   BERR 34:8
filth identical, and so is f.   FORS 116:15
final f. curtain comes down   MAJO 205:4
f. solution   HEYD 147:11
finale Let be be f. of seem   STEV 297:7
finality F. is death   STEP 296:15
finals This is called F.   LODG 193:2

financial with f. acumen   KAUF 167:3
find Someday I'll f. you   COWA 78:11
fine f. romance with no kisses   FIEL 108:6
fines paying f. on sorrow   MAYA 211:5
finest f. hour   CHUR 66:6
our f. shower   OSBO 239:16
finger chills the f. not a bit   NASH 228:12
f. lickin' good   ADVE 3:28
little f. to become longer   SCHO 280:11
Whose f. do you want   NEWS 231:14
fingernails paring his f.   JOYC 164:16
rain rapping like f.   MOOR 221:9
relatively clean f.   MORT 223:4
fingerprints f. across his brain   HEND 146:4
fingers Crumbling between the f.   MACN 203:2
cut their own f.   EDDI 95:6
dabbling their f.   MCGR 200:2
f. do the walking   ADVE 4:8
f. of cold are corpse   LAWR 184:14
Five sovereign f.   THOM 307:5
in your yellow f.   HEAT 144:8
pulled our f. out   PHIL 248:3
finish didn't let me f.   BABE 19:13
f. the job   CHUR 66:10
f. together   BEEC 26:17
Nice guys. F. last   DURO 93:8
started so I'll f.   CATC 58:16
finished book would have been f.   WODE 333:7
f. in the first 100 days   KENN 169:6
poem is never f.   VALÉ 315:13
where England is f.   MILL 215:1
finite knowlege can only be f.   POPP 252:8
finned giant f. cars nose forward   LOWE 195:8
fire every time She shouted 'F.'   BELL 27:15
faith and f. within us   HARD 140:4
f. and the rose are one   ELIO 99:12
f. brigade and the fire   CHUR 65:9
f. into the equations   HAWK 142:10
f. of my loins   NABO 226:13
f. was furry as a bear   SITW 288:3
light my f.   MORR 222:7
shouting f. in a theatre   HOLM 151:3
tongued with f.   ELIO 99:5
with a lake of f.   FLEC 114:3
world will end in f.   FROS 120:6
fires Gorse f.   LONG 194:2
firing faced the f. squad   THUR 309:15
firm family f.   GEOR 126:14
old f., is selling out   OSBO 240:3
first done for the f. time   CORN 77:8
f. Kinnock in a thousand   KINN 173:8
F. things first   CONR 75:9
people who got there f.   USTI 315:7
Safety f.   BALD 21:5
to be called F. Lady   ONAS 235:20
fish colder and dumber than a f.   MULD 225:5
F. are jumpin'   HEYW 148:1

fish (*cont.*):

F. got to swim	HAMM 137:7
F. have their stream	BROO 45:9
f. without a bicycle	STEI 296:12
no longer f. and chips	JEAN 160:4
nose forward like f.	LOWE 195:8
No self-respecting f.	ROYK 270:3
pretty kettle of f.	MARY 209:9
recently dead f.	ORWE 239:10
surrounded by f.	BEVA 36:4
fishbone monument sticks like f.	LOWE 195:9
fishes f. flew and forests walked	CHES 62:4
notes like little f.	MACN 203:8
fish-knives Phone for the f.	BETJ 35:3
fistful for a f. of coins	ZAPA 340:10
fists F. clenched	LOGU 193:7
fit isn't f. for humans now	BETJ 35:12
only the F. survive	SERV 283:2
fitness no test of f. for it	SHAW 283:18
five At f. in the afternoon	GARC 125:1
bombing begins in f. minutes	REAG 262:2
fix don't f. it	SAYI 278:17
looking for an angry f.	GINS 128:7
fixed f. point in a changing age	DOYL 91:12
flabby this f. exterior	LEVA 189:5
flag f. to which you have pledged	BALD 20:13
High as a f.	HAMM 137:17
shall not f. or fail	CHUR 66:5
flagellation Not f.	RATT 260:9
flame Both moth and f.	ROET 266:8
F.-capped, and shout	SHAW 286:10
tongues of f. are in-folded	ELIO 99:12
When a lovely f. dies	HARB 138:7
flames F. for a year	LAMP 179:14
Flanders In F. fields	MCCR 198:8
flappers London wants f.	CAMP 52:3
flat Very f., Norfolk	COWA 78:15
flattering f. and kicking people	TRUM 312:13
think him worth f.	SHAW 284:4
flattery f. hurts no one	STEV 297:18
flavour spearmint lose its f.	ROSE 268:11
flea literature's performing f.	O'CA 234:6
fleas dog that praised his f.	YEAT 339:1
educated f. do it	PORT 252:18
f. that tease	BELL 28:9
fleet whole F.'s lit up	WOOD 334:13
flesh F. perishes. I live on	HARD 139:14
f. was sacramental	ROBI 265:11
flew and they f.	LOGU 193:6
flexible your f. friend	ADVE 3:1
flicker moment of my greatness f.	ELIO 100:8
float f. like a butterfly	ALI 6:2
flooded STREETS F.	TELE 305:6
floor lie on the f. without	MART 209:2
man has just waxed the f.	NASH 228:15
repeat on the Golden F.	LAST 182:15
floors Scuttling across the f.	ELIO 100:7

floppy f. thing in the chair	THAT 306:20
floraisons *mois des f.*	ARAG 12:10
flower cracks into furious f.	BROO 46:6
drives the f.	THOM 307:4
f. of Scotland	WILL 330:11
flowers Beware of men bearing f.	SPAR 292:5
hundred f. blossom	MAO 207:8
Say it with f.	ADVE 4:18
Their f. the tenderness	OWEN 240:16
Where have all the f. gone	SEEG 282:2
wild f., and Prime Ministers	BALD 21:4
fluffy f., just fluffy	HERB 146:9
fluidity *f. of self-revelation*	JAME 159:5
solid for f.	CHUR 65:11
flung f. himself from the room	LEAC 185:8
flushpots f. of Euston	JOYC 164:8
flutter F. and bear him up	BETJ 34:15
fly long-legged f.	YEAT 338:1
show the f. the way out	WITT 332:15
try to f. by those nets	JOYC 164:13
wouldn't hurt a f.	LEAC 185:7
Flying Scotsman F. is no less	BEAV 25:6
foaming f. with much blood	POWE 255:8
foe find a f.	PARK 242:12
His f. was folly	EPIT 105:9
fog f. comes on little cat feet	SAND 274:12
F. in Channel	BROC 44:10
f. that rubs its back	ELIO 100:5
fold f., spindle or mutilate	SAYI 278:12
folded undo the f. lie	AUDE 17:10
Folies-Bergère goes to the F.	STOC 298:12
folk all music is f. music	ARMS 13:3
trouble with a f. song	LAMB 179:9
folk-dancing incest and f.	ANON 12:2
follies f. a man regrets most	ROWL 269:15
folly His foe was f.	EPIT 105:9
lovely woman stoops to f.	ELIO 101:18
food advertise f. to hungry	GALB 123:8
alcohol was a f.	WODE 333:10
Continent have good f.	MIKE 214:4
f. a tragedy	POWE 254:17
F. comes first	BREC 44:2
give f. to the poor	CAMA 52:2
problem is f.	DONL 90:10
fool As any f. kno	WILL 329:2
f. with booze until he's 50	FAUL 107:5
Prove to me that you're no f.	RICE 264:4
when you worked for a f.	SOLZ 290:15
will not laugh is a f.	SANT 275:7
foolish Beware my f. heart	WASH 320:5
more likely to be f.	RUSS 271:14
These f. things	MARV 209:3
fools flannelled f. at the wicket	KIPL 174:7
F.! For I also had my hour	CHES 62:5
fools, the fools, the f.	PEAR 246:4
perish together as f.	KING 172:8
foot foot—f.—sloggin'	KIPL 173:11

I hold Creation in my f.	HUGH	154:2
silver f. in his mouth	RICH	264:7
football excuse not to play f.	LEBO	186:4
fighting Army f. team	RICE	264:2
f. a matter of life	SHAN	283:9
F. and cookery	SMIT	288:15
F. is an art central	GREE	133:6
F.? the beautiful game	PELÉ	246:9
he's f. crazy	MCGR	200:1
like being a f. coach	MCCA	197:6
owe to f.	CAMU	53:5
footfalls F. echo in the memory	ELIO	98:10
footman eternal F. hold my coat	ELIO	100:8
footnotes series of f. to Plato	WHIT	327:4
force combines f. with candour	CHUR	69:3
do not respond to f.	WHIT	327:5
f. that through the green	THOM	307:4
f. with a manoeuvre	TROT	312:5
may the f. be with you	FILM	111:5
Not believing in f.	TROT	312:8
Other nations use 'f.'	WAUG	321:12
reduce the use of f. to	ORTE	237:3
use of *f.* by one class	LENI	187:6
ford F., not a Lincoln	FORD	115:4
my friend F.	WILL	330:9
Nixon gave us F.	ABZU	1:4
foreign call lusty in f. films	WILD	328:11
corner of a f. field	BROO	45:15
f. policy: I wage war	CLEM	71:1
idea behind f. policy	O'RO	236:19
into any f. wars	ROOS	267:12
Life is a f. language	MORL	222:1
past is a f. country	HART	141:13
foreigners f. are fiends	MITF	217:13
Foreign Secretary attacking the F.	BEVA	36:10
F. naked into	BEVA	36:11
Foreland Dawn off the F.	KIPL	174:10
foreplay No f.	BENN	30:12
foreseen What I had not f.	SPEN	293:15
forest burning the rain f.	STIN	298:11
Cutting through the f.	LIND	191:5
In the f.	CHES	63:7
To the f. edge	DURC	93:6
unfathomable deep f.	THOM	308:4
forests fishes flew and f. walked	CHES	62:4
foretell ability to f.	CHUR	68:17
foretold who could have f.	YEAT	338:16
forever diamond is f.	ADVE	3:12
you can see f.	LERN	188:17
forget do not quite f.	CHES	62:13
Don't f. the diver	CATC	57:11
Don't f. the fruit gums	ADVE	3:15
fact that they never f.	DRAB	91:15
f. there was such a thing	WILS	332:8
forgive but do not f.	SZAS	302:5
In violence, we f.	MCCA	197:12
never f. a face	MARX	209:7
forgets f. sooner	CAMU	52:15
forgetting consist in merely f.	MAND	206:2
forgive allows you to f. yourself	SHAW	285:12
do not f. those murderers	WIES	328:4
F. my little jokes	FROS	120:2
f. those who were right	MACL	201:1
wise f. but do not forget	SZAS	302:5
without hope cannot f.	MORR	222:5
woman can f. a man	MAUG	210:5
forgiven f. everything	SHAW	285:10
forgiveness what f.	ELIO	99:14
forgot just f. to duck	DEMP	88:1
forgotten always a f. thing	CHES	62:2
books undeservedly f.	AUDE	18:7
F. Army	MOUN	224:1
f. man at the bottom	ROOS	267:5
learned has been f.	SKIN	288:11
things one has f.	CANE	53:7
fork pick up mercury with a f.	LLOY	192:17
form F. follows function	SULL	301:5
f. the key to organic life	PAST	245:6
formed small, but perfectly f.	COOP	76:9
formerly not what we were f. told	BLUN	39:13
formula 'f.' of the atomic bomb	MEDA	212:1
forsaken utterly f.	BETT	36:3
fortune man who takes your f.	WOOL	336:1
forty fairy when she's f.	HENL	146:5
Life begins at f.	PITK	249:16
Men at f.	JUST	166:11
forty-five At f., what next	LOWE	195:11
forum on the way to the F.	SHEV	286:12
forward looking f. to the past	OSBO	240:4
nothing to look f. to	FROS	120:3
fought to have f. well	COUB	77:10
found man who has f. himself out	BARR	23:16
founding f. a bank	BREC	44:3
four all f.-footed things	CHES	62:4
At the age of f.	USTI	315:8
F. legs good	ORWE	237:11
f.-letter word	ANNA	8:12
f.-year-old child could	FILM	112:2
two plus two make f.	ORWE	238:11
four-legged f. friend	BROO	46:7
fourteen first f. years	GREE	132:11
fourteenth f. earl	HOME	151:7
fox Crazy like a f.	PERE	246:12
F. who was my friend	READ	261:6
mentality of a f. at large	LEVI	189:13
quick brown f. jumps	ANON	11:2
They've shot our f.	BIRC	38:2
foxes second to the f.	BERL	33:5
foxholes no atheists in the f.	CUMM	82:4
signs on the f.	KENN	169:12
fox-hunting prefer f.	HAIL	136:2
fracture f. the Labour party	KINN	173:9
fragrance Has she f.	CAUL	56:4
France F. has lost a battle	DE G	86:8

France (*cont.*):

F. wants you to take part	CHIR 64:11
F. will say	EINS 96:11
I now speak for F.	DE G 86:9
wield the sword of F.	DE G 86:10

frankly F., my dear — FILM 110:6

fraternize beckon you to f. — AUDE 17:8

freckles curiosity, f., and doubt — PARK 242:14

free as soon write f. verse — FROS 121:6

best things in life are f.	DE S 88:12
born f. and equal	ANON 8:15
but it's f.	KRIS 178:5
Comment is f.	SCOT 281:11
condemned to be f.	SART 276:3
Ev'rything f. in America	SOND 291:7
favours f. speech	BROU 46:10
f. again	SOLZ 290:13
F. at last	EPIT 105:3
f. man, an American	JOHN 162:9
f. society is a society	STEV 298:5
F. speech not to be regulated	DOUG 91:9
Give a man a f. hand	WEST 324:9
hungry man is not a f. man	STEV 298:2
I am a f. man	MCGO 199:7
I am not f.	DEBS 86:6
in chains than to be f.	KAFK 166:15
in favour of f. expression	BENN 30:17
Mother of the F.	BENS 31:15
no such thing as a f. lunch	SAYI 279:8
not a f. press but a managed	RADC 259:5
not f. either	SOLZ 290:17
not only to be f.	PANK 242:6
protection of f. speech	HOLM 151:3
truth makes men f.	AGAR 2:7
Universe is a f. lunch	GUTH 135:11
Was he f.	AUDE 18:1

freedom apprenticeship for f. — BARA 22:16

conditioned to a f.	KENY 170:6
condition for f.	FRIE 119:7
cry was for vacant f.	SANT 275:11
efficiencies of f.	GALB 123:13
enemies of f. do not argue	INGE 156:11
first is f. of speech	ROOS 267:14
F. and slavery are mental	GAND 124:10
f. for the one who thinks	LUXE 196:6
F. is not a gift	NKRU 232:10
F. is slavery	ORWE 238:9
F. is the freedom to say	ORWE 238:11
F. of the press	SWAF 301:10
F. of the press guaranteed	LIEB 191:3
F.'s just another word	KRIS 178:5
f. to offend	RUSH 270:11
F., what liberties	GEOR 126:15
f. women were supposed	BURC 48:12
gave my life for f.	EWER 104:12
green f. of a cockatoo	STEV 297:16
I gave them f.	GORB 130:16

means by defending f.	NIEM 231:18
neither equality nor f.	FRIE 119:8
no easy walk-over to f.	NEHR 228:17
Perfect f. is reserved	COLL 73:1
riches and f.	WAŁĘ 318:6
there can be no f.	LENI 187:7
unless f. is universal	HILL 148:6
What stands if f. falls	KIPL 173:17

freedoms four essential human f. — ROOS 267:14

freeze f. my humanity — MACN 203:5

freezes Yours till Hell f. — FISH 109:8

frei *Arbeit macht f.* — ANON 9:2

French F. arrange — CATH 56:3

F. dinner at nine	FLEM 114:8
F. government	COLO 73:5
F. went in to protect	LYNN 196:7
F. widow in every bedroom	HOFF 150:8
F. without tears	RATT 260:8
If the F. noblesse	TREV 311:8
no more F.	ANON 10:14
on speaking F. fluently	COOP 76:8
Paris was F.—and silent	TUCH 313:12
We are not F.	MONT 220:14

Frenchmen Fifty million F. — SAYI 278:14

fresh ever-f. terrain — AMIS 8:1

It's tingling f. — ADVE 4:2

Freud trouble with F. is that — DODD 90:6

Freudian still had her F. papa — LOWE 195:7

friend betraying my f. — FORS 116:19

diamonds a girl's best f.	ROBI 265:6
four-legged f.	BROO 46:7
I lose a f.	SARG 275:15
lay down his wife for his f.	JOYC 165:11
Little F. of all the World	KIPL 175:13
Reagan for his best f.	WARN 319:10
'Strange f.,' I said	OWEN 241:4
think of him as a f.	SMIT 290:5
To find a f.	DOUG 91:6
Whenever a f. succeeds	VIDA 317:9
wish the author was a f.	SALI 274:3

friends best f. are white — DURE 93:7

closest f. won't tell you	ADVE 3:17
deserting f. conciliates	ASQU 14:9
documents and f.	SPAR 292:6
f. are necessarily	USTI 315:7
f. only read the title	WOOL 335:2
f. that have it I do wrong	YEAT 337:13
glory was I had such f.	YEAT 338:4
I have lost f.	WOOL 335:9
lay down his f. for his life	THOR 309:7
little help from my f.	LENN 188:10
Money couldn't buy f.	MILL 216:1
nearly deceiving your f.	CORN 77:9
new f. as you get older	BERN 33:12
no absent f.	BOWE 42:9
no true f. in politics	CLAR 69:13
win f. and influence	CARN 54:2

friendship disease called f.	RENO 263:5
F. without envy	DUNC 92:11
frighten f. the horses	CAMP 52:5
frightened children are f. of me	GEOR 126:11
f. look in its eyes	SITW 288:6
Why should you be f.	WEBB 322:1
frightening never more f.	VAN 315:19
fringe form the lunatic f.	ROOS 268:9
Frodo Let Bingo = F.	TOLK 310:10
frog f. remains	ROST 269:4
frogs F. eat butterflies	STEV 297:8
frontier f. of my Person	AUDE 17:8
new f.	KENN 169:1
frontiers old f. are gone	BALD 21:8
rolled back f. of State	THAT 306:9
frost lovely Morning, rich in f.	DAVI 84:3
frozen F. anger	FREU 119:1
locked and f. in each eye	AUDE 16:13
fruit like a Dead Sea f.	MACM 202:6
trees bear strange f.	HOLI 150:11
fruitcake we want a f.	PARR 244:15
frustrating imagine how f. it is	NOLA 232:12
fuck f. all in between	BENN 30:12
They f. you up	LARK 180:12
zipless f.	JONG 164:1
fudging f. and mudging	OWEN 240:11
fugitive f. from th' law	MAUL 210:14
Führer ein Volk, ein F.	POLI 251:9
fule As any f. kno	WILL 329:2
fun Ain't we got f.	KAHN 166:16
desire to have all the f.	SAYE 277:5
F. is fun but	LOOS 194:8
f. to be in the same decade	ROOS 268:1
Gladstone read Homer for f.	CHUR 68:8
Haute Couture should be f.	LACR 178:11
more f. to be with	NASH 227:16
no reference to f.	HERB 146:16
noted for fresh air and f.	EDGA 95:10
Politics has got to be f.	CLAR 69:16
sex was the most f.	ALLE 6:7
stop people having f.	STRA 300:6
two is f.	SAYI 278:6
wish I thought *What Jolly F.*	RALE 259:10
function Form follows f.	SULL 301:5
frightful word [f.]	LE C 186:15
fundament frigid on the f.	NASH 228:12
fundamental f. things apply	HUPF 154:13
funeral heaping up own f. pyre	POWE 255:7
jolly at my f.	MOUN 224:3
funk in a blue f.	CRAN 79:8
postwar f.	TEBB 303:17
funnier f. than a huge man	THOM 309:4
funny Everything is f.	ROGE 266:12
f. is subversive	ORWE 239:9
f. old world	FILM 110:15
f. old world	THAT 306:16
f. thing happened	SHEV 286:12

funny-ha-ha Funny-peculiar or f.	HAY 142:13
funny-peculiar F. or funny ha-ha	HAY 142:13
fur to make a f. coat	SAYI 278:22
furious time cracks into f. flower	BROO 46:6
furiously green ideas sleep f.	CHOM 64:13
furnish Books do f. a room	POWE 254:18
furnished F. and burnish'd	BETJ 35:13
furniture don't trip over the f.	COWA 79:1
f. on deck of Titanic	MORT 223:11
rearranges the f.	PRAT 256:1
too much of today's f.	LAWR 184:19
furry fire was f. as a bear	SITW 288:3
further f. away than anywhere	RAPH 260:5
f. you got from Britain	CALL 52:1
fury f. and the mire	YEAT 336:14
War hath no f.	MONT 220:9
fuse line is a f.	MAYA 211:4
through the green f.	THOM 307:4
future Back to the f.	FILM 112:5
bridge to the f.	LAWR 183:15
controls the f.	ORWE 238:10
curiosity about the f.	WAUG 321:3
empires of the f.	CHUR 67:7
f. ain't what it used to be	BERR 33:18
F. as a promised land	LEWI 190:2
f. can be promised	TRUD 312:10
F. not for parties	WILS 331:15
f. not what it was	LEVI 189:14
f. refusing to be born	BEVA 36:15
F. shock	TOFF 310:5
lets the f. in	GREE 132:13
never think of the f.	EINS 96:12
once and f. king	WHIT 326:8
past, present and f.	EINS 97:8
perhaps present in time f.	ELIO 98:9
picture of the f.	ORWE 238:15
quick perspective of the f.	SPEN 293:13
seen the f. and it works	STEF 296:1
walking backward into f.	ZHVA 341:4
fuzzy wuzzy f. colony	CAIR 51:5
fwowed Tonstant Weader f. up	PARK 243:11
gadget g.-filled paradise	NIEB 231:16
gadgets worth a thousand g.	SCHU 281:7
Gaels great G. of Ireland	CHES 62:1
gag tight g. of place	HEAN 144:4
Gaia G. a tough bitch	MARG 207:13
gaiety only concession to g.	THOM 308:9
gaily G. into Ruislip gardens	BETJ 35:9
gainful seek g. employment	ACHE 1:7
gaining Something may be g.	PAIG 242:3
gains no g. without pains	STEV 298:1
Galileo G. in two thousand years	PIUS 249:17
status of G. merely	GOUL 131:3
gallant very g. gentleman	EPIT 105:5
gallop G. about doing good	SMIT 289:14

gallows g. in my garden   CHES 62:3
Gallup manifesto written by Dr G.   BENN 30:2
gamble Life is a g.   STOP 299:10
game Anarchism is a g.   SHAW 285:13
  beautiful g.   PELÉ 246:9
  don't like this g.   CATC 58:6
  g. at which two can play   BEER 26:21
  g. is about glory   BLAN 39:9
  how you played the G.   RICE 263:13
  take seriously any g.   STOP 299:15
games dread of g.   BETJ 35:16
  G. people play   BERN 33:14
gamesmanship practice of g.   POTT 253:11
gamut g. of the emotions   PARK 243:13
Gandhi [G.] looms over   THOM 309:3
gangsters nations acted like g.   KUBR 178:8
gap g. between the lace curtains   GREE 132:17
  last g. but one   WHIT 326:5
garage to the full g.   HOOV 151:10
garbage G. in, garbage out   SAYI 278:15
Garbo G.'s visage had a kind of   DE B 85:9
garden at the bottom of our g.   FYLE 122:8
  Back to the g.   MITC 217:6
  England is a g.   KIPL 174:3
  gallows in my g.   CHES 62:3
  g. called Gethsemane   KIPL 173:18
  Glory of the G.   KIPL 174:2
  sunlight on the g.   MACN 203:9
gardenias g. in your hair   HOLI 150:12
garlands they are g.   BENN 30:14
garlic clove of g. round my neck   O'BR 233:8
garter knight of the g.   ATTL 15:8
gas G. smells awful   PARK 243:5
  got as far as poison-g.   HARD 139:6
  remembered to turn the g. off   LEVI 189:10
  ship our masks in case of g.   KIPL 173:18
  when we met the g.   KIPL 174:1
gash be it g. or gold   BROO 46:5
gasworks by the g. crofts   MACC 198:4
gate drops on g.-bars hang   HARD 140:8
  Hun is at the g.   KIPL 173:16
  man at the g. of the year   HASK 142:2
gates at area g.   ELIO 100:11
  g. to the glorious   FORS 116:4
gauze shoot her through g.   BANK 22:13
gay g. man trapped   BOY 42:18
  heart was warm and g.   HAMM 137:10
  second best's a g. goodnight   YEAT 337:14
gazing g. at each other   SAIN 273:8
geese great g. honk northward   WARR 320:3
  Like g. about the sky   AUDE 15:15
gender get My g. right   ARNO 13:8
gene selfish g.   DAWK 84:8
General Motors good for G.   WILS 330:14
generals against the law for g.   TRUM 313:7
  Dead battles, like dead g.   TUCH 313:11
  we're all G.   USTI 315:8

generation beat g.   KERO 170:7
  best minds of my g.   GINS 128:7
  Every g. revolts   MUMF 225:9
  G. X   COUP 78:1
  lost g.   STEI 296:6
  luck of my g.   SHAW 286:11
  never before has a g.   VANE 316:3
  one g. from extinction   CARE 53:15
generations Those dying g.   YEAT 338:9
generosity exercise our g.   SART 276:9
genes what males do to g.   JONE 163:15
genetic g. lottery comes up with   PIML 249:7
  mechanism for g. material   CRIC 80:2
  terrible g. defects   WATS 320:8
genetics geography and g.   WHIT 326:9
genius g. makes no mistakes   JOYC 165:10
  g. of Einstein leads   PICA 249:5
  g. of its scientists   EISE 97:12
  g. with the IQ   VIDA 317:14
  instantly recognizes g.   DOYL 91:14
  Picasso is a g.   DALI 83:2
  talent and g.   KENN 169:11
  think like a g.   NABO 227:4
geniuses G. are the luckiest   AUDE 18:13
gentle Do not go g.   THOM 307:2
gentleman Every other inch a g.   WEST 325:7
  g. in Whitehall   JAY 160:2
  very gallant g.   EPIT 105:5
gentlemen behave like g.   MACK 200:5
  G. do not take soup   CURZ 82:13
  G. go by   KIPL 175:2
  G. prefer blondes   LOOS 194:4
  nation of g.   MUGA 224:7
gentleness only a willed g.   THOM 308:12
genuine place for the g.   MOOR 221:6
geography g. and genetics   WHIT 326:9
  G. is about Maps   BENT 32:2
  too much g.   KING 172:14
George G.—don't do that   GREN 133:11
  G. the Third Ought never   BENT 32:3
Georgia G. on my mind   GORR 131:2
  red hills of G.   KING 172:6
geranium madman shakes a dead g.   ELIO 100:17
geraniums g. (red)   MILN 216:13
  pot of pink g.   MACN 202:15
geriatric years in a g. home   AMIS 8:5
German all a G. racket   RIDL 265:1
  language of poems is G.   CELA 60:1
  Waiting for the G. verb   O'BR 233:13
Germans beastly to the G.   COWA 78:3
  G. . . . are going to be squeezed   GEDD 125:8
  G. classify   CATH 56:3
  G. have historic chance   KOHL 177:11
  G. went in to cleanse   LYNN 196:7
  keep the G. down   ISMA 157:15
  They're G. Don't mention   CLEE 70:12

Germany at war with G.   CHAM 60:5
  Death is a master from G.   CELA 59:22
  G. calling   JOYC 165:15
  G. declare that I am a Jew   EINS 96:11
  offering G. too little   NEVI 229:13
  remaining cities of G.   HARR 141:1
germs Kills all known g.   ADVE 4:6
  Trap the g.   OFFI 235:3
gerund Save the g.   STOP 299:4
gesture Morality's a g.   BOLT 41:4
get G. out as early as you can   LARK 180:13
  g. what you like   SHAW 285:11
  g. where I am today without   CATC 58:5
  hate to g. up in the morning   BERL 32:13
  What you see is what you g.   SAYI 279:13
Gethsemane Garden called G.   KIPL 173:18
Getty Paul G. . . . had always been   LEVI 189:10
ghastly G. good taste   BETJ 36:2
ghost g. asked them to do   O'BR 233:7
  G. in the Machine   RYLE 273:3
  g. of Roger Casement   YEAT 337:15
  g. stories written for ghosts   ALDI 5:10
  If the g. cries   RAIN 259:8
ghosts g. of a nation   PEAR 246:5
  g. outnumber us   DUNN 93:2
giants nuclear g.   BRAD 43:3
  Want one only of five g.   BEVE 37:3
Gibraltar G. may tumble   GERS 127:4
gift Freedom is not a g.   NKRU 232:10
  your g. survived it all   AUDE 16:10
gifted vividly g. in love   DUFF 92:8
  young, g. and black   HANS 138:6
  Young, g. and black   IRVI 157:12
gifts buy g. at Jim Gibson's   LONG 194:1
gigantic America a g. mistake   FREU 119:2
gin get out the g.   REED 262:11
  G. was mother's milk   SHAW 285:20
  Of all the g. joints   FILM 111:11
ginless wicked as a g. tonic   COPE 76:15
Gioconda one isn't the real G.   CRAN 79:8
Gipper Win just one for the G.   GIPP 128:9
gipsies G. are a litmus test   HAVE 142:7
giraffes G.!—a People Who live   CAMP 52:7
girdle helps you with your g.   NASH 228:9
girl can't get no g. reaction   JAGG 158:11
  danced with a g.   FARJ 106:9
  diamonds a g.'s best friend   ROBI 265:6
  do a g. in   ELIO 101:3
  g. at an impressionable age   SPAR 292:10
  g. needs good parents   TUCK 313:13
  g. throwing a ball   WOOL 335:8
  g. with brains ought to   LOOS 194:5
  If you were the only g.   GREY 133:14
  mountainous sports g.   BETJ 35:11
  no g. wants to laugh   LOOS 194:8
  Poor little rich g.   COWA 78:10
  pretty g. is like a melody   BERL 32:14

  say in front of a g.   LEHR 187:2
girls bombers named for g.   JARR 159:18
  G. aren't like that   AMIS 7:11
  g. in slacks remember Dad   BETJ 34:12
  g. who wear glasses   PARK 243:1
  It was the g. I liked   BAIL 20:2
  nude, giant g.   SPEN 293:12
  process whereby American g.   HAMP 138:2
  Thank heaven for little g.   LERN 188:19
  Treaties like g. and roses   DE G 87:4
given I would have g. gladly   JOHN 162:11
glacier g. knocks in the cupboard   AUDE 16:1
glad just g. to see me   WEST 324:13
gladly I would have given g.   JOHN 162:11
Gladstone G. read Homer for fun   CHUR 68:8
glance O brightening g.   YEAT 336:11
glare looked at in merciless g.   WILL 330:4
Glasgow G. Empire on a Saturday   DODD 90:6
  I belong to G.   FYFF 122:7
glass baying for broken g.   WAUG 320:13
  if you break the bloody g.   MACN 203:1
  liked the Sound of Broken G.   BELL 28:4
  No g. of ours was raised   HEAN 143:15
  out of a thin g.   PINT 249:8
glasses girls who wear g.   PARK 243:1
  Such cruel g.   HOWE 153:2
  wears dark g.   ALLE 6:5
gliding g. like a queen   SPEN 293:6
glittering g. prizes   SMIT 289:2
glitters medal g. but   CHUR 67:2
gloaming Roamin' in the g.   LAUD 181:11
global g. thinking   LUCE 196:4
  image of a g. village   MCLU 201:2
globally Think g.   SAYI 279:9
globaloney still g.   LUCE 196:4
globe-trotting g. Madam   YEAT 339:2
glorious Mud! G. mud   FLAN 113:14
glory game is about g.   BLAN 39:9
  G. of the Garden   KIPL 174:2
  g. was I had such friends   YEAT 338:4
  I go to g.   LAST 182:3
  Land of Hope and G.   BENS 31:15
  some desperate g.   OWEN 240:17
  What price g.   ANDE 8:9
glove white g. pulpit   REAG 261:11
gloves brandy and summer g.   JOSE 164:4
  capitalism with the g. off   STOP 299:11
  people in g. and such   CHES 62:7
  through the fields in g.   CORN 77:6
  with my g. on my hand   HARG 140:12
glow g. has warmed the world   STEV 298:8
glow-worm I am a g.   CHUR 69:8
gluttony G. an emotional escape   DE V 88:13
gnomes g. in Zurich   WILS 331:1
go G. ahead, make my day   FILM 110:7
  g. anywhere I damn well please   BEVI 37:7
  good cook, as cooks g.   SAKI 274:1

thousand lost g. balls   ELIO 101:1
gone come out of *G. with the Wind*
    POWE 255:5
gongs Strong g. groaning   CHES 62:9
   struck regularly like g.   COWA 78:17
gong-tormented that g. sea   YEAT 337:1
good anything g. to say   LONG 194:3
   Gallop about doing g.   SMIT 289:14
   g. becomes indistinguishable   DAWS 84:12
   g. fences make   FROS 120:12
   g. in the worst of us   ANON 11:9
   'g. old days' a myth   ATKI 15:2
   g., the bad, and the ugly   FILM 112:10
   G. *Thing*   SELL 282:10
   g. time was had by all   SMIT 290:6
   g. to feel rotten   YESE 339:14
   g. to listen   ADVE 3:29
   g. to talk   ADVE 4:1
   g. unluckily   STOP 299:9
   g. when they do as others do   FRAN 117:8
   G. women always think   BROO 46:1
   Great and the G.   SAMP 274:6
   Greed is g.   FILM 110:8
   Guinness is g. for you   ADVE 3:20
   King John was not a g. man   MILN 216:14
   Lady, be g.   GERS 127:2
   Men have never been g.   BART 24:5
   never had it so g.   MACM 201:17
   not g. but great   VIDA 317:6
   or be thought half as g.   WHIT 327:13
   policy of the g. neighbour   ROOS 267:8
   possibility of g. times   BRAN 43:5
   temptation to be g.   BREC 43:10
   thing is in g. taste   ORTO 237:9
   what was g. for our country   WILS 330:14
   When I'm g.   WEST 324:7
   would be a g. idea   GAND 124:13
goodbye Every time we say g.   PORT 252:13
   G.!—Good-bye-ee   WEST 325:9
   G., moralitee   HERB 146:11
   G. to all that   GRAV 131:14
   Without exactly saying it, g.   FULL 122:1
goodness G. had nothing to do   WEST 324:11
   My G., My Guinness   ADVE 4:11
goodnight G., children   CATC 57:20
   John Thomas says g.   LAWR 183:8
   second best's a gay g.   YEAT 337:14
goods when g. are private   TAWN 303:3
goodwill In peace; g.   CHUR 68:10
goody-goody no better xsample of a g.
    WILL 329:4
goose get g. bumps   JOHN 162:6
gooseberried g. double bed   THOM 307:15
Goose Green on the ground at G.   KINN 173:4
gorse G. fires are smoking   LONG 194:2
gossip in the g. columns   INGH 157:6
got in our case we have not g.   REED 262:10

man g. to do   STEI 296:9
gotcha G.   NEWS 231:6
Gothic cars the great G. cathedrals   BART 24:8
gotta g. use words when I talk   ELIO 101:4
Götterdämmerung G. without the gods
    MACD 199:1
govern cannot g. itself   MCNA 202:12
   g. in prose   CUOM 82:5
   g. New South Wales   BELL 27:13
government art of g. is   SHAW 284:23
   asks you to form a G.   ATTL 15:12
   at g. expense   ARTS 13:9
   conspiracy theory of g.   INGH 157:5
   g. above the law   SCAR 279:18
   G. acquired the tact   WEST 325:1
   G. and public opinion   SHAW 284:15
   g. by discussion   ATTL 15:10
   g. by the uneducated   CHES 64:6
   G. is big enough   FORD 115:6
   G. of laws   FORD 115:5
   G. of the busy   SELD 282:6
   G. to regulate mind   TRUM 312:14
   g. which robs Peter   SHAW 283:19
   have an efficient g.   TRUM 313:4
   important thing for G.   KEYN 170:13
   least g. was the best   FEIN 107:7
   natural party of g.   WILS 331:7
   no British g. should   MACM 202:3
   no go the G. grants   MACN 202:15
   not get all of the g.   FRIE 119:10
   prefer that the g.   O'RO 236:19
   prepare for g.   STEE 295:13
   work for a G. I despise   KEYN 170:10
   working of local g.   THAT 306:19
   worst form of G.   CHUR 67:10
governments G. always want   RADC 259:5
   g. had better get out   EISE 97:14
governor *Jimmy Stewart* for g.   WARN 319:10
Governor-General save the G.   WHIT 327:11
grab all smash and no g.   NICO 230:11
grace g. of a boy   BETJ 35:14
   G. under pressure   HEMI 145:15
gradual g. day weakening   SPEN 293:15
gradualness inevitability of g.   WEBB 322:2
grail g. of laughter   CRAN 79:7
grain rain is destroying his g.   HERB 146:8
grammar destroy every g. school   CROS 80:11
   don't want to talk g.   SHAW 285:18
gramophone g. company   TREE 311:5
   record on the g.   ELIO 101:18
grand g. to be blooming well dead
    SARO 275:16
Grand Canyon down the G.   MARQ 208:13
grandfathers friends with its g.   MUMF 225:9
grandmother We have become a g.
    THAT 306:10
grant OLD CARY G. FINE   TELE 305:5

granted taking things for g. HUXL 155:12
grape G. is my mulatto mother HUGH 154:5
  peel me a g. WEST 324:5
grass g. to graze a cow BETJ 35:12
  g. will grow in the streets HOOV 151:11
  happy as the g. was green THOM 307:3
  I am the g. SAND 274:13
gratuitous autobiography most g. STOP 298:16
grave from the cradle to the g. CHUR 67:5
  into the darkness of the g. MILL 214:8
  send you to the g. ORTO 237:8
  shovel a g. in the air CELA 56:10
  shown Longfellow's g. MOOR 221:8
  stand at my g. and cry ANON 9:9
  years and honour to the g. KIPL 174:8
graves g. of little magazines PRES 256:4
gravitation not believing in g. TROT 312:8
gravy Abominated g. BENT 32:4
grease slides by on g. LOWE 195:8
greasy grey-green, g. Limpopo KIPL 175:12
great All my shows are g. GRAD 131:5
  G. and the Good SAMP 274:6
  g. life if you don't weaken BUCH 47:12
  G. Society JOHN 163:2
  g.—the major novelists LEAV 185:15
  g. things from the valley CHES 63:8
  g. tradition LEAV 185:14
  He Was A G. Man ZIEG 341:5
  live close to g. minds BUCH 47:11
  not good but g. VIDA 317:6
  those who were truly g. SPEN 293:7
Great Britain G. has lost an empire ACHE 1:8
greatest I'm the g. ALI 6:1
greatness g. within them CAMU 52:17
  moment of my g. flicker ELIO 100:8
greed G. is all right BOES 40:6
  G. is good FILM 110:8
  not enough for everyone's g. BUCH 48:1
greedy still selfish, vain, g. COOK 75:13
Greek G. as a treat CHUR 68:6
  half G., half Latin SCOT 281:12
  no more G. ANON 10:14
Greeks G. had a word AKIN 5:6
  G. in this American empire MACM 201:14
green Colourless g. ideas CHOM 64:13
  drives my g. age THOM 307:4
  G. how I love you GARC 125:2
  g. shoots of recovery MISQ 218:6
  Her g. lap WALK 318:11
  How g. was my valley LLEW 192:4
  Make it a *g.* peace DARN 83:5
  My passport's g. HEAN 143:15
  Praise the g. earth BUNT 48:8
  Wherever g. is worn YEAT 337:10
greenery In a mountain g. HART 141:9
greenhouse g. gases MARG 207:13
Greenpeace G. had a ring to it HUNT 154:12

greens healing g. ABSE 1:3
grey but black and g. GREE 132:12
  good g. guardians WILB 328:8
  little g. cells CHRI 65:1
grey-green g., greasy Limpopo KIPL 175:12
grief g. felt so like fear LEWI 190:1
  G. has no wings QUIL 258:12
  g. is like a minefield WARN 319:15
  Of g. I died ROET 266:8
grievance Scotsman with a g. WODE 333:1
groans g. of love LOWR 196:2
grope Group G. THOM 308:16
Groucho G. tendency ANON 10:7
ground G. control to Major Tom BOWI 42:16
  Me here on the g. SOND 291:11
  when I hit the g. SPRI 294:13
grow never g. out of it USTI 315:8
  They shall g. not old BINY 37:13
growing price to pay for g. up STOP 299:13
grown-ups facts about g. JARR 160:1
grumbling rhythmical g. ELIO 102:8
gruntled far from being g. WODE 333:3
guardians good grey g. of art WILB 328:8
guards Brigade of G. MACM 202:7
guerrilla g. wins if he does not KISS 176:2
guessing G. so much and so much CHES 62:7
guest receive an honoured g. AUDE 16:12
guests G. can be delightful ELIZ 103:6
guided g. missiles and misguided KING 172:11
guile squat, and packed with g. BROO 45:12
guilt assumption of g. CROS 81:2
  beggar would recognise g. PARS 244:16
  g. at the obligation LAIN 179:8
  g. of Stalin GORB 130:14
  put on a dress of g. MCGO 199:8
guilty Mortal, g., but to me AUDE 16:17
  Saints should be judged g. ORWE 239:7
guinea g. pigs in laboratory WILL 329:12
Guinness can't drink G. from PINT 249:8
  G. is good for you ADVE 3:20
  My Goodness, My G. ADVE 4:11
guitar blue g. STEV 297:10
gulag G. archipelago SOLZ 290:14
  word 'g.' did not appear WU 336:8
gulf to the G. Stream waters GUTH 135:12
gullet g. of New York MILL 215:8
gum can't fart and chew g. JOHN 163:10
gums Don't forget the fruit g. ADVE 3:15
gun g. in your pocket WEST 324:13
  Happiness is a warm g. LENN 187:13
  no g., but I can spit AUDE 17:8
  out of the barrel of a g. MAO 207:6
  through the door with a g. CHAN 60:13
gun-boat answer is to send a g. BEVA 36:7
gunfire towards the sound of g. GRIM 134:8
guns G. aren't lawful PARK 243:5
  g. not with butter GOEB 129:9

hundred men with g.	PUZO 258:4
monstrous anger of the g.	OWEN 240:14
rather have butter or g.	GOER 129:11
unheroic Dead who fed the g.	SASS 277:2
gush they're oil wells; they g.	PARK 243:18
Gutenberg G. made everybody	MCLU 201:13
gutless sort of g. Kipling	ORWE 239:2
guts Mrs Thatcher 'showed g.'	KINN 173:4
Spill your g. at Wimbledon	CONN 75:4
gutter Journalists belong in g.	PRIE 256:7
walk straight into the g.	SMIT 289:12
guys Nice g. Finish last	DURO 93:8
gym used to seeing in the g.	SULL 301:3
habit entirely different from h.	STRA 300:1
Growing old a bad h.	MAUR 210:15
H. is a great deadener	BECK 26:8
h. is hell for those	HOLI 150:13
habit-forming Cocaine h.	BANK 22:9
haddock hold on sausage and h.	WOOL 335:16
Halg ask for H.	ADVE 3:14
hair And not your yellow h.	YEAT 336:12
part my h. behind	ELIO 100:10
smoothes her h.	ELIO 101:18
your golden h. Margareta	CELA 56:10
half finished in h. the time	WODE 333:7
H. dead and half alive	BETJ 34:14
h. knew my mother	O'BR 233:14
Too clever by h.	SALI 274:5
half-a-crown help to h.	HARD 140:3
hallelujah H.! I'm alive	OSBO 239:19
halo jealousy with a h.	WELL 323:12
life is a luminous h.	WOOL 335:1
What is a h.	FRY 121:11
halt tan with henna hackles, h.	STEV 297:5
Hamlet cigar called H.	ADVE 3:21
had not written H.	WOLP 334:9
H. so much paper and ink	PRIE 256:10
not Prince H.	ELIO 100:9
hammer not a mirror but a h.	GRIE 134:2
hamster Freddie Starr ate my h.	NEWS 231:5
hand by the h. of God	MARA 207:9
Give a man a free h.	WEST 324:9
h. into the Hand of God	HASK 142:2
h. is the cutting edge	BRON 45:3
h. that lays the golden egg	GOLD 130:6
h. that signed the paper	THOM 307:5
h. that signed the treaty	THOM 307:6
Have still the upper h.	COWA 78:12
invisible h. in politics	FRIE 119:6
kiss the h. that wrote	JOYC 165:13
Left h. down a bit	CATC 58:19
Put out my h. and touched	MAGE 204:2
Took me by the h.	TURN 313:17
Wouldst hold my h.	HART 141:10
handbag hitting it with her h.	CRIT 80:7

handclasp h.'s a little stronger	CHAP 61:11
Handel tunes of H.	SITW 288:7
handful fear in a h. of dust	ELIO 101:8
handkerchief feels like a damp h.	MACK 200:6
scent on a pocket h.	LLOY 192:12
state of h. industry	CONN 75:2
hands blood on their h.	SPEN 292:15
has such small h.	CUMM 82:1
Holding h. at midnight	GERS 127:5
handwriting legibility in his h.	HAY 142:14
hang let him h. there	EHRL 96:4
will not h. myself today	CHES 62:3
hanged if they'd been h.	DENN 88:10
hanging cured by h. from a string	KING 173:1
h. garments of Marylebone	JOYC 164:8
hangman fit for the h.	LASK 181:7
happen poetry makes nothing h.	AUDE 16:11
happened after they have h.	IONE 157:11
funny thing h.	SHEV 286:12
happening believe what isn't h.	COLE 72:12
what is *not* h.	TYNA 314:8
happens h. anywhere	LARK 180:8
Nothing h., nobody comes	BECK 26:5
happiness fatal to true h.	RUSS 271:10
H. a cigar	ADVE 3:21
h. alone is salutary	PROU 257:11
H. is an imaginary	SZAS 302:4
H. is a warm gun	LENN 187:13
H. is a warm puppy	SCHU 280:13
h. makes up in height	FROS 120:8
h. was a warm puppy	EPHR 104:3
Last Chance Gulch for h.	STOP 299:12
lifetime of h.	SHAW 284:12
or justice or human h.	BERL 33:6
politics of h.	HUMP 154:10
right to h.	RAYN 261:3
happy ask if they were h.	CHAN 61:2
aware that you are h.	KRIS 178:4
conspiracy to make you h.	UPDI 315:1
fear that someone may be h.	MENC 212:12
h. as the grass was green	THOM 307:3
H. the hare at morning	AUDE 16:4
prevent from being h.	ANOU 12:6
remembers the h. things	LOVE 195:1
remote from the h.	AUDE 15:13
This is the h. warrior	READ 261:7
Was he h.	AUDE 18:1
When I am h. I live	SMIT 289:15
hard h. day's night	LENN 188:6
h. man is good to find	WEST 324:15
h. rain's a gonna fall	DYLA 94:5
not h. enough	GABO 122:12
To ask the h. question	AUDE 17:18
hard-faced h. men who look as if	BALD 21:2
hard-sell h. or soft-sell TV push	NASH 228:7
hare Happy the h. at morning	AUDE 16:4
h. sitting up	LAWR 183:18

hares little hunted h.	HODG 150:5
harlot Prerogative of the h.	KIPL 175:17
Harlow *t* is silent, as in *H.*	ASQU 14:14
harm What h. have I ever done	TAWN 303:5
Harold H. knows best	CROS 80:13
Harpic As I read the H. tin	BENN 31:4
harpsichord describing the h.	BEEC 26:19
harrow H. the house of the dead	AUDE 17:15
harrowing h. clods	HARD 140:1
Harvard glass flowers at H.	MOOR 221:8
hat get ahead, get a h.	ADVE 3:25
hang your h. on a pension	MACN 202:15
puttin' on my top h.	BERL 33:2
think without his h.	BECK 26:6
way you wear your h.	GERS 127:6
hate bother with people I h.	HART 141:8
h. a song that has sold	BERL 33:4
how much men h. them	GREE 133:2
I h. war	ROOS 267:9
letter of h.	OSBO 240:8
man you love to h.	FILM 111:4
not to h. them	SHAW 283:13
People must learn to h.	MAND 206:1
players who h. your guts	STEN 296:14
seen much to h. here	MILL 215:1
you h. something in him	HESS 147:5
hated Make hatred h.	FRAN 117:10
never h. a man enough	GABO 122:9
hates h. dogs and babies	ROST 269:7
man who h. his mother	BENN 31:14
hating h., my boy, is an art	NASH 228:10
hatless H., I take off	LARK 180:4
lands h. from the air	BETJ 35:1
hatred good rancorous h.	WARN 319:14
Great h., little room	YEAT 338:8
h., jealousy, boastfulness	ORWE 239:4
intellectual h.	YEAT 338:7
Make h. hated	FRAN 117:10
Regulated h.	HARD 139:2
What we need is h.	GENE 126:2
Haughey H. buried at midnight	O'BR 233:8
have You can h. it all	PFEI 248:1
hawking h. his conscience round	BEVI 37:6
hay live on h.	HILL 148:12
that's what h. looks like	MARY 209:12
Hays Will H. is my shepherd	FOWL 117:4
hazards h. whence no tears	HARD 140:4
haze Purple h. is in my brain	HEND 146:3
he H. would, wouldn't he	RICE 264:5
Who h.	ROSS 269:3
head if s-E-x rears its h.	AYCK 19:3
If you can keep your h.	KIPL 174:4
Johnny-h.-in-air	PUDN 257:13
keep your h.	PUDN 257:14
should have his h. examined	GOLD 130:8
headmasters H. have powers	CHUR 68:7
headpiece H. filled with straw	ELIO 99:16
head-waiter h. allowed to sit	USTI 315:9
healer compassion of the h.'s art	ELIO 98:18
Time not a great h.	COMP 73:9
health h. of the whole human race	TOYN 310:15
H. Service is safe	THAT 306:2
seriously damage your h.	OFFI 235:11
When you have both, it's h.	DONL 90:10
healthy h. and wealthy and dead	THUR 309:14
hear can't h. what they say	SMIT 289:7
Can you h. me, mother	CATC 57:8
don't h. the cries	MILL 215:15
h. it through their feet	SOUS 292:4
prefer not to h.	AGAR 2:7
want to h. from your sweater	LEBO 186:6
heard h. it's in the stars	PORT 253:3
You ain't h. nuttin' yet	JOLS 163:14
hearing h. without listening	SIMO 287:10
hearse h. horse snicker	SAND 274:14
heart Beware my foolish h.	WASH 320:5
bicycle-pump the human h.	AMIS 7:11
blind side of the h.	CHES 62:2
Bury my h. at Wounded Knee	BENÉ 29:9
committed adultery in my h.	CART 55:3
desires of the h.	AUDE 16:3
ease a h. like a satin gown	PARK 243:6
fed the h. on fantasies	YEAT 338:3
Fourteen h. attacks	JOPL 164:3
get your h.'s desire	SHAW 284:20
h. belongs to Daddy	PORT 253:2
heart-break in the h.	GIBS 127:14
h. grows old	YEAT 338:16
h. in the business	WATS 320:10
h. is a lonely hunter	MCCU 198:9
h. *prefers* to move	UPDI 314:14
h.'s stalled motor	MAYA 211:7
h. to a dog to tear	KIPL 175:1
h. was warm and gay	HAMM 137:10
h. was with the Oxford men	LETT 189:4
known to him by h.	WOOL 335:2
left my h. in San Francisco	CROS 81:3
let your h. be strong	LAUD 181:9
make a stone of the h.	YEAT 337:9
man's h. is small	KIPL 175:4
memory of the h.	CAMU 52:15
rag and bone shop of the h.	YEAT 337:2
waters of the h.	THOM 307:7
heart-beat just a h. away	STEV 298:6
heartbreak h. in the heart	GIBS 127:14
hearthstone squats on the h.	QUIL 258:12
heartless h., witless nature	HOUS 152:8
hearts H. wound up with love	SPEN 293:11
men with Splendid H.	BROO 45:11
queen in people's h.	DIAN 89:7
undeveloped h.	FORS 115:14
heat furnace that gives no h.	RAYM 261:2
If you can't stand the h.	TRUM 313:8

white h. of technology	MISQ 219:4	scream for h. in dreams	CANE 53:7
heather bonnie bloomin' h.	LAUD 181:10	you can't h. it	SMIT 289:3
cries 'Nothing but h.'	MACD 198:14	**helper** mother's little h.	JAGG 158:10
heaven any better in H.	WILL 330:9	**helpless** as h. as everybody else	MAND 206:8
God owns h.	SEXT 283:5	**hen** better take a wet h.	KHRU 171:11
H. would be too dull	EPIT 106:3	**henna** tan with h. hackles	STEV 297:5
Imagine there's no h.	LENN 187:14	**herald** h. angels sing	ANON 9:14
merger between H. and Hell	WELL 323:14	**here** H.'s looking at you	FILM 110:9
Pennies don't fall from h.	THAT 305:8	H. we go	ANON 9:15
pennies from h.	BURK 49:6	If we can't stay h. alive	MONT 220:12
ring the bells of H.	HODG 150:5	Kilroy was h.	ANON 10:8
thirtieth year to h.	THOM 307:8	only h. for the beer	ADVE 3:26
heavenly h. mansion, raging	YEAT 337:4	We're h.	ANON 11:16
heaventree h. of stars	JOYC 165:12	**heretics** H. are the only remedy	ZAMY 340:7
heavy Sob, h. world	AUDE 15:13	**hero** don't want to be a h.	STOP 299:11
Hebrides seas colder than the H.	FLEC 113:17	h. is a man	MAIL 204:10
Hector H. took off his plume	CORN 77:5	h. keeps getting in bed	ROSS 269:1
hedgehog on the back of a h.	LIVI 192:2	Show me a h.	FITZ 113:9
hedgehogs belongs to the h.	BERL 33:5	**Herod** for an hour of H.	HOPE 152:2
throwing h. under me	KHRU 171:12	**heroes** Canadians do not like h.	WOOD 334:12
hedges few surviving h.	BETJ 35:9	fit country for h.	LLOY 192:9
heels like champagne or high h.	BENN 31:10	land that needs h.	BREC 43:11
heigh-ho H., heigh-ho	MORE 221:11	speed glum h.	SASS 276:16
height Happiness makes up in h.	FROS 120:8	**heroing** H. is one of the shortest	ROGE 266:15
someone that h. look regal	AMIE 7:7	**herring** shoals of h.	MACC 198:5
Heinz Beanz meanz H.	ADVE 3:7	**hesitation** Humming, Hawing and H.	
Helen H.'s face in hell	PARK 243:3		CRIT 80:5
hell bells of H. go ting-a-ling	ANON 10:17	**hick** Sticks nix h. pix	NEWS 231:11
do science in h.	VAUG 316:8	**hidden** h. persuaders	PACK 241:8
go to h. like lambs	CHES 62:10	**hide** he can't h.	LOUI 194:12
h. for those you love	HOLI 150:13	h. of a rhinoceros	BARR 24:3
H. full of musical amateurs	SHAW 284:14	nothing to h.	CHUR 69:5
H. is oneself	ELIO 98:5	wise man h. a pebble	CHES 63:7
H. is other people	SART 276:5	**hiding** they got a bloody good h.	GRAN 131:7
H. is to love no more	BERN 33:11	**high** Be ye never so h.	DENN 88:6
If Hitler invaded h.	CHUR 68:13	corn is as h.	HAMM 137:11
I say the h. with it	WHIT 326:1	get h. with a little help	LENN 188:10
made an excursion to h.	PRIE 256:12	Pile it h.	SAYI 279:5
merger between Heaven and h.	WELL 323:14	taking the h. ground	MAND 206:5
not be H. if you are there	EPIT 106:3	**highbrow** What is a h.	WALL 318:13
probably redesigned H.	PRIC 256:6	**higher** find my own the h.	CORN 77:4
they think it is h.	TRUM 313:1	**high-tech** thing with h.	HOCK 150:4
walked eye-deep in h.	POUN 254:1	**high-water** h. mark of my youth	THUR 309:8
War is h., and all that	HAY 142:12	h. mark of Socialist	ORWE 239:2
why they invented H.	RUSS 272:5	**hilarity** h. like a scream	GREE 132:10
working definition of h.	SHAW 285:15	**hill** all gone under the h.	ELIO 98:16
would be h. on earth	SHAW 284:12	**hills** convictions are h.	FITZ 113:1
Yours till H. freezes	FISH 109:8	h. are alive	HAMM 137:15
hellhound h. always a hellhound	WODE 333:4	red h. of Georgia	KING 172:6
hellism It's what-the-h.	COOP 76:8	**hindsight** H. is always twenty-twenty	
hello H., good evening	CATC 58:2		WILD 328:12
help Can't h. lovin' dat man	HAMM 137:7	**hinterland** She has no h.	HEAL 143:8
do something to h. me	LAUR 181:13	**hip** H. is the sophistication	MAIL 204:11
h. and support of the woman	EDWA 95:11	**hippopotamus** h. resolved at any cost	
little h. from my friends	LENN 188:10		WELL 323:3
look on and h.	LAWR 184:13	**hips** armchairs tight about the h.	
present h. in trouble	ANON 8:14		WODE 333:13

hips (*cont.*):

Or Mae West's h.	EWAR 104:11
swing out ungirded h.	SORL 292:1
when your h. stick	NASH 228:9
hipsters angelheaded h. burning	GINS 128:7
hired They h. the money	COOL 76:6
Hiroshima After H.	BOLD 41:3
Einstein leads to H.	PICA 249:5
historian first requisite of h.	STRA 299:16
h. wants more documents	JAME 159:8
historians h. left blanks	POUN 253:16
H. repeat each other	GUED 135:5
history cancer of human h.	SONT 291:15
discerned in h. a plot	FISH 109:4
Does h. repeat itself	BARN 23:7
dustbin of h.	TROT 312:4
end of h.	FUKU 121:17
from the lessons of h.	HUXL 155:4
h. came to a .	SELL 282:14
H. gets thicker	TAYL 303:6
H. is a nightmare	JOYC 165:6
H. is not what you thought	SELL 282:9
h. is now and England	ELIO 99:11
h. is on our side	KHRU 171:10
H. littered with the wars	POWE 255:6
h.-making creature	AUDE 18:4
H. more or less bunk	FORD 115:8
H. started badly	WILL 329:3
H. teaches us that men	EBAN 94:16
h. to the defeated	AUDE 17:17
Human h. becomes more	WELL 323:9
more h. than they can consume	SAKI 273:13
name is h.	THWA 310:2
No h. much	DURR 93:9
no h. of mankind	POPP 252:6
not learning from h.	BLAI 38:12
political h. of the West	HAIL 136:6
rattling good h.	HARD 140:10
reverberates through h.	KOES 177:8
thousand years of h.	GAIT 122:14
too much h.	KING 172:14
What is h.	POWE 255:15
writing h. with lightning	WILS 332:1
hit H. the road, Jack	MAYF 211:9
Hitler H.'s level of accuracy	TAYL 303:8
If H. invaded hell	CHUR 68:13
If I can't love H.	MUST 226:9
kidding, Mister H.	PERR 247:7
like kissing H.	CURT 82:8
Suppose H. had been killed	SCHL 280:3
thank heaven for Adolf H.	BUCH 48:2
When H. attacked the Jews	NIEM 232:1
hitting h. it with her handbag	CRIT 80:7
without h. below it	ASQU 14:12
hoarder h. of two things	SPAR 292:6
Hoares no more H. to Paris	GEOR 126:7
hoary h. sort of land beneath	LAWR 184:12

hobbit lived a h.	TOLK 310:6
hock weak h. and seltzer	BETJ 34:11
hog Not the whole h.	MILL 215:14
hogs Men eat h.	STEV 297:8
hole first h. made through	MOOR 221:4
if you knows of a better h.	BAIR 20:6
In a h. in the ground	TOLK 310:6
making a h. in a sock	EINS 97:11
mint with the h.	ADVE 4:10
holiday perpetual h.	SHAW 285:15
to take a h.	RUSS 271:7
holidays during the h. from Eton	SITW 288:8
hollow We are the h. men	ELIO 99:16
Hollywood H. money isn't money	PARK 243:19
not have been invited to H.	CHAN 60:11
holocaust Somme is like the H.	BARK 23:1
holy H. deadlock	HERB 146:15
h.-water death	MCGO 199:9
home all the comforts of h.	BRYS 47:8
came h. to roost	MILL 215:9
children who leave h.	SLOV 288:12
E.T. phone h.	FILM 110:4
get all that at h.	BENN 30:9
H. is the girl's prison	SHAW 285:9
H. is the place where	FROS 120:4
H. is where you come to	THAT 306:18
H. James	HILL 149:2
house is not a h.	ADLE 2:4
I tank I go h.	GARB 124:15
Keep the H.-fires burning	FORD 115:11
look as much like h.	FRY 121:13
never see any h. cooking	PHIL 248:5
no place like h.	LANC 179:15
Till the boys come h.	FORD 115:11
what is it to be at h.	BECK 25:12
White House or h.	DOLE 90:7
years in a geriatric h.	AMIS 8:5
Homer Gladstone read H. for fun	CHUR 68:8
had the voice of H.	HALD 136:11
homes In h., a haunted apparatus	RAIN 259:8
Stately H. of England	COWA 78:12
homosexual composer and *not* h.	DIAG 89:4
homosexuality If h. were normal	BRYA 47:6
honest buy it like an h. man	NORT 233:2
h. and intelligent	ORWE 239:11
H. to God	ROBI 265:10
poor but she was h.	ANON 11:6
honey h. still for tea	BROO 45:13
Hong Kong H.'s return to China	DENG 88:4
honour Fear God. H. the King	KITC 176:8
for this woman's h.	FILM 111:14
great peaks of h.	LLOY 192:7
h. almost greater than	YOUN 340:5
H. is like a match	PAGN 242:1
Office before h.	POWE 255:10
peace with h.	CHAM 60:4
signed with their h.	SPEN 293:8

years and h. to the grave · KIPL 174:8
honours good card to play for H. · BENN 31:13
hooter because the h. hoots · CHES 62:10
hoover onto the board of H. · GREE 133:5
hope culture without h. · MORR 222:5
  Land of H. and Glory · BENS 31:15
  may we bring h. · THAT 305:7
  Nor dread nor h. attend · YEAT 337:6
  Some blessed H. · HARD 139:11
  there is h. · CROS 81:4
  two thousand years of h. · WEIZ 322:8
  Whatever h. is yours · OWEN 241:4
hopeful with a h. heart · LAWR 183:8
hopefulness Lord of all h. · STRU 300:12
hopeless doctors know a h. case · CUMM 81:15
hopes h. of its children · EISE 97:12
horizon just beyond the h. · KISS 176:7
horizontal h. desire · SHAW 286:6
  Life is a h. fall · COCT 72:3
horn won't come out of your h. · PARK 242:11
horns memories are hunting h. · APOL 12:7
horribilis annus h. · ELIZ 102:12
horror h. of sunsets · PROU 257:6
  h.! The horror · CONR 75:5
horse feeds the h. enough oats · GALB 123:10
  hearse h. snicker · SAND 274:14
  h. designed by a committee · ISSI 158:1
  never heard no h. sing · ARMS 13:3
  Ninety-seven h. power · FLAN 113:16
  old h. that stumbles · HARD 140:1
  On the sightless h. · WALE 318:7
  sick h. nosing around · KAVA 167:8
  sounds like a saddle h. · ONAS 235:20
  torturer's h. scratches · AUDE 17:2
  where's the bloody h. · CAMP 52:9
Horseguards be in the H. · RATT 260:10
horseman H., pass by · YEAT 339:5
horsemen Four H. rode again · RICE 264:2
horses Bring on the empty h. · CURT 82:9
  don't spare the h. · HILL 149:2
  frighten the h. · CAMP 52:5
  if you cannot ride two h. · MAXT 210:17
  I saw the h. · HUGH 154:3
  They shoot h. don't they · MCCO 198:7
horseshoe h. over his door · BOHR 40:9
horticulture lead a h. · PARK 244:2
host I'd have been under the h. · PARK 244:1
hostile h. to the single currency · CLAR 70:9
  universe is not h. · HOLM 151:1
hot English have h.-water bottles · MIKE 214:5
  H. on Sunday · HART 141:12
  how h. the day is · GRAV 131:8
  long h. summer · FILM 112:11
  On a h., hot day · LAWR 184:5
  only in h. water · REAG 261:10
hounds by your own quick h. · MOTI 223:15
hour dark eleventh h. · KIPL 175:5

finest h. · CHUR 66:6
for an h. of Herod · HOPE 152:2
I also had my h. · CHES 62:5
its h. come round at last · YEAT 338:14
matched us with His h. · BROO 45:14
hourglass Egghead weds h. · NEWS 231:4
hours better wages and shorter h. · ORWE 239:1
  see the h. pass · CIOR 69:12
house called a woman in my own h. · WAUG 321:11
  Harrow the h. of the dead · AUDE 17:15
  h. a machine for living in · LE C 186:14
  H. Beautiful is play lousy · PARK 243:12
  h. built upon sand · SAYE 277:4
  h. is not a home · ADLE 2:4
  h. rose like magic · HARG 140:13
  h. seventy years old · JEAN 160:5
  in 'The H. at Pooh Corner' · PARK 243:11
  man in the h. is worth · WEST 324:3
  This H. today is a theatre · BALD 21:9
  With usura hath no man a h. · POUN 253:13
houseful three is a h. · SAYI 278:6
householder think she's a h. · WILD 328:14
housekeeper make a h. think · WILD 328:14
housekeeping good h. to the winds · KEYN 171:6
housemaids damp souls of h. · ELIO 100:11
houses h. are all gone · ELIO 98:16
  h. just as big as · SMIT 289:13
  spaces between the h. · FENT 107:8
housework H. expands to fill · CONR 75:10
  h., with its repetition · DE B 85:12
  no need to do any h. · CRIS 80:3
Houston H., we've had a problem · LOVE 195:2
how H. do they know · PARK 243:17
howitzer h. squatting · GRIG 134:7
howls going to be h. of anguish · HEAL 143:4
Howth H. Castle and Environs · JOYC 164:6
huff leave in a h. · FILM 110:12
Hugo H. was a madman who thought · COCT 72:4
hullo H. Clouds Hullo Sky · WILL 329:4
human affection of the h. animal · SHAW 284:2
  all h. life is there · ADVE 3:3
  dreadful h. beings sitting · NORR 232:13
  emptiness. The h. lack · BOLD 41:1
  err is h. · SAYI 279:10
  fully-rounded h. being · COOK 75:13
  health of the whole h. race · TOYN 310:15
  h. beings are more alike · ANGE 8:11
  H. beings have inalienable · GREE 133:4
  H. kind Cannot bear · ELIO 98:11
  h. nature changed · WOOL 335:3
  H. nature not black and white · GREE 132:12
  H. on my faithless arm · AUDE 16:16
  h. race, to which so many · CHES 63:10
  h. zoo · MORR 222:3

human (*cont.*):

lose its h. face — DUBČ 92:5

love h. beings — GREE 132:7

not a bona fide h. being — SPEC 292:14

not made on a h. scale — MALR 205:8

people are only h. — COMP 74:1

robot may not injure a h. — ASIM 13:11

wish I loved the H. Race — RALE 259:10

humanitarian h. figure — DIAN 89:9

humanity freeze my h. — MACN 203:5

hate 'H.' — CAMP 52:11

h., although born in — JEAN 160:5

H. a work in progress — WILL 329:12

H. i love you — CUMM 81:10

humans isn't fit for h. now — BETJ 35:12

Humean H. predicament — QUIN 258:13

humiliation Art is born of h. — AUDE 18:12

called shame and h. — O'RO 236:17

humility small book on H. — LONG 193:13

humming hear the virus h. — DOTY 91:1

H., Hawing and Hesitation — CRIT 80:5

hummy at that word 'h.' — PARK 243:11

humour deep sense of h. — MCLU 201:4

Good taste and h. — MUGG 224:14

h. for humour — NEIL 229:7

H. is emotional chaos — THUR 310:1

They have no sense of h. — LEAR 185:12

Hun h. is at the gate — KIPL 173:16

hundred h. flowers blossom — MAO 207:8

hunger bodily h. in his eyes — SHAW 284:7

H. allows no choice — AUDE 17:10

h. to be beautiful — RHYS 263:10

hungry advertise food to h. — GALB 123:8

h. for dinner at eight — HART 141:8

h. man is not a free man — STEV 298:2

hunt That dog won't h. — RICH 264:6

hunter heart is a lonely h. — MCCU 198:9

H.'s waking thoughts — AUDE 16:4

Hunter Dunn Miss J. H. — BETJ 35:13

hunting death on the h.-field — MORT 223:2

goddess of h. — SPEN 293:2

hurdles don't really see the h. — MOSE 223:12

hurricane h. on the way — FISH 109:2

hurry H. up please it's time — ELIO 101:13

hurt deliberately tries to h. — BAIN 20:4

never h. a hair — STUD 301:1

no one was to be h. — BROO 46:2

wish to h. — BRON 45:5

Yes it h. — POLI 252:2

hurting eyes are h. me — SWAN 301:11

If the policy isn't h. — MAJO 204:14

once it has stopped h. — BOWE 42:10

husband Bigamy is one h. too many — ANON 9:4

h. is a whole-time job — BENN 31:11

h. what is left of a lover — ROWL 269:13

left her h. because — MURD 225:11

My h. and I — ELIZ 102:11

where I met my h. — MCAL 196:11

husbands Chumps make the best h.

— WODE 332:19

how many h. she had had — GABO 122:11

hush holy h. of ancient sacrifice — STEV 297:16

H.! Hush! Whisper who dares — MILN 217:1

huts still be living in grass h. — PAGL 241:14

hyacinths h. and biscuits — SAND 275:4

hydrogen telescope or h. bomb — LOVE 194:14

hygiene h. of older people — SMIT 289:8

hyphenated h. Americanism — ROOS 268:6

hypocrisy world safe for h. — WOLF 334:2

hypotheses smallest number of h. — EINS 97:6

hypothesis discard a pet h. — LORE 194:11

I I am a camera — ISHE 157:14

I am not I — WAUG 320:11

I plus my surroundings — ORTE 237:2

My husband and I — ELIZ 102:11

IBM for buying I. — ADVE 4:14

ice I. formed on the butler — WODE 333:14

It's fresh as i. — ADVE 4:2

piece of i. on a hot stove — FROS 121:4

skating on thin i. — CAMP 52:6

Some say in i. — FROS 120:6

Vulgarity often cuts i. — BEER 26:22

white lies to i. a cake — ASQU 14:13

iceberg grew the I. too — HARD 139:9

i., you know — DEAN 85:8

ill-concealed i. — LAWS 185:2

ice-cream emperor of i. — STEV 297:7

i. out of the container — BRYS 47:7

iceman i. cometh — O'NE 236:2

id PUT THE I. BACK IN YID — ROTH 269:9

idea better to entertain an i. — JARR 159:20

does get an i. — MARQ 208:9

good i. but it won't work — ROGE 266:16

good i.—son — CATC 57:18

i. And the reality — ELIO 99:18

i. ever to be fashionable — SANT 275:14

i. of death saves him — FORS 116:10

i. whose time has come — SAYI 279:7

more dangerous than an i. — ALAI 5:7

no grand i. was ever born — FITZ 113:8

responsibility for that i. — BIRT 38:4

see it clearly in the i. — STEV 297:12

to whom the i. first occurs — DARW 83:9

would be a good i. — GAND 124:13

ideal i. for which I am prepared — MAND 205:11

i. reader suffering from — JOYC 164:7

idealism morphine or i. — JUNG 166:4

idealist I am an i. — SAND 275:2

idealistic America only i. nation — WILS 332:10

idealists I. are very apt to walk — SMIT 289:12

ideals i. of a nation — DOUG 91:7

shoes with broken high i. — MCGO 199:8

ideas Colourless green i. — CHOM 64:13
 From it our i. are born — GENE 126:2
 hold two opposed i. — FITZ 113:6
 instead of genuine i. — BENT 32:6
 sound and original i. — MACM 202:1
identical they exist, but are i. — FORS 116:15
identify I can i. with her — MADO 203:15
idolatry organization of i. — SHAW 284:23
if I. you can keep your head — KIPL 174:4
igloo improve on the i. — OKPI 234:14
ignorance Disease, I., Squalor — BEVE 37:3
 Don't die of i. — OFFI 235:6
 evil is simply i. — FORD 115:9
 I. is an evil weed — BEVE 37:2
 I. is first requisite — STRA 299:16
 i. is never better — FERM 107:14
 I. is strength — ORWE 238:9
 i. necessarily infinite — POPP 252:8
 i. so abysmal — MEDA 212:1
 sincere i. — KING 172:10
ignorant Asking the i. — ZOBE 341:8
 become an i. man again — STEV 297:12
 everybody is i. — ROGE 266:14
 many i. men are sure — DARR 83:6
ignore nothing to i. — NASH 228:8
ignored because they are i. — HUXL 155:11
ignores poetry i. most people — MITC 217:3
Ike I like I. — POLI 251:12
ill warn you not to fall i. — KINN 173:5
illegal i., immoral, or fattening — WOOL 336:2
 means that it is not i. — NIXO 232:9
 Nothing is i. if — YOUN 340:4
illegitimate no i. children — GLAD 129:1
ill-housed nation i., ill-clad — ROOS 267:10
illness i. identified with evil — SONT 291:12
 i. in stages — GUIB 135:7
 i. the night-side of life — SONT 291:17
 makes i. worthwhile — SHAW 283:12
ill-nourished ill-clad, i. — ROOS 267:10
ills i. of democracy — SMIT 288:13
illuminated i. trouser-clip — MORT 223:9
illusion only an i. — EINS 97:8
illusions life's i. I recall — MITC 217:5
 small change of his i. — WHAR 325:12
image just an i. — GODA 129:6
 live without any i. — MURD 225:12
imagery for their i. — MCEW 199:6
images Fresh i. beget — YEAT 337:1
 i. change as they repeat — WARH 319:8
 i. of life — BERG 32:8
 unpurged i. of day — YEAT 336:13
imagination I. isn't merely — HUGH 154:7
 literalists of the i. — MOOR 221:7
 suspend the i. — HEMI 145:11
 takes a lot of i. — BAIL 20:1
 Television contracts i. — WOGA 333:16
 those that have no i. — SHAW 285:23

 Western i. — STEI 296:13
imaginative any i. exercise — VIDA 317:7
imagine I. there's no heaven — LENN 187:14
imitate i. each other — HOFF 150:6
 Immature poets i. — ELIO 102:2
 never failed to i. them — BALD 20:8
imitation I. lies at the root — FRAN 117:8
 i. without benefit — SANT 275:10
immanent I. Will that stirs — HARD 139:8
immaturity expression of human i. — BRIT 44:9
 symptom of i. — WHAR 325:13
immoral illegal, i., or fattening — WOOL 336:2
immorality i. what they dislike — WHIT 326:16
immortality i. can be assured — GALB 123:15
 i. through my work — ALLE 6:18
 Milk's leap toward i. — FADI 106:6
 Millions long for i. — ERTZ 104:7
 organize her own i. — LASK 181:8
 they gave, their i. — BROO 45:7
impartial i. as between the fire — CHUR 65:9
impartiality i. is bias — REIT 263:1
impatient growing i. to see him — SMIT 290:5
imperialism I. the monopoly stage — LENI 187:5
imperialisms prey of rival i. — KENY 170:6
imperialist Through its i. system — MAND 205:13
impertinent ask an i. question — BRON 45:4
importance belief in the i. — MAUG 210:10
 inversely with the i. — LEVI 189:9
 taking decisions of i. — PARK 244:9
important i. book, critic assumes — WOOL 335:7
 i. to be clever *about* — MEDA 212:5
 think it's i. — MCCA 197:6
 trivial and the i. — POTT 253:5
imported i., elderly American — JENK 160:10
impossible art of the i. — HAVE 142:6
 Dream the i. — DARI 83:4
 i. takes little longer — NANS 227:9
 i. takes longer — SAYI 278:11
 i. to carry the burden — EDWA 95:11
 says that it is i. — CLAR 70:5
 two words, 'i.' — GOLD 130:5
impostors treat those two i. — KIPL 174:5
impotence I. and sodomy — WAUG 321:15
imprecision Decay with i. — ELIO 98:13
 mess of i. of feeling — ELIO 99:1
impressionable at an i. age — SPAR 292:10
improbability high degree of i. — FISH 109:12
 statistical i. — DAWK 84:7
improved i. by death — SAKI 273:12
improvisation I. is too good — SIMO 287:11
impure all things are i. — LAWR 183:5
in KNEW YOU HAD IT I. YOU — TELE 305:3
inadequate how i. intelligence is — EINS 96:14
 not that we are i. — WILL 330:10
inadvertence by chance or i. — HAIL 136:8
inarticulate raid on the i. — ELIO 99:1
inbreeding sick with i. — THOM 308:13

incest i. and folk-dancing	ANON 12:2
inch Every other i. a gentleman	WEST 325:7
inches thirty i. from my nose	AUDE 17:8
include i. me out	GOLD 130:3
inclusion Life being all i.	JAME 159:10
incognito travelling i.	QUEN 258:11
income dread a dead-level of i.	TAWN 303:2
he has i.	NASH 228:2
rises to meet i.	PARK 244:5
income tax I. made more liars	ROGE 266:11
incompatibility i. is the spice	NASH 228:2
incompetence rise to level of i.	PETE 247:11
incomplete i. until he has married	
	GABO 122:10
incomprehensible most i. fact	EINS 97:1
use the i.	ZOBE 341:8
inconceivable i. idea of the sun	STEV 297:12
inconsistency little i. at times	OWEN 240:10
inconvenience i. only an adventure	CHES 63:3
inconvenient cause may be i.	BENN 31:10
lie even when i.	VIDA 317:16
increase who dies fighting has i.	GREN 133:13
incredible i. as if you fired	RUTH 272:14
indecency I.'s conspiracy	SHAW 285:8
indecent for i. behaviour	WAUG 320:14
independence i. of judges	DENN 88:7
India beautiful in I.	NEHR 229:5
Englishman to rule in I.	NEHR 229:6
final message of I.	FORS 116:17
I. will awake to life	NEHR 228:18
Nothing in I.	FORS 116:14
Indians I. are you	BALD 20:13
indifferent It is simply i.	HOLM 151:1
to be i. to them	SHAW 283:13
indignation Moral i. is jealousy	WELL 323:12
Savage i. there	YEAT 338:18
indiscretion cliché and an i.	MACM 201:16
individual cult of the i.	KHRU 171:9
i. men and women	THAT 306:8
i. reader is important	NABO 227:5
individualism system of rugged i.	HOOV 151:9
individuals things i. are doing	KEYN 170:13
indomitable i. Irishry	YEAT 339:4
industrial i. worker would sooner	BLYT 40:3
industrialists die for the i.	FRAN 117:11
industry i. seems inefficient	SCHU 281:4
permit a cottage i.	MARC 207:10
Science finds, i. applies	ANON 11:4
ineffectual Remote and i. Don	BELL 28:2
inefficiencies i. of dictatorship	GALB 123:13
inefficient industry seems i.	SCHU 281:4
inevitability i. of gradualness	WEBB 322:2
inevitable foresee the i.	ASIM 14:1
inexactitude terminological i.	CHUR 65:4
infamy date which will live in i.	ROOS 267:15
infanticide indefensible as i.	WEST 324:20
infants terrors i. go through	DRAB 91:15
infection i. of things gone	LOWE 195:17
inferior make you feel i.	ROOS 267:4
inferno i. of his passions	JUNG 166:2
infinite door to i. wisdom	BREC 43:12
ignorance necessarily i.	POPP 252:8
Space is almost i.	QUAY 258:9
infinitive care what a split i.	FOWL 117:5
when I split an i.	CHAN 60:12
inflation I. one form of taxation	FRIE 119:9
pay to get i. down	LAMO 179:11
inflections beauty of i.	STEV 297:17
influence i. on human life	MULL 225:8
i. people	CARN 54:2
i. to your son	ICE 156:4
in-folded tongues of flame are i.	ELIO 99:12
information lost in i.	ELIO 100:18
ingredients about the basic i.	TANG 302:16
inhale didn't i.	CLIN 71:9
if he doesn't i.	STEV 297:18
inhumanity essence of i.	SHAW 283:13
injustice I. anywhere a threat	KING 172:3
I. is relatively easy to bear	MENC 213:1
i. makes democracy	NIEB 230:13
ink all cough in i.	YEAT 338:12
inn remember an I., Miranda	BELL 28:9
inner have no I. Resources	BERR 34:7
innocence assumption of i. easy	CROS 81:2
business to lose i.	BOWE 42:14
ceremony of i.	YEAT 338:13
i. is like a dumb leper	GREE 132:14
I. no earthly weapon	HILL 148:11
Never such i. again	LARK 180:9
not in i.	ARDR 12:12
speak again of i.	SUTT 301:9
innocent i. and the beautiful	YEAT 337:16
We are i.	ROSE 268:12
innovation i. without reason	SANT 275:10
innuendoes beauty of i.	STEV 297:17
inoperative statements i.	ZIEG 341:6
inorganic now inert and i.	HOUS 152:11
inquisition Spanish I.	MONT 221:3
inscription like a rough i.	YEVT 339:15
insect gigantic i.	KAFK 166:13
insecurity international i.	NIEB 231:16
inside i. the tent pissing out	JOHN 163:7
I've lived i. myself	DAVI 83:11
insignificance of the utmost i.	CURZ 82:11
insincerity great enemy is i.	ORWE 239:5
insomnia suffering from ideal i.	JOYC 164:7
instincts i. already catered for	BENN 30:13
true to your i.	LAWR 183:17
institution change an i.	TUSA 314:1
transformed into i.	SART 276:14
institutional i. collapse	MOYN 224:5
institutions acquiring their i.	HAIL 136:8
instrument State is an i.	STAL 295:4

insubordination i. and insurrection

MACG 199:11
insulted never *hope* to get i.   DAVI 84:4
insults our visible i.   CART 54:8
insurance form of moral i.   BROD 45:1
  National compulsory i.   CHUR 67:5
insurrection insubordination and i.

MACG 199:11
integration policy of European i.   KOHL 177:12
intellect i. of man is forced   YEAT 337:4
  revenge of the i.   SONT 291:13
intellectual I. disgrace Stares   AUDE 16:13
  i. dominion   MAUR 210:16
  i. hatred   YEAT 338:7
  i. is someone whose   CAMU 53:1
  'I.' suggests   AUDE 17:3
  practical i.   STRO 300:9
  wanted to be an i.   SCHW 281:8
intellectuals treachery of the i.   BEND 29:7
intelligence arresting human i.   LEAC 185:6
  bewitchment of i.   WITT 332:14
  first-rate i.   FITZ 113:6
  how inadequate i. is   EINS 96:14
  I. is quickness   WHIT 326:15
  underestimating i.   MENC 213:2
  with so little i.   JENK 161:1
  you pawn your i.   CUMM 81:10
intelligent honest and i.   ORWE 239:11
  Most i., very elegant   BUCK 48:4
  Routine, in an i. man   AUDE 18:10
  rule of i. tinkering   EHRL 96:3
  so i.   ELIO 101:12
  think you must be i.   MIRR 217:2
intensity full of passionate i.   YEAT 338:13
intentions only had good i.   THAT 305:9
interact do not i. at all   UPDI 315:3
interactive greatest i. medium   LYNT 196:9
intercourse positions in i.   KEAT 168:3
interest compete for her i.   LEWI 190:14
interested i. in the arts   AYCK 19:4
  only i. in art   SHAW 286:4
interesting more i. than women   WALL 318:13
  proposition be i.   WHIT 326:13
  Very i. . . . but   CATC 59:10
interests no other subject which i. them

MACM 202:4
international I. life is   DEBR 86:4
Internet I. is an élite   CHOM 64:14
  thanks to the I.   WILE 329:1
interpose i. my body   STRA 299:17
interpretation I. is the revenge   SONT 291:13
intervene i.—before breakfast   HESE 147:4
interviewer i. allows you to say   BENN 30:7
intestine This is the dark i.   HUGH 154:4
intolerance I. of groups   FREU 118:14
intolerant not to tolerate the i.   POPP 252:5
intrusive i. comma on p. 4   HOUS 152:12

invent right to i. themselves   GREE 133:4
invented i. the brake   NEME 229:8
  only lies are i.   BRAQ 43:7
invention Marriage a wonderful i.   CONN 74:10
inverse i. proportion to the sum   PARK 244:7
invisible almost i. literature   BALL 22:1
  i. hand in politics   FRIE 119:6
  i., refined out of   JOYC 164:16
  no i. means of support   BUCH 47:13
  priest of the i.   STEV 297:4
Iraq creating I.   BELL 27:9
Ireland great Gaels of I.   CHES 62:1
  inhabiting island of I.   O'BR 233:7
  I. holds these graves   PEAR 246:4
  I. hurt you into poetry   AUDE 16:10
  I. is the old sow   JOYC 164:14
  now handling I.   WEST 325:1
  Out of I. have we come   YEAT 338:8
  Romantic I.'s dead   YEAT 338:15
  what I have got for I.   COLL 73:3
Irish answer to the I. Question   SELL 282:13
  I. poets, learn your trade   YEAT 339:3
  Let the I. vessel lie   AUDE 16:12
  symbol of I. art   JOYC 165:4
Irishman secondarily, I'm an I.   HEWI 147:10
Irishry indomitable I.   YEAT 339:4
iron he's got i. teeth   GROM 134:11
  i. curtain   CHUR 67:9
  I. Curtain did not reach   SOLZ 291:5
  i. lady   ANON 10:3
  I. Lady   THAT 304:11
irrational i. is rational   STEV 297:13
irrigation numerical i. system   AUGA 18:17
irritation cosiness and i.   PYM 258:5
island at this i. now   AUDE 16:15
  i. made mainly of coal   BEVA 36:4
  soggy little i.   UPDI 314:15
isolated Continent i.   BROC 44:10
isolationist you'll find an i.   RUSK 271:2
it It's just I.   KIPL 175:15
Italy In I. under the Borgias   FILM 110:14
itsy I. bitsy tccnic weenie   VANC 315:17
ivory downstairs from their I. Towers

SMIT 289:12
ivy it was agony, I.   CATC 57:13

jack news of my boy J.   KIPL 174:11
jack-knife j. has Macheath   BREC 44:1
jail dey gits you in j.   O'NE 236:1
  Go to j.   SAYI 278:16
jam j. we thought was for   BENN 29:14
jamais j. triste archy   MARQ 208:7
James Home J.   HILL 149:2
  J. I, James II   GUED 135:4
  J. James Morrison Morrison   MILN 216:12
Jane J., Jane, tall as a crane   SITW 288:2

Jane (*cont.*):

Me Tarzan, you J. — MISQ 218:10
Japan to J.'s advantage — HIRO 149:4
Japanese reconcile J. action — CHUR 66:14
jaw-jaw To j. is always better — CHUR 67:14
jazz If you're in j. — MANN 206:11
  J. music is to be played — MORT 223:10
  J. will endure — SOUS 292:4
  Picasso, sunbathing and j. — WAUG 321:6
jealousy J. is feeling alone — BOWE 42:13
  j. with a halo — WELL 323:12
  To j. nothing is more — SAGA 273:6
jeans blue j. and Coca-Cola — GREE 133:3
jeepers J. Creepers — MERC 213:11
Jeeves J. shimmered out — WODE 333:2
Jefferson when J. ate alone — KENN 169:11
Jellicoe J. was the only man — CHUR 68:16
jelly blasted, j.-boned swines — LAWR 184:9
  shivers like the j. — PIRO 249:13
jellybeans way of eating j. — REAG 262:1
jest laughing at some j. — KIPL 173:14
Jesus blame J. for what was done — BENN 30:1
  J. loves you more — SIMO 287:9
  j. told him; he wouldn't — CUMM 81:13
  J. wants me for a sunbeam — TALB 302:15
  more popular than J. now — LENN 187:16
  thinks he is J. Christ — CLEM 71:2
  When J. came to Birmingham — STUD 301:1
Jew Germany declare that I am a J. — EINS 96:11
  J. and the language — CELA 60:1
  Just J.-*ish* — MILL 215:14
  saved one J. from Auschwitz — AUDE 18:16
jewelled day of the j. epigram — ANNA 8:12
jewellery just rattle your j. — LENN 187:15
jewels death, sex and j. — STRO 300:8
Jewish J. man with parents alive — ROTH 269:8
  murderers of J. children — WIES 328:4
  national home for the J. people — BALF 21:11
  solution of J. question — GOER 129:12
Jews all poets are J. — TSVE 313:10
  But spurn the J. — BROW 46:15
  condition of the J. — SART 276:15
  To choose The J. — EWER 106:4
  When Hitler attacked the J. — NIEM 232:1
jigsaw piece in a j. puzzle — FILM 111:8
Jim worried about J. — CATC 58:12
job circuit learns your j. — MCLU 201:5
  do his j. when he doesn't feel — AGAT 2:10
  easier j. like publishing — AYER 19:7
  finish the j. — CHUR 66:10
  he's doing a grand j. — CATC 59:5
  husband is a whole-time j. — BENN 31:11
  j. working-class parents — ABBO 1:1
  neighbour loses his j. — TRUM 313:3
jogging alternative to j. — FITT 112:17
John King J. was not a good man — MILN 216:14
Johnny J.-head-in-air — PUDN 257:13

joints know the j. — BUTL 50:9
  Of all the gin j. — FILM 111:11
joke every j. a custard pie — ORWE 239:9
  j. must transform real life — BROW 46:12
  j. with a double meaning — BARK 23:2
  not seen the j. — VIDA 317:5
jokes doesn't make j. — IONE 157:9
  Forgive my little j. — FROS 120:2
jolly j. at my funeral — MOUN 224:3
jolt j. in the perspective — WOOL 335:10
journalism but why j. — BALF 21:12
  J.—an ability to — WEST 325:3
  J. largely consists — CHES 64:5
  j. what will be read — CONN 74:11
  Success in j. — GREE 132:16
journalist British j. — WOLF 333:18
  on being a j. — BELO 28:16
  That is for the j. — JOYC 165:14
journalistic j. dirty-mindedness — LAWR 184:15
journalists J. belong in gutter — PRIE 256:7
  j. dabbling — MCGR 200:2
  J. say a thing — BENN 31:12
  tell lies to j. — KRAU 177:14
journey j. *really* necessary — OFFI 235:7
  long day's j. — O'NE 236:3
  now begin the j. — REAG 262:7
  prepare for a j. — MANS 207:4
  such a long j. — ELIO 99:20
journeying sat the j. boy — HARD 140:5
joy from too much j. — GRAV 131:9
  oh! weakness of j. — BETJ 35:14
  Strength through j. — POLI 251:16
Judas boyhood of J. — Æ 2:6
  J. was paid — POWE 255:9
  Whether J. Iscariot — DYLA 94:15
judge Before you j. me — JACK 158:5
  best j. of a run — WHAR 325:10
  Here come de j. — CATC 58:3
  not j. this movement kindly — READ 261:4
judgement nation fit to sit in j. — WILS 332:2
  wait for the last j. — CAMU 52:14
judges independence of j. — DENN 88:7
  J. must follow their oaths — ZOBE 341:9
  justice in the hands of j. — PICA 248:13
jug 'J. Jug' to dirty ears — ELIO 101:10
juggle how to j. work, love, home — FRIE 119:5
July on the Fourth of J. — HAMM 137:17
jumpers Angels in j. — LEWI 190:16
June J. is bustin' out all over — HAMM 137:9
jungle city is not a concrete j. — MORR 222:3
  wise primitive in giant j. — MAIL 204:11
juniper j. talks to the oak — PAUL 245:15
  under a j.-tree — ELIO 98:4
junk J. is the ideal product — BURR 49:10
just j. an image — GODA 129:6
  J. like that — CATC 58:17
  j. one of those things — PORT 252:17

may not be a j. peace	IZET 158:3
rather be British than j.	PAIS 242:4
talk of a j. war	SORL 292:3
justice If this is j.	HISL 149:6
j. and the American way	ANON 9:12
J. denied	MILL 214:11
j. makes democracy possible	NIEB 230:13
J. should not only be done	HEWA 147:7
old line about j.	OSBO 240:6
ounce of j.	TANS 302:17
price of j.	BENN 31:9
pursuit of j.	GOLD 130:2
to order than to j.	KING 172:4
victors' j.	SHAW 286:8
justifiable not a j. act of war	BELL 27:8
Kaiser put the kibosh on the K.	ELLE 103:7
Kalashnikovs didn't have K.	BONO 41:7
Kane of *Citizen K.*	THOM 309:5
Kansas corny as K. in August	HAMM 137:17
Karajan of Herbert von K.	BEEC 26:16
Keats K.'s vulgarity	LEAV 186:1
keep If you can k. your head	KIPL 174:4
some day it'll k. you	WEST 324:4
keeps gave it us for k.	AYRE 19:9
Kennedy President K. was dead	FORS 117:2
you're no Jack K.	BENT 32:7
Kensal Green Paradise by way of K.	
	CHES 62:12
Kentucky Long ago in K.	WARR 320:3
kept I k. my word	DE L 87:17
kettle k.'s breath	HILL 148:10
pretty k. of fish	MARY 209:9
Khrushchev not have married Mrs K.	
	VIDA 317:13
kibosh put the k. on the Kaiser	ELLE 103:7
kick first k. I took	SPRI 294:13
great k. at misery	LAWR 184:10
Nixon to k. around	NIXO 232:2
kicking kissing and k. people	TRUM 312:13
kid comeback k.	CLIN 71:10
Here's looking at you, k.	FILM 110:9
kiddies k. have crumpled	BETJ 35:3
kidding k., Mister Hitler	PERR 247:7
kids don't have any k. yourself	LARK 180:13
how many k. did you kill	POLI 251:11
kill get out and k. something	LEAC 185:7
how many kids did you k.	POLI 251:11
k. a mockingbird	LEE 186:17
k. animals and stick in	NICO 230:10
K. millions of men	ROST 269:6
k. you in a new way	ROGE 266:17
Licensed to k.	MISQ 218:8
Otherwise k. me	MACN 203:6
prepared to k. one another	SHAW 284:11
right to k.	ADAM 2:1

something you k. for	BENN 30:3
we are going to k. it	POWE 255:3
killed don't mind your being k.	KITC 176:9
Go to Spain and get k.	POLL 250:11
I am the enemy you k.	OWEN 241:6
k. in the war	POWE 255:13
k. lots of men	MOYN 224:6
(who k. him) thought	BELL 28:8
killer lover and k. are mingled	DOUG 91:5
killing medal for k. two men	MATL 209:15
kills grip that k. it	TAGO 302:13
K. all known germs	ADVE 4:6
suicide k. two people	MILL 215:2
that which k.	DE B 85:10
Kilroy K. was here	ANON 10:8
Kiltartan My country is K. Cross	YEAT 337:17
kin one's own k. and kith	NASH 227:16
kind k. things I say	COWA 79:3
People will always be k.	SASS 276:17
kindergarten kind of k.	ROBI 265:9
kindliness cool k. of sheets	BROO 45:8
kindness k. of strangers	WILL 330:6
milk of human k.	GUED 135:3
king fight for its K. and Country	GRAH 131:6
five kings did a k. to death	THOM 307:5
God save the K.	MOYN 224:6
If the K. asks you	ATTL 15:12
K. and country need you	SAYI 279:16
K. asked the Queen	MILN 216:15
K. David and King Solomon	NAYL 228:16
k. of banks and stones	KAVA 167:9
K.'s life moving peacefully	DAWS 84:13
K.'s Moll Reno'd	NEWS 231:10
leave without the k.	ELIZ 103:4
once and future k.	WHIT 326:8
unless you're a k.	HULL 154:8
your K. and your Country	RUBE 270:4
kingfish call me the K.	LONG 193:9
kings five k. left	FARO 106:10
k. haul up the lumps	BREC 44:4
Through talk, we tamed k.	BENN 29:16
walk with K.	KIPL 174:6
Kipling K. and his views	AUDE 16:14
kiss cut ribbons and k. babies	MICH 214:3
k. is still a kiss	HUPF 154:13
Kiss K. Bang Bang	KAEL 166:12
k. my ass in Macy's window	JOHN 163:9
k. on the hand	ROBI 265:6
k. the hand that wrote	JOYC 165:13
rough male k. of blankets	BROO 45:8
wanting to k. me	MACD 199:3
When women k.	MENC 212:10
Wouldst k. me pretty	HART 141:10
kissed k. for forty years	ANON 10:12
k. his sad Andromache	CORN 77:5
k. my first woman	TOSC 310:12
never k. an ugly girl	EPIT 105:6

kisses fine romance with no k.   FIEL 108:6
kissing I wasn't k. her   MARX 209:5
  k. your hand   LOOS 194:7
  like k. God   BRUC 47:3
  like k. Hitler   CURT 82:8
Kissinger K. brought peace   HELL 145:4
kit-bag in your old k.   ASAF 13:10
kitchen get out of the k.   TRUM 313:8
  send me to eat in the k.   HUGH 153:11
  whip in k. cups   STEV 297:6
Kitchener K. is a great poster   ASQU 14:10
Kit-Kat have a K.   ADVE 3:22
kitten trouble with a k.   NASH 228:4
kleine eine k. Pause   LAST 182:13
Klondike beer of a man in K.   CHES 63:1
Knebworth Has God played K.   GALL 124:2
knees I don't really like k.   SAIN 273:10
  live on your k.   IBAR 156:2
knew If you looked away, you k.   SERE 282:16
  K. YOU HAD IT IN YOU   TELE 305:3
  told what he k.   AMIS 7:9
knife cannibal uses k. and fork   LEC 186:11
  He who wields the k.   HESE 147:1
knighthoods looking for your k.   KEAT 167:11
knights lances of ancient k.   ROOT 268:10
knitter beautiful little k.   SITW 288:5
knives night of the long k.   HITL 149:10
knocked ruin that Cromwell k. about
              BEDF 26:12
  we k. the bastard off   HILL 149:1
  what they k. down   FENT 107:8
knocking K. on the moonlit door   DE L 87:16
  k. the American system   CAPO 53:10
knot crowned k. of fire   ELIO 99:12
  So the k. be unknotted   ELIO 98:7
know all I k. is what I read   ROGE 266:13
  because we k. how to do them   FOX 117:7
  do not pretend to k.   DARR 83:6
  don't k. what I'm doing   BRAU 43:9
  don't k. where I'm going   SAND 275:2
  He must k. sumpin'   HAMM 137:13
  How do they k.   PARK 243:17
  I do not believe . . . I k.   JUNG 166:9
  I k. what I like   BEER 26:20
  k. a man who can   ADVE 3:9
  k. better what is good   JAY 160:2
  k. the place for the first time   ELIO 99:9
  K. what I mean, Harry   BRUN 47:5
  k. what I think   WALL 319:2
  k. what we are talking about   RUSS 271:15
  k. when I am having a good time
              ASTO 14:15
  not k. what they have said   CHUR 65:5
  Not many people k. that   CAIN 51:4
  things they didn't k.   POUN 253:16
  those who do not wish to k.   RALE 259:9
  to k. what is right   JOHN 163:6

  wanted to k. about sex   REUB 263:6
  We k. too much   ELIO 102:5
  You k. more than you think   SPOC 294:5
  you k. who   ADVE 4:19
  you'll never k.   MISQ 218:9
knowing Bewrapt past k.   HARD 140:5
  lust of k.   FLEC 114:2
  one who INSISTS on k.   POUN 254:12
knowledge After such k.   ELIO 99:14
  k. can only be finite   POPP 252:8
  k. they cannot lose   OPPE 236:9
  k. we have lost   ELIO 100:18
  make k. available   BLAC 38:9
  never better than k.   FERM 107:14
  search for k.   RUSS 271:3
known k. and the unknown   PINT 249:10
  k. unto God   EPIT 105:14
  safer than a k. way   HASK 142:2
knows He k. nothing   SHAW 284:10
  if you k. of a better 'ole   BAIR 20:6
  K. Things   MILN 216:10
  sits in the middle and k.   FROS 120:17
Knox John K. in Paradise   PARK 243:3
koompartoo make a K.   BURN 49:8
Kremlin howl by the K.   AKHM 5:4

laboratory guinea pigs in l.   WILL 329:12
  used to be a l.   RICH 264:10
labour chaos of a L. council   KINN 173:6
  done to the L. Party   TAWN 303:5
  Don't let L. ruin it   POLI 251:19
  fracture the L. party   KINN 173:9
  is L.'s call   POLI 251:10
  is to New L.   LAHR 179:2
  L. isn't working   POLI 251:17
  L. Party owes more   PHIL 248:10
  L.'s double whammy   POLI 251:18
  [L.] the natural party   WILS 331:7
  leader for the L. Party   BEVA 36:12
  never visualised l.   WEBB 321:21
  New L., new danger   POLI 251:20
  not enter the L. Party   BENN 30:2
  Of the L. Party   JENK 161:4
  thousand years of L.   MAJO 205:2
  to live without l.   TAWN 303:4
  trouble with the L. Party   GRIM 134:10
labour-intensive Monarchy is l.   WILS 331:10
lace Nottingham l.   BFTJ 34:11
lacy l. sleeve with vitriol   WOOL 335:18
ladders where all the l. start   YEAT 337:2
ladies l., God bless them   SAYE 277:9
  L., just a little more   TREE 311:4
  L. were ladies   RAVE 261:1
  l. who lunch   SOND 291:9
  worth any number of old l.   FAUL 107:4
lads We are l.   GALL 123:17

law (*cont.*):
l. is above you   DENN 88:6
l. not supported by people   HUMP 154:9
l. of the Yukon   SERV 283:2
liberty under the l.   HAIL 136:6
Nor l., nor duty   YEAT 337:18
One L., one Land, one Throne   KIPL 175:6
whole of the L.   CROW 81:7
lawn Get your tanks off my l.   WILS 331:9
on the l. I lie in bed   AUDE 17:7
scooters off my l.   CLAR 70:8
lawned l. areas with paving   OFFI 235:14
laws Government of l.   FORD 115:5
l. of God will be suspended   SHAW 284:3
neither l. made   JOHN 161:11
scientist's l.   QUIN 258:14
lawyer freely as a l. interprets   GIRA 128:11
l. with his briefcase   PUZO 258:4
to a corporate l.   COMM 73:7
When a l. cashes in   SAND 274:14
lay L. your sleeping head   AUDE 16:16
layout Perfection of planned l.   PARK 244:8
Lazarus L. mystified   HILL 148:9
LBJ All the way with L.   POLI 251:2
Hey, L., how many kids   POLI 251:11
lead can't see who's in the l.   SNAG 290:9
evening l.   CHUR 68:4
l. a horticulture   PARK 244:2
L. Plan Diet   WARR 320:2
leader fanatic a great l.   BROU 46:11
Take me to your l.   CATC 59:8
test of a l.   LIPP 191:10
leadership art of l. is saying no   BLAI 38:11
L. is not about being   KEAT 168:2
leaf wise man hide a l.   CHES 63:7
leap giant l. for mankind   ARMS 13:4
leaping It's l.-before-you-look   COOP 76:8
l. from place to place   HARD 139:14
learn clever ones l. Latin   CHUR 68:6
I l. by going   ROET 266:9
l. how to be aged   BLYT 40:4
Parents l. from children   SPAR 292:8
People must l. to hate   MAND 206:1
learned l. has been forgotten   SKIN 288:11
learning not l. from history   BLAI 38:12
least l. government was the best   FEIN 107:7
leave forever taking l.   RILK 265:2
If you can't l. in a taxi   FILM 110:12
if you l. things alone   CHES 63:15
L. them while you're   LOOS 194:6
l. without the King   ELIZ 103:4
leaves burning of the l.   BINY 38:1
flaps its glad green l.   HARD 139:4
lectures hissed my mystery l.   SPOO 294:9
left L. hand down a bit   CATC 58:19
position was on the l.   MOSL 223:13
left-wing social contract is l.   DEBR 86:4

leg does not resemble a l.   APOL 12:8
like pissing down your l.   JOHN 163:8
legacies l. of empire   SAMP 274:7
legend Your l. ever did   JOHN 162:1
Your l. ever will   JOHN 162:4
legibility dawn of l.   HAY 142:14
legs born with your l. apart   ORTO 237:8
Four l. good   ORWE 237:11
on their own two l.   CASS 55:11
leisure absence of l. to reflect   HAVE 142:3
fill l. intelligently   RUSS 271:11
length for what it lacks in l.   FROS 120:8
Lenin L. was right   KEYN 170:11
Suppose L. had died   SCHL 280:3
lenses beauty and contact l.   PETE 247:12
lent powers l. to me   BENN 30:4
leopard l. does not change   COMP 74:5
leopards three white l. sat   ELIO 98:4
leper innocence is like a dumb l.   GREE 132:14
Lesbia L. with her sparrow   MILL 214:13
less about l. and less   MAYO 211:10
l. in this than meets the eye   BANK 22:10
L. is a bore   VENT 317:1
L. is more   ROHE 267:2
more about l. and less   BUTL 50:6
more and more in l. and less   YATE 336:10
One square foot l.   BENC 29:6
lessons from the l. of history   HUXL 155:4
l. to be drawn   ELIZ 102:13
letter don't think this is a l.   RENO 263:5
l. by strange letter   HEAN 143:9
Someone wants a l.   ADVE 4:20
letters l. get in wrong places   MILN 216:9
l. to a non-existent   LEWI 190:6
levee Drove my Chevy to the l.   MCLE 200:11
levers shan't be pulling the l.   THAT 306:17
leviathan l. retrieving pebbles   WELL 323:3
Levis sold a million pairs of L.   BURR 49:9
lexicons We are walking l.   LIVE 191:14
liar answered 'Little L.'   BELL 27:15
proved l.   HAIL 136:4
liars Income Tax made more L.   ROGE 266:11
liberal first L. leader   STEE 295:13
ineffectual l.'s problem   FRAY 118:6
l. education   BANK 22:12
l. is a conservative who   WOLF 334:4
L. is a man who uses   ROOS 267:11
l. tells other people   BARA 22:15
old l. between the wars   PLOM 250:8
liberals l. can understand   BRUC 47:2
L. have invented   O'RO 236:16
liberation Women's L. is just   MEIR 212:7
liberationists furious about the l.   LOOS 194:9
liberties Freedom, what l.   GEOR 126:15
liberty defence of l.   GOLD 130:2
holy name of l.   GAND 124:9
L. is liberty, not   BERL 33:6

L. is precious · LENI 187:12
L. is unfinished business · ANON 10:9
L. means responsibility · SHAW 285:1
l. under the law · HAIL 136:6
safeguards of l. · FRAN 118:2
survival and success of l. · KENN 169:3
libraries l. of the Commons · CHAN 61:6
library less time in the l. · STRU 300:10
l. is thought in · SAMU 274:8
you have a public l. · BENN 30:6
lice l. on the back · LIVI 192:2
licence l. to act like an asshole · ZAPP 341:1
l. to print money · THOM 309:6
licenced based upon l. premises · O'BR 233:10
licensed L. to kill · MISQ 218:8
licking finger l. good · ADVE 3:28
licorice l. fields at Pontefract · BETJ 35:7
lie definition of a l. · ANON 8:14
Every word she writes is a l. · MCCA 197:14
fall victim to a big l. · HITL 149:14
home to a l. · POUN 254:1
l. even when inconvenient · VIDA 317:16
l. not just a moral category · SOLZ 291:1
l. that makes us realize truth · PICA 249:6
old L.: Dulce et decorum · OWEN 240:17
possible to l. for the truth · ADLE 2:3
undo the folded l. · AUDE 17:10
lied because our fathers l. · KIPL 173:12
I l. to please the mob · KIPL 173:13
lies enough white l. to ice · ASQU 14:13
Here l. Groucho Marx · EPIT 105:6
l. about the Democrats · STEV 297:19
L. are the mortar · WELL 323:8
l. of tongue and pen · CHES 62:8
make l. sound truthful · ORWE 239:6
Matilda told such Dreadful L. · BELL 27:14
only l. are invented · BRAQ 43:7
Without l. humanity would · FRAN 117:9
life actor's l. for me · WASH 320:4
afternoon of human l. · JUNG 166:6
all human l. is there · ADVE 3:3
answers to the meaning of l. · DAWK 84:10
believe in l. · DU B 92:7
believe in the l. to come · BECK 25:14
contempt for l. · VANE 316:3
content to manufacture l. · BERN 33:9
essence of l. · DAWK 84:7
gave my l. for freedom · EWER 104:12
goes through l. holding on · ELLI 103:9
great l. if you don't weaken · BUCH 47:12
images of l. · BERG 32:8
in balance with this l. · YEAT 337:19
isn't l. a terrible thing · THOM 307:17
I've had a wonderful l. · LAST 182:14
lay down his friends for his l. · THOR 309:7
lay down my l. for · HALD 136:13
Lead me from death to l. · KUMA 178:9

l. a glorious cycle of song · PARK 242:13
l. and loves of a she-devil · WELD 322:10
l. a series of images · WARH 319:8
L. a sexually transmitted disease · ANON 10:10
L. begins at forty · PITK 249:16
L. being all inclusion · JAME 159:10
l. exists in the universe · JEAN 160:7
L., friends, is boring · BERR 34:7
l. had been ruined · BROO 46:4
l. happens elsewhere · BENN 31:3
l. is 6 to 5 against · RUNY 270:10
L. is a foreign language · MORL 222:1
L. is a gamble · STOP 299:10
L. is a great surprise · NABO 227:1
L. is a horizontal fall · COCT 72:3
L. is a matter of passing · COOK 75:14
L. is an offensive · WHIT 326:12
L. is a rainbow which · YEVT 340:1
L. is Colour and Warmth · GREN 133:13
L. is doubt · UNAM 314:12
L. is first boredom · LARK 180:5
L. is just one damned · HUBB 153:7
L. is not having been told · NASH 228:15
L. is nothing much to lose · HOUS 152:9
l. is one damn thing · MILL 214:15
L. is the other way round · LODG 193:1
l. is the thing · SMIT 289:10
L. is too short to stuff · CONR 75:8
l. is washed in the speechless · BARZ 24:13
L. just a bowl of cherries · BROW 46:14
l. like a box of chocolates · FILM 111:9
l. like a Christmas cake · TANG 302:16
L. not a series of gig lamps · WOOL 335:1
l. of any important person · PRIE 256:8
L. says: she did this · BARN 23:6
L.'s better with · POLI 251:19
l. sentence goes on · CONL 74:9
l.'s rich pageant · MARS 208:15
l.'s story fills thirty-five pages · ARNO 13:7
L., the Universe and Everything · ADAM 1:12
live out my l. talking · VANZ 316:7
long as you have your l. · JAME 159:6
looked at l. from both sides · MITC 217:5
makes l. worth living · ELIO 101:21
makes us think about l. · DE G 87:8
matter of l. and death · SHAN 283:9
measured out my l. · ELIO 100:6
more a way of l. · ANON 10:16
not a discovery in l. · WOOL 335:14
not in giving l. · DE B 85:10
not the men in my l. that counts · WEST 324:8
one bright book of l. · LAWR 183:14
On l., on death · YEAT 339:5
Our end is L. · MACN 203:10
outer l. of telegrams · FORS 116:8
Perfection of the l. · YEAT 337:4
priceless gift of l. · ROSE 268:12

life (*cont.*):

private l. is a disgrace	ANON 11:3
really don't know l. at all	MITC 217:5
remaining years of l.	MAND 205:12
Reverence for L.	SCHW 281:9
shilling l. will give you	AUDE 17:11
sketchy understanding of l.	CRIC 80:1
some problems with my *l.*	SIMO 287:7
sons and daughters of L.	GIBR 127:11
taking l. by the throat	FROS 121:5
There is l., but not for you	MORT 223:6
there is l. out there	DAWK 84:11
university of l.	BOTT 42:5
warm full blooded l.	JOYC 165:9
Water is l.'s *mater*	SZEN 302:12
What is this l.	DAVI 84:2
whole l. shows in your face	BACA 19:14
Who owns my life	RODR 266:4
Without work, l. goes rotten	CAMU 53:6
Woolworth l. hereafter	NICO 230:6
you lived your l.	JOHN 162:1
lifeless virtue is l.	PAST 245:4
life sentence escape the l.	LAWR 184:16
lifetime l. of happiness	SHAW 284:12
light brief crack of l.	NABO 227:2
dark is l. enough	FRY 121:8
dying of the l.	THOM 307:2
Give me a l.	HASK 142:2
gives a lovely l.	MILL 214:9
I travel l.	FRY 121:10
l. at the end of the tunnel	DICK 89:12
l. at the end of the tunnel	LOWE 195:15
L. breaks where no sun	THOM 307:7
l. has gone out	NEHR 229:1
l. in the darkness	JUNG 166:3
l. my fire	MORR 222:7
speed far faster than l.	BULL 48:6
sudden gust of l.	MOTI 223:14
sweetness and l. failed	FORS 116:2
tried to mend the Electric L.	BELL 28:3
while the l. fails	ELIO 99:11
lightest poor tread the l.	HARR 141:4
lighthouse great l. which stands	JENK 161:6
light-house l. with his eyes	CAMP 52:7
lightly l. skims the midge	BETJ 35:2
take themselves l.	CHES 63:16
lightness unbearable l. of being	KUND 178:10
lightning known the l.'s hour	DAY- 85:3
writing history with l.	WILS 332:1
lights all-the-l.-on man	REED 262:12
turn the l. back on	MOOR 221:9
watching the tail l.	CRAN 79:9
like but you'll l. it	CATC 59:17
don't know whether I l. it	VAUG 316:9
don't l. this game	CATC 58:6
I know what I l.	BEER 26:20
I L. Ike	POLI 251:12

l. everyone else	DE G 87:9
l. is not necessarily good	BELL 27:7
l. what you get	SHAW 285:11
man you don't l.	THOM 307:19
must be l. something	FORS 115:13
No wonder we l. them	AMIS 7:12
liked wish to be l.	RUSS 271:9
would have l. to be Perón	PERÓ 247:4
likely Not bloody l.	SHAW 285:21
likes does know what she l.	RATT 260:7
does what he l. to do	GILL 128:2
lilac l. and the roses	ARAG 12:10
lilacs breeding L.	ELIO 101:6
lily l. rears its gouged face	HILL 148:9
limbs deck your lower l. in pants	NASH 228:14
limelight backing into the l.	BERN 33:15
limited whizzed the L.	CRAN 79:9
limits l. of my language	WITT 332:18
limousine All we want is a l.	MACN 202:14
One perfect l.	PARK 243:2
limp l. father of thousands	JOYC 165:8
Limpopo grey-green, greasy L.	KIPL 175:12
Lincoln Ford, not a L.	FORD 115:4
L. County Road	DYLA 94:12
L. was shovelled	SAND 274:11
L. went to New Orleans	HUGH 153:13
line active l. on a walk	KLEE 176:11
combine to form a l.	LIND 191:4
l. is a fuse	MAYA 211:4
playing on the l.	FORS 116:12
problem of the colour l.	DU B 92:6
through colour and l.	MOND 220:1
lines I plant l.	WALC 318:4
Just say the l.	COWA 79:1
sentiment in short l.	LARK 181:5
lingerie Brevity the soul of l.	PARK 243:9
linguistic form of l. fascism	JAME 159:17
l. philosophy	RUSS 272:10
lining There's a silver l.	FORD 115:11
linoleum shoot me through l.	BANK 22:13
lion nation that had l.'s heart	CHUR 67:17
still a living l.	SOLZ 291:3
lions L. led by donkeys	SAYI 279:1
lips already born before my l.	MAND 206:10
Is it Lombard's l.	EWAR 104:11
My l. are sealed	MISQ 218:11
Read my l.	BUSH 50:4
Red l. are not so red	OWEN 241:2
lipstick bears a l.'s traces	MARV 209:4
too much l.	NASH 228:9
liquid Cats, no less l.	TESS 304:8
let their l. siftings fall	ELIO 101:5
liquidation l. of British Empire	CHUR 67:3
liquor L. is one way out	WILL 330:1
l. is quicker	NASH 228:11
listen don't want to l. to *you*	LEBO 186:6
good to l.	ADVE 3:29

longer (*cont.*):
living lasts l.   ANOU 12:5
longitude l. with no platitude   FRY 121:12
look and l. another   HEDR 144:10
full l. at the worst   HARD 139:12
l. after our people   LAST 182:4
L. back in anger   OSBO 239:18
l. on and help   LAWR 184:13
L., stranger   AUDE 16:15
l. the East End in the face   ELIZ 103:3
L. thy last   DE L 87:15
Stop-l.-and-listen   OFFI 235:12
looked better to be l. over   WEST 324:2
If you l. away, you knew   SERE 282:16
l. at in merciless glare   WILL 330:4
more he l. inside   MILN 216:5
looking Here's l. at you   FILM 110:9
keep l. over his shoulder   BARU 24:12
l. in the same direction   SAIN 273:8
someone may be l.   MENC 212:14
stop other people from l.   BLAC 38:9
while you're l. good   LOOS 194:6
looking glass cracked l.   JOYC 165:4
looking glasses served as l.   WOOL 335:5
looks l. like a duck   REUT 263:7
needs good l.   TUCK 313:13
looney L. Tunes   REAG 262:3
loophole l. through which pervert   BRON 45:5
loose Every which way but l.   FILM 112:9
l. cannon like her   ANON 11:15
man who should l. me   LOWE 195:4
Lorca L. was killed, singing   READ 261:6
lord L. of all hopefulness   STRU 300:12
L. of the Dance   CART 55:5
L. survives the rainbow   LOWE 195:14
Praise the L.   FORG 115:12
saying 'L. Jones Dead'   CHES 64:5
Lord Copper Up to a point, L.   WAUG 321:8
lords L. a matter of controversy   ST J 273:9
L. is the British Outer Mongolia   BENN 29:13
one of the l. of life   LAWR 184:6
lordships good enough for their l.   ANON 11:12
lose hurts to l.   DOLE 90:9
is to l. it   ORWE 239:12
l. them when you are young   BERN 33:12
l. the war in an afternoon   CHUR 68:16
nothing much to l.   HOUS 152:9
nothing to l. but   ORWE 239:3
waste it is to l. one's mind   QUAY 258:10
we don't want to l. you   RUBE 270:4
wins if he does not l.   KISS 176:2
losers no winners, but all are l.   CHAM 60:2
losing l. your sight   SASS 276:17
lost Balls will be l. always   BERR 34:5
France has not l. the war   DE G 86:8
l. an empire   ACHE 1:8
l. boyhood of Judas   Æ 2:6

l. dog somewhere   ANOU 12:6
l. generation   STEI 296:6
not that you won or l.   RICE 263:13
OK. We l.   MAJO 205:3
paradises we have l.   PROU 257:10
Though lovers be l.   THOM 307:1
Vietnam was l. in   MCLU 201:12
what is l. in translation   FROS 121:7
wherever we're l. in   FRY 121:13
lot not a l. . . . but you'll like   CATC 59:17
lottery genetic l. comes up with   PIML 249:7
l. forms a principal part   BORG 42:1
L., with weekly pay-out   ORWE 238:12
Lou lady that's known as L.   SERV 283:4
lousy *House Beautiful* is play l.   PARK 243:12
L. but loyal   SAYI 279:2
l. skin scabbed by cities   BUNT 48:8
lout l.'s game   WEST 324:17
love All you need is l.   LENN 188:1
Any kiddie in school can l.   NASH 228:10
caution in l.   RUSS 271:10
doesn't l. a wall   FROS 120:11
fell in l. with himself   POWE 254:16
for us, it's love   BOUS 42:7
From Russia with l.   FLEM 114:5
God is l., but   LEE 186:16
God si L.   FORS 116:17
greater l. hath no man   THOR 309:7
Greater l. than this   JOYC 165:11
groans of l.   LOWR 196:2
Hearts wound up with l.   SPEN 293:11
Hell is to l. no more   BERN 33:11
If I can't l. Hitler   MUST 226:9
I'll l. you   AUDE 15:15
It's so simple, l.   PRÉV 256:5
Land that I l.   BERL 32:11
Let's fall in l.   PORT 252:18
longing for l.   RUSS 271:3
l. affair with America   MAIL 204:9
l. and work   FREU 118:17
l. boat has crashed   LAST 182:11
L., curiosity, freckles   PARK 242:14
l. does not consist in   SAIN 273:8
L. Flames for a year   LAMP 179:14
L. has pitched his mansion   YEAT 337:5
l. human beings   GREE 132:7
l. is a thing that can never   PARK 242:13
L. is a universal migraine   GRAV 131:12
L. is discovery of reality   MURD 225:15
l. is given over-well   PARK 243:3
l. is here to stay   GERS 127:4
L. is just a system   BARN 23:8
l. is not secure   CHES 62:2
L. is the delusion   MENC 212:11
L. makes the world go round   MACK 200:7
L. means not ever having   SEGA 282:4
L.? most natural painkiller   LAST 182:12

l. one another or die — AUDE 17:10
l. one's country — ANNA 8:13
L. set you going — PLAT 250:5
l. that asks no question — SPRI 294:11
L. the Beloved Republic — FORS 116:20
L.-thirty, love-forty — BETJ 35:14
l. . . . whatever that may — CHAR 61:12
l. will steer the stars — RADO 259:6
l. without the rhetoric — STOP 299:6
l. you for yourself alone — YEAT 336:12
make l. in a canoe — BERT 34:9
Make l. not war — SAYI 279:3
man in l. is incomplete — GABO 122:10
Man's l. is of man's life — AMIS 7:11
man you l. to hate — FILM 111:4
money can't buy me l. — LENN 188:3
Most people l. love — PAST 245:3
My l. and I did meet — BETJ 35:7
Need we say it was not l. — MILL 214:14
never l. a stranger — BENS 32:1
no l. for such — THOM 308:12
programmed to l. completely — BAIN 20:5
right place for l. — FROS 119:15
search for l. — WAŁĘ 318:6
support of the woman I l. — EDWA 95:11
survive of us is l. — LARK 180:3
thought that l. would last — AUDE 16:8
tired of L. — BELL 28:1
vividly gifted in l. — DUFF 92:8
When l. congeals — HART 141:7
Where l. rules — JUNG 166:7
who l., time is eternity — VAN 316:2
wilder shores of l. — BLAN 39:8
Work is l. made visible — GIBR 127:12
You can only l. one war — GELL 126:1
loved l. you, so I drew these tides — LAWR 184:17
thirst to be l. — RHYS 263:10
wish I l. the Human Race — RALE 259:10
loveliness weak from your l. — BETJ 35:14
lovely l. woman stoops to folly — ELIO 101:18
on all things l. — DE L 87:15
so be l. — GRAV 131:11
Wouldn't it be l. — LERN 188:20
lover l. and killer are mingled — DOUG 91:5
l.'s quarrel with the world — FROS 120:10
Scratch a l. — PARK 242:12
what is left of a l. — ROWL 269:13
lovers Though l. be lost — THOM 307:1
wonder if it's l. — MULD 225:6
loves lady l. Milk Tray — ADVE 3:5
life and l. of a she-devil — WELD 322:10
Who l. ya, baby — CATC 59:14
woman whom nobody l. — CORN 77:6
loving Can't help l. dat man — HAMM 137:7
discharge for l. one — MATL 209:15
low l. on whom assurance sits — ELIO 101:17
lowbrow first militant l. — BERL 33:8

lower capitalism of l. classes — SPEN 294:4
l. classes had such white — CURZ 82:17
l. than vermin — BEVA 36:5
While there is a l. class — DEBS 86:6
loyal Lousy but l. — SAYI 279:2
l. to his own career — DALT 83:3
loyalties l. which centre upon — CHUR 68:12
tragic conflict of l. — HOWE 153:1
loyalty I want l. — JOHN 163:9
L. is the Tory's secret — KILM 172:1
l. we feel to unhappiness — GREE 132:8
LSD L.? Nothing much happened — AUDE 18:14
L. reminds me of minks — GRAV 132:1
PC is the L. of the '90s — LEAR 185:10
luck awf'lly bad l. on Diana — BETJ 35:4
believes in l. — STEA 295:12
but it is l. — FORS 116:12
l. of my generation — SHAW 286:11
watching his l. — SERV 283:4
luckiest Geniuses are the l. — AUDE 18:13
lucky l. if he gets out of it — FILM 110:15
lullaby Once in a l. — HARB 138:11
lumps l. in it — STEP 296:15
lunatic all in l. asylums — CHES 63:11
form the l. fringe — ROOS 268:9
lunatics lunatic asylum run by l. — LLOY 192:15
l. have taken charge — ROWL 270:1
lunch cork out of my l. — FIEL 108:9
ladies who l. — SOND 291:9
no such thing as a free l. — SAYI 279:8
unable to l. today — PORT 253:1
Universe is a free l. — GUTH 135:11
luncheon do not take soup at l. — CURZ 82:13
lungs from froth-corrupted l. — OWEN 240:17
lust despair rather than l. — READ 261:8
horrible that l. and rage — YEAT 338:17
l. and calls it advertising — LAHR 178:13
l. and rape and incest — BENN 30:9
l. of knowing — FLEC 114:2
to l. after it — LEWI 190:8
lusty call l. in foreign films — WILD 328:11
luxuries and which l. — WRIG 336:5
luxury Every l. lavished on you — ORTO 237:6
To trust people is a l. — FORS 116:6
lying branch of the art of l. — CORN 77:9
listening, l. in wait — THOM 308:5
One of you is l. — PARK 243:7
Lyonnesse When I set out for L. — HARD 140:9
lyric now it's l. verse — WAUG 321:5

M dreaded four M.'s — STRE 300:7
Maastricht signing the M. treaty — BENN 30:4
MacArthur subordinate of Gen. M. — PERE 246:13
Macavity M. WASN'T THERE — ELIO 100:15
Macbeth Little Nell and Lady M. — WOOL 335:18

m. who should loose me — LOWE 195:4
m. who's untrue to his wife — AUDE 17:3
m. who used to notice — HARD 139:4
m. you love to hate — FILM 111:4
met a m. who wasn't there — MEAR 211:14
more like a m. — LERN 188:14
one small step for a m. — ARMS 13:4
said, ask a m. — THAT 304:10
saw a m. this morning — SHAW 286:9
Sir, no m.'s enemy — AUDE 17:14
Stand by your m. — WYNE 336:9
woman without a m. — STEI 296:12
You'll be a M., my son — KIPL 174:6
managed not a free press but a m. — RADC 259:5
management m. of a balance of power
— KISS 176:1
M. that wants to change — TUSA 314:1
manager m. who gets the blame — LINE 191:8
No m. ever got fired — ADVE 4:14
managing director M.'s chance — WHIT 327:9
man-appeal gives a meal m. — ADVE 4:15
mandarin M. style — CONN 74:15
Manderley dreamt I went to M. — DU M 92:10
mangle my dear Mam's m. — CLOU 71:11
mangrove together by m. roots — BISH 38:5
manhood m. an opportunity — KEIL 168:4
manifesto first powerful plain m. — SPEN 293:6
m. written by Dr Mori — BENN 30:2
manifestoes in the party m. — ROTH 269:11
manilla misery of m. folders — ROET 266:6
man-in-the-street To the m. — AUDE 17:3
mankind giant leap for m. — ARMS 13:4
M. is on the move — SMUT 290:8
M. must put an end to war — KENN 169:9
no history of m. — POPP 252:6
not in Asia, was m. born — ARDR 12:12
study of m. is books — HUXL 155:5
manner All m. of thing shall be — ELIO 99:12
manners automobile changed our m.
— KEAT 168:3
English m. more frightening — JARR 159:19
good table m. — MIKE 214:4
M. the need of the plain — WAUG 321:17
manoeuvre force with a m. — TROT 312:5
manoeuvring could be a m. swine — MCCA 198:1
mansion heavenly m., raging — YEAT 337:4
Love has pitched his m. — YEAT 337:5
mantled M. in mist — AUDE 15:13
manufacture content to m. life — BERN 33:9
manunkind this busy monster, m. — CUMM 81:14
manure liquid m. from the West — SOLZ 291:5
what she lacks: m. — GIDE 128:1
many so much owed by so m. — CHUR 66:7
map m.-makers' colours — BISH 38:6
maps Geography is about M. — BENT 32:2
marathon fought near M. — GRAV 131:10
Politics is a m. — LIVI 192:3

march do not m. on Moscow — MONT 220:13
don't m. as alternative — FITT 112:17
m. my troops towards — GRIM 134:8
m. towards it — CALL 51:9
Men who m. away — HARD 140:4
marching m., charging feet — JAGG 158:12
Marie I am M. of Roumania — PARK 242:13
marijuana experimented with m. — CLIN 71:9
market common m. is a process — MONN 220:4
enterprise of the m. — ANON 9:8
m. has no morality — HESE 147:2
Market Harborough AM IN M. — TELE 305:1
marketing not a m. manager — KOHL 177:13
market-place gathered in the m. — CAVA 56:6
marriage get anywhere in a m. — MURD 225:14
M. a wonderful invention — CONN 74:10
M. is a bribe — WILD 328:14
M. isn't a word — FILM 111:6
M. is popular because — SHAW 285:3
M. is waste-paper basket — WEBB 322:3
So that is m. — WOOL 335:8
three of us in this m. — DIAN 89:8
value of m. is not — DE V 88:14
marriages All the unhappy m. — WODE 332:19
m. selling one's soul — MACK 200:4
thousands of m. — LARK 180:9
married being unhappily m. — PARK 244:10
can't get m. at all — FILM 111:16
getting m. in the morning — LERN 188:13
incomplete until he has m. — GABO 122:10
m. beneath me — ASTO 14:16
m.—to be the more together — MACN 203:3
not getting m. today — GALL 123:16
Onassis would not have m. — VIDA 317:13
marry men we wanted to m. — STEI 296:11
Never m. a man who hates — BENN 31:14
Martha had enough of M. — MACM 202:9
Martians understand than M. — SOLZ 290:12
martinetissimo I am a m. — STOK 298:13
Martini into a dry M. — FILM 111:1
martyr regarded as a m. — KHOM 171:7
martyrdom m. must run its course — AUDE 17:2
M. only way in which — SHAW 283:14
marvel m. my birthday away — THOM 307:9
marvels to credit m. — HEAN 143:13
Marx blame M. for what was done — BENN 30:1
illegitimate child of Karl M. — ATTL 15:9
in M.'s pages — SCHU 281:6
M is for M. — CONN 74:19
Marxism more to Methodism than M.
— PHIL 248:10
Marxist M.—Groucho tendency — ANON 10:7
Mary time for some M. — MACM 202:9
Mary Jane matter with M. — MILN 216:16
Marylebone hanging garments of M.
— JOYC 164:8

Mary Magdalenes Madonnas or M.

WILL 329:11

mask m. that eats into the face UPDI 315:2

masks ship our m. in case of gas KIPL 173:18

masochistic m. a masochistic form

OLIV 235:17

masons Where did the m. go BREC 44:4

mass listen to the B Minor M. TORK 310:11

two thousand years of m. HARD 139:6

Massachusetts denied in M. MILL 214:11

masses calling 'em the m. PRIE 256:11

If it is for the m. SCHO 280:10

Movement of M. CONN 74:19

master Death is a m. from Germany

CELA 59:22

state can be m. of money BEVE 37:4

masterpiece knows, at sight, a m. POUN 254:3

masters never wrong, the Old M. AUDE 17:1

We are not the m. BLAI 39:3

We are the m. now MISQ 219:3

mastery I had m. OWEN 241:5

mastodons like m. bellowing WODE 333:9

masturbation Don't knock m. ALLE 6:8

M. is the thinking HAMP 138:1

m. of war RAE 259:7

match Honour is like a m. PAGN 242:1

matched m. us with His hour BROO 45:14

matches have a box of m. HOME 151:6

with that stick of m. MAND 206:4

materialistic m. of religions TEMP 304:3

really m. people MCCA 197:9

mathematician appear as a pure m.

JEAN 160:8

mathematics avoid pregnancy by m.

MENC 212:15

In m. you don't NEUM 229:12

M. may be defined RUSS 271:15

M., rightly viewed RUSS 271:16

no place for ugly m. HARD 139:3

Matilda M. told such Dreadful Lies BELL 27:14

matrimony critical period in m. HERB 146:17

matter Does it m. SASS 276:17

position of m. RUSS 271:13

What is the m. MILN 216:16

mattering can go on m. BOWE 42:10

matters else you do well m. ONAS 235:19

Nobody that m. MILL 214:7

What can I do that m. SPEN 294:1

mattress crack it open on a m. MILL 215:4

maturing mind is m. late NASH 228:6

maturity M. is a high price STOP 299:13

mausoleum used as its m. AMIS 7:8

may M. month flaps its leaves HARD 139:4

M. to December ANDE 8:8

maybe definite m. GOLD 130:9

mayor tart who has married the M. BAXT 25:2

What did the m. do? GRAV 131:13

MBEs looking for your M. KEAT 167:11

MCC M. ends and the Church PRIE 256:13

McCarthyism M. is Americanism MCCA 197:8

McNamara M.'s War MCNA 202:10

me For you but not for m. ANON 10:17

M. Decade WOLF 334:7

most delight in M. CAMP 52:8

meal gives a m. man-appeal ADVE 4:15

meals cooked a few m. CONR 75:11

mean depends what you m. by CATC 58:13

Down these m. streets CHAN 60:10

even if you don't m. it TRUM 313:5

Know what I m., Harry BRUN 47:5

poem should not m. but be MACL 200:12

They may not m. to LARK 180:12

whatever that may m. CHAR 61:12

meaning Is there a m. to music COPL 77:1

joke with a double m. BARK 23:2

language charged with m. POUN 254:13

m. doubtless objectionable ANON 11:11

missed the m. ELIO 99:4

meanings With words and m. ELIO 98:15

means between ends and scarce m.

ROBB 265:5

decide all m. are permitted DAWS 84:12

end cannot justify the m. HUXL 155:6

Private M. is dead SMIT 290:3

to military m. POWE 255:4

Whatever 'in love' m. DUFF 92:8

meant it's what I m. VAUG 316:9

measles m. of the human race EINS 97:10

measured m. out my life ELIO 100:6

measurements easier to make m. SULL 301:4

meat teeth are in the real m. GRIM 134:9

mechanized m. slaughterhouses VANE 316:4

medal m. for killing two men MATL 209:15

m. glitters, but CHUR 67:2

meddle Do not m. in the affairs TOLK 310:9

media m., I tell pedants INGH 157:7

m. It sounds like STOP 299:1

medical in advance of m. thought

WODE 333:10

medicinal M. discovery AYRE 19:9

medicine mistake m. for magic SZAS 302:7

mediocre middle-aged and m. STRE 300:7

Some men are born m. HELL 145:3

Women want m. men MEAD 211:12

mediocrity M. knows nothing higher

DOYL 91:14

m. of the apparatus TROT 312:6

m. thrust upon them HELL 145:3

meditation light with m. DUNN 93:5

medium call it a m. because ACE 1:5

greatest interactive m. LYNT 196:9

m. is the message MCLU 201:7

mother and m. SZEN 302:12

meet m. 'em on your way down MIZN 217:15

militants m. like cleaning women TRUF 312:12
militarism M. a rusty sword SHAW 286:3
M. . . . is fetish worship TAWN 303:1
military close my m. career MACA 197:3
entrust to m. men CLEM 71:5
M. force MCNA 202:12
m. man approaches SHAW 284:18
to m. means POWE 255:4
milk end is moo, the other, m. NASH 227:13
Gin was mother's m. SHAW 285:20
lady loves M. Tray ADVE 3:5
m. and the yoghurt TRIL 311:12
m. of human kindness GUED 135:3
M.'s leap toward immortality FADI 106:6
m. the cow of the world WILB 328:6
Never cry over spilt m. FIEL 109:1
putting m. into babies CHUR 67:6
milka Drinka Pinta M. Day ADVE 3:16
millennium Bunyan wanted the m. HILL 148:7
end of a m. promises HEWI 147:8
million Fifty m. Frenchmen SAYI 278:14
make a m. ANON 10:2
m. deaths a statistic STAL 295:7
m. million spermatozoa HUXL 155:13
millionaire I am a M. SHAW 284:6
old-fashioned m. FISH 109:10
on a Bradford m. ELIO 101:17
Who wants to be a m. PORT 253:4
millions I will be m. EPIT 105:10
M. long for immortality ERTZ 104:7
that of m. of others LOEW 193:5
minarets Fretted with m. THWA 310:2
mind all in the m. WOLF 334:1
beat at your m. HECH 144:9
Cast your m. on other days YEAT 339:4
could not make up his m. OLIV 235:15
cutting edge of the m. BRON 45:3
don't m. if I do CATC 58:7
empires of the m. CHUR 67:7
forces of the m. PROU 257:11
Georgia on my m. GORR 131:2
If I am out of my m. BELL 28:12
m. begins to roam SOLZ 290:12
M. in its purest play WILB 328:7
m. is just like a spin-dryer NOLA 232:12
m. is maturing late NASH 228:6
m. is not a bed AGAT 2:9
m. moves upon silence YEAT 338:1
M. my bike CATC 59:1
m. of Lord Beaverbrook ATTL 15:5
m. of the oppressed BIKO 37:12
m. the least of possessions WHIT 326:6
m. watches itself CAMU 53:1
m. which reveres details LEWI 190:13
not to have a m. QUAY 258:10
no way out of the m. PLAT 250:2
regulate matters of m. TRUM 312:14

sex in the m. LAWR 184:2
they're wrong. M. it FORS 116:11
travel broadens the m.; but CHES 63:18
Until reeled the m. GIBB 127:9
violence in the m. ALDI 5:11
Why m. being wrong AYER 19:8
would know the m. of God HAWK 142:11
minded m. the opinions of others WOOL 335:6
minds fairly developed m. FORS 115:14
live close to great m. BUCH 47:11
M. like beds always made up WILL 330:7
m. of ordinary men BRON 45:5
paid to have dirty m. TREV 311:10
mine If they are m. or no HOUS 152:8
lovin' dat man of m. HAMM 137:7
M. is the only voice CAMP 52:8
she is m. for life SPAR 292:10
minefield grief is like a m. WARN 319:15
if you're fat, is a m. MARG 207:12
miners like m.' coal dust BOOT 41:9
m. sweat their guts out ORWE 238:17
Minerva owl of M. PAUL 246:1
mines m. reported in the fairway KIPL 174:10
Mineworkers National Union of M. MACM 202:7
minister m. going to run his office HEND 146:2
M. whose stubbornness JENK 161:5
Yes, M.! No, Minister CROS 81:5
ministers 'experts' make the worst M. ATTL 15:11
group of Cabinet M. CURZ 82:10
how much my M. talk THAT 305:10
m. decide THAT 306:12
mink trick of wearing m. BALM 22:6
minks LSD reminds me of m. GRAV 132:1
minor change from major to m. PORT 252:3
minority not enough to make a m. ALTM 7:1
mint m. with the hole ADVE 4:10
minuet constitutional m. SCAR 279:17
minute cannot cage the m. MACN 203:9
fill the unforgiving m. KIPL 174:6
minutes famous for fifteen m. WARH 319:4
have the seven m. COLL 73:4
rate of sixty m. an hour LEWI 190:2
Miranda remember an Inn, M. BELL 28:9
mirror not a m. but a hammer GRIE 134:2
mirrors m. and fatherhood BORG 42:3
misery great kick at m. LAWR 184:10
Man hands on m. to man LARK 180:13
m. of manilla folders ROET 266:6
misfits m., Looney Tunes REAG 262:3
misfortune prodigious siege of m. WOOL 335:12
misguided missiles and m. men KING 172:11
mislead one to m. the public ASQU 14:8
misleading bound to be m. WATS 320:7
misquotation M. is the privilege PEAR 246:6

misrule Thirteen years of Tory m.   POLI 251:22
miss *M.* means respectably unmarried
                                            CART 54:10
missed m. the bus   CHAM 60:6
  Woman much m.   HARD 140:6
misses m. family and friends   EPIT 105:11
missiles guided m. and misguided
                                            KING 172:11
missing M. so much and so much   CORN 77:6
missionaries eaten by m.   SPOO 294:7
Mississippi singing of the M.   HUGH 153:13
mistake America a gigantic m.   FREU 119:2
  author made a m.   DIRA 90:5
  make a m., it's a beaut   LA G 178:12
  m. shall not be repeated   EPIT 105:13
  Shome m., shurely   CATC 59:6
mistakes genius makes no m.   JOYC 165:10
  If he makes m.   CHUR 68:12
  m. of the past   TAYL 303:13
  some of the worst m.   HEIS 144:12
misunderstood through being m.   COCT 72:6
mites with m. of stars   MAYA 211:3
Mitty Walter M., the undefeated   THUR 309:15
moanday m., tearsday, wailsday   JOYC 164:9
mob I lied to please the m.   KIPL 173:13
mockingbird kill a m.   LEE 186:17
model m. of modern Prime Minister
                                            HENN 146:6
moderate white m. devoted to   KING 172:4
moderation m. in the pursuit   GOLD 130:2
  M. the highest virtue   JOHN 163:5
modern called a 'M. Churchman'   WAUG 321:1
  m. Prime Minister   HENN 146:6
modest good deal to be m. about   CHUR 67:15
  M.? My word, no   REED 262:12
mois *m. des floraisons*   ARAG 12:10
molecule inhales one m. of it   JEAN 160:6
molecules cells and associated m.   CRIC 79:13
  without understanding m.   CRIC 80:1
moll King's M. Reno'd   NEWS 231:10
Moloch M., national sovereignty   MEYE 214:1
mom place called M.'s   ALGR 5:14
moment Exhaust the little m.   BROO 46:5
  m. of my greatness flicker   ELIO 100:8
  one brief shining m.   LERN 188:12
momentary Beauty m. in the mind
                                            STEV 297:15
momentum M. part of exhilaration   LAHR 179:1
monarch m. of the road   FLAN 113:16
  relations with the M.   BLAI 39:5
monarchy m. become only popular   ST J 273:9
  M. is labour-intensive   WILS 331:10
  US presidency a Tudor m.   BURG 49:5
Monday Cold on M.   HART 141:12
money ain't got a barrel of m.   WOOD 334:14
  bank will lend you m. if   HOPE 152:3
  Capitalism is using its m.   CAST 56:2

  corrupted by m.   GREE 132:5
  divided up their m.   STEA 295:11
  doing it for m.   PHIL 248:7
  enough m. not to bother   PUNT 258:1
  haven't got the m.   RUTH 272:15
  Having m. like being blonde   QUAN 258:7
  He had m. as well   THAT 305:9
  Hollywood m. isn't money   PARK 243:19
  home for lack of m.   LARK 180:7
  if you can count your m.   GETT 127:7
  If you have m. you spend it   KENN 170:3
  licence to print m.   THOM 309:6
  listen to m. singing   LARK 181:3
  long enough to get m. from   LEAC 185:6
  lost m. by underestimating   MENC 213:2
  m. can't buy me love   LENN 188:3
  M. couldn't buy friends   MILL 216:1
  M. doesn't talk, it swears   DYLA 94:6
  M. gives me pleasure   BELL 28:1
  m. gushes into politics   WHIT 326:11
  M. is like a sixth sense   MAUG 210:8
  m. I spend on advertising   LEVE 189:7
  M. was exactly like sex   BALD 20:11
  must put the m. in   BULL 48:5
  Never ask of m. spent   FROS 120:9
  not having any m.   WHIT 327:7
  not spending m. alone   EISE 97:12
  only interested in m.   SHAW 286:4
  poet can earn more m.   AUDE 18:3
  poetry in m.   GRAV 131:15
  rub up against m.   RUNY 270:8
  sell, and make m.   HARR 141:3
  state can be master of m.   BEVE 37:4
  Take the m. and run   ALLE 6:11
  they have more m.   FITZ 112:18
  They hired the m.   COOL 76:6
  to get all that m.   CHES 64:4
  use the m. for the poor   PERÓ 247:3
  voice is full of m.   FITZ 113:2
  voter who uses his m.   SAMU 274:9
  what to do with their m.   BARA 22:15
  When you have m., it's sex   DONL 90:10
Mongolia British Outer M.   BENN 29:13
mongrels energetic m.   FISH 109:5
monkey attack the m.   BEVA 36:10
  make a m. of a man   BENC 29:2
monkeys m. banging on typewriters
                                            WILE 329:1
  m. strumming on typewriters   EDDI 95:2
  you get m.   SAYI 278:19
monks m. at Clonmacnoise   HEAN 143:14
monogamy M. is the same   ANON 9:4
monologue m. is not a decision   ATTL 15:4
monopoly best of all m. profits   HICK 148:3
  m. stage of capitalism   LENI 187:5
Monroe mouth of Marilyn M.   MITT 217:14

monster this busy m., manunkind

CUMM 81:14

monstrous m. carbuncle CHAR 61:13
M. carbuncles SPEN 293:4
m. either one apart RANS 260:2
With m. head CHES 62:4
month April is the cruellest m. ELIO 101:6
m. of metamorphoses ARAG 12:10
m. of tension LESS 189:2
monument m. sticks like fishbone LOWE 195:9
only m. the asphalt road ELIO 101:1
moo One end is m. NASH 227:13
moocow m. coming down along JOYC 164:12
moon Don't let's ask for the m. FILM 110:2
landing a man on the M. KENN 169:8
land on the m. KOES 177:9
m. belongs to everyone DE S 88:12
m. in lonely alleys CRAN 79:7
m. is in the seventh house RADO 259:6
m. shone bright ELIO 101:14
m. walks the night DE L 87:19
Old Devil M. in your eyes HARB 138:10
only a paper m. HARB 138:9
Only you beneath the m. PORT 252:16
respond to landings on M. STEI 296:13
when the m. was blood CHES 62:4
moonlight m. and music BERL 32:12
M. behind you COWA 78:11
moonlit Knocking on the m. door DE L 87:16
starlit or a m. dome YEAT 336:14
moral demands m. earnestness LEWI 190:9
Englishman thinks he is m. SHAW 284:16
form of m. insurance BROD 45:1
It *is* a m. issue NEWS 231:7
m. as soon as unhappy PROU 257:12
M. indignation is jealousy WELL 323:12
more m. than a wife PHIL 248:7
No m. system can rest AYER 19:5
not just a m. category SOLZ 291:1
party is a m. crusade WILS 331:3
moralist problem for the m. RUSS 271:6
moralists delight to m. RUSS 272:5
morality Goodbye, m. HERB 146:11
know about m. CAMU 53:5
market has no m. HESE 147:2
middle-class m. SHAW 285:19
M. in the novel LAWR 183:11
M.'s a gesture BOLT 41:4
two kinds of m. RUSS 272:2
What is m. WHIT 326:16
morals Food first, then m. BREC 44:2
more believing m. and more YATE 336:10
knows m. and more MAYO 211:10
Less is m. ROHE 267:2
m. and more about less BUTL 50:6
m. equal than others ORWE 237:12
m. Piglet wasn't there MILN 216:5

m. than somewhat RUNY 270:9
M. will mean worse AMIS 8:2
morning autumn arrives in the m. BOWE 42:8
Come, lovely M. DAVI 84:3
getting married in the m. LERN 188:13
Good m., sir CATC 57:19
hate to get up in the m. BERL 32:13
m. again in America POLI 251:14
m. had been golden CHUR 68:4
M. has broken FARJ 106:8
m. light creaks down SITW 288:2
take you in the m. BALD 21:1
what a beautiful m. HAMM 137:12
Mornington present of M. Crescent

HARG 140:13

Morocco we're M. bound BURK 49:7
moron consumer isn't a m. OGIL 234:11
IQ of a m. VIDA 317:14
See the happy m. ANON 11:5
Morris M. Minor prototype NUFF 233:3
mortal M., guilty, but to me AUDE 16:17
mortals startle Composing m. AUDE 15:14
mortar daub of untempered m. HOUS 152:11
Lies are the m. WELL 323:8
Moscow do not march on M. MONT 220:13
mosquito just another m. OKPI 234:15
moss miles of golden m. AUDE 16:7
moth Both m. and flam ROET 266:8
mother artist man and m. woman

SHAW 284:13

Can you hear me, m. CATC 57:8
Did this happen to your m. WALK 318:8
half knew my m. O'BR 233:14
have a beautiful m. WALK 318:11
her m. rather than she SPAR 292:7
I have been a m. to you O'DO 234:9
man who hates his m. BENN 31:14
m. and medium SZEN 302:12
M. died today CAMU 53:4
m. of a great son KENN 170:4
m. of all battles HUSS 155:2
M. of the Free BENS 31:15
m.'s little helper JAGG 158:10
m. taught me as a boy BERR 34:7
M. to dozens HERB 146:12
m. will be there HERB 146:7
plans to resemble: her m. BROO 46:3
rob his m. FAUL 107:4
Took great care of his M. MILN 216:12
mothers Come m. and fathers DYLA 94:14
m. go on getting blamed WHIT 327:6
m. no longer sing MENU 213:7
sorrows of the m. FREN 118:8
mothers-in-law m. and Wigan Pier BRID 44:8
motion Between the m. And the act

ELIO 99:18

poetry in m. KAUF 167:4

motor heart's stalled m.   MAYA 211:7
motorcycle art of m. maintenance   PIRS 249:14
mould frozen in an out-of-date m.   JENK 161:3
mountain Climb ev'ry m.   HAMM 137:8
  go up to the m.   KING 172:9
  In a m. greenery   HART 141:9
mountains m. to the prairies   BERL 32:11
  river jumps over the m.   AUDE 15:15
mourn no cause to m.   OWEN 241:4
mourning Don't waste time in m.   HILL 148:13
  M. becomes Electra   O'NE 236:4
mouth Englishman to open his m.

                                                                        SHAW 285:16
  Keep your m. shut   OFFI 235:13
  m. of Marilyn Monroe   MITT 217:14
  m.. used as a latrine   AMIS 7:8
  My m. went across   NERU 229:9
  silver foot in his m.   RICH 264:7
  z is keeping your m. shut   EINS 97:4
mouthful filling in a m. of decay   OSBO 240:7
mouthless millions of the m. dead   SORL 292:2
mouths examining his wives' m.   RUSS 271:12
  poets keep our m. shut   YEAT 338:5
  stuffed their m. with gold   BEVA 37:1
movable Paris is a m. feast   HEMI 145:12
move feel the earth m.   HEMI 145:10
moved We shall not be m.   SAYI 279:11
moves If it m., salute it   SAYI 278:18
movie could direct a m.   HYTN 156:1
  on the m. set   REAG 262:6
movies M. should have a beginning

                                                                        GODA 129:7
  pay to see bad m.   GOLD 130:7
  thing that can kill the m.   ROGE 266:10
Mozart Children are given M.   SCHN 280:5
  en famille, they play M.   BART 24:7
  no female M.   PAGL 241:16
  when M. was my age   LEHR 187:1
MP Being an M.   ABBO 1:1
  Being an M.   PARR 244:14
MPs healthy cynicism of M.   CREW 79:12
Mrs M. respectably married   CART 54:10
Ms M. means nudge, nudge   CART 54:10
much Missing so m. and so much   CORN 77:6
  M. as you said you were   HARD 139:13
  not m. for them to be   COMP 74:1
  Sing 'em m.   MELB 212:8
  so m. owed by so many   CHUR 66:7
muckrakes men with the m.   ROOS 268:5
mud M.! Glorious mud   FLAN 113:14
  pure clay of time's m.   MALA 205:5
muddle beginning, a m.   LARK 181:6
  middle-of-the-road m.   WILS 331:13
mudging fudging and m.   OWEN 240:11
mug drink Guinness from thick m.   PINT 249:8
mulatto Grape is my m. mother   HUGH 154:5

mum fuck you up, your m. and dad

                                                                        LARK 180:12
  oafish louts remember M.   BETJ 34:12
mumble When in doubt, m.   BORE 41:10
murder about a m.   ORWE 237:15
  brought m. into the home   HITC 149:8
  commit a m.   VAN 316:1
  m. by the throat   LLOY 192:11
  M. is a serious business   ILES 156:6
  m. respectable   ORWE 239:6
  m. the thinker   WESK 323:17
  not m. but the restoration   JAME 159:16
  stick to m. and leave art   EPST 104:5
  to m., for the truth   ADLE 2:3
  We hear war called m.   MACD 199:2
murderer m. for fancy prose style   NABO 226:14
  shoot your m.   ACHE 1:6
murderers m. of Jewish children   WIES 328:4
Murdoch wrapped in a M. newspaper

                                                                        ROYK 270:3

Muscles M. better and nerves more

                                                                        CUMM 82:2
muse Can a m. of fire exist   OLIV 235:18
  tenth American m.   BRON 45:6
  Why does my M. only speak   SMIT 289:15
museum ace caff with a nice m.   ADVE 3:2
  m. inside our heads   LIVE 191:14
mush m. and slush   OWEN 240:11
mushroom supramundane m.   LAUR 181:14
  too short to stuff a m.   CONR 75:8
music all m. is folk music   ARMS 13:3
  Beauty in m.   IVES 158:2
  body swayed to m.   YEAT 336:11
  'classic' m. eliminates   STRA 300:2
  Classic m. is th'kind   HUBB 153:8
  dance to the m. of time   POWE 254:20
  Darling of the m. halls   SMIT 289:4
  day the m. died   MCLE 200:10
  don't like my m.   LOEW 193:5
  English may not like m.   BEEC 26:14
  Good m. is that which   BEEC 26:13
  how potent cheap m. is   COWA 78:16
  I got m.   GERS 127:1
  Is there a meaning to m.   COPL 77:1
  Let's face the m. and dance   BERL 32:12
  most civilized m.   USTI 315:6
  M. begins to atrophy   POUN 254:8
  m. business is not   MORR 222:10
  m. expresses itself   STRA 300:5
  M. is feeling, then   STEV 297:14
  M. is your own experience   PARK 242:11
  M. makes you feel   HARB 138:14
  m. that excels   FISH 109:9
  m. the brandy of the damned   SHAW 284:14
  My m. is best understood   STRA 300:3
  sound of m.   HAMM 137:15
  twang, and you've got m.   VICI 317:4

music (*cont.*):
  What do you think about m.   VAUG 316:10
  What m. is more enchanting   SMIT 289:7
  worth expressing in m.   DELI 87:22
musical kind of m. Malcolm Sargent
                        BEEC 26:16
musician m., if he's a messenger   HEND 146:4
Muslims zealous M. to execute   KHOM 171:7
must m. do what they most want   AUDE 18:13
  you m. go on   BECK 25:15
mute any part except that of m.   MACM 202:2
mutilate fold, spindle or m.   SAYI 278:12
mutton what m. tastes like   MAUG 210:11
myriad There died a m.   POUN 254:2
myself m. that I remake   YEAT 337:13
mystery grasped m. of the atom   BRAD 43:2
  I had m.   OWEN 241:5
  riddle wrapped in a m.   CHUR 66:1
myth m. not a fairy story   RYLE 273:1
myths Science must begin with m.   POPP 252:7
  where m. Go when they die   FENT 107:10

nabobs nattering n.   AGNE 5:1
nagging N. is the repetition   SUMM 301:7
nail I n. my pictures together   SCHW 281:10
  walks away with the n.   LAWR 183:10
nailing n. his colours   FIEL 108:4
nails n. upon the cross   SITW 288:4
naive children are n.   NASH 227:12
  n. domestic Burgundy   THUR 309:12
  n. forgive and forget   SZAS 302:5
naked n. ape   MORR 222:4
  n. into the conference chamber   BEVA 36:11
name by a scribbled n.   THOM 307:6
  In the n. of God, go   AMER 7:5
  know, yet can't quite n.   LARK 180:10
  n. at the top of the page   CHUR 68:5
  n. is history   THWA 310:2
  n. liveth for evermore   EPIT 105:15
  n. of a man is numbing blow   MCLU 201:8
  n. of the goddess   SPEN 293:2
  prefer a self-made n.   HAND 138:4
  problem that has no n.   FRIE 119:3
  problem that has no n.   FRIE 119:5
  spell my n. right   COHA 72:10
  state with the prettiest n.   BISH 38:5
  what was done in his n.   BENN 30:1
  with n. and nation   BUNT 48:8
  writing our n. there   HEAN 143:9
nameless intolerably n. names   SASS 277:1
names confused things with n.   SART 276:7
  in love with American n.   BENÉ 29:8
  n. of all these particles   FERM 107:13
naming n. of parts   REED 262:9
napalm smell of n. in the morning   FILM 110:13
Napoleon thinks he is N.   CLEM 71:2

Napoleons Caesars and N.   HUXL 155:7
nastier how much n. I would be   WAUG 321:19
nastiest n. thing in nicest way   GOLD 129:13
nasty n. in the woodshed   GIBB 127:8
  when we turn n.   PARR 244:13
NATO N. exists for three reasons   ISMA 157:15
nation AMERICA thus top n.   SELL 282:14
  broad mass of a n.   HITL 149:14
  create a n. Europe   MONN 220:6
  exterminate a n.   SPOC 294:6
  ghosts of a n.   PEAR 246:5
  n. at his service   POMP 250:13
  n. engaged in heaping up   POWE 255:7
  n. fit to sit in judgement   WILS 332:2
  n.'s collective memory   POWE 255:15
  N. shall speak peace   REND 263:3
  n. talking to itself   MILL 215:10
  n. that had lion's heart   CHUR 67:17
  one-third of a n.   ROOS 267:10
  take a n.'s pulse   WHIT 326:2
  terrorize a whole n.   MURR 226:4
  what our N. stands for   BETJ 35:6
  with name and n.   BUNT 48:8
national N. Debt a very Good Thing
                        SELL 282:12
  n. dish no longer   JEAN 160:4
  n. home for the Jewish people   BALF 21:11
nationalism N. is an infantile   EINS 97:10
  n. is a silly cock   ALDI 5:9
nations Europe of n.   DE G 87:1
  n. acted like gangsters   KUBR 178:8
  n. which have put mankind   INGE 157:1
  Other n. use 'force'   WAUG 321:12
native England's n. people   BURN 49:8
  our ideas about the n.   LESS 189:1
nattering n. nabobs   AGNE 5:1
natural n. party of government   WILS 331:7
  N. selection a mechanism   FISH 109:12
nature Defying n., it surpasses   PAGL 241:13
  deposes Mother N.   HUGH 154:6
  heartless, witless n.   HOUS 152:8
  interpreted n. as freely   GIRA 128:11
  left-wing, like n.   DEBR 86:4
  n. cannot be fooled   FEYN 108:2
  N., Mr Allnutt, is what   FILM 111:10
  n. replaces it with   WILL 329:11
  n.'s way of telling you   SAYI 278:10
  n. turns girls into women   STEV 297:2
  whatever N. has in store   FERM 107:14
naught n. for your comfort   CHES 61:18
naughty N. but nice   FILM 112:12
naval N. tradition   CHUR 67:13
navy head of the N.   CARS 54:6
Neanderthal of N. man   STRA 299:19
necessarily ain't n. so   HEYW 147:12
  Not n. conscription   KING 172:15
necessary journey *really* n.   OFFI 235:7

sometimes it is n.   ADAM 2:1
necessities which were n.   WRIG 336:5
neck at last wrings its n.   RUSS 271:17
    Some chicken! Some n.   CHUR 67:1
necklace with our n.   MAND 206:4
need All you n. is love   LENN 188:1
    enough for everyone's n.   BUCH 48:1
    face of total n.   BURR 49:11
    People who n. people   MERR 213:15
    things that people don't n.   WARH 319:7
    Will you still n. me   LENN 188:9
negative Europe the unfinished n.
      MCCA 197:10
    n. waiting to be slipped   WILS 330:15
    prefers a n. peace   KING 172:4
negotiate n. out of fear   KENN 169:5
    not here to n.   TRIM 312:1
negotiating N. with de Valera   LLOY 192:17
Negro American N. problem   BALD 20:10
    life of the N. race   DARR 83:7
    N.'s great stumbling block   KING 172:4
    one drop of N. blood   HUGH 153:14
    places where the average N.   DAVI 84:4
Negroes culture of the N.   PADE 241:9
neighbour policy of the good n.   ROOS 267:8
neighbourhood narrow into a n.   JOHN 162:13
neighbours make good n.   FROS 120:12
    will the n. say   HARD 139:4
Nell Little N. and Lady Macbeth   WOOL 335:18
nerve do not lose my n.   NEHR 229:2
    n. has been extracted   ROWL 269:13
nerves Muscles better and n. more   CUMM 82:2
nervous approaching n. breakdown
      RUSS 271:7
nessun N. *dorma*   ADAM 1:10
net surfing the N.   ELIZ 103:2
nets try to fly by those n.   JOYC 164:13
nettles dust on the n.   THOM 308:7
neurosis n. is a secret   TYNA 314:11
    N. is a way of avoiding   TILL 310:4
neurotics come to us from n.   PROU 257:7
neuter aggressively n.   BETJ 35:10
neutral apart, studiously n.   WILS 332:4
neutrality Armed n.   WILS 332:6
    Just for a word 'n.'   BETH 34:10
    N. helps the oppressor   WIES 328:2
neutrinos N., they are very small   UPDI 315:3
never N. explain   FISH 109:7
    n. had it so good   MACM 201:17
    N. in the field   CHUR 66:7
    N. knowingly undersold   ADVE 4:12
    N. mind the quality   POWE 255:17
    N. on Sunday   FILM 112:13
    N. to have lived is best   YEAT 337:14
    second things n.   CONR 75:9
    We n. closed   VAN 315:18
new beginning of a n. month   MANN 206:13

Few n. truths have ever won   BERL 33:7
    is to N. Labour   LAHR 179:2
    kill you in a n. way   ROGE 266:17
    n. clichés   GOLD 130:10
    n. deal   ROOS 267:6
    New Labour, n. danger   POLI 251:20
    n. world order   BUSH 50:5
    no n. thing has ever arisen   LAWR 183:13
    no n. truths   MCCA 197:13
    nothing n. in dying   LAST 182:8
    shock of the n.   DUNL 93:1
    so quite n. a thing   CUMM 82:2
    wrote MAKE IT N.   POUN 253:14
    Youth is something very n.   CHAN 61:3
Newcastle No more coals to N.   GEOR 126:7
New England charge against N.   KRUT 178:6
news good n. yet to hear   CHES 62:12
    HERE IS THE N.   HEAN 144:3
    how much n. there is   DOUG 91:8
    man bites a dog, that is n.   BOGA 40:8
    n. into sausage factory   PAXM 246:2
    news that STAYS n.   POUN 254:11
    only n. until he's read it   WAUG 321:10
    that ain't n.   SIMP 287:13
    told bad n. to American   KEIL 168:5
New South Wales govern N.   BELL 27:13
newspaper n. is a nation talking   MILL 215:10
    n. is to be Accurate   SWOP 301:12
    n. touches a story   MAIL 204:12
    Whenever I see a n.   MENU 213:6
    wrapped in a Murdoch n.   ROYK 270:3
newspapers All succesful n.   MENC 212:16
    don't actually read n.   MCLU 201:11
    n. I can't stand   STOP 299:2
    n. paid too much   MURD 226:3
    read the n. avidly   BEVA 36:14
    writing for the n.   LEWI 190:14
Newton another N., a new Donne   HUXL 155:13
    N. in his garden   AUDE 17:5
New York gullet of N.   MILL 215:8
    to the N. Island   GUTH 135:12
New Yorker N. will be   ROSS 269:2
next At forty-five, what n.   LOWE 195:11
    n. thing I do   DIAN 89:10
    n. to god america   CUMM 81:9
Nibelungen N. is for the European
      LANG 179:16
nice involving not very n. people   FRAN 118:2
    Naughty but n.   FILM 112:12
    N. guys   PARR 244:13
    N. guys. Finish last   DURO 93:8
    N. one, Cyril   ADVE 4:13
    n. to people on your way up   MIZN 217:15
    N. to see you   CATC 59:2
    N. work if you can get it   GERS 127:5
    not about being n.   KEAT 168:2
    thoroughly n. people   PYM 258:5

nicely That'll do n.	ADVE 3:4	love the n. it makes	BEEC 26:14
nicens n. little boy	JOYC 164:12	n.! And the people	ANON 10:13
nicest nastiest thing in n. way	GOLD 129:13	n. is an effective means	GOEB 129:10
niche your n. in creation	HALL 137:3	prisoners of n.	MORE 221:10
nigger n. of the world	ONO 236:7	**noisy** into the n. crowd	TAGO 302:14
night blue of the n.	CROS 80:9	**non-being** avoiding n.	TILL 310:4
dark n. of the soul	FITZ 113:7	**non-combatant** no fury like a n.	MONT 220:9
fit n. out for man or beast	FIEL 108:11	**non-cooperation** n. with evil	GAND 124:12
gentle into that good n.	THOM 307:2	**nonexistent** obsolescent and n.	BREN 44:6
hard day's n.	LENN 188:6	**nonsense** firm anchor in n.	GALB 123:5
Illness the n.-side of life	SONT 291:17	**non-violence** N. the first article	GAND 124:11
journey into n.	O'NE 236:3	**Norfan** N., both sides	WELL 323:6
moon walks the n.	DE L 87:19	**Norfolk** bear him up the N. sky	BETJ 34:15
n. after tonight	AMIS 8:1	Very flat, N.	COWA 78:15
N. and day, you	PORT 252:16	**normal** n. and easy	JAME 159:3
N. Mail crossing the Border	AUDE 17:4	N. is the good smile	SHAF 283:7
n. of the long knives	HITL 149:10	we're n.	OSBO 239:16
n. starvation	ADVE 3:24	**north** answer from the N.	KIPL 175:6
returned on the previous n.	BULL 48:6	heart of the N. is dead	LAWR 184:14
something of the n.	WIDD 328:1	He was my N., my South	AUDE 16:8
night-club taking the floor in n.	MUGG 224:10	to us the near n.	MENZ 213:8
nightgowns tweed n.	GING 128:3	**northern** N. reticence	HEAN 144:4
nightingale n. sang in Berkeley	MASC 209:13	**nose** blow his n. without	CONN 75:2
nightingales n. are singing near	ELIO 101:5	run up your n. dead against	BALD 21:10
nightmare History is a n.	JOYC 165:6	thirty inches from my n.	AUDE 17:8
In the n. of the dark	AUDE 16:13	very shiny n.	MARK 207:14
national n. is over	FORD 115:5	what lies under one's n.	AUDE 18:9
third act in a n.	BEER 26:23	**noses** where the n. would go	HEMI 145:9
Nile looked upon the N.	HUGH 153:13	**nostalgia** N. isn't what it used	ANON 10:15
nineties n. is a good time to die	SPEN 294:3	**not** find out what you are *n.*	LOY 196:3
ninety live to be over n.	ABBO 1:2	n. I, but the wind	LAWR 184:7
Nineveh temple, poets, N.	MEYN 214:2	N. so much a programme	ANON 10:16
nix Sticks n. hick pix	NEWS 231:11	N. while I'm alive	BEVI 37:10
Nixon N. impeached himself	ABZU 1:4	say 'Why n.'	SHAW 283:11
no art of leadership is saying n.	BLAI 38:11	**note** longest suicide n.	KAUF 167:2
can't say N. in any of them	PARK 243:14	**notebook** in a little n.	LASK 181:8
It's n. go the merrygoround	MACN 202:14	**notes** n. I handle no better	SCHN 280:8
land of the omnipotent N.	BOLD 41:2	small *quantity* of the n.	SCHN 280:5
man who says n.	CAMU 53:2	**nothing** don't believe in n.	CHES 64:7
N.! No! No	THAT 306:14	Emperors can do n.	BREC 43:14
she said 'n.'	ALLE 6:14	individually can do n.	ALLE 6:6
Noah N. he often said to his wife	CHES 63:2	N. ain't worth nothin'	KRIS 178:5
one poor N.	HUXL 155:13	N. happens, nobody comes	BECK 26:5
Nobel dinner for N. Prizewinners	KENN 169:11	N. is ever done	SHAW 284:11
nobility n. without pride	DUNC 92:11	N., like something	LARK 180:8
noble days of the N. Savage	BIKO 37:11	N. to be done	BECK 26:1
nobody N. came	GINS 128:6	n. to look backward to	FROS 120:3
n.'s going to stop 'em	BERR 34:1	n. to say	CAGE 51:2
n.'s perfect	FILM 111:16	resent having n.	COMP 74:2
n. tells me anything	GALS 124:5	whatever you say, say n.	HEAN 144:4
n. will come	SAND 275:3	You ain't heard n. yet	JOLS 163:14
Nothing happens, nobody comes	BECK 26:5	**nothingness** N. haunts being	SART 276:2
there is n. there	KEYN 171:5	**notice** has not escaped our n.	CRIC 80:2
nod Old N., the shepherd	DE L 87:18	man who used to n.	HARD 139:4
one great n. after the other	NOLA 232:12	**noun** verb not a n.	FULL 122:2
noise Go placidly amid the n.	EHRM 96:5	**novel** got the n.	HILL 148:7
loud n. at one end	KNOX 177:3	Morality in the n.	LAWR 183:11

n. gets up and walks away   LAWR 183:10
n. is the one bright book   LAWR 183:14
n. tells a story   FORS 115:15
n. was self-administered   O'BR 233:11
novelist n. must preserve   MAUG 210:10
novelists great—the major n.   LEAV 185:15
novels ideal reader of my n.   BURG 49:4
  sex in yesterday's n.   WELD 322:11
  you lose two n.   MCWI 203:11
now We are the masters n.   MISQ 219:3
nowness n. of everything   POTT 253:5
nuclear n. arms race has no   MOUN 224:2
  n. giants   BRAD 43:3
nudge nudge n., snap snap   MONT 221:1
nuisance exchange of one n.   ELLI 103:11
  n. in time of war   CHUR 67:8
nuisances small n. of peace-time   HAY 142:12
NUM against the Pope or the N.   BALD 21:10
number best n. for a dinner party   GULB 135:8
  called the wrong n.   THUR 309:13
  I am not a n.   MCGO 199:7
  n. of the question   CHUR 68:5
  very interesting n.   RAMA 260:1
numbers Noting the n. of trains   MAXW 211:1
  n. that rocket the mind   WILB 328:5
numerical n. irrigation system   AUGA 18:17
Nuremberg of the N. trials   SHAW 286:8
  prosecution at N.   JACK 158:6
nurse always keep a-hold of N.   BELL 27:12
nursery century's cool n.   AKHM 5:5
nuts N.   MCAU 197:5

oafish o. louts remember Mum   BETJ 34:12
oafs muddied o. at the goals   KIPL 174:7
oak juniper talks to the o.   PAUL 245:15
  O., and Ash, and Thorn   KIPL 175:3
  o. would sprout in Derry   HEAN 144:2
oasis If O. are bigger than God   CHIS 64:12
oaths Judges must follow their o.   ZOBE 341:9
oats feeds the horse enough o.   GALB 123:10
obit turning up on the o. pages   SULL 301:3
obituary except your own o.   BEHA 27:4
  o. in serial form   CRIS 80:4
objectification o. of feeling   LANG 180:1
objectionable meaning doubtless o.
                                          ANON 11:11
objective o. correlative   ELIO 102:1
obligation o. goes unrecognized   WEIL 322:4
obliteration policy is o.   BELL 27:8
oblivion over o.   HARD 139:14
obscenity 'o.' is not a term   RUSS 272:6
observer keen o. of life   AUDE 17:3
obsolescence planned o.   STEV 297:3
obsolescent o. and nonexistent   BREN 44:6
obsolete war is o. or men are   FULL 122:4
occurred Ought never to have o.   BENT 32:3

ocean drop in the o.   TERE 304:5
  Earth when it is clearly O.   CLAR 70:6
  love you till the o.   AUDE 15:15
oceans To the o. white with foam   BERL 32:11
October O., that ambiguous month
                                          LESS 189:2
octopus dear o.   SMIT 289:1
odd But not so o.   BROW 46:15
  How o. Of God   EWER 106:4
  must think it exceedingly o. KNOX 176:17
odds how am I to face the o.   HOUS 152:5
  mass of o. and ends   WOOL 335:11
odium lived in the o.   BENT 32:4
Odysseus O. was a bastard   CROS 80:13
offence I was like to give o.   FROS 120:13
  only defence is in o.   BALD 21:7
offend freedom to o.   RUSH 270:11
offensive extremely o.   SMIT 289:3
  Life is an o.   WHIT 326:12
  what is merely o.   EPHR 104:4
offer o. he can't refuse   PUZO 258:3
office holding public o.   ACHE 1:7
  in o. but not in power   LAMO 179:12
  O. before honour   POWE 255:10
  O. builds up a man only if   BENN 29:15
  o. is going to run him   HEND 146:2
  o. party is not   WHIT 327:9
  Whichever party is in o.   WILS 331:12
official No sane local o.   SMIT 288:14
  This high o., all allow   HERB 146:13
officialism Where there is o.   FORS 116:16
officials O. take different view   ROTH 269:10
  persistence of o.   LEVI 189:9
offspring human animal for its o.   SHAW 284:2
oil as providers they're o. wells   PARK 243:18
  foreign o. controlling   DYLA 94:13
  like an o. painting   INGH 157:7
  sound of o. wells   FISH 109:9
oiled O. his way around the floor   LERN 188:21
OK O. We lost   MAJO 205:3
Okie O. means you're scum   STEI 296:10
old attendance on my o. age   YEAT 338:17
  die before I get o.   TOWN 310:14
  first sign of o. age   HICK 148:4
  Growing o. a bad habit   MAUR 210:15
  Growing o. is like   POWE 255:2
  heart grows o.   YEAT 338:16
  HOW O. CARY GRANT   TELE 305:5
  I grow o. . . . I grow old   ELIO 100:10
  make me conservative when o. FROS 120:14
  no country for o. men   YEAT 338:9
  not bored is never o.   CASA 55:8
  now am not too o.   BLUN 39:13
  o. age always fifteen years BARU 24:10
  O. age is the most unexpected TROT 312:7
  O. age should burn   THOM 307:2
  o. age, the last gap but one WHIT 326:5

old (*cont.*):

o. heads on young shoulders SPAR 292:9
o. is having lighted rooms LARK 180:10
o. Lie: Dulce et decorum OWEN 240:17
o. man in a dry month ELIO 99:13
O. man river HAMM 137:13
O. soldiers never die FOLE 114:12
outrageous o. fellow HOYL 153:5
planned by o. men RICE 264:1
that horror—the o. woman COLE 72:16
They shall grow not o. BINY 37:13
they were o. too MAUG 210:1
too o. to rush up to the net ADAM 1:13
warn you not to grow o. KINN 173:5
When I am an o. woman JOSE 164:4
older Another day o. TRAV 311:3
ask somebody o. than me BLAK 39:6
for us o. ones ELIZ 102:14
grow o. and older SAYE 277:7
O. men declare war HOOV 151:12
so much o. then DYLA 94:11
old-fashioned o. millionaire FISH 109:10
omelettes make o. properly BELL 28:11
omens grievous o. SUTT 301:9
omnibus horse power o. FLAN 113:16
omnipotent land of the o. No BOLD 41:2
Onassis O. would not have married
VIDA 317:13
once o. and future king WHIT 326:8
one But the O. was Me HUXL 155:13
centre upon number o. CHUR 68:12
How to be o. up POTT 253:9
o. for my baby MERC 213:12
square root of minus o. BECK 26:11
oneself Hell is o. ELIO 98:5
only If you were the o. girl GREY 133:14
It's the o. thing SAND 275:6
O. connect FORS 116:9
O. the lonely ORBI 236:12
onwards o. and upwards YORK 340:3
oozing O. charm from every pore LERN 188:21
open in the great o. spaces MARQ 208:6
O. covenants of peace WILS 332:9
opera o. ain't over SAYI 279:4
O. is when a guy gets GARD 125:3
operas German text of French o. WHAR 325:11
operatic so romantic, so o. PROU 257:6
operations o. we can perform WHIT 327:2
opinion form a clear o. BONH 41:6
Government and public o. SHAW 284:15
o. has been widely held RUSS 271:14
what is my o. LOEW 193:5
whole climate of o. AUDE 16:9
opinions men who have no o. CHES 63:6
minded the o. of others WOOL 335:6
opponents o. eventually die PLAN 250:1
opportunity maximum of o. SHAW 285:3

o. for achievement KEIL 168:4
unfettered o. of remaining MADA 203:12
when he had the o. ROWL 269:15
opposite o. of people STOP 299:7
opposites o. are obviously absurd BOHR 40:11
opposition effective means of o. GOEB 129:10
oppressed mind of the o. BIKO 37:12
oppression violence and o. SOLZ 291:2
oppressor Neutrality helps the o. WIES 328:2
weapon in hands of o. BIKO 37:12
opprobrium term of o. MOYN 224:4
optimist o. is a guy MARQ 208:4
o. proclaims CABE 50:13
optimistic o. for the moment BROD 44:11
opulence private o. GALB 123:6
oracles earth's green o. SUTT 301:9
oral o. contraception ALLE 6:14
orange clockwork o. BURG 49:1
happen to be an o. ALLE 6:4
oratory Parliamentary o. CRIT 80:5
orchestra golden rules for an o. BEEC 26:17
o. play as they like BEEC 26:15
o. playing to the rich AUDE 16:2
signals to the o. SZEL 302:10
orchestration o. of platitudes WILD 328:15
order cannot bring o. MCNA 202:12
inspire o. in the world THOM 309:4
more devoted to o. KING 172:4
new world o. BUSH 50:5
not necessarily in that o. GODA 129:7
o. of the acts is planned PAST 245:7
restoration of o. JAME 159:16
war creates o. BREC 43:13
wretched rage for o. MAHO 204:4
ordinariness religion of *o.* WHIT 326:7
ordinary learn to see the o. BAIL 20:1
O. made beautiful SHAF 283:7
see God in the o. things AWDR 19:2
warn you not to be o. KINN 173:5
organ o. grinder is present BEVA 36:10
organic form the key to o. life PAST 245:6
organization about the o. man WHYT 327:14
o. of idolatry SHAW 284:23
organize o. her own immortality LASK 181:8
waste time mourning—o. HILL 148:13
organized it's got to be o. HOCK 150:3
organizing Only an o. genius BEVA 36:4
organs o. have been transplanted HARB 138:12
orgasm o. has replaced the Cross MUGG 224:12
original o. is unfaithful BURG 42:2
saves o. thinking SAYE 277:6
sound and o. ideas MACM 202:1
originality O. is deliberate HOFF 150:6
orphan defeat is an o. CIAN 69:10
O., both sides WELL 323:6
Oscar assume that O. said it PARK 243:4

other happens to *o.* people	CART 54:9	**paces** open an oyster at sixty p.	WODE 333:6
O. is ourselves	THOM 308:15	**pacifist** absolute p.	EINS 96:10
o. people are reading	NAIP 227:8	militant p.	EINS 96:13
o. people's children	CLIN 71:8	quietly p. peaceful	WALK 318:10
O. voices, other rooms	CAPO 53:11	**pack** changed the form of the p.	TROT 312:3
wonderful for o. people	KERR 170:9	p., and take a train	BROO 45:11
others woman who lives for o.	LEWI 190:3	p. up your troubles	ASAF 13:10
Otis Miss O. regrets	PORT 253:1	running with the p.	BUTL 50:11
ought didn't o. never to have	BEVI 37:8	**Paganini** village fiddler after P.	NICO 230:8
something o. to be done	WELL 323:13	**page** allowed P. 3 to develop	MURD 226:2
ours O. is the land	MAYA 211:8	**pageant** life's rich p.	MARS 208:15
ourselves Other is o.	THOM 308:15	**pages** life's story fills thirty-five p.	ARNO 13:7
out best way o. is always through	FROS 120:19	**paid** attention must be p.	MILL 215:5
counted them all o.	HANR 138:5	Judas was p.	POWE 255:9
get o. while we're young	SPRI 294:14	p. far too much	MURD 226:3
include me o.	GOLD 130:3	**pain** intoxication with p.	BRON 45:5
truth is o. there	CATC 59:9	she hasn't a p.	MILN 216:16
outcast o. on the world	HEWI 147:9	**painkiller** most natural p.	LAST 182:12
outer o. life of telegrams	FORS 116:8	**pains** no gains without p.	STEV 298:1
outlaw attacks from o. states	REAG 262:3	**paint** can't pick it up, p. it	SAYI 278:18
outlaws o. Russia forever	REAG 262:2	p. objects as I think them	PICA 249:3
outrageous o. old fellow	HOYL 153:5	p. with my prick	MISQ 218:7
outside just going o.	LAST 182:6	**painted** unreality of p. people	UPDI 315:5
just going o.	MAHO 204:3	**painter** I am a p.	SCHW 281:10
nothing o. of the text	DERR 88:11	paintbrush in hands of p.	PICA 248:13
ovaltine want art to be like o.	READ 261:9	**painting** essence of p.	MOND 220:1
Ovaltineys We are the O.	ADVE 4:26	like an oil p.	INGH 157:7
over ain't o. till it's over	BERR 33:17	no matter what you're p.	HOCK 150:3
oversexed, and o. here	TRIN 312:2	P. is saying 'Ta'	SPEN 293:5
O. there	COHA 72:9	p. not made to decorate	PICA 249:1
They think it's all o.	WOLS 334:10	**paints** God p. the scenery	HART 141:9
overcome We shall o.	SAYI 279:12	**pale** whiter shade of p.	REID 262:15
overlooked looked over than o.	WEST 324:2	**Palestine** establishment in P.	BALF 21:11
overpaid grossly o.	HERB 146:13	**pallor** p. of girls' brows	OWEN 240:16
O., overfed, oversexed	TRIN 312:2	**palms** p. before my feet	CHES 62:5
over-prepared o. the event	POUN 254:7	**paltry** aged man is but a p. thing	YEAT 338:10
oversexed o., and over here	TRIN 312:2	**Pam** P., I adore you, Pam	BETJ 35:11
overstated save by being o.	BERL 33:7	**Pandora** open that P.'s Box	BEVI 37:9
owed so much o. by so many	CHUR 66:7	**panic** Don't p.	ADAM 1:11
owl o. of Minerva	PAUL 246:1	with wonderful p.	HECH 144:9
own apart from my o.	GABO 122:11	**panther** Black P. Party	NEWT 230:1
for what they o.	TAYL 303:9	**pants** deck your lower limbs in p.	NASH 228:14
money and a room of her o.	WOOL 335:4	**paparazzi** p. dogs of war	DENE 88:2
only to those who o. one	LIEB 191:3	p. pictures	MURD 226:3
To each his o.	ANON 10:6	**paper** at a piece of tissue p.	RUTH 272:14
owner I am the o.	MAND 206:6	both sides of the p.	SELL 282:15
ownership common o.	ANON 11:14	By the evening p.	MACN 203:3
Oxford academia in O.	AUNG 18:18	keep the p. work down	ORTO 237:7
either O. or Cambridge	SNAG 290:9	only a p. moon	HARB 138:9
heart was with the O. men	LETT 189:4	personality than a p. cup	CHAN 60:8
secret in the O. sense	FRAN 118:5	ran the p. for propaganda	BEAV 25:8
sends his son to O.	STEA 295:12	reactionaries are p. tigers	MAO 207:7
Oxford University Press by the O.	YOUN 340:5	scrap of p.	BETH 34:10
oxygen o. of publicity	THAT 306:7	truth-divulging p.	GREE 132:16
oyster eye that can open an o.	WODE 333:6	worth the p. it is written	GOLD 130:4
world is an o.	MILL 215:4	**papers** go to the p.	CLAR 70:1
		He's got my p.	PINT 249:9

pennies P. don't fall from heaven | THAT 305:8
  p. from heaven | BURK 49:6
penny Not a p. off the pay | COOK 75:12
pension hang your hat on a p. | MACN 202:15
  spend my p. on brandy | JOSE 164:4
pentagon P., immense monument | FRAN 118:3
people as if p. mattered | SCHU 281:2
  hate *p. and children* | CAMP 52:11
  law not supported by p. | HUMP 154:9
  look after our p. | LAST 182:4
  Most p. ignore most poetry | MITC 217:3
  noise! And the p. | ANON 10:13
  no petty p. | YEAT 339:9
  Not many p. know that | CAIN 51:4
  p. are only human | COMP 74:1
  p. are the masters | BLAI 39:3
  p. as a source of power | SCAR 279:17
  People p., but books never | ROOS 267:16
  P.'s Princess | BLAI 39:4
  p. were a kind of solution | CAVA 56:7
  People who need p. | MERR 213:15
  P. you know, yet can't | LARK 180:10
  Power to the p. | POLI 251:21
  same as if they was p. | DURE 93:7
  we are the p. of England | CHES 62:13
  What kind of a p. | CHUR 66:14
Peoria It'll play in P. | POLI 251:13
pepper Sergeant P. | TYNA 314:10
percentage reasonable p. | BECK 26:3
perdition led to *p.* by a man | WEST 325:6
perestroika [p.] combines | GORB 130:15
  started the process of p. | GORB 130:16
perfect ever more p. eyes | TEIL 304:1
  nobody's p. | FILM 111:16
  Nothing is p. | STEP 296:15
  One p. rose | PARK 243:2
perfection P. of planned layout | PARK 244:8
  P. of the life | YEAT 337:4
perfectly small, but p. formed | COOP 76:9
perform p. without thinking | WHIT 327:2
period p. of silence on your part | ATTL 15:6
periphrastic p. study | ELIO 98:15
perish p. together as fools | KING 172:8
perished Now that love is p. | MILL 214:14
permanent less p. than thought | BUNT 48:10
permissive p. society | TEBB 303:17
Perón not been born P. | PERÓ 247:4
perpendicular p. expression | SHAW 286:6
persecuted because he is p. | GOUL 131:3
Persians Truth-loving P. | GRAV 131:10
persistence p. of officials | LEVI 189:9
  take the place of p. | COOL 76:7
person frontier of my P. | AUDE 17:8
  no more than a p. | AUDE 16:9
  P. from Porlock | SMIT 290:5
personal P. relations | FORS 116:8
  warm p. gesture | GALB 123:9

personalities meeting of two p. | JUNG 166:5
  p. of the two sexes | MEAD 211:11
personality From 35 to 55, good p. | TUCK 313:13
  no more p. than | CHAN 60:8
  powerful political p. | JENK 161:1
  product of his own p. | FROM 119:12
perspective jolt in the p. | WOOL 335:10
  quick p. of the future | SPEN 293:13
perspiring city of p. dreams | RAPH 260:4
persuaders hidden p. | PACK 241:8
pertinent way to a p. answer | BRON 45:4
perverse real life in some p. way | BROW 46:12
perversion War the universal p. | RAE 259:7
perversity p. is the soul's | UPDI 314:14
pervert loophole through which p. | BRON 45:5
pessimist p. fears this is true | CABE 50:13
  p. waiting for rain | COHE 72:11
petal dropping a rose p. | MARQ 208:13
petals P. on a wet, black bough | POUN 254:4
Peter government which robs P. | SHAW 283:19
Peter Pan Slightly in *P.* | TYNA 314:5
pets hate a word like 'p.' | JENN 161:8
pettiness to expiate: a p. | LAWR 184:6
petty no p. people | YEAT 339:9
pews faith of those in the p. | AUST 18:20
phagocytes stimulate the p. | SHAW 283:16
phallic P. and ambrosial | POUN 253:17
phallus future is the p. | LAWR 183:15
Pharisees P.'s hypocrisy | PAST 245:7
Philadelphia living in P. | EPIT 105:7
  went to P., but | FIEL 108:15
philistine run by a p. | KAUF 167:3
philistinism our yawning P. | PRIT 257:4
philosophers separation of p. | QUIN 259:1
philosophical p. tradition | WHIT 327:4
philosophy advantage for a p. | SANT 275:13
  linguistic p. | RUSS 272:10
  P. is a battle | WITT 332:14
  P. is the replacement | RYLE 273:2
phoenix expect a p. hour | DAY- 85:2
phone answer the p. | THUR 309:13
  call him up on the p. | SALI 274:3
  E.T. p. home | FILM 110:4
  never even made a p. call | CHOM 64:14
  P. for the fish-knives | BETJ 35:3
  p. is for you | LEBO 186:8
photograph p. is a secret | ARBU 12:11
photographer p. is like the cod | SHAW 286:2
  to be a good p. | BAIL 20:1
photography p. is all right if | HOCK 150:2
  P. is truth | GODA 129:5
phrase p. becomes current | HOLM 151:4
  p. is born into the world | BABE 19:10
physical lightly called p. | COLE 72:14
physician p. can bury mistakes | WRIG 336:6
physicians P. of the Utmost Fame | BELL 27:11

physicists p. have known sin	OPPE 236:9	seas of p. lie	AUDE 16:13
physics no democracy in p.	ALVA 7:2	unbearable p.	RUSS 271:3
p. or stamp collecting	RUTH 272:12	**pix** Sticks nix hick p.	NEWS 231:11
talk about quantum p.	WILC 328:9	**pixie** some vanilla-flavoured p.	PARR 244:15
pianists no better than many p.	SCHN 280:8	**place** at the wrong p.	BRAD 43:4
piano help with moving the p.	WEST 325:4	In p. of strife	CAST 56:1
playing a p. in a brothel	MUGG 225:1	know your p. in the set-up	KING 173:3
Picardy Roses are flowering in P.	WEAT 321:20	**places** all p. were alike to him	KIPL 175:10
Picasso abhorred plastics, P.	WAUG 321:6	been things and seen p.	WEST 324:6
P. is a genius	DALI 83:2	distance between two p.	WILL 330:2
pick p. it up	SAYI 278:18	**placidly** Go p. amid the noise	EHRM 96:5
P. yourself up	FIEL 108:8	**plagiarism** one author, it's p.	MIZN 219:7
pickle weaned on a p.	ANON 11:13	**plagiarist** No p. can excuse	HAND 138:3
picklocks p. of biographers	BENÉ 29:10	**plagiarize** P.! Let's no one	LEHR 186:18
picnic attempt a p. in Eden	BOWE 42:14	**plain** need of the p.	WAUG 321:17
Teddy Bears have their P.	KENN 168:9	no p. women on television	FORD 115:3
picture no go the p. palace	MACN 202:15	pint of p.	O'BR 233:12
One p. is worth	BARN 23:3	'p.' cooking	MORP 222:2
pictures I nail my p. together	SCHW 281:10	**plan** by his p. of attack	SASS 276:22
P. are for entertainment	GOLD 130:11	coherent p. to the universe	HOYL 153:6
p. didn't have beginning	POLL 250:12	cunning p.	CATC 58:9
p. that got small	FILM 112:4	wagon of his 'P.'	PAST 245:9
pie Miss American P.	MCLE 200:11	**plane** It's a p.	ANON 9:12
p. in the sky when you die	HILL 148:12	only two emotions in a p.	WELL 323:2
pig p. got up and walked away	BURT 49:12	**planet** hanging from a round p.	EDDI 95:4
pigeon crooning like a bilious p.	SHAW 285:17	**plank** landing on a p. travelling	EDDI 95:4
pigeon-holed branded, p.	PRES 256:2	**planned** order of the acts is p.	PAST 245:7
pigs P. treat us as equals	CHUR 69:1	p. obsolescence	STEV 297:3
Pilate water like P.	GREE 132:3	**planning** p. is indispensable	EISE 98:1
pile P. it high	SAYI 279:5	**plans** p. are useless	EISE 98:1
P. the bodies high	SAND 274:13	**plant** I p. lines	WALC 318:4
pilgrims land of the p.	CUMM 81:9	**plantation** still working on a p.	HOLI 150:12
pill little yellow p.	JAGG 158:10	**planter** Ulsterman, of p. stock	HEWI 147:10
Protestant women may take the p.		**plants** talk to the p.	CHAR 61:14
	THOM 308:10	**plasterer** agog at the p.	HEAN 143:9
pillar p. of the State	SOLZ 291:1	**plastic** cannot pass through p.	JOHN 161:15
pillow like the feather p.	HAIG 135:13	**plastics** abhorred p., Picasso	WAUG 321:6
pimples scratching of p.	WOOL 335:13	**platitude** longitude with no p.	FRY 121:12
pinkly p. bursts the spray	BETJ 35:8	p. is simply a truth	BALD 21:3
pinko-grey really p.	FORS 116:13	stroke a p. until	MARQ 208:12
pinstripe come in a p. suit	FEIN 107:6	**platitudes** orchestration of p.	WILD 328:15
pint p. of plain	O'BR 233:12	**Plato** P. told him: he couldn't	CUMM 81:13
p.—that's very nearly	GALT 124:6	series of footnotes to P.	WHIT 327:4
pinta Drinka P. Milka Day	ADVE 3:16	**play** Did that p. of mine send out	YEAT 338:2
pips until the p. squeak	GEDD 125:8	every time I p. it	JOHN 162:6
piss worth a pitcher of warm p.	GARN 125:4	game at which two can p.	BEER 26:21
pissed p. in our soup	BENN 30:11	Games people p.	BERN 33:14
pissing inside the tent p. out	JOHN 163:7	It'll p. in Peoria	POLI 251:13
like p. down your leg	JOHN 163:8	P. it again, Sam	FILM 110:11
pistol I reach for my p.	JOHS 163:13	P. it again, Sam	MISQ 218:12
p. in your pocket	WEST 324:13	p. it over again	LAMB 179:9
pistol-shot echo of a p.	DURR 93:9	p. things as they are	STEV 297:10
pistons black statement of p.	SPEN 293:6	p. was consumed in wholesome	O'BR 233:11
pitchfork use my wit as a p.	LARK 180:14	structure of a p.	MILL 215:9
pity P. the feeling which arrests	JOYC 164:15	work, rest and p.	ADVE 4:9
p. this busy monster	CUMM 81:14	y is p.	EINS 97:4
Poetry is in the p.	OWEN 240:12	**played** p. our cards	SCHE 280:1

players p. who hate your guts   STEN 296:14
playing p. on the line   FORS 116:12
  work terribly hard at p.   MORT 223:3
plays enjoyed going to p.   UPDI 315:5
  Shaw's p.   AGAT 2:8
please not here to p. myself   HEND 146:1
  try to p. everyone   SWOP 302:1
pleasure For physical p.   WAUG 321:13
  give that sort of p.   GLEN 129:4
  greater than the p.   YOUN 340:5
  No p. worth giving up   AMIS 8:5
  P.'s for those who are bad   YESE 339:14
pleasures p. of the senses   ESHE 104:9
pleats witty little p.   BAIL 20:2
plebiscite justice by p.   ZOBE 341:9
plot discerned in history a p.   FISH 109:4
plumage If you have bright p.   CLAR 69:15
plumber choose to be a p.   EINS 97:7
  getting a p. on weekends   ALLE 6:15
  p. comes to unblock   GLEN 129:4
plume in blast-beruffled p.   HARD 139:10
plums p. and orange peel   RALE 259:11
plural Incorrigibly p.   MACN 203:7
pluralism p. in social attitudes   BOWI 42:17
pneumatic promise of p. bliss   ELIO 101:20
pocket gun in your p.   WEST 324:13
  picking his p.   JOHN 162:10
  pound in your p.   WILS 331:8
pockets young man feels his p.   HOUS 152:6
poem Every good p. is a bridge   DAY- 85:6
  figure a p. makes   FROS 121:2
  p. is never finished   VALÉ 315:13
  p. lovely as a tree   KILM 171:13
  p. must ride on its own melting   FROS 121:4
  p. should not mean but be   MACL 200:12
  write a p. after Auschwitz   ADOR 2:5
poems P. are made by fools   KILM 171:14
  p. should be Clyde-built   DUNN 93:3
poet All a p. can do is warn   OWEN 240:13
  ask a p. to sing   BOLD 41:3
  Fat-head p. that nobody   CHES 62:7
  hate what every p. hates   KAVA 167:9
  No p. ever interpreted   GIRA 128:11
  p. can earn more money   AUDE 18:3
  p. is always indebted   MAYA 211:5
  p. is the priest   STEV 297:4
  p. seems most himself   YEAT 339:7
  p.'s hope: to be   AUDE 17:13
  p.'s inward pride   DAY- 85:3
  p.'s voice need not merely   FAUL 107:3
  p. will give up writing   CELA 60:1
  there is a p. indulging   MAHO 204:4
  worst tragedy for a p.   COCT 72:6
poetry campaign in p.   CUOM 82:5
  deeper intimacy with p.   NERU 229:10
  Emptied of its p.   AUDE 16:12
  Ireland hurt you into p.   AUDE 16:10

  p. begins to atrophy   POUN 254:8
  p. ignores most people   MITC 217:3
  p. in money   GRAV 131:15
  p. in motion   KAUF 167:4
  P. is a way to taking life   FROS 121:5
  [P.] is capable of saving   RICH 264:9
  P. is in the pity   OWEN 240:12
  P. is not most important   THOM 307:20
  P. is the achievement   SAND 275:4
  P. is the supreme fiction   STEV 297:9
  P. is to prose   WAIN 318:1
  P. is what is lost   FROS 121:7
  p. makes nothing happen   AUDE 16:11
  P. must be *as well written*   POUN 254:15
  P. not a turning loose   ELIO 102:4
  p. should be alive   ZEPH 341:3
  p. strays into my memory   HOUS 152:10
  P. unearths from among   HILL 148:9
  power corrupts, p. cleanses   KENN 169:14
  quarrel with ourselves, p.   YEAT 339:6
  saying it and that is p.   CAGE 51:2
  Writing a book of p.   MARQ 208:13
poets all p. are Jews   TSVE 313:10
  impossible to hold the p.   GIRA 128:10
  Irish p., learn your trade   YEAT 339:3
  mature p. steal   ELIO 102:2
  Nor till the p. among us   MOOR 221:7
  p. are their own patients   THOM 308:11
  P. do not go mad   CHES 63:12
  P. hope too much   LAWR 184:18
  p. keep our mouths shut   YEAT 338:5
  P. must be *difficult*   ELIO 102:7
  Should p. bicycle-pump   AMIS 7:11
  think all p. were Byronic   COPE 76:15
point still p.   ELIO 98:12
  Up to a p., Lord Copper   WAUG 321:8
points P. have no parts   LIND 191:4
poison got as far as p.-gas   HARD 139:6
  put p. in your coffee   CHUR 69:2
  Slowly the p.   EMPS 104:1
poisoned may have been p.   FIEL 109:1
polecat semi-house-trained p.   FOOT 115:2
polemic don't watch BBC for p.   SIMP 287:12
police among p. officers   ORTO 237:7
  citizen or the p.   AUDE 17:10
  p. are those who arrest   HARR 140:17
  p. can beat you   SHAW 285:13
  p. were to blame   GRAN 131:7
policeman become the world's p.   HEAL 143:5
  p. and a pretty girl   CHAP 61:9
  p. is there to preserve   DALE 83:1
  terrorist and the p.   CONR 75:6
policemen aren't enough p.   LEC 186:12
  how young the p. look   HICK 148:4
  sadists become p.   CONN 74:12
policies but rarely p.   HURD 154:14
policy home p.: I wage war   CLEM 71:1

If the p. isn't hurting | MAJO 204:14
instrument of national p. | BRIA 44:7
My [foreign] p. | BEVI 37:7
p. of the good neighbour | ROOS 267:8
polite no allies to be p. to | GEOR 126:12
politeness suave p. | KNOX 176:15
political fear of P. Economy | SELL 282:12
half your p. life | THAT 305:15
match p. expectations | POWE 255:4
not a p. figure | DIAN 89:9
points to a p. career | SHAW 284:10
p. correctness can be | JAME 159:17
P. language is designed | ORWE 239:6
p. lives end in failure | POWE 255:16
p. will | LYNN 196:8
powerful p. personality | JENK 161:1
test of any p. decision | TREN 311:6
politician my life as a p. | POWE 255:14
p. does get an idea | MARQ 208:9
p. is an arse upon | CUMM 81:12
p. is a statesman who | POMP 250:13
p. never believes | DE G 87:3
p. to complain about | POWE 255:12
p. urges them to rebel | PERU 247:9
p. was a person | LLOY 192:16
statesman is a p. | TRUM 313:2
politicians Conviction p. | BANC 22:8
die for p. | THOM 309:2
p. complain that TV | MURR 226:6
p. hear the word 'culture' | ESHE 104:8
P. often believe | ROTH 269:10
to be left to the p. | DE G 86:13
politics Being in p. is like | MCCA 197:6
between p. and equations | EINS 97:9
do not go in for p. | CAMU 52:17
In p., if you want anything | THAT 304:10
invisible hand in p. | FRIE 119:6
Men enter local p. | PARK 244:10
no true friends in p. | CLAR 69:13
parties 'playing p.' | WILS 331:15
p. and little else | CAMP 52:10
P., executive expression | BRIT 44:9
P. has got to be fun | CLAR 69:16
P. is a marathon | LIVI 192:3
P. is not the art | GALB 123:14
P. is the Art | BUTL 50:10
P. is war without bloodshed | MAO 207:5
p. of happiness | HUMP 154:10
p. of Versailles | MONN 220:5
P. supposed to be | REAG 261:12
p. the art of impossible | HAVE 142:6
P. the art of preventing | VALÉ 315:12
p. to a spectator sport | GALB 123:11
P. too serious a matter | DE G 86:13
their p. usually stink | LAWR 184:18
want to succeed in p. | LLOY 192:13
week a long time in p. | WILS 331:6

poll-taking science of p. | WHIT 326:2
poll tax of the p. | THAT 306:19
pollution engine of p., the dog | SPAR 292:13
p. of democracy | WHIT 326:11
polyester p. sheets | FARR 106:11
pond have their stream and p. | BROO 45:9
ponies Five and twenty p. | KIPL 175:2
p. have swallowed | BETJ 35:4
wretched, blind, pit p. | HODG 150:5
Pontefract licorice fields at P. | BETJ 35:7
poodle in a p. parlour | PARR 244:12
right hon. Gentleman's p. | LLOY 192:5
pool Walk across my swimming p. | RICE 264:4
poor For the urban p. the police | HARR 140:17
give food to the p. | CAMA 52:2
help the many who are p. | KENN 169:4
how expensive it is to be p. | BALD 20:9
I've been p. | TUCK 313:14
My countrymen Kiltartan's p. | YEAT 337:17
p. but she was honest | ANON 11:6
p. don't know that | SART 276:9
p. get children | KAHN 166:16
P. little rich girl | COWA 78:10
p. people in rich countries | BAUE 25:1
p. tread the lightest | HARR 141:4
p. who die | SART 276:1
p. wot gets the blame | ANON 11:6
rich richer and the p. poorer | NEHR 229:4
trampled on faces of p. | NICO 230:9
undeserving p. | SHAW 285:19
Pope against the P. or | BALD 21:10
anyone can be p. | JOHN 161:13
P.! How many divisions | STAL 295:6
poppies In Flanders p. | MCCR 198:8
poppy not to wear a p. | MCAL 196:10
porcupines throw p. under you | KHRU 171:12
Porlock Person from P. | SMIT 290:5
pornography give p. a dirty name | BARN 23:4
p. is really about | SONT 291:14
p. of war | RAE 259:7
P. the attempt to | LAWR 183:12
porridge consistency of cold p. | TURI 313:15
Porsches friends all drive P. | JOPL 164:2
Porson P. sober | HOUS 152:13
portal fitful tracing of a p. | STEV 297:15
porter shone bright on Mrs P. | ELIO 101:14
portrait Every time I paint a p. | SARG 275:15
family p. not too stale | PLOM 250:8
p. of the artist | JOYC 164:11
position altering the p. | RUSS 271:13
Every p. must be held | HAIG 136:1
only p. for women | CARM 53:16
p. of the artists | THOM 307:13
positive ac-cent-tchu-ate the p. | MERC 213:10
power of p. thinking | PEAL 246:3
possessed much p. by death | ELIO 101:19
possessions least of p. | WHIT 326:6

possibility p. of suicide — CIOR 69:11
possible Art of the P. — BUTL 50:10
  not the art of the p. — GALB 123:14
  says that something is p. — CLAR 70:5
possum said the Honourable P. — BERR 34:8
postal p. districts packed — LARK 181:2
poster Kitchener is a great p. — ASQU 14:10
posterity P. as likely to be — BROU 46:9
postern latched its p. behind — HARD 139:4
Post-Impressionist term P. — WINT 332:12
postman p. always rings twice — CAIN 51:3
  think I am, a bloody p. — BEHA 27:3
posts fenced in with p. — WINT 332:12
postures lie down in clean p. — FOWL 117:4
postwar p. funk — TEBB 303:17
pot chicken in every p. — HOOV 151:10
  Look at p. — NASH 228:7
potato p.-gatherers like — KAVA 167:7
  You like p. — GERS 127:3
potent how p. cheap music is — COWA 78:16
pound p. in your pocket — WILS 331:8
poured p. into his clothes — WODE 333:15
poverty implication of dreary p. — WEST 324:18
  setting him up in p. — NAID 227:7
  struggled with p. — BALD 20:9
  war on p. — JOHN 163:1
  worst of crimes is p. — SHAW 284:5
power All p. to the Soviets — POLI 251:1
  balance of p. — KISS 176:1
  Black P. — HAMI 54:1
  corridors of p. — SNOW 290:10
  cult added to p. — ANON 11:17
  have sidled back to p. — KIPL 174:9
  have the p. to end it — SASS 277:3
  in office but not in p. — LAMO 179:12
  Johnson's instinct for p. — WHIT 326:10
  no will to p. — JUNG 166:7
  only have p. over people — SOLZ 290:10
  p. corrupts, poetry cleanses — KENN 169:14
  p. grows out of the barrel — MAO 207:6
  P. is not a means — ORWE 238:14
  P. is the great aphrodisiac — KISS 176:4
  P.? It's a Dead Sea fruit — MACM 202:6
  p. of suppress — NORT 233:1
  p.-state — TEMP 304:2
  P. to the people — POLI 251:21
  P. without responsibility — KIPL 175:17
  responsibility without p. — STOP 298:17
  rob it of its p. — SZAS 302:8
  standing armies of p. — RADC 259:4
  teacher have minimal p. — SZAS 302:3
  they confer p. — RUSS 272:4
  Treasury is in p. — WILS 331:12
  Wealth and p. are much more — LEBO 186:9
  What p. have you got — BENN 30:5
powerful fear is that we are p. — WILL 330:10
powers Headmasters have p. — CHUR 68:7

high contracting p. — BRIA 44:7
  p. lent to me — BENN 30:4
  real separation of p. — DENN 88:7
practical p. intellectual — STRO 300:9
  P. men, who believe — KEYN 171:2
practise preach but do not p. — RUSS 272:2
prairies mountains to the p. — BERL 32:11
praise countryman must have p. — BLYT 40:3
  highest p. of God — PROU 257:8
  P. the green earth — BUNT 48:8
  P. the Lord — FORG 115:12
  they only want p. — MAUG 210:7
praised dog that has p. his fleas — YEAT 339:1
praising always p. the past — SMIT 290:2
pram p. in the hall — CONN 74:14
pray Often when I p. — LEWI 190:6
  Work and p. — HILL 148:12
prayer Conservative Party at p. — ROYD 270:2
  wing and a p. — ADAM 2:2
  wish for p. is a prayer — BERN 33:10
prayers saying his p. — MILN 217:1
prays family that p. together — SAYI 278:13
preach p. but do not practise — RUSS 272:2
precedent is a dangerous p. — CORN 77:8
precious p. it must be rationed — LENI 187:12
predicament is the human p. — QUIN 258:13
  It is a p. — BENN 31:2
predict only p. things after — IONE 157:11
prefaces Shaw's p. — AGAT 2:8
preference special p. for beetles — HALD 136:12
pregnancy avoid p. by mathematics
  — MENC 212:15
pregnant If men could get p. — KENN 168:8
prejudices deposit of p. laid — EINS 97:5
  proprietor's p. — SWAF 301:10
premier P. for years to come — CHAN 61:7
premises based upon licenced p. — O'BR 233:10
prepare not to p. for life — PAST 245:2
prepared BE P. — BADE 19:15
  p. for all emergencies — FORS 116:7
prerogative p. of the eunuch — STOP 298:17
  P. of the harlot — KIPL 175:17
prescription p. of a quick dip — WESL 323:18
presence posted p. of the watcher — JAME 159:9
present know nothing but the p. — KEYN 170:12
  no p. in Wales — THOM 308:13
  not able to be p. for him — BROD 44:12
  past, p. and future — EINS 97:8
  perpetuates the p. — DE B 85:12
  p. of Mornington Crescent — HARG 140:13
  p., yes, we are in it — LOWE 195:17
  Time p. and time past — ELIO 98:9
  When the P. has latched — HARD 139:4
  who controls the p. — ORWE 238:10
presents all those p. — WILL 329:5
preserve do not p. myself — ORTE 237:2
  there to p. disorder — DALE 83:1

Whom God P.   MORT 223:9
presidency cancer close to the P.   DEAN 85:7
  heart-beat from the P.   STEV 298:6
  I will seek the p.   DOLE 90:7
  messenger-boy P.   SCHL 280:2
  pursuit of the P.   JOHN 163:5
  Teflon-coated P.   SCHR 280:12
  US p. a Tudor monarchy   BURG 49:5
  vice-p. isn't worth   GARN 125:4
president All the P. is   TRUM 312:13
  All the P.'s men   BERN 33:16
  anybody could become p.   DARR 83:8
  any boy may become P.   STEV 298:4
  choose to run for P.   COOL 76:4
  going to be your next p.   CART 55:1
  more than any other P.   MENC 213:4
  P. is a crook   NIXO 232:7
  P. should not wear   MCAL 196:10
  P.'s spouse   BUSH 50:1
  P.'s task is   JOHN 163:6
  security around the p.   MAIL 204:13
  to hide from the P.   CHUR 69:5
  vote for the best P.   PETE 247:13
  We are the P.'s men   KISS 176:5
  When the P. does it   NIXO 232:9
press complain about the p.   POWE 255:12
  Freedom of the p.   SWAF 301:10
  Freedom of the p. guaranteed   LIEB 191:3
  lose your temper with the P.   PANK 242:5
  not a free p. but a managed   RADC 259:5
  popular p. is drinking   MELL 212:9
  power of the p.   NORT 233:1
  p. is ferocious   DIAN 89:11
  p. still hounded you   JOHN 162:2
  p. would kill her   SPEN 292:15
  with you on the free p.   STOP 299:2
pressed p. out of shape   FROS 120:18
pressure Grace under p.   HEMI 145:15
prestige doesn't work without p.   DE G 87:6
presumption amused by its p.   THUR 309:12
pretender Old P.   GUED 135:4
pretending p. to be someone else   PAQU 242:9
pretty lived in a p. how town   CUMM 81:8
  policeman and a p. girl   CHAP 61:9
  p. can get away with   WAUG 321:17
  p. girl is like a melody   BERL 32:14
prevent not knowing how to p.   RUSS 272:11
preventing Politics the art of p.   VALÉ 315:16
price love that pays the p.   SPRI 294:11
  pay any p.   KENN 169:3
  p. of championing human   OWEN 240:10
  p. of justice   BENN 31:9
  p. well worth paying   LAMO 179:11
  What p. glory   ANDE 8:9
  Wot p. Selvytion nah   SHAW 284:8
prices reduce the rise in p.   HEAT 144:5
prick paint with my p.   MISQ 218:7

prickly go round the p. pear   ELIO 99:17
pride here have P. and Truth   YEAT 338:6
  lacks a proper p.   MACD 198:11
  London P. handed down to us   COWA 78:6
  look backward to with p.   FROS 120:3
  save its p.   MEYE 214:1
priest p. of the invisible   STEV 297:4
  p. persuades humble people   PERU 247:9
prig not too much of the p.   CROS 80:12
priggish p. schoolgirl   GRIG 134:5
prime One's p. is elusive   SPAR 292:11
Prime Minister best P. we have   BUTL 50:8
  HOW DARE YOU BECOME P.   TELE 305:4
  modern P.   HENN 146:6
  next P. but three   BELL 27:13
  No woman will be P.   THAT 304:9
  on the P.'s jet   SELF 282:7
  P. has nothing to   CHUR 69:5
  P. has to be a butcher   BUTL 50:9
  P. is like the banyan   PATI 245:10
  P. should be intimidating   THAT 306:20
  P. shuffling along   HEAL 143:7
  Unknown P.   ASQU 14:7
  would have become P.   CONN 74:16
Prime Ministers Disraeli school of P. BLAI 39:5
  P. dissatisfied   JENK 161:7
  P. have never yet been   CHUR 68:7
  wild flowers, and P.   BALD 21:4
primitive call it a 'p. society'   GREG 133:8
  wise p. in giant jungle   MAIL 204:11
prince Advise the p.   ELIO 100:9
  danced with the P. of Wales   FARJ 106:9
  P. of Wales not a position   BENN 31:2
princess People's P.   BLAI 39:1
  P. of Wales was   DOWD 91:10
principle little of the p. left   REIT 262:16
  rise above p.   LONG 193:12
  standing up for a p.   O'RO 236:15
  useful thing about a p.   MAUG 210:3
principles instead of p., slogans   BENT 32:6
print licence to p. money   THOM 309:6
  when you read the fine p.   SEEG 282:3
priorities language of p.   BEVA 36:6
  p. have gone all wrong   BEVA 36:13
prison at home in p.   WAUG 321:2
  Home is the girl's p.   SHAW 285:9
  while there is a soul in p.   DEBS 86:6
  world not a 'p. house'   ROBI 265:9
prisoner thoughts of a p.   SOLZ 290:17
  your being taken p.   KITC 176:9
prisoners p. of addiction   ILLI 156:7
  p. of noise   MORE 221:10
  weapons of all p.   COLE 72:15
private P. faces in public places   AUDE 17:6
  p. life is a disgrace   ANON 11:3
  P. Means is dead   SMIT 290:3
  p. opulence   GALB 123:6

psychopath p. is the furnace   RAYM 261:2
psychotherapy waste money on p.
                                                    TORK 310:11
public Desolation in immaculate p. places
                                                    ROET 266:6
   give the p. something   SKEL 288:9
   I and the p. know   AUDE 17:9
   one to mislead the p.   ASQU 14:8
   Private faces in p. places   AUDE 17:6
   p. rallies around an idea   ASIM 14:2
   p. squalor   GALB 123:6
   respect p. opinion   RUSS 271:8
   tell the p. which way   SULZ 301:6
publications previous p.   HILB 148:5
publicity history of p.   LEAV 186:2
   justice is eternal p.   BENN 31:9
   no such thing as bad p.   BEHA 27:4
   now called p.   O'RO 236:17
   oxygen of p.   THAT 306:7
   qualities which create p.   ATTL 15:7
public relations glorified p. man   TRUM 312:13
   precedence over p.   FEYN 108:2
public school to an English p.   WAUG 321:2
   with a p. accent   LEAV 186:1
publish p. and be sued   INGR 157:8
published before this book is p.   RUNC 270:7
publisher makes everybody a p.   MCLU 201:13
publishers become p.   CONN 74:12
publishing easier job like p.   AYER 19:7
   p. faster than you think   PAUL 245:13
pudding Take away that p.   CHUR 69:7
Pulitzer P. Prize ready to be won   CHIL 64:10
pull P. down thy vanity   POUN 254:6
pulpit faith of those in the p.   AUST 18:20
   such a bully e.   ROOS 268:8
   white glove p.   REAG 261:11
pulse take a nation's p.   WHIT 326:2
   two people with the one p.   MACN 203:4
punch p. above its weight   HURD 155:1
punctual Aunt Minnie always p.   WILD 328:13
punctuality P. is the virtue   WAUG 321:16
punished [wickedness] is not p.   COMP 74:8
punk Gert's writings are p.   ANON 9:16
punt better fun to p.   SAYE 277:5
puppy Happiness is a warm p.   SCHU 280:13
   happiness was a warm p.   EPHR 104:3
pure p. as the driven slush   BANK 22:11
purify p. the dialect   ELIO 99:8
Puritan to the P. all things are   LAWR 183:5
Puritanism not P. but February   KRUT 178:6
   P. The haunting fear   MENC 212:12
purity Science lost its virgin p.   GRAV 131:16
purple colour p.   WALK 318:12
   deep p. falls   PARI 242:10
   I shall wear p.   JOSE 164:4
   P. haze is in my brain   HEND 146:3
purpose happy sense of p.   O'RO 236:15

   want a sense of p.   MACM 202:5
purrs p. like an epigram   MARQ 208:12
pursuit common p.   LEAV 185:13
push without trying to p. it   O'CA 234:7
pushed and he p.   LOGU 193:6
put up with which I will not p.   CHUR 67:11
pygmies peace like retarded p.   PEAR 246:8
pyjamas in p. for the heat   LAWR 184:5
pylons P., those pillars bare   SPEN 293:12
pyramid bottom of the economic p.
                                                    ROOS 267:5
pyre heaping up own funeral p.   POWE 255:7

quad No one about in the Q.   KNOX 176:17
quaint q. and curious war is   HARD 140:3
qualification only great q.   CARS 54:6
quality knowing you gave them q.
                                                    SOLZ 290:15
   Never mind the q.   POWE 255:17
quantum of q. mechanics   BOHR 40:10
quarks Three q. for Muster Mark   JOYC 164:10
quarrel lover's q. with the world   FROS 120:10
   no q. with the Viet Cong   ALI 6:3
   q. in a far away country   CHAM 60:3
   q. with ourselves, poetry   YEAT 339:6
   takes one to make a q.   INGE 156:13
Quebec Long Live Free Q.   DE G 87:5
queen dying for Q. and country   THOM 309:2
   have the Q. as their aunt   MARG 207:11
   Q. has the quality   PHIL 248:8
   q. in people's hearts   DIAN 89:7
   To toast *The Q.*   HEAN 143:15
queer q. old dean   SPOO 294:8
queerer q. than we suppose   HALD 136:9
questing passes the q. vole   WAUG 321:9
question Answer to the Great Q.   ADAM 1:12
   ask an impertinent q.   BRON 45:4
   asked any clear q.   CAMU 52:12
   mere asking of a q.   FORS 116:14
   q. is absurd   AUDE 18:1
   q. why we died   KIPL 173:12
   secretly changed the Q.   SELL 282:13
   To ask the hard q.   AUDE 17:18
   what is the q.   LAST 183:2
questions *all* q. were stupid   WEIS 322:7
   ask q. of those   RALE 259:9
   q. the distempered part   ELIO 98:18
queue orderly q. of one   MIKE 214:6
quick q., and the dead   DEWA 89:1
quiet is a q. life   HICK 148:3
   never have a q. world   SHAW 285:14
   q. flows the Don   SHOL 286:14
   q. on the western front   REMA 263:2
   should be kept very q.   LOOS 194:9
quieten q. your enemy by talking   CEAU 56:9
quietly q. pacifist peaceful   WALK 318:10

quit try again. Then q. — FIEL 108:14
quotation always have a q. — SAYE 277:6
  considered worthy of q. — COWA 79:3
  get a happy q. anywhere — HOLM 151:5
  q. is a national vice — WAUG 321:5
  q. what a speaker wants — BENN 30:7
quotations read books of q. — CHUR 68:9
quote man is to q. him — BENC 29:2
quoted very seldom q. correctly — STRU 300:11
quotes q. give us acquaintance — WILL 329:8

rabbit r. has a charming face — ANON 11:3
  r. in a snare — STEP 297:1
race play the r. card — SHAP 283:10
  r. between education — WELL 323:9
  white r. *is* the cancer — SONT 291:15
races so-called white r. — FORS 116:13
racket all a German r. — RIDL 265:1
  Once in the r. — CAPO 53:9
  r. of the female — OSBO 240:1
radar writer's r. — HEMI 145:17
radical dared be r. when young — FROS 120:14
  R. Chic — WOLF 334:8
  R. is a man — ROOS 267:11
radio had the r. on — MONR 220:7
  R. and television — SARR 275:17
  r. expands it — WOGA 333:16
rag foul r. and bone shop — YEAT 337:2
  Shakespeherian R. — ELIO 101:12
rage horrible that lust and r. — YEAT 338:17
  r. against the dying of the light — THOM 307:2
  r. to live — VANE 316:3
  wretched r. for order — MAHO 204:4
rages weight of r. — SPOO 294:10
ragged pair of r. claws — ELIO 100:7
raging r. in the dark — YEAT 337:4
raid r. on the inarticulate — ELIO 99:1
railway big r. station — NABO 227:3
  by r. timetables — TAYL 303:7
  lying across a r. line — JENK 161:4
  R. termini — FORS 116:4
rain buried in the r. — MILL 214:12
  glazed with r. water — WILL 330:8
  hard r.'s a gonna fall — DYLA 94:5
  not even the r. — CUMM 82:1
  r. in Spain — LERN 188:18
  r. is destroying his grain — HERB 146:8
  r. rapping like fingernails — MOOR 221:9
  Singin' in the r. — FREE 118:7
  Still falls the r. — SITW 288:4
  waiting for it to r. — COHE 72:11
  waiting for r. — ELIO 99:13
  wedding-cake in the r. — AUDE 18:15
rainbow Follow ev'ry r. — HAMM 137:8
  Lord survives the r. — LOWE 195:14
  r. and a cuckoo's song — DAVI 83:12

  R. gave thee birth — DAVI 84:1
  r. which includes black — YEVT 340:1
  real r. coalition — JACK 158:4
  Somewhere over the r. — HARB 138:11
raineth R. drop and staineth slop — POUN 253:12
rains r. pennies from heaven — BURK 49:6
Ramsbottom Mr and Mrs R. — EDGA 95:10
rape procrastinated r. — PRIT 257:2
  you r. it — DEGA 86:7
raped r. and speaks English — ANON 9:1
Raphael draw like R. — PICA 249:2
rapist r. bothers to buy a bottle — DWOR 94:2
rapists all men are r. — FREN 118:9
rapper to your son as a r. — ICE 156:4
rappers first r. of Europe — BJÖR 38:8
rascality prudence on r. — SHAW 285:6
rat anthropomorphic view of r. — KOES 177:6
  Anyone can r. — CHUR 65:8
  creeps like a r. — BOWE 42:12
  giant r. of Sumatra — DOYL 91:11
  r. swimming *towards* — CHUR 69:4
  You dirty r. — MISQ 219:6
rational irrational is r. — STEV 297:13
  make life more r. — AYER 19:6
rationed precious it must be r. — LENI 187:12
rats r.' alley — ELIO 101:11
rattle Shake, r. and roll — CALH 51:6
ray and a r. of sunshine — WODE 333:1
razor arse full of r. blades — KEAT 167:10
reach I r. for my pistol — JOHS 163:13
  other beers cannot r. — ADVE 3:23
  r. the promised land — CALL 51:9
reaction can't get no girl r. — JAGG 158:11
  if there is any r. — JUNG 166:5
reactionaries r. are paper tigers — MAO 207:7
reactionary R. is a somnambulist — ROOS 267:11
read cannot *r.* a book — NABO 226:11
  don't actually r. newspapers — MCLU 201:11
  Don't r. too much now — LARK 180:11
  his books were r. — BELL 28:7
  not r. Eliot, Auden — RICH 264:12
  only news until he's r. it — WAUG 321:10
  people who can't r. — ZAPP 341:2
  r. any good books lately — CATC 58:1
  r., much of the night — ELIO 101:7
  R. my lips — BUSH 50:4
  r. one book in my life — MITF 217:12
  r. The Hunter's thoughts — AUDE 16:4
  r. the life of any important — PRIE 256:8
  r. too widely — PEAR 246:6
  suffered in learning to r. — WEST 325:5
  superfluous to r. — HILB 148:5
  what I r. in the papers — ROGE 266:13
  What we used to r. — CROS 81:1
  who don't r. the books — BYAT 50:12
reader ideal r. of my novels — BURG 49:4
  ideal r. suffering from — JOYC 164:7

individual r. is important | NABO 227:5
no tears in the r. | FROS 121:3
not to inform the r. | ACHE 1:9
one r. in a hundred years | KOES 177:10
readers so many of my r. belong | CHES 63:10
reading careful of his r. | LEWI 190:4
get nowadays from r. | GREE 132:11
lie in a hot bath r. | THOM 307:20
Like R., only farther | FLEM 114:7
other people are r. | NAIP 227:8
Peace is poor r. | HARD 140:10
prefer r. | SMIT 289:10
R. isn't an occupation | ORTO 237:7
than they are of r. | LEBO 186:9
what is worth r. | TREV 311:9
readmission r. to the human race | LYNN 196:7
real home to a r. world | TURK 313:16
joke must transform r. life | BROW 46:12
never did anything r. | DOLE 90:8
their world is the r. one | ROTH 269:10
washed in the speechless r. | BARZ 24:13
realism I don't want r. | WILL 330:5
realistic make a 'r. decision' | MCCA 197:11
reality art is but a vision of r. | YEAT 337:11
Cannot bear very much r. | ELIO 98:11
employs r. as little | MOND 220:2
idea And the r. | ELIO 99:18
Love is discovery of r. | MURD 225:15
other people's r. | SONT 291:16
principal part of r. | BORG 42:1
R. beats fiction | CONR 75:7
R. goes bounding past | COCK 72:1
r. take precedence | FEYN 108:2
really be a R. Useful Engine | AWDR 19:1
what I r. really want | ROWB 269:12
reaping No, r. | BOTT 42:6
reason Blotting out r. | GRAV 131:12
for the wrong r. | ELIO 100:13
R. and Progress | OSBO 240:3
reasonable be right than be r. | NASH 227:17
r. man adapts | SHAW 285:7
They were r. people | BROO 46:2
reasons r. for the rule change | STRA 300:4
We want better r. | RUSS 272:11
rebel die like a true-blue r. | HILL 148:13
R. without a cause | FILM 112:14
What is a r. | CAMU 53:2
rebellion r. and revivalism | THOM 308:8
rebels One final tip to r. | NICO 230:12
receipt Applause is a r. | SCHN 280:7
receiver left the r. off the hook | KOES 177:7
recession r. when your neighbour | TRUM 313:3
spend way out of a r. | CALL 51:8
recherche A la r. du temps perdu | PROU 257:5
recipes r. always successful | VALÉ 315:14
recirculation vicus of r. | JOYC 164:6
recognize only a trial if I r. it | KAFK 166:14

reconciliation bridge of r. | RUNC 270:5
True r. does not | MAND 206:2
record as fast as the world r. | COLE 72:13
not merely be the r. | FAUL 107:3
red Better r. than dead | POLI 251:5
not even r. brick | OSBO 240:2
R. lips are not so red | OWEN 241:2
r. wheel barrow | WILL 330:8
reds honour the indomitable R. | DUNN 93:3
redundancy handing out r. notices | KINN 173:6
redwood From the r. forest | GUTH 135:12
reeled Until r. the mind | GIBB 127:9
referee having two you are a r. | FROS 119:14
refined Englishwoman is so r. | SMIT 290:4
refinement r. scrapes at vainly | BEER 26:22
reformers All R. live in houses | SMIT 289:13
refreshes r. the parts | ADVE 3:23
refuse offer he can't r. | PUZO 258:3
regal someone that height look r. | AMIE 7:7
regrets Miss Otis r. | PORT 253:1
regulated R. hatred | HARD 139:2
speech is not to be r. | DOUG 91:9
rehearsal r. I let the orchestra | BEEC 26:15
reheat cannot r. a soufflé | MCCA 198:3
Reich Ein R., ein Volk | POLI 251:9
reindeer Herds of r. move | AUDE 16:7
Red-nosed R. | MARK 207:14
rejoice r. at that news | THAT 305:14
relations God's apology for r. | KING 173:2
in personal r. | RUSS 271:9
Personal r. | FORS 116:8
relationship human r. suffers | FORS 116:16
Their r. consisted | GUNN 135:10
relationships our r. begin | AUDE 18:5
R., relationships | FISH 109:3
relative one day in a r. way | BULL 48:6
Success is r. | ELIO 98:6
relaxed feel terribly r. | DAYA 85:1
religion Art and R. are two roads | BELL 27:5
as great a regard for r. | O'CA 234:4
can't talk r. to | SHAW 284:7
r. has always been to me | POTT 253:6
R. is the frozen thought | KRIS 178:2
r. of Socialism | BEVA 36:6
r. weak | SZAS 302:7
r. without science | EINS 96:6
start your own r. | ANON 10:2
substitute for r. | ELIO 102:5
That is my r. | SHAW 284:6
tourism is their r. | RUNC 270:6
trust the old r. | LOWE 195:16
wisest r. | HAIL 136:2
religions materialistic of r. | TEMP 304:3
they who found r. | PROU 257:7
religiose r. And mystic | DUNN 93:5
religious commit to any r. belief | WAUG 321:1
great r. art | CLAR 70:2

Rhine think of the R.	BALD 21:8	r. goes unrecognized	WEIL 322:4
rhinoceros hide of a r.	BARR 24:3	r. to happiness	RAYN 261:3
Rhodesia majority rule in R.	SMIT 289:6	r. to kill	ADAM 2:1
rhubarb blancmange and r. tart	KNOX 176:16	scientists are probably r.	ASIM 14:2
rhyme r. is a barrel	MAYA 211:4	Self-government is our r.	CASE 55:9
R. is still most effective	GIRA 128:10	to *know* what is r.	JOHN 163:6
still more tired of R.	BELL 28:1	Two wrongs don't make a r.	SZAS 302:9
rhythm I got r.	GERS 127:1	Women would rather be r.	NASH 227:17
sweet, soft, plenty r.	MORT 223:10	**righteous** seen the r. forsaken	BLUN 39:13
rhythmical r. grumbling	ELIO 102:8	**rights** Bill of R. seems	COMM 73:7
ribbon changing a typewriter r.	BENC 29:1	championing human r.	OWEN 240:10
ribbons cut r. and kiss babies	MICH 214:3	equal in dignity and r.	ANON 8:15
Ribstone Pippin Right as a R.	BELL 27:16	Stand up for your r.	MARL 208:1
rice *r. pudding for dinner*	MILN 216:16	talked about equal r.	JOHN 162:12
rich all the r. people	STEA 295:11	your r. become only	CASE 55:10
by chance grow r.	THOM 308:3	**right-wing** life is r.	DEBR 86:4
never be too r. or too thin	WIND 332:11	**rime** r. was on the spray	HARD 140:9
not really a r. man	GETT 127:7	**ring** One R. to rule them all	TOLK 310:8
orchestra playing to the r.	AUDE 16:2	r. with Mr Tolstoy	HEMI 145:16
parish of r. women	AUDE 16:10	**rings** postman always r. twice	CAIN 51:3
people r. enough to pay	HEAL 143:4	**riot** r. is the language of	KING 172:12
Poor little r. girl	COWA 78:10	**ripper** no female Jack the R.	PAGL 241:16
poor people in r. countries	BAUE 25:1	**rise** Early to r.	THUR 309:14
r. are different	FITZ 112:18	into this world to r. above	FILM 111:10
r. are the scum of the earth	CHES 63:4	resistible r. of Arturo Ui	BREC 43:16
r. get rich	KAHN 166:16	r. at ten thirty	HARG 140:12
r. is better	TUCK 313:14	**risen** r. without trace	MUGG 224:8
r. richer and the poor poorer	NEHR 229:4	**rises** sun also r.	HEMI 145:14
r. wage war	SART 276:1	**rising** r. expectations	CLEV 71:6
r. wot gets the gravy	ANON 11:6	**risks** just one of the r. he takes	STEV 298:4
save the few who are r.	KENN 169:4	We took r.	SCOT 281:14
sincerely want to be r.	CORN 77:3	**ritual** body building is r.	PAGL 241:13
to tax r. people	LLOY 192:14	**river** guy who cleans the r.	PERO 247:5
riches titled for r.	PEAR 246:7	Ol' man r.	HAMM 137:13
rid time we got r. of Him	BALD 20:12	r. Is a strong brown god	ELIO 99:3
riddle r. of the sands	CHIL 64:9	r. jumps over the mountains	AUDE 15:15
r. wrapped in a mystery	CHUR 66:1	Sleepless as the r.	CRAN 79:10
ride if you cannot r. two horses	MAXT 210:17	**riverrun** r., past Eve and Adam's	JOYC 164:6
r. on a tiger	ANON 11:10	**rivers** I've known r.	HUGH 153:12
She's got a ticket to r.	LENN 188:8	**road** ads and not the r.	NASH 228:5
ridiculous heart of the r.	MAHO 204:3	along the r. of evening	DE L 87:18
sense of the r.	PAGE 241:11	Follow the yellow brick r.	HARB 138:13
Riga young lady of R.	ANON 11:10	Golden R. to Samarkand	FLEC 114:2
right convinced that they are r.	VAN 315:19	Goodbye yellow brick r.	JOHN 162:5
curst conceit o' bein' r.	MACD 198:10	Hit the r., Jack	MAYF 211:9
exclusively in the r.	HUXL 155:10	in the middle of the r.	BEVA 36:8
forgive those who were r.	MACL 201:1	one more for the r.	MERC 213:12
it's all r. with me	BELL 28:12	on to the end of the r.	LAUD 181:9
just not r.	PARK 244:11	r. through the woods	KIPL 175:7
man of the r.	MOSL 223:13	rolling English r.	CHES 62:11
no r. in the circus	MAXT 210:17	**roads** By r. not adopted	BETJ 35:15
not only to be r.	SZAS 302:2	How many r.	DYLA 94:3
one WAS r.	POUN 254:10	Two r. diverged	FROS 120:16
questioned its r. to exist	SCHU 281:3	without fear the lawless r.	MUIR 225:2
R. as a Ribstone Pippin	BELL 27:16	**roam** mind begins to r.	SOLZ 290:12
R. but Repulsive	SELL 282:11	**roaming** R. in the gloamin'	LAUD 181:11
r. deed for the wrong	ELIO 100:13	**roar** called upon to give the r.	CHUR 67:17

roar (*cont.*):
r. of London's traffic — ANON 11:1
roareth that r. thus — GODL 129:8
roast R. beef and Yorkshire — ORWE 237:15
rob r. his mother — FAUL 107:4
robbed We was r. — JACO 158:7
robber-state vast parasite r. — HOPE 152:1
robbing r. a bank — BREC 44:3
Robey R. is the Darling — SMIT 289:4
Robinson here's to you, Mrs R. — SIMO 287:9
robot r. may not injure a human — ASIM 13:11
robotics Rules of R. — ASIM 13:11
robs government which r. Peter — SHAW 283:19
rock I'm dealing in r. and roll — SPEC 292:14
like the R. of Gibraltar — GAMO 124:7
r. around the clock — DE K 87:11
R. journalism is people — ZAPP 341:2
Sex and drugs and r. and roll — DURY 94:1
simple r. and roll reasons — GELD 125:9
rocked r. the system — ROBI 265:12
rocket numbers that r. the mind — WILB 328:5
Rockies R. may crumble — GERS 127:4
rocks r. remain — HERB 146:14
rode r. madly off — LEAC 185:8
role not yet found a r. — ACHE 1:8
roll R. over, Beethoven — BERR 34:4
Shake, rattle and r. — CALH 51:6
rolled bottoms of my trousers r. — ELIO 100:10
rolling jus' keeps r. along — HAMM 137:13
Like a r. stone — DYLA 94:8
r. English road — CHES 62:11
Roman Before the R. came to Rye — CHES 62:11
romance fine r. with no kisses — FIEL 108:6
music and love and r. — BERL 32:12
romantic R. Ireland's dead — YEAT 338:15
'r.' music — STRA 300:2
ticket to r. places — MARV 209:4
Wrong but R. — SELL 282:11
romantics We were the last r. — YEAT 337:3
Rome Treaty [of R.] is like — DENN 88:5
roof cat on a hot tin r. — WILL 329:13
roof-wrecked r.; damps there drip — HARD 139:5
rooks r. in families homeward go — HARD 140:8
room about to enter a r. — EDDI 95:4
All I want is a r. — LERN 188:20
Books do furnish a r. — POWE 254:18
boys in the back r. — LOES 193:3
Great hatred, little r. — YEAT 338:8
money and a r. of her own — WOOL 335:4
smoke-filled r. — SIMP 287:14
rooms boys in the back r. — BEAV 25:7
lighted r. inside your head — LARK 180:10
Other voices, other r. — CAPO 53:11
roost came home to r. — MILL 215:9
roots drought destroying his r. — HERB 146:8
rope fourfold r. of nerves — HEAT 144:8
rose English unofficial r. — BROO 45:10

fire and the r. are one — ELIO 99:12
Goodbye, England's r. — JOHN 162:3
I know the colour r. — ABSE 1:3
One perfect r. — PARK 243:2
R. is a rose — STEI 296:5
Roves back the r. — DE L 87:12
scent of the summer r. — GRAV 131:8
white r. of Scotland — MACD 198:12
rosebud R. is just a piece — FILM 111:8
rose-garden Into the r. — ELIO 98:10
roses ash the burnt r. leave — ELIO 99:6
Everything's coming up r. — SOND 291:8
lilac and the r. — ARAG 12:10
R. are flowering in Picardy — WEAT 321:20
r. in December — BARR 24:1
Treaties like girls and r. — DE G 87:4
rot As artists they're r. — PARK 243:18
it must be all r. — NICH 230:3
r. the dead talk — ASQU 14:11
rots liquid which r. braces — MORT 223:8
rotted simply r. early — NASH 228:6
rotten good to feel r. — YESE 339:14
You r. swines — CATC 59:18
rottenness r. of our civilization — READ 261:4
rotting big r. log — WHIT 326:4
rough children who were r. — SPEN 293:9
round R. and round the circle — ELIO 98:7
R. up the usual suspects — FILM 111:3
rounded fully-r. human being — COOK 75:13
Roundheads R. (Right but) — YEAT 282:11
Rousseau R. was the first — BERL 33:8
routine R., in an intelligent man — AUDE 18:10
royal If you have a R. Family — PIML 249:7
My children are not r. — MARG 207:11
needed no r. title — SPEN 293:1
royalty R. the gold filling — OSBO 240:7
rub r. up against money — RUNY 270:8
rubble crushed by the r. — SOLZ 291:4
rubs fog that r. its back — ELIO 100:5
Rudolph R., the Red-nosed — MARK 207:14
rugby R. Union which is — THOM 308:8
rugged system of r. individualism — HOOV 151:9
rugs like a million bloody r. — FITZ 113:5
ruin r. himself in twelve months — GEOR 126:8
r. that Cromwell knocked about — BEDF 26:12
ruined They r. us — DUNN 93:4
Ruislip Gaily into R. gardens — BETJ 35:9
rule golden r. is — SHAW 284:22
One Ring to r. them all — TOLK 310:8
reasons for the r. change — STRA 300:4
R. I, on page I — MONT 220:13
r. by amateurs — ATTL 15:11
You work, we r. — DUNN 93:4
rules disregard of all the r. — ORWE 239:4
keep making up these sex r. — SALI 274:4
R. of Robotics — ASIM 13:11
rum It's a R. Go — VAUG 316:10

r., sodomy, prayers	CHUR 67:13	Sloane turned secular s.	BURC 48:13
what a R. Go everything is	WELL 323:7	**saints** S. should be judged guilty	ORWE 239:7
run best judge of a r.	WHAR 325:10	**sake** Art for art's s.	DIET 89:14
born to r.	SPRI 294:14	**salad** turn to chicken s.	JOHN 162:8
He can r.	LOUI 194:12	**salary** s. of the chief executive	GALB 123:9
In the long r.	KEYN 171:3	**sales** equation would halve the s.	HAWK 142:8
Now Teddy must r.	KENN 170:5	**salesman** Death of a s.	MILL 215:3
Take the money and r.	ALLE 6:11	s. is got to dream	MILL 215:6
They get r. down	BEVA 36:8	**salmon** primordial as a s.	WHIT 326:10
runaway r. Presidency	SCHL 280:2	s. sing in the street	AUDE 15:15
runner long-distance r.	SILL 287:4	s. standing on its tail	TYNA 314:7
running r. with the pack	BUTL 50:11	smoked s. and tinned	WILS 331:4
Ruskin art needed R.	STOP 299:14	**saloon** in the last chance s.	MELL 212:9
Russia forecast the action of R.	CHUR 66:1	**salt** s. rubbed into their wounds	WEST 324:19
From R. with love	FLEM 114:5	**salute** If it moves, s. it	SAYI 278:18
innocent R. squirmed	AKHM 5:3	**salvation** Wot prawce s. nah	SHAW 284:8
outlaws R. forever	REAG 262:2	**Sam** Play it again, S.	FILM 110:11
R. an empire or democracy	BRZE 47:9	Play it again, S.	MISQ 218:12
Russian embrace the R. bear	CHAN 61:8	**Samaritan** remember the Good S.	THAT 305:9
R. literature saved	RATU 260:11	**Samarkand** Golden Road to S.	FLEC 114:2
Russians keep the R. out	ISMA 157:15	**Samarra** tonight in S.	MAUG 210:9
Rutherford R. was a disaster	BULL 48:5	**same** doing the s. thing	PHIL 248:7
rye Before the Roman came to R.	CHES 62:11	s. the whole world over	ANON 11:6
catcher in the r.	SALI 274:2	**sanctions** Baldwin denouncing s.	BEAV 25:6
		sanctuary classes which need s.	BALD 21:4
		sands riddle of the s.	CHIL 64:9
Sacco S.'s name will live	VANZ 316:6	smoothed down like silly s.	BUNT 48:10
sack S. the lot	FISH 109:6	**sandwich** cheaper than a prawn s.	RATN 260:6
sacrament abortion would be a s.	KENN 168:8	raw-onion s.	BARN 23:7
sacramental flesh was s.	ROBI 265:11	**sane** if he was s. he had to fly	HELL 145:2
sacrifice final s.	SPRI 294:11	**San Francisco** left my heart in S.	CROS 81:3
great pinnacle of S.	LLOY 192:7	**sang** s. his didn't he	CUMM 81:8
holy hush of ancient s.	STEV 297:16	s. within the bloody wood	ELIO 101:5
Too long a s.	YEAT 337:9	**sanity** ain't no S. Claus	FILM 110:16
you refused a lesser s.	MARY 209:11	**sank** s. my boat	KENN 169:16
sacrificed be s. to expediency	MAUG 210:3	Sighted sub, s. same	MASO 209:14
never s.	DOLE 90:8	**Santa** shoot S. Claus	SMIT 288:14
sacrifices forgive him for the s.	MAUG 210:5	**sap** dried the s. out of my veins	YEAT 337:12
sad all their songs are s.	CHES 62:1	**sardines** s. will be thrown	CANT 53:8
sadistic source of s. conduct	PAGE 241:12	**Sargent** kind of musical Malcolm S.	
sadists repressed s.	CONN 74:12		BEEC 26:16
safe Health Service is s.	THAT 306:2	**sat** everyone has s. except a man	CUMM 81:12
made s. for democracy	WILS 332:7	**Satan** casting out S. by Satan	SORL 292:3
S. is spelled D-U-L-L	CLAR 69:16	saint or incarnation of S.	MADO 203:15
s. to be unpopular	STEV 298:5	**Satanic Verses** author of *The S.*	KHOM 171:7
s. to go back in the water	ADVE 4:4	**satellite** With s. TV	O'DO 234:8
world s. for hypocrisy	WOLF 334:2	**satiable** full of s. curtiosity	KIPL 175:11
safer s. than a known way	HASK 142:2	**satin** ease a heart like a s. gown	PARK 243:6
safety S. first	BALD 21:5	**satire** S. is what closes Saturday	KAUF 167:1
strike against public s.	COOL 76:1	**satirist** bounding past the s.	COCK 72:1
sagas frosty s.	CRAN 79:5	**satisfaction** can't get no s.	RICH 158:11
peoples who memorized s.	BJÖR 38:8	**Saturday** closes S. night	KAUF 167:1
said if you want anything s.	THAT 304:10	Glasgow Empire on a S.	DODD 90:6
not know what they have s.	CHUR 65:5	**sausage** hold on s. and haddock	WOOL 335:16
sailed I have s. the seas	YEAT 338:11	news into s. factory	PAXM 246:2
saint call me a s.	CAMA 52:2	s. machine	CHRI 65:2
s. or incarnation of Satan	MADO 203:15	**savage** days of the Noble S.	BIKO 37:11

savage (*cont.*):

has not wept is a s.	SANT 275:7
savaged s. by a dead sheep	HEAL 143:6
save destroy the town to s. it	ANON 10:4
God s. the King	MOYN 224:6
helped s. the world	KEYN 171:6
s. the Governor-General	WHIT 327:11
through life trying to s.	ROGE 267:1
To s. your world	AUDE 16:5
saved could have s. sixpence	BECK 25:13
only s. the world	CHES 62:6
saving capable of s. us	RICH 264:9
saw *I s. you do it*	STOP 299:7
say anything good to s.	LONG 194:3
don't s. nothin'	HAMM 137:13
has nothing to s.	TAYL 303:12
more to s. when I am dead	ROBI 265:8
nothing to s.	CAGE 51:2
S. it with flowers	ADVE 4:18
s. *something* about me	COHA 72:10
see what I s.	FORS 116:1
see what I s.	WALL 319:2
way I s. it	WEST 324:16
what circumstances we s. it	HAVE 142:4
whatever you s., say nothing	HEAN 144:4
wink wink, s. no more	MONT 221:1
scale not made on a human s.	MALR 205:8
puts his thumb in the s.	LAWR 183:11
scales someone is practising s.	MACN 203:8
scallywags Women love s.	BAIL 20:3
scandal because of a s.	HAIL 136:4
scare s. myself with my own	FROS 120:5
scarlet His sins were s.	BELL 28:7
scenery among savage s.	HOFF 150:8
God paints the s.	HART 141:9
scent how hot the s.	GRAV 131:8
s. on a pocket handkerchief	LLOY 192:12
scepticism s. kept her	SART 276:10
schedule my s. is already full	KISS 176:3
schizophrenia S. cannot be	LAIN 179:4
schizophrenic s. is a special	LAIN 179:6
you are a s.	SZAS 302:6
school At s. I never minded	MORT 223:3
destroy every grammar s.	CROS 80:11
learned about in s.	JARR 159:18
schoolchildren What all s. learn	AUDE 17:9
schoolgirl priggish s.	GRIG 134:5
s. complexion	ADVE 4:5
schoolmaster becoming a s.	WAUG 320:14
schoolmasters write for the s.	FITZ 113:11
schoolteacher s. underpaid	OSBO 240:9
science aim of s.	BREC 43:12
All s. is either physics	RUTH 272:12
do s. in hell	VAUG 316:8
essence of s.	BRON 45:4
grand aim of all s.	EINS 97:6
In s. the credit goes	DARW 83:9

Modern s. largely conceived	LEBO 186:5
no less true than s.	DAY- 85:6
plundered this new s.	MCEW 199:6
redefined the task of s.	HAWK 142:9
S. aggregate of recipes	VALÉ 315:14
S. Fiction no more written	ALDI 5:10
S. finds, industry applies	ANON 11:4
S. is an edged tool	EDDI 95:6
S. is part of culture	GOUL 131:4
s. is satisfying the curiosity	ARTS 13:9
s. is strong	SZAS 302:7
S. lost its virgin purity	GRAV 131:16
S. may have found a cure	KELL 168:6
S. must begin with myths	POPP 252:7
S. offers best answers	DAWK 84:10
S. proceeds to destroy	HUGH 154:6
s. reassures	BRAQ 43:6
S. without religion	EINS 96:6
separation of state and s.	FEYE 108:1
triumph of modern s.	WAUG 321:18
understand how s. works	ASIM 13:12
science fiction becoming s.	BALL 22:1
S. writers foresee	ASIM 14:1
scientific *empirical s. system*	POPP 250:14
importance of s. work	HILB 148:5
new s. truth	PLAN 250:1
scientist distinguished s. says	CLAR 70:5
exercise for research s.	LORE 194:11
not try to become a s.	EINS 97:7
s.'s laws	QUIN 258:14
s. thinks of a method	PERU 247:9
s. were to cut his ear	MEDA 212:2
We believe a s.	RICH 264:8
scientists in the company of s.	AUDE 18:6
s. are probably right	ASIM 14:2
than most young s.	MEDA 212:5
scissors end up using s.	HOCK 150:4
scooters s. off my lawn	CLAR 70:8
score time required to s. 500	COMP 73:8
scorer One Great S.	RICE 263:13
Scotch as a S. banker	DAVI 83:10
Mary, ma S. Bluebell	LAUD 181:10
Scotland flower of S.	WILL 330:11
our infinite S.	MACD 198:14
S., land of omnipotent No	BOLD 41:2
white rose of S.	MACD 198:12
Scotsman S. on the make	BARR 23:15
S. with a grievance	WODE 333:1
Scotty Beam me up, S.	MISQ 218:1
scouts s.' motto	BADE 19:15
scrabble s. with all the vowels	ELLI 103:8
scrap s. of paper	BETH 34:10
scrape s. your strings darker	CELA 59:21
scratch S. a lover	PARK 242:12
scratching s. of pimples	WOOL 335:13
scream like a s. from a crevasse	GREE 132:10
s. till I'm sick	CROM 80:8

scum Okie means you're s.   STEI 296:10
  rich are the s. of the earth   CHES 63:4
  They are s.   MAUG 210:12
scuttling S. across the floors   ELIO 100:7
scythe sighs like s.   WALC 318:3
sea all gone under the s.   ELIO 98:16
  complaining about the s.   POWE 255:12
  In a solitude of the s.   HARD 139:7
  in our s. of confusion   GAMO 124:7
  like bathing in the s.   LEIG 187:3
  Put out to s.   MACN 203:10
  s.-change in politics   CALL 51:12
  s. hates a coward   O'NE 236:5
  s.-worm crawls—grotesque   HARD 139:7
  serpent-haunted s.   FLEC 114:1
  snotgreen s.   JOYC 165:3
  very much at s.   CARS 54:6
seagulls When s. follow a trawler   CANT 53:8
seal heard a s. bark   THUR 309:10
sealed My lips are s.   MISQ 218:11
seals aroma of performing s.   HART 141:7
seams Amusing little s.   BAIL 20:2
search in s. of an author   PIRA 249:12
  s. for a voice of his own   MORT 223:1
seas floors of silent s.   ELIO 100:7
  s. colder than the Hebrides   FLEC 113:17
  s. roll over   HERB 146:14
season dry brain in a dry s.   ELIO 99:15
  man has every s.   FOND 114:13
seat-belts Fasten your s.   FILM 110:5
second grow a s. tongue   MONT 220:10
  not a s. on the day   COOK 75:12
  s. best's a gay goodnight   YEAT 337:14
  s. oldest profession   REAG 261:12
  s. profession in reserve   NICO 230:12
  s. things never   CONR 75:9
  when you come s.   HILL 148:8
second-best s. is anything but   LESS 188:22
second-hand s. Europeans   HOPE 152:1
secret girls that have no s.   SPEN 293:12
  neurosis is a s.   TYNA 314:11
  photograph is a s.   ARBU 12:11
  s. diary of Adrian Mole   TOWN 310:13
  s. in the Oxford sense   FRAN 118:5
  S. sits in the middle   FROS 120:17
secretive make sex less s.   SZAS 302:8
secrets privacy and tawdry s.   LEAC 185:3
  throw their guilty s.   PRIE 256:7
security otherwise styled s.   MADA 203:14
  s. around the president   MAIL 204:13
seduction In s., the rapist   DWOR 94:2
see come up and s. me sometime   MISQ 219:5
  day I was meant not to s.   THAT 306:5
  I'll s. you again   COWA 78:5
  I shall never s.   KILM 171:13
  Nice to s. you   CATC 59:2
  s. and hear nothing   THOM 308:5

  s. clearly what lies under   AUDE 18:9
  s. it clearly in the idea   STEV 297:12
  s. the hours pass   CIOR 69:12
  s. things and say 'Why'   SHAW 283:11
  s. what I say   WALL 319:2
  wait and s.   ASQU 14:5
  What you s. is what you get   SAYI 279:13
seeing s. what everybody has seen
                                       SZEN 302:11
seem Let be be finale of s.   STEV 297:7
seen being s. for what one is   DRAB 92:3
  I have s. war   ROOS 267:9
  s. one city slum   AGNE 4:30
  should be s. to be done   HEWA 147:7
  when you've s. one Western   WHIT 327:10
  You've never s. this country   PURD 258:2
segregation S. now   WALL 318:14
selection discrimination and s.   JAME 159:10
  Natural s. a mechanism   FISH 109:12
self divided s.   LAIN 179:3
self-assertion s. abroad   WAUG 321:7
self-contempt S., well-grounded   LEAV 186:3
self-defence it was in s.   MARL 208:2
self-denial S. is not a virtue   SHAW 285:6
self-esteem proper measure of s.   BENN 30:10
self-government S. is our right   CASE 55:9
self-indulgence life of s.   BENN 31:5
selfish s. gene   DAWK 84:8
  small and s. is sorrow   ELIZ 103:5
  still s., vain, greedy   COOK 75:13
self-made s. man is one who   STEA 295:12
  s. man may prefer   HAND 138:4
self-respect starves your s.   PARR 244:14
self-revelation *fluidity of s.*   JAME 159:5
  s., whether it be   LANC 179:15
self-sufficiency S. at home   WAUG 321:7
sell I'll s. him   LEAC 185:5
  s., and make money   HARR 141:3
  s. it cheap   SAYI 279:5
  s. Jack like soapflakes   KENN 170:1
  to s. time   TAWN 303:4
selling old firm, is s. out   OSBO 240:3
  s. cosmetic cream   RODD 266:2
  S. off the family silver   MISQ 218:13
seltzer weak hock and s.   BETJ 34:11
semen no frozen s. ever read a story
                                       WILL 329:10
semi-house-trained s. polecat   FOOT 115:2
senator S., and a Democrat   JOHN 162:9
senators s. burst with laughter   AUDE 16:6
sensations easy prey to s.   TREV 311:9
sense Money is like a sixth s.   MAUG 210:8
  talk s. to American people   STEV 298:1
senseless kind of s. wit   WILB 328:7
senses pleasures of the s.   ESHE 104:9
sensibility dissociation of s.   ELIO 102:6
  informed by s.   READ 261:5

sensual to be Catholic and s.   CHAN 61:4
sensuality s., rebellion   THOM 308:8
sentence it's a s.   FILM 111:6
     life s. goes on   CONL 74:9
sentenced s. to death in my absence
                                   BEHA 27:2
sentences Backward ran s.   GIBB 127:9
sentiment corrupted by s.   GREE 132:5
sentimental s. value   FRY 121:10
sentimentality S. the emotional   MAIL 204:7
separation real s. of powers   DENN 88:7
     s. of state and science   FEYE 108:1
September When you reach S.   ANDE 8:8
seraglio s. of eunuchs   FOOT 115:1
serene that unhoped s.   BROO 45:7
serenity called the s. of age   BLIS 39:10
sergeant S. Pepper   TYNA 314:10
serial obituary in s. form   CRIS 80:4
serious Murder is a s. business   ILES 156:6
     War is too s. a matter   CLEM 71:5
     You cannot be s.   MCEN 199:5
seriously S., though   CATC 59:5
sermon rejected S. on the Mount   BRAD 43:2
serpent s. ate Eve   HUGH 154:4
     s.-haunted sea   FLEC 114:1
servant answer to the s. problem   LEBO 186:5
     as a humble s.   MAND 205:12
     become the s. of a man   SHAW 284:1
     lookingglass of a s.   JOYC 165:4
     One s. worth a thousand gadgets
                                     SCHU 281:7
     s. to the devil   SISS 288:1
servants equality in the s.' hall   BARR 23:9
     wish your wife or s.   GRIF 134:4
serve love to s. my country   GIBR 127:10
served s. to him course by course   CHUR 65:13
service at the s. of the nation   POMP 250:13
     devoted to your s.   ELIZ 102:10
     Pressed into s.   FROS 120:18
     s. of my love   SPRI 294:11
     s.? The rent we pay   CLAY 70:10
serviettes crumpled the s.   BETJ 35:3
servility savage s.   LOWE 195:8
sesquippledan S. verboojuice   WELL 323:5
seven have the s. minutes   COLL 73:4
     s.-stone weakling   ADVE 4:3
     S. types of ambiguity   EMPS 104:2
seventh moon is in the s. house   RADO 259:6
seventies s. started 21st century   BOWI 42:17
seventy Oh, to be s. again   CLEM 71:4
sewer s. in a glass-bottomed boat   MIZN 219:8
sewing job of s. on a button   BROU 46:8
sex attempt to insult s.   LAWR 183:12
     Battles and s.   MCAR 196:12
     call you darling after s.   BARN 23:8
     Continental have s. life   MIKE 214:5
     death, s. and jewels   STRO 300:8

     have s. with a man   WESL 324:1
     if s. rears its ugly head   AYCK 19:3
     isn't s. but death   SONT 291:14
     Is s. dirty   ALLE 6:9
     make s. less secretive   SZAS 302:8
     men think. S., work   FISH 109:3
     Money was exactly like s.   BALD 20:11
     mostly about having s.   LODG 193:1
     No s. please—we're British   MARR 208:14
     only unnatural s. act   KINS 173:10
     portray this [s.] relation   ROBI 265:11
     practically conceal its s.   NASH 227:10
     S. and drugs and rock and roll   DURY 94:1
     S. and taxes are   JONE 163:15
     s. business isn't worth   LAWR 185:1
     s. in the mind   LAWR 184:2
     s. in yesterday's novels   WELD 322:11
     S. is something I really   SALI 274:4
     S. never been act of freedom   WILC 328:9
     s. on the basketball court   SEIK 282:5
     s. that brings forth   DE B 85:10
     s. was the most fun   ALLE 6:7
     s. with someone I love   ALLE 6:8
     she has herself no s. at all   GREE 133:1
     wanted to know about s.   REUB 263:6
     what age the s. drive goes   BLAK 39:6
     When you have money, it's s.   DONL 90:10
sexes difference within the s.   COMP 74:7
     personalities of the two s.   MEAD 211:11
sexophones s. wailed   HUXL 155:3
sexual car crash as a s. event   BALL 22:2
     draws so oddly with the s.   GUNN 135:9
     s. continence requires   PAGE 241:11
     S. intercourse began   LARK 180:2
     S. Object sought by all men   GREE 133:1
     shock of s. astonishment   WESL 323:18
sexuality relinquish their s.   WOLF 333:17
sexually Life a s. transmitted disease
                                     ANON 10:10
shabby s. equipment   ELIO 99:1
shackles Memories are not s.   BENN 30:14
shad-blow Cowslip and s.   CRAN 79:6
shade sitting in the s.   KIPL 174:3
     whiter s. of pale   REID 262:15
shadow also casts a s.   CHUR 67:2
     Falls the S.   ELIO 99:18
     live under the s. of a war   SPEN 294:1
     s. stands over us   ALLI 6:20
shadows less liquid than their s.   TESS 304:8
     long s. on county grounds   MAJO 204:16
     s. and twilights   Æ 2:6
shafts Its s. remain   ROET 266:5
shake S., rattle and roll   CALH 51:6
shaken S. and not stirred   FLEM 114:4
Shakespeare Even if I could be S.   HUXL 155:15
     If S. had not written   WOLP 334:9
     read S.   WELL 323:4

reproduce works of S.   WILE 329:1
S., another Newton   HUXL 155:13
S. is like bathing   LEIG 187:3
S. is so tiring   HULL 154:8
S.—the nearest thing   OLIV 235:16
When I read S.   LAWR 184:8
When you do S.   MIRR 217:2
Shakespearian That S. rag   BUCK 48:4
Shakespeherian S. Rag   ELIO 101:12
shall picked the was of s.   CUMM 81:16
shambles accountable s.   HUNT 154:11
shame all a bleedin' s.   ANON 11:6
   called s. and humiliation   O'RO 236:17
   secret s. destroyed   RICH 264:12
   terrible s. for me   YOKO 340:2
shamrock Apart from the s.   MCAL 196:10
shape pressed out of s.   FROS 120:18
   s. of Lord Hailsham   PAGE 241:11
   s. of things to come   WELL 323:10
shareholder sole s.   MAND 206:6
shares Fair s. for all   POLI 251:10
shark s. has pretty teeth   BREC 44:1
sharks s. circling, and waiting   CLAR 69:13
shaves s. and takes a train   WHIT 326:3
Shaw S.'s plays   AGAT 2:8
shed disused s. in Co. Wexford   MAHO 204:5
she-devil life and loves of a s.   WELD 322:10
sheep eat a whole s.   MAUG 210:11
   mere s.-herding   POUN 254:12
   savaged by a dead s.   HEAL 143:6
   s. in sheep's clothing   CHUR 69:6
   s. to pass resolutions   INGE 156:13
sheet brought in the white s.   GARC 125:1
sheets cool kindliness of s.   BROO 45:8
   polyester s.   FARR 106:11
shelf s. life of the modern   TRIL 311:12
shell aggressive s.   MCLU 201:10
   fired a 15-inch s.   RUTH 272:14
shells choirs of wailing s.   OWEN 240:15
shepherd Old Nod, the s.   DE L 87:18
sheriff I shot the s.   MARL 208:2
sherry first-rate s. flowing   PLOM 250:9
shift s. in what the public wants   CALL 51:12
shilling s. life will give you   AUDE 17:11
shimmered Jeeves s. out   WODE 333:2
shimmy s. like my sister Kate   PIRO 249:13
shine that's where I s.   BENC 29:4
ship as the smart s. grew   HARD 139:9
   desert a sinking s.   BEAV 25:10
   like a sinking s.   WOOL 335:17
   s. appeared in the air   HEAN 143:14
   towards a sinking s.   CHUR 69:4
ships little s. of England   GUED 135:2
   s. have been salvaged   HALS 137:6
   s. sail like swans asleep   FLEC 114:3
   wrong with our bloody s.   BEAT 25:4
shire rambles round the s.   CHES 62:11

shires bugles calling from sad s.   OWEN 240:15
shit chicken s. can turn   JOHN 162:8
   ocean of s.   TANS 302:17
   shock-proof s. detector   HEMI 145:17
shivering s. human soul   PAST 245:5
shivers s. like the jelly   PIRO 249:13
shoals s. of herring   MACC 198:5
shock Future s.   TOFF 310:5
   s. of the new   DUNL 93:1
   sudden s. of joy   BLIS 39:10
shocked not s. by this subject   BOHR 40:10
shocking something s.   PORT 252:10
shocks s. the magistrate   RUSS 272:6
shoe embrace a woman's s.   KRAU 177:15
shoes Englishwomen's s.   HALS 137:4
   in cheap s.   AMIE 7:6
   mind it wipes its s.   THOM 307:16
   s. with broken high ideals   MCGO 199:8
shoeshine smile and a s.   MILL 215:6
shoestring runs it into a s.   WOOL 336:1
shook Ten days that s. the world   REED 262:14
shoot s. me in my absence   BEHA 27:2
   s. me through linoleum   BANK 22:13
   s. Santa Claus   SMIT 288:14
   s. your murderer   ACHE 1:6
   They s. horses don't they   MCCO 198:7
   they shout and they s.   INGE 156:11
   You'd s. a fellow down   HARD 140:3
shooting war minus the s.   ORWE 239:8
shoots green s. of recovery   MISQ 218:6
   man who s. him gets caught   MAIL 204:13
shop foul rag and bone s.   YEAT 337:2
shopping main thing today—s.   MILL 215:7
   Whole families s.   GINS 128:8
shore To the other s.   PAUL 245:14
shores wilder s. of love   BLAN 39:8
short long and the s.   HUGH 153:10
shorts Eat my s.   CATC 57:12
shot Certain men the English s.   YEAT 338:2
   I s. the sheriff   MARL 208:2
   They've s. our fox   BIRC 38:2
shots take pot s. at you   CLAR 69:15
shoulder keep looking over his s.   BARU 24:12
shoulders City of the Big S.   SAND 274:10
   old heads on young s.   SPAR 292:9
   s. held the sky   HOUS 152:7
shout they s. and they shoot   INGE 156:11
show wrong if someone can s. you   AYER 19:8
show business no business like s.   BERL 33:1
   s. with blood   BRUN 47:4
shower haven't had a bath or s.   NEWT 230:2
   sweetness of a s.   THOM 308:7
showing review without s. off   AUDE 18:8
showman great s. whose technique

     TAYL 303:14
shows All my s. are great   GRAD 131:5
shrimp s. learns to whistle   KHRU 171:8

shrined bower we s. to Tennyson   HARD 139:5
shrink discussed it with his s.   FARR 106:11
shroud stiff dishonoured s.   ELIO 101:5
   striped s.   THOM 308:9
shudder s. in the loins engenders   YEAT 337:20
shuffle All s. there   YEAT 338:12
shy life has made me s.   BERG 32:8
sick kingdom of the s.   SONT 291:17
   Pass the s. bag, Alice   CATC 59:4
   scream till I'm s.   CROM 80:8
   think we're s.   WOLF 334:1
Sid Tell S.   ADVE 4:22
Sidcup get down to S.   PINT 249:9
side S. by side   WOOD 334:14
   which s. do they cheer for   TEBB 303:18
sides both s. of the paper   SELL 282:15
   everyone changes s.   CONN 75:1
   holding on to the s.   ELLI 103:9
   looked at life from both s.   MITC 217:5
   Norfan, both s.   WELL 323:6
siege She kept the s.   HILL 148:10
Siegfried washing on the S. Line   KENN 168:10
siesta Englishmen detest a s.   COWA 78:8
siftings let their liquid s. fall   ELIO 101:5
sigh s. is just a sigh   HUPF 154:13
sight Beauty at first s.   SHAW 284:19
   neatly out of s.   CRAN 79:9
sights few more impressive s.   BARR 23:15
sign God would give some s.   ALLE 6:16
signed hand that s. the paper   THOM 307:5
   I s. my death warrant   COLL 73:3
significance s. of its own   JUNG 166:6
signposts s. to socialist Utopia   CROS 80:10
signs no 'white' or 'coloured' s.   KENN 169:12
   s. of his awareness   BLUN 40:1
silence chequered s.   AKHM 5:5
   clamour of s.   TAGO 302:14
   conspiracy of s.   SHAW 285:8
   Deep is the s.   DRIN 92:4
   Go to where the s. is   GOOD 130:13
   mind moves upon s.   YEAT 338:1
   period of s. on your part   ATTL 15:6
   private s.   PRIT 257:3
   s., exile, and cunning   JOYC 165:1
   S. like a cancer grows   SIMO 287:10
   stain upon the s.   BECK 26:10
   world of s.   EPIT 105:1
silent mornings are strangely s.   CARS 54:7
   one must be s.   WITT 332:16
   Paris was French—and s.   TUCH 313:12
   s. majority   NIXO 232:4
   t is s., as in Harlow   ASQU 14:14
silk s. hat on a Bradford   ELIO 101:17
silkworm of s. size or immense   MOOR 221:5
silly You were s. like us   AUDE 16:10
silver About a s. lining   COWA 78:13
   in her s. shoon   DE L 87:19

Selling off the family s.   MISQ 218:13
s. foot in his mouth   RICH 264:7
spread your s. sunsets   DAVI 84:3
There's a s. lining   FORD 115:11
thirty pieces of s.   BEVA 36:9
simple C'est tellement s.   PRÉV 256:5
   hard question is s.   AUDE 17:18
   I'm a s. man   LOWR 196:1
simplify s. me when I'm dead   DOUG 91:4
Simpson I'm Bart S.   CATC 58:10
   Mrs S.'s pinched   ANON 9:14
sin My s., my soul   NABO 226:13
   physicists have known s.   OPPE 236:9
   researches in original s.   PLOM 250:10
   what did he say about s.   COOL 76:5
   worst s. towards our fellow   SHAW 283:13
sincere Always be s.   TRUM 313:5
   s. ignorance   KING 172:10
sincerely s. want to be rich   CORN 77:3
sinecure gives no man a s.   POUN 254:3
sing I, too, s. America   HUGH 153:11
   I will s. of the sun   POUN 253:15
   never heard no horse s.   ARMS 13:3
   no longer s. to the babies   MENU 213:7
   S. 'em muck   MELB 212:8
   S. whatever is well made   YEAT 339:3
   Soul clap its hands and s.   YEAT 338:10
   souls can s. openly   SPEN 293:3
   that they will s. to me   ELIO 100:10
singer s. not the song   ANON 11:7
singing always a secret s.   SAND 274:14
   listen to money s.   LARK 181:3
   Lorca was killed, s.   READ 261:6
   S. in the rain   FREE 118:7
   s. will never be done   SASS 276:21
   suddenly burst out s.   SASS 276:20
sings fat lady s.   SAYI 279:4
   instead of bleeding, he s.   GARD 125:3
sinister strange and s.   JAME 159:3
sinking desert a s. ship   BEAV 25:10
   like a s. ship   WOOL 335:17
   that s. feeling   ADVE 3:8
   towards a s. ship   CHUR 69:4
sinned people s. against   COMP 74:4
sins half the s. of mankind   RUSS 271:6
   His s. were scarlet   BELL 28:7
   not the s. of the fathers   FREN 118:8
   s. are attempts to fill   WEIL 322:5
   s. of despair   READ 261:8
sir S., no man's enemy   AUDE 17:14
sister Did your s. throw up   WALK 318:8
   trying to violate your s.   STRA 299:17
sisterhood S. is powerful   MORG 221:13
Sistine on the S. Chapel roof   YEAT 339:2
Sisyphus imagine that S. is happy   CAMU 52:16
   like the torture of S.   DE B 85:12
sit allowed to s. down   USTI 315:9

small (*cont.*):

S. is beautiful	SCHU 281:2
s. states—Israel, Athens	INGE 157:1
they are very s.	UPDI 315:3

small-talking Where in this s. world

	FRY 121:12

smash all s. and no grab — NICO 230:11
English never s. in a face — HALS 137:5
smashed s. it into because — CUMM 81:16
smell s. and hideous hum — GODL 129:8
s. of napalm in the morning — FILM 110:13
Sweet s. of success — FILM 112:16
smile Cambridge people rarely s. — BROO 45:12
faint fleeting s. — THUR 309:15
good s. in a child's eyes — SHAF 283:7
has a nice s. — GROM 134:11
Is it Colman's s. — EWAR 104:11
s. and a shoeshine — MILL 215:6
S. at us, pay us — CHES 62:13
s. dwells a little longer — CHAP 61:11
s. of a cosmic Cheshire cat — HUXL 155:16
s. on the face of the tiger — ANON 11:10
s., smile, smile — ASAF 13:10
smiled only the dead s. — AKHM 5:2
smith Chuck it, S. — CHES 61:17
smoke rise then as s. to the sky — CELA 59:21
S. gets in your eyes — HARB 138:7
watching people s. in old films — WELD 322:11
smoked s. my first cigarette — TOSC 310:12
smoke-filled s. room — SIMP 287:14
smoking S. can seriously damage — OFFI 235:11
smoky burnt-out ends of s. days — ELIO 100:16
snake s. came to my water-trough — LAWR 184:5
snakes S. eat frogs — STEV 297:8
snare rabbit in a s. — STEP 297:1
snaring s. the poor world — CRAN 79:8
snatching s. his victuals from — CHUR 65:13
sneaky snouty, s. mind — NICO 230:7
sneeze like having a good s. — LAWR 184:11
sneezes Coughs and s. spread — OFFI 235:3
snicker hold my coat, and s. — ELIO 100:8
snipe could shoot s. off him — POWE 255:1
snobbery bereaved if s. died — USTI 315:10
S. with Violence — BENN 31:1
snobs bad Brits are s. — SHAF 283:8
snored Coolidge only s. — MENC 213:4
snotgreen s. sea — JOYC 165:3
snouty s., sneaky mind — NICO 230:7
snow congealed s. — PARK 243:19
dark over the s. — THOM 308:6
first fall of s. — PRIE 256:9
like the s. geese — OKPI 234:15
s. falling faintly — JOYC 164:5
woods fill up with s. — FROS 120:20
wrong kind of s. — WORR 336:3
snowed s. for six days — THOM 307:11
snows more it s. (Tiddely pom) — MILN 216:4

Snow White used to be S. — WEST 324:14
so And s. do I — HARD 140:7
soaked s. to the skin — COHE 72:11
soapflakes sell Jack like s. — KENN 170:1
sob S., heavy world — AUDE 15:13
sober covered by s. journalists — O'RO 236:14
Porson s. — HOUS 152:13
sees in Garbo s. — TYNA 314:6
tomorrow I shall be s. — CHUR 69:9
social s. and economic experiment

	HOOV 151:8

S. Contract nothing more — WELL 323:8
s. progress, order — JOHN 161:12
socialism Democracy and s. — NEHR 229:3
lots of ways to get s. — KINN 173:9
really believe in S. — GRIM 134:10
religion of S. — BEVA 36:6
S. can only arrive — VIER 317:17
S. does not mean — ORWE 239:1
S. nothing but capitalism — SPEN 294:4
s. would not lose — DUBČ 92:5
socialist build a s. society — NYER 233:6
In the blood of the s. — CROS 80:12
signposts to s. Utopia — CROS 80:10
S. literature — ORWE 239:2
socialists s. throw it away — CAST 56:2
socially often s. impressive — WILL 329:8
society affluent s. — GALB 123:2
call it a 'primitive s.' — GREG 133:8
class-ridden s. — KING 173:3
Great S. — JOHN 163:2
litmus test of civil s. — HAVE 142:7
No s. can survive — GING 128:4
no such thing as S. — THAT 306:8
prosperous or caring s. — HESE 147:3
shape of s. — ORWE 238:2
so-called affluent s. — BEVA 36:13
s. founded on trash — SAYE 277:4
S. needs to condemn — MAJO 204:15
s. to make boys into men — STEV 297:2
s. where it is safe — STEV 298:5
sock making a hole in a s. — EINS 97:11
sockets candles burn the s. — HOUS 152:6
Socratic S. manner is not a game — BEER 26:21
soda wash their feet in s. water — ELIO 101:14
sodium having discovered S. — BENT 32:4
sodomy Impotence and s. — WAUG 321:15
rum, s., prayers — CHUR 67:13
sofa s. upholstered in panther — PLOM 250:10
soft s. under-belly of Europe — MISQ 219:1
softly S. along the road — DE L 87:18
softness s. of my body — LOWE 195:4
soggy s. little island — UPDI 314:15
soldier British s. stand up to — SHAW 283:15
s. of the Great War — EPIT 105:14
s.'s life is terrible hard — MILN 216:11
s. trying to violate — STRA 299:17

who had the s. singled | DOUG 91:5
soldiers brought its s. home for lack of | LARK 180:7
Old s. never die | FOLE 114:12
old s. never die | MACA 197:3
S. are citizens | SASS 276:18
young Argentinian s. | RUNC 270:5
soldiery Emperor's drunken s. | YEAT 336:13
sole nothing can be s. or whole | YEAT 337:5
solid s. for fluidity | CHUR 65:11
solidity appearance of s. | ORWE 239:6
s. was knocked out | LEAC 185:4
solitary s. confinement inside our own skins | WILL 330:3
solitude endure our own s. | PRIT 257:3
feel his s. more keenly | VALÉ 315:15
Solomon S.'s temple, poets | MEYN 214:2
S. wrote the Proverbs | NAYL 228:16
soluble art of the s. | MEDA 212:4
solution can't see the s. | CHES 63:17
either part of the s. | CLEA 70:11
final s. | HEYD 147:11
people were a kind of s. | CAVA 56:7
total s. | GOER 129:12
solutions s. are not | ASIM 14:1
sombrero in a s. speaking English | PHIL 248:4
some S. mishtake, shurely | CATC 59:6
somebody life of s. else | DAVI 83:11
someday S. I'll find you | COWA 78:11
someone fear that s. may be happy | MENC 212:12
S. wants a letter | ADVE 4:20
something must be like s. | FORS 115:13
say s. about me | COHA 72:10
s. completely different | CATC 57:2
S. may be gaining | PAIG 242:3
S. must be done | MISQ 219:2
s. of the night | WIDD 328:1
Time for a little s. | MILN 216:8
was there s. | CATC 57:19
sometime come up and see me s. | MISQ 219:5
woman is a s. thing | HEYW 148:2
somewhat more than s. | RUNY 270:9
somewhere S. over the rainbow | HARB 138:11
Somme S. is like the Holocaust | BARK 23:1
son good idea—s. | CATC 57:18
mother of a great s. | KENN 170:4
s. was killed while laughing | KIPL 173:14
song carcase of an old s. | THOM 308:13
hate a s. that has sold | BERL 33:4
only s. where I get | JOHN 162:6
s. is ended (but the melody) | BERL 32:15
s. makes you feel a thought | HARB 138:14
s. was wordless | SASS 276:21
spur me into s. | YEAT 338:17
trouble with a folk s. | LAMB 179:9
When ever I remake a s. | YEAT 337:13

songs all their s. are sad | CHES 62:1
sonnets ten passably effective s. | HUXL 155:8
sons s. and daughters of Life | GIBR 127:11
sophistication Hip is the s. | MAIL 204:11
Sorbonne one day at the S. | STEV 297:13
sorrow paying fines on s. | MAYA 211:5
small and selfish is s. | ELIZ 103:5
S. in all lands | SUTT 301:9
S. is tranquillity | PARK 243:8
sorrows s. of the mothers | FREN 118:8
sorry having to say you're s. | SEGA 282:4
S. for itself | LAWR 184:4
soteriological In s. terms | FENT 107:9
soufflé cannot reheat a s. | MCCA 198:3
sought least s. for | CRAN 79:11
soul dark night of the s. | FITZ 113:7
engineers of the s. | GORK 131:1
give his own s. | BOLT 41:5
God rest his s. | SMIT 290:3
literature saved my s. | RATU 260:11
Lord take my s. | LAST 182:10
not engineers of the s. | KENN 169:15
object is to change the s. | THAT 305:13
open channel to the s. | BELL 28:14
owe my s. to the company store | TRAV 311:3
selling one's s. | MACK 200:4
shivering human s. | PAST 245:5
S. clap its hands and sing | YEAT 338:10
s. swooned slowly | JOYC 164:5
soulless when work is s. | CAMU 53:6
souls damp s. of housemaids | ELIO 100:11
engineers of human s. | STAL 295:5
live in furnished s. | CUMM 82:3
only in men's s. | STEV 298:3
stuff of other people's s. | MCGR 200:2
sound feeling, then, not s. | STEV 297:14
s. and original ideas | MACM 202:1
s. of music | HAMM 137:15
s. of surprise | BALL 22:5
with s. turned down | HARR 141:2
soundbite s. all an interviewer | BENN 30:7
sounds similar s. at their ends | LARK 181:5
soup do not take s. at luncheon | CURZ 82:13
pissed in our s. | BENN 30:11
s. is chaos | WARN 319:11
south go s. in the winter | ELIO 101:7
I want to go s. | LAWR 184:14
Yes, but not in the S. | POTT 253:10
South Africa S., renowned | CAMP 52:10
southern S. trees bear strange | HOLI 150:11
souvenirs s. sont cors de chasse | APOL 12:7
sovereign change for a s. | NESB 229:11
sovereignties addition of s. | MONN 220:3
Soviet S. power plus electrification | LENI 187:10
Soviets All power to the S. | POLI 251:1
Soviet Union S. has indeed | FULB 121:18
sow old s. that eats her farrow | JOYC 164:14

space abandoned s. station	THOM 309:3	
art of how to waste s.	JOHN 163:12	
cantos of unvanquished s.	CRAN 79:5	
filling the s.	WEST 325:3	
more s. where nobody is	STEI 296:3	
S. is almost infinite	QUAY 258:9	
S. is blue	HEIS 145:1	
S. isn't remote	HOYL 153:4	
untrespassed sanctity of s.	MAGE 204:2	
spaces s. between the houses	FENT 107:8	
spaceship S. Earth	FULL 122:3	
Spain Go to S. and get killed	POLL 250:11	
nor leave S.	JUAN 165:17	
permanence and unity of S.	JUAN 165:16	
spain rain in S.	LERN 188:18	
Spaniards not the power of the S.	SCHU 281:1	
Spanish in a bowler speaking S.	PHIL 248:4	
spanner their throats with a s.	BETJ 35:4	
spare Brother can you s. a dime	HARB 138:8	
do in his s. time	GILL 128:2	
spark-gap s. mightier than pen	HOGB 150:9	
sparrow Lesbia with her s.	MILL 214:13	
sparrows pass through for the s.	GALB 123:10	
speak I now s. for France	DE G 86:9	
s. before you think	FORS 116:18	
s. for Britain	BOOT 41:8	
S. for England	AMER 7:4	
s. ill of everybody except	PÉTA 247:10	
S. softly	ROOS 268:3	
whereof one cannot s.	WITT 332:16	
speaker as a public s.	NICO 230:8	
speaking talking without s.	SIMO 287:10	
spearmint s. lose its flavour	ROSE 268:11	
special all s. cases	CAMU 52:13	
specialist definition of a s.	MAYO 211:10	
spectacle global s.	DEBO 86:3	
spectacular assured by a s. error	GALB 123:15	
spectator politics to a s. sport	GALB 123:11	
speech dead had no s. for	ELIO 99:5	
gift of articulate s.	SHAW 285:17	
make a s. on conservation	STEV 298:9	
making a s. on economics	JOHN 163:8	
our concern was s.	ELIO 99:8	
s. from Ernest Bevin	FOOT 114:14	
S. is civilization	MANN 207:2	
speeches all the easy s.	CHES 62:8	
speechless from among the s. dead	HILL 148:9	
washed in the s. real	BARZ 24:13	
speed s. far faster than light	BULL 48:6	
s. glum heroes	SASS 276:16	
Unsafe at any s.	NADE 227:6	
What good is s.	KRAU 177:16	
spell utter inability to s.	HAY 142:14	
spelling s. is Wobbly	MILN 216:9	
spend If you have money you s. it	KENN 170:3	
s., and spend, and spend	NICH 230:4	
s. more time with my family	FOWL 117:6	

s. your way out	CALL 51:8	
spender big s.	FIEL 108:5	
spent Never ask of money s.	FROS 120:9	
spermatozoa million million s.	HUXL 155:13	
spice of the S. girls	HARR 141:2	
spider s. is sole denizen	HARD 139:5	
s. trying to hide	NERU 229:9	
spiders No more s. in my bath	ANON 10:14	
spill let them not s. me	MACN 203:6	
S. your guts at Wimbledon	CONN 75:4	
spin Sob, as you s.	AUDE 15:13	
spinach I say it's s.	WHIT 326:1	
spindle fold, s. or mutilate	SAYI 278:12	
spin-doctors s. in spin clinics	BENN 30:8	
spin-dryer mind is just like a s.	NOLA 232:12	
spinner S. of the Years	HARD 139:9	
spires grey s. of Oxford	LETT 189:4	
spirit appeals to the Dunkirk s.	WILS 331:2	
forge his s. spirit	GUEV 135:6	
sacramental of the s.	ROBI 265:11	
spirits S. of well-shot woodcock	BETJ 34:15	
spiritual approach the s. in art	MOND 220:2	
Music is s.	MORR 222:10	
not being a s. people	MANC 205:10	
skip his s. struggles	LIBE 191:2	
spiritualist you are a s.	SZAS 302:6	
spiritualists convention of s.	STOP 299:1	
spit no gun, but I can s.	AUDE 17:8	
spite In S. of Everything	ZIEG 341:5	
spiteful write when I feel s.	LAWR 184:11	
spitter he was a poor s.	WODE 333:12	
splinters teeth like s.	CAUS 56:5	
split care what a s. infinitive	FOWL 117:5	
when I s. an infinitive	CHAN 60:12	
spoiled Story the s. child of art	JAME 159:4	
spoke s. for a hundred and seventeen	BENN 31:8	
spoken never have s. yet	CHES 62:13	
spongy on s. shoes	WILB 328:8	
sponsored s. film work	GRIE 134:3	
spontaneous S. joy	YEAT 337:12	
spoons world locks up its s.	SHAW 284:18	
sport owe to s.	CAMU 53:5	
Serious s.	ORWE 239:4	
Serious s.	ORWE 239:8	
thing about s.	GREA 132:2	
sports mountainous s. girl	BETJ 35:11	
sportsman s. is a man who	LEAC 185:7	
spots s. rather a credit	COMP 74:5	
spotted s., silent, unfancied	MORT 222:13	
spouse President's s.	BUSH 50:1	
spray pinkly bursts the s.	BETJ 35:8	
rime was on the s.	HARD 140:9	
spread S. ALARM AND DESPONDENCY	PENI 246:10	
spring easing the S.	REED 262:10	
first hour of s.	BOWE 42:8	

stays prays together s. together · SAYI 278:13

steak not the meat of the s. · PRIE 257:1

steaks smell of s. in passageways · ELIO 100:16

steal s. from many, it's research · MIZN 219:7

s. more than a hundred men · PUZO 258:4

stealing For de little s. · O'NE 236:1

steamers little holiday s. · PRIE 256:12

steaming wealth of s. phrases · SCHU 281:6

steel s. canisters hurtling about · CASS 55:11

surgeon plies the s. · ELIO 98:18

steeple lone religious s. · CAMP 52:7

steeples dreary s. of Fermanagh · CHUR 65:7

Stein don't like the family S. · ANON 9:16

step one small s. for a man · ARMS 13:4

step-parents especially s. · POWE 254:19

stick are we going to make it s. · MACG 199:11

carry a big s. · ROOS 268:3

rattling of a s. inside · ORWE 239:14

tattered coat upon a s. · YEAT 338:10

Work was like a s. · SOLZ 290:15

sticks S. nix hick pix · NEWS 231:11

stiff woman can be proud and s. · YEAT 337:5

stiffen had time to s. · ORWE 239:10

stigma Any s. to beat a dogma · GUED 135:1

still S. falls the rain · SITW 288:4

s. point · ELIO 98:12

stimulate s. the phagocytes · SHAW 283:16

sting s. like a bee · ALI 6:2

sting-a-ling-a-ling where is thy s. · ANON 10:17

stink their politics usually s. · LAWR 184:18

stirred Shaken and not s. · FLEM 114:4

stocking glimpse of s. · PORT 252:10

stole son of a bitch s. my watch · FILM 111:15

stolen s. his wits away · DE L 87:13

stone bomb them back into S. Age · LEMA 187:4

Let them not make me a s. · MACN 203:6

Like a rolling s. · DYLA 94:8

make a s. of the heart · YEAT 337:9

through a piece of s. · MOOR 221:4

stones stained s. kissed · OWEN 241:2

stony more s. than a shore · WILL 330:7

stood should of s. in bed · JACO 158:8

stop full s. at the right place · BABE 19:11

nobody's going to s. 'em · BERR 34:1

s. everyone from doing it · HERB 146:10

S.-look-and-listen · OFFI 235:12

S. me and buy one · ADVE 4:21

S. the world · NEWL 229:14

stopped s. the engine · JENK 161:2

stops buck s. here · TRUM 313:6

storage thought in cold s. · SAMU 274:8

stork S. from butter · ADVE 3:10

storm carry you through the s. · EWAR 104:11

stormy S. weather · KOEH 177:4

story life's s. fills thirty-five pages · ARNO 13:7

novel tells a s. · FORS 115:15

s. is ephemeral and doomed · FAUL 107:2

S. the spoiled child of art · JAME 159:4

St Paul's Say I am designing S. · BENT 32:5

straight nothing ever ran quite s. · GALS 124:3

strain train take the s. · ADVE 4:7

Words s. · ELIO 98:13

strand never alone with a S. · ADVE 4:30

walk down the S. · HARG 140:12

strange s. and sinister · JAME 159:3

'S. friend,' I said · OWEN 241:4

stranger I, a s. and afraid · HOUS 152:5

Look, s. · AUDE 16:15

never love a s. · BENS 32:1

S., unless with bedroom eyes · AUDE 17:8

wiles of the s. · NASH 227:16

You may see a s. · HAMM 137:14

strangers kindness of s. · WILL 330:6

s. in the Capitol · HEWI 147:9

straw Headpiece filled with s. · ELIO 99:16

strawberry S. fields forever · LENN 188:7

stream cool as a mountain s. · ADVE 3:11

Fish have their s. · BROO 45:9

long-legged fly upon s. · YEAT 338:1

street at the end of the s. · MACN 203:2

don't do it in the s. · CAMP 52:5

inability to cross the s. · WOOL 335:9

s. fighting man · JAGG 158:13

sunny side of the s. · FIEL 108:7

talking at s. corners · VANZ 316:7

worth two in the s. · WEST 324:3

streets children died in the s. · AUDE 16:6

Down these mean s. · CHAN 60:10

grass will grow in the s. · HOOV 151:11

S. FLOODED · TELE 305:6

s. that no longer exist · FENT 107:8

Streltsy like wives of the S. · AKHM 5:4

strength full of the s. of five · BETJ 35:11

no s. to respond · BROD 44:12

S. through joy · POLI 251:16

stretch s. the human frame · SCAR 277:10

strife In place of s. · CAST 56:1

strike s. against public safety · COOL 76:1

s. it in anger · SHAW 285:4

strings scrape your s. darker · CELA 59:21

striped s. shroud · THOM 308:9

stroke at a s., reduce the rise · HEAT 144:5

strong nature of s. people · BONH 41:6

only the S. shall thrive · SERV 283:2

realize how s. she is · REAG 261:10

river Is a s. brown god · ELIO 99:3

struck s. regularly like gongs · COWA 78:17

structuralists S. constructed · WOLF 334:6

struggle s. between artist man · SHAW 284:13

s. continues · LAST 182:10

s. towards the heights · CAMU 52:16

to-day the s. · AUDE 17:16

stubbornness self-righteous s. · JENK 161:5

student two classes of s. · PUNT 258:1

studiously apart, s. neutral — WILS 332:4
study proper s. of mankind — HUXL 155:5
stuff too short to s. a mushroom — CONR 75:8
stuffed We are the s. men — ELIO 99:16
stump mount the s. — STEV 298:9
stupid *all* questions were s. — WEIS 322:7
  interesting . . . but s. — CATC 59:10
  It's the economy, s. — POLI 251:15
  on the part of the s. — WARN 319:14
  pretend to be more s. — STAR 295:9
  s. enough to want it — CHES 64:4
  s. neither forgive nor — SZAS 302:5
stupidvision It is S. — TOYN 311:2
style cut, the s., the line — LOES 193:4
  has no real s. — PICA 249:4
  Mandarin s. — CONN 74:15
  murderer for fancy prose s. — NABO 226:14
sub Sighted s., sank same — MASO 209:14
subject not shocked by this s. — BOHR 40:10
  uninteresting s. — CHES 63:5
sublime most s. noise — FORS 116:5
  ridiculous, the s. — MAHO 204:3
subordinate s. of Gen. MacArthur — PERE 246:13
substitute no s. for talent — HUXL 155:9
  no s. for victory — MACA 197:2
substitutes Ours is the age of s. — BENT 32:6
subtle s. but not malicious — EINS 96:8
suburb new s. beyond the runway — BETJ 35:1
suburbia come from s. — RAPH 260:5
subversive funny is s. — ORWE 239:9
subway in a New York s. — STRA 299:19
succeed How to s. in business — MEAD 211:13
  If at first you don't s. — FIEL 108:14
  not enough to s. — VIDA 317:11
  not going to s. — MORT 223:6
  possible to s. — RENO 263:4
succeeds Whenever a friend s. — VIDA 317:9
success guarantee s. in war — CHUR 66:8
  If *A* is a s. in life — EINS 97:4
  no s. like failure — DYLA 94:9
  S. in journalism — GREE 132:16
  s. is disgraceful — MENC 213:3
  S. is relative — ELIO 98:6
  s. only a delayed failure — GREE 132:15
  Sweet smell of s. — FILM 112:16
successful recipes always s. — VALÉ 315:14
successors dissatisfield with s. — JENK 161:7
sucker give a s. an even break — FIEL 108:10
sue s. its parents — WATS 320:8
sued publish and be s. — INGR 157:8
suet-pudding cold, black s. — LEWI 190:15
Suez S.—a smash and grab raid — NICO 230:11
  S. Canal flowing through — EDEN 95:9
suffer men s. as badly — COPE 76:11
suffered never s. — DOLE 90:8
suffering About s. they were — AUDE 17:1
  not true that s. ennobles — MAUG 210:4

sufferings constant in human s. — JOYC 164:15
sufficient S. conscience — LLOY 192:18
sugar no s. cane for miles — HOLI 150:12
suicide alter the s. rate — WHIT 327:12
  it is s. — MACD 199:2
  longest s. note — KAUF 167:2
  possibility of s. — CIOR 69:11
  s. 25 years after — BEAV 25:9
  s. kills two people — MILL 215:2
  s. to avoid assassination — TRUM 312:14
  s. to be abroad — BECK 25:12
sui generis say I am s. — LONG 193:11
suitable s. case for treatment — MERC 213:9
sum s. of all the choices — DIDI 89:13
Sumatra giant rat of S. — DOYL 91:11
summer long hot s. — FILM 112:11
  on a hot s. afternoon — ANON 11:12
  s. afternoon — JAME 159:15
  S. time and the livin' — HEYW 148:1
sun At the going down of the s. — BINY 37:13
  Before you let the s. in — THOM 307:16
  Born of the s. — SPEN 293:8
  inconceivable idea of the s. — STEV 297:12
  I will sing of the s. — POUN 253:15
  staring at the s. — BELL 27:10
  s. also rises — HEMI 145:14
  s. has gone in — SMIT 289:11
  S. Wot Won It — NEWS 231:9
  watched the s. going down — VAN 316:1
  where no s. shines — THOM 307:7
sunbathing Picasso, s. and jazz — WAUG 321:6
sunbeam Jesus wants me for a s. — TALB 302:15
sunbeams fatuous s. — OWEN 241:1
Sunday feeling of S. is the same — RHYS 263:11
  Hot on S. — HART 141:12
  Never on S. — FILM 112:13
  rainy S. afternoon — ERTZ 104:7
  S., bloody Sunday — FILM 112:15
  this is S. morning — MACN 203:8
  working week and S. best — AUDE 16:8
sundial s., and I make a botch — BELL 28:6
sunlight s. on the garden — MACN 203:9
sunlit broad, s. uplands — CHUR 66:6
sunny lived in a warm, s. climate — COWA 78:14
  some s. day — PARK 244:4
  s. side of the street — FIEL 108:7
sunset make a fine s. — MADA 203:13
  s. of my life — REAG 262:7
sunsets Autumn s. exquisitely — HUXL 155:14
  horror of s. — PROU 257:6
  spread your silver s. — DAVI 84:3
sunshine and a ray of s. — WODE 333:1
superior S. people never make — MOOR 221:8
  s. persons can remain — ORWE 238:17
Superman It's S. — ANON 9:12
superseded has not been s. — LONG 193:13
superstition main source of s. — RUSS 272:8

supplies just bought fresh s.	BREC 43:15	**swine** could be a manoeuvring s.	MCCA 198:1
support depend on the s. of Paul	SHAW 283:19	**swines** You rotten s.	CATC 59:18
no invisible means of s.	BUCH 47:13	**swing** ain't got that s.	MILL 216:3
s. of the woman I love	EDWA 95:11	s. for it	KING 172:16
suppose queerer than we s.	HALD 136:9	s. our ungirded hips	SORL 292:1
suppress power of s.	NORT 233:1	**switching** sanction of s. off	EYRE 106:5
surely Shome mishtake, s.	CATC 59:6	**Switzerland** In S. they had	FILM 110:14
surface looks dingy on the s.	PIRS 249:15	S. is proud of this	GIDE 128:1
surfaces queen of s.	DOWD 91:10	**sword** bank mightier than the s.	PLOM 250:8
surf-boarding s. along the new	MCLU 201:3	I gave them a s.	NIXO 232:8
surfing s. the Net	ELIZ 103:2	Militarism a rusty s.	SHAW 286:3
We are s. food	MACK 200:8	s. the axis of the world	DE G 87:7
surgeon s. plies the steel	ELIO 98:18	wield the s. of France	DE G 86:10
surprise get a big s.	DIAN 89:10	**swords** either dreams or s.	LOWE 195:5
Life is a great s.	NABO 227:1	paper hats and wooden s.	USTI 315:8
Live frugally on s.	WALK 318:9	**syllable** never used one s.	JAY 160:3
No s. for the writer	FROS 121:3	**syllogism** conclusion of your s.	O'BR 233:10
sound of s.	BALL 22:5	**sympathy** messages of s.	AYCK 19:4
surrender we shall never s.	CHUR 66:5	Tea and s.	ANDE 8:10
surroundings I plus my s.	ORTE 237:2	**symphony** Beethoven's Fifth S.	FORS 116:5
survival s. is all there is	FULL 122:5	**system** rocked the s.	ROBI 265:12
there is no s.	CHUR 66:4		
we are their s. machines	DAWK 84:9		
survive Dare hope to s.	HUXL 155:13	**t** t is silent, as in *Harlow*	ASQU 14:14
know they can s.	HART 141:5	**ta** saying 'T.' to God	SPEN 293:5
Only the paranoid s.	GROV 134:12	**table** patient etherized upon a t.	ELIO 100:3
s. of us is love	LARK 180:3	**tablet** keep taking The T.	THOM 308:10
s. to consume	VANE 316:5	**tactful** t. in audacity	COCT 72:5
survivors more the s.' affair	MANN 207:1	**tail** salmon standing on its t.	TYNA 314:7
old, old s.	SHAW 286:11	**tails** Brushin' off my t.	BERL 33:2
suspects Round up the usual s.	FILM 111:3	**Taisez-vous** T.! *Méfiez-vous*	OFFI 235:13
Sussex S. by the sea	KIPL 175:4	**take** big enough to t. away	FORD 115:6
swallow speed of a s.	BETJ 35:14	can't t. it with you	HART 141:11
swamp botanize in the s.	CHES 64:1	can't t. that away from me	GERS 127:6
swamps across primeval s.	WODE 333:9	T. me to your leader	CATC 59:8
swans ships sail like s. asleep	FLEC 114:3	t. you in the morning	BALD 21:1
swarm S. over, death	BETJ 35:12	**takes** t. just like a woman	DYLA 94:7
swear Don't s., boy	BENN 30:16	**talcum** bit of t. is always walcum	NASH 227:11
swearing s. is part of it	GREA 132:2	**tale** most tremendous t. of all	BETJ 34:13
swears Money doesn't talk, it s.	DYLA 94:6	Trust the t.	LAWR 183:16
sweat blood, toil, tears and s.	CHUR 66:2	**talent** no substitute for t.	HUXL 155:9
s. of its labourers	EISE 97:12	no t. for writing	BENC 29:5
sweater want to hear from your s.	LEBO 186:6	nothing to do with t.	HARR 141:3
sweeps beats as it s.	ADVE 3:27	t. instantly recognizes	DOYL 91:14
sweet dead thing that smells s.	THOM 308:2	t. to amuse	COWA 78:4
suck on a boiled s.	WESL 324:1	tomb of a mediocre t.	SMIT 289:9
S. smell of success	FILM 112:16	**talents** t. and our expectations	DE B 86:2
S., soft, plenty rhythm	MORT 223:10	**talk** Careless t. costs lives	OFFI 235:1
technically s.	OPPE 236:10	good to t.	ADVE 4:1
sweetness s. and light failed	FORS 116:2	how much my Ministers t.	THAT 305:10
s. of a shower	THOM 308:7	If you t. to God	SZAS 302:6
sweets bag of boiled s.	CRIT 80:6	Money doesn't t., it swears	DYLA 94:6
swell s. a progress	ELIO 100:9	people who can't t.	ZAPP 341:2
Thou s.! Thou witty	HART 141:10	rot the dead t.	ASQU 14:11
What a s. party	PORT 253:3	t. about the rest of us	ANON 11:9
swift S. has sailed into his rest	YEAT 338:18	t. like a lady	SHAW 285:18
swimmers as s. into cleanness	BROO 45:14	t. to the plants	CHAR 61:14

Through t., we tamed kings	BENN 29:16	**tea-cup** crack in the t. opens	AUDE 16:1
use words when I t. to you	ELIO 101:4	**tea-girl** t.'s chance to kiss	WHIT 327:9
ways of making you t.	CATC 59:12	**teapot** old t., used daily	WARN 319:13
talking ain't t. about him	GLAS 129:2	warming the t.	MANS 207:3
Enough of t.	BLAI 39:2	**tear** Wipe the t., baby dear	WEST 325:9
nation t. to itself	MILL 215:10	**tears** blood, toil, t. and sweat	CHUR 66:2
opposite of t. is waiting	LEBO 186:7	enough of blood and t.	RABI 259:3
quieten your enemy by t.	CEAU 56:9	French without t.	RATT 260:8
stop people t.	ATTL 15:10	hazards whence no t.	HARD 140:4
t. without speaking	SIMO 287:10	No t. in the writer	FROS 121:3
talks t. frankly only with his wife	BABE 19:12	t. I cannot hide	HARB 138:7
tall short and the t.	HUGH 153:10	**tearsday** moanday, t., wailsday	JOYC 164:9
t. as a crane	SITW 288:2	**tease** fleas that t.	BELL 28:9
tambourine Mr T. Man	DYLA 94:10	**technically** t. sweet	OPPE 236:10
tango Takes two to t.	HOFF 150:7	**Technik** *Vorsprung durch T.*	ADVE 4:25
tank tiger in your t.	ADVE 4:17	**technique** t. improved as the real situation	
tanks Get your t. off my lawn	WILS 331:9		TAYL 303:14
tanstaafl acronym T.	SAYI 279:8	**technology** advanced t. is	CLAR 70:4
tarnished neither t. nor afraid	CHAN 60:10	in relation to our t.	BERR 34:3
tart t. who has married the Mayor	BAXT 25:2	into the Sixties t.	LEVI 189:11
tarts action of two t.	MACM 202:3	T. just a tool	GATE 125:6
Tarzan Me T., you Jane	MISQ 218:10	T. . . . the knack	FRIS 119:11
tasks dear unfinished t.	ANON 10:1	white heat of t.	MISQ 219:4
taste bouquet better than the t.	POTT 253:8	**teddy** Now T. must run	KENN 170:5
doubt and good t.	BROD 45:2	T. Bears have their Picnic	KENN 168:9
ghastly good t.	BETJ 36:2	**tedious** What makes men so t.	COPE 76:14
Good t. and humour	MUGG 224:14	**teenager** as a t.	LEBO 186:8
have very bad t.	ORTO 237:9	**teenie** Itsy bitsy t. weenie	VANC 315:17
tasted t. your worm	SPOO 294:9	**teeth** clean their t. in the dark	JENK 160:9
tastes if it t. good, it's bad	ASIM 14:3	he's got iron t.	GROM 134:11
t. may not be the same	SHAW 284:21	old bitch gone in the t.	POUN 254:2
tattered t. coat upon a stick	YEAT 338:10	shark has pretty t.	BREC 44:1
wars have t. his ears	HUGH 154:1	t. are in the real meat	GRIM 134:9
tax to t. rich people	LLOY 192:14	t. like splinters	CAUS 56:5
taxation Inflation one form of t.	FRIE 119:9	women have fewer t.	RUSS 271:12
taxes Death and t. and childbirth	MITC 217:7	**Teflon** T.-coated Presidency	SCHR 280:12
little people pay t.	HELM 145:8	**telegrams** life of t. and anger	FORS 116:8
no new t.	BUSH 50:4	**telephones** Tudor monarchy with t.	
Sex and t. are	JONE 163:15		BURG 49:5
taxi If you can't leave in a t.	FILM 110:12	**telescope** t. or hydrogen bomb	LOVE 194:14
t. throbbing waiting	ELIO 101:15	**televised** first live t. war	O'RO 236:14
taxi-cab look like a t.	HUGH 153:9	**television** daytime t.	TOYN 311:2
taxis hiring t. to scuttle round	KINN 173:6	I hate t.	WELL 323:1
taxpayer at the t.'s expense	MENC 213:5	It's t., you see	HOWE 153:3
Tchaikovsky If I play T.	LIBE 191:2	no plain women on t.	FORD 115:3
tea honey still for t.	BROO 45:13	of t.	WILD 328:10
Like having a cup of t.	GALL 124:1	on t. as an agent	EYRE 106:5
T., although an Oriental	CHES 62:14	On t. I feel like	MUGG 225:1
T. and sympathy	ANDE 8:10	Radio and t.	SARR 275:17
t. for two	CAES 51:1	see bad t. for nothing	GOLD 130:7
t.'s out of the way	REED 262:11	Some t. programmes	ANON 11:8
teabag woman is like a t.	REAG 261:10	T. brought brutality	MCLU 201:12
teach change the people who t.	BYAT 50:12	T. closer to reality	PAGL 241:15
T. us to care	ELIO 98:3	T. contracts imagination	WOGA 333:16
teacher t. have maximal authority	SZAS 302:3	T. has brought murder	HITC 149:8
t. is the most important	GATE 125:6	T. has made dictatorship	PERE 247:1
teaches He who cannot, t.	SHAW 285:2	T. is for appearing on	COWA 79:2

publishing faster than you t.   PAUL 245:13
speak before you t.   FORS 116:18
tell what I t.   FORS 116:1
t. globally   SAYI 279:9
T. like a wise man   YEAT 339:10
t. of yourself one way   HEDR 144:10
t. only this of me   BROO 45:15
t. what other people think   YEAT 338:12
t. with our wombs   LUCE 196:5
t. without his hat   BECK 26:6
we've got to t.   RUTH 272:15
what death makes us t.   DE G 87:8
whether machines t.   SKIN 288:10
You know more than you t.   SPOC 294:5
thinker murder the t.   WESK 323:17
thinking lateral t.   DE B 86:1
  not t. accurately   HOLM 151:4
  our modes of t.   EINS 97:3
  power of positive t.   PEAL 246:3
  saves original t.   SAYE 277:6
  t. about themselves   MACM 202:4
  t. man's crumpet   MUIR 225:4
  t. what nobody has thought   SZEN 302:11
thinks t. he knows everything   SHAW 284:10
third t. of my life over   ALLE 6:19
thirteen clocks were striking t.   ORWE 238:7
  T. years of Tory misrule   POLI 251:22
thirtieth t. year to heaven   THOM 307:8
thirty bus over the age of t.   WEST 325:8
  t. pieces of silver   BEVA 36:9
thorn Oak, and Ash, and T.   KIPL 175:3
thorns crown of t.   BEVA 36:9
thou t. art not he or she   WAUG 320:11
  T. swell! Thou witty   HART 141:10
  Through the T.   BUBE 47:10
thought beautiful clean t.   LAWR 183:18
  forced into a state of t.   GALS 124:4
  frozen t. of men   KRIS 178:2
  song makes you feel a t.   HARB 138:14
  T. does not crush   ROET 266:5
  t. in a concentration camp   ROOS 267:16
  t. in cold storage   SAMU 274:8
  troubled seas of t.   GALB 123:5
  What was once t.   DÜRR 93:10
  where a t. might grow   MAHO 204:5
thoughts bring my t. to an end   SMIT 290:5
  censor one's own t.   WALE 318:7
  Hunter's waking t.   AUDE 16:4
  One has to multiply t.   LEC 186:12
  t. of a prisoner   SOLZ 290:17
thousand ditch a t. years   MAJO 205:2
  first t. days   KENN 169:6
  lasts for a t. years   CHUR 66:6
  not in a t. years   SMIT 289:6
  one bullet in ten t.   SPEN 293:14
  t. years of history   GAIT 122:14
thousands limp father of t.   JOYC 165:8

threaten only t. and be angry   KIPL 174:9
three Though he was only t.   MILN 216:12
  t. is a houseful   SAYI 278:6
  T. o'clock always too late   SART 276:12
  t. o'clock in the morning   FITZ 113:7
  t. of us in this marriage   DIAN 89:8
thriftily men who left them t.   KIPL 174:8
throat in the city's t.   LOWE 195:9
  murder by the t.   LLOY 192:11
  taking life by the t.   FROS 121:5
  t. 'tis hard to slit   KING 172:16
throne One Law, one Land, one T.   KIPL 175:6
  t. of bayonets   INGE 157:2
  t. of bayonets   YELT 339:11
through best way out is always t.   FROS 120:19
  live t. someone else   FRIE 119:4
throwing t. themselves off it   MAND 206:5
thrown All *this* t. away   MARY 209:10
thrush aged t., frail, gaunt   HARD 139:10
thumb puts his t. in the scale   LAWR 183:11
Tiananmen tanks into T. Square   ANON 11:17
Tiber River T. foaming   POWE 255:8
ticket She's got a t. to ride   LENN 188:8
  take a t. at Victoria   BEVI 37:7
  t. for the peepshow   MACN 202:14
tickets t. in their hands   BONO 41:7
tickled t. to death to go   WEST 325:9
tiddely more it snows (T. pom)   MILN 216:4
tide *Not this t.*   KIPL 174:11
  Treaty like an incoming t.   DENN 88:5
tides drew these t. of men   LAWR 184:17
  Push in their t.   THOM 307:7
tidy Keep Britain t.   OFFI 235:8
tiger atom bomb is a paper t.   MAO 207:7
  ride on a t.   ANON 11:10
  t. in your tank   ADVE 4:17
tigers ride to and fro upon t.   CHUR 65:12
  tamed and shabby t.   HODG 150:5
tight t. gag of place   HEAN 144:4
tile not red brick but white t.   OSBO 240:2
time As t. goes by   HUPF 154:13
  at the wrong t.   BRAD 43:4
  Cathedral t.   ANON 9:7
  dance to the music of t.   POWE 254:20
  devote more t. to them   FOWL 117:6
  expands to fill the t.   CONR 75:10
  gave its victims t. to die   GUIB 135:7
  Get me to the church on t.   LERN 188:13
  good t. was had by all   SMIT 290:6
  Hurry up please it's t.   ELIO 101:13
  idea whose t. has come   SAYI 279:7
  leave exactly on t.   MUSS 226:8
  may be some t.   LAST 182:6
  no enemy but t.   YEAT 337:16
  peace for our t.   CHAM 60:4
  say you're ahead of your t.   MCGO 199:10
  something to do with the t.   ROGE 267:1

time (*cont.*):

spend more t. with family	THAT 306:13
That passed the t.	BECK 26:7
t. cracks into furious flower	BROO 46:6
t. for a change	DEWE 89:2
T. for a little something	MILN 216:8
t. has come	LONG 193:12
T. has no divisions	MANN 206:13
T. has too much credit	COMP 73:9
T. has transfigured them	LARK 180:3
t. is running out	KOES 177:7
T. is too slow	VAN 316:2
T. present and time past	ELIO 98:9
t.'s arrow	EDDI 95:1
T. spent on any item	PARK 244:7
t. the longest distance	WILL 330:2
T. was away and somewhere	MACN 203:4
to fill the t. available	PARK 244:6
to sell t.	TAWN 303:4
very good t. it was	JOYC 164:12

time-lag comfortable t. — WELL 323:13

times bad t. just around — COWA 78:13

one year's experience 30 t.	CARR 54:3
possibility of good t.	BRAN 43:5
t. they are a-changin'	DYLA 94:14
Top people take *The T.*	ADVE 4:24

timetables by railway t. — TAYL 303:7

timid inclined to be t. — WEBB 322:1

timing real bad sense of t. — MCGO 199:10

Timothy T. has passed — EPIT 106:1

T. Winters comes — CAUS 56:5

tin cat on a hot t. roof — WILL 329:13

on a corrugated t. roof — BEEC 26:19

Tina acronym T. — THAT 305:11

ting-a-ling-a-ling bells of hell go t. — ANON 10:17

tingling It's t. fresh — ADVE 4:2

tinker don't matter a t.'s cuss — SHIN 286:13

to t. with his car — MACN 203:8

tinkering rule of intelligent t. — EHRL 96:3

tinned smoked salmon and t. — WILS 331:4

tiny My t. watching eye — DE L 87:20

Tipperary long way to T. — JUDG 166:1

tipster racing t. who only — TAYL 303:8

tiptoe Dance t., bull — BUNT 48:9

tired I was t. of it — PARK 244:11

t. of Love — BELL 28:1

Tiresias T., old man — ELIO 101:16

tiring Shakespeare is so t. — HULL 154:8

Wooing, so t. — MITF 217:11

titanic furniture on deck of T. — MORT 223:11

t. wars had groined — OWEN 241:3

title friends only read the t. — WOOL 335:2

I love the t.	COPE 76:13
needed no royal t.	SPEN 293:1

titles rich for t. — PEAR 246:7

toad Give me your arm, old t. — LARK 181:1

let the t. work — LARK 180:14

toads gardens with real t.	MOOR 221:7
today get where I am t. without	CATC 58:5
Mother died t.	CAMU 53:4
standing here t.	JOHN 162:11
T. the last day	YELT 339:13
t. the struggle	AUDE 17:16
T. we have naming of parts	REED 262:9
we gave our t.	EPIT 106:2
will not hang myself t.	CHES 62:3

toe big t. ends up making a hole — EINS 97:11

toff Saunter along like a t. — HARG 140:12

toil blood, t., tears and sweat — CHUR 66:2

told I t. you so — EPIT 105:4

like to be t. the worst	CHUR 66:11
not what we were formerly t.	BLUN 39:13
plato t. him: he couldn't	CUMM 81:13

tolerance such a thing as t. — WILS 332:8

T. the essential — PHIL 248:8

tolerant being t. for nothing — GREG 133:9

tolerate not to t. the intolerant — POPP 252:5

tolerated women not merely t. — AUNG 18:19

Tolstoy ring with Mr T. — HEMI 145:16

Tom Ground control to Major T. — BOWI 42:16

tomato You like t. — GERS 127:3

tomb t. of a mediocre talent — SMIT 289:9

tombs in the cool t. — SAND 274:11

tomcat t. lies stretched flat — HUGH 154:1

tomorrow For your t. we gave — EPIT 106:2

Leave t. behind	COWA 78:2
T. for the young	AUDE 17:16
t. is another day	MITC 217:9
we thought was for t.	BENN 29:14

tomorrows from time's t. — SASS 276:18

tongue grow a second t. — MONT 220:10

lies of t. and pen	CHES 62:8
tip of the t. taking	NABO 226:13

tons Sixteen t. — TRAV 311:3

tool Science is an edged t. — EDDI 95:6

Technology just a t. — GATE 125:6

tools Give us the t. — CHUR 66:10

toothache Venerable Mother T. — HEAT 144:8

toothpaste t. is out of the tube — HALD 136:14

top T. of the world — FILM 110:1

T. people — ADVE 4:24

topography T. displays — BISH 38:6

torch t. passed to new generation — KENN 169:2

Tories potential T. — ORWE 238:2

tormented cries of the t. — MILL 215:15

tornado set off a t. in Texas — LORE 194:10

torso remain only a t. — ERHA 104:6

torture self-imposed t. — MILL 215:12

So does t. — AUDE 18:2

torturer t.'s horse scratches — AUDE 17:2

Tory hatred for the T. Party — BEVA 36:5

Thirteen years of T. misrule	POLI 251:22
T.'s secret weapon	KILM 172:1

total t. solution — GOER 129:12

totalitarian lead to the t. state   DENN 88:8
totalitarianism name of t.   GAND 124:9
totem t.-symbol in his hand   KOES 177:9
totter t. towards the tomb   SAYE 277:7
tough in t. joints   RUNY 270:9
   t. get going   SAYI 279:14
   T. on crime   BLAI 38:10
toughness T. doesn't have to come   FEIN 107:6
tourism t. is their religion   RUNC 270:6
   What an odd thing t. is   BRYS 47:8
tourist makes everyone a t.   SONT 291:16
   t. of wars   GELL 125:11
town destroy the t.   ANON 10:4
   Dirty old t.   MACC 198:4
   go down to the end of the t.   MILN 216:12
   lived in a pretty how t.   CUMM 81:8
trace risen without t.   MUGG 224:8
tracing fitful t. of a portal   STEV 297:15
tracks hungry on the t.   CRAN 79:9
   stopped engine in its t.   JENK 161:2
trade half a t. and half an art   INGE 157:4
   Irish poets, learn you t.   YEAT 339:3
   There isn't any T.   HERB 146:13
traders into the hands of t.   GRAV 131:16
Trade Unionist British T.   BEVI 37:5
tradition great t.   LEAV 185:14
   T. different from habit   STRA 300:1
   T. means giving votes   CHES 63:13
   t. objects to their   CHES 63:14
traffic reckless motor t.   DEWA 89:1
   roar of London's t.   ANON 11:1
tragedies two t. in life   SHAW 284:20
tragedy comedy is t. that happens   CART 54:9
   convenient in t.   ANOU 12:3
   first time as t.   BARN 23:7
   food a t.   POWE 254:17
   I will write you a t.   FITZ 113:9
   t. is clean   ANOU 12:4
   t. of a man   OLIV 235:15
   t. of a man who has found   BARR 23:16
   T. ought to be a great kick   LAWR 184:10
   weak, washy way of true t.   KAVA 167:8
   what t. means   STOP 299:9
tragic essentially a t. age   LAWR 183:7
   I acted so t.   HARG 140:13
   t. consciousness   FUEN 121:16
trahison t. des clercs   BEND 29:7
trail t. has its own stern code   SERV 282:17
train biggest electric t. set   WELL 322:14
   headlight of an oncoming t.   DICK 89:12
   light of the oncoming t.   LOWE 195:15
   like a runaway t.   CONL 74:9
   moving t. needs passenger   STOP 299:14
   pack, and take a t.   BROO 45:11
   Runs the red electric t.   BETJ 35:9
   shaves and takes a t.   WHIT 326:3
   Shaw is like a t.   LEIG 187:3

   t. is arriving on time   MUSS 226:8
   t. of events   AMER 7:3
   t. take the strain   ADVE 4:7
trains Noting the numbers of t.   MAXW 211:1
traitors form of our t.   WEST 324:17
tramp must imitate the t.   GREE 132:16
   why the lady is a t.   HART 141:8
trampled t. on faces of poor   NICO 230:9
tranquillity remembered in t.   THUR 310:1
   T. Base here   ALDR 5:12
   t. remembered   PARK 243:8
tranquillized t. *Fifties*   LOWE 195:10
translated T. Daughter, come   AUDE 15:14
   t. into Italian   WHAR 325:11
translation unfaithful to the t.   BORG 42:2
   what is lost in t.   FROS 121:7
transplanted organs have been t.   HARB 138:12
transsexuals aspiring male t.   LEBO 186:4
trash society founded on t.   SAYE 277:4
travel I t. light   FRY 121:10
   t. broadens the mind   CHES 63:18
   t. in the direction of   BERR 34:6
   two classes of t.   BENC 29:3
travelled care which way he t.   BEAV 25:11
   took the one less t.   FROS 120:16
traveller said the T.   DE L 87:16
trawler When seagulls follow a t.   CANT 53:8
treachery t. of the intellectuals   BEND 29:7
treason greatest t.   ELIO 100:13
   Shakespeare the word t.   BENN 30:11
treasury T. is in power   WILS 331:12
   T. to fill old bottles   KEYN 171:1
treat t. if met where any bar is   HARD 140:3
treaties T. like girls and roses   DE G 87:4
treatment suitable case for t.   MERC 213:9
treaty hand that signed the t.   THOM 307:6
   not a peace t.   FOCH 114:11
   T. like an incoming tide   DENN 88:5
tree billboard lovely as a t.   NASH 228:13
   cut down a redwood t.   STEV 298:9
   finds that this t.   KNOX 176:17
   only God can make a t.   KILM 171:14
   poem lovely as a t.   KILM 171:13
trees apple t. will never get   FROS 120:12
   think of the poor t.   MENU 213:6
   t. bear strange fruit   HOLI 150:11
   t. that grow so fair   KIPL 175:3
tremulous behind my t. stay   HARD 139:4
trespass t. there and go   HOUS 152:8
trial only a t. if I recognize it   KAFK 166:14
tribal t., intimate revenge   HEAN 144:1
tribalism It is pure t.   FITT 112:17
tribe dialect of the t.   ELIO 99:8
   Our t.'s complicity   HEAN 143:11
trick conjuring t. with bones   JENK 160:11
trickle-down T. theory   GALB 123:10
tried Christian ideal not been t.   CHES 64:2

tried (*cont.*):

he t. to do something	MAND 206:8
one I never t. before	WEST 324:10
trigger do you want on the t.	NEWS 231:14
triglyph now that t.'s here	CUMM 81:11
trip Clunk, click, every t.	OFFI 235:2
don't t. over the furniture	COWA 79:1
triple-towered t. sky	DAY- 85:2
tripwire touch the t.	WARN 319:15
triste jamais t. archy	MARQ 208:7
tristesse *Bonjour t.*	ÉLUA 103:13
triumph his revolutionary t.	TAYL 303:11
our career and our t.	VANZ 316:7
than when they t.	WOOL 335:12
T. and Disaster	KIPL 174:5
t. of the embalmer's art	VIDA 317:12
trivial such t. people	LAWR 184:8
t. and the important	POTT 253:5
trivialities contrast to t.	BOHR 40:11
Trojan T. 'orses will jump out	BEVI 37:9
troops t. towards the sound	GRIM 134:8
trouble *business* to get him in t.	ROBI 265:13
it is not our t.	MARQ 208:8
present help in t.	ANON 8:14
There may be t. ahead	BERL 32:12
When in t., delegate	BORE 41:10
troubled bridge over t. water	SIMO 287:8
troubles From t. of the world	HARV 142:1
pack up your t.	ASAF 13:10
t. seemed so far away	LENN 188:11
trousers bottoms of my t. rolled	ELIO 100:10
cloud in t.	MAYA 211:2
trucking Keep on t.	CATC 58:18
trucks learn about t.	AWDR 19:1
true always t. to you, darlin'	PORT 252:9
And is it t.	BETJ 34:13
believe is not necessarily t.	BELL 27:7
long enough it *will* be t.	BENN 31:12
no matter how t.	VIDA 317:7
than that it be t.	WHIT 326:13
to be substantially t.	SANT 275:13
what we are saying is t.	RUSS 271:15
You are not t.	WILB 328:6
trust Never t. the artist	LAWR 183:16
To t. people is a luxury	FORS 116:6
trusted t. neither of them	WODE 333:12
truth Art is not t.	PICA 249:6
Believing T. is staring	BELL 27:10
economical with the t.	ARMS 13:5
forsake this t.	ROSE 268:12
here have Pride and T.	YEAT 338:6
how many people know the t.	WEST 325:2
just tell the t.	TRUM 313:1
keep t. safe in its hand	TAGO 302:13
know the t. at last	EPIT 105:12
lawyer interprets the t.	GIRA 128:11
mistook disenchantment for t.	SART 276:6

new scientific t.	PLAN 250:1
possesses not only t.	RUSS 271:16
simply a t. repeated	BALD 21:3
stop telling the t.	STEV 297:19
to lie for the t.	ADLE 2:3
t. 24 times per second	GODA 129:5
t. cannot be told	SOLZ 290:12
T. exists, only lies	BRAQ 43:7
T. is a pathless land	KRIS 178:3
T. is never undone	ROET 266:5
t. is out there	CATC 59:9
t., justice and the American way	ANON 9:12
T.-loving Persians	GRAV 131:10
t. makes men free	AGAR 2:7
T. not merely what we are thinking	
	HAVE 142:4
t. that has lost its temper	GIBR 127:13
unpleasant way of saying t.	HELL 145:6
truths all t. are half-truths	WHIT 326:14
Few new t. have ever won	BERL 33:7
no new t.	MCCA 197:13
old universal t.	FAUL 107:2
profound t. recognized	BOHR 40:11
repetition of unpalatable t.	SUMM 301:7
t. being in and out	FROS 120:1
try t., try again	FIEL 108:14
We t. harder	ADVE 4:27
trying I am t. to be	SMIT 289:3
just goes on t.	PICA 249:4
without really t.	MEAD 211:13
tsar no t., but the slaves remain	ZAMY 340:8
T-shirt got the T.	SAYI 278:3
tube lovely t. of delight	POTT 253:7
toothpaste is out of the t.	HALD 136:14
tuckoo little boy named baby t.	JOYC 164:12
Tudor US presidency a T. monarchy	
	BURG 49:5
tumour aspirin for a brain t.	CHAN 60:9
ripens in a t.	ABSE 1:3
tumult t. and the shouting dies	KNOX 176:16
tune guy who could carry a t.	EPIT 105:8
thinkin'll turn into a t.	HUBB 153:8
turn on, t. in and drop out	LEAR 185:9
tunes t. of Handel	SITW 288:7
tunnel back down the time t.	KEAT 167:11
light at the end of the t.	DICK 89:12
light at the end of the t.	LOWE 195:15
some profound dull t.	OWEN 241:3
turkeys t. vote for Christmas	CALL 51:11
turn and quickly t. away	YEAT 337:14
Because I do not hope to t.	ELIO 98:2
t. on, tune in and drop out	LEAR 185:9
T. that off	WILL 330:4
world t. by itself	O'CA 234:7
turning lady's not for t.	THAT 305:12
point of the t. world	ELIO 98:12
turnip candle in that great t.	CHUR 67:12

turtle t. lives 'twixt plated	NASH 227:10	**unable** unwilling or u.	WILL 330:7
TV blight has hit the T. industry	STRE 300:7	**unacceptable** u. face	HEAT 144:6
by T. stupor	SOLZ 291:2	**unaware** And I was u.	HARD 139:11
T.—a clever contraction	ACE 1:5	**unbearable** in victory u.	CHUR 68:2
T. turns their proceedings	MURR 226:6	u. lightness of being	KUND 178:10
twang t., and you've got music	VICI 317:4	**unbeatable** In defeat u.	CHUR 68:2
twangs something t. and breaks	MACN 203:2	**unbeautiful** are u. and have	CUMM 82:3
tweed t. nightgowns	GING 128:3	**unborn** possible to talk to the u.	BARZ 24:13
twelve snowed for t. days	THOM 307:11	**uncertainty** u. principle	HAWK 142:9
twentieth close of the t. century	HEWI 147:8	**uncomfortable** thinks he is u.	SHAW 284:16
half of the t. century	QUAN 258:6	**uncommon** owes existence to u. men	
horror of the T. Century	MAIL 204:8		COWA 78:19
language of the t. century	BEVA 36:7	**unconscious** investigate the U.	BELL 28:13
reality of the t. century	BALL 22:1	royal road to the u.	MISQ 218:4
t. century belongs	TRUD 312:10	u. cerebration	JAME 159:7
t. century decorates	TANG 302:16	**undecided** five who are u.	STEN 296:14
t. century have looked	SCHL 280:3	u. whether to desert	BEAV 25:10
t. century will be	TOYN 310:15	**under** got you u. my skin	PORT 252:15
twenty at T. I tried to vex	AUDE 17:12	I'd have been u. the host	PARK 244:1
T. men crossing a bridge	STEV 297:11	**under-belly** soft u. of Europe	MISQ 219:1
twenty-first started t. century	BOWI 42:17	**underdogs** Englishman among the u.	
twenty-twenty Hindsight is always t.			WAUG 321:4
	WILD 328:12	**underestimating** u. intelligence	MENC 213:2
twice Don't think t.	DYLA 94:4	**underneath** U. the Arches	FLAN 113:12
must do t. as well as men	WHIT 327:13	**undersexed** happy u. celibate	COFF 72:8
postman always rings t.	CAIN 51:3	**undersold** Never knowingly u.	ADVE 4:12
twilights shadows and t.	Æ 2:6	**understand** child could u.	FILM 112:2
twist almost invisible t.	BABE 19:10	don't u. things	NEUM 229:12
t. slowly in the wind	EHRL 96:4	don't u. too hot	SALI 274:4
twisted You silly t. boy	CATC 59:20	failed to u. it	BOHR 40:10
two game at which t. can play	BEER 26:21	Grown-ups never u.	SAIN 273:7
Takes t. to tango	HOFF 150:7	I do not u.	FEYN 108:3
tea for t.	CAES 51:1	liberals can u.	BRUC 47:2
t. cultures	SNOW 290:11	much that I did not u.	ORWE 237:18
t. glasses and two chairs	MACN 203:4	Nor can anyone u. Ein	ANON 9:16
t. is fun	SAYI 278:6	smart enough to u.	MCCA 197:6
t. plus two make four	ORWE 238:11	u. a little less	MAJO 204:15
We're number t.	ADVE 4:27	u. how science works	ASIM 13:12
worth t. in the street	WEST 324:3	u. nothing	CORN 77:2
types Seven t. of ambiguity	EMPS 104:2	u. the situation	MURR 226:7
typewriter changing a t. ribbon	BENC 29:1	What you can't u.	DYLA 94:14
t. separated me from	NERU 229:10	**understanding** sketchy u. of life	CRIC 80:1
typewriters banging on million t.	WILE 329:1	**understood** I have u. you	DE G 86:11
monkeys strumming on t.	EDDI 95:2	music u. by children	STRA 300:3
tyranny against a monstrous t.	CHUR 66:3	**undertaking** no such u.	CHAM 60:5
conditions of t.	AREN 13:2	**undeservedly** books u. forgotten	AUDE 18:7
unnecessary t.	RUSS 271:8	**undeserving** u. poor	SHAW 285:19
tyrants restrained t.	BENN 29:16	**undo** u. the folded lie	AUDE 17:10
tyres concrete and t.	LARK 180:6	**undone** death had u. so many	ELIO 101:9
		uneconomic shown it to be 'u.'	SCHU 281:3
		uneducated government by the u.	CHES 64:6
ugly Bessie, you're u.	CHUR 69:9	u. man to read books	CHUR 68:9
good, the bad, and the u.	FILM 112:10	**unemployment** leave it to u.	KEYN 171:1
no place for u. mathematics	HARD 139:3	rising u.	LAMO 179:11
Ulster betrayal of U.	CAIR 51:5	**unexpected** most u. of all things	TROT 312:7
Ulsterman U., of planter stock	HEWI 147:10	**unexplained** you're u. as yet	HALL 137:3
umbrella u. might pacify	PLOM 250:8	**unfaithful** original is u.	BORG 42:2

unfathomable u. deep forest THOM 308:4
unfinished Liberty is u. business ANON 10:9
unfit chosen from the u. SAYI 278:7
unforgiveness alp of u. PLOM 250:7
unforgiving fill the u. minute KIPL 174:6
unfree Ireland u. shall never be at peace
  PEAR 246:4
unhappily bad end u. STOP 299:9
unhappiness loyalty we feel to u. GREE 132:8
  putting-off of u. GREE 132:4
  u. develops the forces of the mind
  PROU 257:11
  U. is best defined DE B 86:2
  vocation of u. SIME 287:6
unhappy Men who are u. RUSS 271:5
  moral as soon as u. PROU 257:12
  only speak when she is u. SMIT 289:15
  U. the land that needs BREC 43:11
unheard language of the u. KING 172:12
unhurt U. people not much good STAR 295:10
uninspiring may be u. GEOR 126:9
uninteresting u. subject CHES 63:5
union u. has been guiding star CARS 54:5
unions Hitler attacked the u. NIEM 232:1
  would have been no u. BALD 21:6
unique conscious of being u. USTI 315:12
United States drawn to the U. DENN 88:9
unity u. of our fatherland KOHL 177:11
universe Architect of the U. JEAN 160:8
  coherent plan to the u. HOYL 153:6
  fact about the u. EINS 97:1
  good u. next door CUMM 81:15
  Life, the U. and Everything ADAM 1:12
  repetitious mechanism of the U. WHIT 326:12
  u. go to all the bother HAWK 142:10
  U. is a free lunch GUTH 135:11
  u. is not hostile HOLM 151:1
  u. is not only queerer HALD 136:9
  u.'s existence made known PENR 246:11
  u. sleeps MAYA 211:3
  visible u. an illusion BORG 42:3
universities men who go to the u.
  MAUG 210:12
university able to get to a u. KINN 173:8
  u. of life BOTT 42:5
  u. of the air WILS 331:5
  u. training AMIS 8:2
unknowable decide on the u. ZOBE 341:8
unknown glorious and the u. FORS 116:4
  known and the u. PINT 249:10
  tread safely into the u. HASK 142:2
  U. Prime Minister ASQU 14:7
  Woman is the great u. HARD 139:1
unluckily good u. STOP 299:9
unlucky It was his u. night MCHA 200:3
  so u. that he runs into MARQ 208:10
unmaking things are in the u. KING 172:13

unnatural only u. sex act KINS 173:10
unnecessary to to the u. SAYI 278:7
unofficial English u. rose BROO 45:10
unpalatable disastrous and the u. GALB 123:14
unplayable another u. work SCHO 280:11
unpleasant u. to meet Mr Eliot ELIO 98:8
unpopular safe to be u. STEV 298:5
unprepared Magnificently u. CORN 77:7
unprincipled sold by the u. CAPP 53:12
unreality u. of painted people UPDI 315:5
unreason Television thrives on u. DAY 84:14
unreasonable depends on u. man SHAW 285:7
unreliable Even death is u. BECK 26:11
unsafe U. at any speed NADE 227:6
unsayable say the u. RUSH 270:12
unscathed u. tourist of wars GELL 125:11
unselfishly U. so we might have MCHA 200:3
unsoiled delicately and u. CHUR 68:3
unspeakable speak the u. RUSH 270:12
untalented product of the u. CAPP 53:12
unthought never be u. DÜRR 93:10
untouchable dying from being u. HEGG 144:11
untried difficult; and left u. CHES 64:2
untrue man who's u. to his wife AUDE 17:3
  u. in the House WALD 318:5
unwanted feeling of being u. TERE 304:7
unwell Jeffery Bernard is u. WATE 320:6
unwilling group of the u. SAYI 278:7
  u. or unable WILL 330:7
up nice to people on your way u. MIZN 217:15
  U. to a point, Lord Copper WAUG 321:8
uplands broad, sunlit u. CHUR 66:6
upper Like many of the U. Class BELL 28:4
  prove the u. classes COWA 78:12
uppity feeling a bit u. CLOU 71:11
upstanding clean u. chap like you KING 172:16
upwards car could go straight u. HOYL 153:4
  onwards and u. YORK 340:3
uranium element u. may be turned EINS 97:2
urban u., squat, and packed BROO 45:12
urges stirs and u. everything HARD 139:8
urine red wine of Shiraz into u. DINE 90:3
Uruguay big she is in U. THOM 308:14
USA Born in the U. SPRI 294:12
use u. words as they are used COMP 74:6
used ain't what they u. to be PERS 247:8
  buy a u. car POLI 252:1
  get u. to them NEUM 229:12
useful be a Really U. Engine AWDR 19:1
  what is apparently u. WHIT 327:3
useless plans are u. EISE 98:1
USSR Back in the U. LENN 188:2
usual Business carried on as u. CHUR 65:6
usura With u. hath no man a house
  POUN 253:13
usury u. is contrary to Scripture TAWN 303:4
uterus what your u. looks like EPHR 104:3

we w. it now	MORR 222:8
What does a woman w.	FREU 118:16
what I really really w.	ROWB 269:12
war After each w.	ATKI 15:1
ain't gonna be no w.	MACM 201:15
anyone who wasn't against w.	LOW 195:3
at w. with Germany	CHAM 60:5
Austria is going to the w.	CHES 62:9
beating of w. drums	KOES 177:8
bungled, unwise w.	PLOM 250:7
cold w.	BARU 24:9
cold w. warrior	THAT 304:11
condemn recourse to w.	BRIA 44:7
day w. broke out	CATC 57:9
devil's madness—w.	SERV 283:3
done very well out of the w.	BALD 21:2
Don't mention the w.	CLEE 70:12
easier to make w.	CLEM 71:3
enable it to make w.	WEIL 322:6
European w. might do it	REDM 262:8
first live televised w.	O'RO 236:14
First World W. had begun	TAYL 303:7
for w. like precocious giants	PEAR 246:8
France has not lost the w.	DE G 86:8
guarantee success in w.	CHUR 66:8
here to see the w. through	HEND 146:1
home policy: I wage w.	CLEM 71:1
if someone gave a w.	GINS 128:6
I hate w.	ROOS 267:9
I have seen w.	ROOS 267:9
involve us in the wrong w.	BRAD 43:4
In w., no winners	CHAM 60:2
In w.: resolution	CHUR 68:10
I renounce w.	FOSD 117:3
I will not have another w.	GEOR 126:10
killed in the w.	POWE 255:13
live under the shadow of a w.	SPEN 294:1
lose the w. in an afternoon	CHUR 68:16
Make love not w.	SAYI 279:3
Mankind must put an end to w.	KENN 169:9
McNamara's W.	MCNA 202:10
no declaration of w.	EDEN 95:7
not a justifiable act of w.	BELL 27:8
nuisance in time of w.	CHUR 67:8
Older men declare w.	HOOV 151:12
Once lead this people into w.	WILS 332:8
page 1 of the book of w.	MONT 220:13
paparazzi dogs of w.	DENE 88:2
pattern called a w.	LOWE 195:4
quaint and curious w. is	HARD 140:3
rich wage w.	SART 276:1
seek no wider w.	JOHN 163:3
seven days w.	MUIR 225:3
soon as w. is declared	GIRA 128:10
subject is W.	OWEN 240:12
talk of a just w.	SORL 292:3
tempered by w.	KENN 169:2

they'll give a w.	SAND 275:3
understood this liking for w.	BENN 30:13
wage w. against	CHUR 66:3
w. and peace in 21st century	KOHL 177:12
W. being deliberately prolonged	SASS 277:3
w. between men and women	THUR 309:11
w. creates order	BREC 43:13
w. has used up words	JAME 159:12
W. hath no fury	MONT 220:9
w. in which everyone	CONN 75:1
W. is capitalism with	STOP 299:11
W. is hell, and all that	HAY 142:12
w. is obsolete or men are	FULL 122:4
W. is peace	ORWE 238:9
w. is politics with bloodshed	MAO 207:5
W. is too serious a matter	CLEM 71:5
W. makes good history	HARD 140:10
w. minus the shooting	ORWE 239:8
w. on poverty	JOHN 163:1
w. run to show the Third World	BERR 34:3
W.'s annals will cloud	HARD 140:2
w. situation has developed	HIRO 149:4
w. that will end war	WELL 323:11
w. that would not boil	TAYL 303:10
W. the most exciting thing	DAYA 85:1
W. the universal perversion	RAE 259:7
W. too serious a business	BUCH 48:3
w. wasn't fought that way	ROSS 269:1
w. which existed to produce	HOBS 150:1
W. will cease when	POLI 251:24
waste of God, w.	STUD 301:2
way of ending a w.	ORWE 239:12
We hear w. called murder	MACD 199:2
what a lovely w.	LITT 191:11
what did you do in the W.	SAYI 278:9
win an atomic w.	BRAD 43:1
without having won the w.	YOKO 340:2
You can only love one w.	GELL 126:1
wardrobe open your w.	WELD 322:12
warfare Armed w. must be preceded	
	ZINO 341:7
warm lived in a w., sunny climate	COWA 78:14
man who's w. to understand	SOLZ 290:16
w. full blooded life	JOYC 165:9
warn All a poet can do is w.	OWEN 240:13
w. you not to be ordinary	KINN 173:5
War Office except the British W.	SHAW 283:15
warrior cold war w.	THAT 304:11
This is the happy w.	READ 261:7
wars all their w. are merry	CHES 62:1
came to an end all w.	LLOY 192:8
end to beginnings of all w.	ROOS 268:2
History littered with the w.	POWE 255:6
how do w. start	KRAU 177:14
into any foreign w.	ROOS 267:12
not armaments that cause w.	MADA 203:14
old liberal between the w.	PLOM 250:8

weekends getting a plumber on w.	ALLE 6:15
weight one and half times own w.	UPDI 314:13
punch above its w.	HURD 155:1
w. of rages	SPOO 294:10
welcome good evening, and w.	CATC 58:2
welfare lead to the w. state	DENN 88:8
W. became a term	MOYN 224:4
w.-state	TEMP 304:2
well alive and w.	ANON 10:5
all shall be w.	ELIO 99:12
country where nobody is w.	AUDE 18:11
Didn't she do w.	CATC 57:10
doing w. that which should not	VIDA 317:10
w. of loneliness	HALL 137:2
wept young man who has not w.	SANT 275:7
west face neither East nor W.	NKRU 232:11
in the gardens of the W.	CONN 74:20
liquid manure from the W.	SOLZ 291:5
political history of the W.	HAIL 136:6
W. of these out to seas	FLEC 113:17
where the W. begins	CHAP 61:11
western delivered by W. Union	GOLD 130:11
quiet on the w. front	REMA 263:2
W. is not only history	LANG 179:16
When you've seen one W.	WHIT 327:10
Westerners W. have aggressive	KAUN 167:5
West Indian I am a W. peasant	MCDO 199:4
wet out of these w. clothes	FILM 111:1
so w. you could shoot snipe	POWE 255:1
Wexford disused shed in Co. W.	MAHO 204:5
whale Save the w.	SAYI 279:6
screw the w.	STOP 299:4
whales W. play	WILL 329:7
whammy Labour's double w.	POLI 251:18
wharf sit on the w. for a day	BEAV 25:10
what know what's w.	WEST 324:12
W. is to be done	LENI 187:8
W.'s up, Doc	CATC 59:13
wheat packed like squares of w.	LARK 181:2
wheel breaks a butterfly on a w.	NEWS 231:13
created the w.	APOL 12:8
invented the w.	NEME 229:8
red w. barrow	WILL 330:8
wheels w. of black Marias	AKHM 5:3
when forgotten to say 'W.!'	WODE 333:15
where w. do they all come from	LENN 188:4
W. OUGHT I TO BE	TELE 305:1
whereof w. one cannot speak	WITT 332:16
whimper Not with a bang but a w.	ELIO 99:19
whimsical say something w.	LOVE 194:13
whin three w. bushes rode across	KAVA 167:6
whisky good old boys drinkin' w.	MCLE 200:11
W. makes it go round	MACK 200:7
whisper my w. was already born	MAND 206:10
W. who dares	MILN 217:1
whispering just w. in her mouth	MARX 209:5
whistle shrimp learns to w.	KHRU 171:8
W. while you work	MORE 221:12
You know how to w.	FILM 111:7
white American w. man to find	BALD 20:10
best friends are w.	DURE 93:7
be the w. man's brother	KING 172:2
dreaming of a w. Christmas	BERL 33:3
enough w. lies to ice	ASQU 14:13
fat w. woman	CORN 77:6
lowest w. man	JOHN 162:10
no 'w.' or 'coloured' signs	KENN 169:12
say this for the w. race	GREG 133:8
shake a bat at a w. man	GREG 133:10
so-called w. races	FORS 116:13
W.-Anglo Saxon-Protestant	BALT 22:7
w. heat of technology	MISQ 219:4
w. race *is* the cancer	SONT 291:15
white-collar not the w. people	WHYT 327:14
Whitehall condottiere through W.	
	HURD 154:14
gentleman in W.	JAY 160:2
White House W. or home	DOLE 90:7
whitewash at the W.	NIXO 232:6
whiter Persil washes w.	ADVE 4:16
w. shade of pale	REID 262:15
whitewash w. at the White House	NIXO 232:6
Whitman daintily dressed Walt W.	CHES 64:1
Walt W.—	CRAN 79:6
whizzing W. them over the net	BETJ 35:11
who W. am I going to be today	WELD 322:12
W. he	ROSS 269:3
w. the hell are you	CATC 58:10
W.? Whom	LENI 187:11
whole nothing can be sole or w.	YEAT 337:5
whom Who? W.	LENI 187:11
whore like a chaste w.	MUGG 224:14
w. in the bedroom	HALL 137:1
whores parliament of w.	O'RO 236:18
second-rate w.	PLOM 250:9
Who's Who been in W.	WEST 324:12
why about the wasp, except w.	THOM 307:12
but also w., to whom	HAVE 142:4
finding only w.	CUMM 81:16
see things and say 'W.'	SHAW 283:11
W. not? Why not? Yeah	LAST 183:4
w. people laugh	FIEL 108:13
Would this man ask w.	AUDE 16:5
wicked August is a w. month	O'BR 233:9
wickedness [w.] is not punished	COMP 74:8
wicket flannelled fools at the w.	KIPL 174:7
wider seek no w. war	JOHN 163:3
w. still and wider	BENS 31:15
widow French w. in bedroom	HOFF 150:8
W. The word consumes itself	PLAT 250:6
width feel the w.	POWE 255:17
wields He who w. the knife	HESE 147:1
wife If I were your w.	CHUR 69:2
lay down his w. for his friend	JOYC 165:11

wife (*cont.*):

man who's untrue to his w.	AUDE 17:3
more moral than a w.	PHIL 248:7
nobody's w.	HERB 146:12
riding to and from his w.	WHIT 326:3
she is your w.	OGIL 234:11
talks frankly only with his w.	BABE 19:12
that is the w.	CURR 82:7
wish your w. or servants	GRIF 134:4
your w. and your dog	HILL 148:8

Wigan mothers-in-law and W. Pier — BRID 44:8

road to W. Pier — ORWE 238:16

wild call of the w. — LOND 193:8

never saw a w. thing — LAWR 184:4

walk on the w. side — ALGR 5:13

wilder w. shores of love — BLAN 39:8

wilderness Women have no w. — BOGA 40:7

will Immanent W. that stirs — HARD 139:8

political w. — LYNN 196:8

w. to carry on — LIPP 191:10

wrote my w. across the sky — LAWR 184:17

willed only a w. gentleness — THOM 308:12

willingness w. to be deceived — MEDA 212:3

wilt Do what thou w. — CROW 81:7

Wimbledon Spill your guts at W. — CONN 75:4

win From w. and lose — MITC 217:5

spend it, and w. — KENN 170:3

that's to w. — MALR 205:7

To w. in Vietnam — SPOC 294:6

w. an atomic war — BRAD 43:1

W. just one for the Gipper — GIPP 128:9

wind answer is blowin' in the w. — DYLA 94:3

candle in the w. — JOHN 162:1

how the w. doth ramm — POUN 253:12

not I, but the w. — LAWR 184:7

Not with this w. blowing — KIPL 174:11

sifted by the w. — BUNT 48:10

solidity to pure w. — ORWE 239:6

twist slowly in the w. — EHRL 96:4

wash the w. — ELIO 100:14

w. of change is blowing — MACM 201:19

windbags W. can be right — FENT 107:11

window argument of the broken w.

PANK 242:8

back upon the w.-panes — ELIO 100:5

doggie in the w. — MERR 213:14

Good prose like a w.-pane — ORWE 237:13

has not one w. — JAME 159:9

hole in a stained glass w. — CHAN 60:7

kiss my ass in Macy's w. — JOHN 163:9

windows open the w. of the Church

JOHN 161:14

wine doesn't get into the w. — CHES 63:2

red sweet w. of youth — BROO 45:7

red w. of Shiraz into urine — DINE 90:3

w. was a farce — POWE 254:17

wing knowst'ou w. from tail — POUN 254:6

w. and a pray'r — ADAM 2:2

wings Grief has no w. — QUIL 258:12

on laughter-silvered w. — MAGE 204:1

wink wink w., say no more — MONT 221:1

winners no w., but all are losers — CHAM 60:2

winning more fun w. — DOLE 90:9

W. is everything — HILL 148:8

w. isn't everything — SAND 275:6

wins Who dares w. — SAYI 279:15

w. if he does not lose — KISS 176:2

Winston W. is back — ANON 12:1

winter furious w. blowing — RANS 260:2

go south in the w. — ELIO 101:7

rich and lovely W.'s Eve — DAVI 84:3

very dead of w. — ELIO 99:20

W. is icummen in — POUN 253:12

w. of discontent — CALL 51:10

W. of discontent — NEWS 231:15

wisdom conventional w. — GALB 123:3

door to infinite w. — BREC 43:12

W. was mine — OWEN 241:5

w. we have lost — ELIO 100:18

wise Astrologers or three w. men — LONG 194:1

w. forgive but do not forget — SZAS 302:5

wisecrack w. played Carnegie Hall — LEVA 189:6

wisecracking w. and wit — PARK 243:16

wisely nations behave w. once — EBAN 94:16

wish If otherwise w. I — SHAW 286:9

w. for prayer is a prayer — BERN 33:10

w. I loved the Human Race — RALE 259:10

wishes compliance with my w. — CHUR 68:14

wit his weapon w. — EPIT 105:9

use my w. as a pitchfork — LARK 180:14

W. has truth in it — PARK 243:16

witch-doctors Accountants are w.

HARM 140:15

witches burnt at the stake as w. — SMIT 290:2

without get where I am today w. — CATC 58:5

witnesses w. to the desolation — GEOR 126:6

wits stolen his w. away — DE L 87:13

witty Thou swell! Thou w. — HART 141:10

wives left the w. and joined — WELD 322:9

wizards affairs of W. — TOLK 310:9

wobbly spelling is W. — MILN 216:9

wolf afraid of the big bad w. — CHUR 65:3

w. of a different opinion — INGE 156:13

Wolsey W.'s Home Town — NEWS 231:10

woman artist man and mother w.

SHAW 284:13

As you are w. — GRAV 131:11

Being a w. — LEBO 186:4

called a w. in my own house — WAUG 321:11

comfort about being a w. — STAR 295:9

done, ask a w. — THAT 304:10

embrace a w.'s shoe — KRAU 177:15

Every w. adores a Fascist — PLAT 250:3

fat white w. — CORN 77:6

words (*cont.*):

w. you couldn't say	LEHR 187:2
worth ten thousand w.	BARN 23:3
wrestle With w.	ELIO 98:15
you can drug, with w.	LOWE 195:5

Wordsworth daffodils were for W.   LARK 181:4

W. drunk	HOUS 152:13

work good idea but it won't w.   ROGE 266:16

got my w. cut out	SQUI 295:3
Go to w. on an egg	ADVE 3:19
immortality through my w.	ALLE 6:18
in w. does what he wants	COLL 73:1
let the toad w.	LARK 180:14
looked for w.	TEBB 303:16
love and w.	FREU 118:17
Man grows beyond his w.	STEI 296:8
men think. Sex, w.	FISH 109:3
men w. more and dispute less	TAWN 303:3
most of my w. sitting down	BENC 29:4
never have to w. again	TWIG 314:4
Nice w. if you can get it	GERS 127:5
off to w. we go	MORE 221:11
of the life, or of the w.	YEAT 337:4
slaughterhouses of w.	VANE 316:4
Whistle while you w.	MORE 221:12
Without w., life goes rotten	CAMU 53:6
W. and pray	HILL 148:12
W. expands	PARK 244:6
W. is love made visible	GIBR 127:12
W. is of two kinds	RUSS 271:13
w. is terribly important	RUSS 271:7
W. is the call	MORR 222:6
W. is x	EINS 97:4
W. liberates	ANON 9:2
w., rest and play	ADVE 4:9
W. seethes in the hands	PAST 245:8
w. terribly hard at playing	MORT 223:3
W. to survive	VANE 316:5
W. was like a stick	SOLZ 290:15
You w., we rule	DUNN 93:4

worked yes it w.   POLI 252:2

worker weapon with w. at each end

    POLI 251:4

w. is the slave	CONN 75:3

workers not the w.   WHYT 327:14

organized w. of the country	SHIN 286:13
secure for the w.	ANON 11:14
W. all demand	SERV 283:3

workhouse woman's w.   SHAW 285:9

working in his w. time   GILL 128:2

it isn't w.	MAJO 204:14
killin' meself w.	O'CA 234:1
Labour isn't w.	POLI 251:17
start their w. lives	KIPL 174:3
w. like a dog	LENN 188:6

working class into the w.   ORWE 239:3

working-class job w. parents want   ABBO 1:1

working classes worst fault of w.   MORT 223:6

works seen the future and it w.   STEF 296:1

w. and is not bored	CASA 55:8
w. even if you don't	BOHR 40:9

world adventure in the w. of Aids   PERK 247:2

all the towns in all the w.	FILM 111:11
become the w.'s policeman	HEAL 143:5
blamed for worsening the w.	JAME 159:1
decide the fate of the w.	DE G 86:12
Feed the w.	GELD 125:10
funny old w.	THAT 306:16
Hog Butcher for the W.	SAND 274:10
in 1915 the old w. ended	LAWR 183:6
In a w. I never made	HOUS 152:5
limits of my w.	WITT 332:18
Little Friend of all the W.	KIPL 175:13
loosed upon the w.	YEAT 338:13
Love makes the w. go round	MACK 200:7
new w. order	BUSH 50:5
Oh, w., Oh, death	SPEN 293:14
only girl in the w.	GREY 133:14
only saved the w.	CHES 62:6
point of the turning w.	ELIO 98:12
put the w. to sleep	MUIR 225:3
Sob, heavy w.	AUDE 15:13
Stop the w.	NEWL 229:14
sword the axis of the w.	DE G 87:7
Ten days that shook the w.	REED 262:14
Their w. gives way	MACN 203:2
Top of the w.	FILM 110:1
war run to show the w.	BERR 34:3
way the w. ends	ELIO 99:19
We want the w.	MORR 222:8
woods against the w.	BLUN 39:12
w. empty of people	LAWR 183:18
w. is an oyster	MILL 215:4
w. is becoming like asylum	LLOY 192:15
w. is changing	ELIZ 102:14
w. is everything that is	WITT 332:17
w. must be made safe	WILS 332:7
w. of silence	EPIT 105:1
w. safe for hypocrisy	WOLF 334:2
w.'s in a state o' chassis	O'CA 234:3
w.'s worst wound	SASS 277:1
w. turn by itself	O'CA 234:7
w. will end in fire	FROS 120:6
W., you have kept faith	HARD 139:13

worlds best of all possible w.   CABE 50:13

destroyer of w.	OPPE 236:8

worm tasted your w.   SPOO 294:9

worms diet of w.   FENT 107:9

We are all w.	CHUR 69:8

worried may not be w. into being   FROS 121:4

w. about Jim	CATC 58:12

worry I w., I worry   COPE 76:11

worrying What's the use of w.   ASAF 13:10

worse bad against the w.   DAY- 85:5

don't feel w.   FRAY 118:6
fear of finding something w.   BELL 27:12
If my books had been any w.   CHAN 60:11
More will mean w.   AMIS 8:2
worsening blamed for w. the world
                                                 JAME 159:1
worship second is freedom to w.   ROOS 267:14
worst full look at the w.   HARD 139:12
  good in the w. of us   ANON 11:9
  intellectual hatred the w.   YEAT 338:7
  like to be told the w.   CHUR 66:11
  While the w. are full   YEAT 338:13
  world's w. wound   SASS 277:1
  w. form of Government   CHUR 67:10
  w. is yet to come   JOHN 163:11
  w. time of the year   ELIO 99:20
  You do your w.   CHUR 66:12
worth confident of their own w.   AUNG 18:19
  makes life w. living   ELIO 101:21
  w. doing badly   CHES 64:3
Worthington on the stage, Mrs W.   COWA 78:9
wotthehell w. archy   MARQ 208:7
would He w., wouldn't he   RICE 264:5
wound Hearts w. up with love   SPEN 293:11
  world's worst w.   SASS 277:1
  w., not the bandage   POTT 253:6
Wounded Knee Bury my heart at W.
                                                 BENÉ 29:9
wounds salt rubbed into their w.   WEST 324:19
wren Sir Christopher W. Said   BENT 32:5
wrestle w. With words   ELIO 98:15
wrestled w. for perhaps too long   HOWE 153:1
wrings at last w. its neck   RUSS 271:17
wrinklies not because ageing w.   STRA 300:6
write attempt to w. on both sides   SELL 282:15
  people who can't w.   ZAPP 341:2
  restraint with which they w.   CAMP 52:9
  w. about the extraordinary   JOYC 165:14
  w. all the books   EDDI 95:2
  w. every other day   DOUG 91:8
  w. for the youth   FITZ 113:11
  w. like distinguished author   NABO 227:4
  w. when I feel spiteful   LAWR 184:11
writer best fame is a w.'s fame   LEBO 186:10
  For a w., success is   GREE 132:15
  I'm a w.   WALC 318:4
  modern hardback w.   TRIL 311:12
  more interested in the w.   AMIS 8:6
  No tears in the w.   FROS 121:3
  No w. can give that   GLEN 129:4
  obsesses a w. starting   MORT 223:1
  protect the w.   ACHE 1:9
  things a w. is for   RUSH 270:12
  w. must refuse   SART 276:14
  w. people think other   NAIP 227:8
  w.'s ambition should be   KOES 177:10
  w.'s only responsibility   FAUL 107:4

w.'s radar   HEMI 145:17
w. to eat a whole sheep   MAUG 210:11
writers dead w. are remote   ELIO 102:3
writes w. when it grows dark   CELA 56:10
writing get it in w.   LEE 186:16
  little point in w.   AMIS 8:3
  live and despise w.   SMIT 289:15
  no talent for w.   BENC 29:5
  obstacle to professional w.   BENC 29:1
  thought *nothing* of her w.   SITW 288:5
  W. is not a profession   SIME 287:6
written *as well w. as prose*   POUN 254:15
  being w. about   BELL 28:15
  W. English is now inert   HOUS 152:11
wrong as likely to be w.   BROU 46:9
  but also to be w.   SZAS 302:2
  called the w. number   THUR 309:13
  customer is never w.   RITZ 265:3
  different kinds of w.   COMP 74:4
  Eating people is w.   FLAN 113:15
  excuse the w. by showing   HAND 138:3
  Fifty million Frenchmen can't be w.
                                                SAYI 278:14

  Had anything been w.   AUDE 18:1
  involve us in the w. war   BRAD 43:4
  I was w.   AUDE 16:8
  majority are w.   DEBS 86:5
  never w., the Old Masters   AUDE 17:1
  not always to be w.   EDEN 95:8
  only an accumulated w.   CASE 55:10
  ran w. through all the land   MUIR 225:2
  right deed for the w.   ELIO 100:13
  something has gone w.   POTT 253:9
  thought it w. to fight   BELL 28:8
  very probably w.   CLAR 70:5
  We were w.   MCNA 202:11
  Why mind being w.   AYER 19:8
  W. but Wromantic   YEAT 282:11
  w. decision isn't forever   GALB 123:12
  w. kind of snow   WORR 336:3
  w. members in control   ORWE 238:4
  w. side of the door   CHES 62:2
  w. with our bloody ships   BEAT 25:4
wrongs Two w. don't make a right   SZAS 302:9
Wykehamist rather dirty W.   BETJ 36:1
wysiwyg shortened to w.   SAYI 279:13

X Generation X   COUP 78:1
xerox X. makes everybody   MCLU 201:13
XXXX wouldn't give a X.   ADVE 3:6

Yale libel on a Y. prom   PARK 243:15
Yanks Y. are coming   COHA 72:9
year man at the gate of the y.   HASK 142:2
  one y.'s experience 30 times   CARR 54:3

year (*cont.*):

thirtieth y. to heaven	THOM 307:8
years gave up the y. to be	BROO 45:7
house seventy y. old	JEAN 160:5
nor the y. condemn	BINY 37:13
two thousand y. of hope	WEIZ 322:8
y. to come seemed waste	YEAT 337:19
Yeats Y. is laid to rest	AUDE 16:12
yellow And not your y. hair	YEAT 336:12
banana man, y. outside	PAGE 241:10
Follow the y. brick road	HARB 138:13
Goodbye y. brick road	JOHN 162:5
y. polkadot bikini	VANC 315:17
yes getting the answer y.	CAMU 52:12
Y., but not in the South	POTT 253:10
Y.; I remember Adlestrop	THOM 308:1
Y. it hurt	POLI 252:2
Y., Minister! No, Minister	CROS 81:5
Y.! we have no bananas	SILV 287:5
yesterday Evil visited us y.	TAYL 303:15
I believe in y.	LENN 188:11
keeping up with y.	MARQ 208:3
Y.'s men	POLI 252:3
yid PUT THE ID BACK IN Y.	ROTH 269:9
York Duchess of Y. is a vulgarian	CHAR 61:15
you For y. but not for me	ANON 10:17
'Y.' your joys and sorrows	CRIC 79:13
young angry and defrauded y.	KIPL 173:13
as I was y. and easy	THOM 307:3
Being y. is not minding	WHIT 327:7
Being y. is overestimated	QUAN 258:8
denunciation of the y.	SMIT 289:8
get out while we're y.	SPRI 294:14
how y. the policemen look	HICK 148:4
I have been y.	BLUN 39:13
I'll die y.	BRUC 47:3
resolute, the y.	KIPL 174:8

too y. to fall asleep	SASS 276:19
too y. to take up golf	ADAM 1:13
voices of y. people	SMIT 289:7
Women never have y. minds	DELA 87:21
y., gifted and black	HANS 138:6
Y., gifted and black	IRVI 157:12
y. had discovered	MAUG 210:1
y. men think it is	HOUS 152:9
y. regard me as outrageous	HOYL 153:5
y. whom I hope to bother	AUDE 17:12
younger curse of the y. generation	
	MACM 202:4
y. than that now	DYLA 94:11
y. with time	CASA 55:7
youngster going out a y.	FILM 112:3
yours Y. till Hell freezes	FISH 109:8
yourself love you for y. alone	YEAT 336:12
youth belongs to Y.	QUAN 258:6
it is y. who must fight	HOOV 151:12
red sweet wine of y.	BROO 45:7
shake their wicked sides at y.	YEAT 338:6
write for the y.	FITZ 113:11
Y. is something very new	CHAN 61:3
Y. is vivid	LOVE 195:1
Y., which is forgiven	SHAW 285:10
Y. would be an ideal state	ASQU 14:6
yuppie y. version of bulimia	EHRE 96:2

zeal tempering bigot z.	KNOX 176:15
Zen Z. and the art	PIRS 249:14
zip Children and z. fasteners	WHIT 327:5
zipless z. fuck	JONG 164:1
zones retain our z. erogenous	HARB 138:12
zoo human z.	MORR 222:3
Zurich gnomes in Z.	WILS 331:1